D1752435

Irish English as Represented in Film

Bamberger Beiträge zur Englischen Sprachwissenschaft

Bamberg Studies in English Linguistics

Begründet von / founded by Wolfgang Viereck

Herausgegeben von / edited by Manfred Krug,
Heinrich Ramisch und / and Wolfgang Viereck

Bd./Vol. 53

PETER LANG

Frankfurt am Main · Berlin · Bern · Bruxelles · New York · Oxford · Wien

Shane Walshe

Irish English as Represented in Film

PETER LANG
Internationaler Verlag der Wissenschaften

Bibliographic Information published by the Deutsche Nationalbibliothek
The Deutsche Nationalbibliothek lists this publication in the Deutsche Nationalbibliografie; detailed bibliographic data is available in the internet at http://dnb.d-nb.de.

Zugl.: Bamberg, Univ., Diss., 2009

Veröffentlichung einer Dissertation
der Otto-Friedrich-Universität, Bamberg

Erstgutachter: Prof. em. Dr. Wolfgang Viereck
Zweitgutachter: Prof. Dr. Gabriele Knappe

Tag der mündlichen Prüfung: 24. Juli 2009

D 473
ISSN 0721-281X
ISBN 978-3-631-58682-2
© Peter Lang GmbH
Internationaler Verlag der Wissenschaften
Frankfurt am Main 2009
All rights reserved.

All parts of this publication are protected by copyright. Any utilisation outside the strict limits of the copyright law, without the permission of the publisher, is forbidden and liable to prosecution. This applies in particular to reproductions, translations, microfilming, and storage and processing in electronic retrieval systems.

www.peterlang.de

Contents

Acknowledgments ix

1 Introduction 1
2 Film as literary dialect 5
3 The notion of authenticity 9
4 Irish English 15
    4.1 Terminology 15
    4.2 The history of the English language in Ireland 16
    4.3 Irish English in the context of this study 20
5 Methodology 21
    5.1 Establishing the corpus 21
    5.2 Analysing the data 26
6 Irish English dialect in the film corpus 37
    6.1 Grammar 45
        6.1.1 The verb phrase 45
            6.1.1.1 Habitual aspect 45
            6.1.1.2 Perfect markers 48
            6.1.1.3 Non-standard verb forms 60
            6.1.1.4 Lack of *do* support 65
            6.1.1.5 *Will* for *shall* 67
            6.1.1.6 The overuse of the progressive form 68
            6.1.1.7 Imperatives with progressive form 69
            6.1.1.8 Plural subject – verb concord 71
            6.1.1.9 Singular existential 73
            6.1.1.10 *For to* infinitives 73
        6.1.2 The noun phrase 74
            6.1.2.1 Plurals of quantity nouns 74
            6.1.2.2 The non-standard use of the definite article 76
            6.1.2.3 Reflexive pronouns 87
            6.1.2.4 Adverb marking 89
        6.1.3 Negation 92
            6.1.3.1 Negative concord 92
            6.1.3.2 Lack of negator contraction 93
        6.1.4 Questions 94
            6.1.4.1 Word order in indirect questions 94
            6.1.4.2 Responses to *Yes/No* questions 96
        6.1.5 The complex sentence 100
            6.1.5.1 Relative clause marking 100
            6.1.5.2 Focusing devices 102
            6.1.5.3 'Subordinating *and*' 109
            6.1.5.4 'Subordinating *till*' 112
        6.1.6 Morphology 113
            6.1.6.1 Second person plural 113
            6.1.6.2 Negation of auxiliary *am* 116
            6.1.6.3 *Them* as a demonstrative pronoun 117
        6.1.7 Summary of findings for grammar features 119
    6.2 Discourse features 121
        6.2.1 *Sure* 121
        6.2.2 Sentence-final markers 123

- 6.2.2.1 *But* 123
- 6.2.2.2 *What* 124
- 6.2.2.3 *Like* 125
- 6.2.2.4 *So* 127
- 6.2.2.5 Repetition for emphasis 128
- 6.2.3 *Come here* 128
- 6.2.4 Religious expressions 129
- 6.2.5 *Arrah* 137
- 6.2.6 *Musha* 138
- 6.2.7 Summary of findings for discourse markers 138
- 6.3 Lexicon 139
  - 6.3.1 Labels/Terms of address 140
    - 6.3.1.1 *Ma*, *Mam* and *Mammy* 140
    - 6.3.1.2 *Da* 141
    - 6.3.1.3 *Lad* and *Lads* 141
    - 6.3.1.4 *Your man/woman/one* 144
    - 6.3.1.5 *One* as a referent for females 145
    - 6.3.1.6 *Guard(s)* 146
  - 6.3.2 Irish English pronunciations which have become lexicalised 147
    - 6.3.2.1 *Eejit* 147
    - 6.3.2.2 *Oul(d)* 147
    - 6.3.2.3 *Shite* 148
    - 6.3.2.4 *Feck*, *feckin'* and *fecker* 149
  - 6.3.3 Swear words or vulgarisms 150
    - 6.3.3.1 *Arse* 150
    - 6.3.3.2 *Bollocks/bollix* 150
    - 6.3.3.3 *Bleedin'* 152
    - 6.3.3.4 *Gobshite* 152
    - 6.3.3.5 *Shag*, *shaggin'* and *shagger* 153
  - 6.3.4 Adjectives/adverbs with meanings different to those of Standard English 153
    - 6.3.4.1 *Grand* 153
    - 6.3.4.2 *Bold* 154
    - 6.3.4.3 *Desperate* 155
  - 6.3.5 Summary of findings for lexical items 155
- 6.4 Results 157
- 7 Accent perception 172
  - 7.1 Is everybody able to perceive accent? 172
  - 7.2 Can some people judge accent better than others? 173
  - 7.3 What, and how much, input is actually necessary for one to perceive accent? 178
  - 7.4 Vowels versus consonants 180
  - 7.5 Suprasegmentals 181
  - 7.6 Voice setting 182
- 8 Dialect coaches and the factors influencing accent acquisition 185
  - 8.1 The role of dialect coaches 185
  - 8.2 Factors which determine successful accent learning 192
    - 8.2.1 The influence of the learner's first language 192
    - 8.2.2 The learner's age 193
    - 8.2.3 Amount of exposure to the target accent 194
    - 8.2.4 The amount and type of prior pronunciation instruction 195
    - 8.2.5 The actor's phonetic ability 195
    - 8.2.6 The learner's attitude and sense of identity 197

- 8.2.7 The learner's motivation ... 198
- 8.3 Defining successful accent acquisition ... 199
- 9 Irish English accents in the film corpus ... 202
  - 9.1 Consonants ... 202
    - 9.1.1 /θ/ and /ð/ ... 202
    - 9.1.2 [t̪] and [d̪] for /t/ and /d/ ... 205
    - 9.1.3 Additional realisations of alveolar plosives ... 208
    - 9.1.4 [ʃ] for /s/ ... 209
    - 9.1.5 [ʒ] for /z/ ... 213
    - 9.1.6 [ʍ] for /w/ ... 213
    - 9.1.7 Clear [l] in all positions ... 214
    - 9.1.8 Yod deletion ... 215
    - 9.1.9 Rhoticism ... 216
    - 9.1.10 Nasal alveolarisation ... 217
  - 9.2 Vowels ... 217
    - 9.2.1 Raising of /ɛ/ to /ɪ/ ... 217
    - 9.2.2 Retention of /eː/ for Early Modern English <-ea-> words ... 219
    - 9.2.3 /oː/ and /eː/ as monophthongs ... 222
    - 9.2.4 Occasional pronunciation of /oː/ as /aʊ/ ... 223
    - 9.2.5 /ɑː/ in BATH set ... 224
    - 9.2.6 [ɑː] for /ʌ/ ... 225
    - 9.2.7 Occasional pronunciation of [ɛ] for /a/ ... 225
    - 9.2.8 [ʊ] for /ʌ/ ... 226
    - 9.2.9 Occasional pronunciation of /ʊ/ as [uː] ... 226
    - 9.2.10 [ə] or [i] for the unstressed /oʊ/ ... 227
    - 9.2.11 [ai] for /ɔi/ ... 229
    - 9.2.12 [ɔi] for /ai/ ... 230
    - 9.2.13 [i] for /ai/ ... 230
    - 9.2.14 Merger of CAUGHT and COT ... 231
    - 9.2.15 Epenthesis ... 231
    - 9.2.16 Metathesis ... 233
  - 9.3 Features of local Dublin pronunciation ... 234
    - 9.3.1 [uː] or [ɛː] for /ɜː/ ... 234
    - 9.3.2 Vowel breaking ... 236
    - 9.3.3 Fronting of /au/ ... 237
    - 9.3.4 Fortition of dental fricatives ... 237
- 10 Evaluating accents ... 240
- 11 Dialect coach handbooks as sources of poor accents ... 250
  - 11.1 Perpetuation of cultural stereotypes ... 250
  - 11.2 Respellings of sound changes ... 252
  - 11.3 Misinformation ... 253
  - 11.4 Recommendations of media representations of the accent ... 257
- 12 Additional reasons for the perception of poor accents in film ... 260
  - 12.1 Stereotypical expressions or pat phrases ... 260
  - 12.2 Non-linguistic factors ... 265
  - 12.3 Accent hallucination ... 266
- 13 Conclusions ... 267
- 14 Bibliography ... 270

15	Appendix 1	295
16	Appendix 2	297
17	Appendix 3	298

Acknowledgments

Although my name appears as the author of this book, numerous people have had a hand in its creation. To thank everybody by name is, unfortunately, impossible, but I would like to take this opportunity to express my gratitude to the following:

First of all, my sincere thanks to my supervisor Prof. Wolfgang Viereck for his guidance and patience throughout this project. He has always given generously of his time and experience and he has honoured me greatly by including this volume in his series *Bamberger Beiträge zur Englischen Sprachwissenschaft*.

Prof. Gabriele Knappe for her continuous support and her valuable feedback. Her keen eye for detail and her incisive comments throughout have greatly improved the quality of this work.

Prof. Manfred Krug for his infectious enthusiasm and for creating a regular forum for academic debate at the University of Bamberg in the form of his *Oberseminar*.

My colleagues, friends and students at the Chair of English Linguistics at the University of Bamberg, especially Dr. Heinrich Ramisch, Katrin Sell, Anna Rosen and Ole Schützler. Their comments and suggestions throughout the writing process were extremely helpful and greatly appreciated. Kenneth Wynne for his humour and friendship all these years. Our shared experiences in the world of practical language teaching are amongst my fondest memories.

Prof. Carlo Milan, Prof. Thomas Becker and Dr. Andreas Weihe for their interest and support at important stages of the examination process.

The staff at the English Seminar at the University of Zürich for welcoming me so warmly into their family and for their support during the final stages of my thesis.

Dialect coaches Brendan Gunn and Poll Moussoulides for taking so much time out of their hectic schedules to give me a fascinating insight into their work in film.

The ETA-Hoffmann Theater, the New Triad Theatre Company and the Bamberg University English Drama Group for giving me the opportunity to work with them as a dialect coach. The experience gained over the course of those projects has enriched this volume. Special thanks also to Dr. Mark Ferguson of Wofford Theatre, South Carolina, for his comments, interest and motivation.

The library staff at the Irish Film Institute for their generous assistance during my too brief stays in Dublin. John Commons, Harris King, Kay Boulware and Tracey Nesselrote for sourcing elusive DVDs, books and articles overseas. Felix Knöchel for his technical support and input on dubbing, subtitling and sound.

My parents, Tony and Carmel, and my sisters, Lorna, Brenda and Trish, for their unwavering support and encouragement. I really was working when you thought I was just watching TV. I dedicate this book to ye.

And, finally, Lorena for her love and encouragement.

Shane Walshe

Stage Irishman – A term for stereotypical Irish characters on the English-Language Stage from the 17th cent. It is also applied to characters in fiction (and, exceptionally, in real life) in whom Irish national characteristics are emphasised or distorted.

(*The Oxford Companion to Irish Literature*)

Paddyism – A term of mild abuse or self-irony to describe an action or speech that is perceived as being Stage Irish or based on an exaggerated display of so-called national characteristics, such as excessive drinking, the gift of the gab or the Irish Bull.

(*Brewer's Dictionary of Irish Phrase and Fable*)

Oirish – Paddyism connoting excessive or exaggerated display of perceived national characteristics.

(*Slanguage. A Dictionary of Irish Slang*)

1 Introduction

The whole concept of cinema is based on artifice, on what is often called "the suspension of disbelief". For the duration of their stay in the cinema, audiences are expected to enter into a silent pact, whereby they essentially agree to accept what they see and hear without question. However, modern audiences are becoming increasingly difficult to satisfy, and are unwilling to enter into this unwritten contract unconditionally. Rather than suspending their disbelief, they instead want to be made to believe, and, thus, filmmakers must rise to the challenge by providing them with the most believable cinematic world possible. Whereas certain types of rear-screen projection were quite commonplace in the early days of cinema, audiences today would probably laugh at an actor sitting in a car pretending to drive, jerking the steering wheel occasionally from side to side, while the scenery whizzes past on an obviously fake backdrop behind him. Modern audiences, it seems, are simply more demanding and they expect, and insist on, authenticity in sets, costumes, stunts, special effects and, increasingly, language.

For example, when people watch a film, they want to hear the actors speak with the accents and dialects which are typical of the place in which the film is set. When this is not the case, they are quick to voice their dismay, as can be seen in the following review of John Ford's *The Informer* and in a letter to the editor regarding Alan Parker's *Angela's Ashes*:

> Gallagher, the rebel leader, played by a youthful Preston Foster, speaks in accurate American, punctuated with an occasional, inaccurate concession to an Irish brogue. Mulligan and the strange inhabitants of the brothel are phony lapses into Paddyisms, perpetrated from Hollywood, USA.
>
> (*Films and Filming*, Vol. 6 (10), July 1960)

> Sir, - I don't wish to appear regionalistic, but does anyone find it odd that, despite the setting of Alan Parker's film *Angela's Ashes*, there is hardly a Limerick accent to be heard? A slight quibble perhaps, but can you imagine a Scorsese gangster film set in New York in which the protagonist speaks with a pronounced Texas drawl? Oh well, not to worry, the Yanks won't notice anyway! - Yours, etc., J.G. Byrne, Crescent Villas, Limerick.
>
> (*The Irish Times*, 20 January, 2000)

In light of these and similar comments, this book aims to explore the authenticity of portrayals of Irish English in film. To do so, I shall examine the language in 50 movies set in Ireland, ranging from John Ford's *The Informer* (1935) to Lenny Abrahamson's *Garage* (2007), firstly, searching them for a selection of typical grammar, discourse and lexical features, before approaching them from a phonological perspective.

With regard to the dialect features, I believe that the speech that we hear in film is a construct and can, thus, be regarded as a form of literary dialect, in the same way as the dialogue in a novel or play can. After all, like a play, it, too, is written down to be performed. My main aim here will therefore be to explore how Irish English is constructed in film and to discover to what extent it is faithful to what linguists consider Irish English to be. In order to do so, I will begin by offering a brief summary of the state of research in the core fields which have influenced this study, namely Irish English, literary dialect and Irish film (Chapter 1), before taking a more in-depth look at the concepts of literary dialect, Stage Irishness and the notion of authenticity which are central to this work (Chapters 2 and 3). Having addressed the main concepts and terminology behind this study, I will concentrate briefly on the history and current state of the English language in Ireland (Chapter 4), and then outline the methodology employed when compiling and analysing the corpus (Chapter 5). Using existing research on Irish English as my guide, I will then search the 50 films for the presence of 67 recognised features (39 grammar, 10 discourse and 18 lexical) of the variety. The findings will be compiled in tables and the results compared with those of a study by Raymond Hickey (2004a) in order to establish how "authentic" the representation of Irish English in the corpus is. These findings will also be examined to establish whether trends in feature occurrence are visible depending on when the film was produced, when it is set, where it is set, and, finally, depending on whether or not it is an Irish production (Chapter 6).

Having looked at the authenticity of the dialect features, I will then turn my attention to accents in Irish film, the area which receives the greatest amount of criticism regarding its authenticity (or lack thereof). The reason for such criticism is that non-Irish actors regularly play Irish characters in films, thereby assuming "Irish" accents which are often less than convincing. I will begin by addressing the phenomenon of accent perception in general, as it will be important to find out just what it is that these critical audiences are honing in on (Chapter 7). Once this has been established, I will illustrate how experts known as dialect coaches assist actors in acquiring new accents for their roles, and I will reveal the key factors which determine the successful acquisition of such accents (Chapter 8). I will then proceed to search the films for examples of, what are recognised as, the typical phonological features of Irish English (Chapter 9). Having done so, I will offer instances of where actors' accents have faltered through their inclusion of erroneous features, thus, betraying the actors' true origins (Chapter 10). Sometimes these erroneous features are not remnants of the performers' own accents, but rather something which has been learned, under the assumption that it was Irish. I will therefore look for the sources of these incorrect pronunciations in dialect coach handbooks (Chapter 11), before, finally, investigating whether other linguistic, or even non-linguistic, factors might be involved in people's judging accents to be inauthentic (Chapter 12). I shall conclude the study by providing a summary of my findings and offering some suggestions for future research.

State of research

While there have been numerous studies on Irish English, as well as on literary dialect and on stereotyping in film, this work is the first of its kind to reconcile the various disciplines. To that end, it was, of course, necessary to explore each field in considerable depth, and the following pages serve to bring the reader up to speed on the current state of research in each area.

Irish English (or Anglo-Irish or Hiberno-English) only became a major field of research at the beginning of the twentieth century, when a number of works appeared which concerned themselves with the idiosyncrasies of English as it is spoken in Ireland. The first of these were of an anecdotal nature and include Mary Hayden and Marcus Herzog's 1909 study "The Irish Dialect of English: Syntax and Idioms" (Hayden and Hertog 1909: 933-47) and P.W. Joyce's popular book *English as we Speak it in Ireland* from 1910 (Joyce 1988). The first more serious linguistic study of Irish English came in 1927, with the publication of James Hogan's *The English Language in Ireland* (Hogan 1927), which examined the history of

English in Ireland, as well as various grammar features and phonology. This was followed in 1957 by P.L Henry's *An Anglo-Irish Dialect of North Roscommon. Phonology, Accidence, Syntax* (Henry 1957), which proved to be influential in its exploration of the phonology of Irish English, as well as controversial in its attributing any non-standard English forms to substrate influences. Such substratal claims have since been keenly debated by a host of scholars, including John Harris, Markku Filppula, Jeffrey Kallen and Raymond Hickey. Together with Alan J. Bliss, Michael V. Barry, Roger Lass, John M. Kirk, Terence P. Dolan, Karen Corrigan and Kevin McCafferty, these scholars make up the core group of academics who since the 1970s have examined the many features of Irish English in great detail. Between them, they have written extensively on the phonology, morphology, syntax, tense, mood, aspect and lexicon of Irish English, but rather than summarising their individual contributions to the subject at this point, I shall instead return to them when discussing the various features of the variety in Chapter 6.

Although literary dialect has long been used as a stylistic device to distinguish between characters from different regions, classes or countries, the actual analysis of literary dialect has played merely a peripheral role for those who study literature, with the majority of scholars (perhaps understandably) focussing instead on what a character says rather than how he says it, i.e. on content rather than form. For the linguist, however, literary dialect can be extremely useful, since it is a form of preserving extinct or dying dialects which otherwise may never have been recorded for posterity[1]. Moreover, it can also be examined to explore stereotypes and prejudices which are often expressed in subtle (and sometimes not so subtle) ways in the language of the characters.

As outlined in Chapter 2, two of the most important works published on literary dialect are those written by George Philip Krapp and Sumner Ives in 1925 and 1950 respectively[2]. They serve as reference points for all subsequent works and examine the problems of accuracy and the potential for misunderstanding which all writers who convey dialect in literature face. These aspects have been addressed by a number of scholars since, with many focussing on dialect literature of the American South, particularly the writing of William Faulkner, Alice Walker, Joel Chandler Harris and Mark Twain.[3] One such study, by Lisa Cohen Minnick (2004), proved to be of particular interest for the current study, particularly with regard to methodology, and it will be referenced again over the course of the book.

Examinations of literary dialect related to Irish English also exist, and include Alan Bliss' "The Language of Synge" (1971), Jiro Taniguchi's *A Grammatical Analysis of Artistic Representation of Irish English with a Brief Discussion of Sounds and Spelling* (1972), James P. Sullivan's "The Validity of Literary Dialect: Evidence from the Theatrical Portrayal of Hiberno-English Forms" (1980), Richard Wall's "Dialect in Irish Literature: The hermetic

---

[1] See Brook (1965).
[2] Both Krapp's "The Psychology of Dialect Writing" and Ives' "A Theory of Literary Dialect" were republished in *A Various Language. Perspectives on American Dialects* (Williamson and Burke 1971: 22-29 and 145-177).
[3] See Williamson and Burke (1971) for a collection of essays on the use of literary dialect in works by Joel Chandler Harris, Mark Twain, Edgar A. Poe and Eugene O'Neill. *Dialect and Dichotomy. Literary Representations of African American Speech* (Lisa Cohen Minnick 2004) also extensively examines literary dialect in works by Mark Twain, William Faulkner and Zora Neale Hurston, while "Two Views of One Place: The Dialect of Putnam County, Georgia, in the Works of Joel Chandler Harris and Alice Walker" by Ellen Johnson and Stephanie Chastain (2003) explores the works of the aforementioned authors.

core" (1990), John M. Kirk's "Irish English and Contemporary Literary Writing" (1997) and Carolina Amador Moreno's *An Analysis of Hiberno-English in the Early Novels of Patrick MacGill. Bilingualism and Language Shift from Irish to English in County Donegal* (2006). A further study of literary dialect in an Irish English context, and one which initially inspired the shape of the current study, is Anna Asián and James McCullough's "Hiberno-English and the Teaching of Modern and Contemporary Irish Literature in an EFL Context" (1998). The paper, which is aimed at teachers of English as a Foreign Language, describes certain linguistic features of Irish English and shows their presence in John Millington Synge's play *The Tinker's Wedding*, as well as in Roddy Doyle's novel *The Snapper* and in its subsequent film adaptation. To my knowledge, this is the only study prior to my own which in any way examines, albeit very briefly, Irish English in the context of film. Any other research into literary dialect in Ireland has examined its use in poetry, prose and drama, yet never explored the medium of film. Indeed, studies on the use of *any* sort of dialect in film are also extremely rare. To date, I have discovered only three such works, one of which remains unpublished. In the first, "Teaching Children How to Discriminate: What we Learn from the Big Bad Wolf", Rosina Lippi-Green (1997) examines the way that accent and dialect are used in Disney films to portray characters as good or bad, or to assign them stereotypes, while, in the second, "Accent, Linguistic Discrimination, Stereotyping and West Virginia in Film", Teresa L. O'Cassidy (2004) conducts a similar investigation, in which she examines ten films featuring West Virginia characters for accent and stereotyping[4]. The third, which was published just before this book went to press, is by Kizzi Edensor and is entitled "Dialect in Films: Examples of South Yorkshire Grammatical and Lexical Features From Ken Loach Films". It investigates the presence of a variety of dialect features in three films set in Yorkshire over a thirty year period and in that respect is the study which is most similar to my work.

The present book, however, is much broader in its scope, analysing not only the grammatical, lexical and discourse features of a total of 50 films produced in Ireland over the course of seventy years, but also offering examples of a variety of phonological features of Irish English which occur in these movies. By providing a comprehensive linguistically-based analysis of Irish film, I aim to open up new avenues of exploration for other scholars of Irish English, while at the same time contributing something new to the emerging canon of works on Irish film, established by the pioneering research of Kevin Rockett, John Hill, Luke Gibbons, Terry Byrne, Martin McLoone, Lance Pettitt, and Ruth Barton[5].

---

[4] I am very grateful to Teresa L. O'Cassidy for granting me access to her work.
[5] See, for example, Rockett, Kevin., Hill, John., and Gibbons, Luke. *Cinema and Ireland*, Routledge, London, 1988; Byrne, Terry. *Power in the Eye. An Introduction to Contemporary Irish Film*, The Scarecrow Press, Inc. Lanham, MD. & London, 1997; McLoone, Martin. *Irish Film. The Emergence of a Contemporary Cinema*, British Film Institute, London, 2000; Pettitt, Lance. *Screening Ireland. Film and television representation*. Manchester University Press, 2000; Barton, Ruth. *Irish National Cinema*, Routledge, London and New York, 2004.

2 Film as literary dialect

As already outlined in the introduction, this study purports that the dialect spoken in films can be regarded as a form of literary dialect. Before we can judge whether this is the case, it is necessary to examine what literary dialect actually is. According to Sumner Ives, literary dialect is:

> ... an author's attempt to represent in writing a speech that is restricted regionally, socially, or both. His representation may consist merely in the use of an occasional spelling change, [...] or he may attempt to approach scientific accuracy by representing all the grammatical, lexical and phonetic peculiarities that he has observed.
>
> (Ives 1950: 146)

The phenomenon of literary dialect is certainly nothing new. It was already evident in the works of Geoffrey Chaucer, Edmund Spenser and William Shakespeare (cf. Ives 1950: 146) and it continues to be a prominent feature of literature today. Nevertheless, it had received relatively little scholarly attention until recently, with the two most cited works in the field still being those by George Philip Krapp and Sumner Ives, which date back to 1925 and 1950 respectively and which set out the key theories relating to the phenomenon.

Subsequent studies of literary dialect have generally tended to focus on American varieties, particularly Southern and African American ones, with works by Joel Chandler Harris, Mark Twain, William Faulkner and Alice Walker proving to be the usual suspects for analysis. For this reason, many of the examples used in the following pages to explain this phenomenon are also from American literature[6]. Irish literature, in contrast, has spawned relatively few in-depth studies on the use of literary dialect[7], with more attention instead being paid to what the characters do rather than what they say. Thus, while there is a proliferation of texts which analyse the portrayals of the Irish as drunkards, fighters and various comic figures[8], few examine the related aspect of the language of these Irish characters[9]. The most influential works with regard to the latter are arguably Taniguchi's *A Grammatical Analysis of Artistic Representation of Irish English with a Brief Discussion of Sounds and Spelling* (1972) and Sullivan's "The Validity of Literary Dialect: Evidence from the Theatrical Portrayal of

---

[6] This is not to say that there is no tradition of literary dialect in Great Britain. In fact, it features prominently in the work of many British authors (cf. Page 1981; Blake 1981). However, as Shorrocks observes, the field is often neglected by academics. The same applies to the related field of dialect literature. Shorrocks distinguishes between the two, stating that literary dialect is "the representation of non-standard speech in literature that is otherwise written in standard English (for instance, some of the dialogue in the works of such writers as Eliot, Dickens and Hardy) and aimed at a general readership" whereas (non-standard) dialect literature refers to "works composed wholly (sometimes partly) in a non-standard dialect, and aimed essentially, though not exclusively, at a non-standard-dialect-speaking readership" (1996: 386).

[7] Raymond Hickey's *A Source Book for Irish English* (2002) attests only a small number of studies on Irish literary dialect. Some of the more relevant ones from a linguistic perspective are: Taniguchi (1972), Garvin (1977), Bliss (1979), Sullivan (1980) and Asián and McCullough (1998). An important recent work on literary dialect from an Irish perspective is that by Amador Moreno (2006). In addition to her examination of Irish English features in fictional texts, she also provides an updated summary of previous studies on literary dialect.

[8] See: *The Stage Irishman – A History of the Irish Play and Stage Characters from the Earliest Times* (Duggan 1937), "The Development of a Stock Character: The Stage Irishman to 1800" (Bartley 1942), *Teague, Shenkin and Sawney. Being an Historical Study of the Earliest Irish, Welsh and Scottish Characters in English Plays* (Bartley 1954), *Apes and Angels. The Irishman in Victorian Caricature* (Perry Curtis, Jr. 1971) and *The Comic Irishman* (Waters 1984) for in depth accounts of the history of "Stage Irish" characters.

[9] A notable exception is "Pre-Nineteenth Century Stage Irish and Welsh Pronunciation" (Bartley and Sims 1949).

Hiberno-English Forms" (1980). Both works examine Irish literature for evidence of features of Irish English, with Sullivan's proceeding one step further by questioning whether literary dialect constitutes a reliable source of linguistic evidence[10]. He comes to the important conclusion that the theatrical portrayals of the variety, on the whole, tend to reflect the dialect quite accurately (cf. Sullivan 1980: 195). This notion will prove to be of interest to the current study.

However, although Sullivan's examination proved fruitful, literary dialect still has its detractors when it comes to accuracy. Many experts criticise it, arguing that writers focus on stereotypical features to poke fun at ethnic groups and those from other regions or social classes. Others denounce its authenticity, claiming that the respellings[11] of pronunciations are erroneous. Still more condemn its inconsistencies. Given these criticisms, it is worth looking at the aforementioned arguments in a little more detail.

It is true that literary dialect often serves a comedic function, making outsiders the butt of the joke. Indeed, Maureen Waters, who has researched the role of the comic Irishman, argues that this is not surprising as "deviation from the standard, whether it be in matters of language or behavior is a subject for humor the world over" (1984: 1).

Nonetheless, not all literary representations of speech make fun of the speakers or are intended to be sources of laughter. In her analysis of the African American English spoken by Jim in *Huckleberry Finn*, Lisa Cohen Minnick points out that although there are "a number of credible critical accounts that argue that Jim is in some ways represented unfairly or stereotypically", if the results of her analysis are considered, "such a representation is not created by way of Twain's depiction of Jim's actual linguistic behavior" (Cohen Minnick 2004: 68). She shows that there is nothing actually inherent in the literary dialect which leads one to conclude that the character of Jim is being stereotyped and, thus, that readers must have drawn such conclusions based solely on Jim's behaviour or perhaps on others' behaviour towards him. She goes on to prove that far from being stereotypical, Twain's literary dialect is actually realistic. This is in keeping with one of Ives' key arguments, which states that although some writers have, of course, tried to exploit the possibilities of humour in their representations of dialect, others have had more noble aims and have used literary dialect as a means of realism – "to show actual speech as actually used" (Ives 1950: 146).

This remark leads to the second criticism levelled at literary dialect, namely that dialect representations are often erroneous and do not show speech as it is actually used. This criticism can prove to be problematic for two reasons: firstly, in order to judge whether these *representations* of the dialect are accurate or not, one must first be very well acquainted with

---

[10] Taniguchi does not engage in questions of literary dialect being authentic, instead acknowledging that the dialogue used in novels and plays is very different from that heard in real life: "The speech of daily life is dull, disjointed, full of repetitions, inconclusive, and in order to have any literary quality, needs a great deal of grafting and pruning" (Taniguchi 1972: i).

[11] According to Wolfram (1991: 262-3), respellings in literary dialect can take two forms. The first type, known as eye dialect, consists of respellings that do not reflect actual phonological differences of real dialects, but instead uses the respellings to simply convey dialect to the reader's eye. Examples include <wunce> for *once*, <duz> for *does*, <nite> for *night* etc. Although the respellings are pronounced exactly the same as the correctly spelled words, the impression the reader gets is that the speaker speaks differently to the norm. The second type of respelling does actually portray real phonological variation, with words like *them* being rewritten as <dem> to reflect the alveolar realisation of the initial consonant, or *easy* being written as <aisy> to show that it is pronounced with [e:]. These are the types of respellings which are generally used with regard to Irish English. For more on the phenomenon of respellings see Wolfram (1991).

the *actual* dialect, that is, one must be aware of the phonological peculiarities of this speech, as well as the appropriate lexicon, grammar structures, etc. What is more, when it comes to respellings, one must also be familiar with the phonology of the person who has written the dialect. After all,

> an author, seeking spellings to represent pronunciations that differ from his own, will select those which 'stand for' the deviant sounds in his own speech type, not in that of other varieties of English. Hence, in order to interpret his dialect spelling, it is necessary to know how these spellings would be pronounced in the region to which the author belongs.
>
> (Ives 1950: 162)

Unless one is aware of this fact, one is likely to misunderstand the author's intention, as is probably the case for many readers who are so quick to dismiss the accuracy of certain authors' literary dialects. Perhaps they are familiar with the pronunciation of the actual dialect, yet the spellings that they themselves would use to represent those sounds are not the same as those the author uses and, thus, they deem the pronunciation to be incorrect. For those native to the author's region, on the other hand, those respelling perfectly capture the intended pronunciation.

This is not to say that all literary dialect is accurate and that it is just the reader who is to blame when it does not appear authentic. On the contrary. In the hands of amateurs, literary dialect can be reduced to a series of clichéd sayings and expressions which in no way reflect reality. This has often been the case in portrayals of Irish English, particularly on the stage. The following quotation from Annelise Truninger's *Paddy and the Paycock* describes how Irish English has been represented for the theatre and highlights its progression, or rather regression, from faithful to facile to farcical.

> There are various ways of disclosing an Irish character's nationality through his speech: he may speak broken English, or pronounce English sounds incorrectly; he may use ordinary English interspersed with Gaelic words, notably exclamations; or use cliché expressions over and over again, especially in emphatic phrases. Each of these devices has been employed by English as well as Irish playwrights for centuries. But right from the beginning these forms were more or less arbitrary. Because they were used as a means to nationalize a character they tended to stagnate and to lose any connection with reality. Finally, they became convenient patterns for any dramatist. Certain striking features were isolated and repeated, and the language degenerated into a stage dialect.
>
> (1976: 20)

Such features are not restricted to the stage, but also appear in novels and short stories. Below is an example from the short story collection *Darby O'Gill and the Good People*, originally from 1926, which features incorrect English forms, such as *sociabler*, English sounds pronounced "incorrectly", such as *niver* and *baste*, the inclusion of Gaelic exclamations, such as *arrah*, *musha* and *agra*[12], and the repetition of clichéd expressions, such as *so it is, so I do*.[13]

---

[12] *Agra* (or *a ghrá*) is a term of endearment which means 'my love'. *Arrah* and *musha* will be addressed with the discourse markers in Chapter 6.

[13] Other features such as imperatives with the progressive form, the use of non-standard verb forms, such as *broke*, the use of the indefinite anterior perfect and the lexical item *lad* will all be examined later.

> Arrah, don't be blaming me, Char-les, me poor lad! Don't look at me that way! Me heart's fair broke, so it is. Haven't I raised you since you were the size of that hand? An' a sociabler, civiler-mannered baste I niver saw. Musha, I wisht you were a cow, so I do; then you wouldn't be a pig an' have to be kilt. Heigh, ho! Sorrows the day! Come along up with me, agra, an' we'll have a petatie.
>
> (Templeton Kavanagh 2003: 106)

A further criticism of literary dialect is the number of inconsistencies which appear in many of the respellings, with a word being spelled one way on one occasion and another the next. These inconsistencies may be intentional or may be attributed to mere slovenliness or an oversight on the part of the writers, most of whom did not have the luxury of modern word processing capabilities with spell check and search functions. Either way, many of the errors, whether intended or not, are not as problematic as one might imagine. In her analysis of the literary dialect employed in Eugene O' Neill's work, Ruth Blackburn acknowledges that on very close examination it is indeed possible to find inconsistencies, but that language by its very nature is not consistent and "therefore, consistency itself cannot be said unreservedly to be a criterion by which to judge a representation of a dialect" (1971: 238).

While references to literary dialect typically refer to novels, short stories and plays, it is my contention that the term literary dialect can also be applied to the dialect used in fiction films. After all, despite how natural the speech in the films may sound, the fact of the matter is that it is scripted in exactly the same manner as other written texts, with the screenwriter employing typical grammatical and lexical features to lend the dialogues more authenticity. Like the playwright[14], the screenwriter can also choose to forego the phonological respellings which often appear in novels or short stories, as in the end it is likely that only the actors will read the script and they are often already trained in applying dialect pronunciations to a given text or else they have a dialect coach on hand to teach them the authentic pronunciation. What exactly "authentic" pronunciation might be is examined next.

---

[14] In the first few pages of *Pygmalion*, for example, Shaw hints at how Elisa speaks: "Ow, eez, yɔ-ooa san, is e? Wal, fewd dan y' d-ooty bawmz a mather should, eed now bettern to spawl a pore gel's flahrzn than ran away athaht pyin. Will ye-oo py me f'them?" and then lets the reader or actor simply continue to apply the pronunciation throughout, writing "here, with apologies, this desperate attempt to represent her dialect without a phonetic alphabet must be abandoned as unintelligible outside London" (2003: 16-17).

3 The notion of authenticity

The terms "authenticity" and "authentic" are frequently used by critics when judging the quality of the representations of dialect or accent in film. However, these terms, and indeed the concept itself, prove to be quite problematic. Let us take, for example, the notion of a dialect or accent that is supposed to be "authentically" Irish. Before examining what exactly such an accent or dialect might sound like, it is necessary to first question what exactly is meant by the term "authentically" Irish. Who or what is "authentically" Irish?

In his book, *Inauthentic*, Vincent J Cheng poses that very question, wondering what it is that defines Irishness. Is one Irish by virtue of being born there[15] (thus exempting immigrants of all ages)? Does one have to live there to be Irish (thus exempting emigrants of all ages)? "What are the essentials or essences needed to qualify as 'Irish'? And who gets to say what qualifies as genuinely Irish?" (Cheng 2004: 28)[16]. Cheng states that we generally have preconceived notions which we ascribe to a place and to a people, attributes which somehow capture their spirit. These can be seen as a checklist of authenticity, on which we cross off our preconceptions as they are fulfilled.

> I daresay that we each carry with us certain personal assumptions about the Irish spirit, such as Gaelic inflections and influences; the rural and peasant West; the Connemara hills; folk traditions; pub culture and a communal life of bibulous, even drunken, joviality; music, dance, and the arts; the gift of gab [sic]; an emotional and temperamental, sometimes sentimental mind-set; a brooding and poetic imagination; a quality of mists, fairies, spirits, and an ineffable mystique or otherworldliness. All of these and more are perhaps part of the cultural baggage we take with us on our travels to Ireland, looking for the real, the authentic, the hidden Ireland.
> (Cheng 2004: 29)

Based on Cheng's criteria, the film *Darby O'Gill and the Little People* (Robert Stevenson, 1959) would appear to encapsulate Irishness, as all of the aforementioned features are present in abundance in that movie. However, in reality, *Darby O'Gill and the Little People* is seen by most Irish people as the epitome of Stage Irish hokum[17], which would imply that the "cultural baggage" which Cheng and other non-Irish people use to shape their perception of Ireland and Irishness is invariably different from that of the Irish themselves. Or is it? While I think I can say with some degree of certainty that "mists, fairies, spirits" etc.

---

[15] It would appear that being born in Ireland is apparently not enough to guarantee "authenticity" in the eyes of film audiences. Pierce Brosnan is a case in point. The Irish actor was born and raised in Navan, Co. Meath but moved to London at the age of 11, where he changed his accent to fit into his new surroundings – "to sound like one of the lads" (O'Connor 1996: 125). It worked, so much so that the actor, who is best known for playing the role of the suave and sophisticated British spy James Bond, is not seen as Irish, not even by (or especially not by) Irish people. In her book *Acting Irish in Hollywood*, Ruth Barton discusses the problems the Navan-born actor encountered when playing the role of the Irish character Rory O'Manion in the mini-series, *The Manions of America* (ABC, 1981), stating that "the actor's authenticity in the part is complicated by his accent [...]; for Brosnan has never managed to acquire a convincing local Irish accent" (Barton 2006: 183). Other commentators have been less diplomatic in their evaluation of Brosnan's Irishness and Barton quotes one *Irish Times* critic whose review of the film *Laws of Attraction* (Peter Howitt, 2004) is particularly stinging, citing Brosnan as "the English lad who thinks he's from Naas or Newbridge or wherever" (Barton 2006: 197).
[16] For further discussion on defining national identity, see: O'Mahony and Delanty (1998: 2-3).
[17] Indeed, the label Darby O'Gill is frequently used pejoratively in Ireland when referring to stereotypical portrayals of the Irish. Film critic Stephen Walsh describes it as "a catch-all put-down designed to elicit a knee-jerk reaction to foreigners telling stories set in Ireland and, supposedly, making a holy show of us all" (Walsh 1999: 17).

would not feature on Irish people's checklist of Irishness, some of the other elements are more difficult to dismiss, and deserve closer inspection, particularly the role of "the rural and peasant West".

History would suggest that also among the Irish there is a commonly-held belief that the rural West of Ireland is the quintessence of Irishness. This ideology was fostered at the beginning of the twentieth century by Douglas Hyde's Gaelic League movement, whose members essentially set out the terms of what even today constitutes Irish identity, with regard to culture, the Irish language, Gaelic sports, traditional music and dance, and so on. These parameters of Irish identity were refined even further by the "Irish Ireland" movement, which was led by Daniel Corkery and which "tended to exclude as un-Irish any thing or anyone that lay outside of its categories of Irishness" (Cheng 2004: 42). If, as Corkery suggested, the real "Irish Ireland" was "a peasant nation, with no urban existence and no middle class" (Foster 1987: 195), then there would clearly be no place for cities, or for those who lived in them, in the real Ireland.

This understanding of "rural Ireland as real Ireland" (Kiberd 1996: 5) also inevitably found its expression in the arts, with the Abbey Theatre Company, also known as the Irish Players, being founded to "present an authentic image of Irishness"[18] (Barton 2004: 23). The following excerpt from an interview with one of the Irish Players, Fred O'Donovan, reflects the commonly-held opinion on what was thought to exemplify the "real Irishman" of that time:

> The Irish Players wanted to put on the stage the real Irishman of today – to reveal the real Irish conditions and real Irish character. Now, to reach the real Irish character, the poets and dramatists had to deal with the life of the peasantry, those who lived close to the soil and obtained their subsistence from it. The upper classes are veneered with English thought and manners, hence few plays which the Irish Players have presented deal with life in the cities – with business and social circles.
>
> (O'Donovan 1988: 101)

According to Cheng, the result of such thinking was "a construction of Irish national identity around the idealization of a rural and primitive West, the sentimentalized national mythology about rural Ireland as the authentic Ireland" (Cheng 2004: 48). This in turn implies that "the real thing, the authentic culture and ethos of the tribe/people, can be found only in the rural and primitive countryside of an Aran or a Connemara, and certainly not in the modern cityscape of a Dublin" (Cheng 2004: 48-9)[19].

The implications of such a statement are enormous and also controversial. If the Irish (and others) do indeed regard rural Ireland, and, particularly, the primitive West, as the "authentic" Ireland, then one could be forgiven for thinking that by extension the "authentic" Irish dialect or accent must be that of rural Ireland[20]. This, however, would imply that all urban accents and dialects (and those who speak them) are inauthentic and thus not really "Irish". It would also mean that only films set in rural Ireland like *The Field* (Jim Sheridan,

---

[18] The Irish Players also brought their brand of authentic Irishness to a number of films produced by Ireland's first indigenous film company, the Film Company of Ireland (cf. Barton 2004: 23-33).
[19] Of course, the notion of the rural or pastoral as authentic is by no means merely an Irish phenomenon. British poets in the First World War regularly extolled the authentic virtues of rural England.
[20] This notion is reinforced by Willie Fay, the director of the original Abbey Theatre company, "beating the Dublin accents out of his players", thereby forcing them "to learn to talk like peasants" (O'Toole 1985: 112).

1990), *The Quiet Man* (John Ford, 1952) and *Ryan's Daughter* (David Lean, 1970) are bona fide, while films dealing with urban life, such as *The Commitments* (Alan Parker, 1991), *The General* (John Boorman, 1998) or *Angela's Ashes* (Alan Parker, 1999) are somehow fake. Such statements are, of course, preposterous and should highlight the aforementioned problems inherent in the whole concept of authenticity.

Even if we, for argument's sake, assume that all Irish actors (and for that matter, all Irish people) are equally "authentic", then we are still only touching the tip of the iceberg regarding the authenticity of Irish English being spoken in film. As one could expect, when it comes to the plethora of non-Irish actors who assume an accent for their roles in Irish films, then the concept of authenticity becomes even more absurd and murky.

Firstly, no matter how good their performances are, non-Irish actors passing themselves off as Irish characters are still not Irish. Their Irish English is therefore not authentic, not genuine. Their performances amount to little more than imitation, and no matter how good an imitation is, it remains fake and, thus, not "authentic". After all, a copy of a Van Gogh remains a copy no matter how indistinguishable it is from the real thing. Thus, an impersonation of an Irish accent is merely an impersonation and cannot be described as "authentic".

A second problem arises when people ascribe degrees of authenticity to performances of dialects or accents. They may speak of a certain British or American actor as having a very authentic Irish accent or perhaps suggest that one actor's speech is more authentic than another's, maybe even the most authentic they have ever heard. However, in his analysis of authenticity and authentication in language learning, Stuart Amor correctly states that "there can be no comparative and superlative of the adjective authentic in the sense of genuineness" (2002: 97)[21]. Something is either authentic or it is not. There are no shades of authenticity. Bearing this in mind, if we return to the Van Gogh analogy, two paintings by the artist must therefore be regarded as equally authentic, in that they both stem from his brush, even if we may find one to be more typical of his style and thus label it as more "Van Goghian". The same applies when people assert that one Irish accent is more authentic or more "Irish" than another; what they are actually referring to is how typical it is of what they believe Irish English to be. This is in keeping with an idea set out by Sarah Rubidge in her essay on authenticity in the performing arts, in which she claims that authenticity is "not a property *of*, but something we ascribe *to* a performance" (1996: 219). This notion is also very much reflective of Eleanor Rosch's notion of prototypes (Rosch 1973 and 1978). She suggests that if our concept of a bird is a creature which is small, has feathers and is able to fly, then a robin is a better example of a bird than an ostrich, which is big and cannot fly. By the same token, if we believe Irish English to sound a certain way or to consist of expressions like *Top of the mornin'* and *Begorrah* because that is what existing representations in the media have led us to expect, then performances which sound that way and which feature those expressions will be deemed authentic by us. Those, on the other hand, which do not meet our perceptions or expectations of what Irish English is will be judged to be unauthentic and we will not accept them as credible.

---

[21] He is echoing the words of Werner Beile, whom he also quotes, who also stated that genuineness is an absolute quality: "Verschiedene Grade von Authentizität [= genuineness] kann es aber nicht geben." Beile, Werner quoted in Amor (2002: 97).

This was one of the conflicts which became apparent with the release of the movie *Far and Away* (Ron Howard, 1993), where opinions regarding the performances of both Tom Cruise and Nicole Kidman varied greatly on either side of the Atlantic. In the United States, the film was felt to realistically portray Irish speech, no doubt because it met the expectations of an audience raised on what one British magazine has ironically called that "wonderfully fantastical vocabulary by which American cinema has consistently celebrated Irishness from *The Quiet Man* to *Finian's Rainbow*" (Strick 1993: 53)[22]. In addition, American audiences were taken in by the Irish accents of the two leads. Indeed, on two occasions in her handbook aimed at teaching actors to perform dialect roles, American dialect coach[23] Ginny Kopf describes the accents of the lead characters as "convincing" and "admirable" and recommends that students watch the film as it is "an excellent film to study the culture and attitudes of the Irish people" (2003: 50 and 131). In Ireland, on the other hand, the film is widely regarded as Stage Irishness incarnate, "with its clichés and speech anachronisms" (Malcolm 1992: 30), and Tom Cruise's accent, the self-same one which Kopf had lauded as convincing and admirable, was in fact voted the worst Irish accent in the movies in a poll conducted by an Irish radio station in 2006[24]. This disparity clearly indicates that the way a performance is received is strongly influenced by what the viewer accepts as "authentic".

As we have seen, these perceptions of what is authentic can be very different depending on an audience's experience and expectations. Therefore, filmmakers may run the risk of disappointing Irish audiences if the accents or dialects in Irish films are not accurate, or of alienating non-Irish audiences if they are, but are difficult to understand. Since films are generally produced to be exposed to as large an audience as possible, the last thing filmmakers want is to alienate audiences just because the actors are speaking some incomprehensible dialect[25] and thus in order to ease comprehension for a wider audience,

---

[22] Although *Finian's Rainbow* (Francis Ford Coppola, 1968) is not included in the film corpus, as it is set in the United States, it is worth noting that *Glocca Morra*, the emigrants' fictional Irish homeland in the movie, has become somewhat of a byword for "Oirishness", and may appear in reviews of other movies (cf. Dwyer 1998, Ingle 2007). The use of the name of a fictional town as a critique of a false image of national identity is not unique to an Irish context. The same applies to *Brigadoon*, the hamlet from the Scottish movie of the same name (Vincente Minnelli, 1954), which stands for a fantastical notion of Scottishness. According to McArthur, the name *Brigadoon* appears "regularly in Scottish broadsheet journalism, often in contexts quite unconnected with cinema, as shorthand for all that is twee and regressive" (2003: 3).
[23] The role of a dialect coach is described in greater detail in Chapter 8.
[24] The poll surveyed listeners to the *Breakfast Express* show on Dublin's youth radio station *Spin* and the results were published on the *Irish Independent* affiliate http://www.unison.ie on January 26, 2006. (Retrieved: January 30, 2006).
[25] Of course, this is less of a problem in certain film markets, such as the German one, which tend to dub films into the audience's mother tongue. Nevertheless, problems can still occur when trying to translate dialect or heavily accented pronunciation into a foreign language for the purposes of dubbing or subtitling. Indeed, this is even evident in the English subtitling of some of the Irish films featured in this book. For example, compare the two versions of the following exchange from *When the Sky Falls* (John MacKenzie, 2000). It takes place between a drug addict and some Dublin thugs, one of whom is named Keegan, but called Keego, the familiarizing suffix *-o* being common in colloquial Dublin speech. It appears on the soundtrack as follows (my transcription):
Thug 1: *Ah look who it is.*
Thug 2: *Go on, ya waster!*
Drug Addict: *Alright, Keego?*
Thug 1: *You alright, tinfoil head?*
Thug 2: *Ya scumbag ya, keep walkin'.*
The subtitles, however, read as follows:
Thug 1: *Look who it is.*

dialect and accent are often modified. To that end, dialect coach Robert Blumenfeld offers the following words of advice to actors (note again, however, the troubling reference to degrees of authenticity!):

> As an actor you must be understood by your audience. Do not, for instance, do such a thoroughly authentic Cockney or Glasgow accent that most of your audience will find everything you say utterly incomprehensible. Instead do an authentic-sounding version, and always keep your diction clear by articulating consonants strongly.
> (Blumenfeld 2000: 24)

Blumenfeld's words are echoed by a fellow dialect coach who suggests that "sometimes you have to "cheat" and do a lighter or more generic accent if you think your audience would have trouble easily accepting the true one" (Kopf 2003: 51)[26]. However, these suggestions seem to imply that authentic automatically means incomprehensible, and that authenticity and intelligibility are mutually exclusive. Dialect coach Poll Moussoulides states that it is not necessary to sacrifice authenticity for the sake of being understood and he stresses that the focus should be on intelligibility or clarity as he calls it.

> You're not reducing the authenticity to get the clarity. There is that fear that you lose one for the other one. You can find a working-class Dublin accent which is clear, you can find a working-class Cork accent which is clear, you can find a rural Tipperary accent which is clear, but, of course, you'll also find people where you can't understand a word they're saying. One isn't more 'authentic' than the other, but for the purposes of a film, clarity must be a priority.
> (Personal communication 2005)

A further reason why authenticity is a problematic concept when analysing speech in film is that film dialogue is basically just another form of literary dialect, and thus the speech we hear cannot really be regarded as "authentic".

> Speech, after all is regularly non-fluent, with numerous breakdowns and minor repairs, as any genuine transcription reveals; by contrast, literary representations are invariably polished and idealised reflecting only a selection of salient markers. Literary dialect is thus never unplanned spontaneous speech.
> (Kirk 1999: 47)

If there can be any doubt about that, then Sarah Kozloff's *Overhearing Film Dialogue* dramatically shows just to what extent film dialogue differs from spontaneous everyday speech.

Thug 2: *On your ways.*
Drug Addict: *All right, Keego.*
Thug 1: *You are, rude tinfoil head.*
Thug 2: *You scumbag, keep walking.*
Clearly, the person responsible for subtitling had difficulty understanding the Dublin pronunciation and, thus, two of the five lines of the exchange are incorrect.

[26] A fine example of this school of thought is evident in the case of the Newcastle-set film *The One and Only* (Simon Cellan Jones, 2002). According to the local newspaper *The Northern Echo*, the producers were so worried about foreign audiences not understanding the dialogue in the movie that they hired a dialect coach, Majella Hurley, "to create the 'Geordie Light' accent". Producer Leslie Udwin later apologised to locals for having made such a compromise regarding the language, but justified it by saying: "we believed we could either please local people and lose an international audience, or make it accessible to everyone." http://archive.thenorthernecho.co.uk/2003/2/20/103201.html (Retrieved: June 10, 2008).

> In narrative films, dialogue may strive mightily to imitate natural conversation, but it is always an imitation. It has been scripted, written and rewritten, censored, polished, rehearsed, and performed. Even when lines are improvised on set, they have been spoken by impersonators, judged, approved, and allowed to remain. Then all dialogue is recorded, edited, mixed, underscored, and played through stereophonic speakers with Dolby sound. The actual hesitations, repetitions, digressions, grunts, interruptions, and mutterings of everyday speech have either been pruned away, or, if not, deliberately included.
>
> (Kozloff 2000: 18)

Thus, based on this information, film dialogue would appear to be anything but "authentic", whatever that means.

Having seen the problems which arise through the term "authenticity"[27], I would suggest that a more appropriate term be found, one which is not absolute, but which offers degrees of comparison. This is in keeping with the work of Regina Bendix, who also advocated the removal of, what she jocularly termed, "the A-word" from "the vocabulary of the emerging global script" (cf. Bendix 1997: x and 7).

For the purposes of this study and for future similar works, I propose replacing the word "authenticity" with another "A-word", namely "accuracy". Unlike "authenticity", it stakes no claims to originality, suggesting fidelity instead. Indeed, in this regard, a native accent (or dialect) can be compared with a text which is to be translated: just as a translation of a text is not the original but can be rendered with greater or lesser degrees of fidelity to the original, depending on how "accurately" it is translated, so too can an actor's accurate accent (or dialect) be regarded as nothing more than a copy, albeit a faithful one.

---

[27] The problems arising from the term "authentic" and "authenticity" are perennial topics in academia, with at least three new books on the topic being published in Germany alone in 2007 (see Sponsel, Knaller and Fischer-Lichte). However, the issue also entered public consciousness in December 2007 when the Hamburg Museum of Ethnology became embroiled in a scandal for unwittingly exhibiting fake Chinese terracotta warriors. The Centre of Chinese Arts and Culture (CCAC) in Leipzig, which had supplied the exhibits and guaranteed the museum that they were "authentic", was forced to explain itself when it turned out that the figures were merely copies. A spokesperson claimed that the CCAC had never used the term "original" and that the contract with the museum had merely stipulated that the figures would be "authentic". "For us, 'authentic' means ceramic, life-sized and comparable with the originals," he said. This strange scandal caused *Spiegel* magazine to ask the questions on everybody's lips regarding what effectively had been reduced to semantic hair-splitting: "What does it mean to be 'authentic'? How is that different from 'original'? And can a fake also be authentic?" http://www.spiegel.de/international/germany/0,1518,523341,00.html (Retrieved: June 10, 2008) The language in these questions echoes that used by Umberto Eco over thirty years earlier in his seminal text "Travels in Hyperreality". There he describes the phenomenon of Ripley's "Believe It or Not" Museums, writing that "some of the curiosities in the Ripley's Museums are unique; others, displayed in several museums at once, are said to be authentic duplicates. Still others are copies" (Eco 1975/1986: 15). The confusion in such terminology is also tackled by Rouvel (1997).

4 Irish English

4.1 Terminology

When it comes to labelling the type of English which is spoken in Ireland, one must tread carefully through what has become a potential semantic minefield. Terms such as *brogue*, *Anglo-Irish* and *Hiberno-English* have each found favour with linguists and lay people alike at some point or another, yet have all in turn been displaced and replaced by a seemingly more appropriate term, the most recent of which is *Irish English*.

The term *brogue* first appeared in 1689 (cf. Bliss 1977: 7-19); yet, from the beginning, it posed a problem by virtue of the fact that it referred specifically to the particularly Irish pronunciation of English[28] and, thus, completely ignored the other features of the variety, namely morpho-syntax and lexis, which so clearly set it apart from Standard English[29]. Not only that, but in addition to describing an Irish accent, *brogue* also refers to the "exaggerated stereotype of such an accent" (Wells 1982b: 434) and, thus, possesses inherent negative value judgements. These negative associations towards the Irish pronunciation of English are often exacerbated by the folk etymology which is attributed to the word *brogue* as coming from the Irish *bróg*, meaning 'shoe', and which suggests that Irish people speak their words so clumsily that it sounds as though they are speaking with a shoe in their mouths[30]. In the following excerpt, Jonathan Swift expresses the nature of the prejudice which Irish speakers of English encountered:

> How is it possible that a gentleman who lives in those parts where the *townlands* (as they call them) of his estate produce such odious sounds from the mouth, the throat, and the nose, can be able to repeat the words without dislocating every muscle that is used in speaking, and without applying the same tone to all other words, in every language he understands; as it is plainly to be observed not only in those people of the better sort who live in Galway and the Western parts, but in most counties of Ireland?...What we call the Irish *brogue* is no sooner discovered, than it makes the deliverer, in the last degree, ridiculous and despised; and from such a mouth, an Englishman expects nothing but bulls, blunders and follies.
>
> (Swift 1728: 346)

The term *Anglo-Irish*, which replaced *brogue*, enjoyed much more longevity and was retained until relatively recently, as it was deemed to be more apt insofar as it was not disparaging and it served as an umbrella term for all of the salient features of the variety. However, it too came with its fair share of baggage, both political and semantic. Firstly, the term *Anglo-Irish* is quite a loaded one and has long been used to refer to both the literature written in English by Irish authors and to political dealings between Ireland and England, as in the Anglo-Irish Treaty of 1921 or the Anglo-Irish Agreement of 1985. Secondly, the term

---

[28] The Oxford English Dictionary (OED) defines *brogue* as "a strongly-marked dialectal pronunciation or accent; now particularly used of the peculiarities that generally mark the English speech of Ireland" (OED s.v. brogue, n. 3). All references to the OED refer to the online edition.
[29] For the purpose of this study, Standard English refers to the dialect of English with the greatest prestige and the one which is generally used in books and newspapers (cf. Trudgill 1994: 5)
[30] An alternative etymology suggested that *brogue* means 'impediment', and that it came from *barróg* which is homophonous with *bróg* in Munster Irish. However, research indicates that the word for 'impediment' is actually *bachlóg* and that the term *brogue* to describe speech is known to Irish speakers in Munster only as an English word (cf. Murphy 1943: 231-6).

itself is actually a misnomer. As Hickey points out, "strictly speaking, the term refers to a variety of Irish, if one interprets the modifier 'Anglo-' as qualifying the head 'Irish'" (2002: xiii). Bearing these facts in mind, one cannot help but wonder today how the term ever survived so long in the first place.

To sidestep these problems, that is, to find a term which had no previous connotations and which did not actually refer to a variety of Irish, scholars such as Alan Bliss began to use the term *Hiberno-English* in the 1970s[31]. The term, which simply combined a form of the Latin word for Ireland, *Hibernia*, with the word *English*, aimed to clear up the confusion once and for all. Sadly, and perhaps inevitably, this was not the case, as the Latin origin of the word proved too perplexing for many people and did not necessarily suggest connotations of Ireland. What is more, a debate between linguists arose as to what they were actually labelling. Some saw *Anglo-Irish* and *Hiberno-English* as completely different varieties and felt it was therefore totally inappropriate to replace the former term with the latter. Patrick. L. Henry, for example, regarded *Anglo-Irish* as referring to the rural variety of English comprised of Irish and English or Irish and Scots, while for him *Hiberno-English* applied to the urban standard variety which can be traced back to the British settlers of the 17th century (cf. Henry 1977: 20-36). Loreto Todd, on the other hand, took the entirely opposite view and suggested that *Anglo-Irish* described the varieties derived from English, whereas *Hiberno-English* related to those varieties which were strongly influenced by Irish (1992: 529-30). The majority of linguists either agreed with Henry or were of the opinion that no distinction between the varieties was really necessary when trying to find a cover term for the English spoken in Ireland. Thus, the search for a better term continued.

In the end, in keeping with the terminology used to describe other national varieties of English worldwide, such as Australian English or Canadian English, the term *Irish English* was born. This term succeeds where the others failed: it fulfils the criteria of being an all encompassing umbrella term, unlike *brogue*, but does not have the ambiguity or the potential of complete bewilderment inherent in *Anglo-Irish* and *Hiberno-English*[32] respectively.

However, even this seemingly perfect label for English as it is spoken in Ireland needs to be qualified further, since it does not account for the fact that two main varieties of *Irish English*, with very different origins, exist on the island. These are *Southern Irish English* and *Northern Irish English* respectively. A brief look at the history of the English language in Ireland will illustrate the differences in origins of these varieties and by extension the differences between their manifestations even today.

4.2 The history of the English language in Ireland

The English language is traditionally said to have been introduced to Ireland in 1169, when a band of Anglo-Norman soldiers from Pembroke in Wales landed in Wexford at the

---

[31] Although the term *Hiberno-English* gained currency in the 1970s, Hickey (2007: 4) observes that the label had already occasionally been used in the past by T.F. O'Rahilly (1932) and Arthur Hutson (1947).

[32] Some scholars, however, still prefer to use the term Hiberno-English. In an interview with Carolina Amador Moreno, Terence Dolan, explained the logic behind this: "The term *Irish English* is a misnomer, because it works on the principle that 'Irish English' is similar to Australian English, American English or Canadian English, which it isn't. English was transported to these countries, but did not mix with the native languages. In Ireland, Hiberno-English means that you have two languages in a kind of unruly shotgun marriage together, fighting all the time over the centuries, for syntax, pronunciation, vocabulary, idiom. 'Hiberno-English', therefore, exactly symbolises this very healthy connexion between the two disparate and independent languages" (Amador Moreno 2007: 214).

invitation of Dermot MacMurrough, the former King of Leinster. MacMurrough, who was engaged in a battle with rival kings could find no military support in Ireland and was forced to seek help from overseas, in the form of the Anglo-Normans (cf. Simms 1989: 55-6).

Although these Norman lords and soldiers themselves spoke French, their entourage were English-speaking English, Welsh and Flemish, who spoke a southwestern English dialect (cf. Barry 1982: 84). Despite this, neither English nor French were really able to establish themselves as languages among the common people of Ireland in the 12th and 13th centuries, due to the fact that the very people who brought them there became "more Irish than the Irish themselves"[33], adopting Irish dress, customs and, most importantly, the Irish language.

To counteract this negative assimilation of the Anglo-Normans into Irish society, the Statutes of Kilkenny were introduced by the English government in 1366. They aimed to force everybody, including the French-speaking lords and the native Irish to speak English and, through a system of discriminatory laws[34], hoped to ensure that a social gulf developed between the native population and the "English", as they were now known. However, the Statutes proved impossible to enforce and "the English language continued to give way to the Irish" (Bliss 1979: 13).

The situation remained so until the 16th century when the English began a process of "plantations", whereby settlers from England were relocated in Ireland. The first of these plantations, in Laois and Offaly from 1549 to 1557 and in Munster from 1586 to 1592, did not prove to be successful, as once again the English were either assimilated into the Irish communities or, if they were upper class, distanced themselves to such an extent from the local population that their language never took hold. However, in the 17th century, two large scale plantations of farmers and soldiers were undertaken and these actions profoundly shaped what is considered to be Irish English today.

From about 1607, James I orchestrated the "Plantation of Ulster" in the north of the country, in which he transported large numbers of Scottish soldier-farmers and settled them in the northeastern parts of Ulster, while settlers from England occupied central and southern areas of the province. Kallen notes that "these settlement patterns are still a powerful force in determining dialect differentiation in the zone of Ulster speech" (1997: 14).

The rest of Ireland did not escape the effects of plantation, either. Following Oliver Cromwell's military victory over Ireland in 1649-1650, he was obliged to reward those who had fought for him. Lacking the money to pay his soldiers wages, Cromwell instead decided to offer them tracts of land in Ireland which were to be taken from the Irish natives and the "Old English". Those he displaced he famously told to go "to Hell or to Connacht" and forced them to accept the far-inferior, infertile land in the western part of the country, while their property was settled by those loyal to him.

According to Bliss, the Cromwellian Settlement was instrumental in establishing the English language in Ireland. It ensured that the landowners in three of the four provinces were English-speaking and that as a result their tenants and servants had to learn the language in order to communicate with their masters. A further consequence was that:

---

[33] This oft cited description of the descendents of the Anglo-Norman invaders comes from the Latin "Hiberniores ipsis hibernis" (cf. Hickey 2002: 9).
[34] The Statutes made it unlawful for the English and Irish to intermarry, and for the English to sell food or horses to the Irish in times of war or weapons in times of peace (cf. Simms 1989: 88).

The masters themselves, isolated as they were from frequent converse with their own kind, were soon affected by the gaelicized English of the native Irish with whom they spoke every day, as Swift's evidence shows. The English spoken in most parts of Ireland today is descended from the English of Cromwell's planters, and since the early part of the eighteenth century no other type of English has been spoken in any part of Ireland except in Ulster.

(Bliss 1979: 19-20)

Be that as it may, the survival of the English language in Ireland was in no way guaranteed in the 18th century, but, having learnt from their previous mistakes, the English were certainly not going to take the risk again that the settlers in Ireland would become "more Irish than the Irish themselves". They therefore introduced further punitive measures, along the lines of the Statutes of Kilkenny in order to again create some sort of gulf between the natives and the new settlers. The Penal Laws or Popery Bills of 1703-4 were aimed at Catholics, who at that time comprised 75% of the population but owned only 14% of the land, and ensured that they remained excluded from all areas of public life by refusing them, among other things, the right to vote or the right to education (cf. Simms 1989: 164-5).

Since they were barred from formal education, Catholics were forced to seek their schooling elsewhere and so they turned to what are known as "hedge schools". As the name suggests, classes, which were taught by wandering school-masters, were held in the open air in order to allow pupils and teachers the chance to make a quick getaway, should the authorities appear (cf. Hickey 2002: 15). Despite what they may have thought of the English, the Catholic Irish still recognised the importance of the English language for social mobility and, thus, English was also taught at these schools. However, the school masters were very often self taught and therefore the English they taught often bore the marks of Irish interference in syntax and phonology, or involved mispronunciation or unorthodox stress patterning for unknown lexemes[35]. These "errors" were perpetuated further and passed down from learner to learner, resulting in many of the distinctive features which are associated with Irish English even today.

When the Catholic Irish finally were allowed access to formal education after the passing of the Act of Union in 1800 and the establishment of the National School system in the 1830s, one of the preconditions was that they be taught through English, with any use of Irish being severely punished. Children who spoke Irish in school had a stick, known as a *tally-stick* or a *bata scóir*, hung around their necks and each time they dared speak their native tongue the teacher carved a notch into the stick. At the end of the day, these notches were tallied up and the child was duly punished (cf. Dolan 2006: 234)[36].

It would be incorrect to assume, however, that the English language was only able to establish itself in Ireland on the basis of such draconian measures as those just described. The fact of the matter is that, as already mentioned, the desire for social mobility was essential in

---

[35] For more, see Hickey (2004b: 70). Examples of such unorthodox stressing patterns are evident in the Irish English pronunciations of the words *discipline* (second syllable), *committee* (first syllable), *concentrate* and *educate* (final syllable) (cf. Pennington 1996: 133).

[36] Dolan further adds that "in Mayo, a piece of string, with knots as markers, was used as an alternative to the stick." In Donegal, a *cingulum*, a thick straw collar resembling that worn by a donkey or horse was used to humiliate those who spoke Irish. An example of a pupil being punished in this manner is visible in the film *The Secret of Roan Inish* (John Sayles, 1993).

encouraging the Irish natives to learn English. This was never so apparent, or so necessary, as during the Great Famine.

When potato crops failed annually in the mid 1840s due to a potato blight, millions of Irish people were left without their main form of sustenance. One million died of hunger or disease and another million emigrated, mostly to Britain, Australia, Canada, and particularly the USA (cf. Foster 1989: 161-212 and 202-03). Faced with the choice between death and emigration, those who could afford it chose the latter and realised then, at the latest, the importance of being able to speak English. Their own native tongue, on the other hand, was becoming "increasingly associated with rural backwardness, poverty and an unsophisticated peasantry" (Edwards 1984: 494) and it soon began to fall into decline. This shift in the linguistic status quo was certainly not welcomed by everybody, and, indeed, in some circles this negative attitude to the English language reverberates even today. This is reflected in John Montague's poem *A Grafted Tongue*, which laments the negative impact the English language has had in Ireland:

> To grow
> a second tongue, as
> harsh a humiliation
> as twice to be born.

The poet then goes on to describe the aforementioned tally-stick as being:

> Like a bell
> on a cow, a hobble
> on a straying goat.

(1974: 344-45)

However, Montague's sentiment aside, the reality was that it was the Irish language itself at that time which was the "hobble", the stumbling block, which impeded the progress of the Irish, both in Ireland and, especially, in the English-speaking countries they emigrated to.

Therefore, it is no surprise that after the Famine there was a gradual move towards bilingualism, and then later towards what has essentially become English monolingualism. The Irish language has, thus, been relegated to merely a peripheral role in Irish society, and not even the fact that it is nominally the first language of the State or that it is a compulsory subject in school can change that.[37]

The English language, on the other hand, has continued to thrive in Ireland. Just as it was instrumental in affording people the prospect of upward mobility via emigration, both

---

[37] On January 1, 2007, Irish became an official working language of the European Union much to the dismay of many taxpayers, both in Ireland and abroad. The implementation of the language across all EU institutions cost an estimated €3.5 million. The belief by many people that this gesture was a waste of time and money was underscored a year later in an *Irish Examiner* report which noted that "Less than 30 minutes of Irish was spoken in the European Parliament in the first full year as an official language – working out at a little less than €13,000 a minute". The report continued that the parliament's four interpreters of Irish cost €30,000 a month, and that "two interpreters are needed at a time in case there is an 'overflow', or two MEPs speaking Irish in succession". However, "records show that an overflow is unlikely, with an average of 30 seconds of Irish spoken for each day the parliament sits" (Mary Regan, *Irish Examiner*, 21 January, 2008). For more information, see: http://archives.tcm.ie/irishexaminer/2008/01/21/story53174.asp (Retrieved: January 23, 2008).

after the Famine and throughout the twentieth century, it was also crucial in the rise of the "Celtic Tiger" - Ireland's economic upturn in the 1990s, with the presence of the country's educated English-speaking workforce often being cited by major US companies as one of the main reasons for locating there.

However, the variety of English spoken by Irish people is now also under threat, with the increasing influence of American and British English in the media and it remains to be seen whether or not the typical features of Irish English will endure.

4.3 Irish English in the context of this study

In the majority of studies on English as it is spoken in Ireland, scholars have divided the island of Ireland into two linguistic areas, that of Ulster English and that of Southern English, for the reasons outlined above, namely that the varieties display considerable differences both in their origins and in their manifestations today. For the purpose of the present study, a similar distinction will be made. Unfortunately, on this occasion, due to space constraints, the northern varieties will have to be excluded from the analysis[38]. I am, nevertheless, under no illusions that what remains is one homogenous dialect with uniform features or pronunciation. Indeed, at least six distinct accents are generally recognised for the island of Ireland, five of which belong to the category of Southern Irish English.[39] Having said that, there is widespread agreement among linguists that Southern Irish English dialects have more similarities than differences. Bliss, for example, has observed that "perhaps the most remarkable feature of the present-day Anglo Irish dialects is their relative uniformity. Of course there are regional differences; it is usually possible to recognise from a man's accent what part of the country he comes from. Yet in the three southern provinces, at least, there are fewer basic differences than one might expect" (1977: 18-19).

Thus, in keeping with the work set out by Bliss (1977), Wells (1982a/b) and Hickey (2004a), I will focus on the features which these southern varieties share and which together define what we regard today to be Southern Irish English. It should be noted that wherever the term Irish English is used in the following, it refers to the southern variety, unless expressed otherwise.

---

[38] For an excellent overview of English in the north of Ireland, see Harris (1984b: 115-34).
[39] Delahunty lists these five as: Dublin, Cork, Kerry, Midlands and Standard Hiberno-English. The sixth refers to Northern Ireland and Donegal (cf. 1977: 127-149).

5 Methodology

5.1 Establishing the corpus

In order to examine the accuracy of representations of Irish English in film, it was first necessary to establish an appropriate corpus. To that end, I used a process of elimination which excluded all films which fit into the following categories:

Documentaries

Filled as they are with examples of natural, spontaneous speech samples, documentaries would certainly appear to be perfect sources of material for a linguist intending to examine dialect in film. After all, natural[40], spontaneous speech is one of the foundations of linguistic research, with linguists regularly recording such speech in the field. The analysis of documentaries would therefore certainly be in keeping with standard linguistic practice, in that the linguist's tape-recorder would merely be replaced by a camera, and the resulting authentic speech samples – the "overheard exchange" of a fly-on-the-wall documentary or the "testimony" of an interview[41] – would be akin to those found in the field.

However, seeing as this study is concerned with the artistic representation of speech, rather than with natural and spontaneous speech itself, films which typically feature the latter are excluded from the corpus.

Silent Films

Since this book examines Irish English speech in film, it snould go without saying that one can automatically exclude films in which no speech can be heard[42]. By eliminating such films, one also establishes a time frame into which the films can be put, namely from 1930 (when sound films or "talkies" were first produced[43]) to the present day.

Irish Language Films

As in the case of silent films, the fact that this study focuses on Irish English in film means that Irish language films can be dismissed.

Films not set in Ireland

Irish characters regularly appear in films set abroad, often in the roles of police officers, firemen, priests, nuns, chamber maids, gangsters, terrorists, boxers, politicians or any of the other walks of life in which the Irish diaspora have tended to find their calling. While many of these figures may be "fresh-off-the-boat" Irishmen and women, others are second or third generation Irish and, thus, of no interest from the perspective of Irish English, as their speech will be very much influenced by their upbringing abroad. Therefore, to avoid any confusion and to limit the corpus even further, films which are not set in Ireland will be excluded[44].

---

[40] The term "natural" is used quite loosely here, of course; one should not lose sight of Labov's "observer's paradox" that people modify their language when they are conscious that they are being observed (cf. Labov 1978: 209 or Chambers 1995: 19).

[41] These terms are taken from Corner (1996: 29).

[42] In theory, one could, of course, analyse the language in the inter-titles for elements of Irish English grammar, lexis and possibly phonology. However, like the commentary in documentaries, the language of such inter-titles is often formal and consists of expository information rather than dialogue.

[43] See: Rockett, Kevin (ed.). *The Irish Filmography. Fiction Films 1896-1996*. Red Mountain Media, Dublin, 1996: iii.

[44] *Far and Away* (Ron Howard, 1992) is somewhat of an exception. Although only 40 minutes of the 2 hour 14 minute film are set in Ireland, those 40 minutes are all at the beginning and establish that the protagonists are indeed Irish. Therefore, despite the fact that the film is ostensibly about emigrants to the United States, it has

Films set in Ulster

Due to the fact that this study explores southern varieties of Irish English, those films which are set in areas where the northern varieties are spoken will not be analysed. This not only eliminates films set in Northern Ireland, such as *Some Mother's Son* (Terry George, 1996) and *Resurrection Man* (Marc Evans, 1998), but also films such as *Dancing at Lughnasa* (Pat O'Connor, 1998), *The Playboys* (Gillies MacKinnon, 1992), and *The Butcher Boy* (Neil Jordan, 1997) which are set in Donegal and the border counties of Cavan and Monaghan respectively. This division is in keeping with the recognised linguistic boundary between northern and southern varieties of Irish English which stretches roughly from Dundalk and Drogheda in the East to Bundoran and Sligo in the West[45]. In instances where characters from Ulster, the region north of this linguistic boundary, appear in films set in "the South", the films will still be analysed, yet the speech of the northern characters ignored[46].

Films not widely available on DVD

For the purpose of this study, only films which are widely available on DVD have been included[47]. This format, like its predecessor the video cassette, enables one to pause at will to transcribe speech samples and, more importantly, facilitates repeated viewing, thus ensuring the most accurate analysis possible. One could, of course, argue that the films available on this medium are not necessarily representative and that only big budget films, or at least those which have the backing of a major distributor, are able to secure a DVD release. One could also claim that it might be more useful to seek out less well-known films elsewhere, such as in the archive of the Irish Film Institute (IFI). However, my motivation to choose films which were readily available in a digital format was merely a logistical one. I found that films on DVD which could be viewed anywhere and at any time were more feasible. Furthermore, the fact that all of these films are readily available on DVD means that the lay reader can also find them quite easily, should he/she desire. An additional advantage to using only those films which are available on DVD is that they are also often equipped with subtitles, commentaries and special features which can prove to be both useful and interesting[48].

Films made after 2007

To ensure the study was as up-to-date as possible, films which were produced up to, and including, 2007 are present in the corpus. Productions from 2008, on the other hand, have been excluded, as, at the point of writing, they were not yet available on DVD.

---

been included. It should be noted, however, that only the speech of those characters whose Irish credentials have been established in the first 40 minutes of the film is analysed. The speech of supposedly "Irish" characters who Shannon and Joseph meet in Boston is therefore disregarded, as it is unclear how long these people have been in America and to what extent their language has been shaped by contact with others.

[45] Cf. Tilling (1985: 20) and Viereck, Viereck, and Ramisch (2002: 143).

[46] Characters whose speech is ignored as their accents betray that they come from Ulster include Malachy McCourt Sr. in *Angela's Ashes*, Liam Mercier and a number of the other boys in *Song for A Raggy Boy*, Rose in *The Magdalene Sisters*, and Martin Plunkett in *High Spirits*. In cases where Ulster actors have attempted a southern accent (no matter how poorly), their speech is analysed.

[47] Not all DVDs are readily available in Europe, and thus many were purchased in the United States. Since the special features or running time may differ according to where the DVD has been produced, the origin of each DVD, either Region 1 (North America) Region 2 (Europe) or Region Free (Worldwide) is included in the list of films on page 24.

[48] In the case of subtitles, the most interesting examples from a linguist's perspective were those in which the person responsible for the subtitling completely misunderstood the Irish English dialect and wrote something else which made no sense in the context (cf. page 24 and page 43 for some examples).

Having established a corpus based on the criteria outlined above, it was also important, for the purposes of this study, to subdivide the films into two categories: those which are Irish-made, and those which are set in Ireland, but produced, financed and directed by non-Irish groups or individuals. There is good reason for doing this, as it is widely accepted among scholars and critics that representations of the Irish in non-Irish films have often been less than accurate; some might say laughable or even offensive (cf. Byrne 1997: 200). These films tend to trade in stereotypes based on the Stage Irish[49] tradition, and they reduce the Irish to mere figures of fun. As early as in 1930, a reporter for the *Dublin Evening Mail* commented that "no race has suffered more at the hands of American and English film and stage producers than has ours[50]". Almost seventy years later, in her review of *Waking Ned* (Kirk Jones, 1998)[51], film critic Kathleen Murphy highlighted how little had changed with regard to outsiders' views of the Irish. She described the film as "odious" and wrote:

> A rural 'Irish' romp filmed on the Isle of Man, featuring a village-full of rib-ricklingly *(sic)* retrograde 'Irish' types headed by British Ian Bannen under the direction of an Englishman who cut his teeth on TV commercials, this Gaelic *Amos 'n' Andy* is contemptibly dumb, 'shamrock and blarney' cartooning, the likes of which Dublin-born Swift savaged several hundred years ago.
> (Murphy, cited by Dwyer 1998: 6)

Such stereotypical representations of the Irish by foreign directors and producers would probably not be taken so seriously by critics or audiences, were there sufficient indigenous representations of the Irish on film to balance them out. Kevin Rockett points out, however, that this is certainly not the case and that, in fact, "more fiction films were produced about the Irish by American film-makers before 1915, when the first indigenous Irish fiction film was made, than in the whole 100 year history of fiction film-making in Ireland" (Rockett 1996: i).

The most famous of these films by American film-makers are undoubtedly *The Quiet Man* (John Ford, 1952) and *Darby O' Gill and the Little People* (Robert Stevenson, 1959). Between them these staples of St Patrick's Day television have shaped entire generations' perceptions of the Irish, both in the United States and beyond, with the average Irishman being portrayed as "a country bumpkin with a homespun-and-tweed wardrobe, blackthorn stick, and clay pipe", who always speaks with a "ridiculous brogue (the like of which never passed the lips of any living Irishman)", and who has "a fondness for whiskey and a violent temper" (Byrne 1997: 6).

It is clear therefore that the most significant and iconic representations of Irishness, and by extension the most deep-seated perceptions of the way Irish people speak, are those created abroad. Thus, when the corpus of films is examined for the presence of Irish English features, it will be interesting to see whether the language used in them is accurate from a linguist's perspective, or whether, just as in their general portrayal of the Irish, these films resort to caricatures in speech too.

In order to divide these films into the two aforementioned categories, I have adopted the methodology set out by Anthony Kirby and James MacKillop in their "Selected Filmography of Irish and Irish-Related Feature Films" (1999). In keeping with their parameters, an "Irish

---

[49] For more on Stage Irish, see Chapter 2.
[50] Source: *Dublin Evening Mail*, 12/08/1930: 7 (cf. Rockett 1996: 333).
[51] *Waking Ned* was released in the USA under the title *Waking Ned Devine*.

film" is here defined as: (a) one made in Ireland, with (b) an Irish director, (c) produced or backed by an Irish company, and (d) based on a text by an Irish writer, or a compelling minority of those four elements[52] (cf. Kirby and MacKillop 1999: 182-231). Films, on the other hand, which do not fit into the category of "Irish films" are labelled "Irish-related".[53]

Irish films
- *My Left Foot* (1989), 103 min, col. Region 1.
- *The Field* (1990), 107 min, col. Region 1.
- *The Commitments* (1991), 117 min, col. Region 2.
- *Into the West* (1993), 97 min, col. Region 1.
- *A Man of No Importance* (1994), 99 min, col. Region 2.
- *Circle of Friends* (1995), 110 min, col. Region 2.
- *Last of the High Kings* (1996), 95 min, col. a.k.a. *Summer Fling* Region 1.
- *The Van* (1996), 100 min, col. Region 2.
- *Michael Collins* (1996), 135 min, col. Region 2.
- *Trojan Eddie* (1996), 105 min, col. Region 2.
- *The General* (1998), 124 min, b/w. Region 1.
- *A Very Unlucky Leprechaun* (1998), 92 min, col. Region 1.
- *The Nephew* (1998), 106 min, col. Region 1.
- *A Love Divided* (1999), 98 min, col. Region 1.
- *Agnes Browne* (1999), 92 min, col. Region 2.
- *Angela's Ashes* (1999), 145 min, col. Region 2.
- *When the Sky Falls* (2000), 107 min, col. Region 1.
- *When Brendan met Trudy* (2000), 95 min, col. Region 2.
- *About Adam* (2000), 105 min, col. Region 2.
- *Ordinary Decent Criminal* (2000), 93 min, col. Region 1.
- *Nora* (2001), 106 min, col. Region 1.
- *Rat* (2001), 89 min, col. Region 2.
- *How Harry Became a Tree* (2001), 100 min, col. a.k.a. *Bitter Harvest* Region 1.
- *Mystics* (2002), 90 min, col. Region 2.
- *Veronica Guerin* (2003), 98 min, col. Region 2.
- *Intermission* (2003), 105 min, col. Region 2.
- *Song for a Raggy Boy* (2003), 100 min, col. Region 2.
- *Goldfish Memory* (2003), 85 min, col. Region 2.
- *The Boys and Girl from County Clare* (2003), 90 min, col. Region 2.
- *Cowboys and Angels* (2003), 89 min, col. Region 2.
- *Adam and Paul* (2004), 83 min, col. Region 2.
- *Inside I'm Dancing* (2004), 104 min, col. a.k.a. *Rory O'Shea was Here* Region 2.
- *Dead Meat* (2004), 80 min, col. Region 1.
- *Garage* (2007), 85 min, col. Region-free.

---

[52] The definition of "a compelling minority" is open to interpretation, but Kirby and MacKillop explain it using the following example: "John Ford's *Rising of the Moon* (1958), adapting three short works by Irish writers and produced at Ardmore Studios, is here classed as 'Irish'; Ford's *The Quiet Man* (1952), shot largely in Ireland for Republic Pictures, is here 'Irish Related' (sic)" (1999: 182). Although both films were based on Irish material and made in Ireland by the same American director, the producer (Republic Pictures from the USA) proves to be the deciding factor in labeling the latter film Irish-related.

[53] The abbreviations given in the descriptions are as follows: min. (minutes), col. (colour), b/w. (black and white), and a.k.a. (also known as). Region refers to the part of the world where it is possible to view the DVD using the standard technology sold in that region (Region 1 includes the USA, Canada, US territories and Bermuda; Region 2 includes Western and Central Europe, Western Asia and much of Africa. Some discs are Region-free and can be viewed worldwide.). It is now possible to buy DVD players which decode DVDs from all regions, thus rendering the viewing of encoded films unproblematic.

Irish-related films
- *The Informer* (1935), USA, 91 min, b/w. Region 2.
- *The Quiet Man* (1952), USA, 129 min, col. Region 1.
- *Darby O'Gill and the Little People* (1959), USA, 90 min, col. Region 1.
- *Ryan's Daughter* (1970), UK, 206 min, col. Region 1.
- *The Dead* (1987), UK/USA, 83 min, col. Region 2.
- *High Spirits* (1988), USA, 97 min, col. Region 1.
- *Far and Away* (1992), USA, 140 min, col. Region 2.
- *The Snapper* (1993), UK, 91 min, col. Region 1.
- *Widows' Peak* (1994), UK, 101 min, col. Region 1.
- *The Matchmaker* (1997), USA, 97 min, col. Region 1.
- *This is my Father* (1998), US/Canada, 120 min, col. Region 2.
- *Waking Ned* (1998), UK, 91 min, col. a.k.a. *Waking Ned Devine* Region 2.
- *The Magdalene Sisters* (2002) UK, 119 min, col. Region 2.
- *Evelyn* (2002), USA, 94 min, col. Region 2.
- *Irish Jam* (2004), USA, 94 min, col. Region 1.
- *The Wind that Shakes the Barley* (2006), UK, Spain, Germany, 127 min, col. Region 2.

When one examines these lists, a number of details are immediately striking.

1). It may seem odd that there is not a single film on the "Irish" list which predates 1989. However, there are two good reasons for the absence of indigenous films before this date. Firstly, as outlined above, very few fiction films were actually produced by the Irish during the first century of cinema, due to what Pettit calls "cultural and macro-economic factors" (2000: 35)[54]. Indeed, the Irish film industry was such a late bloomer that, as recently as 1988, in the introduction to his seminal book *The Cinema and Ireland*, Anthony Slide wryly observed that, to many readers, the idea of a book devoted to Irish cinema would be comparable to a volume on the snakes of Ireland, in that "there were none of the latter and little of the former" (1988: vi.). A second reason for the absence of early indigenous films from the list is that those films which *were* produced in Ireland before 1989 have not yet been widely released in DVD format and have therefore been excluded from the corpus.

At this stage, it is also important to point out that the boom in Irish film production since 1989 can be attributed to two major factors: on the one hand, a series of tax incentives which were introduced by the Irish government from 1987 to encourage investment in film production in Ireland[55], and, on the other hand, the unexpected success of Jim Sheridan's *My Left Foot* at the Oscars in 1990, where the film garnered Academy awards for both best actor and best supporting actress[56]. This achievement and the subsequent Oscar nominations for *The Field* (Jim Sheridan, 1990), *The Crying Game* (Neil Jordan, 1992), and *In the Name of the Father* (Jim Sheridan, 1993) put the Irish film industry on the map and inspired future film-production, which again would probably not have been possible without the aforementioned incentives.

---

[54] Luke Gibbons attributes this lack of a film industry to "the lack of an economy of scale and adequate industrial base; the hostility to mass culture, fuelled by cultural protectionism in the early decades of the state; the existence of an anglophone audience which made a fledgling Irish cinema unduly susceptible to Anglo-American influence; and – not least – the absence of a strong visual tradition" (2005: 207).

[55] Under Section 481 of the Finance Act (formerly Section 35), a tax deduction is available to Irish investors who buy shares in Irish film production companies, with 80% of the amount invested being written off for tax purposes. For further information on these tax incentives, see http://www.filmboard.ie/section_481.php (Retrieved: June 19, 2005)

[56] Daniel Day Lewis and Brenda Fricker respectively.

2). It is also apparent that, despite the fact that sound films existed from 1930, the first film on the "Irish-related" list dates from 1935. This is once again due to the fact that it was not possible to find films from before this period on DVD.

3). Finally, one cannot help but notice the unusually high percentage of literary adaptations which appear in the corpus[57]. For a study like this which is concerned with literary dialect, this proves to be of great interest when comparing sentences in the screen and text versions[58].

5.2   Analysing the data

The present study is corpus-based and employs methods from the fields of empirical and computational linguistics with the aim of offering reliable data on the presence of certain features of Irish English in film. In addition to this quantitative analysis of the grammar, discourse and lexical features of the dialect, a qualitative analysis of the phonological features of the variety will also be offered.

The corpus itself consists of 50 films, which were chosen according to the criteria outlined above. While this sample aims to be as representative as possible, with efforts having been made to try to include at least one movie from every decade since the 1930s, the majority of these films were, nevertheless, produced after 1990, as prior to that the development of an Irish film industry was deemed "neither economically viable nor ideologically desirable" (McLoone 2006: 88)[59]. The purpose of trying to provide such a representative selection of films is to facilitate some form of diachronic analysis in order to examine whether certain Irish English features have become less common over time due to supraregionalisation[60], globalisation and the influence of the media, or whether an increase in regionalism, as is evident in other countries, has also led to a pride in local dialects and thus a retention of dialect features.

Simply examining the films chronologically, according to the year they were produced, will not necessarily help in testing this hypothesis, as some of the films which were produced recently are set in the past and would, thus, be expected to display more traditional features than films made at the same time, but set in modern Ireland. Ordering the films according to the year of their production (see Table I), therefore, is not the only way of conducting a diachronic analysis. Thus the films will also be organised chronologically according to when they are set (see Table II), and the frequency and type of typical features will be investigated as they appear. The results will then be compared with those from the first analysis.

In addition to these diachronic analyses, the films will also be examined synchronically for features which occur in films made at the same time (all the films from the 1990s, for example) or set in the same period (all the films set in the 1950s).

---

[57] *My Left Foot, The Field, The Commitments, The Snapper, The Van, Circle of Friends, Last of the High Kings, The General, Agnes Browne, Angela's Ashes, The Informer, The Quiet Man, Darby O'Gill and the Little People, The Dead, Song for a Raggy Boy, Nora* and *Evelyn* all are based on novels, plays, short stories, memoirs or biographies.
[58] Examples of such comparisons include those on pages 84, 89, 125 and 127.
[59] For more on the cultural and macroeconomic factors which transformed the Irish film industry after 1990, see Chapter 5.1
[60] Hickey suggests that a supraregional variety is establishing itself as a national standard in Ireland, and that the changes which took place in Dublin English in the 1990s have become widespread in the rest of the country as well (cf. 2005: 208).

Furthermore, films set in one particular locale will be analysed to see how frequently certain features appear there. For example, one can focus on films set in Dublin and explore the type and number of features which appear in *The Commitments*, *The Van*, *The General*, *Ordinary Decent Criminal*, *Agnes Browne*, *My Left Foot* etc. (see Table III). Unfortunately, the setting of many of the films is never explicitly mentioned, leaving one to guess where they are set, based perhaps on possible landmarks, topographical details or the accents of the characters featured. Relying on landmarks, famous buildings or landscape as an indicator of place is, however, very problematic, as filmmakers often use numerous locations, sometimes in different parts of the country or even different parts of the world, and pass these off as being one place. For example, *The Quiet Man*, was famously filmed at various locales throughout counties Galway and Mayo[61], as well as in a Hollywood studio, while *Ryan's Daughter* seamlessly blends footage from numerous locations both at home and abroad to create the fictional setting of Kirarry: the film begins on top of what are unmistakably the Cliffs of Moher in County Clare, with subsequent scenes of the beach below being compiled from material shot on various beaches in County Kerry and even from footage filmed months later on beaches in South Africa.

Trying to determine the setting of the film based on accents (or based on accents and topography) would therefore seem to be a more reliable alternative. However, this strategy is also extremely problematic. For example, in the case of the film *The Nephew*, set on the fictional island of Inis Dara, I had already categorised the accent as a general West of Ireland accent, because it was logical to place Inis Dara somewhere along the western seaboard between Sligo and Clare, due to the fact that the majority of habitable islands are off the west coast of Ireland. Then, listening to the accents on offer, I classified them as "neutral" West of Ireland accents, since they do not possess the more instantly recognisable sounds associated with accents from Donegal, Cork or Kerry, for example[62]. However, on viewing the film for the second time, I made a discovery which totally contradicted my classification, yet which, strangely, was also completely at odds with the rest of the evidence in the film. In the movie, Chad, the eponymous nephew, finds letters written by his mother to her ex-boyfriend Joe Brady. These letters come as a surprise to Chad because he realises that his uncle Tony has kept them from their intended recipient for all these years. However, the real surprise, for the linguist at least, is that the address on these letters places Inis Dara in County Cork, despite the fact that only one member of the cast, Niall Toibin, bears anything resembling a Cork accent[63].

The film *Darby O'Gill and the Little People* poses similar problems. It is set in the fictional village of Rathcullen, which topographically could be anywhere in Ireland[64]. The books on which the film was based were set near Sleive-na-mon, presumably Sliabh na mBan (Slievenamon) in Tipperary, yet this information is not necessarily helpful as the unrealistically large variety of accents on display in this small nineteenth century hamlet make

---

[61] For the precise geography of the locations in *The Quiet Man*, see MacHale (2000).

[62] It is interesting to note that Rains (2007: 89) also reaches the same conclusion with regard to the location of Inis Dara, stating that "the film concerns the arrival on an island off the west coast of Ireland of Chad, a black Irish-American teenager".

[63] Indeed, the film has a number of inconsistencies regarding accents, with the shopkeeper's two young sons displaying very strong Dublin accents, which are certainly not in keeping with the supposed locale nor with the accents of the rest of their family or community.

[64] "Anywhere in Ireland" turns out to be "nowhere in Ireland", as the film was actually shot in California.

it virtually impossible to pinpoint it to any one location. Finally, an hour and eleven minutes into the film, a letter arrives bearing an address which helps to place the fictional community in a real Irish county, while, at the same time, undermining the accents which appear in the film, as it turns out that Rathcullen is actually in County Kerry. In light of these findings, the results for some of the films in Table III may need to be taken with a pinch of salt. Indeed, it would be more reliable to group them by province rather than by county, as this would allow for greater freedom when dealing with films with ambiguous settings. This will also prove useful for making comparisons with other studies, as we shall see in Chapter 6.4.

Finally, as outlined above, the films will also be subdivided into Irish and Irish-related films[65], with a view to examining whether there are significant differences between indigenous films and foreign productions regarding the amount and type of features present (see Tables IV and V). One would typically expect that the Irish films would display more features and that the non-Irish films would perhaps even include some clichéd or erroneous language.

---

[65] For the differences between these two labels, see Chapter 5.1.

Table I

Films ordered according to the year of their production
The Informer (1935)
The Quiet Man (1952)
Darby O'Gill and the Little People (1959)
Ryan's Daughter (1970)
The Dead (1987)
High Spirits (1988)
My Left Foot (1989)
The Field (1990)
The Commitments (1991)
Far and Away (1992)
The Snapper (1993)
Into the West (1993)
A Man of No Importance (1994)
Widows' Peak (1994)
Circle of Friends (1995)
Last of the High Kings (1996) also known as *Summer Fling* (USA)
The Van (1996)
Michael Collins (1996)
Trojan Eddie (1996)
The Matchmaker (1997)
The Nephew (1997)
This is my Father (1998)
Waking Ned (1998) also known as *Waking Ned Devine* (USA)
The General (1998)
A Very Unlucky Leprechaun (1998)
A Love Divided (1999)
Agnes Browne (1999)
Angela's Ashes (1999)
When the Sky Falls (2000)
About Adam (2000)
Ordinary Decent Criminal (2000)
When Brendan Met Trudy (2000)
Nora (2001)
Rat (2001)
How Harry Became a Tree (2001) also known as *Bitter Harvest* (USA)
The Magdalene Sisters (2002)
Mystics (2002)
Evelyn (2002)
Intermission (2003)
Song for a Raggy Boy (2003)
Veronica Guerin (2003)
Goldfish Memory (2003)
The Boys and Girl from County Clare (2003)
Cowboys and Angels (2003)
Adam and Paul (2004)
Dead Meat (2004)
Inside I'm Dancing (2004) also known as *Rory O'Shea Was Here* (USA)
Irish Jam (2004)
The Wind that Shakes the Barley (2006)
Garage (2007)

Table II

Period	Films ordered according to the period they are set in
1800-1900	*Darby O'Gill and the Little People* (1959)
	Far and Away (1992)
1900-1910	*The Dead* (1987)
	Nora (2001)
1920-1930	*Ryan's Daughter* (1970)
	Michael Collins (1996)
	The Informer (1935)
	The Wind that Shakes the Barley (2006)
	How Harry Became a Tree (2001) a.k.a. *Bitter Harvest* (USA)
1930-1940	*Widows' Peak* (1994)
	The Quiet Man (1952)
	This is my Father (1998)
	Song for a Raggy Boy (2003)
1950-1960	*Circle of Friends* (1995)
	My Left Foot (1989)
	The Field (1990)
	Angela's Ashes (1999)
	A Love Divided (1999)
	Evelyn (2002)
1960-1970	*Agnes Browne* (1999)
	The Magdalene Sisters (2002)
	A Man of No Importance (1994)
	The Boys and Girl from County Clare (2003)
1970-1980	*Last of the High Kings* (1996) a.k.a. *Summer Fling* (USA)
1980-1990	*High Spirits* (1988)
	The Commitments (1991)
1990-2000	*The Snapper* (1993)
	Into the West (1993)
	The Van (1996)
	Trojan Eddie (1996)
	The Matchmaker (1997)
	The Nephew (1997)
	Waking Ned (1998) a.k.a. *Waking Ned Devine* (USA)
	A Very Unlucky Leprechaun (1998)
	The General (1998)
	Ordinary Decent Criminal (2000)
	When the Sky Falls (2000)
	Veronica Guerin (2003)
2000- Present	*About Adam* (2000)
	When Brendan Met Trudy (2000)
	Rat (2001)
	Mystics (2002)
	Intermission (2003)
	Goldfish Memory (2003)
	Cowboys and Angels (2003)
	Adam and Paul (2004)
	Dead Meat (2004)
	Inside I'm Dancing (2004) a.k.a. *Rory O'Shea Was Here* (USA)
	Irish Jam (2004)
	Garage (2007)

Table III

	Films ordered according to the locale they are set in
LEINSTER	
Dublin (and surrounding areas)	*The Informer*; *Michael Collins*; *The Dead*; *Agnes Browne*; *Evelyn*; *My Left Foot*; *A Man of No Importance*; *Last of the High Kings* a.k.a. *Summer Fling*; *The Snapper*; *Into the West*; *The Commitments*; *The Van*; *The General*; *Ordinary Decent Criminal*; *When the Sky Falls*; *Veronica Guerin*; *About Adam*; *When Brendan Met Trudy*; *Rat*; *How Harry Became a Tree* a.k.a. *Bitter Harvest*; *Mystics*; *Intermission*; *Adam and Paul*; *Goldfish Memory*; *Inside I'm Dancing* a.k.a. *Rory O'Shea Was Here*; *Nora*
Wexford	*A Love Divided*
Midlands[66]	*This is my Father*; *Circle of Friends*; *Widows' Peak*; *The Magdalene Sisters*; *Song for a Raggy Boy*; *Trojan Eddie*; *Garage*
MUNSTER	
Clare	*The Boys and Girl from County Clare*
Limerick	*Angela's Ashes*; *Cowboys and Angels*
Cork	*The Wind that Shakes the Barley*; *The Nephew*
Kerry	*Far and Away*; *Ryan's Daughter*; *Darby O'Gill and the Little People*
CONNAUGHT	
Leitrim	*Dead Meat*
West of Ireland (Unspecified)	*The Field*
	The Quiet Man
	A Very Unlucky Leprechaun
	The Matchmaker
	High Spirits
	Waking Ned a.k.a. *Waking Ned Devine*
	Irish Jam

---

[66] In keeping with the general use of the term, the Midlands roughly refers to the following counties: "Westmeath, Longford, Offaly, Laois along with west Kildare and Meath, south Roscommon and north Tipperary" (Hickey 2004b: 75).

Table IV

Irish films
My Left Foot (1989)
The Field (1990)
The Commitments (1991)
Into the West (1993)
A Man of No Importance (1994)
Circle of Friends (1995)
Last of the High Kings (1996) a.k.a. *Summer Fling* (USA)
The Van (1996)
Michael Collins (1996)
Trojan Eddie (1996)
The Nephew (1997)
The General (1998)
A Very Unlucky Leprechaun (1998)
A Love Divided (1999)
Agnes Browne (1999)
Angela's Ashes (1999)
When the Sky Falls (2000)
About Adam (2000)
Ordinary Decent Criminal (2000)
When Brendan Met Trudy (2000)
Nora (2001)
Rat (2001)
How Harry Became a Tree (2001) a.k.a. *Bitter Harvest* (USA)
Mystics (2002)
Intermission (2003)
Song for a Raggy Boy (2003)
Veronica Guerin (2003)
Goldfish Memory (2003)
The Boys and Girl from County Clare (2003)
Cowboys and Angels (2003)
Inside I'm Dancing (2004) a.k.a. *Rory O'Shea Was Here* (USA)
Adam and Paul (2004)
Dead Meat (2004)
Garage (2007)

Table V

Irish-related films
The Informer (1935)
The Quiet Man (1952)
Darby O'Gill and the Little People (1959)
Ryan's Daughter (1970)
The Dead (1987)
High Spirits (1988)
Far and Away (1992)
The Snapper (1993)
Widows' Peak (1994)
The Matchmaker (1997)
This is my Father (1998)
Waking Ned (1998) a.k.a. *Waking Ned Devine* (USA)
Evelyn (2002)
The Magdalene Sisters (2002)
Irish Jam (2004)
The Wind that Shakes the Barley (2006)

In order to conduct an analysis of the dialect features of Irish English which appear in the corpus, it was first necessary to ascertain which features are actually regarded as characteristic of Southern Irish English. The list of features selected is based predominantly on those identified by Hickey in his *A Survey of Irish English* (Hickey 2004a: 121-32)[67] and supplemented by those which appeared in Filppula's *The Grammar of Irish English* (1999) and in an article of the same name by Harris (1993)[68]. These sources proved to be particularly useful, as Hickey had already examined the acceptability of 57 Irish English vernacular features[69] among the Irish population, thus giving an indication about the prevalence of such features today, whilst Filppula and Harris had also identified additional features, particularly discourse features, which were likely to appear in literary dialect, and thus in film scripts. Further discourse features were garnered from Amador Moreno's "Discourse Markers in Irish English: An Example from Literature" (2005), whilst examples of lexical items were sourced from Dolan's *A Dictionary of Hiberno-English* (2006) and Share's *Slanguage* (2003). Together, these sources provided a comprehensive list of features to search for in the corpus. As I watched the films, I also remained vigilant for possible further features not included in the list, but which occurred so frequently in the films that they warranted a special mention. This resulted in a total of 67 features (39 grammar, 10 discourse and 18 lexical) which I examined across all 50 films.

Each film was viewed a minimum of three times for the presence of the aforementioned features, with all of the utterances which displayed these items being

---

[67] The survey itself was carried out in 2002 but appeared as a CD-Rom in Hickey's *A Sound Atlas of Irish English* in 2004. All page references and references to the study in this book refer to the survey as it appeared in the Sound Atlas, i.e. Hickey 2004a.

[68] This article had previously been published as a booklet commissioned by the Economic and Social Research Council (ESRC). However, all references in this study refer to the amended version published in Milroy and Milroy (eds.) (1993) *Real English. The Grammar of English Dialects in the British Isles*. London and New York: Longman. 139-86.

[69] Not all of Hickey's original 57 features are examined here, since some of them are more typical of northern varieties of Irish English.

transcribed into *Excel* files in order to facilitate speedy searches again in the future[70]. As one would expect, utterances which were in Standard English were simply disregarded for this part of the study.

For the purposes of transcription, each speaker received an abbreviated codename which consisted of their gender, initial(s) (or in cases where characters shared initials, some other descriptor, such as the first two letters of their name), the decade in which the film is set, and an indication of the setting. Thus, in the film *The General*, for example, the codename MMC1990D stands for Male Martin Cahill 1990 Dublin, while in the same film MIK1990K stands for Male Inspector Kenny 1990 Kerry. Frances Cahill, one of Martin Cahill's wives, has the codename FFC1990D, with the first "F" standing for Female. These markers of period and locale will prove useful in conducting both the synchronic and diachronic analyses, where dates and places are of importance. However, the relatively low frequency of female characters in many of the films renders the gender descriptor redundant for this study.[71]

As outlined in Chapter 5.1, the speech of characters who do not speak Southern Irish English was disregarded; this includes, for example, the words spoken by American tourists or returned emigrants in *The Quiet Man*, *The Matchmaker*, *High Spirits*, *This is my Father*, *The Last of the High Kings*, *The Boys and Girl from County Clare* or those of Northern Irish English speaking characters in *Angela's Ashes*, *Song for a Raggy Boy* and *The Magdalene Sisters*.

Where narrators are used in the films, I decided to also include their utterances. This is a variation of the methodology employed by Lisa Cohen Minnick[72] in her analysis of literary dialects, and has been altered to fit the contrasting conventions of the medium of film[73]. In general, narrators are used sparingly in the films, due to the movie maxim that one should show and not tell, but when they do appear, they are characters who also appear in the story and they use the same speech style in their narration as elsewhere in the film. It is therefore justifiable to include their voiceover narratives. Some examples of such narrators include Frank in *Angela's Ashes*, Benny in *Circle of Friends*, Father Lonergan in *The Quiet Man*, Frankie in *The Last of the High Kings*, and Mrs Carney in *This is my Father*.

A further variation from Cohen Minnick's methodology, and one which I believe makes my results all the more representative, is that I searched for the same 67 features across all 50 films. Cohen Minnick has admitted that one of the shortcomings of her study is that the

---

[70] While the screenplays of some of the films are available in book format, I did not rely on those as my guide while transcribing. In most cases, these are merely the shooting scripts and do not correspond to the final cut of the film, as actors sometimes improvise lines or are given last minute scene changes which often deviate greatly from what is already written. Paul Laverty's screenplay for *The Wind that Shakes the Barley*, for example, is quite different to the film that made it to the screen (cf. Laverty 2006).

[71] Other sociolinguistic factors, such as class, were also discounted from this study, as assumptions about the class of the speakers would just have been speculation. Whereas in traditional sociolinguistic studies questionnaires can be distributed to determine education, occupation, income, etc. (and even then the categorization of the various classes is often controversial), this is not possible in a fictional world and any classification would have had to be based on appearances or the way characters spoke, which, needless to say, in the case of the latter is counterproductive.

[72] Cf. Chapter 2.

[73] In the case of novels with a narrator who uses Standard English, Cohen Minnick disregarded the narrator's language and analysed solely the direct speech of the characters, also ignoring indirect or reported speech, due to concerns about how one character might reproduce the speech of another. If, however, the narrator recounted the entire story in his own dialect, thereby reproducing the speech of a variety of characters "without any differentiation among the varieties of speech those characters might be imagined to speak," (Cohen Minnick 2004: 47) then she analysed the narrator's language.

final list of features for each of her analyses "varies somewhat from one text to the next according to what is in each text and also because the methodology continued to refine itself" (2004: 53) as she became more adept at analysing texts.

However, one of the strengths of Cohen Minnick's work was her decision to use a binary coding system when looking at the individual features (2004: 44), and this methodology is something which has been retained for this study. Thus, the various features of Irish English have been noted as either *occurring* or *not occurring* in the films. The actual number of occurrences of individual features per film was not measured, as frequency is not necessarily a measure of the accuracy of the dialect. Just because a feature appears numerous times in one film does not make the language in that film any more Irish than that in another where it appears relatively rarely, or not at all. Indeed, on some occasions, high frequency may even suggest that a particular scriptwriter is resorting to pat phrases, as is the case in *Circle of Friends* where the frequency of the tag *altogether* is so conspicuous[74] that it gave one critic yet another reason to criticise the film:

> The screenplay has its fair share of tourist board Irishry too: the breathless giggling of trios of brash young Irish women is becoming something of a cliché post Roddy Doyle, and I'm not sure how convincing everybody saying "altogether" at the end of every sentence is as a signifier of Gaelic warmth. More worrying [...] is the fact that only one of the six main roles is played by an Irish actor.
>
> (Thompson 1995: 42)

By extension, the absence of particular features in a film does not necessarily make the language in that film less Irish than that in films in which such features occur. As we shall see, some features are restricted regionally and, thus, do not appear in movies set in other parts of the country[75]. Similarly, some features are restricted to certain classes[76] and, thus, may not appear in films concerned with other social groups, just as films set in the past may display features which have become obsolete in modern speech and thus do not appear in films set today, and vice versa. Moreover, it is important to remember that a feature may just not appear in a film simply because the circumstance never arises in the plot to warrant it.

---

[74] In order to show just how exaggerated the use of *altogether* is in *Circle of Friends*, I have included the examples from the film below. The overuse of this word is all the more obvious given that at one point it occurs three times in just over 4 minutes.

00:07:38	FNM1950D	Come on, you look gorgeous **altogether**.
00:16:44	FBH1950D	Oh, he's awful **altogether**, Father. I could never love him.
00:20:49	FBH1950D	Oh, it was a great film **altogether**.
00:23:44	FBH1950D	Thanks Nan. You're a brilliant person **altogether**.
00:25:00	FBH1950D	It's perfect **altogether**.
00:37:35	FEM1950D	He was great **altogether**.

An examination into the use of *altogether* at the end of clauses or sentences in the rest of the corpus reveals that it only occurs in nine other films and even then rarely on more than one or two occasions per film. An exception is *Trojan Eddie*, in which the form appears four times. However, even though the frequency is quite high there (the examples all appear within a twenty-minute spell), they do not stand out to the same extent as those in *Circle of Friends*.

[75] For example, the use of *youse* or *yez* for second person plural is more likely to be found in Dublin and along the east coast (Hickey 2007: 18), whereas *ye* is used with greater frequency outside of the Pale. In the Middle Ages, the Pale referred to the territory around and including Dublin which was "the only part of Ireland where the crown's writ unquestionably ran" (McMahon and O'Donoghue 2004: 650). The term is still frequently used today.

[76] Kallen, for example, suggests that middle class speakers are less likely to use the *'after' perfect* in public contexts than working class speakers (1991: 61-74).

Perhaps a character never actually addresses two or more people at one time and therefore does not need to employ the *ye*, *yiz* or *youse* forms which mark the second person plural in Irish English. Perhaps he or she has no call to report what has just happened and thus does not make use of the *'after' perfect*. These factors also need to be borne in mind when examining the results of this study[77].

In theory, once a list of grammar, discourse and lexical features has been compiled, they should be relatively easy to detect in the films. Phonetic analysis of the speech samples, on the other hand, is more difficult and is an area always open to criticism, as objectivity can never be completely guaranteed. However, every possible measure has been taken to ensure that the transcriptions are as accurate as possible.

Firstly, just as with the grammar, discourse and lexical elements, it was necessary to consult the existing research on Irish English, in order to establish what exactly the typical sounds of the variety are. Particularly salient phonological features were identified from works by Taniguchi (1972), Bliss (1984), Wells (1982b), Moylan (1996) and Hickey (2004a, 2004b and 2005) and then searched for in the films. Rather than conduct a quantitative analysis of these features by recording their appearance in every film, it was deemed more appropriate to simply select some particularly good examples of each one from the corpus. These were transcribed using broad phonetic transcriptions, based on the International Phonetic Alphabet (IPA) used by Wells (1982a/b) and adapted by Hickey (2004a). What is more, transcriptions of cases in which actors who are imitating an Irish accent do a particularly poor job are also included, in order to offer the listener a means of comparison.

Since I am aware that it has been suggested that "scholars purposely bias their transcripts in order to make them fit preconceived notions" (Bailey *et al.* 1991: 17), the reader should always regard the films themselves as the definitive sources and the transcriptions merely as a guide. Indeed, the fact that these films are widely available in the public domain, and not merely a series of interviews conducted privately by the author and stored away from prying eyes (or rather ears), should also ensure greater transparency (cf. Bailey *et al.* 1991: 2).

I am also conscious of the fact that listeners react differently depending on the information they have regarding the identity of the speaker they are to judge. Duncan Markham, commenting on this phenomenon regarding speakers of a second language (L2), states that it is not uncommon that "a native speaker treats an L2 speaker as native until such time as the L2 speaker reveals that she is non-native, whereupon the native speaker claims to have heard a number of non-native characteristics" (1997: 99)[78]. The same could be said to apply to cinemagoers evaluating foreign actors speaking with an Irish accent. If one knows that the actors are British or American, then one is more likely to focus on their pronunciation, scouring it for traces of something foreign. Bearing this in mind, I have tried to conduct my analysis as objectively as possible, disregarding biographical details of the actors and letting them "speak for themselves", so to say.

---

[77] Unlike in surveys or interview situations, where one can elicit desired features by questioning respondents, in a study of this kind, there can, of course, be no guarantee that one will encounter a certain feature for all films.
[78] For more on the phenomenon of accent hallucination, see Chapter 12.3.

6　Irish English dialect in the film corpus

The first part of this study, the quantitative part, deals with the dialect features of Irish English, focussing on a host of grammar[79], discourse and lexical features, whereas the second part, the qualitative part, deals with Irish accents. As already outlined in the methodology, the features of Irish English searched for in the films were predominantly compiled from three sources: Hickey's *A Sound Atlas of Irish English* (2004a) and two works which share the same title, *The Grammar of Irish English*, by Filppula (1999) and Harris (1993). Hickey's work examines the acceptability of a host of Irish English features in present-day Ireland, while Filppula and Harris explore both the grammar of the variety and some of the discourse features which one would expect to encounter in a corpus compiled almost entirely of dialogues[80]. A small number of additional features were taken from Taniguchi's *A Grammatical Analysis of Artistic Representation of Irish English with a Brief Discussion of Sounds and Spelling* (1972), which, as the title suggests, looks at literary dialect representations of Irish English.

Although the grammar features chosen are all regarded as *typical* of Irish English, this in no way suggests that they are *exclusive* to this variety. This is a point which has also been stressed by other linguists. Kallen, for example, has qualified the notion of typicality meaning exclusivity, stating that "the term 'characteristic' does not necessarily mean 'unique'" (1994: 163). Indeed, all of the grammar features dealt with in this book also appear in other varieties of English throughout the world[81]. Not even the famous *'after' perfect* can be attributed to Irish English alone, as it also appears in Scottish Highland and Island English (cf. Sabban 1982), where it is based on substratal influence from Scots Gaelic rather than from Irish (see Bliss 1972, 1977, 1984; Harris 1984b, 1991a; Filppula 1986). The presence of the other non-standard grammar features of Irish English can likewise be found elsewhere and can be explained by the substratist approach, the retentionist theory (Harris 1983, 1984a, 1991a, 1991b and 1993; Lass 1990) or the conservative nature of the variety (Kallen 1991, 1994; Lass 1990). Irish English, like any variety, therefore has to be seen as the sum of its parts. In this respect, it is useful to remember Ives' definition of a dialect as "the use in one locality of speech traits that may be individually found somewhere else, but nowhere else in exactly the same combination" (1950: 152).

In order to examine the presence of the features in the corpus, all 50 films were viewed at least three times each, with features finally being noted as either *occurring* or *not occurring*[82]. This does not mean, however, that during the viewing of the films, only the first instance of the appearance of a particular feature was recorded. In fact, many films displayed several examples of the same feature, and these were also recorded in order to have a greater selection of examples from which to choose when compiling the tables for the Appendix.

---

[79] In keeping with the terminology employed in other studies, I shall refer to morphosyntactic features simply as grammar features (cf. Hickey 2007: 169). As well as encompassing the syntax of Irish English, this also includes the second person plural forms, the negation of auxiliaries and the use of non-standard demonstrative pronouns, which often belong to morphology.

[80] Since Filppula deals with the features in considerably more depth, I shall generally use his terminology and his inventory of grammatical features as my guideline. However, in cases where he does not address a particular feature or where I find his terminology problematic, I shall turn to either Hickey or Harris.

[81] These features are often what Chambers (2001) has labelled "vernacular universals" or what Mair (2003) calls "angloversals".

[82] See Chapter 5 on methodology.

These additional sentences, the ones which were not included in the final tables, often make an appearance as examples in the main text, thus offering the reader access to an even more comprehensive collection of examples. For the presentation of the results and examples of the individual features, the films are presented chronologically in the tables according to the year of their production. To the right of the title of each film is a column indicating the time in the film at which the feature or utterance appears[83], and to the right of that again is the abbreviated codename[84] for the character who uses the feature in the film, followed in the next column by the feature itself in a sentence. I have tried to include examples which are understandable without one having to have seen the films, and in cases where an utterance may have been unclear standing in isolation, I have also included preceding or subsequent utterances in order to provide the reader with as much context as possible. However, I hope the reader will appreciate the fact that it is not always possible to include lengthy excerpts within the confines of a narrow table. The tables are numbered 1 to 67 and can be found in the Appendix.

Although the findings of the tables are certainly interesting, by themselves they are not necessarily very revealing with regard to how representative the number of appearances of a feature per film is when compared with its frequency in everyday speech. After all, how frequent is frequent? Depending on one's expectations, 17 examples of a non-standard feature in 50 films could be regarded as either very high or very low, and, therefore, in order to contextualise these findings, it was necessary to compare my results with those from other corpora. Unfortunately, this was not so easy, as my corpus is compiled entirely of non-standard utterances, something which no other corpus of Irish English reflects, and thus comparing their results with mine would not have been representative.

Due to the absence of comparable corpora with appropriate speech data, I decided to use Hickey's *A Survey of Irish English Usage* (2004a) as my frame of reference. Hickey's survey tested the acceptability of certain structures in colloquial speech among the younger generation of the Irish population in 2002, and, by comparing my findings with his, I hope to show that the frequency of a feature in a film should correspond to its acceptability among the population, i.e. the more acceptable a feature was in Hickey's survey, the more likely it would be to appear in each film in my corpus. In addition to consulting the *Survey of Irish English Usage*, I also cross referenced my results with those found by Filppula in his "Hiberno-English corpus" (1999) and, where appropriate, I have presented his findings as well. The following is a brief description of both Hickey's and Filppula's corpora, followed by an observation relating to the film corpus.

A Survey of Irish English Usage

Hickey's study was based on a questionnaire of 57 sample sentences (see Appendix 1), each of which displayed a feature known to appear in some form of Irish English. As outlined earlier, the majority of these sentences were subsequently used as reference points in my compilation of a list of grammar structures. The respondents, most of whom were in the 18-30 age bracket, were requested to evaluate the sentences in terms of their acceptability in casual

---

[83] These times are approximate and should be used as a guideline for where to find the utterances on the relevant DVD.
[84] For more information on the codenames, see Chapter 5.1. In some cases, the names of the characters were not apparent and thus they were given labels like OM=Old Man, MIB=Man in bar, B1–Boy 1 etc.

speech among friends and to label them either as "no problem", "a bit strange" or "unacceptable" (Hickey 2004a: 115).

In total, 1017 questionnaires were used and compiled to form an excellent, user-friendly database which offers results for all 32 counties of Ireland, and which can be analysed on a county by county basis or can be subdivided according to the 4 provinces: Ulster, Munster, Leinster and Connaught[85]. The fact that one can be so selective regarding the data was very convenient and meant that I could exclude the findings for Ulster from Hickey's survey just as I had done for my films[86], leaving a total of 815 informants and an area which corresponded perfectly to that of my own corpus. Having selected the appropriate databases, I could then choose the parameters for which they were to be examined, namely, whether a feature was regarded as "no problem", "a bit strange" or "unacceptable". As with the provinces and counties, these parameters can be combined, so that one can, for example, group the first two categories together to check for positive values or the last two factors together for negative ones[87]. For my purposes, however, I felt it more appropriate to choose simply the "no problem" category alone, as I believed that the degree of acceptance of a feature would signal its likelihood to appear in the films. Those Irish English features which were regarded as "no problem" should be so common as to have been picked up by screenwriters and thus used in films, whereas those which were met with some degree of opposition (i.e. those which were deemed "a bit strange" or "unacceptable" even by Irish informants) would, in contrast, not be expected to occur frequently in my corpus, particularly since the audience for the films is a global one.

All of the findings for Hickey's survey and for my film corpus were originally presented as both pure numbers and as percentages. For example, in the case of Hickey's sentence *There was two men on the road*, containing the singular existential form, the "no problem" responses totalled 385 out of 815 or 47.24% in the *Survey of Irish English Usage*, while in the film corpus the singular existential form appeared in 33 of the 50 movies or 66% of the time. To simplify comparisons between the findings, however, I have omitted the pure numbers from the *Survey* part entirely and have converted those percentages into full percentages by rounding them up or down to the nearest full number. Thus, in the example above the degree of acceptability of the singular existential form is 47% among young Irish people.

The Hiberno-English corpus

The other corpus which I use for comparative purposes is Filppula's Hiberno-English (HE) corpus[88]. In order to have some data to conduct an analysis of Irish English speech, Filppula compiled a corpus from interviews conducted in the late 1970s and early 1980s with informants from counties Clare, Kerry, Wicklow and Dublin. While the HE corpus itself is quite small, amounting to approximately 158,000 words and featuring only 24 speakers, all of whom were elderly, and most of whom were male, it nevertheless provides some useful data

---

[85] For more on Hickey's corpus, see Hickey (2004a: 115-16).
[86] For a justification of the omission of all films which were set in Ulster, see Chapter 5.1.
[87] The gender of the respondents could also have been entered separately as a criterion for the analyses, if desired. However, as I do not break down the results from the film corpus by gender, such a comparison was not necessary.
[88] It should be noted that the corpus itself is not available for examination by the public, and thus the results cited are always those given by Filppula himself in his *The Grammar of Irish English* (1999).

on a wide range of features in different parts of the country and serves as an interesting counterpoint to Hickey's survey, particularly when one bears in mind that Filppula's respondents are considerably older and the results are by now almost 30 years old[89].

Potential discrepancies within the film corpus

It is worth pointing out in advance that while there would appear at times to be large discrepancies between the frequency and type of features which appear in individual films within the corpus, it is useful to remember something which Cohen Minnick remarked on with regard to her findings for African American English (AAE) in *Huckleberry Finn*, namely that

> (n)o speaker of AAE, real or fictional, will incorporate every possible feature associated with AAE into his or her speech, produce speech that contains no non-AAE features or AAE features shared with other American English varieties, or produce speech that contains the same AAE features as every or even any other speaker.
> (Cohen Minnick 2004: 64)

Needless to say, the same applies to speakers of Irish English. The occasional use of the Standard English present perfect rather than, what is regarded as, the more typically Irish '*after' perfect* in a screenplay need not imply carelessness or a lack of consistency on the part of the screenwriter. In fact, Blackburn, defending the inconsistencies she found in the literary dialect used by Eugene O'Neill, argues that language, by its very nature, is not consistent, as dialects of whole communities of speakers are always susceptible to change. The same applies to the idiolects of the individuals within those groups. Therefore, although a language remains systematic, some dialect features remain stable while others vary between competing forms (cf. 1971: 238).

However, as convenient as it would be to claim that the inconsistencies or inaccuracies in the language in the films were merely a matter of free variation and, therefore, examples of art imitating life, this would just not be true. In a great number of cases, the inaccuracies or inconsistencies present in the films cannot simply be glossed over or played down as minor anomalies, due to the fact that they are often so systematic or so conspicuous that they catch the eye, or rather ear, of even the non-linguist. In fact, features do not even have to be erroneous to draw attention to themselves. In some cases, a perfectly acceptable Irish English feature can be so overused in a film as to render it a stereotype. In *Waking Ned*, for example, the lexical item *mighty*, meaning 'great'[90], is used excessively[91] – appearing 7 times over the course of the film, although otherwise it only appeared in 3 of the 50 films in the corpus, and then only on one occasion per film. Indeed, the frequency of its usage in *Waking Ned* was so high as to even force the *Irish Times* film critic, Michael Dwyer, to comment on it when reviewing the film. He wrote that the plot involves "the villagers consuming vast amounts of alcohol at all hours of the day and night and saying 'mighty' a lot, as in 'murder is a mighty word to use at this time of the [sic][92] night …'" (Dwyer 1998)[93]. Research into the

---

[89] For more about Filppula's HE corpus, see Filppula (1999: 37-9).
[90] Dolan also offers the words *intensive, enjoyable, exciting, strong* and *hard* as synonyms (2006: 155).
[91] Ives has commented on this tendency for authors "to regularize" the frequency of particular dialectal forms to such an extent that the features, inevitably, become exaggerated and noticeable (1950: 159).
[92] Dwyer's erroneous insertion of the word *the* into the film quote is an interesting example of the non-standard use of the definite article which is prevalent in Irish English and will be discussed on page 76.

background of the film uncovers a very likely reason for this overuse of the expression. It turns out that, until shortly before shooting, the film was not even supposed to be set in Ireland. In an interview with *The Canadian Journal of Irish Studies*, Rod Stoneman, the former Chairman of the Irish Film Board, admitted that "*Waking Ned Devine* is a profoundly ambiguous film in Irish terms. It was made on the Isle of Man and up to a month before it was shot it was set in Cornwall; then they decided to reset it in Ireland and recast it in Irish[94]. Of course, it's dreadful paddy-whackery[95]" (McIlroy 2003b: 56). The last-minute change in setting implies that a script change had to happen quickly and thus that the screenwriter may have simply resorted to the use of pat phrases to lend the script, what he perceived to be, an extra dimension of "Irishness".

Throughout the film corpus, one can find many similarly interesting examples of anomalies. Sometimes they are film-specific, as in the case above, and, thus, shall be addressed individually under the heading of "unusual examples" whenever they appear. However, in the majority of cases, they can usually be attributed to one of a number of reasons, so in order not to have to repeatedly offer the same reasons for the appearance of features in places where, or at times when, one would not expect them in the tables, I shall explain the presence of such inaccuracies/inconsistencies now in some detail.

The role of the scriptwriter

Despite all the efforts made by moviemakers to ensure that the dialogue in their films is as appropriate as possible to time and place, shortcomings in a film's language are not uncommon. When inaccuracies or inconsistencies do appear, the most obvious person to point the finger at would seem to be scriptwriters. After all, if we regard film language as literary dialect, they are the ones who put the words into the mouths of the actors. Thus, if screenwriters are not sensitive to the language of the setting or period of the film, they may include features which seem out of place in the region or time portrayed.

Lexical items could potentially pose the greatest danger here, with words typical of a certain region of Ireland possibly being used elsewhere (for example, *bleedin'* being used as an adverb outside of Dublin is extremely rare), or, worse still, words which are not used in

---

[93] The overuse of the word *mighty* in this film is particularly conspicuous, as it appears three times in three minutes in one portion of the movie and again three times within five minutes at another point. The examples are as follows:

00:05:20	MJ2000W	Hold on there now…I've some **mighty** news.
00:06:14	MM2000W	God, it's **mighty**, Jackie!
00:07:56	FA2000W	That's **mighty**, for I've an idea I know myself.
00:24:50	FA2000W	There'd have been a **mighty** party.
00:27:21	MN2000W	There would have been a **mighty** party, Jackie.
00:29:10	MM2000W	Murder is a **mighty** word to use at this time of night, Jackie.
01:03:26	MD2000W	It's not easy cashing such a **mighty** cheque.

Mighty occurs in three other films (*The General*, *High Spirits* and *Angela's Ashes*) but only one time in each.

[94] Last minute changes of this nature are more common than one would think. For example, Scottish actor James McAvoy's character in *Inside I'm Dancing* was originally supposed to have been from County Cork. Indeed, McAvoy even spent a month learning the Cork accent. "Four weeks I'm doing this Cork accent and I was really loving it. We were doing a really thick accent, but the producers thought it was too alienating. So it was changed to Dublin" (*The Irish Times*, October 8, 2004). Knowing this background detail makes James McAvoy's impeccable Dublin accent in the movie all the more impressive.

[95] According to Share (2003: 235), *paddywhackery* is "Stage Irish goings-on; exaggeration of national characteristics, customs or behaviour; employment of such alleged characteristics in a racist context".

Ireland at all being used in an Irish setting. While there are no examples of the former in the film corpus, there is an example of the latter. In *The Wind that Shakes the Barley*, Indian-born scriptwriter Paul Laverty employs the term *chicken coop* (01:16:40, FP1920C), although Cork locals would most certainly say *hen house*[96].

Similar problems can arise with regard to using terms which are not in keeping with the period of the film. In the case of anachronisms, one could perhaps argue that a term deemed to be obsolete or old-fashioned may have survived in a particular dialect, or even idiolect, and, thus, could be justified in a particular film. However, in the case of neologisms which appear before their time, before they have even been coined, then even the most creative of minds will have difficulty defending them. For example, in *How Harry Became a Tree*, Harry tells his son Gus to "Get out of that scratcher!" (00:15:29, MH1920WW), which in Dublin English is a perfectly acceptable form of telling somebody to get out of bed. However, the term *scratcher* (meaning 'bed') only came into use following the scabies epidemic which swept through Dublin in the 1940s (Share 2003: 281), and is thus out of place in a film set some twenty years previously. Another obvious example of an anachronism is evident in *The Informer*. Early in the film, Frankie tells his mother and sister that he was so homesick to see them that he would have come out of hiding as a fugitive and "walked down the middle of O'Connell Street" (00:16:32, MFMP1920D) just to get a glimpse of the two of them. However, O'Connell Street still bore the name Sackville Street in 1922, the year the film is set; its name was not actually changed until 1924 (cf. McMahon and O'Donoghue 2004: 605).

While these types of errors tend to occur most often in the case of foreign writers, who are less likely to be versed in the nuances of Irish English, or Irish history, they can also happen to even the most experienced of Irish writers. For example, in the film *Widows' Peak*, written by the renowned Dublin playwright Hugh Leonard, a number of the characters use the second person plural form *youse* which is typical of Dublin usage[97], although the film is set outside of the capital and the characters do not show any other evidence of coming from there, such as a Dublin accent. This unexpected usage of the term can thus perhaps be traced back to an oversight on the part of the screenwriter, who may have used this term unconsciously as it is second nature to him as a Dubliner.

The role of the actor
It would be unfair, however, to place the blame for any inconsistencies or inaccuracies which appear in the final cut of the film solely on the shoulders of the screenwriter. When one compares the shooting script with the finished cut of the film, there are often numerous discrepancies, and many of these can be attributed to the actor or, perhaps, the director. In the case of the actor, there appears to be a tendency for actors to ad lib, meaning that, for better or worse, they deviate from the script they have been given. In the best cases, an actor who is sensitive to the idiom of a particular place and/or time can actually lend the script a greater degree of realism by changing the occasional word. This is evident in Sean McGinley's

---

[96] Writing at the end of the nineteenth century, Wright suggested that the term *coop* was used for 'a chicken-hutch' in Scotland, the North Country, Yorkshire, Lancashire, Lincoln, Worcester, Shropshire, Gloucester, Hertford, East Anglia and the Isle of Wight, but he did not offer any evidence for Ireland (EDD s.v. coop, *sb.*[1].).
[97] The form is also a feature of Northern Irish English, but in any case it would be inappropriate in this locale.

addition of the Dublin slang term *dirt bird*[98] to his character Gary's courtroom outburst in *The General*[99], when he shouts, "Martin Cahill. He's a murderer, a drug dealer and a dirt bird!"[100].

However, in other cases, whether consciously nor not, actors distort what originally was written and add features which are inappropriate for their character or place. This is most likely to be unconscious and happens when an actor forgets himself and uses terms that come naturally to him, the actor, rather than those that would come naturally to his character. An example of this is evident with regard to the use of the second person plural form *yez*[101] in *The Quiet Man*, where Feeney, played by Jack MacGowran, says "Attention, attention please, Squire...Squire Danaher has the floor; in other words he's got something to say to *yez* all." In his in-depth analysis of the film, MacHale states that this line is not in the original script and that Feeney's "use of 'yez' for 'you' (plural) is not authentic West of Ireland usage and betrays Jack MacGowran's Dublin background" (2000: 174). However actors need not necessarily hail from Dublin for them to introduce this second person plural form which is not in keeping with the locale. Indeed, MacHale (2000) cites another example from *The Quiet Man*, this time of an American actor, Ward Bond, using the Dublin form *yez* in his role as a West of Ireland priest. This time, unlike in the previous example, the actor is obviously not automatically resorting to the phrase that comes most naturally to him. However, perhaps the slip can be explained by the actor's exposure to people, like his co-star MacGowran, who use that feature regularly or by his erroneous belief that that is a feature which is common in the West of Ireland. In any case, Bond's character Fr Lonergan says "I want *yez* all to cheer like Protestants" whereas the original line was "Now remember! I want you all to cheer him as if you were Protestants" or in another draft "Now remember! I want you to cheer him as though you mean it" (MacHale 2000: 239). Neither of the original sentences from the script includes the *yez* form, nor indeed the *ye* form which would have been most in keeping with the West of Ireland setting. Nevertheless, as outlined above, I would argue that in this context even the use of Standard English *you* would still have been more appropriate than *yez/yiz*.

The role of the producer/director

As outlined in the section on authenticity, producers and directors are also often responsible for the fact that the dialects or accents in Irish films do not really sound Irish at all. In a bid to secure their bottom line, producers often ask actors, writers and dialect coaches to compromise the strength of an accent or dialect in order to make the film more accessible to a larger English-speaking audience, with Middle America[102] often being referred to as the lowest common denominator which needs to be appeased. Likewise, directors often decide to

---

[98] Bernard Share's *Slanguage - A Dictionary of Irish Slang* compares *dirt bird* to the US terms *dirt bag* and *dirt ball* and defines it as a 'contemptible individual' (Share 2003: 86).

[99] A different example from the same film has already been commented on by Ruth Barton. She praises the quality of Brendan Gleeson's improvised lines, stating that "Cahill's quip to a Garda next to him as Gary assaults the camera operator: 'Desperate, isn't it?' is an unscripted ad lib by Gleeson that is in character and perfect Dublin vernacular" (Barton and O'Brien 2004: 37).

[100] Cf. John Boorman's original script which merely has the line, "Martin Cahill is a murderer and a drug dealer" (Boorman 1998: 45). Interestingly, the word *dirt bird* delivered in a strong Dublin accent proved to be too much for whoever subtitled the film. He/she misunderstood it and therefore has Gary say that Martin Cahill is "a murderer, a drug dealer and a dart board!" For more on this potential for misunderstanding, see Chapter 9.3 on vowels in Irish English.

[101] This and other second person plural forms will be addressed later when dealing with morphology.

[102] Middle America does not refer to Central America, but instead describes conservative middle-class Americans who live in small towns or suburbia.

make last-minute changes to the script during shooting and are, thus, responsible for cutting, adding and editing lines of dialogue. If they are not familiar with the dialect at hand, they too may further compromise the faithfulness of the dialect to the original (cf. Herman and Herman 1997: 9-10).

From the above, it should be clear that numerous factors are at play which can add to or detract from the accuracy of the language which appears in the final cut of a film. Bearing these factors in mind, let us now proceed to look at the language in the films in detail.

6.1 Grammar

In keeping with the approach taken by Filppula (1999) and Harris (1993), the features of Irish English have been divided up into those which occur as parts of the verb phrase, the noun phrase, negation, questions, the complex sentence and morphology. Since there was not always agreement between these two authors, nor with Hickey, regarding what should go into each category, I have grouped the features in a way which allows a certain amount of overlap.

6.1.1 The verb phrase

6.1.1.1 Habitual aspect

Irish English has three ways of marking habitual aspect. These are 1) the use of an unstressed form of *do* with the infinitive of another verb[103], 2) the use of an unstressed form of *do* with the infinitive of the verb *be* plus a *progressive construction* and 3) the use of habitual *be*, either as an uninflected form (*be*) or with non-standard inflection (*bees*). These forms can be seen in the following examples from the film corpus:

1) People do pay me compliments on my roses. I **do tell** them there's not a ha'porth[104] of skill involved.
(*Widows' Peak*, 00:08:45, MOH1930M)

2) They **do be peepin'** from the gorse bushes.
(*Dead Meat*, 00:41:28, FF2000LM)

3) You'd wonder what **bees** scraping through their heads[105].
(*Dead Meat*, 00:42:16, MC2000LM)

Many scholars, such as Sullivan (1980), attribute the use of these habitual aspect forms in Irish English to influence from the Irish language, which possesses a tense form which has no equivalent in Standard English, namely the consuetudinal or habitual present (Sullivan 1980: 203). The suggestion is that the first Irish learners of English simply

---

[103] Hickey suggests that the first way of indicating habitual aspect involves "the use of an unstressed form of *do* with *be*" (2004a: 123). However, results from the films show that the unstressed form of *do* need not necessarily be followed by the verb *be*, but, in fact, can be used with any verb in the infinitive to suggest habitual use. These findings are in keeping with those by Harris, who also offers examples of a form of *do* together with the infinitives of other verbs, such as "He does plough the field for us" or "A lot of them does cut them on into June" (1993: 163). Henry (1957: 169) also offers the form *does be*, as in "There does be fairies in it" or "There doesn't only be three or four people in it". The lack of agreement between subject and verb, as evidenced in these examples, will be dealt with later in the book. In his recent *Irish English*, Hickey does indeed acknowledge that unstressed *do* can occur with lexical verbs, although the observation is still reduced to a footnote (cf. 2007: 216).
[104] *Ha'porth* (sometimes *ha'p'orth*) stands for 'ha'penny's worth' or 'halfpennyworth' and means 'as much as a halfpenny will purchase; hence a very small quantity' (OED s.v. halfpennyworth, *n*.). An example is to be found in the play *Arrah na Pogue* by Boucicault - Fanny: "It was not you, then, that robbed Feeny on Derrybawn?" Shaun: "Me, miss – devil a ha'porth" (Krause 1964: 146).
[105] In his *Survey of Irish English Usage*, Hickey describes only an uninflected form of *be*, although his example is actually of the inflected *bees* form. Unfortunately, there are no examples of the uninflected form of habitual *be* in the film corpus. Examples of what this structure might look like are offered by Filppula: "A lot of them *be* interested in football matches" (1999: 136) and Taniguchi: "They be sayin' Farrelly bought it for a song [...]" (1972: 80). It should be noted that Filppula (1999) offers a further category in his division of habitual aspect forms, seeing clear distinctions between all of the aforementioned forms, and a negative imperative form *don't be + verb (-ing form)* (131). However, I shall address this last form later on page 69 when looking at imperatives.

transferred this aspect to English by creating a habitual aspect form with the verb *be* as they would in Irish. This argument is certainly credible, particularly when one is aware that although the Irish verb *tá* (*be*) is the only one to possess a habitual form (*bíonn*), it can be used together with other verbs to create habitual present constructions for these verbs as well. Sullivan illustrates this with the Irish example *bíonn sé ag crú* which in Standard English means "he (always) does the milking" (1980: 203) but in Irish English would likely be expressed as "he bees[106] milking" or "he does be milking". This explanation would certainly account for the constructions which occur in sentence 3), and possibly 2), above, in which the verb *be* is actually present, but this would not explain the structures in sentence 1) in which the verb *be* does not even appear[107].

An explanation for these elusive forms could be that the use of the habitual with the periphrastic *do* is a feature of English in the South West and West Midlands of England which was brought to Ireland. This idea was corroborated in research by Ihalainen in East Somerset in the 1970s. He discovered that *do* is also used there to signify habitual aspect in affirmative sentences and he observed that even if this periphrastic use of *do* is now considered a provincialism, it was common in Standard English until the end of the eighteenth century (cf. Ihalainen 1991: 148). He was also quick to point out the phonological difference between the periphrastic *do* and the emphatic *do*. The first is unstressed, whereas the second carries stress to indicate emphasis. This distinction is very important in Irish English as well, and is duly noted by Asián and McCullough (1998: 47) as a potential stumbling block for the uninitiated when reading literary dialect aloud. A perfect example of this pitfall is evident in the film *Rat* (Steve Barron, 2000), where British actress Imelda Staunton, whose Dublin accent is otherwise impeccable, on one occasion stresses the *do*, resulting in the emphatic form (example 4a below) rather than the periphrastic form (example 4b) which one would expect.

4a) They 'do say if a budgie escapes, the wild birds will kill him. (emphatic *do*)
(*Rat*, 00:44:12, FC2000D)

4b) They do 'say if a budgie escapes, the wild birds will kill him. (periphrastic *do*)

The contrast in pronunciation of the emphatic *do* and the periphrastic *do* is further highlighted by two excellent examples from the film corpus, in which both forms happen to appear in the same sentence. In each case, the first use of *do* is emphatic and the second periphrastic. The exchanges are as follows:

5) *Agnes*: All right youse, what's wrong with Mark?
Cathy: Maybe he has worms.
Agnes: Don't be so disgusting, you!
Cathy: But, Mammy, people **do get** worms in their pooh. Mary Dowdall told me. And they **do be** mad long.
(*Agnes Browne*, 00:17:34, FCB1960D)

---

[106] This feature is sometimes also spelled *be's* (cf. Harris 1984b: 162).
[107] That is not to say that the verb *be* cannot appear in such structures. On the contrary, it appears in three of the examples in Table 2. However, the point being made is that the verb *be* is not obligatory in such cases, as the other examples testify.

6) *Mrs Doyle-Counihan*: Good morning Ms O'Hare. I hope I didn't hunt your visitor.
Ms O'Hare: Oh, Mrs Doyle-Counihan, not at all. Mr Clancy was just admiring my roses.
Mrs Doyle-Counihan: Sure, why wouldn't he?
[...]
Ms O'Hare: People **do pay** me compliments on my roses. I **do tell** them there's not a ha'porth of skill involved. A weenie bit of loving care maybe.
(*Widows' Peak*, 00:08:45, FMOH1930M)

With regard to the corpus, the habitual aspect with an unstressed form of *do* plus the infinitive of a verb appears in 6 of the 50 films (12%) [see Table 1]. This finding corresponds very well with the results of Hickey's *Survey of Irish English Usage*, for which the average acceptability rate nationwide was 10%[108]. Interestingly all of the films which display this feature are set in Leinster, where informants also showed a 12% acceptance rate for this aspect form in Hickey's survey. This finding is in keeping with those of Filppula's *HE corpus* (1999). Although he made a distinction between the *do* plus the infinitive of the verb and the *do* plus the verb *be* construction, he found that in total the frequency of these features was highest in Leinster. Nevertheless, that is by no means to say that this feature does not appear elsewhere in everyday speech.

The use of an unstressed form of *do* with the infinitive of the verb *be* plus a progressive construction is extremely rare in the film corpus and features in only 1 of the 50 films (2%) [see Table 2]. This result is, on the one hand, very surprising, as intuition and much of the literature published on Irish English would suggest that the progressive form would be far more common than the form with the periphrastic *do* and *the infinitive of a verb*. This notion is also supported by Hickey's survey, for which the *do + be + verb (-ing form)* feature was regarded considerably more favourably than the previous example, with 25% of those surveyed, on average, regarding the progressive construction as being "no problem".

On the other hand, the fact that the *do + be + verb (-ing form)* hardly features at all in the film corpus is in keeping with corpus-based studies by Kallen (1985 and 1989) and Filppula (1999). They made very similar discoveries which also went against their intuition regarding this supposedly typical Irish English feature. They too discovered that the *do/does + be + verb (-ing)* occurred far less frequently than expected and was greatly outnumbered by the *do/does + infinitive* construction. This led them to conclude that the former feature which has often been regarded as one of the "classics" of Irish English "appears to be rare enough in actual usage" (Filppula 1999: 132)[109].

---

[108] It may be important to note that the acceptability of this feature in Hickey's survey was for a *do + be* construction (due to the nature of the sentence he provided) and not for a general *do + infinitive* structure, as was the case in the films. Whether or not these would have met with differing degrees of acceptability in his study is unclear, although one could compare the results with Filppula's in which the *do + V* outnumbered the *do + be* form by a ratio of 2:1 (1999: 132). If one were to divide up the two forms as they appear in the films, there would, however, be no difference, with appearances in 3 out of the 50 (6%) films each for both the *do + V* form and the *do + be* structure.

[109] The feature may be more common in Northern Irish English, however, as Amador Moreno's study of the language in Patrick MacGill's Donegal-set novels, showed the *do + be + V-ing* form to be "the most salient expression of the habitual aspect in HE" (2006: 92).

The only film to display this feature, namely *Dead Meat* (Conor McMahon, 2004), is set in County Leitrim, which is located in Connaught, the province which showed by far the highest acceptability for this feature (35%) in Hickey's survey.

Similarly low results to those of the *do + be + verb (-ing)* construction were found for the aspect form involving the inflected form of the verb *be*. This, too, appears in only 1 of the 50 movies (2%) [see Table 3], and, again, the film in question is the Leitrim-based[110] *Dead Meat*. Such a low frequency rate is not so surprising and is certainly in keeping with the results of Hickey's survey, which show a mere 3% acceptability rating, both in Connaught and nationwide, for this form of habitual aspect. The low frequency in the film corpus and the low approval rate in the *Survey of Irish English* can both be explained by the fact that, according to Harris, the *bees/bes/be's* form is actually "more typically northern" (1993: 162). This is a notion which is also supported by Bliss (1984: 143) and is further borne out in the acceptability of the feature among the Ulster cohort in Hickey's study, where 13% of the respondents regarded it as "no problem".[111]

6.1.1.2 Perfect markers

Irish English has six different ways of marking perfect aspect. These are the Standard English *present/past perfect*, formed with a form of the verb *have* and a past participle, as well as five non-standard forms: the *'after' perfect*, the *'medial-object' perfect*, the *'be' perfect*, the *'extended-now' perfect* and the *'indefinite anterior' perfect*. I will not address the Standard English *present perfect* in this study, although there is ample evidence of its presence in the film corpus. Instead, I shall focus on the non-standard forms, which in a study by Ronan (2005) were found to appear 41.5% of the time in Irish English speech and writing[112]. The frequencies of the non-standard perfect forms in the film corpus will again be compared with the acceptability ratings from Hickey's survey, where possible. Unfortunately, the *'indefinite anterior' perfect* did not feature in the *Survey of Irish English Usage*, but, since it appears frequently in the film corpus, I have also included it below.

The 'after' perfect

The *'after' perfect*, also known as the *'immediate perfective'* (Hickey 2004a), the *'hot news' perfect* (McCawley 1971) or the *PI* (Greene 1979), is one of the most frequently discussed features of Irish English, and refers to an action which has just taken place, or, to be more precise, to an event "occurring immediately prior to the time of speaking or time of reference" (Asián and McCullough 1998: 47). It is generally found in the form, *be + after + verb (-ing form)*, as is the case in all of the examples from the corpus, although it can also appear with a noun phrase, as will be seen below.

---

[110] Henry found evidence of this same form in neighbouring Roscommon: "The cattle bees wanderin' around the fields lookin' for water" (1957: 170).

[111] It might be of interest for a future study to also analyse the use of this feature in films set in Ulster to see whether it appears more frequently there as well, particularly since the results of Amador Moreno's recent study of the literary dialect in Patrick MacGill's novels proved to be counter-intuitive, showing the inflected *be* "to have been quite rare in Donegal" (2006: 91).

[112] Ronan's corpus consisted of a selection of spoken and written Irish English data in which she specifically investigated the various forms of perfect marking in Irish English. As stated above, she found that the various non-standard perfect markers appeared 41.5% of the time and she broke these down further to find the ratio of their respective appearances. Her results are given on page 60.

The reason that this feature has received so much attention in the past is that it is the only one whose origins can unequivocally be traced back to a substratal influence from the Irish language (or, where it appears in Scotland, to Scots Gaelic). This is because there is no verb *have* in Irish, and the perfect tenses are instead formed with parts of the verb *be* and the preposition *after* (*tar éis* or *tréis*). The first Irish speakers of English simply transferred this structure onto their new language, so that, for example, the Irish sentence *Tá mé tar éis mo dhinnéar a ithe* became the Irish English "I'm after eating my dinner" (cf. Dolan 2006: 3). This structure, which in Standard English means 'I have just had my dinner', has a great chance of being misunderstood by those who are not familiar with Irish English, as they may see the *after* as implying a desire or intention to do something[113], and thus interpret the sentence as "I want to eat my dinner"[114]. This potential for misunderstanding is even greater when the participle is omitted as in *He is after his dinner* (Hickey 1983: 41), which, again, means 'He has just had his dinner' and not 'He wants his dinner', as one might think[115].

It is perhaps the aforementioned potential for misunderstanding which accounts for the complete absence of the *be* + *after* + *noun phrase* perfective structure from the film corpus. Instead, all of the examples from the corpus are of the *be* + *after* + *verb* (*-ing form*) variety. Having said that, it is likely that sentences with a verb phrase, such as the following, are not necessarily any less confusing for the uninitiated.

7) I think **that's him after coming** in[116].

(*Rat*, 00:12:47, FC2000D)

The flexibility of the *'after' perfect* can be seen in the fact that, by changing the tense of the verb *be*, this perfective form can be used across different tenses, creating the equivalent of Standard English's 8) *present perfect*, 9) *past perfect* and, what appears to be, 10) *future perfect* respectively[117].

8) **I'm after getting** a tip for a horse at Leopardstown.

(*Mystics*, 00:10:07, ML2000D)

---

[113] One of the examples from the film corpus, "Someone's after poaching rabbits" (*Darby O'Gill and the Little People*, 00:13:17, MMB1800D), could very well reflect this meaning of desire or intention, particularly if the American screenwriter was not familiar with the true use of the *'after' perfect*. However, since this is just speculation on my part, I have given the sentence the benefit of the doubt and included it as meaning 'Someone has been poaching rabbits'.

[114] In a study by Harris (1982: 111), two groups – one consisting of native speakers of Irish English and the other of speakers of British English – were asked to interpret the sentence "I'm after getting a cup of tea". The results differed greatly, with all but 2 of the 145 Irish English speakers (98.6%) understanding the sentence to convey a "hot news" meaning. 51 of the 63 British speakers (81%), on the other hand, understood the sentence to mean 'I want to go for a cup of tea now'.

[115] However, it would be wrong to assume that all noun phrases in Irish English which feature the word *after* in them imply a perfective form. They very often do convey the sense of wanting something. In the case of the sentence "I'm not after a bleedin' postcard. I'm after urban decay" (*The Commitments*, 01:13:10, MJR1990D), Jimmy Rabbitte is describing the effect he wants to capture in the photograph of the band. In "It's the drink you're after, is it?" (*Angela's Ashes*, 00:08:36, MIRA1930D) the IRA man is not asking Malachy McCourt whether he has just had a drink, but rather recognises that McCourt is looking for money to buy alcohol. Furthermore, in *Darby O'Gill and the Little People*, the sentence "And if it's music you're after, how about a song?" (*Darby O'Gill and the Little People*, 00:37:35, MKB1800K) is also an expression of desire. The *front clefting* evident in the last two sentences is dealt with on page 102.

[116] The sentence can be roughly translated as "I think that must be him who has just come in."

[117] For more on the use of the perfective across all tenses, see Hickey (1982: 41).

9) I left that fella fencin' this mornin'; when I went back **he was after shaggin' off** on me.

(*The Nephew*, 00:34:01, MT1990C)

10) **He'll be after catching** a few flounders.

(*Ryan's Daughter*, 01:01:13, MFR1920W)

However, future uses of the *'after' perfect*, i.e. sentences featuring *will* + *be* + *after* + *verb* (*-ing form*) have traditionally been regarded as problematic and are often dismissed as "Stage Irish" (cf. Bartley 1954: 130), even if there is also some evidence of their use by Irish writers (cf. McCafferty 2003: 299)[118]. In this regard, it should also be noted that the use of *will* together with an *'after' perfect* does not necessarily imply future use. For example, while sentence 10 above from *Ryan's Daughter* ostensibly looks like a case of future use, due to the presence of a *will* form, it does not actually convey future meaning. Instead, it is more in keeping with Taniguchi's observation that "the auxiliary is often used before 'be', to denote possibility, inference, probability, conviction and so forth" (1972: 57)[119]. This explanation fits example 10, as Fr Collins just assumes or infers that Michael has been out fishing because he sees him in his boat.

Unusual examples

The fact that Irish English utilises the *'after' perfect* form does not mean that the Standard English forms are unheard of there. In fact, they are used increasingly in everyday life and are also evident in the film corpus. Surprisingly, the Standard English present perfect and the *'after' perfect* are even used *together* on two occasions in the film corpus[120].

11) **He's done it** again. Matt, **he's after doin'** it again.

(*Rat*, 01:13:04, MP2000D)

12) What **have I done**? What **am I after doing**?

(*About Adam*, 01:22:36, FA2000D)

It is unclear whether the repetition in these examples is for the benefit of a non-Irish audience, or just simply an emphatic means of expressing one's disbelief at what has just happened[121].

---

[118] Hickey's recent findings have confirmed that the *'after' perfect* "had genuine future reference in its earliest attestations" (2007: 201). What is more, he offers an acceptable use of *will*+ *the 'after' perfect* in modern Irish English: "By the time you get there he'll be after drinking the beer" (2007: 198).

[119] Taniguchi is echoing what Quirk *et al.* describe as "the present predictive sense of will". They go on to state that the structure is "similar in meaning to *must* in the 'logical necessity' sense" and they offer the examples "She will have had her dinner by now" or "That'll be the postman [on hearing the doorbell ring]" (1985: 228). This structure would also appear to be the one referred to by Kallen as "non-factual", "hypothetical" or "counterfactual", for which he gives the somewhat unsatisfactory example: "A student will be after accomplishing an academic task" (1991: 66).

[120] It is unclear whether a third sentence "Teddy O'Donovan's after takin' Mister Sweeney off us. He's taken/takin' him out the front door of the court" from *The Wind that Shakes the Barley* (see Table 4) is also evidence of the mixing of the two forms, as it could either be an example of a present perfect with contraction of "He has taken" or simply a shortened form of "He is taking". Unfortunately, the screenplay does not clarify the matter, as the line is not included there at all, suggesting that it was improvised on the set (cf. Laverty 2006: 92).

[121] While Taniguchi also sometimes found both perfect forms occurring in the same speech in his corpus of literary texts, the verbs used were never repeated. This can be seen in the following example, in which two

In addition to this unusual use of both the present perfect and the *'after' perfect* in the same sentence, *The Snapper* offers another interesting variation on *'after' perfect* usage in the following example:

> 13) Your **da's after being defending** your honour.
>
> (*The Snapper*, 00:58:26, FKay1990D)

Here one finds the insertion of an additional participle form between the *after* and *verb (-ing form)* construction which one would normally expect in Irish English, namely "Your da's after defending your honour". The insertion of *being* could perhaps be seen as an example of hypercorrection on the part of the speaker who knows that some form of the verb *be* (*been*) is required to construct the present perfect progressive in Standard English, yet who applies the Irish English rule of *be* + *after* + *verb (-ing form)* to it, resulting in the example above. This sentence is all the more interesting when one compares it with the corresponding one from the Roddy Doyle novel on which the film is based. Although the novel features numerous examples of Irish English in literary dialect (cf. Asián and McCullough 1998), this particular sentence is actually in Standard English in the book, employing the present perfect, and reads: "Your father's been defending your honour. Isn't he great?" (Doyle 1992: 276).

Examples like number 13 above, with the insertion of an additional participle form between the *after* and *verb (-ing form)* construction, are extremely rare in the literature on Irish English, although Kallen does include a couple in his essay on *after* as a Dublin variable (1991)[122]. Having compiled a total corpus of 114 tokens of *after* obtained from 74 speakers in Dublin, he found a total of 7 verbs which take, what he refers to as, "being" used as an "auxiliary" (1991: 64), two of which he includes in the article.

> 14) That's where **I'm after bein looking**.
>
> (Kallen 1991: 65)

> 15) **We're after bein livin** there for the past 21 years.
>
> (Kallen 1991: 62)

The first of these examples is quite similar to the example from *The Snapper*, in that it refers to an event that has just taken place. The second, however, sounds a little strange due to the time reference. Admittedly, *'after' perfects* do not always have to express something which has just taken place (see Asián and McCullough's definition on page 48); nonetheless, the fact that it expresses something durative, such as living somewhere for the past 21 years, makes it a very unlikely use of the structure. It would be interesting to subject this type of *'after' perfect* structure to further testing, including an acceptability test, much like that used by Hickey.

---

different verbs, *read* and *hear*, appear. "And now that I*'m after reading* the Bishop's Letter, for ye, I hope – I hope that – ye *have heard* the Bishop's Letter and …" (Taniguchi 1972: 56). This is in contrast to the film examples, which use the same verb twice.

[122] The structure also appears as a footnote in Hickey (2007: 206), who includes an example of the *'after' perfect* with a continuous form uttered by an old man in County Wicklow: "We're after bein' removin' rocks".

The *be + after + verb (-ing form)* appears in 24 of the 50 films (48%) [see Table 4], which, as we shall see, makes it one of the most frequent Irish English grammar features in the film corpus. Having said that, this percentage is quite low, when one considers the *'after' perfect*'s high acceptability rate among the Irish population (90%), as can be seen in Hickey's study. With such a large discrepancy, it is necessary to examine the potential reasons for such results.

Research has shown that it is not unusual for this most Irish of features to appear less frequently than one would expect in a corpus. Indeed, Harris (1984a: 316) and Filppula (1999: 100) also found this to be the case. However, in their studies, the low frequency of this feature was attributed to the formal interview situation used to elicit information (cf. also Sabban 1982: 158-9), as well as to the fact that the interview itself "precluded questions dealing with the immediate context (including hot-news past)" (Harris 1984a: 316). These arguments, of course, do not apply to the film corpus, which suggests that the aforementioned potential for misunderstanding among an international audience may very well play a determining role in the decision of whether or not to include the *'after' perfect* in films.

When it comes to the geographical distribution of this feature, Filppula's findings were also quite revealing, as they showed that the *'after' perfect* was considerably more common in the eastern dialects than in the (south) western ones (1999: 101). This would seem to go against all expectations, particularly if one bears in mind that the structure is a calque on the Irish *tar éis* construction and that the influence of the Irish substratum is supposed to be greatest on the west coast, and, thus, in Kerry and Clare in his corpus. However, by consulting Irish language scholars (cf. Ó Sé 1992), Filppula was able to discover a plausible reason for this seeming anomaly. It would seem that the Irish *PI*, a similar structure in the Irish language, is relatively uncommon in Munster and Connaught Irish and that, by extension, the *'after' perfect* is therefore less common in the Irish English in those regions (cf. Filppula 1999: 102). It is worth noting that, although the results of Hickey's survey are not as clear cut as Filppula's, the feature also received marginally less approval in Connaught than elsewhere, which suggests that there may be some merit to this argument.

Bearing these results in mind, it is useful to look at the distribution of the *'after' perfect* in the film corpus to see whether similar geographical trends arise. In order to do this, it is not only necessary to see where the film is set but also to bear in mind where the speaker who uses the form is from. For example, although the *'after' perfect* occurs in *Nora*, a film originally categorised as one set predominantly in Leinster[123], it is used by the character Nora Barnacle who hails from Galway and, thus, it should be filed under the Connaught category. Similarly, although *Darby O'Gill and the Little People* is ostensibly set in Munster[124], the speaker who uses the *'after' perfect* is the Dubliner Michael McBride and thus the example should go on the Leinster list. The opposite applies for the example from *When Brendan Met Trudy*: although the film is set in Dublin, Trudy who uses the form is from Cork and therefore the feature is attributed to Munster. Having divided the films accordingly, one does indeed see exciting parallels to both Filppula's and Hickey's findings. The *'after' perfect* again appears most often on the Leinster list and least often on the Connaught one. The results for the films are broken down as follows: the *'after' perfect* appears in 18 of the 34 films (53%) attributed

---

[123] Admittedly, a large part of the film takes place in Trieste. Dublin, however, is the setting for the largest Irish portion of the film.
[124] See page 28 for this controversial categorisation.

to Leinster, in 4 of the 8 (50%) accredited to Munster and 2 of the 8 (25%) assigned to Connaught. These findings, while by no means conclusive, lend a certain amount of support to the theory that the substratal influence is greatest in areas where this is a newer feature of Irish and thus also of Irish English.

As outlined above, the *be + after + noun phrase* perfective structure does not appear in the film corpus, perhaps due to the inherent potential for misunderstanding which arises when this appears without a verb form. Unfortunately, there are no comparable results for this form for Hickey's study, as it was not one of the features included in his survey. Nonetheless, perhaps its omission from his questionnaire in the first place can be seen as an indicator of its supposed rarity. After all, no tokens appeared in Filppula's HE corpus either, suggesting that the form could be far less common than originally thought[125].

The 'medial-object' perfect

The second non-standard perfective aspect form in Irish English is the *'medial-object' perfect* (Filppula 1999), which is also known as the *resultative perfective* (Hickey 2004a) or *PII* (Greene 1979). It is basically a standard perfect construction, but with the object before the past participle rather than after it. Filppula suggests that this perfective form "is best described as 'stative' and/or 'resultative': the construction focuses on the end-point, result, or resulting state, of the action rather than the action itself" (1999: 108).

The following examples from the film corpus show the past perfect (example 16) and present perfect forms (example 17) of this construction:

> 16) I **had** a drop **taken** before I came here and I didn't know what I was sayin', but now I remember.
>
> (*The Informer*, 01:08:43, MG1920D)

> 17) I **have** four crates of lemonade bottles **collected**. You can have them; that's ten bob.
>
> (*Agnes Browne*, 00:48:42, MT21960D)

The *'medial-object' perfect* is evident in 10 of the 50 films (20%) [see Table 5] in the corpus[126], which again is very low compared to the 93% acceptability rate for this feature in Hickey's survey. Seeing as there were similarly large discrepancies between the frequency rate of the *'after' perfect* in the film corpus and that of Hickey's survey, it is perhaps interesting to compare the findings for this form and the *'after' perfect* across a number of corpora to see whether there is a noticeable trend. In the *Survey of Irish English Usage*, the *'medial-object' perfect* was regarded as marginally more acceptable than the *'after' perfect* (93% versus 90%). The *'medial-object' perfect* was also found to be more common than the *'after' perfect* in Filppula's HE corpus, although the difference in his study was by no means

---

[125] On the other hand, my mother, a native of County Mayo, uses the form regularly on the telephone, informing me that they are "just after the dinner".

[126] Filppula warns that "it is important to keep the MOP ['medial object' perfect S.W.] apart from superficially identical constructions with different readings" (1999: 109). Such structures generally have a passive meaning, such as the following examples from the film corpus: "He has them X-rayed as they clock out, in case they swallow one" (*The General*, 01:04:32, MMC1990D), "Ah, don't mind that old shite Carson. He had me transferred" (*A Man of No Importance*, 01:29:47, MRo1960D), "So, in the heel of the hunt, I went to Dublin and had her adopted" (*Widows' Peak*, 01:14:20, FMOH1930M).

marginal. In fact, he found that the *'medial-object' perfect* occurred almost twice as often as the *'after' perfect* (cf. Filppula 1999: 109). In the film corpus, however, this ratio is reversed, with the *'after' perfect* actually occurring over twice as many times as the *'medial-object' perfect* (48% versus 20%)[127].

It is also useful to examine the types of verb used in the *'medial-object' perfect* construction. Filppula (1999) observes that they are transitive, since an object is involved and that they are generally dynamic verbs of activity or accomplishment. The five most common verbs in Filppula's HE corpus (1999) were *do, make, build, get,* and *forget*, while in Harris' (1984b) and Kallen's (1989) studies of Northern Irish English and Southern Irish English respectively, *do* and *make* were also the most common verbs. These findings are not really reflected in the film corpus. Only one of the aforementioned verbs, namely *make*, appears, albeit as a phrasal verb *make up*. What is more, none of the verbs given in Filppula's other examples, namely *skip, shoot, see, miss* and *forget* – appear at all in *'medial-object' perfect* structures in the film corpus, not even in those films which exhibited more than one example of this perfect form. Instead the verbs which appear are the aforementioned *make up*, as well as *break, take, save, plan, fool, put, collect, destroy, mesmerise* and *rob*, with *break, take* and *plan* appearing in two films each. In this respect, these findings are slightly more in keeping with those of Taniguchi, who also cites examples with *break* and *take* (1972: 59)[128].

The *'be' perfect*

A further method of expressing the perfect in Irish English is the use of what Filppula calls the *'be' perfect* (1999: 116). Also known as a *quasi-perfect* (Bliss 1984: 145) or the *'be' auxiliary* (Hickey 2004a: 125)[129], this form involves the substitution of *be* for *have* to create the perfect. It is similar to the *'after' perfect* and the *'medial-object' perfect* in that it favours verbs with dynamic meaning, but, in contrast to the other types, it occurs with intransitive verbs (cf. Filppula 1999: 116). Filppula also stresses that "the focus is clearly on the end-point or result of some prior activity or event" (1999: 117). The verbs which are most likely to occur with the *'be' perfect* are mutative verbs, such as *go, leave, change* and *die* (cf. Harris 1984a: 308). In her study dedicated to the perfect forms in Irish English, Ronan also includes the verb *finish* in this category (cf. 2005: 256), while Filppula discovered instances of *come, vanish, wear, wither, fade, dry,* and *break up* in his corpus. Amador Moreno, on the other hand, could only find examples with *come, go* and *change* in her novels (2006: 107)[130].

Some examples of this structure from the literature include: "The amusements are gone quite expensive", "They're certainly changed for the better", "They're finished with the repairs now" (Hickey 2007: 178); "The sergeant is gone up to the barracks", "You were only gone out of sight when I came on your book" (Bliss 1984: 145); "All the tourists are gone

---

[127] To show the complete lack of consistency that exists across corpora, it is worth mentioning that in Amador Moreno's study of the literary dialect of Patrick MacGill's novels, which are set in Donegal at the turn of the twentieth century, there was absolutely no evidence of the *'medial-object' perfect* (2006: 101).
[128] He also includes instances with *hide* and *sicken*.
[129] The *'be' perfect* has also been recorded in other varieties, such as in the Shetland Islands where *be* is used for *have*, as in "ye're burnt the broth" (cf. EDD § 441). Wright adds that this *'be' perfect* could sometimes be heard in Rutland, Northampton, Warwick, Bedford, Hertford and southern Norfolk.
[130] Some examples of the *'be' perfect* from Bliss' corpus of literature include "di Lady is runne away from dee", I am come a great vay of miles", "the wind is turn'd, the wind was turn'd" (1979: 294).

back now", "I know they're gone mad" (Filppula 1999: 90) and "The children are gone back to school" (Dolan 2006: xxv).

Despite the availability of such examples for comparison, the classification of potential *'be' perfect* structures for this study was quite problematic. This is because some authors also included cases of *be* being used with a past participle as an adjective rather than as a *'be' perfect* per se. Ronan (2005: 254) and Filppula (1999: 120), for instance, offer the sentences "He is gone now" and "This was s'posed to be a Gaeltacht area, but = all the Irish, they *are* all *gone* out of it, they *are* all *gone*" respectively. It is not clear whether these authors also included such sentences in their calculations, but I decided to err on the side of caution and have thus excluded sentences in which *gone*, *finished* etc can be regarded as adjectives. What is more, despite the fact that Bliss claims that '*s* is always the contracted form of *is* and not *has* in Irish English (cf. Bliss 1971: 61), I have dismissed examples of such contractions, except in instances such as example 21, where confirmation of the contracted form being *is* is offered by the tag "isn't it".[131] Below are examples of the *'be' perfect* from the film corpus:

18) Now that Dad **is gone** to England, surely our troubles would be over.
    (*Angela's Ashes*, 01:15:02, MN1990L)

19) Mammy, **is** Daddy **gone** to Heaven forever?
    (*Agnes Browne*, 00:21:06:FCB1960D)

20) Ah, Jaysus, Marian! **I'm gone** blind.
    (*Agnes Browne*, 00:56:49, FAB1960D)

21) It**'s gone cold** now, **isn't it**?
    (*Adam and Paul*, 01:12:47, FJ2000D)

22). **You're** not even **changed**, Billy.
    (*The Commitments*, 01:13:37, MJR1990D)

The *'be' perfect* appears in 7 of the 50 films (14%) [see Table 6]. This compares with an 84% acceptability rating for Hickey's sentence "They're finished the work now", which once again reveals that there is quite a disparity between the findings from the film corpus and the results of Hickey's survey.

'Extended-now' perfect

Despite the fact that it has the appearance of a present tense form, the *'extended-now' perfect* (Filppula 1999: 123) or the *extended present*, as Hickey calls it (2004a: 124), is a further method of expressing the perfect in Irish English. This structure involves the use of a present tense form, very often of the verb *be*, where Standard English would use *have* and an appropriate participle. In addition, these structures are recognisable by the "obligatory presence of a time adverbial expressing duration" (Filppula 1999: 123). Therefore, although

---

[131] If examples of '*s* contractions and of *gone* and *finished* as adjectives had been regarded as instances of the *'be' perfect*, the total number of occurrences in the film corpus would have been 30 out of 50 (60%). Here are some of these omitted examples: "She's gone from you, and small wonder" (*The Quiet Man*, 01:46:43, MMF1930W), "Are you finished in here?" (*Michael Collins*, 00:28:04, MNB1910M) and "They're gone" (*Dead Meat*, 00:51:49, MD2000LM).

example 23) below might appear to have similarities with the *'be' perfect* above, it is actually an 'extended now' perfect, due to the absence of the participle *been* and the presence of the time adverbial expressing duration. Below are some examples from the film corpus:

23) **They're gone** about six hours.
(*Into the West*, 01:01:08, FK1990M)

24) How long **are** you **married**?
(*Intermission*, 00:26:14, FSa2000D)

25) Bang on time. **We're not long here** ourselves.
(*The Wind that Shakes the Barley*, 00:17:41, MC1920C)

The example from *Garage* below is particularly interesting in that it shows that, surprisingly, a verb is not even necessary to express the *'extended-now' perfect*.

26) **Pauline all right since**?
(*Garage*, 00:48:55, MJ2000M)

The verb which is omitted is *be*, but it is clear that the omitted form is not the present perfect, but rather the simple present. After all, Josie's question is not "Pauline *been* all right since?" a shortened form of "*Has* Pauline *been* all right since (the break up)?" but rather "Pauline all right since?" a shortened form of "*Is* Pauline all right since (the break up)?".

Like the *'be' perfect*, the *'extended-now' perfect* is included in Hickey's survey and, thus, I was able to compare its frequency in the film corpus with its acceptability among the Irish respondents. In total, the *'extended-now' perfect* form appears in 22 of the 50 films[132] (44%) [see Table 7]. However, if one were to examine only sentences containing the verb *know*, as in the example from the *Survey of Irish English Usage*, namely "I know her for five years now", then the number would be considerably lower at 3 out of 50 (6%). Like Hickey's example, which received an 80% acceptability rating nationwide, those three examples were all in the present tense[133], they were all accompanied by a time phrase, and their meaning was always undoubtedly the equivalent of the present perfect in Standard English. Examples are:

27) **I know** Chris Reilly since he was a child.
(*The Wind that Shakes the Barley*, 00:52:10, MD1920C)

28) **I know** him years, love. Never seen him look so bad. Dead. Definitely dead.
(*Agnes Browne*, 00:03:04, FM1960D)

---

[132] Unlike Filppula's findings (1999: 128), there is no indication to suggest that the *'extended-now' perfect* is more frequently used in areas adjoining the *Gaeltachtaí* (regions, predominantly in the west of Ireland, in which Irish is still spoken) than in the east.

[133] Filppula suggests that one can use either the present or the past tense in creating this structure. He offers the example: "I didn't hear him playin' with years an' years. Maybe he isn't able to play at all now" (1999: 122) to show that a past tense form can be used to create what would be a present perfect form in Standard English. However, the fact that he uses the simple past in the example would seem to relegate it to his *'indefinite anterior' perfect* category, which, as we will see, uses preterite forms, and not present forms, in contexts where one would use the present perfect in Standard English. After all, his sentence echoes sentences 36) and 37) on page 58 in their use of a simple past form of the auxiliary verb *do*.

29) Sure, **you** hardly **know** him more than a day.
(*The Boys and Girl from County Clare*, 01:12:04, FM1960Cl)

The 'indefinite anterior' perfect

The final form of perfect marking is the *'indefinite anterior' perfect*. Although it was not included on Hickey's questionnaire, it appears frequently in the literature on Irish English, as well as in the film corpus and will therefore be discussed here briefly.

The *'indefinite anterior' perfect* involves the use of the preterite in contexts where standard British English would usually require the perfect. Again, this feature is by no means unique to Irish English, but is a recognised form in both standard and non-standard American English. Harris, for example, compares the standard British English "Have you eaten yet?" with the American "Did you eat yet?" (1984a: 309).

What follows is just a selection of examples which feature the *'indefinite anterior' perfect*. In examples 30 and 31 below from the film corpus, the preterite is utilised to express indefinite anterior time, whereas in standard British English one would normally use the past perfect (cf. Taniguchi 1972: 66; Trudgill and Hannah 1994: 106).

30) We thought you **died**, Da.
(*Far and Away*, 00:07:09, MJD1890W)

31) If I **wasn't** in there, sure, you wouldn't have got your eyesight back.
(*How Harry Became a Tree*, 00:45:48, MH1920WW)

Sentences 32, 33 and 34 show that the *'indefinite anterior' perfect* can also occur even in situations where a signal word, such as *since* or the adverbials *ever*, or *never* would usually preclude this form[134].

32) Since when **were** you a smoker?
(*Last of the High Kings*, 00:56:33: MF1970D)

33) You're the most stubborn man I ever **met**.
(*The Wind that Shakes the Barley*, 00:35:40, MD1920C)

34) All I can say is I never **heard** her sing half as well as long as I'm coming here[135].
(*The Dead*, 00:31:30, MF1900D)

---

[134] The time adverbials *always, often, until/till, before* and *yet* can also appear in this context (Filppula 1999: 93), and there is evidence of some of these in the film corpus. "**Did** you **always** work here, Josie?" (*Garage*, 00:33:38, MD2000M), "And you can have your own pigeon loft like you **always wanted**" (*The General*, 00:15:26, FFC1990D), "'Some time!' I **heard** that **before**, Mary. Why is it always some fuckin' time?" (*My Left Foot*, 01:33:48, MCB1950D), "I **never seen** him **before** in me life!" (*The General*, 00:33:39, MMC1990D), "I **didn't go** to him **yet**" (*Agnes Browne*, 00:36:00, FM1960D), "We **never died** of winter **yet**" (*Evelyn*, 00:05:08, MG1950D). Note that the last sentence involves both the use of *never* and *yet*. This would appear to be a set phrase, as it also appears in *Mystics*. "Look, oul son, we **never died** o' winter **yet**. Haven't you all the names?" (*Mystics*, 00:18:13, MD2000D).
[135] The *'extended-now' perfect* form "as long as I'm coming here" would, of course, also be a present perfect form in Standard English. For more on the *'extended-now' perfect* see page 55.

Moreover, according to Filppula, adverbial phrases such as "three times", "in the last ten years", or "in my life", which are associated with a perfect form in Standard English, can be used with the preterite in Irish English (cf. 1999: 93). Examples 35, 36, 37 and 38 feature similar adverbial phrases used in conjunction with this form.

> 35) Kieran only went dancing the odd time, but to bring a girl with him ... sure, it was the first time he **took** a girl anywhere and he wanted to make a good impression.
> *(This is my Father*, 00:27:02, FT2000M)

> 36) He **didn't send** us a penny in months, Sir.
> *(Angela's Ashes*, 01:22:59, FA1930L)

> 37) Oh, yeah. **Didn't see** him in a while actually.
> *(The Wind that Shakes the Barley*, 00:28:12, MCh1920C)

> 38) You're a bad boy. I **told** you time and time again not to be playing with matches[136].
> *(Waking Ned*, 00:38:43, MB2000W)

Filppula found that the most common verbs used with the *'indefinite anterior' perfect* were (in decreasing order of frequency) *hear, see, be, have, go, get, know, do, come* and *tell* (1999: 92). A number of these verbs are also evident in the examples from the film corpus. What is more, in Filppula's study, two-thirds of the instances involved an adverbial of time, especially *never* and *ever*, which again corresponds to the findings of the film corpus. In those cases, where an adverbial of time is not present, the time is clear from the context of the film.

A further observation by Filppula was that the use of the *'indefinite anterior' perfect* was so widespread, that "not even the interviewers' use of the standard have perfect was able to tease out the same structure in the informants' replies" (1999: 95)[137]. Evidence of this is also visible in the film corpus in which the interlocutor uses the standard form, but the reply is in the *'indefinite anterior' perfect*.

> 39) [**We've done** the minutes.]
> Oh, yes. So **we did**.
> *(A Man of No Importance*, 00:55:41, MFR1960W)

This mismatch of tenses also applies in the other direction when the addressee, who, in these examples, is generally a character who is better educated, replies to an 'indefinite anterior' perfect statement using the present perfect form.

> 40) [Strange. I never even **heard** of him.]
> **Haven't you**, D'arcy?
> *(The Dead*, 00:43:09, MMG1900D)

---

[136] For more on habitual *be* see Chapter 6.1.1.1.
[137] Failure to elicit the present perfect in the informants' replies does not always result in answers involving the 'indefinte anterior' form. Fryd also displays evidence of an interviewer using the present perfect but the respondent replying with a different non-standard form, in this case the *'extended-now' perfect*: "Field-worker. Have you always lived here? *Answer.* We're living here seventeen years" (1992: 53).

41) [Howaya, Father? **Did** you **talk** to the committee?]
   I have, yes, and they've agreed in principle.
   (The Commitments, 00:45:08, MFR1990D)

Unusual examples

Example 42, from *This is my Father*, is particularly interesting as it displays instances of the 'indefinite anterior' perfect and the present perfect within the speech of a single character. In the example, Fiona is telling Kieran about the doomed date she had planned for them in Galway, which included going to the cinema to see *Camille* (Edmund Goulding, 1932), a film which she has already seen five times. The 'indefinite anterior' perfect appears at both the beginning and end of the passage, while the Standard English present perfect is in the middle.

42) I **saw** it five times[138]. And afterwards I wanted to teach you to dance in the Grand Ballroom with the biggest band you've ever seen[139] plays the most beautiful music you ever **heard**.
   (This is my Father, 00:50:00, FF1930M)

This mixture of forms lends some support to Harris' suggestion that some Irish English speakers "show evidence of having acquired the standard perfect form but less than complete control over its function" (1984a: 315). However, the above example does not justify his assertion that "such speakers frequently overgeneralize the form [i.e. the standard present perfect S.W.] by using it in past anterior contexts" (1984a: 315). Indeed, the film corpus only displays one example of what one could call an overgeneralization of the standard perfect construction in a past anterior context[140].

43) Since I **have been** thirteen years old, I have been in love with the films.
   (The Magdalene Sisters, 01:24:18, FSB1960D)

Harris regards such instances as examples of hypercorrection which "reflect the difficulty of acquiring a non-native grammatical distinction between indefinite and past definite within the anterior category" (1984a: 315).

In total, the *'indefinite' anterior perfect* appears in 44 of the 50 films (88%) [see Table 8]. Unfortunately, as already mentioned, this perfect form was not surveyed in the *Survey of Irish English Usage* and thus there are no figures for comparison. However, it is possible to compare the relative frequency of the *'indefinite' anterior perfect* and, indeed, that of all of the perfect forms in the film corpus with their frequency in two other corpora, namely Filppula (1999) and Ronan (2005), in order to get an impression about whether there are parallels in the ratio of the features across corpora. Although Hickey did not survey the *'indefinite' anterior perfect*, I have, nonetheless, included his results for the *'be' perfect*, the *'after' perfect*, the *'medial-object' perfect* and the *'extended-now' perfect*, to offer further

---

[138] A similar example of the *'indefinite anterior' perfect* rather than the present perfect being used with the verb *see* is evident in the example from *Intermission* in Table 9.
[139] For more on the omission of relative pronouns, see page 100.
[140] For further examples of these hypercorrections, see Harris (1984a: 315).

comparison. If one were to rank all of these perfect forms in descending order of frequency per corpus, the results would be as follows:

Table VI

	Ronan	Hickey	Filppula	Film corpus
1	'after' perfect	'medial-object' perfect	'indef.' anterior perfect	'indef.' anterior perfect
2	'indef.' anterior perfect	'after' perfect	'be' perfect	'after' perfect
3	'be' perfect	'be' perfect	'medial-object' perfect	'extended-now' perfect
4	'medial-object' perfect	'extended-now' perfect	'extended-now' perfect	'medial-object' perfect
5	'extended-now' perfect		'after' perfect	'be' perfect

As Table VI shows, there is very little agreement across corpora with regard to the frequency of the alternative perfect forms, and, thus, this is an area which certainly warrants a great deal of future study, ideally with much larger corpora. It should be noted, however, that size is not everything. For example, the largest corpus of Irish English, the International Corpus of English (ICE) Ireland, which consists of one million words but which was not yet available to the public at the time of writing, may not have been ideal for comparative purposes anyway, seeing as it is compiled from both written and oral Irish English from both the North and South of Ireland[141].

6.1.1.3   Non-standard verb forms

The film corpus shows numerous examples of speakers of Irish English who appear not to have acquired complete mastery of the grammar of English, particularly with regard to past-tense and past-participle forms. The reason for this is that Irish English, like a number of other dialects, uses a more simplified strong verb system than that of Standard English. The standard two-form and three-form patterns of Standard English become non-standard one-form and two-form patterns. For example, the three-form pattern *do/did/done* becomes *do/done/done*, while the two-form pattern *come/came/come* is reduced to *come/come/come*[142]. Although Hickey only addresses the verbs *do* and *see* with regard to simplified verb patterns in his survey, many other examples of simplified strong verb patterns are evident in the film corpus and therefore they deserve to be mentioned briefly here. Let us first take a look at the standard three-form pattern which is reduced to a two-form one in Irish English. Harris (1993: 153) lists a number of verbs which are likely to undergo this transformation.

---

[141] For more information on issues arising from the compilation of ICE-Ireland, see Kirk *et al.* (2003).
[142] As outlined above, this phenomenon is not restricted to Irish English, but is found in the UK and beyond. Eisikovits found very similar changes in Inner Sydney English, for example. More importantly, she found that "almost all variation (89.9 per cent) occurs with only five verbs *do, see, come, give* and *run*" (1991: 126). As can be seen in the tables and the sample sentences given, the majority of examples in the film corpus also feature these verbs, either as non-standard two-form pattern verbs or as one-form pattern verbs.

Standard English			Irish English	
bite	bit	bitten	bite	bit
hide	hid	hidden	hide	hid
sing	sang	sung	sing	sung
do	did	done	do	done
drink	drank	drunk	drink	drunk
break	broke	broken	break	broke
see	saw	seen	see	seen
take	took	taken	take	took
tear	tore	torn	tear	tore
grow	grew	grown	grow	grew
fall	fell	fallen	fall	fell
go	went	gone	go	went

The film corpus provides numerous examples of this pattern change, as well as evidence of other verbs which were not included in Harris' list, such as *wear*, *speak*, *ride*, *write*, and *eat*:

44) And I was **bit**[143] be a rat once in the bakery. That could have done it.
(*Rat*, 01:13:48, MH2000D)

45) She has me **wore**[144] out, that one. Always wanting her hair plaited.
(*Adam and Paul*, 00:12:09, FM2000D)

46) Me fuckin' arms are **tore**[145] out of me with this thing. I'm not bleedin' waiting.
(*Adam and Paul*, 00:58:50, MTV2000D)

47) Oh, Katie, many a girl has **spoke**[146] these words and lived to rue them.
(*Darby O'Gill and the Little People*, 01:03:50, MKB1800K)

48) It's only an oul cup got **broke**[147]. It'd be worse if it was your heart.
(*A Man of No Importance*, 01:08:45, FW1960D)

49) Must be **broke**. Come on, we'll take the stairs.
(*Adam and Paul*, 01:01:28, MK2000D)

50) Pardon me for sayin' it, Felix, but you're lookin' a bit **shook**[148].
(*Rat*, 01:01:00, MM2000D)

---

[143] *Bit* has also been found as a past participle form on the Isle of Man and in Shropshire (cf. EDD § 430).

[144] The verb form *wore* as a past participle has also been attested in Scotland, Ulster, Berkshire, East Anglia, Surrey, West Sussex, Dorset and Cornwall (cf. EDD § 434). This sentence is also a further example of the *'medial-object' perfect* described on page 53.

[145] This form is also known in Scotland, the Isle of Wight, Dorset and Devon (cf. EDD § 430).

[146] *Spoke* is recorded as a past participle in Scotland, Down, south Stafford, Shropshire, Berkshire, Devon and Cornwall (EDD § 430).

[147] This use of *broke* as a past participle has also been noted in Cheshire, Lincoln, Northampton, Gloucester, Oxford, Hampshire and the south west (EDD § 430).

[148] *Shook*, the irregular past participle of *shake*, has become lexicalised in Irish English and means 'disturbed, in bad shape' (Hickey 2005: 136) or 'showing signs of having been through a stressful experience' (Dolan 2006: 210).

51) She must have **went**[149] somewhere else.
(*Trojan Eddie*, 00:32:57, MTE1990M)

52) The man has drink **took**[150].
(*Widows' Peak*, 01:32:31, FDC1930M)

53) I suppose I'm the only man alive today to have **rode**[151] in the cóiste bodhar and come back to tell it.
(*Darby O'Gill and the Little People*, 01:27:23, MDOG1800K)

54) I've **wrote**[152] down here the name and address of a decent woman, who'll ask six shillings a week for a dry room and a clean bed.
(*Ryan's Daughter*, 01:32:01, MFR1920W)

55) You're not moving from that seat till **you've ate**[153] that egg.
(*Rat*, 00:05:54, FC2000D)

In order to examine how common these types of simplification are in Irish English, it is possible to again compare data from the film corpus with results from Hickey's *Survey of Irish English Usage*. Hickey offered his respondents the sentences "I seen him yesterday" and "They done all the work for us" (Hickey 2004a: 131) and therefore the frequency of the two-form pattern for the verbs *see* and *do* was also examined in the films. The *seen* form appears in 12 of the 50 films (24%) [see Table 9], while the *done* form features in 10 of the 50 (20%) [see Table 10]. It is to be expected that the frequency of these features would be relatively low, as Hickey notes that, unlike for other features, Irish speakers are conscious of these particular forms being "wrong" (2004a: 21). In Hickey's own survey, the forms had acceptability ratings of 39% and 38% respectively.

It is important to note that not all of the examples of *seen* or *done* in the film corpus are simple past tense forms as in Hickey's first example. Some of them are simplified two-form patterns used in present perfect contexts, but without the use of the auxiliary *have*[154]. This could also be a possible reading of Hickey's second sentence, which would then be "They have done all the work for us." There are, of course, less ambiguous instances, which

---

[149] *Went* is also a common past participle form in north Lincoln, Leicester, south Worcester, Hereford, south Pembroke, Gloucester, Berkshire, Dorset, west Somerset and Devon (EDD § 432).

[150] This sentence is an example of the aforementioned *'medial-object' perfect*. Unlike the example from *The Informer* on page 53, this form displays the simplified form *took* rather than *taken*. *Took* has also been found in this form in the British Midlands and in the east and south country (EDD § 430).

[151] *Rode* is also recorded as a past participle in Scotland, Cumberland, Shropshire, west Somerset and Devon (cf. EDD § 430).

[152] The past participle form *wrote* has also been found in Edinburgh, Warwick and Somerset (cf. EDD § 430).

[153] The simplified two-pattern form *ate* is quite common in Irish English, and also recorded in Warwick, Shropshire, Gloucester, the Isle of Wight, Dorset, Somerset and Devon (cf. EDD § 425). It is generally pronounced [et] as in this example from the film, *Rat*. An example of *ate* being used in the simple past tense and also being pronounced [et] can be found shortly beforehand in the same film. "But he ate the black pudding" (*Rat*, 00:05:44, FM2000D).

[154] According to Wright, the auxiliary *have* is often omitted in expressing the present perfect in affirmative sentences in those dialects of English which have preserved the old strong past participles, particularly in affirmative sentences in which the subject is a personal pronoun followed immediately by the verb. He confirms that in the midland, eastern and southern dialects, this construction is sometimes used to express the preterite, as can be seen in many of the examples from the film corpus (EDD § 441).

include a reference to time, such as *already*, *just*, etc. that signifies the need for the present perfect.

> 56) **I seen** it three times already.
> *(Angela's Ashes*, 00:41:36, MMM1930L)

> 57) I know **I done** some quare things on[155] you in me time and all, Eddie, but there was things I didn't do on you too, ya know?
> *(Trojan Eddie*, 01:23:55, MR1990M)

The simplification of the two-pattern form to a one-pattern form is also possible in Irish English. The result is a verb with identical forms for the base, past tense and past participle. Harris offers a list of verbs which assume this pattern: *run, come, give, beat, loss* (= standard *lose*) (1993: 153). Again, the film corpus exhibits some examples of these forms. Interestingly, they all feature either the verb *come* or *run* and they all appear when characters are recounting a story about the past.

> 58) They were so pissed off they couldn't get the better of me the Lord Mayor of Dublin himself **come** out to see your da.
> *(Ordinary Decent Criminal*, 00:12:51, MML1990D)

> 59) I worked on till about half past three, or maybe a quarter to four it was, when Charlie Corrigan **come** in and said his brother Dave was just out of prison after being on hunger strike for 18 days.
> *(The Informer*, 01:10:38, MM1920D)

> 60) Then I **run** down home, put on me overcoat - this same one it was, second-hand as it is - and I went out into the chapel.
> *(The Informer*, 01:10:55, MM1920D)

> 61) He took Gina, very gently, and he brought her into the bathroom and he **run** her under the tap.
> *(The Commitments*, 01:04:50, ML1990D)

Unfortunately, no figures are available for the acceptability of these forms in the *Survey of Irish English Usage*.

Not all participle forms from the corpus which one would regard as grammatically non-standard in Standard English can be conveniently explained by the two-form or one-form patterns. There are also examples in which the participle form does not correspond with the expected form for Irish English. For example, sentence 54 above featured the expected two-form pattern for the verb *write*, namely *wrote*. However, the sentence below features an alternative form of the verb.

---

[155] The non-standard use of the preposition *on* rather than *to* is a further feature of Irish English and is used to indicate that the person is "affected by some (usually negative) action" (cf. Filppula 1999: 223). Further examples are visible in *How Harry Became a Tree* and *The General*: "George, now, what has he ever done **on** you?" (*How Harry Became a Tree*, 00:11:42, MG1920WW); "I don't know what I done **on** Maeve" (*The General*, 01:42:06, Mga1990D).

62) Oh, mam, what's **writ** on it[156].

(*Widows' Peak*, 00:48:38, FMad1930M)

This form is described by Eisikovits as a 'coined' form which follows the pattern of another irregular verb class and is also a feature in Inner-Sydney English. She offers the following examples from that variety: *brang, brung, git, writ, rid* (*ride*) (Eisikovits 1991: 129)[157]. Of course, it is not necessary to go as far afield as Australia to find such forms. Wright's *The English Dialect Dictionary* (EDD), compiled between 1898 and 1905, also includes numerous examples of such forms throughout the British Isles. The following example from *Angela's Ashes* shows a similar pattern in an Irish context.

63) What happened[158] your face? It's all **swole**[159].

(*Angela's Ashes*, 01:45:12, MPat1950L)

Many Irish English speakers also use what appears to be a redundant double past tense form, *drownded*, as the participle form of the verb *drown*. Interestingly, they use the Standard English past tense form, *drowned*, as the base form of the verb for expressing the present tense and then construct the past tense by adding the suffix *–ed* to it. These are the older English forms of the verb and, according to Taniguchi, are still common in popular and dialectal speech (cf. 1972: 107). They were also traditionally evident in British dialects in the north country and north midlands (cf. EDD § 428). Examples of both the present and past tense forms are evident in the film corpus:

64) I'll throw you in the river and **drowned** you like a kitten.

(*Darby O'Gill and the Little People*, 01:00:31, MDOG1800K)

65) Ah, get him out, Ma. He'll be **drownded**.

(*Rat*, 00:26:58, FM2000D)

Some further irregular verb forms involve the addition of a regularised *–ed* suffix to the base form of an irregular verb. This form is then used as the past tense or the participle form, as in the following examples from the film corpus[160]:

66) I **hurted**[161] Jimmy when I shouldn't have.

(*The General*, 00:57:28, MMC1990D)

67) It'd be easy **stealed**[162].

(*Adam and Paul*, 00:42:23, MA2000D)

---

[156] The non-standard nature of this expression is even commented on by a non-Irish character in the movie. The American Mrs. Broom replies: "'Writ'? What do you mean 'writ'? You mean 'written'? Written where?" (*Widows' Peak*, 00:48:40, FEB1930US).
[157] Also see Taniguchi (1972: 106-09).
[158] In Irish English *happen* is often found with a direct object instead of a prepositional object and *to* (cf. Hickey 2007: 174).
[159] This form was also found in Inverness (cf. EDD § 430).
[160] Again, there is ample evidence of these structures throughout the British Isles (cf. EDD § 427 and § 428).
[161] This is an archaic form which is also found in other dialects (cf. Taniguchi 1972:108 and EDD § 428).
[162] *Stealed* was also attested to Scotland, Lincoln, Oxford, Berkshire, Devon and Cornwall in the 19th century (cf. EDD § 427).

68) It's **busted**[163], Charles.

(*Ryan's Daughter*, 01:04:42, MFR1920W)

A further example of an unexpected verb form is evident in the following sentence. Although, the accepted non-standard two-form pattern for the verb *see* is *seen*, as outlined above and as can be seen in Table 9, the example below displays something different.

69) Ah, Katie, you should have **saw** the turf the two of us cut this afternoon.
(*Darby O'Gill and the Little People*, 00:17:31, MDOG1800K)

Like the *writ* example above, this non-standard form of the verb *see* may appear in the film to illustrate the fact that the character who uses it is poorly educated.

6.1.1.4 Lack of *do* support

Unlike in Standard English, the Irish variety does not require the auxiliary verb *do* when forming the interrogative with *have* or when marking negation (cf. Hickey 2004a: 126). While it is not unheard of in other varieties to also omit the *do* support, this omission is generally compensated for by the addition of *got* to the sentence. Therefore, instead of asking "Do you have a cat?", as is the case in American English, Standard British English speakers will more likely ask "Have you got a cat?" in informal speech (cf. Quirk *et al.* 1985: 131-2 and Tottie 2002: 153). In Irish English, however, no such substitution with *got* takes place and, thus, the likely Irish English question will be "Have you a cat?".[164] The lack of *do* support applies equally to interrogatives and to negation, meaning that the Standard American English "I don't have a cat" and the Standard British English "I haven't got a cat" take the form "I haven't a cat" in Irish varieties. Here are some examples of both questions and negative sentences from the film corpus:

Interrogatives:

70) **Have you** a desk for this one, Anna?
(*A Love Divided*, 00:24:31, FS1950WX)

71) **Have you** a pen?
(*About Adam*, 00:05:24, MA2000D)

72) **Have you** coffee?
(*Garage*, 00:24:26, MD2000M)

73) What right **has he** to land that he's never worked?
(*The Quiet Man*, 00:24:18, MRW1930W)

---

[163] This verb is not addressed in the literature, although a similar verb *burst* does appear and was recorded by Wright as having the past tense form *bursted* in Scotland, Lancashire, south Cheshire, Derby, Lincoln, Northampton, Warwick, Worcester, Shropshire, Hereford, Gloucester, Berkshire, Hampshire and Devon (cf. EDD § 427).

[164] Tottie notes that *have* can be used without *do* in formal and somewhat old-fashioned British English.

Negatives:

> 74) **I hadn't** the balls to do anything different.
> (*Cowboys and Angels*, 00:30:38, MJ2000L)
>
> 75) But **he hasn't** a chance to be bad. Benny, we don't let him out of our sight.
> (*Circle of Friends*, 01:04:11, FNM1950D)
>
> 76) Now, if I had a horse, which **I haven't**, I'd go for it myself, which I won't.
> (*Darby O'Gill and the Little People*, 00:11:46, MFR1800K)
>
> 77) **I haven't** the heart for it.
> (*Into the West*, 00:46:16, MPR1990D)

In total, there is a lack of *do* support in 32 of the 50 films (64%) [see Table 11]. Unfortunately, there are no comparable numbers for the *Survey of Irish English Usage*, which focuses instead on the acceptability of a Standard English sentence with *do* support, *Do you have any matches on you?*, rather than on a non-standard one. 90% of respondents found the standard feature to be "no problem".

This lack of *do* support also extends to the negative and interrogative forms of the verb *use*, when referring to the habitual past tense form, i.e. *used to*. Whereas in Standard English, the interrogative form would typically be "Didn't you use to cycle to school?" and the negative form would be "I didn't use to cycle to school in winter" (cf. Quirk *et al.* 1985: 140), in Irish English, the auxiliary *do* is not used (cf. Hickey 2004a: 129), giving the forms "Usedn't you cycle to school?" and "I usedn't cycle to school in winter". Unfortunately, although there are a number of instances of the habitual past being used in a positive sense in the film corpus, i.e. "We used to be climbing up those rocks" (*Trojan Eddie*, 00:20:12, MJP1990M), there are no examples of the verb *use* in negative sentences, and only two examples in interrogatives, one of which is actually the standard form.

> 78) **Usedn't he** be pals with Frankie McPhillip who was shot by the Black and Tans tonight?
> (*The Informer*, 00:42:28, MOS1920D)
>
> 79) **Didn't they use** to do a tour during the summer?
> (*Mystics*, 00:17:11, MCC22000C)

These two sentences do not really offer much insight into the acceptability of the non-standard form *usedn't*, as, with one standard example and one non-standard example, the situation is very much a case of six of one and half a dozen of another. While it might be tempting to speculate that the non-standard form may have died out between its appearance in *The Informer* (1930) and the appearance of the standard form in *Mystics* (2000), this would be unwise, particularly when one only has two films on which to base this assumption. What is more, intuition would suggest that the non-standard form is still far more prevalent in Irish speech today.

This supposition is also borne out by evidence from Hickey's *Survey of Irish English Usage*. Although he, unfortunately, did not test the acceptability of the non-standard form *usedn't*, he did check Irish people's reaction to the standard form, eliciting some very interesting results. On average, only 7% of respondents found the Standard English "Did you use to cycle to school?" to be "no problem". Approximately 57%, on the other hand, found the sentence to be "a bit strange," while as many as 35% felt the standard form was actually "unacceptable"[165]. These results are very revealing and suggest that, given the underwhelming approval for the standard form, the non-standard form is likely to be alive and well in Irish English today.

6.1.1.5 *Will* for *shall*

Just as in other varieties, such as Scottish and American English, Irish English does not adhere to the rules which govern the use of *will* and *shall* in Standard British English. Whereas Standard British English differentiates between the normal future for prediction (*I shall, you will, he/she/it will, we shall, you will, they will*) and the emphatic future for volition (*I will, you shall, he/she/it shall, we will, you shall, they shall*), Irish English speakers are more likely to employ *will* in all contexts (cf. Dolan 2006: xxv and Harris 1993: 158). This is nicely illustrated in the following examples from the film corpus:

    80) **Will** I take care of this, Sergeant, or will you?
                                  (*The Field*, 00:19:01, MBMC1950W)

    81) **Will** I put the kettle on?
                                      (*The Boys and Girl from County Clare*, 00:51:12, FMS1960L)

    82) **Will** I shoot him, Inspector Bolger?
                                      (*Into the West*, 00:23:49, MAG1990D)

    83) Lads, **will** we go to the ould dance? Ah, say we will.
                                      (*Widows' Peak*, 01:01:35, FCG11930M)

In the interest of clarity, all of the examples given are in the interrogative, as that is the form which most clearly shows that it is the *will* form and not the *shall* form that is being used. The reason for this is that in affirmative sentences *I will* and *we will* are more likely to be contracted to *I'll* and *we'll*.[166]

The use of *will* for *shall* can be found in 21 of the 50 films (42%) [see Table 12] and is widespread from both a geographical and temporal perspective. In his *Survey of Irish English Usage*, Hickey did not examine the acceptability of the use of *will* for *shall*, but he did test the acceptability of the Standard English *shall* among the Irish population and came up with the following findings. His sample sentence "I shall have to leave soon" was regarded as "no problem" by 59% of the population, as "a bit strange" by 35% and as "unacceptable" by 6%.

---

[165] This number was as high as 44 % in Connaught.
[166] For the sake of consistency, I have thus also discounted interrogative sentences which themselves feature contractions, such as "What'll I do?" (*A Love Divided*, 01:15:34, MS1950WX) or "What'll we drink to?" (*My Left Foot*, 01:40:07, MCB1950D), even if from a phonotactic perspective the contracted form is, of course, more likely to arise from the reduction of the semi-vowel /w/ from *will* rather than from the fricative /ʃ/ of *shall*. This notion has been confirmed by Quirk *et al.* who state that "from the semantic point of view, as well as from the historical point of view, *'ll* and *'d* are to be regarded as contractions of *will* and *would* respectively, rather than of *shall* and *should*" (1985: 228).

67

These results reflect those of the film corpus quite well, in that the approximately 41% of those people who found the *shall* form "a bit strange" or "unacceptable" in the *Survey of Irish English Usage* are probably those who use the *will* form themselves in such situations. This is a comparable number to those from the film corpus.

Unusual examples

In his section on the use of *will* for *shall*, Taniguchi also addresses a similar phenomenon in Irish English, namely the substitution of *would* for *should*. He states that *would* is often used in place of *should* "in passing a judgement of an emotional character on some occurrence, implying wonder, surprise, indignation, and so forth" (Taniguchi 1972: 72). Some examples of this from the film corpus include:

    84) I'm going to live with her. And why **wouldn't** I?
                        (*Widows' Peak*, 01:30:51, FMOH1930M)

    85) Sure, why **wouldn't** I? Sure, my daughter has the most lovely little house there at the edge of the city. Just where the tram starts.
                        (*The Dead*, 00:14:40, FMM1900D)

    86) [Jaysus, that dog loves you, Marion.]
        And why **wouldn't** he? Don't I always think of you, Spartacus?
                        (*Agnes Browne*, 00:08:28, FM1960D)

    87) [He was looking at you!]
        And why **wouldn't** he?
                        (*The Nephew*, 00:10:11, FA1990C)

    88) [So she moved back home then. Hasn't trusted a man since.]
        Jesus, why **would** ya?
                        (*Intermission*, 00:29:15, MSa2000D)

6.1.1.6   The overuse of the progressive form

Research has shown that speakers of Irish English have a tendency to overuse the progressive forms of verbs (cf. Bliss 1984; Harris 1993; and Ronan 2001). Whereas Standard English typically only permits the use of the progressive form with dynamic verbs, in Irish English the progressive is often found with stative verbs, especially those of perception and cognition, such as *hear*, *want*, *wonder*, *know*, *think* and *believe* (cf. Harris 1993: 164). While these forms can occur in other dialects of English, Taniguchi's comparison of the form in literature from different countries confirmed that "Irish English accords much greater preference to the expanded form than any other English dialect" (1972: 75). Progressive structures contain some part of the verb *be* together with the present participle form of the verb in question. This non-standard progressive form can be applied across tenses, as can be seen from the examples below, which are in the present, past, future[167] and conditional tenses respectively.

---

[167] Despite the presence of the contracted *will* form, this sentence does not really express the future tense, but rather a supposition on the part of the speaker. In this regard, it is similar to the *'after' perfect* sentence from *Ryan's Daughter*, which was addressed on page 50: "He'll be after catching a few flounders" (*Ryan's Daughter*,

89) What more **are** you **wanting** now?
(Ryan's Daughter, 01:02:30, MFR1920W)

90) Well, what is it you **were wanting** to show me?
(The Magdalene Sisters, 00:02:47, FM1960D)

91) Let me guess. You**'ll be wanting** to know where I stashed the diamonds?
(Mystics, 00:22:27, MLA2000D)

92) **Wouldn't** you **be wanting** mercy then? And won't you be giving it to me now?
(The Informer, 01:26:09, FK1920D)

Based on the findings in the film corpus, it would appear that the overuse of the progressive form is not restricted to stative verbs alone, but also occurs far more frequently than one would expect for dynamic verbs. In total, 30[168] of the 50 films (60%) [see Table 13] in the corpus display unusual use of the progressive form, where one would normally expect the standard form. Unfortunately, neither Hickey nor Filppula offer any comparative figures.

6.1.1.7　Imperatives with progressive form

Further evidence of the overuse of the progressive form in Irish English is visible in the use of a continuous verb form in imperatives. Whereas Standard English simply uses the infinitive of a verb to create the imperative, as in "Sit down", Irish English has traditionally employed a construction consisting of *be* and an *ing*-participle, resulting in the expression "Be sitting down". According to Taniguchi (1972: 63), this use of the progressive for positive imperatives was a common feature of Elizabethan English. However, Hickey (2007: 223) states that a substratal influence is at play here, since in order to create the imperative in Irish, one must always take the habitual verb form *bí* "be" together with a continuous form of the lexical verb which follows it. This usage extends to negative imperatives, where *bí* is preceded by the negator *ná*. Hickey argues that there is a prosodic equivalence between the Irish and the Irish English structures, both of which have two stressed syllables at the beginning:

93) *Ná bí ag labhairt mar sin.*
[not be-IMPERATIVE at speaking like that]
'Don't be talking like that.'

(Hickey 2007: 223)

In Irish English today, the progressive form generally only occurs in negative imperatives involving the auxiliary verb *do*, as in example 93. Indeed, there is only one example of a positive imperative in the entire film corpus:

01:01:13, MFR1920W). In both cases, the auxiliary is used before *be* to indicate possibility, or inference (cf. Taniguchi, 1972: 57).

[168] At first glance, the example from *Agnes Browne* (see Table 13) may seem to be a standard use of the progressive form. However, given the context, a woman being asked whether her husband has a job rather than whether he is at work at present, the form belongs in the table.

94) Ah, it's Inisfree you want. **Be saving** your breath, Mister Malouney, let me direct the gentleman.

(*The Quiet Man*, 00:02:40, MB1930W)

This example from *The Quiet Man* can be seen to be somewhat of an antiquated or possibly even Stage Irish construction. MacHale supports the latter notion, stating that the line is delivered in "what Irish-Americans fondly imagine is an Irish accent", while "the 'Oirish' grammar employed is one never heard outside the United States" (2000: 55).

The rest of the examples of imperatives with the progressive form are of negative imperatives, some of which also include the second-person pronoun, something which is only implicit in imperatives in Standard English usage[169] (cf. Harris 1993:157). According to Taniguchi, the retention of the pronoun is a survival of older English and is still common in some other dialects such as Scottish English (Taniguchi 1972: 65). Examples of this retention of second person pronouns in the film corpus include:

95) And **don't you be pretending** you know what Captain Moonlight means, coz you don't.

(*Far and Away*, 00:12:20, MDD1800W)

96) **Don't youse be hangin'** round here, do you hear me?

(*Adam and Paul*, 00:57:56, MN2000D)

In total, imperatives with the progressive form appear in 22[170] of the 50 films (44%) [see Table 14]. As already mentioned, all 22 films display forms with the *don't be + verb(-ing)* constructions, which is quite convenient for comparative purposes, as this was also the structure which Hickey surveyed among his respondents. His sentence *Don't be teasing your brother* received a 90% 'no problem' rating nationwide, which places it among the most highly acceptable structures in the *Survey of Irish English Usage*, and on a par with the *'after' perfect*, for example. These findings are mirrored in the film corpus, where despite its not even coming close to anything like a 90% frequency, this imperative form is nonetheless one of the most frequent grammatical features.

Harris (1993: 157) also describes a further means of constructing imperatives in Irish English, namely through the use of the words *let* or *leave*.[171] He offers two examples, "Let you all go now!" and "Let you not be making noise"[172], both of which, strangely enough, feature solely the *let* form. His omission of the *leave* form would suggest that the feature is

---

[169] There are, however, some exceptions in Standard English cf. Quirk *et al.* (1985: 828-31).

[170] The form actually appears in 23 films, but I have discounted the sentence "Sure, I have a great life; only **don't be telling** the wife, yeah" (*Garage*, 00:07:25, MTD2000UK), as it is uttered by a British character, or at least by an actor with a strong North of England accent. The typically Irish use of *sure*, the imperative with the progressive form and the use of the definite article by the British truck driver in the movie could be explained as examples of accommodation by the outsider with the local, or could simply be seen as an oversight on the part of the Irish screenwriter, who did not distinguish carefully enough between the speech of the characters.

[171] The use of *let* as an imperative is also possible in Standard English, but not in the same way as in Irish English. According to Quirk *et al.* (1985: 829), it occurs in sentences like "Let us all work hard" and "Let no one think that a teacher's life is easy". They stress, however, that "there are no second person imperatives with *let*", and they offer an unacceptable example "*Let you have a look" (1985: 830). This unacceptable example is acceptable in Irish English, as outlined above.

[172] Harris' sample sentences are modified versions of those given in Henry (1957: 180-1). Henry's original sentences featured *ye* rather than *you*.

not actually that common, and this assumption is borne out by the absence of this form in the film corpus as well[173]. Indeed, the *let* form of the imperative is also very rare and appears in only 2 of the 50 films[174]. What is more, it is worth noting that in both examples the *let you/let yiz* part of the imperative is actually redundant.

> 97) Now, **let yiz** fuck off for yourselves, alright?
> (*Adam and Paul*, 01:14:12, MW2000D)
>
> 98) **Let you** get in so, and we'll head over.
> (*Garage*, 01:02:10, MSgt2000M)

Despite the fact that the aforementioned *leave* does not appear as an imperative in the same way as *let*, it is noticeable from the film corpus that the two verbs are often used interchangeably in other contexts. This substitution, which is common in many British dialects[175], was also observed in Ireland by Dolan (cf. 2006: xxvi) and can be seen in the following examples from the film corpus:

> 99) **Leave** me go. Let me out!
> (*Darby O'Gill and the Little People*, 00:44:27, MKB1800K)
>
> 100) **Leave** her through.
> (*The Field*, 00:42:47, MBMC1950W)
>
> 101) Now, shut up and **leave** me do this.
> (*Adam and Paul*, 01:02:32, MK2000D)
>
> 102) Maybe you should drop it by and **leave** her see it for herself.
> (*Darby O'Gill and the Little People*, 01:10:23, FWIP1800K)
>
> 103) Own up, and I'll **leave** you off with a hiding.
> (*The General*, 00:52:40, MMC1990D)
>
> 104) It's all right, Barney. **Let** him alone. He didn't mean any harm.
> (*The Informer*, 00:24:18, FK1920D)

6.1.1.8   Plural subject – verb concord

Like many other dialects of English, Irish English does not always adhere to the rules of subject-verb concord exhibited in Standard English. One of the most common deviations

---

[173] Interestingly, Bliss (1984: 145) does exactly the same thing. He too suggests that "in Munster *let* is often replaced by *leave*" in such imperative structures, yet he fails to give an actual example of it.

[174] It is telling that the only two films which feature this form were in fact written by the same screenwriter, County Clare native, Mark O'Halloran. Indeed he includes a second example of this structure in *Garage* "Let ya put that blanket on the back seat: the dogs are sheddin'" (*Garage*, 00:40:06, MMS2000M). Note that all three of the examples from the films are of the type "positive imperative with simple form of a verb" (Taniguchi 1972: 61). Other possible types and the corresponding examples from Taniguchi are: "positive imperative with expanded form of a verb" ("Let ye be watching for a light in it"), "negative imperative with simple form of a verb" ("Let you not say anything") and "negative imperative with expanded form of a verb" ("Let you not be expecting anything from me"). For more on this feature, see Taniguchi (1972: 61-3).

[175] Wright attributes the use of *leave* for 'to allow, permit, to let' to speakers from Scotland, Ireland, Cumberland, Yorkshire, Cheshire, Nottingham, Shropshire, Hereford, Pembroke, Kent, Devon, Cornwall and Guernsey (cf. EDD s.v. leave, $v.^2$. 1.).

from the norm is that plural subjects can receive singular inflection[176], albeit only in certain contexts. Harris writes that bare plural pronouns almost never take the *s*-ending in verbs, thus rendering structures such as **they knows/is/was* "ungrammatical by the rules of Irish English" (Harris 1993: 155)[177]. This rule also applies to constructions with first- and second-person plural pronouns, which means that a structure such as *we was*, which is possible in other dialects of English, does not appear frequently in Irish English[178]. In contrast, as we shall see in the morphology section, the third-person demonstrative plural form *them* regularly occurs with *s*-inflection. The other contexts in which, according to Harris (1993: 154-6), this inflection may occur are listed below, together with some relevant examples from the film corpus, where possible.

a) with subjects which are full nouns (as opposed to pronouns):

105) **Country girls is** very lax in their morals. It's all that loose straw lying around.
(*A Man of No Importance*, 01:02:00, FRW1960D)

b) after relative pronouns:

106) The **men that is** now **is** only all palaver[179] and what they can get out of ya.
(*The Dead*, 00:07:46, FL1900D)

c) with 'collective' noun phrases, which have plural meaning but contain no grammatically plural noun[180]:

107) Devil take me if **the lot of you is** not possessed and damned.
(*Ryan's Daughter*, 00:13:34, MFR1920W)

d) in questions with subject-verb inversion:

108) **Is that tins** of corned beef you have there?
(*Ordinary Decent Criminal*, 01:27:23, MML1990D)

Although Harris suggests that "the most favourable context for a verbal *s*-ending to occur with a plural subject appears to be in questions where we get subject verb inversion, e.g. Is my hands clean?" (1993: 156), there is only one example of this form in the film corpus, namely example 108 taken from *Ordinary Decent Criminal*.

---

[176] For more on the Northern Subject Rule, see Ihalainen (1994).
[177] Filppula, however, observes that these rules are not set in stone in Southern Irish English, and he cites some findings from his corpus which prove this. For example, although he too could not find any evidence of a *they is…* construction, "the rate of occurrence of the past tense *they was…*(at just over 10 per cent) and the occasional occurrence of nonconcord with other verbs involving pronoun subjects suffice to show that the Subject-Type Constraint is not categorically observed in southern H[iberno]E[nglish]" (1999: 156). Indeed, there is also evidence to support this in the film corpus. The following example is taken from *Ryan's Daughter*: "You'd think **they was** announcing the coming of Christ" (*Ryan's Daughter*, 00:24:12, MFR1920W).
[178] However, although the feature does not appear frequently, that is not to say that there is no evidence of this structure in the film corpus. The following sentence is taken from *The Field*: "**We wasn't** rich enough to be priests or doctors" (*The Field*, 00:56:15, MBMC1950W).
[179] *Palaver* means 'idle talk' (cf. Share 2003: 236).
[180] Harris offers the following examples of this construction: "The whole six of us was sitting…" and "Most of the hard core's all older men" (1993: 156).

In total, the lack of *plural subject-verb concord* appears in 30 out of 50 films[181] (60%) [see Table 15]. This figure is quite high compared to the acceptability rate in Hickey's survey. A reason for that may be the fact that the results for the film corpus are all-encompassing and examine the presence of *plural subject-verb concord* in any of the aforementioned contexts, whereas Hickey's respondents were judging only two sentences: *Some farmers has little or no cattle* and *John and his wife plays bingo at the weekend*, which both featured full nouns as the subjects. The average acceptability rates for those sentences were 11% and 21% respectively.

6.1.1.9 Singular existential

A structure which is very similar to the *plural subject-verb concord* is the *singular existential*, which involves the use of a singular verb in existential sentences even when there is a plural reference. An example is "There was two men on the road" (Hickey 2004a: 131). Such structures are not exclusive to Ireland but are very common in English varieties world wide. For example, Cheshire *et al.* (1989: 194-5) established that, with an average frequency rate of 83%[182], the *singular existential* form was among the most common non-standard grammatical forms in teenage speech throughout Britain (cf. also Krug 2007). Below are a couple of examples from the film corpus.

> 109) We've got three kids now, so **there's always aunties and uncles and cousins** coming over wanting to visit.
> (*Waking Ned*, 00:45:55, MLM2000D)

> 110) **There was about eight or nine of them**.
> (*The Wind that Shakes the Barley*, 00:18:14, FS1920C)

In total, the *singular existential* occurs in 33 of the 50 films (66%) [see Table 16], with the present tense forms clearly outnumbering the past tense forms. In Hickey's *Survey of Irish English Usage*, the feature has a 47% acceptability rating. This percentage, unfortunately, only reflects the acceptability of his example sentence, which is in the past tense. It would be very interesting to see if there were similar discrepancies between the frequency of past and present tense forms, as was the case in the film corpus, or whether they were only marginally different as in Cheshire's findings. This is certainly a point worthy of future study.

6.1.1.10 *For to* infinitives

The formation of infinitives with *for to* is a further feature of Irish English which is well attested in the literature. As with so many of the features of Irish English, there is disagreement over the origin of this construction. Joyce (1988), for example, points out the parallels to the Irish structure *chun* 'for (the purpose of)', yet also acknowledges the presence of *for to* infinitives in England. An English origin would, indeed, appear to be more likely, as Taniguchi observes that the form was very common in Early Modern English, but has been

---

[181] If one reads the example from *The Snapper* in Table 15 out of context, it does not appear to be an example of *plural subject-verb concord*, as it is unclear what the "yours" in the utterance "Not bad, how's yours?" refers to. However, the fact that it is an answer to a nurse's question, "How are your movements?", justifies its inclusion in the table.
[182] The rates were 85% for the past tense form and 82.5% for the present tense form.

disappearing ever since, and now is only found "in vulgar or dialectal speech" (1972: 99)[183]. In any case, this archaic structure, with its non-standard use of the two prepositions side by side, is generally thought to be used with verbs of purpose, and can be seen to have a similar function to the phrase 'in order to', as in Hickey's sample sentence *He went to Dublin for to buy the car*. However, as Harris points out, it can also be used in other contexts, as in "He was asked for to loosen the rope" or "It wouldn't do for to say that" (1993: 167)[184]. In these examples, purpose is not implied, meaning that the *for to* structure cannot be replaced by *in order to*. This would appear to be the litmus test for distinguishing between the two types. While in both cases above the *for to* structure can be replaced by Standard English *to*, only those sentences which involve verbs of purpose can be replaced by the *in order to* structure.

The *for to* infinitive structure appears in only 2 of the 50 films (4%) [see Table 17], but it is interesting to see that even with so few appearances, there is still evidence of each type of structure, the latter being the one in which *for to* cannot be replaced by *in order to*.

111) [Run and get a turf creel. A big one.]
[What for?]
For to hold the gold.
(*Darby O'Gill and the Little People*, 01:12:47, MIP1800K)

112) Me sister's third young one is living at Inisfree, and she'd be only too happy **for to show** you the road.
(*The Quiet Man*, 00:03:42, FBW1930W)

It is interesting to note that the two films in which the structure occurs are among the oldest, both from a production point of view (1959 and 1952 respectively) and from a setting standpoint (the 1800s and the 1930s), thus lending weight to the notion that this feature is indeed archaic. This idea is further supported by the fact that even as early as in 1909, Hayden and Hartog regarded the structure as "antiquated" (1909: 777).

In Hickey's *Survey of Irish English Usage*, the *'for to'* infinitive was greeted with an approval rate of 8%. Coincidentally, the acceptability rate was marginally higher in Connaught and Munster, the areas in which the two films above are set. Seeing as Hickey's survey only tested the acceptability of the *in order to* meaning of the structure, it would be interesting in any future studies to also test the other form.

6.1.2 The noun phrase
6.1.2.1 Plurals of quantity nouns

A feature which Irish English shares with many other non-standard forms of English is the omission of the plural *s*-ending on nouns which indicate quantities of weight, time, measure, mass, cost, etc. (cf. Harris 1993: 146). Such words include *pound, mile, tonne, year* etc. Some examples from the film corpus include:

113) Then, I'll just take some potatoes. **Five pound**.
(*Ryan's Daughter*, 00:22:32, FR1920W)

---

[183] The *for to* infinitive is also attested to Northern Irish English (cf. Harris 1984b: 131 and Henry 1992).
[184] Harris' examples are from Henry, who calls this construction the 'pleonastic' *for* + infinitive (1957: 190).

114) That'll be **sixty-four pound** in old money.

(*Mystics*, 00:41:32, MCh2000D)

115) I've known him now **twenty year**. 'Twasn't an aisy thing to do either.

(*Dead Meat*, 00:42:34, MC2000LM)

The absence of the *s*-ending on nouns which indicate quantities of time, weight, cost, mass, measure, etc. is evident in 12 of the 50 films (24%) [see Table 18]. Strikingly, 11 of these involved the noun *pound*[185], either referring to currency, as in the majority of the cases, or, as in the example from *Ryan's Daughter*, relating to a measure of weight. The only other example of a quantity noun without a plural *s*-ending is that from *Dead Meat* (see sentence 115 above), which refers to a period of time[186].

Hickey's survey found that on average 61% of respondents found the omission of the s-ending on plurals of quantity nouns to be "no problem". The sentence being analysed was "He paid twenty pound for the meal" which, as we have seen from the film corpus, is a context in which this feature typically occurs. A reason for the disparity between the results from the film corpus and those from the *Survey of Irish English Usage* is that quantities simply were not talked about all that frequently in the films or, when they were, the nouns were often omitted. i.e. "She'll be lookin' for a hundred a week for it anyway, I'd say" (*Trojan Eddie*, 01:11:23, MA1990M) rather than "She'll be lookin' for a hundred pound(s) a week for it anyway, I'd say".

Unusual examples

With regard to the creation of plural forms, Taniguchi notes that speakers of Irish English still often observe plural forms from older English. For example, the suffix -*n* which was a plural marker in Old English was redundantly added to the word *childer* in Middle English, although *childer* itself was actually already the plural of *child* (cf. Taniguchi 1972: 9). In Irish English, this earlier plural form *childer* is still often used[187].

116) Do you think, lady, you could spare a few coppers for the **childer**?

(*This is my Father*, 00:40:58, FT1930M)

---

[185] It is interesting to note that since the introduction of the euro as the unit of currency in Ireland on January 1, 2002, the most likely context for this feature to occur, namely with regard to pounds, has therefore disappeared. Indeed, the structure has only appeared in this context in one film since then (see example 114), and in that instance it was while Irish people were still becoming accustomed to the new currency. The fact that the "official" plural of *euro* is *euro* means that the omission of the plural *s*-ending is no longer an issue. The term "official" is used here with caution. There has been some debate about what the real plural of euro actually is. Although the European Commission's Translation Service has recommended that the regular English language plurals *euros* and *cents* be used in non-legal documents intended for the general public, the official policy of the Department of Finance in Ireland and of Irish broadcasters and print media has been to use *euro* and *cent* as both the singular and plural forms. For more on this issue, see http://www.evertype.com/standards/euro/open-letter.pdf. (Retrieved: March 30, 2008).

[186] It is worth mentioning that despite the introduction of the metric system to Ireland in the late 1960s, a very large percentage of the population still use the imperial system when referring to their height (six foot two), their weight (twelve stone), distances (four mile outside of Dingle) etc. Indeed, road signs showing the speed limit in kilometres per hour were first introduced in Ireland as recently as in January 2005. The consequence of this survival of the imperial system in the minds of the people is that the lack of the plural *s*-ending is therefore more likely to occur with regard to *pound, foot, stone*, etc. rather than *gramme, metre* or *kilo*.

[187] This is also the case in other parts of the British Isles (cf. EDD § 380 and EDD s.v. childer, *sb. pl.*).

Both Dolan and Taniguchi also draw attention to double plural forms (or what Taniguchi calls "vulgar" forms) which also occasionally appear in Irish English. These involve the addition of /əz/ to existing plurals which end in –s[188]. Dolan offers the examples of *bellowses* for *bellows* and *galluses* for *gallus*, an obsolete form of the word *gallows* meaning 'braces' (2006: xxvii and 102). Taniguchi, on the other hand, cites *newses* as a plural for *news* (1972: 10). While I have not encountered the latter form, I have frequently heard other forms, such as *pantses* and *knickerses*[189]. What is more, the film corpus displays the forms *chipses* and *barrackses*, as in the examples below.

117) Right, queue up for your **chipses**.
(*The Van*, 00:54:50, MB1990D)

118) Two **barrackses** burnt down? That's brilliant.
(*The Wind that Shakes the Barley*, 00:55:00, MC1920C)

6.1.2.2 The non-standard use of the definite article

Irish English uses the definite article far more extensively and in cases that one would not find it in Standard English. While this is not an exclusively Irish English feature[190], it is certainly characteristic of the variety and thus worthy of attention. It has been discussed to varying degrees by Henry (1957: 117-8), Bliss (1984a: 149) and Harris (1993: 144-5), and having consulted these sources, Filppula (1999: 56) compiled a list of contexts in which the non-standard use of the definite article is most likely to occur. What follows is that list accompanied by relevant examples from the film corpus.

a) plural count nouns with generic reference
In Standard English, plural count nouns with generic reference appear with zero article. In Irish English, however, a definite article is often placed before them, as in these examples:

119) Sure, yes, yes, he's a millionaire you know, like all **the Yanks**.
(*The Quiet Man*, 00:22:15, MMF1930W)

120) They buy **the vegetables** off[191] you.
(*A Man of No Importance*, 00:06:51, MA1960D)

---

[188] The "vulgar" addition of /əz/ is not restricted to plural –s. It can also be found when <-s> is used to indicate possession, most famously in the name of the public holiday which falls on December 26th, namely, St Stephen's Day, which is regularly termed *Stephens's Day* by Irish people.

[189] *Knickerses* also makes an appearance in an example sentence from *For Focal Sake*, a non-academic guide to Irish Slang, compiled from online contributions and published in 2008. The sentence in question is: "I caught de dirty minker robbing knickerses off the nuns (sic) line again! Ah now!" (Foley 2008: 39).

[190] There is also evidence of non-Standard use of the definite article in Scottish dialects (cf. Miller and Brown 1982:17 and Sabban 1982: 380-418).

[191] *Off* is very frequently used instead of *from* in such contexts. Some examples include: "I borrowed money **off** Mr Billy" (*Agnes Browne*, 01:11:42, MFB1960D), "Is it ok if I get nappies **off** ya?" (*The General*, 00:50:57, FK1990D), "I got this big oul antique wardrobe **off** them a couple of weeks ago there" (*Trojan Eddie*, 00:09:56, MR1990M), "I've someone who'll take them **off** me" (*When Brendan Met Trudy*, 00:39:27, FT2000C), "Can I get a few cans **off** you there, Val?" (*Garage*, 00:28:50, MJ2000M). "He took a bite out of my Gus's leg that'll leave him crippled for the rest of his days. And you want money **off** me?" (*How Harry Became a Tree*, 01:20:31, MH1920WW). Joyce suggests that the word is actually *of* rather than *off*, in keeping with the Irish preposition *de* which is conjugated as *diom/diot/de/di/dinn/dibh/diobh* and literally means 'of me/of you/of him/of her' etc. Be that as it may, the pronunciation is certainly that of *off* [ɑf] (1988: 30).

121) If we knew how to keep **the women** happy, sure, we'd still be in Paradise.
(*The Field*, 00:05:52, MBMC1950W)

122) You're way off the mark, Veronica. Martin Cahill isn't into **the drugs**. Neither am I.
(*Veronica Guerin*, 00:16:45, MJT1990D)

b) non-count abstract nouns and concrete mass nouns
As was the case for plural count nouns with generic reference, non-count abstract nouns and concrete mass nouns do not take a definite article in Standard English, but do so in the Irish variety (cf. Harris 1993: 144; Taniguchi 1972: 49).

123) Look at the state of ya - eyes falling out of your head with **the drink**.
(*Last of the High Kings*, 00:05:02, FMG1970D)

124) I said he takes **the snuff**.
(*Widows' Peak*, 00:06:45, FMG1930M)

125) And forcing Eve to eat **the stirabout**[192], the poor child, she simply hates the sight of it.
(*The Dead*, 00:09:42, FG1900D)

126) Nothing pleases a rat more than potato skins, the peelings of onions, the scrapings of porridge, so you'll be saving on **the grub**.
(*Rat*, 00:14:14, MM2000D)

127) Where would you be without **the social welfare**?
(*Ordinary Decent Criminal*, 00:08:07, MML1990D)

128) Sir, we'd like the address, sir, to claim for **the assistance**.
(*Into the West*, 00:07:00, MMM1990D)

129) Well, when you've got **the music**, you've got friends for life. It's why I'm never alone.
(*The Boys and Girl from County Clare*, 01:14:12, MJJ1960Cl)

130) Anyone with a drop of **the buccaneering spirit**, like meself, ...
(*When the Sky Falls*, 00:05:45, MS1990D)

c) quantifying expressions involving *most, both, half* and *all*
While Filppula found evidence of all of these words being used with the definite article in his HE corpus, they were not very common in the films. The following are some examples:

131) Ach, you don't know **the half** of it.[193]
(*A Very Unlucky Leprechaun*, 00:24:35, ML1990W)

---

[192] *Stirabout* is a dialect term for *porridge* (cf. Dolan 2006: 227, Share 2003: 314 and Bliss 1979: 274).
[193] These examples may be regarded as somewhat controversial, as these expressions with "the half of it" are also common in Standard English. I have included them, nonetheless, as they correspond with Filppula's and Henry's examples: "He has a room there, and be = I don't know what **the half** of it is, err, full of medals, and plaques, [...]" (1999: 58) and "You didn't see **the half** of it" (1957: 119).

132) Sure, that's only **the half** of it.
(*When Brendan Met Trudy*, 00:42:28, FT2000C)

133) Quiet now, **the both**[194] of yiz.
(*Mystics*, 00:05:41, ML2000D)

134) There's no point in **the both** of us getting caught.
(*When Brendan Met Trudy*, 01:13:10, FT2000C)

135) I don't want your father's job at all, not unless I can have **the both** of you along with it.
(*Darby O'Gill and the Little People*, 01:12:18, MMB1800D)

Interestingly, the form *the most*, which occurred most frequently in Filppula's corpus[195], was not evident at all in the film corpus. The same applies to the *all* form, which is nothing like the other quantifying expressions mentioned, in that it precedes the definite article. This is evident in Filppula's example: "I haven't = I never had trouble, but I hear people at it = that they'd be around the house *all the night*, wakenin' 'em out of the bed" (1999: 58).

d) the numerals *one* and *two* used in the senses 'same' and 'both', respectively

136) Did you ever in your life see such a collection of dossers, knackers, gougers and gurriers all in **the one** place?[196]
(*Rat*, 00:24:49, FC2000D)

137) A bunch of more vicious bastards in **the one** room you can't imagine.
(*The Wind that Shakes the Barley*, 01:23:42, MTe1920C)

138) Me dada was very disappointed, I think. Raging with himself really for dawdling too long in **the one** spot.
(*Trojan Eddie*, 00:20:42, MJP1990M)

139) There's eighteen of us in **the one** area phone book[197].
(*The Van*, 00:16:52, MG1990C)

140) Worked in the bookies all his life, talked through his nose, all **the one** note.
(*Mystics*, 00:08:36, MD2000D)

---

[194] See Taniguchi (1972: 51) for similar examples. The form *the both of* also appears in Broad Scots, as can be seen in Miller and Brown (1982: 17). Interestingly, Henry (1957: 117) suggests that in Irish English *both* occurs, as in Shakespeare, in the sense of 'more than two'. He offers the examples, "Good evening to ye both" (three people addressed) and "both he and they and you". However, there is no evidence in the film corpus to suggest that this is still the case.

[195] Filppula offers the example: "The most of the farms were three cows and four" (1999: 58).

[196] In his list of Dublin terms, Hickey glosses the words *dossers, knackers, gougers* and *gurriers* as 'lazy good for nothing(s)', 'itinerant(s)' 'thug(s)' and 'lout(s)' (2005: 138).

[197] This particular sentence could be seen to have another meaning, particularly if one takes the film's Dublin setting into account. Since the area code for telephoning Dublin is 01, one could understand that the speaker is suggesting that there are eighteen people with the name Gerry McCarthy in the Dublin area. This is also reflected in the film's subtitles: "There's 18 of us in **the 1-area** phone book". However, given that locals generally speak of the "oh one area", the latter meaning is unlikely.

The film corpus does not display any evidence of *the two* being used in the sense described by Filppula. His example was: "But the two parishes were the one, one time. Mullagh and Milltown were the one parish" (1999: 58).

e) names of languages and branches of learning

The names of languages[198] and other branches of learning are another category which takes the definite article in Irish English. Examples provided in Filppula (1999: 59) and Bliss (1984: 149) would seem to suggest that this "rule" applies more with reference to Irish than to other languages, and, indeed, the only language in the film corpus to take the definite article before it was also Irish[199].

> 141) Father, could I...could I tell you in **the Irish**?
> (*The Quiet Man*, 01:33:55, FMK1930L)

While there are no references to branches of learning as such, the following example from *Angela's Ashes* can be included in this category:

> 142) And **the Shakespeare**. I love **the Shakespeare**.
> (*Angela's Ashes*, 01:31:39, FMP1940L)

f) physical sensations or states

A further non-standard use of the definite article is before physical states or sensations. Filppula (1999: 59) notes that these states or sensations are often unpleasant, and this notion is borne out by the examples which appear in the film corpus. It is perhaps no surprise that all of the examples come from *Angela's Ashes*, a film which features such a great deal of death and despair.

> 143) We were going back to Ireland where there was no work and people were dying of **the starvation** and the damp.
> (*Angela's Ashes*, 00:06:30, MN1990L)

> 144) Is there any possibility of somebody singing something to liven up the proceedings before I'm driven to the drink with **the sadness**[200].
> (*Angela's Ashes*, 02:10:28, MUP1930L)

> 145) Holy Blessed God, you're freezing with **the cold**, boy![201]
> (*Angela's Ashes*, 01:31:00, FMP1940L)

---

[198] The use of the definite article with regard to names of languages is also a feature of Guernsey English (cf. Ramisch 1988: 113), Hebridean English and Scottish English (cf. Filppula 1999: 69-71).

[199] It should, of course, be noted that not all uses of the definite article before "Irish" are non-standard. The film corpus provides an apt example: "It's a translation from the Irish by Lady Gregory" (*The Dead*, 00:23:35, MMG1900D). This usage is in keeping with the optional use of the definite article, which is possible in Standard English, as in Quirk *et al.*'s example "a word borrowed from (the) French/(the) Italian" (1985: 287).

[200] This sentence offers particularly good evidence of the overuse of the definite article, in that it attests three different instances where the definite article would not appear in standard usage.

[201] The related field of the weather also attests non-standard definite article usage, as in the following examples: "And I can tell ya, It gets fairly powerful here in **the warm weather**. So powerful you'll be calling for a gas mask". (*Angela's Ashes*, 00:29:37, MMWB1930L), "A few more steps and a good night's sleep and you'll be as right as **the rain**". (*Widows' Peak*, 01:04:38, MMC1930M).

g) names of diseases and ailments

The category of diseases and ailments is quite similar to the previous category, and so it should again be no surprise to find some examples from *Angela's Ashes*[202].

> 146) Oh, God, Malachy, we're surely going to catch our death out here, and you'll be getting **the pneumonia**.
> (*Angela's Ashes*, 00:12:39, FA1930L)

> 147) Only I'm worried about sleeping in beds that people might have died in. Especially if they died of **the consumption**.
> (*Angela's Ashes*, 00:27:50, FA1930L)

> 148) You can die from **the flu**.
> (*The Magdalene Sisters*, 00:56:01, FCr1960D)

This phenomenon is not restricted merely to human medical conditions, but also includes animal diseases, as in the following example from *Darby O'Gill and the Little People*.

> 149) Your cows will die of **the Black Leg** [203] and your sheep of **the Red Water**, and in every cradle in town there'll be a changeling[204].
> (*Darby O'Gill and the Little People*, 01:00:44, MKB1800K)

h) names of social and 'domestic' institutions

This title of this category is quite vague, as it is not immediately apparent what such "institutions" might be. Filppula adapted the category from Quirk *et al.* (1985: 277), who had used the label "'institutions' of human life and society". Unfortunately, the latter name is equally unclear and, thus, in selecting my examples, I have taken my lead from both of the aforementioned studies. Filppula (1999: 60) offers examples featuring *school*, *work* and *bed*, while Quirk *et al.* also include *church*, *class* and *college*.

> 150) They want me to go to **the university** but they want me to stay their little child as well.
> (*Circle of Friends*, 00:16:35, FBH1950M)

> 151) He'll have to go back to **the fifth class**.
> (*Angela's Ashes*, 01:07:31, MHOH1930L)

> 152) I thought you were supposed to delay him at **the customs**.
> (*The Boys and Girl from County Clare*, 00:23:19, MJJ1960Cl)

---

[202] This phenomenon is well-attested in Irish English (Joyce 1988: 83; Taniguchi 1972: 51 and Moylan, 1996: 275), but it also occurs in Hebridean English and Scottish English (Filppula 1999: 69-71).
[203] Filppula also encountered *the Black Leg* in his corpus (1999: 59-60).
[204] While *black* and *red* are used in a literal sense regarding the diseases above, it is worth pointing out that in other contexts these colours also serve as intensifiers in Irish English (cf. Moylan 1996 and Amador Moreno 2006). *Black* is a negative intensifier, meaning 'evil, malevolent, bigoted or fatal' (cf. Amador Moreno 2006: 205), while *red* is more neutral. The following examples from the film corpus show these colours as intensifiers: "And now we know the sort of black business it was." (*Widows' Peak*, 01:22:17, FDC1930M). Here the *black* business refers to murder. "Never had a red cent on him. Wouldn't give you the steam off his piss, if you'll excuse my French." (*Last of the High Kings*, 00:37:59, MTD1970D). Here *red* means 'single' (cf. Share 2006: 119).

153) Where the hell is she goin'? She only got out of **the hospital** a couple of days ago.
(*Veronica Guerin*, 00:50:25, MGS1990D)

154) That's it. In from the pub, off to **the bed**.
(*Rat*, 00:03:43, FC2000D)

i) names of geographical areas and localities, public institutions, buildings, monuments, and streets

155) Seventy years ago, me grandfather, Hubert Flynn I, set out from his home in **the County Wexford**[205] and journeyed north over the hills and valleys of Wicklow until he came to Dublin City.
(*Rat*, 00:00:17, MH2000D)

156) The ould panto in **the Francis Xavier Hall**.
(*Mystics*, 00:53:55, FF2000D)

j) expressions involving reference to body parts or items of clothing
Expressions referring to body parts occur quite frequently in the film corpus and include the following:

157) Oh, and he has these four sisters with **the enormous breasts**.
(*Angela's Ashes*, 00:53:24, MF1940L)

In many instances referring to parts of the body, the definite article takes the function of a possessive adjective (cf. Henry 1957: 118; Ó hÚrdail 1997: 194). In the examples below, *the* represents the possessive adjective *my* in the first three cases, *your* in the fourth and *her* in the final one.

158) No, I have **the mind** made up and it's not working out with all of us on top of each other like this.
(*Nora*, 00:57:42, MSJ1900D)

159) Drop me off here, Michael. I'll walk the rest of the way. Stretch out **the hip**.
(*Garage*, 01:07:36, MJ2000M)

160) I'll take it in **the hand**, Josie. We're headin'.
(*Garage*, 00:59:20, MDec2000M)

161) Morning, boys, how's **the heads**?
(*Waking Ned*, 00:12:14, MD2000W)

162) That one? Not likely, and her with **the freckles** and her temper.
(*The Quiet Man*, 00:13:38, MMF1930W)

---

[205] The use of the definite article before the names of counties will be familiar to many people, as the phenomenon is quite common in the opening lines of traditional Irish songs, such as "The Galway Shawl" ("In Oranmore, in **the** County Galway...") and "The Star of the County Down" ("Near Banbridge town, in **the** County Down...").

k) terms for members of the family

As was the case for many of the examples referring to parts of the body, the definite article here takes the function of a possessive adjective. In the examples below, *the* represents the possessive adjective *my* in the first two examples, *your* in the next five and *your* and *her* in the last one[206].

163) **The wife** told me that.
(*Evelyn*, 00:32:38, MBM1950D)

164) **The mammy** and I live up the hill from you.
(*Widows' Peak*, 00:13:58, MGDC1930M)

165) And where's **the husband**?
(*Angela's Ashes*, 01:22:53, MSVDP1940L)

166) She's a peculiar woman, **the mother**. She's led me a quare[207] life all these years.
(*The Field*, 01:04:30, MBMC1950W)

167) Where's **the nephew**?
(*The Nephew*, 00:09:23, MP1990C)

168) Get up there beside **the uncle**.
(*The Nephew*, 00:09:29, MP1990C)

169) Woman of the house, I've brought **the brother** home to supper[208].
(*The Quiet Man*, 02:06:10, MST1930US)

170) [Is she minding them on her own since **the missus** died?]
Ah, it won't do her no harm. **The granny** comes in during the day.
(*The General*, 01:34:08, Mga1990D)

l) terms for parts of the day, week or year

171) What a surprise! Out and about at this time of **the night**.
(*Mystics*, 00:53:20, MD2000D)

172) This is a fine time of **the night** to be comin' in.
(*My Left Foot*, 00:33:47, FMB1950D)

---

[206] According to Amador Moreno, the definite article also replaces the possessive in Northern Irish English (cf. 2006: 69). It has traditionally also been found in this context in a number of northern British dialects (cf. EDD s.v. the, *dem*. II. 1.).
[207] The word *quare* representing the Irish English pronunciation of *queer* has also become lexicalised. In addition to its traditional meaning of 'strange' as in the example above, it can also be used as an intensifier, as in "I'll tell yeh one thing Conway he's trainin' queer hard for it" (Dolan 2006: 187). It also appears in the term *the quare stuff*, a reference to illicit whiskey or poteen (cf. Share 2003: 259).
[208] This sentence is an interesting example of speech accommodation, since the speaker, who is an American, uses the definite article before the noun in typical Irish fashion. Minutes before he also mockingly pronounces *tea* as *tay* to show he is trying to become one of the locals: "Woman of the house, where's me tay?" (*The Quiet Man*, 01:46:38, MST1930US). *Woman of the house* is an anglicised version of the Irish term *bean a' tí* (cf. Dolan 2006: 18-19).

173) He'd as soon put his clob of a fist in me teeth as bid me the time of **the day**.
(*The Quiet Man*, 00:38:52, MMF1930W)

174) They won't notice the paintings are missin' till **the mornin'**.
(*The General*, 01:10:52, MMC1990D)

175) A fine soft day in **the spring** it was, when the train pulled into Castletown, three hours late as usual, and himself got off.
(*The Quiet Man*, 00:02:04, MFL1930W)

176) And in **the winter**, they did a panto.
(*Mystics*, 00:17:15, MCC22000C)

m) names of festive days or seasons[209]

177) Just helpin' the sister's husband[210] to make a few extra bob over **the Christmas**.
(*The Dead*, 00:57:28, MTD1900W)

178) Thanks again for coming out on **the Christmas Eve**.
(*Rat*, 00:55:20, FC2000D)

n) expressions involving the -*ing* form of verbs, used to refer to trades and professional or general activities

179) She'd been at **the teaching** for over 50 years.
(*Ryan's Daughter*, 00:18:34, MS1920W)

180) And about that horse for **the ploughing**, we could sell that black hunter of yours.
(*The Quiet Man*, 01:28:05, FMK1930W)

181) If me mates saw me making a pure eejit out of meself at **the Irish dancing**, I'd be disgraced forever.
(*Angela's Ashes*, 00:49:12, MN1990L)

182) Ah there she is. Still at **the oul writin'**.
(*The General*, 01:18:49, MMC1990D)

183) Ah now, don't be sending the poor man to Knockanore, sure **the fishing** is finished there entirely.
(*The Quiet Man*, 00:03:00, MMC1930W)

184) I thank you anyway, Sean Thornton, for **the asking**.
(*The Quiet Man*, 00:45:58, FMK1930W)

---

[209] By seasons, Filppula means festive seasons, such as Christmas and Easter, which often take the definite article in Irish English, e.g. "He's coming home for the Christmas".

[210] The aforementioned use of the definite article in place of a personal pronoun when referring to family members is also evident in this sentence from *The Dead*.

185) Well, we've just started **the courtin'** and next month we...we start **the walking out** together, and the month after that, there'll be the threshing parties and the month after that there'll be...
(The Quiet Man, 01:07:25, FMK1930W)

186) Just in here, like. Bit of **the oul skills training** with the young fella.
(Adam and Paul, 00:09:39, MG2000D)

Filppula notes that expressions involving the *-ing* form of verbs are often followed by an *of*-genitive and are addressed by Harris (1993: 148) under the heading 'nominalisation'[211]. Moylan (1996: 348-9) refers to this as 'gerundial formation'. Below are some examples:

187) Then why did you let her believe that I was brought here only for **the cuttin' of** the turf?
(Darby O'Gill and the Little People, 00:19:35, MMB1800D)

188) Look here, Father Hugh, **the stripping of** her was an accident.
(Ryan's Daughter, 01:11:10, ML1920W)

o) names of persons when qualified by an adjective or a title

It is important to note that the adjectives in question are not those which in Standard English would also take the definite article, such as *young, former* etc., as in "the young Goethe" or "the former Miss World".

189) And how's **the bould Gus**[212], and the new daughter-in-law?
(How Harry Became a Tree, 00:42:19, FOW1920WW)

190) Oh, God, there's my da, with **the creepy Sean Walsh**.
(Circle of Friends, 00:05:17, FBH1950M)

191) At least my grandpa in the North sent us five pounds for **the baby Alphie**[213].
(Angela's Ashes, 00:58:24, MN1990L)

192) That's from **the Lord Fitzpatrick**, I'd know his fist anywhere.
(Darby O'Gill and the Little People, 01:09:46, FWIP1800K)

193) The wealthiest woman in Inisfree was **the Widow Tillane**.
(The Quiet Man, 00:14:00, MFL1950W)

---

[211] Note, however, that not all examples of nominalisation need take the *-ing* form, nor indeed a definite article. This can be seen in the following examples from the film corpus. "They're all going to know we got **the eviction**. Will you be quiet?" (*Angela's Ashes*, 01:34:26, FA1930L), "But, faith, I **have need** for it now" (*Darby O'Gill and the Little People*, 00:18:51, MDOG1800K).

[212] *Bould* in this case means 'brave' (cf. page 154). A synonymous construction, featuring the definite article before an adjective, is evident in the title of the famous song "The gallant John Joe".

[213] While this example from *Angela's Ashes* may seem out of place and appear as though a pause (or in the written form, a comma) should occur between *baby* and *Alphie*, this is not the case. This is also substantiated by comparing the same line from the novel: "Grandpa in the North sends a telegram money order for five pounds for the baby Alphie" (McCourt 1996: 206).

194) I have an announcement to make. With me own two eyes, I saw Gypo knock **the Scrapper Maloney** flyin' across the road like a man divin' off the bull wall.

(The Informer, 00:42:11, MSP1920D)

The insertion of the definite article would also appear to be able to apply to non-proper nouns when qualified by an adjective, as can be seen from the following example:

195) Ye're **the busy men** this hour on a Sunday mornin'.

(Garage, 01:01:41, MJ2000M)

p) reference to means of transport
Filppula suggests that whereas Standard English speakers elect to use zero article and the preposition *by* when referring to means of transport, Irish English speakers opt for constructions with the definite article and a different preposition, such as *in* or *on*. He offers the example: "They'll come out there *on the bus* to where I'm telling you, down the road" (1999: 63). Unfortunately, there are no such examples in the film corpus.

q) sentences containing nouns with a strong emotional content
Filppula states that a further use of the definite article in Irish English is in "sentences containing definite nouns with a strong 'emotional colour'" where it is used for "the purpose of rhetorical effect" (1999: 63). Here he is echoing Bliss' observation that the definite article is used in Irish English "in ejaculations and in general in sentences with a strong emotional colour" (1984: 149). However, what exactly is meant by "strong emotional colour" remains unclear and, unfortunately, the examples offered, particularly those from Filppula, are not all that helpful in clarifying the matter.

Filppula's two examples are: "And who was there, only the fellow. And I said to him then, I said to him, behind of that, I said, 'You are the pig!' says I. 'Outside with it!' 'You are the pig,' says I" (1999: 63-4) and "And I had to bring it [turf] out there by lorry, by tractor [...] Whatever was in it was the good share of turf an' all right" (1999: 64). While the notion of 'emotional colour' can be inferred from the first sentence, due to the name-calling, the second sentence does not seem to fulfil this criterion.

Bliss, in contrast, offers the sentences: "That's the grand morning, thank God!" and "It was the sorry day I ever let you come into this house" (1984: 149). Again, the "emotional colour" is really only evident in one sentence, namely the latter one.

While there are no cases of such "emotional" sentences in the film corpus, there are examples of sentences which are similar in structure, i.e. like the examples given, they involve the substitution of the definite article for the indefinite article. These have been included in the first of the additional categories below.

r) taking the place of the indefinite article
In their studies of Irish English, Henry (1957: 118), Harris (1993: 145), Bliss (1984: 149) and Amador Moreno (2006: 67 and 123) also include the category of the definite article taking the place of the indefinite article. Evidence of this usage can be seen in the examples from the film corpus below, the first of which is very much like an example offered by Harris.

196) Oh, you're **the thinkin' man**.
                (*Darby O'Gill and the Little People*, 00:08:30, MKB1800K)

197) Well, you're **the comical girl**, Molly.
                (*The Dead*, 00:34:03, FG1900D)

198) Well now, aren't you **the clever girl**?
                (*Darby O'Gill and the Little People*, 00:49:00, MMB1800D)

199) **The woman** is incomplete until himself is six feet under.
                (*Widows' Peak*, 00:03:59, MMC1930M)

s) the names of meals/mealtimes

Ó hÚrdail (1997: 194) makes a fleeting reference to the fact that the word *dinner* often takes the definite article in Irish English, and, indeed, evidence from the film corpus shows this to be the case. What is more, this phenomenon is not just restricted to that particular mealtime. Thus, in keeping with Taniguchi (1972: 50) we can also add the category of meals/mealtimes to the list of contexts in which the definite article is likely to appear[214].

200) Mr McBride is coming to resort with us for a fortnight, so throw a couple of extra spuds in the pot for **the supper**, and make up the bed in the loft.
                (*Darby O'Gill and the Little People*, 00:15:57, MDOG1800K)

201) It'd want to be better than that heap of shite you gave me for **the breakfast**.
                (*Trojan Eddie*, 00:17:56, MGG1990M)

202) Wouldn't you feel very nervous closing your eyes for the[215] short kip after **the dinner** with Vulturus monachus perched on the mantelpiece.
                (*Rat*, 00:13:51, MM2000D)

As can be seen above, there are numerous examples of non-standard usage of the definite article in the film corpus. Indeed, it appears in some form or other in 42 of the 50 films (84%) [see Table 19]. However, even though it can appear in so many contexts, it is apparent from the previous pages that there are clearly contexts which are much preferred, such as before non-count abstract nouns and concrete mass nouns or terms for members of the family, and those which are quite rare, such as before reference to means of transport. The variety in frequency is also reflected in the results from Hickey's *Survey of Irish English Usage* which investigated respondents' approval of the definite article in the following sentences: "He likes the life in Galway", "She has to go to the hospital", and "He is good at the maths". These sentences received acceptability ratings of 77%, 95% and 39% respectively, with acceptance of the definite article before an abstract noun, in this case *life*, being twice as high as that of the definite article before a branch of learning, in this case *maths*.

---

[214] See also Sabban (1982: 380-418).
[215] This is another example of the aforementioned non-standard use of the definite article where one would normally expect an indefinite article.

6.1.2.3 Reflexive pronouns

The non-standard use of reflexive pronouns, especially *himself* and *herself*, must be regarded as one of the most salient features of Irish English, especially to the ears of non-Irish people. Indeed, the feature is so strongly associated with Irish English that it has even motivated a series of his and hers souvenir mugs, socks and T-shirts, bearing the motifs *himself* and *herself* respectively. Whereas in Standard English the use of reflexive pronouns is dependent on the presence of a nominal element in the same clause or sentence, in Irish English this is not the case. Here, they can be used independently, and are, thus, also known as unbound reflexives or UBRs (cf. Filppula 1999: 77-8). They can appear in subject, object or prepositional complement position, as can be seen in the following examples:

> 203) A fine soft day in the spring it was, when the train pulled into Castletown, three hours late as usual, and **himself** got off.
> (*The Quiet Man*, 00:02:04, MFL1930W)

> 204) It'd be a real honour to reunite **yourself** and Big Mac across the great divide.
> (*Mystics*, 00:14:01, MD2000D)

> 205) I know there have been various allegations made about **meself**. And I know the names of all the allegators.
> (*Last of the High Kings*, 01:01:28, MJF1970D)

Throughout much of the literature on Irish English, the unbound reflexives *himself* and *herself* are thought to refer to "an individual who is regarded as being the person in charge or the person in a leading position" (Hickey 2004a: 128) or to the "mistress or master of the house" (Joyce 1988: 47). These meanings are borne out in the following two film examples, in which the pronouns do, indeed, refer to a landlord and a woman of the house respectively.

> 206) And we are pretty sure that **himself** is up to something.
> (*Irish Jam*, 00:02:45, MFR2000W)

> 207) Oh, and remember, next time you see me with **herself**, don't let on to her that I'm such a handyman.
> (*Widows' Peak*, 00:17:46, MGDC1930M)

However, although there is evidence of these forms in the film corpus, it would simply be wrong to suggest that this is the only context in which the unbound reflexives *himself* and *herself* can appear. Filppula echoes this notion, also finding evidence to prove that "the 'master/mistress of the house' reading of UBRs is far too narrow" (1999: 81)[216]. A more accurate description of the meaning of these unbound reflexives would be Harris' definition that "rather than the person being mentioned explicitly in the immediate linguistic context (for instance, in a preceding sentence), the reference draws on the shared knowledge of the

---

[216] Amador Moreno also found that the notion of reflexives simply alluding to power structures was inaccurate. In fact, the use of *himself/herself* to refer to the master/mistress did not apply to any of the novels she examined (cf. 2006: 77).

speaker and hearer"[217] (1993: 147). This explanation is certainly borne out by examples in the film corpus. In the first, Damien, a doctor, is called to examine a sick child and is asked whether he would like a drink of water while he is there. He politely declines and replies:

> 208) Maybe a drop for **himself**.
> *(The Wind that Shakes the Barley*, 01:34:39, MD1920C)

Here there is a clear understanding between Damien and the boy's mother/grandmother that *himself* refers to the boy and not to some unseen "person in charge or in a leading position". In example 209, Foxy meets the retired entertainers Dave and Locky and their performing dog. She thinks she recognises the dog from having seen him perform tricks many decades earlier and questions whether this can still possibly be the same animal:

> 209) This can't still be **himself**.
> *(Mystics*, 00:54:25, FF2000D)

Again, Dave and Locky implicitly understand that Foxy is referring to the famous dog of yesteryear and so they tell her that this is not the famous dog but rather its grandson. These two examples should clearly show that the notion that unbound reflexives automatically refer to someone in some sort of position of power is an inaccurate one, and even more so when the person being referred to by *himself* is a little boy or a even a Jack Russell terrier.

While most attention has been given to *himself* and *herself*, it would be extremely short-sighted to focus solely on these reflexive pronouns, as other forms are equally, if not more, popular in Irish English. This can be seen in Table 21 which displays examples of *myself, yourself* and *yourselves* used in contexts where one would normally expect other pronouns in Standard English usage. While Standard English speakers do sometimes also use reflexive pronouns in contexts where one would expect the objective or subjective pronoun, – Quirk et al., for example, offer the sentence: "My brother and I/myself went sailing yesterday" (1985: 213) – Irish English usage allows the reflexive in considerably more contexts. Furthermore, Filppula also observes that when unbound reflexives are used, the order of constituents in conjoined subjects is quite striking in Irish English, in that the reflexive pronoun generally came first in the sentence (1999: 84). Thus sentences of the "Myself and John" variety would be expected to outnumber those beginning "John and myself". This is, indeed, the case in the film corpus, in which the reflexive comes first in examples from 10 of the films, whereas the reverse is the case for only 4 movies.[218]

For instances of *himself* or *herself* in a context which echoes that of Hickey's sample sentence "Himself is not in today", the number of occurrences is 12 out of the 50 films (24%) [see Table 20]. This is in keeping with the findings for Hickey's sentence, which as it happens also had an average acceptability rate of 24%. Other non-standard reflexive pronouns (*myself, yourself, yourselves*) are evident in 29 of the 50 films (58%) [see Table 21].

---

[217] This notion of drawing on the shared knowledge of the speaker and hearer also applies to the structures *your man/your woman/your one* which are dealt with in Chapter 6.3.1.4.

[218] According to Filppula, this reflexive-first trend is also evident in the Irish language, particularly with the first person, and also features strongly in Hebridean English (cf. 1999: 84 and Odlin 1997: 44-5), suggesting a Celtic substratum is at play. Indeed, the use of reflexives in Hebridean English in general is very similar to that in Irish English (cf. Filppula 1999: 85).

An additional feature which is usually only referred to briefly in the literature on Irish English is the use of the reflexive pronoun *itself* (cf. Hayden and Hartog 1909: 945; Joyce 1988: 36-37; Taniguchi 1972: 29-32; Filppula 1999: 82; and Amador Moreno 2006: 79). According to Taniguchi, *itself* can be glossed as either "even", "at all" or "so" (cf. 1972: 29-32). A reason for this is that *itself* is a translation of the Irish term *féin,* which can mean 'even/only' and 'self', and therefore these terms were also perceived as synonymous by early speakers of English in Ireland (cf. Dolan 2006: 127)[219].

The feature, which is common in Synge's dramas, occurs only once in the film corpus:

210) To take a pick **itself** after all your dancing[220].
(*The Dead*, 00:33:45, FMJ1900D)

Despite the low frequency of the feature in the corpus and the dearth of research on it, I believe it to still be quite a common feature of Irish English, particularly in the West of Ireland. In my experience, the reflexive *itself* is actually pronounced *inself* in such contexts, as in my constructed examples below:

211) *Guy*: Do you know where Paula is?
Girl: No, and if I did **inself**[221], I wouldn't tell you. You broke her heart. She doesn't want to see you.

212) *Host*: Will you have something to eat?
Guest: No, I won't thanks. I'm only after eating.
Host: Ah, go on. You'll have a cup of tea **inself**[222].

However, there does not appear to be any mention of *inself* as a variant of *itself* anywhere in the research on Irish English to date. The closest thing to it is to be found in Taniguchi (1972). There he states that "the corrupted form, 'aself' for 'itself' is occasionally found occurring in Irish English" and he offers the following example from Sean O'Casey's play *Juno and the Paycock*:

213) An', if I get up **aself**, how am I going to get down agen?
(Taniguchi 1972: 26)

In light of the relatively little attention which has been paid to this feature, it would be very useful to conduct further research to discover Irish people's recognition and acceptance of these *inself, aself* and *itself* structures.

6.1.2.4   Adverb marking

Hickey (2004a: 128) observes that Irish English uses a large number of intensifying adverbs without the *-ly* inflection[223] which one would expect in Standard English, and he cites the

---

[219] Stockwell observes a similar structure in Indian English, in which *itself* also means 'only'. He gives the example: "Can I meet with you tomorrow itself?" (2007: 26). In Irish English, this sentence would probably be glossed: 'Can I at least meet with you tomorrow?' or 'Can I meet with you tomorrow anyway?'.
[220] This line is taken directly from Joyce's short story *The Dead* (1914) – To take a pick itself, said Mary Jane, after all your dancing (Schwarz 1994: 37).
[221] "And if I did inself" can be paraphrased as 'and even if I did'.
[222] "You'll have a cup of tea inself" can be paraphrased as 'you'll have a cup of tea anyway/at least'.

example "The work is real difficult" which he gave to his respondents to evaluate. The lack of -*ly* inflection for intensifying adverbs is also evident in the film corpus, with the most common occurrences being with the intensifiers *awful, terrible* and *real*[224].

214) I do love them, Father, but I'm finding it **awful** hard to honour them.
(*Circle of Friends*, 00:16:56, FBH1950M)

215) Oh, Lord, this is getting **awful** serious.
(*Waking Ned*, 00:52:51, MJ2000W)

216) He looks **terrible** angry too.
(*High Spirits*, 01:07:31, MDMC1980W)

217) Well, it did look **terrible** smashed about, Father.
(*Ryan's Daughter*, 00:22:29, MS1920W)

218) Jaysus, I'm **terrible** sorry about this, John. Disgraced the family, she did. And as for that other fella…he's dead.
(*Trojan Eddie*, 00:58:44, MG1990M)

219) Do you know, Matt, he's got **terrible** dirty?
(*Rat*, 00:15:15, FC2000D)

220) Faith, I never saw dancin' so fine or heard pipin' so **shockin'** sweet or touched a fiddle so grand and never in me wildest dreams did I dream I'd be sitting on diamonds.
(*Darby O'Gill and the Little People*, 00:35:48, MDOG1800K)

221) I was **real** cut up when I heard the news.
(*Mystics*, 00:04:43, MB2000D)

However, the dropping of -*ly* inflection is not limited to intensifying adverbs but also appears in other contexts. For example, sentence 222 from *Dead Meat* below displays the lack of -*ly* inflection in both the intensifying adverb *really* and the adverb *badly*, while the other examples show that this lack of -*ly* inflection can occur with a number of adverbs which either premodify a verb, as in examples 227 and 228 with *nearly*, or which postmodify it, as in the other examples[225]. The adverbs *badly, nearly,* and *differently* all appear more than once in the film corpus.

222) They hurt my dad **real bad**.
(*Dead Meat*, 00:37:18, FLG2000LM)

223) He might take it **bad**.
(*A Man of No Importance*, 00:19:03, MCB1960D)

---

[223] The use of the adjectival form for the adverbial is a common feature of other dialects of English (cf. EDD § 444).
[224] The tendency to omit –*ly* from the adverbs *really* and *awfully* has also been observed in American English (cf. Tottie 2002: 169).
[225] Example 229 is an exception in that it premodifies "200 years".

224) My mother took it really **bad**.
(*Cowboys and Angels*, 00:41:28, MS2000L)

225) If someone hurt you, and I was there, I'd hurt them back so **bad**, I'm telling you.
(*Nora*, 00:39:16, FN1900G)

226) You promised that no one in the town would ever mention it or think **bad** of me, that it would be looked after.
(*Widows' Peak*, 01:13:53, FMOH1930M)

227) Some young fellas are after robbin' a car. **Near** fuckin' killed us they did.
(*Adam and Paul*, 00:57:28, MA2000D)

228) He **near** had me plugged when I went back to report.
(*The Informer*, 00:12:02, MG1920D)

229) You gave me my first moment of peace in **near** 200 years.
(*High Spirits*, 00:50:00, FMP1980W)

230) It's spelled completely **different**.
(*Last of the High Kings*, 00:45:25, MF1970D)

231) I know that. I never said **different**.
(*The Van*, 00:29:38, MB1990D)

232) I love you. I can't help it if I can't say it **different** to other people. Even writers have to use the same words as other people.
(*Nora*, 01:17:25, FN1900G)

233) Does she think he killed himself **deliberate**?
(*Ryan's Daughter*, 01:23:30, MFR1920W)

234) We'll both write **regular**.
(*Ryan's Daughter*, 01:28:17, FR1920W)

235) The floor will need to be cleaned **proper** before we go.
(*Waking Ned*, 00:31:23, MM2000W)

236) Nothin', Frankie. You came up to me so **sudden**, like[226].
(*The Informer*, 00:10:10, MG1920D)

237) I seen him humpin' her out the back window but I'd no shoes or pants on, so I couldn't get to them **quick** enough.
(*Garage*, 00:30:25, MSul2000M)

238) But I know you won't judge me too **harsh**.
(*A Man of No Importance*, 00:44:00, FA1960M)

---

[226] The possibility of *like* rather than *-ly* being used to create an adverb in this example is discussed in 6.2.2.3.

Unusual examples
To this list, one can add a structure identified by Joyce (1988: 89). It involves the use of the adjective *cruel* in place of the intensifier *very*. Joyce offers the examples "This is a cruel wet day", "that old fellow is cruel rich", and "that's a cruel good man"[227]. In the example below from *Darby O'Gill and the Little People*, the structure is used to suggest that the *poteen*, the illicit alcohol which the characters are drinking, is very easy to drink or that it goes down smoothly.

239) Ah it drinks **cruel aisy**[228], so it does.
(*Darby O'Gill and the Little People*, 00:37:04, MKB1800K)

A similar adjective to *cruel* which can also take the place of the intensifier *very*, particularly in Cork and Kerry, is *fierce* (cf. Dolan 2006: 92). It can also be glossed as *terribly* or *awfully*.

240) We were **fierce** close as young fellas, the two of us.
(*The Wind that Shakes the Barley*, 00:40:42, MD1920C)

241) Jesus, boy, I'm getting **fierce** hungry just looking at them.
(*When Brendan Met Trudy*, 01:05:32, FT2000C)

As can be seen from the examples above, there is ample evidence of non-standard adverb forms in the film corpus. However, there is a potential for this picture to become somewhat skewed if one makes a comparison with the results of Hickey's survey. On his questionnaire, respondents were judging the lack of *-ly* inflection for just one intensifying adverb, namely *really*, which resulted in an average acceptability rate of 37% nationwide. For the film corpus, the rate for that particular adverb is considerably lower, due to the fact that the aforementioned intensifying adverb *really* only occurs in 2 of the 50 films (4%). If, on the other hand, one were to include other intensifying adverbs, such as *awfully* and *terribly*, as well as non-standard adverbs in general, then the rate for the film corpus would increase accordingly to 29 out of 50 movies (58%) [see Table 22].

6.1.3 Negation
6.1.3.1   Negative concord

Another feature which Irish English shares with many other forms of non-standard English is negative concord. This means that "any element within a clause which can occur in the negative will do so if the entire clause is negative, e.g. He isn't interested in no cars" (Hickey 2004a: 126). Such structures are sometimes referred to as *double negatives* in layman's terms, although, according to Harris (1993: 169) a more appropriate term would be *multiple negation* as, in theory, more than two negatives can appear in a sentence featuring negative concord. This is evident in his example: "She never lost no furniture or nothing"

---

[227] For further examples, see Taniguchi (1972: 41).
[228] In addition to the use of the intensifier *cruel*, this example also exhibits the absence of the *-ly* inflection on the adverb *easily* – here spelled <aisy> and pronounced ['e:zi]. However, not all instances of non-standard adverb usage need necessarily involve the omission of *-ly* inflection. The film corpus also shows evidence of the non-standard use of *good* for *well* in a comparative sense, as in the following example: "I can track as **good** as me brother" (*Into the West*, 00:56:33, FK1990M).

(1993: 169). Hickey's suggestion that *negative concord* does not occur in the supraregional form of Irish English is borne out to a certain extent by both the results of the film corpus and those of his own survey.

In the film corpus, *negative concord* is evident in 10 of the 50 films (20%) [see Table 23], with 8 of those being set in Leinster, while the remaining ones are set in Connaught and Munster respectively. There is no evidence of *multiple negation*, as defined above, with all of the examples being of the double negative variety, such as:

242) **Nothing** mad goin' on or **nothin'**?
(Adam and Paul, 00:04:04, MA2000D)

243) All right so, I'll ask her, sure. It **don't** cost **nothin'** to ask, do it? Huh?
(Trojan Eddie, 01:12:27, MA1990M)

In Hickey's survey, the acceptability rate for *negative concord* was even lower than was the frequency in the films, with an average of 6% nationwide and a low of 3% in Connaught. The low acceptability rate in Hickey's survey can probably be accounted for by the fact that, despite it being a common feature of vernacular language in general, it is one of the features with the highest degree of "folk awareness" (cf. Chapter 7.2). From a young age, people are made aware of this structure being "wrong" and thus negative concord is exposed to a degree of prescriptivism that does not apply to most other features of Irish English, with the exception perhaps of *I done/I seen* and the use of *them* as a demonstrative pronoun (cf. Hickey 2004a: 21).

6.1.3.2 Lack of negator contraction

Although it is a feature most often associated with Scottish English, a lack of negator contraction is still reasonably common in Ireland. Whereas in Standard English one typically finds contracted negators, as in "I won't" or "I haven't", in Irish English the corresponding structure often takes the form "I'll not" or "I've not". Some examples include:

244) **I'll not** wish for the gold.
(Darby O'Gill and the Little People, 01:12:50, MDOG1800K)

245) **We've not** done anything.
(Ryan's Daughter, 00:13:24, FMC1920W)

Examples of a lack of negator contraction appear in 14 of the 50 films (28%) [see Table 24], and it is interesting to note that all but four of the films in which this feature appears are set prior to 1990. This is quite significant, and supports Hickey's notion that, although this feature was used in the early half of the twentieth century (cf. the plays by Sean O'Casey), it is not expected to occur in supraregional varieties of Irish English today (cf. Hickey 2004a: 127). Nevertheless, when asked to judge the sentence "I'll not wait any longer for him", approximately 36% of Hickey's informants still regarded the lack of negator contraction as perfectly acceptable.

6.1.4 Questions

6.1.4.1 Word order in indirect questions

Unlike in Standard English, Irish English displays inversion of word order even in indirect questions[229]. Since the terminology here can be somewhat confusing, I shall first of all briefly explain what is meant by inversion, using some examples from Standard English. In order to ask a direct question in Standard English, one inverts the word order of a given statement, thus "He is going home" becomes "Is he going home?" in the interrogative. However, although this inversion takes place in direct questions, there is no such inversion in indirect questions or in reported speech in Standard English, as the following example shows "I asked him whether he was going home". In Irish English, in contrast, indirect questions retain the inversion of direct questions, resulting in sentences such as "I asked him was he going home". According to Bliss (1984: 148), indirect questions can take two forms. The first kind, as shown above, are indirect simple questions, which in Standard English require an introductory *if* or *whether* and which can often be answered by a simple *yes* or *no*[230]. In Irish English, however, the *if* or *whether* is omitted and the inversion, also known as "embedded inversion" (Filppula 1999: 167), is retained. As can be seen in the examples from the film corpus, typical verbs which introduce this type of indirect question include *ask*, *wonder*, *know*[231] and *see* (cf. Filppula 1999: 167).

246) Read out the part where he asks **is Giorgio really his son**.
(*Nora*, 01:02:29, FN1900G)

247) I wonder **has he any taste in clothes**?
(*About Adam*, 01:03:52, FA2000D)

248) He wants to know **do you want to have an abortion**.
(*The Snapper*, 00:04:28, FKC1990D)

249) We were just waitin' to see **is what's-his-name around**.
(*Adam and Paul*, 00:20:43, MP2000D)

The second form these indirect questions can take is as indirect complex questions. These preserve the interrogative word (*who*, *what*, *when*, *where*, *which* and *how*[232]) and unlike in Standard English they again retain the word order of a direct question.

250) Inspector, the press want to know **why was there no Gardaí presence**.
(*The General*, 00:02:14, MI1990D)

---

[229] Again, this is by no means an exclusively Irish feature. Filppula (1999: 170-2) offers examples of it from Tyneside, Scottish and Hebridean English. In this regard, Sabban suggests that the high frequency of the feature in Scotland, Ireland and the Hebrides can be attributed to the influence from Gaelic, which, irrespective of sentence type, places the verb at the beginning of the sentence. This pattern also applies to both direct and indirect questions (1982: 479).

[230] Filppula calls these simple questions "Yes/No questions" (1999: 167).

[231] Bliss (1984: 148) suggests that *know* is used in the negative, as in "I didn't know did anybody try to find out". However, as can be seen in example 248 from *The Snapper* this form can also be used in questions.

[232] Despite the presence of *how* in this list, these questions are generally termed "WH-questions" (cf. Filppula 1999: 67).

251) May I ask **what are you doing sitting at my table?**
(Far and Away, 00:40:34, FSC1890W)

252) I don't know **what's the matter with the youngsters in this place.**
(Ryan's Daughter, 00:15:19, MFR1920W)

253) You'll find out **who's the knowledgeable one.**
(Darby O'Gill and the Little People, 00:34:10, MDOG1800K)

Based on his Hiberno-English corpus, Filppula observed that embedded inversion was more likely to occur in simple *Yes/No* questions than in complex WH-questions. His findings were corroborated by those of the *Survey of Irish English Usage*[233], in which Hickey gave his respondents the questions "She asked him was he interested" and "He asked who had she spoken to", and found that 86% of them felt that the first sentence, the *Yes/No* question, was "no problem", while 60% felt the same way about the second sentence, the WH-question. The notion of embedded inversion appearing more frequently in *Yes/No* questions was also supported in the film corpus where the *Yes/No* form appears in 10 of the 50 films (20%) [see Table 25] compared to the 7 of the 50 (14%) [see Table 26] for the more complex form. The numbers for the former could be seen to be even higher, depending on one's tolerance of a slight pause before the indirect question itself. In the following examples, I felt that the pause was too long, suggesting that it was the equivalent of a colon or comma in punctuation, which in Standard English would then also allow the subsequent question to have inversion. The reader may like to consult the movies to draw his or her own conclusions.

254) And the only question I want you to answer today is: **are ye men of your word?**
(The Wind that Shakes the Barley, 01:25:24, MR1920C)

255) So he asked me if I would come down here to ask you, **would you like to come and have tea with us tonight?**
(A Man of No Importance, 00:38:08, FL1960D)

256) Christine asked me to ask you, **would you mind looking after Tom and Shane tomorrow?**
(Ordinary Decent Criminal, 00:15:15, MML1990D)

257) Listen, I was just wonderin', **do you think I could maybe leave my stuff with you for a little while, while I go and look at a flat?**
(Goldfish Memory, 00:43:45, MB2000D)

However, what is even more striking than the disparity in the frequency rates of the different inversion types is the fact that there is not a single example of embedded inversion in WH-questions in any of the 26 most recent films in the corpus. While this certainly does not mean that the structure has disappeared, it is nonetheless very striking, particularly since there are so few cases of features appearing in only one half of the tables in the film corpus and not

---

[233] This higher frequency of embedded inversion in *Yes/No* questions than in WH-questions can also be witnessed in other non-standard varieties (cf. Erdmann 1979: 8f), and even though Sabban (1982: 479) found the opposite to be the case, she suggests that her findings can be attributed to chance.

in the other. When this does happen, there is usually a good reason for it, as in the case of the *'for to' infinitive* or *musha* (see Chapter 6.2.6), which have both disappeared as they are regarded as old-fashioned or clichéd. In the case of embedded inversion, however, no such explanation is available and, thus, further research into the current status of the feature needs to be conducted.

Another reason for further research is that there was no evidence in the film corpus nor in Hickey's survey to support Filppula's findings that there is a strong rural-urban divide regarding embedded inversion. Filppula (1991) had found that there were fewer instances of the form in Dublin speech, but Hickey discovered that at 88%, the acceptability rate for the *Yes/No* form was actually slightly higher in Dublin than the aforementioned national average of 86%. Hickey's findings were corroborated in the film corpus, for which the instances of embedded inversion in *Yes/No* questions in Dublin films also outnumbered the cases elsewhere. However, it is worth noting that with regard to WH-questions embedded inversion does indeed appear less frequently in Dublin than elsewhere. This was the case in both the film corpus and in Hickey's survey, where the feature had a 57% acceptability rate compared to the national average of 60%. It would be interesting to conduct further research into these features to see whether a different type of rural-urban divide exists than the one originally suggested by Filppula. Perhaps the rural-urban divide regarding embedded inversion does not apply across the board, but rather depends upon the type of questions involved.

6.1.4.2   Responses to *Yes/No* questions

A feature of Irish English which has received a great degree of attention is the fact that answers to *Yes/No* questions are very rarely a simple *yes* or *no* for Irish people. Indeed, according to Biggar, this feature is one which often "strikes English people as peculiar and amusing" (1897: 62). The reason for this phenomenon is that the Irish language "has no exact equivalents of the affirmative and negative particles *yes* and *no*" (Filppula 1999: 160). Instead, the verb of the question is repeated in the answer, usually in the shortest form possible. Filppula cites an example of this Irish pattern from MacEoin (1993: 141):

>   258) Question: *An dtiocfaidh tú?* 'Will you come?'
>   Answer: *Tiocfad* (1 sg.) or *Tiocfaidh* (3 sg. or personless form) 'I will.'

This pattern has also carried over into Irish English, albeit not necessarily in such a rigid fashion. Filppula (1999: 164-6), for example, points out that speakers use a variety of methods for answering such questions, but that in the end it is important to remember that they are rarely confined to just *yes* and *no*.

Even when respondents do use the words *yes* and *no* in their answer, these initial response words are invariably accompanied by additional information. This is known as "elaboration" (cf. Stenström 1984: 180-1) and usually involves repeating part of the clause given in the question - the repeated part being known as the "Modal element" (cf. Halliday and Hasan 1976: 209). Examples of this from the film corpus include:

>   259) [Do you know where your boys are?]
>   No, I don't know where they are, sir. I don't know.
>   (*Into the West*, 00:37:00, MPR1990D)

260) [Evelyn, did Jesus have a big sister?]
   No, Dermot, he didn't. He wasn't as lucky as you.
   (*Evelyn*, 00:01:49, FE1950D)

261) [Do ya want me to?]
   Aye[234], I do.
   (*Trojan Eddie*, 01:12:23, MTE1990M)

Filppula also notes that the modal element can be replaced by some other structure which serves the same function of elaboration, thus avoiding a simple *yes* or *no* response.

262) [And do you have any family, Ned?]
   No, there's just meself now[235].
   (*Waking Ned*, 00:37:43, MJ2000W)

However, the most common forms of response would appear to be those which echo the Irish pattern of having the modal element and which do not include *yes* or *no*. These appear throughout the film corpus, and include the wonderful exchange from *This is my Father* (below), which is an invitation to sexual intimacy (Irish-style!).

263) [Do you want to?]
   I do. [Do you?]
   I do.
   (*This is my Father*, 01:18:26, FF1930M)

264) [Do you remember that linoleum the mother bought for that room a way back?]
   I do.
   [Do you know how much it cost a square yard?]
   I do not.
   (*The Field*, 00:21:05, MT1950W)

265) [Was she a nurse?]
   She was.
   (*Dead Meat*, 01:01:17, MC2000LM)

266) [Are you Frances Cahill?]
   I am.
   (*Veronica Guerin*, 00:18:31, FFC1990D)

Occasionally, the modal element in such responses is expanded on further by a follow-up, as can be seen in example 267 (cf. Filppula 1999: 165).

---

[234] As can be seen from this example, *aye* sometimes takes the place of *yes*, much like in Scottish English and other British dialects (cf. Dolan 2006: 11).

[235] It should be noted that *now* is not a temporal referent in the above sentence. Instead, it is used, as is often the case in Irish English, as a discourse marker at the end of a clause or sentence. To date, the feature has not received much scholarly attention. For example, although Hickey includes some sentences which feature *now* as a discourse marker (cf. 2007: 373), he never explicitly identifies it as such.

267) [Was Janine there, Marian? This morning?]
   She was. Not that it's any of your business.
   (*Adam and Paul*, 00:17:06, FM2000D)

Rather than repeating merely the verb from the question, as in the previous examples, Irish speakers will sometimes echo the question in their response, i.e. they repeat the appropriate affirmative or negative form, often in its entirety, or they repeat an adjective rather than the verb like in example 271 (cf. Filppula 1999: 165):

268) [Do you mean it?]
   I mean it.
   (*A Love Divided*, 00:02:50, MS1950WX)

269) [Did you tell the tinkers about the donkey, Bird?]
   I did not tell the tinkers.
   (*The Field*, 00:20:10, MBi1950W)

270) [Is that it over there?]
   Oh, that's it over there now[236].
   (*A Very Unlucky Leprechaun*, 00:07:45, MPM1990W)

271) [Isn't that a grand class of a day?]
   Grand, thank God.
   (*Widows' Peak*, 01:08:35, FMOH1930W)

Filppula has also identified two additional types of responses which can be given to *Yes/No* questions, namely "the occurrence of yes/no in the follow-up move, i.e. after the elaboration part and thus outside the primary response" and "direct responses with structures other than those listed so far" (1999: 165).

In the first of these types, the *yes* (sometimes *yeah* or *aye*) or the *no* element is not the initial response word, but rather comes later in the reply in the follow-up move, as in examples 272-274 (cf. Filppula 1999: 165).

272) [Is that its real name?]
   It is, yeah.
   (*Goldfish Memory*, 00:45:51, FK2000D)

273) [Isn't she, Orla?]
   Oh, she is, yeah. Total straight and narrow. Very healthy.
   (*Adam and Paul*, 00:17:12, FO2000D)

274) [Well, you'll be away early in the morning, I suppose?]
   We will, yes, Mr Ryan.
   (*Ryan's Daughter*, 00:47:34, MS1920W)

The second type, direct responses with structures other than the aforementioned ones, is quite common and can be structured as follows:

---

[236] Here again is an excellent example of *now* being used as a discourse marker rather than as a temporal referent. See page 97.

275) [You're the doctor?]
    That's right.
        (*The Wind that Shakes the Barley*, 00:31:30, MD1920C)

276) [Did you get a fright?]
    I'm grand.
        (*The Wind that Shakes the Barley*, 00:18:16, FS1920C)

It should be noted that, in addition to these structures which are very much in keeping with Filppula's patterns[237], the film corpus shows evidence of the use of a further structure: *indeed* or *that* followed by the modal element. The latter, the emphatic use of *that*, has also been observed by Taniguchi (1972: 25)[238] and Amador Moreno (2006: 149)[239].

277) [It was a hard oul year's work all the same, what?]
    Indeed and it was.
        (*How Harry Became a Tree*, 00:19:38, MG1920WW)

278) [Will you not be putting up your bonnet, Mary Kate?]
    Indeed I will not.
        (*The Quiet Man*, 00:50:00, FMK1930W)

279) [We're set so?]
    Indeed we are set. We're set. We're ready for anything
        (*Garage*, 00:03:02, MJ2000M)

280) [Do you remember Kitty?]
    Indeed I do. How are you, Kitty? Do you remember me?
        (*Michael Collins*, 00:21:48, MMC1910C)

281) [Did you sleep well?]
    That I did, thank you.
        (*Darby O'Gill and the Little People*, 00:45:10, MMB1800D)

282) [So you told him all that, did you?]
    That I did.
        (*The Quiet Man*, 00:16:34, MRW1930W)

---

[237] Filppula's examples were: "[Now, you were sayin' that there were two sorts of fairies there?] That's right" and "[Yeah. And does it (fall of snow) happen very often then?] Well, not very often. But when it does come, it does be wicked here sometimes" (cf. 1999: 165-6).

[238] The emphatic use of *that* need not necessarily come as a response to a question. It can also come as a sign of agreement, as in the following examples from the film corpus: [He sure seems to like roses.] "Oh, that he does" (*A Very Unlucky Leprechaun*, 00:07:20, MPM1990W), [Mayor McGreedy won't like that.] "That he won't" (*A Very Unlucky Leprechaun*, 01:21:07, MPM1990W), [Your Jessy would have been proud of you!] "That she would, God Bless her!" (*Waking Ned*, 00:53:12, MM2000W). This usage is also common in Scotland (cf. Taniguchi 1972: 25).

[239] The use of *that* as an emphatic reiteration or assertion is also a feature of other dialects of English, such as Yorkshire, Lancashire and Lincolnshire (cf. EDD s.v. that II. 4.). *That* can also appear after the modal element, as in the following example from the film corpus: [Does it suit me, Maggie?] "It does at that." (*Waking Ned*, 00:06:54, FM2000W). To my ears, this structure sounds quite unnatural and, indeed, MacHale identifies a similar structure in *The Quiet Man* as bearing "more than a hint of stage-Irish language" (2000: 159). The example is as follows: [Nice day.] "It is that, Mr Thornton" (*The Quiet Man*, 01:02:50, FMK1930W).

In total, the film corpus exhibits examples of this avoidance of a simple *yes* or *no* in 43 of the 50 films (86%) [see Table 27], with the majority favouring the modal element response modelled on Irish usage. While there are no comparable results for Hickey's survey, this is quite understandable, as, given the nature of the survey, such information would have been difficult to elicit.

6.1.5 The complex sentence
6.1.5.1 Relative clause marking

Something which has been remarked on by many scholars of Irish English is that when it comes to marking relative clauses, *wh*-relative forms, such as *who* and *which* are not particularly frequent in the variety (cf. Harris 1993; Hickey 2004a). Indeed, Hickey (2004a) observes that the most common method of introducing relative clauses in Irish English is to use *that* in place of the *wh*-forms, irrespective of whether the referent is animate or not[240]. Some examples from the film corpus include:

> 283) There are those here **that** will tell you that Liam Mercier died of an illness.
> (*Song for a Raggy Boy*, 01:25:03, MMF1930)

> 284) During the recent Troubles, Dublin Castle had an intelligence network **that** was only legendary.
> (*Widows' Peak*, 00:16:45, MGDC1930M)

A further method of marking the relative clause is to use a *zero relative*, i.e. no relative pronoun at all[241]. According to Taniguchi, the omission of the relative pronoun is most frequently found "when 'be' or 'have' is used either in the main clause or in the dependent clause or in both of them" (Taniguchi 1972: 35-6). Numerous examples of this are evident in the film corpus and include:

> 285) It was him Ø came at me with the gun, what was I to do? What, in the name of God, was I to...?
> (*How Harry Became a Tree*, 01:25:20, MF1920WW)

> 286) I did in me arse! Dozy bollocks! It was the queers Ø robbed him. They're always at it.
> (*A Man of No Importance*, 01:14:00, MIC1960D)

These examples also nicely illustrate the fact that the omission of the relative pronoun very often occurs in conjunction with *it*-clefting, which is discussed on page 102.

Hickey (2004a: 127) states that the word *what* can also be used as a relative marker for an animate referent in Irish English, and offers the example: "I know a farmer what rears sheep". There are, indeed, two instances of *what* being used as a relative marker in the film

---

[240] The use of *that* as a relative pronoun is, of course, also a feature of Standard English (cf. Quirk *et al.* 1985: 366-7). However, it tends to be used more frequently in Irish English.
[241] As was the case for *that*, zero relative clauses are also possible in Standard English. However the frequency of zero relative pronouns is higher in Irish English due to their regular co-occurrence with *it*-clefting, a very common feature of English in Ireland.

corpus, although only one of them refers to an animate object. That sentence is taken from *Ryan's Daughter*:

> 287) Well, it's not the cuttlefish **what** I told you to look for.
> (*Ryan's Daughter*, 00:03:21, MS1920W)

The other sentence comes from *Garage*, and the inanimate object being referred to is a display stand for cans of oil. The utterance is given below with two preceding sentences to aid comprehension.

> 288) [Will I move them oils then?]
> [What?]
> Them oils onto the new stand **what** I got off the rep.
> (*Garage*, 00:03:55, MJ2000M)

In total then, *what* appears as a relative marker in only 2 of the 50 films (4%) [see Table 30], which is very much in keeping with Hickey's findings regarding the feature. Nationwide, the average acceptability rate for his sample sentence was also merely 4%, while the proportion of respondents who found the form totally "unacceptable" was 77%. The reason for such a high degree of opposition to this feature is that *what*, especially with regard to animate objects, is widely regarded as a stereotypical feature of Irish English, with many of the respondents in Hickey's survey referring to its use as being Stage Irish (cf. Hickey 2007: 260). Although Hickey's sentence featured an animate referent, it would be interesting to see whether the outcome would have been any different, had it featured an inanimate one like the second example from the film corpus.

In contrast to *what*, the other relative markers appear quite often in the film corpus with the *that* form appearing in 35 of the 50 films (70%) [see Table 28] and the zero relative occurring in 20 of the movies (40%) [see Table 29]. In Hickey's survey, the *that* form met with a 76% acceptability rate, while the *zero relative* was deemed "no problem" by 16% of respondents.

While watching the films, I discovered an additional means of relative marking which does not appear in any of the literature on Irish English. It involves the use of *as* as a substitute for *that*, *who* or *which* and appears in two of the films in the corpus.

> 289) Well, if there's one of that lot **as** is fit for her, maybe you'll point him out, Father.
> (*Ryan's Daughter*, 00:16:10, MTR1920W)

> 290) Them **as** I heard it from give it no name[242].
> (*Darby O'Gill and the Little People*, 00:18:11, MDOG1800K)

While this form is not usually associated with Irish English, it is a feature of other dialects in the British Isles, with Wright (EDD § 423) and Viereck/Ramisch (1991 S8, S9, S10) finding that it is used quite extensively throughout England. Kortmann and Szmrecsanyi (2004: 1151)

---

[242] The use of *them* as a demonstrative pronoun, as is the case here, is discussed in Chapter 6.1.6.3.

have since noted that the feature is recessive, but can, nonetheless, still be found in the North, Southeast and Southwest of England.

6.1.5.2 Focusing devices

Speakers of Irish English make extensive use of focusing devices in their discourse, employing them to give prominence to a certain element of an utterance. Such focusing devices can take the form of either *'it' clefting* or *topicalisation*.

'It' clefting

'It' clefting involves the splitting of a clause into two subclauses, each of which has its own verb. The first of these subclauses can be introduced by *it* and either the present or past tense forms of the copula, namely *it is*/*it's*/ *'tis*[243]/*is it?*/*it was*/ *'twas*/*was it?*, followed by the element to be fronted. The second subclause comes after that and has the appearance of a *that* relative clause, although in Irish English the relative pronoun itself is very frequently omitted (cf. Harris 1993: 173 and Taniguchi 1972: 155). It is important to note here that the introductory *it is*, *it was* etc. remain unstressed in these structures.

Although *'it' clefting* is a phenomenon which is also employed in both written and spoken Standard English (cf. Quirk *et al.* 1985: 504), it does not appear there with anything like the frequency with which it occurs in the Irish variety. For example, Filppula (1999) found that clefts occurred in his HE corpus at a rate of 21.3 per 10,000 words, in contrast to frequencies of 4.1 and 6.7 for the southwestern and Yorkshire spoken corpora respectively (cf. Filppula 1999: 248-9). A possible reason for *'it' clefting* being so widespread in Irish English is the substratal influence of the Irish language, which allows clefting to be used in a much wider variety of environments than Standard English does (cf. Filppula 1999: 256) [244]. Over time, this flexibility of usage has also manifested itself in Irish English. Research by Taniguchi (1972) shows the extent of this, revealing that *'it' clefting* can be used to introduce any part of speech: nouns, pronouns, adjectives, past participles, *-ing* forms, bare infinitives, *to* infinitives, prepositional phrases, and adverbs. Below are some examples of usage of each:

Nouns:

> 291) If it's **a drink** you want, it's down there. Good lad.
> (*Widows' Peak*, 01:03:00, MMC1930M)

> 292) 'Twas **a rabbit** I saw.
> (*Darby O'Gill and the Little People*, 00:56:32, MMB1800D)

> 293) I did in me arse! Dozy bollocks! It was **the queers** robbed him. They're always at it.
> (*A Man of No Importance*, 01:14:00, MIC1960D)

---

[243] *'tis* and *'twas* are contractions of *it is* and *it was* and are commonly used in Irish English. *'tis* is a very frequent feature in both the novel and the film version of Frank McCourt's *Angela's Ashes*, so much so that McCourt titled his second book *'Tis*.
[244] Furthermore, the role of the substratum in clefting can also be seen in Scottish Highland and Island English, which also has greater scope for clefting thanks to influence from Gaelic (cf. Shuken 1984: 155).

294) It's **a rabbit** she is, that Angela.

(Angela's Ashes, 00:15:16, FAA1930L)

295) It was **Lester** told me.

(The Snapper, 00:28:56, MDC1990D)

296) Sure, 'tis **a great judge** that you'd be and you from the land of Perry Mason and all.

(The Matchmaker, 00:41:52, MSea2000W)

297) It's **a bold one** you are. And who gave you leave to be kissing me?

(The Quiet Man, 00:31:00, FMK1930W)

Pronouns:

298) It was **him** came at me with the gun, what was I to do? What, in the name of God, was I to....

(How Harry Became a Tree, 01:25:20, MF1920WW)

299) 'Twas **I** informed on your son, Mrs McPhillip. Forgive me.

(The Informer, 01:30:13, MG1920D)

300) Come on now, Dennis. It was **you** that drew the match. Don't be afraid.

(The Informer, 01:27:45, MT1920K)

Filppula observed that, at least on the basis of his database, "clefts involving UBRs [unbound reflexives S.W.][245] are rare in HE speech" (1999: 86). This assumption also holds true for the film corpus. There are only two examples of clefts involving UBRs, but, since they also include prepositions, I felt they fit best into the prepositional phrase category below (cf. examples 326 and 327). These examples show, however, that it is also possible to have an unbound reflexive pronoun in the focus position[246] and are, thus, in keeping with findings by Henry (1957: 120), Taniguchi (1972: 150) and Amador Moreno (2006: 78).

Adjectives:

According to Quirk *et al.* (1985: 1385), informal Irish English is the only variety which allows either subject complement nouns or adjectives in focus position (Filppula 1999: 251).

301) Is it **afraid** of the commandant you are?

(The Informer, 00:31:14, MT1920K)

302) What ails ya, lad? Is it **blind** you are?

(Darby O'Gill and the Little People, 00:55:35, MDOG1800K)

303) Is it **drunk** you are?

(Darby O'Gill and the Little People, 01:16:50, MDOG1800K)

---

[245] See page 87.

[246] The fact that unbound reflexives can stand in the focus position is also evident in the title of Irish actress Maureen O'Hara's autobiography *'Tis Herself* (2004).

304) Ah, it's **better** you're getting.
   (*A Man of No Importance*, 00:52:02, MCB1960D)

305) You've been a grand adversary. 'Tis **sorry** I am to see you come to this.
   (*Darby O'Gill and the Little People*, 01:25:24, MKB1800K)

306) It's true. It's **ashamed** you should be.
   (*The Quiet Man*, 00:25:21, MDT1930W)

Past participle:

Taniguchi (1972: 150) includes past participles such as *pleased* in this category, even if they technically function as adjectives and, thus, probably should have been included in the previous category. However, in keeping with his categorisation, I shall also include such adjectives in the past participle category.

307) Well, Darby O'Gill, 'tis **pleased** and **delighted** I am to see you again.
   (*Darby O'Gill and the Little People*, 00:24:27, MKB1800K)

- *ing* form:

It is in its use of '*it*' *clefting* before the verb phrase that Irish English really sets itself apart from Standard English. According to both Harris and Filppula, this form of clefting is not possible in standard usage (cf. Harris 1993:175 and Filppula 1999: 250). Having said that, it is not all that common in the film corpus either, appearing only on three occasions:

308) Is it **puttin'** the coward's name on me you are?
   (*Darby O'Gill and the Little People*, 01:03:08, MMB1800D)

309) It's **training** he wants.
   (*Rat*, 00:15:28, MM2000D)

310) It's **makin'** too free with them Darby is!
   (*Darby O'Gill and the Little People*, 01:09:33, FWIP1800K)

Bare infinitive:

Unfortunately, there are no examples of this form in the film corpus. However, Taniguchi (1972: 152) offers the following examples from Irish literature:

311) Is it **have** her back here you would in all this misery and she happy walkin through the green fields of Heaven.
   (Murtagh, Donovan)

312) "I'm going on to Carraunbeg," said Priscilla; I'll steer with an oar." "Is it **steer** with an oar, Miss?"
   (Birmingham, Sanctuary-200)

To-infinitive:

As was the case with the bare infinitive, the film corpus does not offer any examples of the *to*-infinitive. However, some examples from Taniguchi (1972: 152) are listed below:

    313) Is it **to blame** Peter yer askin' me?

                                                                     (O'Flaherty, Tent-137)

    314) Is it **to slaughter** him (= the calf) you bought him?

                                                                       (O'Flaherty, Beasts)

Prepositional phrases:

Prepositional phrases can occur with clefting in two different contexts: a) with the preposition appearing before the verb or b) with it after the verb. In 1972, Taniguchi argued that the placing of the preposition in end position was "gaining currency, presumably in accordance with the general practice, in colloquial speech, of placing prepositions at or towards the end of the sentence" (1972: 153). This statement has proven to be true, as the majority of examples of prepositional phrases in clefts occur after the verb, as can be seen in examples 319-327.

    315) I was on me way back home, and I says to meself, "Brian", says I, "'tis **at his side** you should be."
                    (*Darby O'Gill and the Little People*, 01:25:13, MKB1800K)

    316) It's **off to the cinema** the First Communion boys will go to wallow in the disgusting filth spewed across the world by the Devil's henchmen in Hollywood.
                                      (*Angela's Ashes*, 00:40:59, MMB1930L)

    317) It's **out on the pavement** you'll be with the sky peeing on your furniture.
                                          (*Angela's Ashes*, 01:33:17, ML1940L)

    318) It's **like the bleedin' fire of hell** that one is.
                                          (*My Left Foot*, 00:30:00, MBB1950D)

    319) It's him I'm here **about**, Mrs Tillane.
                                          (*The Quiet Man*, 00:15:35, MRW1930W)

    320) Is it us they're **after**?
                                          (*Into the West*, 00:34:50, MOR1990D)

    321) It's a hospital we're goin' **to**, not the pine forest!
                                          (*The Snapper*, 01:22:20, MDC1990D)

    322) It's Frigid Brigid you've got to watch out **for**. She could put the fear of death into a corpse, so she could.
                                          (*Evelyn*, 00:18:44, FM1950D)

323) It's Mammy I'm sorry **for**.

(*Mystics*, 01:18:55, MMic2000D)

324) Is it your mouth those words are coming **out of**?

(*The Field*, 01:35:24, MBMC1950W)

325) It's you she seems to have taken a liking **to**.

(*Irish Jam*, 01:01:44, MMOM2000W)

326) It's not meself I'm worried **for**, Felix. It's the children.

(*Rat*, 00:22:44, FC2000D)

327) So it's himself you're named **after**.

(*The Quiet Man*, 00:21:07, MDT1930W)

Adverbs:

Irish English is also different to other varieties of English in that it allows clefts with certain types of adverbs (cf. Filppula 1999: 252). Examples include:

328) It's **always** me that's caught.

(*Nora*, 00:06:10, MC1900D)

329) Oh, it's **well** I know it.

(*The Quiet Man*, 00:38:51, MMF1930W)

'*It*' *clefting* appears in 26 of the 50 films (52%) [see Table 31] and is quite equally distributed both chronologically and geographically. In the *Survey of Irish English*, in contrast, the acceptance rate was quite low, with the sample sentence, "It's to Glasgow he's going tomorrow", only being regarded as "no problem" by an average of 18% of respondents. 46% of those surveyed, on the other hand, found the sentence "a bit strange", while the remaining 36% found it "unacceptable". A possible reason for the relatively low acceptability rate for Hickey's sentence could be, as already explained above, that the placing of the preposition towards the end of the sentence has become more popular in sentences with '*it*' *clefting* in Irish English, and, thus, a sentence more likely to have received a favourable rating would probably have been "It's Glasgow he's going to tomorrow". This would be something to bear in mind for future surveys of this kind.

Unusual examples

Taniguchi observed that, whereas *it was* generally precedes the preterite in Standard English, in Irish English the preterite can be preceded by the present tense form *it is*. As examples he offers the following sentences: "'*Tis* too good for this world he *was* entirely" or "'*Tis* too long she *thought* he *was* away from her" (Taniguchi 1972: 157). However, although I am certainly familiar with similar examples from personal experience, there was only one[247] instance in the film corpus of the preterite being preceded by *it is*, namely:

---

[247] There is, actually, a second example of the preterite being preceded by *it is* in the movie *The Dead*. However, since the example appears as part of a recitation which is being performed at a party and is cited as being an Irish

330) **It's** only an oul cup **got broke**. It'd be worse if it was your heart.
(*A Man of No Importance*, 01:08:45, FW1960D)

For Taniguchi, examples like this, which show that the preterite does not need to be preceded by the corresponding past tense form *it was*, are proof that the introductory *it is* in Irish English is "nothing but a meaningless phrase" (Taniguchi 1972: 157). Indeed, Amador Moreno offers further support for what she calls this "indifference" regarding the need for consistency of tenses by pointing out that *it is* can also appear with the future tense (2006: 117). Evidence of this is also available in the film corpus:

331) If you don't pay more attention, **it's** the Last Rites **you'll** be getting', not your Holy Communion.
(*Angela's Ashes*, 00:39:53, MMB1930L)

332) I'll volunteer. After all, **it's** a real man **she'll** be needing, O'Malley.
(*Irish Jam*, 00:15:15, MBMN2000W)

333) And **it's** more than talk **you'll** be getting if you step a step closer to me.
(*The Quiet Man*, 00:31:10, FMK1930L)

While the above examples all display the future tense being used together with the progressive forms, it should be noted that it can also occur with the infinitive, as in the following example:

334) **It's** off to the cinema the First Communion boys **will** go to wallow in the disgusting filth spewed across the world by the Devil's henchmen in Hollywood.
(*Angela's Ashes*, 00:40:59, MMB1930L)

Topicalisation

The other form of focussing in Irish English is topicalisation (Filppula 1999: 260-270). This phenomenon, which is also referred to in the literature as "left dislocation" or "fronting" (Harris 1993: 173-5), involves detaching an object or adverbial complement from its verb, and repositioning it before the subject and verb[248]. Some examples from the film corpus include:

335) **Doin' very well for herself she is** now.
(*Adam and Paul*, 00:17:09, FM2000D)

336) **The world champion he is**, Uncle Pat.
(*Angela's Ashes*, 01:45:43, MOF1950L)

337) **Bold and cunning they are**, but I'm up to them.
(*Darby O'Gill and the Little People*, 00:18:39, MDOG1800K)

---

love poem translated by Lady Gregory, I did not include it as an example of natural speech. The sentence in question is: "It **is** late last night the dog **was** speaking of you" (*The Dead*, 00:21:02, MMG1900D).
[248] Fronting is also a very common feature in Welsh English (cf. Thomas 1985: 215-16).

338) **Throttling me he was.**
(Evelyn, 01:09:43, FSr1950D)

339) **Seven pounds five shillings and sixpence he owed**, Missus.
(My Left Foot, 01:20:15, MBM1950D)

340) **Spending money like water he was**, Bull.
(The Field, 01:01:13, MBi1950W)

341) **Fresh and well she's looking.**
(Widows' Peak, 00:03:51, MMC1930M)

342) Shocking. **Filthy dirty it is.**
(The Van, 00:53:46, MOM1990D)

343) **A fine ill-tempered pair they were.** It was only a matter of time before one or other of them broke their neck.
(The Quiet Man, 00:47:16, MFL1930W)

In his study of Irish English in literature, Taniguchi raised the question of whether there is a connection between the aforementioned *it* clefting and topicalisation, namely whether "the dropping off of the introduction 'it is' is one of the vital factors – if not the exclusive factor – in the growth and development of the inverted word-order in Irish English" (1972: 175). He found that while it was not the key factor, it was partly responsible for the high number of occurrences. He also questioned whether the use of the preterite with an auxiliary in the past tense was still in actual currency in Ireland, and offered the sentence "Just *battled* it out I *did* – just battled it out" from Lady Gregory's *The Image* (Taniguchi 1972: 60) as an example. Based on the evidence from the film corpus, the structure would appear to be alive and well, occurring in four films from the present day.

344) Jaysus, I'm terrible sorry about this, John. **Disgraced** the family, she **did**. And as for that other fella…he's dead.
(Trojan Eddie, 00:58:44, MG1990M)

345) Fuckin' **idolised** them two, Matthew **did**. Idolised.
(Adam and Paul, 00:15:51, FO2000D)

346) Fuckin' **pegged**[249] it he **did**.
(Intermission, 00:31:50, MBD2000D)

347) Only **said** it to a pal he **did** and then word got round and then his mother heard.
(Garage, 01:07:58, MSgt2000M)

In total, topicalisation can be found in 27 of the 50 films (54%) [see Table 32]. Again, these occurrences are well spread amongst the films. Unfortunately, there are no comparable numbers for Hickey, as topicalisation was not a feature examined in his survey. Based on

---

[249] The verb *peg* means 'throw' (usually with force) in Irish English (cf. Dolan 2006: 174).

other sources, however, the general trend appears to be that topicalisation occurs less frequently than clefting. In Filppula's HE corpus, for example, topicalisation was found to be less common than clefting in all of the four dialects examined (1999: 263). The same applied to Taniguchi's study (1972: 173). Those findings are not reflected in the film corpus, however, in which, at 54%, topicalisation is marginally more frequent than *it* clefting, with 52%.

6.1.5.3 'Subordinating *and*'

Another well-attested feature of Irish English is the use of *and* to introduce a subordinate (rather than a coordinate) clause which lacks a finite verb. According to Filppula (1999: 196-7), these 'subordinating *and*' constructions can take different forms depending on the form of the *and*-clause. In the first instance, they can consist of a non-finite verb phrase, which may be either a present participle or a past participle, as in these examples from the film corpus:

> 348) It's the best friend I have this night **and** me dodging down dark streets to get here.
> (*The Informer*, 00:16:28, MFMP1920D)

> 349) How can I give the order **and** me tied up in a sack?
> (*Darby O'Gill and the Little People*, 01:00:30, MKB1800K)

The second type of 'subordinating *and*' structure involves either an adjective or a noun phrase in the predicate position, as can be seen in the following film corpus example:

> 350) Ma found her, it was like two or three days later, and "the stink" she said, flies crawling over her **and** her hysterical.
> (*Intermission*, 00:29:02, FD2000D)

A third kind of 'subordinating *and*' construction permits the predicate of the *and*-clause to take the form of a prepositional phrase. This can be seen in these examples:

> 351) Dancin' like an animal **and** your children out on the road without a mother to look after them.
> (*Into the West*, 00:53:10, MSgt1990D)

> 352) Sure, 'tis a great judge that you'd be **and** you from the land of Perry Mason and all.
> (*The Matchmaker*, 00:41:52, MSea2000W)

As can be seen from these examples and from those in Table 33, this 'subordinating *and*' can have a number of different meanings. According to Harris (1993: 166), the most likely function of this construction is to express a temporal relation of two actions occurring simultaneously, and, thus, this *and* form can be replaced by the words *while*, *as* or *when* in Standard English. However, according to Filppula (1999: 197), another function of this structure is to express "a relation of causal or concessive dependence between the actions or states of affairs expressed in the two clauses connected by *and*". In such contexts, the *and* can be glossed by the Standard English *although, since, because, seeing as*[250] or perhaps *with* or *what with*[251]. In examples 348, 349 and 351 above, then, the word *while* can take the place of the 'subordinating *and*', while in 352 the words *because* and *since* can take this role[252]. Example 350 is much more difficult to paraphrase using the conjunctions listed above[253]. Nonetheless, it is clear that the "relation of causal or concessive dependence between the actions or states of affairs expressed in the two clauses connected by *and*" still applies.

Many scholars trace the origin of this feature back to the influence of the Irish substratum[254], where a similar structure exists. To illustrate this, Harris (1984a: 305) provides an example of an Irish English sentence and the possible Irish source from where it came:

> 353) He fell **and** him crossing the bridge (i.e. '… while he was crossing the bridge').
> *Thit sé **agus** é ag dul thar an droichead.*
> 'Fall + PAST he and he at go over the bridge.'

Looking at these sentences, it is interesting to compare the Irish and the Irish English versions, particularly with regard to the personal pronouns used. Filppula (1999: 196) observes that the use of the objective form of personal pronoun in Harris' Irish English example is in marked contrast to the pronoun in the original Irish. More significantly, it is in marked contrast to all the pronouns evident in the 'subordinating *and*' constructions in Filppula's own HE corpus, which were all in the subjective case, e.g. "I only thought of him there and **I** cooking my dinner", "I often got them [pheasants] dead out in the middle of the field and **they** not torn up or anything" or "He said you could hear them [strange noises] yet, inside in his own house late at night and **he** in the bed" (emphasis S.W.).

However, Harris (above) was not alone in finding examples in the objective case. Henry (1957: 206) also offers: "We were listenin' to them an' **them** talkin'" or "You put in your nose an' **us** churning". Such evidence suggests that both subjective and objective forms are possible in Irish English[255], and this notion is upheld in the film corpus. Examples include:

Subjective:

> 354) Isn't that a nice way for a girl to talk to her father and **she** me one and only.
> (*Darby O'Gill and the Little People*, 01:00:00, MDOG1800K)

---

[250] Bliss (1984: 147) also offers *if* and *seeing that* as possible substitutes.
[251] The parallels with the circumstantial *what with* structure (cf. Quirk *et al.* 1985: 1106) are particularly evident with regard to the example above from *The Matchmaker*, in which *what with* can replace the subordinating *and*: "Sure, 'tis a great judge that you'd be, **what with** you (being) from the land of Perry Mason and all".
[252] For further examples, see Taniguchi (1972: 130-41).
[253] The difficulty of paraphrasing Irish English sentences which feature the 'subordinating *and*' is evident in much of the literature on the subject. In addition to the aforementioned possibilities, Filppula also suggests that the *and*-clause can be replaced by a relative clause (1999: 197), while Taniguchi (1972: 130-41) purports that the meaning of *and* can also extend to the subordination of "condition" and the subordination of, what he calls, "attendant circumstances", in which case the *and* stands for *if* for the former but again remains untranslatable for the latter.
[254] 'Subordinating *and*' has also been found in other dialects of English in both the United States and Great Britain, thus casting some doubt on the validity of the substratum account. For more on the discussion see Amador Moreno (2006: 134).
[255] See Joyce (1988: 33-35) for more examples and discussion.

355) Ah there ya go, there ya go talking about Katie and **we** havin' a fine little jamboree.
(*The Informer*, 00:48:10, MSP1920D)

Objective:

356) Oh be the holy, where did ya get it, Gypo? There's enough there to choke a horse, and **me** joking you about it a few minutes ago.
(*The Informer*, 00:49:05, MSP1920D)

357) He'll be back in a few years with a new suit and fat on his bones like any Yank. And a lovely girl with pearly white teeth, and **her** hanging from his arm.
(*Angela's Ashes*, 02:11:57, MUP1930L)

358) He don't dare raise his eyes to you, and **him** the catch of the town.
(*Darby O'Gill and the Little People*, 00:02:46, FMS1800K)

359) And for a stranger to move in, says I, and what would she to be doing that for, and **us** so close to an understanding, as you might say.
(*The Quiet Man*, 00:16:31, MRW1930W)

As can be seen from just these few examples, there are more instances of different pronouns in the objective case[256] than those in the subjective case in the film corpus. This is in keeping with observations made by Joyce (1988: 34) and is in stark contrast to Filppula's findings, which, as mentioned above, were all in the latter case.

In total, the 'subordinating *and*' construction appears in 10 of the 50 films[257] (20%) [see Table 33]. While it is quite well spread throughout the corpus, there are many more individual examples of it in the first three films in the table, namely *The Informer* (1935), *The Quiet Man* (1952) and *Darby O'Gill and the Little People* (1959), suggesting that the feature may have been more common back then or perhaps was overdone by the respective screenwriters.

Hickey's *Survey of Irish English Usage* reveals a 15% acceptability rating for the 'subordinating *and*' construction, or rather for the example of the structure the respondents were given, namely "We went for a walk and it raining". While Hickey's result is slightly below that of the film corpus, the sentence itself was well-chosen and was likely to receive the highest acceptance possible for this construction, as it fulfilled the two most important criteria which determine the frequency of this feature: a) the use of *and* to express a temporal relation of simultaneity, as determined by Harris (above), and b) the use of a present participle as predicate, as observed by Filppula (1999: 202), who discovered that about half of his

---

[256] It should be noted that these pronouns in the objective case can also include unbound reflexive pronouns, such as *himself* and *herself*. Evidence of this is apparent in the example from *Ryan's Daughter* which due to space constraints appears in a shortened form in Table 33. The full sentence reads as follows: "Red Tim himself that 1,000 secret policemen have been hunting for these last five years, and himself no doubt at this very moment walking the broad streets of Dublin" (*Ryan's Daughter*, 00:40:57, MTR1920W).
[257] Subordination can also occur without the *and*, particularly when spoken quickly. For example, *The Nephew* features a sentence which formally displays the structure of a 'subordinating *and*', but which does not actually feature the word *and*. The sentence in question is: "Ah would you stop. Me husband not cold in his grave" (*The Nephew*, 00:03:20, FB1990C) and is uttered by a widow who feels that it is inappropriate to have been asked on a date.

examples took the latter form. Unfortunately, the use of the pronoun *it* rather than a different personal pronoun means that no information is available regarding the issue of preference for the objective or subjective case.

6.1.5.4 'Subordinating *till*'

And is not the only conjunction which may have an additional function in Irish English. The same applies to *till*[258]. Unlike in Standard English, *till* can have much more than a temporal meaning in Irish English and is commonly used in the sense of "in order that" or "so that I may" (cf. Hickey 2004a: 128; Taniguchi 1972: 118; Harris 1993: 165 and Dolan 2006: 239). According to Dolan, these extended meanings of *till* enable it to approximate the sense of the Irish conjunction *go* (cf. 2006: 239). Where it occurs in Irish English, *till* is very often preceded by the phrase *come here*[259] or *come on*, as can be seen in the following examples from the film corpus:

    360) Come here **till** I tell ya.
                                          (*A Love Divided*, 00:10:18, MP1950WX)

    361) Come here **till** I see ya, Hubert.
                                            (*Rat*, 00:28:11, FD2000D)

    362) Come on **till** I show you, Felix.
                                            (*Rat*, 00:10:26, FC2000D)

    363) Come on in now, Josie, **till** I get rid of you.
                                            (*Garage*, 00:09:15, FC2000M)

Dolan, however, does offer a number of other examples which show just how flexible this conjunction is: "Stand still, Mary, till I comb your hair", "Where is he till I murder him?" and "Tell me who's to blame will yeh til I tear his friggin' head off" (2006: 239-40). This flexibility is also reflected in the only examples from the film corpus which do not involve *come here* or *come on*, both of which come from *Adam and Paul*.

    364) Right, out you that side, **till** we stand guard.
                                            (*Adam and Paul*, 00:54:12, MA2000D)

    365) Climb onto the front there **till** we open it from the outside.
                                            (*Adam and Paul*, 00:54:35, MA2000D)

Again these meanings are not temporal. The speaker, Adam, orders his friend, Paul, to get out of the car so that they can keep watch during a raid on a shop. However, when the doors of the car turn out to be fitted with child-locks, Paul is instructed to climb into the front of the car and to go out one of the front doors, in order to open the back door from the outside. As can be seen from the table, *till* is used in the sense of "in order that" in 8 of the 50 films (16%)

---

[258] *Till* is also sometimes spelled *til*, as in the final example given by Dolan above.
[259] The film corpus also displays an example of *and* (rather than *till*) being used together with *come here*. The meaning, however, is the same, and it should be noted that this usage is also very common in Ireland. The example sentence is as follows: "Come here and I tell ya!" (*Intermission*, 00:11:48, MIW2000D).

[see Table 34]. In Hickey's *Survey of Irish English*, in contrast, the structure was regarded as perfectly acceptable by an average of 72% of respondents nationwide. The reason for such a large discrepancy between the results from the film corpus and Hickey's survey may be that the Irish English use of *till* in films may just lead to confusion among non-Irish audiences, who are only aware of the conjunction's temporal meaning, and, thus, screenwriters choose to omit it. Accordingly, the 8 films which do feature this Irish English use of *till* are all Irish productions.

6.1.6 Morphology

In addition to addressing the syntax of Irish English, scholars have also identified different categories as being typical of morphological usage in the variety. These are: s*econd person plural forms, negation of auxiliaries*, and *demonstrative pronouns*[260].

6.1.6.1 Second person plural

The presence of a distinct second person plural form is by no means unique to Irish English. It appears in many guises in many other varieties of English worldwide, such as in the American South where it takes the form *y'all* and sometimes *you 'uns*, or in the dialect of East Anglia where it is manifested as *you...together*, as in *"Come you on together"* (Cheshire 1981: 8). However, the fact that the Irish language also has a second person plural form, *sibh*, has led some scholars to argue that the adoption of ways to express the second person plural in Irish English arose from the additional need of early Irish speakers of English to find a way to express in their new language what they were familiar with from their native tongue (cf. Dolan 2006: 258).

In Irish English, the second person plural can be indicated in three different ways. The first is through the use of *ye*, a pronoun which indicated second person plural in English up until the thirteenth century (cf. Baugh and Cable 1993: 237). This is the most common form of Irish English second person plural and is used throughout Ireland (cf. Hickey 2005: 116). The second form is *youse* or *yous*, which is a constructed plural most likely to have been created during a period when Irish learners were first encountering the English language. In order to create a distinction between second person singular and plural, they simply tagged on a plural *-s* to the word *you*. The third form *yez*, sometimes written *yiz*, is an amalgam of the two other forms and, like *yous/youse*[261], its use is more commonly associated with Dublin and surrounding areas[262]. Indeed, Hickey adds that these forms "are stigmatised and more typical of strongly local varieties of Dublin English" (Hickey 2005: 116).

---

[260] A further feature which could be included under the heading of morphology is the addition of *the diminutive ending –een* (from the Irish –in) to English words to indicate smallness, endearment or sometimes disparagement (cf. Asián and McCullough 1998). However, I will not include *the diminutive ending –een* in this section on morphology, but instead will address it briefly later under lexicon as many of the instances of it which appear in the film corpus can be regarded as lexicalised forms rather than examples of productive morphology per se.

[261] Sources, and also the subtitles in the films, vary in their spelling of the second and third forms of the second person plural, thus again reflecting the problems inherent in trying to transcribe dialect features. However, despite the fact that the terms are often spelled differently, this should not necessarily be seen as an indicator of different pronunciations. *Youse* and *yous* are both generally pronounced [juːz] with a voiced consonant at the end, while *yiz*, *yis* and *yez* are pronounced [jɪz] or [jɔz], again with a voiced consonant at the end. Hickey, however, suggests that these can also be voiceless when they come before voiceless consonants (1983: 48).

[262] *Yiz/yez* also appears in Northern Irish English but that variety is beyond the scope of this study.

The *ye* form, pronounced [jiː], and not [jə] or [je] as some people who encounter it in written literary dialect may think[263], appears in 26 of the 50 films (52%) [see Table 35] and, as expected, its use is most frequent in films set outside of Dublin. The occasional usage of *ye* in movies set in the capital can, on the one hand, be attributed to characters who are not originally from Dublin, such as Papa Reilly, the King of the Travellers in *Into the West*, who went against traveller tradition and became a member of the settled community there when his children were born, or Fr Geraldo in *Rat* or Fr Kenny in *A Man of No Importance* whose accents betray that they hail from elsewhere. On the other hand, the use of the *ye* form by characters who are clearly Dubliners and who use *yiz* or *youse* in other circumstances, like Janine in *Adam and Paul*, can simply be attributed to the fact that, as outlined by Blackburn (see page 40), speakers sometimes vary in their choice between competing forms[264]. Further evidence of the potential for variation is evident in the following examples which display both the Standard English plural pronoun *you* and the non-standard *ye* form in the same sentence.

> 366) Do **you** want to go into the dancing first or do **ye** want to have a refreshment?
> (*The Dead*, 00:05:30, FAK1900D)

> 367) Oh, I was so homesick to see **you**, I'd have walked down the middle of O'Connell Street to get a glimpse of the two of **ye**.
> (*The Informer*, 00:16:32, MFMP1920D)

In Hickey's *A Survey of Irish English Usage*, the *ye* form is regarded by 91% of the respondents as being "no problem". This percentage is almost twice that of the frequency in the film corpus (52%) and the disparity can, in part, be explained by the fact that a large portion of the films in the corpus are set in Dublin or parts of Leinster where the *yiz* or *youse* forms are more frequently used than the *ye* form. This assumption is further strengthened by the fact that on a province by province basis the acceptability of *ye* decreases from Munster (97% of those surveyed there) to Connaught (95%) to Leinster (86%).

The *youse* form is evident in 18 of the 50 films (36%) [see Table 36]. The fact that 14 of these 18 appearances are in the 27 films set in or around Dublin[265] supports the thesis that

---

[263] A good example of the correct pronunciation is evident in *A Man of No Importance*, where in Fr Kenny's question, "So, *ye're* trying it again this year?" the words *ye're* and *year* are homophones. A further related homophone is *yeer*, which is the Irish English form of the possessive adjective *your*. Dolan describes it as being "formed from ye by analogy with your" and he cites an example of its use in the novel *Angela's Ashes*: "What are ye having for yeer dinner?" (Dolan 2006: 257). This particular example, however, does not appear in the film adaptation of the book, but the structure does appear elsewhere in the film corpus: "If I hear one more report of any of our boys fallin' down yeer stairs, you'll be shot. Is that clear?" (*The Wind that Shakes the Barley*, 00:21:17, MF1920C). On a related issue, Hickey observes that when constructing reflexive forms, "no distinction is usually made in the first vowel as singularity or plurality is indicated at the end of the word" (1983: 49) and, thus, by implication that the form *yeerselves* will not be found. The form *yizerselves*, sometimes *yisser selves* (cf. Share 2006: 64, 79), on the other hand, does appear in the film corpus and is a fine example of a combination of the pronoun *yiz* with the possessive adjective *yourselves*. "Suit yizerselves" (*Adam and Paul*, 00:11:42, MG2000D).
[264] I believe, however, that, at least with regard to this feature, the argument only applies in one direction, i.e. for non-Dubliners *yez* and *youse* are not really seen as viable competing forms for *ye*. Evidence of these features in films set outside of the Pale can usually be explained (see page 43).
[265] As outlined in the methodology, it is very difficult to pinpoint the setting of some of these films. For example in *Circle of Friends* and *Trojan Eddie*, some characters venture into Dublin frequently, with Benny in the former

youse is predominantly a Dublin feature. The single appearance of the form in a film set elsewhere by characters who do not appear to be from Dublin can perhaps be attributed to an oversight on the part of the screenwriter. The film in question is *Widows' Peak*, penned by Dublin dramatist Hugh Leonard, which might explain why the feature is used on several occasions by a number of different non-Dublin characters.

With regard to the *youse* form, the *Survey* shows a 60% acceptability rating nationwide, compared to the 36% rate for the film corpus. As expected, the acceptability rate is highest in Leinster (74% of those surveyed there), compared to Connaught (44%) and Munster (42%). The relatively high acceptability rate of *youse* in both Connaught and Munster, where traditionally the *youse* form is rarely used, may be connected with the wording of Hickey's questionnaire. By asking the informants about the acceptability of features among their friends, he seems to have overlooked the fact that Irish people are becoming increasingly mobile, both geographically and socially, and, thus, their friends may include university friends or colleagues from other parts of the country. Therefore, the fact that 4 of the 7 respondents from Leitrim[266], for example, regarded *youse* as no problem, says very little about Leitrim speech per se, but could just as well mean that these speakers may have friends from elsewhere who use this feature. The outcome is a statistic that states that for 57% of Leitrim respondents the feature is "no problem", and, by implication, whether intended or not, that it is used by 57% of the population there. This, of course, is problematic. Rather than using Hickey's question: "How do you find the following sentences (in casual speech among friends)" (Hickey 2004a: 130), a more telling question for eliciting information on a regional basis would be something like: "How do you find the following sentences (in casual speech among your family or in your locality)?"[267]

---

commuting to university daily and Eddie in the latter carrying out his "business" in the city. However, in both cases the majority of the action appears to take place away from the city and, thus, I have placed these films somewhere in the Midlands not very far from Dublin. It has to be said that in the case of *How Harry Became a Tree*, another film which displays the *youse* form, the setting is also very ambiguous and could really be anywhere in rural Ireland. However, based on topographical details, and the fact that the main character is a cabbage farmer, I have placed this film in Wicklow, which appropriately has the nickname "the garden of Ireland". Additional research has confirmed that the film was indeed shot in Wicklow, the county directly south of Dublin, and, thus, a region likely to use the *youse* form. However, as pointed out earlier, relying on where a film was made can be problematic.

[266] The unequal number of respondents per county is somewhat troubling. Admittedly, one could argue that Ireland's least populated county, Leitrim, should only have a fraction of the respondents of its most populous county, Dublin. However, 7 informants for one and 205 for the other is quite a substantial difference. Hickey has since acknowledged this shortcoming in his methodology and warned against reading too much into results from those counties where fewer than 15 questionnaires were completed (2007: 172). There are, however, some other methodological problems evident in Hickey's survey, such as the fact that the "questionnaires of those informants who inserted prescriptive comments were ignored" (Hickey 2004a: 115). In itself, this is well and good and is arguably accepted methodological practice. However, if that is the case, then one should certainly not invite informants to offer their comments in the first place. By including an additional column entitled "something else, short comment" beside the categories, Hickey did just that (cf. Hickey 2004a: 130). Finally, there is the important point that the respondents were judging the acceptability of written sentences, even though the features they were evaluating are ones which they would predominantly only be familiar with as oral forms. This difference between what is acceptable to our eye and what is acceptable to our ear should not be underestimated and should be borne in mind when reading the results.

[267] The problems of using friends as points of reference when trying to elicit data about regional dialects was recently discussed as part of the University of Bamberg's approach to compiling questionnaires on English as it is spoken in Malta, the Channel Islands and Gibraltar. Nowadays, "friends" may not serve as appropriate points of reference for regional dialect among young people, particularly students, as there is so much mobility in modern life that friends are less likely to come solely from the locality being studied.

The third form, *yiz*, is the most common of the second person plural forms which feature in the corpus, appearing in 30 of the 50 films (60%) [see Table 37]. As before, its frequency can be explained by the fact that the majority of the films are set in or close to the capital city, and, as before, its presence in films set outside the Pale can generally be explained by similar reasons. For example, an actor may forget himself and use terms that come naturally to him, the actor, rather than those that would come naturally to his character, as in the example from *The Quiet Man* discussed on page 43. Another reason for the *yez* form appearing in films not set in Dublin is that, for plot reasons, some of the films set in other parts of Ireland feature Dublin characters. For example, Liam Cunningham's character, Dan, in *The Wind that Shakes the Barley* is clearly identified as being from Dublin, and his participation in the Dublin Lockout of 1913 is an important element in the story, since it adds a socialist dimension to the struggle for freedom.

Hickey's study shows a 51% acceptability rate for the *yez* form in the three provinces studied. This compares with a 60% frequency in the films. It is surprising that the most common second person plural form in the films is the one which receives the least favourable responses nationwide: Leinster (63%), Connaught (38%) and Munster (35%). This can perhaps be attributed to the fact that the respondents received the questionnaire in written form and may have misread the word *yez* as [jiːz], some non-existent variant of [jiː], rather than as [jɪz] or [jəz] and, thus, they regarded it as strange or unacceptable.

6.1.6.2 Negation of auxiliary *am*

The next morphological feature of Irish English listed by Hickey is the contraction of *am* and *not* to produce *amn't*. W. Nelson Francis attributes the use of the *amn't* form to what he calls the "notorious 'hole in the pattern' which many standard speakers encounter when faced with the need of using a first person singular negative-interrogative form" and he quotes Quirk *et al*. who state that "there is no universally accepted colloquial question form corresponding to the stiltedly formal 'Am I not beautiful?'" (Nelson Francis 1985: 141).

Again, this is not a feature which is exclusive to Irish English, but is also common in some Scottish English dialects, where it is also a syncopated form (cf. Cheshire 1981: 56). Alternative forms of auxiliary negation, such as *ain't* and *aren't*, which appear frequently in other varieties, are, however, unusual in Irish English (Hickey 2004a: 123).

Amn't appears in 4 of the 50 films (8%) [see Table 38], and is spread widely across the decades, occurring in films set in the 1930s, 60s, 90s and the present day. It is interesting to note that in each case, it is used in an interrogative situation. This is particularly noteworthy when one bears in mind that in Cheshire's study of the use of a similar auxiliary negation, *ain't* in Reading English, the occurrences of the form in interrogative sentences were so minimal as to disqualify them from the analysis. Instead, she noted the occurrence of *ain't* in declarative sentences and tag questions, finding that the frequency of occurrence was consistently higher in the latter (Cheshire 1981: 58). In the films, however, there are no examples of declarative sentences featuring *amn't*, while the only tag question in which the structure appears is not a typical tag question (according to the rules set out by Quirk *et al*. 1985: 810), but rather can be regarded as an "invariant tag question". These differ from standard tag questions, in that they take the form, "am I right?", "isn't that so?", "don't you think?", or "wouldn't you say?", and they have the same form irrespective of whether the statement they follow is positive or negative (cf. Quirk *et al.* 1985: 814). The example from the film corpus is as follows: "Now, we're all feckin' refugees. Amn't I right?" (*When Brendan Met Trudy*, 00:55:52, MHM2000D).

On the whole then, *amn't* would appear to behave differently to the related form *ain't*, in that, unlike the latter, it almost solely appears in interrogatives. This notion is supported by the fact that the example sentence, "Amn't I leaving soon anyway?", provided by Hickey for his survey, is also in the interrogative, and Dolan's *A Dictionary of Hiberno-English* offers five examples of the use of *amn't* in different sentences, all of which are, again, interrogative sentences (2006: 7).

In Hickey's *A Survey of Irish Usage*, *amn't* is regarded as "no problem" by 38% of the population, with the greatest acceptability being among Connaught respondents (55% of those surveyed there), followed by those from Munster (36%) and Leinster (33%). Based on the findings in the film corpus, one could perhaps regard these results as surprising, particularly since 3 of the 4 examples in the film corpus are from Dublin (Leinster). However, those with a knowledge of Irish English would not be surprised by Hickey's results, since the majority of non-standard features, with the exception of "typical" Dublin features, would generally be expected to occur in exactly that order: Connaught, Munster and Leinster.

6.1.6.3 *Them* as a demonstrative pronoun

The use of *them* as a demonstrative pronoun, in place of the Standard English *those*, has long been a common feature of many varieties of English (EDD § 420), and Irish English is no exception, with *them* appearing as a demonstrative pronoun in 25 of the 50 films (50%) [see Table 39]. While the majority of cases involve *them* before a noun, there are other cases in which it appears on its own. However, it is always clear from the context and, particularly, from the intonation that *them* is being used where *those* is meant. In sentences 368 and 369 below, for example, which involve transactions in shops, the speakers are pointing to or showing objects[268].

368) And, listen, I'll throw in one of **them** as a little gift.
(*The Matchmaker*, 00:51:13, MG2000W)

369) Three of **them**, Mr Carney.
(*A Man of No Importance*, 00:12:18, MB1960D)

It is interesting to also note that, despite the fact that it is a plural marker, *them* is followed in some of the examples by a singular verb form. Examples include:

370) You listen to me. **Them boys is** stayin' here.
(*Into the West*, 00:10:23, MPR1990D)

371) **Them** flats is right opposite the cop shop.
(*The General*, 00:06:03, MMC1990D)

---

[268] There are other similar examples in the film corpus. Again, it is important to note that the stress is on the word *them* in each case: "Oh, they're lovely. Did you do **them** yourself?" (*Inside I'm Dancing*, 00:14:48, MMOS2000D), "What's **them**, then?" (*Ryan's Daughter*, 00:22:40, FR1920W), "You brought 400 of **them** back from Dublin" (*Cowboys and Angels*, 00:55:15, MBU2000L).

372) And if **them two's tinkers**, I'm the Bishop of Cork.
(*Ryan's Daughter*, 00:39:21, MFR1920W)

The "ungrammatical" nature of these examples could perhaps be justified by the fact that *them*, as a demonstrative pronoun, is also regarded as a marker of "the illiterate" (OED s.v. *them* III. 5 'Now only dialect or illiterate'), and that the screenwriter may have wanted to create the impression that the speakers were in some way uneducated. This would certainly apply in the case of the first example, as the speaker, Pa Reilly, is a member of the travelling community, an ethnic group with a history of poor literacy, and he is actually ostracised by the police for the fact that he is not able to read or write. In the latter examples, however, both characters can read and write, with one of them being a priest and therefore someone whom one would expect to be educated. Based on these facts, it is difficult to justify the "illiterate" theory. When one looks at other examples of the use of *them* followed by a singular verb form in *Ryan's Daughter*, the situation becomes even more unclear, as even the village schoolmaster, Charles Shaugnessy, who is regarded by everyone as the most intelligent and cultivated man in the community, uses *them* followed by a singular verb form:

373) **Them fellas has** an elegant sense of humour.
(*Ryan's Daughter*, 00:50:58, MS1920W)

Given the fact that educated characters in the films also use this feature, the presence of the singular verb form after *them* need not be seen as a mark of the illiterate, but can instead be regarded simply as an example of dialect usage, and, thus, something which is not all that unusual.

What is unusual, however, is the use of *them* in the following sentence from *The Commitments* in which Bernie tells Jimmy to move the laundry which is on the chair beside the ironing board.

374) Move **them** washing there if you want to sit down.
(*The Commitments*, 00:42:58, FB1990D)

This strange usage can possibly be explained by Bernie's regarding *washing* as a plural noun just like *clothes*. Indeed, one can just as easily imagine her saying "Move them clothes there if you want to sit down".

In the *Survey of Irish English Usage*, *them* is regarded by 28% of the population as a perfectly acceptable demonstrative pronoun. Again, as in all categories there is a disparity between the provinces, with Connaught displaying 38% acceptance, Leinster 28% and Munster 25%. Interestingly, the frequency of this form in the films is considerably higher than the approval rate is among the population. This disparity can be justified by the fact that the use of *them* as a demonstrative pronoun is actually one of the two[269] features singled out by Hickey as having been "very salient" to his respondents, as they felt they were either "'strange' 'wrong' or 'particularly Irish'" (2005: 130). In light of such facts, it is not surprising that they were not very likely to deem it "no problem".

---

[269] The other feature was the use of the past participle as a preterite, as in *I seen* and *I done* (cf. Chapter 6.1.1.3).

6.1.7 Summary of findings for grammar features

Before moving on to look at the discourse markers associated with Irish English, it is useful to briefly review the findings from the film corpus, thus far. To that end, I have compiled a Top 10 of the most frequent non-standard grammar features as they appeared in the corpus.

Top 10 Non-standard grammar features

Feature	% of films which display the feature
Indefinite anterior perfect	88
Responses to *Yes/No* questions	86
Non-standard use of definite article	84
That as a relative pronoun	70
Singular existential	66
Lack of *do* support	64
Yez	60
Singular verb concord	60
Overuse of *–ing* form	60
Use of reflexive pronouns	58

If one looks at the rankings, it becomes apparent that the most common features are not necessarily those which immediately spring to mind when one thinks of Irish English. In fact, many of them (the indefinite anterior perfect, singular existential, and the non-standard use of the definite article) are also very common in other varieties of vernacular English. Those features, on the other hand, which have traditionally been listed as being characteristic of Irish English, namely the *after* perfect (48%), the medial object perfect (20%), the use of the progressive imperative (44%), the use of habitual aspect forms (2%, 2% and 12%) or *it* clefting (52%) and topicalisation (54%) are less common, all appearing outside of the Top 10.

While it might be tempting based on these findings to claim that traditional Irish English features are in decline or are being replaced by vernacular forms from the US, this would be unwise. The forms in the Top 10 are not new, but rather have long been regarded as typical features of Irish English, even if they are not exclusive to the variety. They are also included in studies by Filppula, Harris and Hickey and are proof that a dialect is made up of features which are typical but not unique.

Looking beyond the Top 10, some general observations can be made on the state of Irish English grammar in the corpus. On the whole the features are quite well spread across all periods and places, with few visible trends. Those trends which do exist are, thus, all the more striking and include the following.

The most noticeable finding is that habitual aspect proved to be very rare in the film corpus, confirming what researchers had found in other studies (cf. Kallen 1985 and 1989; Filppula 1999; Hickey 2004a). This dearth of examples in the movies was even true of the *do/does + be + verb (-ing)* form, which for a long time was regarded as one of the "classics" of Irish English (Filppula 1999: 132), and can be attributed to the feature being stigmatised and regarded as "rural and backward" (Hickey 2007: 18).

Secondly, although the *'after' perfect* is quite common in the film corpus, it is interesting to note that it never occurs with a noun phrase, i.e. "I'm after my dinner". This, one could argue, could be because screenwriters fear that the latter structure would confuse international audiences, who might understand it as implying a desire or intention to do something. However, this argument is weakened by the fact that the 'after' perfect appears numerous times in the form *be + after + verb (-ing form)*, a structure which is probably equally confusing to outsiders, with the sentence "I'm after getting a cup of tea", for example, having been misunderstood by 81% of British people surveyed by Harris in 1982. It would, thus, be interesting in future studies to examine whether the reason for the absence of the *'after' perfect* with the noun phrase can be attributed to something other than good will and consideration on the part of the screenwriter. Perhaps the structure is simply less common in Irish speech than was previously thought and for that reason does not appear in the films.

With regard to the *singular existential*, present tense forms were found to outnumber past tense forms in the film corpus. Seeing as Hickey's *Survey of Irish English Usage* only tested the acceptability of the past tense form, it would be pertinent in future surveys to also include a sentence in the present tense to see whether there are similar discrepancies in frequency. Findings could then also be compared with those of Cheshire (1989) and Krug (2007).

Not only did the *'for to' infinitive* prove to be a rare and very old-fashioned feature in the corpus, it also prompted some interesting questions regarding its usage, with its meaning being shown to go beyond the *in order to* function which has long been associated with the structure.

Questions about usage also arose with regard to *amn't*. Although it rarely appears in the film corpus, when it does it is always in interrogatives. To that end, it would be worthwhile to check whether the approval rating for a declarative sentence, such as "I amn't", is lower than that for the feature in questions. This again could be done through the addition of a sentence to *A Survey of Irish English Usage*.

A further trend which is visible with regard to usage also happens to be strongly linked with time. The lack of an *-s* ending for plural quantity nouns rarely occurs after 2000, as the introduction of the euro ensured that the most likely context for its (non)occurrence, namely *pound*, was gone.

Another interesting development relating to time is that there are no examples of embedded inversion in WH- questions in any of the 26 films made since the new Millennium. There is no obvious explanation for this trend and, thus, the matter certainly warrants further research.

The above offers a sampling of some of the most striking findings from the film corpus with regard to grammar features. However, as we shall see, there are additional ways of marking dialect in speech, namely through discourse and lexical features.

6.2 Discourse features

While a great deal of attention has been paid to the grammar features of Irish English in literary dialect, the role of discourse features in the variety should by no means be underestimated. Indeed Johnstone has observed that

> (f)eatures such as these are often more responsible for the regional and social speech stereotypes on which writers draw than are differences in pronunciation and grammar, and their representation in fiction may convey as much or even more about a character, setting and regional culture as do traditionally-studied dialect respellings and nonstandard grammatical usages.
>
> (Johnstone 1991: 461-2)

Before investigating the merits of this claim, it is necessary to first define what discourse features are in the context of this study. According to Amador Moreno (2005: 74) *discourse markers* are "expressions such as *well*, or *but*, which are used in conversation to indicate how a message should be interpreted". She offers a list of general examples from Schiffrin (2001), which show just how varied these structures can be, in that they can include "conjunctions (e.g., *and, but, or*), interjections (*oh*), adverbs (*now, then*), and lexicalised phrases (*y'know, I mean*)" (Schiffrin 2001: 57). For the purpose of this study, I shall adopt Amador Moreno's definition, although I shall adapt it slightly to include religious expressions and repetitions, which were also included in studies by Asián and McCullough (1998) and Harris (1993) respectively. To that end, I shall also use the broader term *discourse features*. As far as the structures themselves are concerned, they include adverbs (*sure, but, like, so*), pronouns, (*what*), and lexicalised phrases (*come here, arrah, musha*), as well as the aforementioned religious expressions and repetitions as emphatic markers. In order to test Johnstone's statement, I took these discourse features, which are recognised as being typical of Irish English, and I carried out a similar quantitative and qualitative study of them as I had with the grammar features. The hypothesis was that if discourse features do indeed "convey as much or even more about a character, setting and regional culture as do traditionally-studied dialect respellings and non-standard grammatical usages" then it would be likely that the percentages of their appearances in film would on average be higher than those of the grammar features. In order to ensure a level-playing field, I decided not to find the total averages, but rather the averages for the ten most common grammar and discourse features respectively, thus excluding some of the many minor grammar features which would have distorted the overall picture. The discourse features investigated were as follows: *sure, but, what, like, so, repetitions, come here, religious expressions, arrah* and *musha*[270].

6.2.1 Sure

Sure is the most typical discourse marker in Irish English, but its use in the variety is very different from its uses in other varieties of English. The OED states that *sure* is used to qualify a statement and is synonymous with *assuredly, undoubtedly* and *for a certainty*, and it

---

[270] In her article on discourse features, Amador Moreno also included the need for a reinforcing element to support affirmative or negative answers to *yes/no* questions (2005: 88). However, as I have already included these in the section on questions on page 96, they shall not be readdressed here. The same applies for *it clefting* and *topicalisation*, which Harris (1993: 173-76) and Asián and McCullough (1998: 49) included among their discourse features, but which I have dealt with elsewhere.

attributes this usage to Irish and North American colloquial English where, supposedly, it is frequently introduced between the subject and verb (cf. OED, s.v. sure, *adv.* 3a). While this may be the case for American English, as also testified by Tottie (2002: 169), who describes *sure* as being used colloquially as a sentence adverb in the same way as *certainly*, for which she offers the examples: "I sure can tell", "I sure do" and "He sure likes to drink", this is most certainly not the way *sure* is used in Irish English. To prove this, one can switch the word order of a sample sentence from the film corpus, so that *sure* is between the subject and verb. The sentence "But, **sure**, I can't act." from *A Man of No Importance* (see sentence 382) would thus become "But, I **sure** can't act." While the first sentence implies a certain amount of surprise on the part of the speaker, the latter places a strong emphasis on the fact that while the speaker might be able to do other things, there is one thing he certainly cannot do. What is more, Irish English also permits one to place *sure* at the end of the clause, i.e. "But, I can't act, **sure**.", while still retaining the meaning of the first sentence. One of the most obvious indicators that there is a clear distinction between the Irish and the American uses of *sure* is that Irish people pronounce the words differently depending on the context they appear in. When *sure* appears as a discourse marker, as in the first and third examples, Irish English speakers pronounce it as [ʃʌr], whereas when it appears as an adverb, as in the second example, it is pronounced [ʃuər].

The versatility of *sure* as a discourse marker has also been pointed out by Amador Moreno, who notes that it can occur in affirmative, negative and interrogative sentences (2005: 85), with its versatility also extending to its meaning. While in the majority of instances *sure* is simply used as an emphatic marker (see examples 375-80), it can also suggest contrast like the Standard English *but* (cf. Dolan 2006: 231). However, it is worth noting that, despite their similarity in meaning, *sure* can also be used in conjunction with *but* for even further emphasis as in examples 381 and 382 below. In other cases, *sure* can be used as a tag, as in examples 383 and 384. Furthermore, Amador Moreno has also observed the use of *sure* as a marker of cause which can be paraphrased with *because*, as in example 385, or, as a means of diffusing or playing down a situation, when it is used together with *ah*, as in example 386. As already mentioned above, it is important to note that in all of the examples *sure* is always pronounced [ʃʌr] and not [ʃuər][271].

> 375) **Sure**, don't you know I'll be there? **Sure**, amn't I always there when you're having a good time?
>
> (*Agnes Browne*, 00:54:41, FM1960D)
>
> 376) That's Sunday. **Sure**, we'll have to get Mass first. **Sure**, we might as well leave it off till Monday then.
>
> (*This is my Father*, 01:25:50, MGard1930M)
>
> 377) Ah, musha, me son, **sure** you must be starvin'.
>
> (*The Informer*, 00:16:37, FFM1920D)

---

[271] There are examples of non-Irish actors pronouncing *sure* as [ʃuər] rather than [ʃʌr]. Such pronunciations sound very unnatural to Irish ears and betray the fact that the actor is not Irish. Examples include the following: "**Sure**, I said to him, Packy MacFarlane, you'll never make me believe that Sarah Tillane would be selling White O'Morn" (*The Quiet Man*, 00:16:19, MRW1930W) and "Oh, **sure**, I'm full of surprises" (*About Adam*, 00:09:09, FL2000D).

378) She was in a tearin' rage at me and **sure** it was your fault for not telling her the truth in the first place.
(*Darby O'Gill and the Little People*, 01:17:13, MMB1800D)

379) Now, tell me. You're after blowing your cover, **sure**.
(*Intermission*, 01:21:09, ML2000D)

380) They wouldn't kill me in my own county, **sure**.
(*Michael Collins*, 00:07:06, MMC1910C)

381) I know, but **sure** looks aren't everything.
(*A Very Unlucky Leprechaun*, 00:05:11, MPM1990W)

382) But, **sure**, I can't act.
(*A Man of No Importance*, 00:10:21, FA1960M)

383) If you died of the flu, it wouldn't be your fault, **sure** it wouldn't?
(*The Magdalene Sisters*, 00:59:45, FCr1960D)

384) He doesn't really like me, **sure** he doesn't?
(*The Van*, 00:57:14, FM1990D)

385) [Trudy: You're from Galway, aren't you?]
[Guard: I am.]
[Trudy: See now! Where abouts?]
[Guard: Athenry.]
[Trudy: Do you know the Joyces?]
[Guard: Yeah, I'm one of them. How do you know?]
Trudy: **Sure**, they're all called Joyce in that kip!
(*When Brendan Met Trudy*, 01:15:29, FT2000C)

386) **Ah, sure**, after the Great War, I don't think anyone'd be foolish enough to do that ever again.
(*This is my Father*, 00:56:00, MK1930M)

Sure is one of the most frequent features of Irish English in the film corpus, appearing in 46 of the 50 movies (92%) [see Table 40]. This high frequency can perhaps be explained by the fact that, as outlined above, it is such a versatile discourse marker, and can appear in many different positions and with many different meanings. Unfortunately, this feature was not examined by Hickey and thus there are no figures available for comparison.

6.2.2 Sentence-final markers

In addition to *sure*, which as illustrated above, can also be employed as a sentence-final marker, Irish English employs a number of similar markers, such as *but*, *what* and *like* to achieve focus at the end of a sentence (cf. Harris 1993: 176).

6.2.2.1 *But*

The first of these, the conjunction *but*, proves to be quite interesting, particularly with regard to where it is most likely to be heard. One the one hand, McMahon and O'Donoghue (2004:

136) suggest that *but*, meaning 'though' or 'however', is a typical feature of Dublin English and, what is more, that the final *-t* is often not pronounced. This attestation to Dublin is indeed borne out by the evidence in the film corpus, with *but* as a sentence-final marker[272] appearing in 5 of the 50 films (10%) [see Table 41], all 5 of which are set in the capital.

> 387) You have to hand it to the Vietnamese, **but**.
>
> (*The Van*, 00:15:48, ML1990D)

> 388) They're goin' to fuckin' kill us. Not lookin' out was bad, then stealin' their car, **but**.
>
> (*Adam and Paul*, 00:56:05, MP2000D)

> 389) Just wanted to make sure he wouldn't get up, **but**.
>
> (*Michael Collins*, 00:38:10, MA1910D)

> 390) I tell you, **but**, I gave as good as I got.
>
> (*The Snapper*, 00:57:50, MDC1990D)

> 391) He used to like them pan-fried, **but**.
>
> (*The General*, 01:16:29, MMC1990D)

However, Hickey and Harris attest the feature to northern Irish English (cf. Hickey 2004a: 128 and Harris 1984b: 132) and again Hickey's corpus offers strong evidence to support this notion. His sentence "He's gone to the races, but?" received its highest acceptability rating in Ulster (35%) compared to the average rate of 20% for the other three provinces[273]. What makes these results all the more interesting is that Dublin, the area which so clearly dominated the findings in the film corpus, lags far behind other parts of the country in Hickey's survey, displaying an acceptability rating of just 13%, which is lower than the national average. This lack of agreement between Hickey's results and those from the film corpus is interesting and suggests that further research is warranted to find out whether this is more likely to be a Belfast or a Dublin feature. Dolan's *A Dictionary of Hiberno-English* does not help to clarify the situation, as with examples attested to both the Belfast poet Tom Paulin and the Dublin author Roddy Doyle (2006: 39), the situation remains equally unclear.

6.2.2.2   *What*

The word *what*, sometimes pronounced without the final *-t*, particularly in Dublin English, is a common sentence final marker and is a way of seeking assent or confirmation about what the speaker has just said. There are numerous examples of it in the film corpus:

> 392) This is the life, **what**?
>
> (*The Van*, 01:06:06, ML1990D)

> 393) Yeah, she's some chick, **what**?
>
> (*Goldfish Memory*, 00:26:46, MC2000C)

---

[272] In example 390, *but* appears at the end of the clause rather than at the end of the sentence.
[273] This feature received a surprisingly high acceptability rating of 31% in Connaught, despite the fact that none of the literature has claimed that it is a common feature there.

394) Yeah, well. See you tomorrow, **wha'**?

(*Agnes Browne*, 00:27:22, MMB1960D)

395) Grand, now I'm sucking diesel, **wha'**?

(*Dead Meat*, 00:40:58, MC2000LM)

This structure is far more prevalent in the film corpus than was *but* as a sentence final marker and it can be found in the speech of characters from Cork, Wexford, Wicklow, Leitrim, the Midlands and, of course, Dublin, where it is most common. In total, it appears in 19 of the 50 films (38%) [see Table 42], compared to the 10% for *but* above. Unfortunately, no numbers are available for comparison from Hickey's study.

6.2.2.3   *Like*

Like as a sentence-final focus marker, on the other hand, does appear in the *Survey of Irish English Usage* and, thus, we can compare its results with those from the film corpus. It is important in this regard, however, to distinguish between it and the filler *like*, which has by now become quite common in Irish English, and which is often described as being an Americanism stemming from people's exposure to US television shows[274]. The important difference between the two forms is the positioning of the word *like* in the sentence.

In the case of the traditional Irish English usage, the adverb *like* appears at the end of a clause or sentence[275], and can be glossed with the words "as it were" (Dolan 2006: 140; Share 2003: 192). Below are examples from the corpus which show *like* in its favoured position:

396) Nothin', Frankie. You came up to me so sudden, **like**[276].

(*The Informer*, 00:10:10, MG1920D)

397) We were only young, **like**.

(*Nora*, 00:55:48, FN1900G)

398) Ah, Jesus Christ, lads. He's only a young fella, **like**.

(*The Wind that Shakes the Barley*, 00:51:06, MC1920C)

---

[274] This use of *like* as a filler is often thought to go hand-in-hand with the use of another Americanism, namely upspeak. This notion is reflected in the title of an *Irish Times* opinion piece from August 16th, 2005, entitled "Leave upspeak to the, like, Americans?" (Behan 2005). What is more, the author of the article attributes these phenomena, rightly or wrongly, to the American TV shows *Friends* and *Sex in the City*. There may be some merit to the argument that *like* is spreading from America, particularly when one bears in mind that Tottie discovered that *like* is used as a discourse marker about 1,300 times per million words in American English speech compared with 325 times per million words in British English speech (cf. Tottie 2002: 204).

[275] *Like* is also traditionally used as a focussing device in clause-final position in dialects in the North-east of England (cf. Beal 2004: 136) and can also be found in this context in the South-east of England (cf. Anderwald 2004: 192).

[276] This particular example may be ambiguous. According to Taniguchi, *like* can also be suffixed to the adjective instead of *-ly* to create an adverb. In his examples from Irish English literature, he offers the words "careless-like" and "jovial-like". What is more, he also offers an English dialect example from a novel by Thomas Hardy which is almost identical to that in *The Informer*. "She is off to foreign lands again at last – hev made up her mind quite sudden like – and it is thoughted she'll leave in a day or two" (Taniguchi 1972: 42). By consulting the novel, *The Informer*, one does not necessarily gain any further insights into the intended use of *like* in the film, as in the book the line is "But it's how ye've come in on me so sudden, an I don't know right what I'm talkin' about" (O'Flaherty, 1925/1999: 22). However, given the lack of the *-ly* ending for both *sudden* and *right*, and the absence of *like* in the sentence from the novel, the chances are that the *like* used in the film is, indeed, more likely to be a sentence-final focus marker rather than some sort of alternative adverb form.

On the few rare occasions when *like* is not in final position, it is followed, at most, by a filler, such as *you know*, which serves a similar purpose.

> 399) So I always had the kind of a notion of joining the navy, **like**, ya know.
> (*This is my Father*, 00:51:57, MK1930M)

> 400) Oh, I don't know. Sure, they came from near and far, **like**, ya know.
> (*Trojan Eddie*, 00:49:33, MTE1990M)

> 401) Ah, just hangin' around, **like**, you know. Just layin' low, **like**.
> (*Adam and Paul*, 00:10:57, MP2000D)

The "American" filler *like* on the other hand, can be employed in a variety of different environments and according to Tottie (2002) can precede the following types of words: a) nouns, b) numerals, c) adjectives, d) and e) adverbs, f) verbs, g) prepositional phrases and h) even other hedges or vocalizations. She offers the following American English examples as evidence of its versatility:

> a) Are you taking **like** a college course?
> b) He's **like** six foot seven tall ...
> c) He's **like** tall ...
> d) No, I mean **like**, **like** even Nadia gets annoying ...
> e) Men were **like** literally throwing themselves at me ...
> f) So you just **like** try different things out ...
> g) Anything **like** with a brand name on it.
> h) But, but maybe **like** uh, Michael ...
>
> (Tottie 2002: 188)

Although the feature is gaining currency in Irish English, particularly among young people (cf. Dolan 2006: 140), it is less common in the film corpus. Below, however, are some examples:

> 402) Ma found her, it was **like** two or three days later, and "the stink" she said, flies crawling over her and her hysterical.
> (*Intermission*, 00:29:02, FD2000D)

> 403) Could I just say that, **like**, it's entirely up to himself.
> (*Mystics*, 00:20:30, MD2000D)

> 404) Well, I mean, **like**, even though I always knew that Tom was a bit of a fuckin' eejit, you know, he was sound.[277]
> (*Ordinary Decent Criminal*, 00:27:48, MT1990D)

In total, *like* appears as a final focus marker in 21 of the 50 films (42%) [see Table 43]. This rate is very similar to that of the *Survey of Irish English*, in which Hickey's sentence "She's hard-working, like" had an acceptability rating of 43%.

---

[277] This example nicely illustrates a variety of discourse markers (*well*, *I mean*, *like* and *you know*) all in one sentence.

6.2.2.4 *So*

A further discourse marker used for emphasis is the use of *so* in a sentence tag (cf. Joyce 1988: 10 and Harris 1993: 176). This sentence tag generally involves the use of *so* together with the verb which was used in the main clause (or an auxiliary, as in example 411), resulting in structures which basically affirm what has come before, as in the following examples:

> 405) Sure, you're practically one of the family now, **so you are**.
> (*Circle of Friends*, 00:38:47, FAH1950D)

> 406) I can make up a thousand songs, **so I can**.
> (*Darby O'Gill and the Little People*, 00:37:45, MKB1800K)

> 407) Ah, stop! She would mind mice at the crossroads for ya, **so she would**.
> (*Nora*, 01:00:14, FN1900G)

> 408) Frankie Browne, get outta that and go to school or I'll tell Mammy on ya, **so I will**.
> (*Agnes Browne*, 00:27:38, FCB1960D)

> 409) It's Frigid Brigid you've got to watch out for. She could put the fear of death into a corpse, **so she could**.
> (*Evelyn*, 00:18:44, FM1950D)

> 410) I wouldn't argue with you, **so I wouldn't**.
> (*Into the West*, 00:26:04, MPR1990D)

> 411) Now, we gave her every chance, **so we did**.
> (*Widows' Peak*, 00:09:34, FDC1930M)

> 412) Dad said he would get a job soon, **so he will**[278], and buy her dresses of silk and shoes with silver buckles.
> (*Angela's Ashes*, 00:04:04, MN1990L)

So appears as a sentence tag in 11 of the 50 films (22%) [see Table 44]. As can be seen from the examples in the table, this structure would seem to appear slightly more frequently in films set prior to the 1970s. Although there are some examples in *Trojan Eddie*, *Into the West*, *The Van* and *Rat*, which are set in the early 1990s or at the turn of the new millennium, there is evidence to suggest that, in films set in the last two decades, the sentence final tag is also likely to occur without the use of the word *so*, particularly in Dublin. Some examples include:

> 413) He's been a great help to me lately, **he has**.
> (*Adam and Paul*, 00:47:38, FJ2000D)

---

[278] This example from *Angela's Ashes* is unusual in that there is a shift in the speech of the narrator from reported speech to present tense. The expected pattern would be: "Dad said he would get a job soon, **so he would**, and buy her dresses of silk and shoes with silver buckles". The sentence as it appears in the film may be an error on the part of the actor or perhaps something which was overlooked by the screenwriters when adapting the original line from the novel, which reads: "He'll get a job soon, so he will, and she'll have dresses of silk and shoes with silver buckles" (McCourt 1996: 24).

414) Yeah, we're rides, **we are**.

(*About Adam*, 01:23:19, FD2000D)

415) They freak me out, **they do**.

(*The Snapper*, 01:02:36, FJ1990D)

6.2.2.5 Repetition for emphasis

In general, there is a strong tendency for Irish English speakers to use repetition for emphasis. As seen above, this occurs through the use of structures like *so* (and sometimes *sure*), as well as through a repetition of the verb or an auxiliary verb in the final tag. While this structure has so far been evident in declarative sentences, it also frequently occurs in interrogatives, as can be seen in the following examples from the corpus.

416) **Will** I kick the ball, **will** I?

(*Adam and Paul*, 00:11:19, MP2000D)

417) **Will** we take a look at this ocean, **will** we?

(*This is my Father*, 00:50:28, MK1930M)

418) **Will** I bring them back then, **will** I?

(*The General*, 00:03:57, MYMC1960D)

419) **Do** I know you, **do** I?

(*The Wind that Shakes the Barley*, 00:31:17, MD1920C)

In total, repetitions of this nature in questions appear in 17 of the 50 films (34%) [see Table 45], but there are no comparative results for the *Survey of Irish English Usage*.

It should be noted that the general tendency of Irish people to use repetitions was identified as early as in the 19th century by Stoney. In his prescriptive pamphlet on English usage, he writes: "don't, Pat, ever say, 'at all at all' unless you wish to proclaim your nationality from the house-top" (Stoney 1885: 41). It is worth mentioning that the use of this particular repetition has developed a reputation as being somewhat of a Stage Irish feature, and, indeed, Share (2003: 7) describes it as a "Paddyism"[279]. The same also applies to the expression *to be sure, to be sure*[280]. Having said that, *at all, at all* only appears once in the corpus (see below), while *to be sure, to be sure* does not appear at all.

420) I'm not interested **at all, at all**.

(*The Matchmaker*, 00:33:16, MFis2000W)

6.2.3 *Come here*

While *come here* is often used in conjunction with 'subordinating *till*', as was evident in chapter 6.1.5.4., it is also used in its own right as a discourse marker, particularly when requesting attention to a story or question (cf. McMahon 2004: 181). In this respect, it is used

---

[279] Share offers the following humorous example of the use of *at all at all* being used with regard to the rules of the road: "One yellow line means no parking at all; two yellow lines means no parking atallatall *(sic)*"(2003: 7).
[280] The standing of *to be sure, to be sure* as an Irish expression has been immortalised in the well-known joke: Question: "Why did the Irishman wear two condoms?" Answer: "To be sure, to be sure."

in the same way as one might use *listen* or *look*.[281] It is important to note, however, that despite the fact that the speaker says *come here*, there is rarely a spatial distance between him and the addressee which would necessitate the listener actually coming physically closer. This notion is best exemplified in sentence 427, which is said on the telephone, with the speaker in Dublin and the addressee in Clare. As can be seen from the examples below, *come here* is often shortened to *here* or lengthened to *come here to me*. While the majority of the examples below are from Dublin speakers, the form can be heard all over Ireland.

421) **Come here**, Wexford isn't that bad, is it?
(*Intermission*, 00:07:25, FSG2000D)

422) **Come here**, the way it was told, it's the way it has to be.
(*Intermission*, 01:31:27, MG2000D)

423) Yeah, it is, and, **come here**, if nothing happens and he's still acting the prick, we go ahead and do it, ok?
(*The Snapper*, 01:02:28, FJ1990D)

424) **Here**, do you hear that?
(*Dead Meat*, 01:03:12, MD2000LM)

425) **Here**, what colour socks are you wearing?
(*The Van*, 01:06:11, ML1990D)

426) **Come here to me**, listen, go on upstairs, right, and I'll be with you in a few minutes. All right, chicken?
(*Ordinary Decent Criminal*, 00:26:48, MBi1990D)

427) **Come here to me**, your brother is on his way.
(*The Boys and Girl from County Clare*, 00:23:11, MCO1960D)

In total, *come here* and its variants are to be found in 20 of the 50 films (40%) [see Table 46], with all but two of those occurrences being in Irish productions. Unfortunately, there are no comparable figures from Hickey's survey.

6.2.4 Religious expressions

Irish people's propensity to swear, often using religious expressions, has long been recognised. In the 1950s, Bartley observed that there was certainly rather more profane swearing in Ireland than in the rest of the British Isles, and that this seemed to have been the case for centuries. He also cites Camden as having said of the Irish in 1610 that

---

[281] Hickey (2005: 145-6) also offers *look here* and *look it*, often written as *lookit* or *looka* (cf. McMahon and O'Donoghue 2004: 480), as discourse markers which share the same function. Examples of these are also evident in the film corpus: "**Lookit**, if I buy a house, the tax people'll get me" (*The General*, 00:14:48, MMC1990D), "**Lookit**, I changed my mind" (*When Brendan Met Trudy*, 00:13:10, FT1990C), "**Lookit**, you mustn't mind himself this day, Mary Kate" (*The Quiet Man*, 00:18:37, MFe1930D), "**Look here**, Father Hugh, the stripping of her was an accident" (*Ryan's Daughter*, 01:11:10, ML1920W).

[a]t every third word it is ordinary with them to lash out with an oth, namely by the Trinity, by God, by S. Patrick, by S. Brigid, by their Baptisme, by Faith, by the Church, by my God-fathers hand, and by thy hand.

(Camden cited in: Bartley 1954: 34)

Asián and McCullough's 1998 study of Irish English in literary dialect also showed that the use of religious expressions is a very salient discourse marker in the variety, and can range from one-word forms to much more elaborate oaths and exclamations. Some good examples of the varying length of such expressions are evident in the movie *Far and Away*:

428) **Jesus!**

(*Far and Away*, 00:22:21, MJD1890W)

429) **Jesus and the saints preserve us!**

(*Far and Away*, 00:07:05, MJD1890W)

430) **Sweet Mary and Jesus and all the saints preserve us!**

(*Far and Away*, 01:51:55, MJD1890W)

In addition to their use in such exclamations, religious expressions in Irish English can take the form of greetings, salutations, marks of respect when speaking about the deceased, and expressions of sympathy or thanks. What follows below are examples of each type.

Greetings and salutations:
In the past, speakers of Irish English preserved the Irish language tradition of extending a general greeting or blessing on entering a house or public house. Joyce lists a number of these greetings, including what he regarded as "the commonest of all our salutes" *God save you* or (for a person entering a house) *God save all here*. He also gives the appropriate response to these greetings, namely *God save you kindly* (cf. 1988: 15). However, these expressions and others like them are by now quite archaic, and when they do occur in the film corpus, they appear in movies set prior to the 1940s. Examples include:

431) **God bless all in this house!**

(*Far and Away*, 00:15:03, MJD1890W)

432) **God bless all here!**

(*The Quiet Man*, 01:23:41, MFe1930D)

433) **God save all here!**

(*This is my Father*, 00:41:44, FT1930M)

Just as they used religious blessings in their greetings, speakers of Irish English in the past also did so in salutations, on parting company with somebody. While the examples from the film corpus below are also from films set in the early to mid part of the last century, this salutation can still be heard to a certain degree in Ireland.

> 434) One way ticket now, lads. Have a safe journey and **God bless to all of ye**.[282]
>
> *(The Wind that Shakes the Barley*, 01:30:57, MC1920C)
>
> 435) Good man, you're a grand man, good night, **God bless**.
> *(Evelyn*, 00:58:50, MDES1950D)

When speaking about the deceased:
Taniguchi also observed that when speaking about the deceased, Irish people often use religious expressions as a mark of respect (1972: 212-3). This usage is also evident in the film corpus, with one character in *The Informer* even reprimanding another for failing to show due respect:

> 436) Hey, when you mention the dead, you might add "**May the Lord have mercy on his soul**".
> *(The Informer*, 00:42:39, MG1920D)

Other means of expressing the same sentiment are given in the examples below:

> 437) When I was a young lad, knee high to a sod of turf, me grandfather Podge, **God be good to him**, he told me there was only one man in the town who was happy altogether - the village eejit.
> *(Darby O'Gill and the Little People*, 01:13:20, MDOG1800K)
>
> 438) This isn't the way Mary would have raised them, **God rest her**.
> *(Into the West*, 00:10:12, MGR1990D)
>
> 439) As my Annie, **God rest her soul**, always said, "The future of this country, if it has any future at all, lies in cabbages".
> *(How Harry Became a Tree*, 00:17:02, MH1920WW)
>
> 440) **God bless your soul**, poor Joe Donnelly.
> *(Far and Away*, 00:06:38, MDD1980W)
>
> 441) Aye, I married a Traveller – ould Kitty, **the Lord be good to her**.
> *(Trojan Eddie*, 00:21:13, MJP1990M)
>
> 442) And when poor Miss O'Hare, **the Lord have mercy on her**, got suspicious, that was her death warrant.
> *(Widows' Peak*, 01:26:36, FDC1930M)

Expressions of sympathy:
Religious expressions can also take the form of expressions of sympathy:

> 443) To the zoo. **God love them**, they could do with a day out.
> *(Agnes Browne*, 00:21:29, FAB1960D)

---

[282] The blessing in this particular example could be seen to be tongue in cheek, as the speaker is actually saying goodbye (and good riddance) to the British soldiers who had been stationed in Ireland prior to the foundation of the Irish Free State.

444) **God help him**, he's in the hall with that bastard Stafford.
(*A Love Divided*, 01:25:44, MA1950WX)

445) **God help her**, he's a terrible cross to the poor woman.
(*My Left Foot*, 00:14:42, FWN1950D)

446) Ah, sure, **God love him**. Sure, he wasn't so bad this year.
(*The Dead*, 00:55:03, FAK1900D)

447) Well, **God bless her**, she thinks that I'm like the rest of the men. A bit helpless, a bit of a namby pamby.
(*Widows' Peak*, 00:14:40, MGDC1930M)

Requests for divine intervention or forgiveness:
A further instance in which religious expressions can appear is in requests for divine intervention or forgiveness:

448) But, sure, maybe it'll all work out all right in the end, **with the help of the Lord**.
(*Trojan Eddie*, 00:53:20, MJP1990M)

449) He'll be spared for many years, **God willin'**.
(*Darby O'Gill and the Little People*, 00:03:25, FMS1800K)

450) **God protect us**, Daniel. Here they come!
(*Far and Away*, 01:59:35, FMC1890W)

451) **Oh, Jesus have Mercy**! Oh, Jesus Christ!
(*The Wind that Shakes the Barley*, 00:07:38, FB1920C)

452) **Lord save us**!
(*This is my Father*, 00:52:26, MK1930M)

453) **Lord bless us and save us**. You'd nearly... you'd nearly say they were better off dead.
(*Dead Meat*, 00:42:13, MC2000LM)

454) **God help us all**!
(*Goldfish Memory*, 01:03:33, FP2000D)

455) I beat her today, **God forgive me**. Jesus, I nearly killed her.
(*How Harry Became a Tree*, 01:07:54, MG1920WW)

456) It was then I arrived with me family, and **may God forgive me**, I didn't make things any better.
(*This is my Father*, 00:40:33, FT2000M)

457) So we formed a little conspiracy, the Reverend Mister and Mrs Playfair, Michaleen Oge and, **saints forgive us**, myself.
(*The Quiet Man*, 00:49:00, MFL1930W)

As an expression of thanks:
Gratitude in Irish English is also expressed through the use of religious expressions:

> 458) Well, we don't live in Hollyfield now, **thanks be to God**.
> (*The General*, 01:43:12, FMD1990D)

> 459) Well it's the spare-room for me tonight, **thank Christ**!
> (*About Adam*, 01:09:21, FA2000D)

> 460) Nothing changes, **thank God**.
> (*Agnes Browne*, 00:24:51, MB1960D)

> 461) **Thank the Lord**, you've arrived.
> (*The Dead*, 00:07:07, FAK1900D)

> 462) **Thanks be to Jesus**!
> (*Far and Away*, 01:01:35, MJD1890W)

As a blessing:
Religious expressions also appear as a means of wishing someone well:

> 463) Ah, **God bless you**, Alfred!
> (*A Man of No Importance*, 00:12:45, MMC1960D)

> 464) **God send youse good luck**.
> (*Widows' Peak*, 00:59:39, MMC1930M)

As a curse or a threat:
Just as they can be used to wish someone well, religiously-motivated expressions can also be employed to express ill will or to intensify an oath:

> 465) **God's curse on them**.
> (*Michael Collins*, 00:32:55, MMC1910C)

> 466) **By Jaysus**, if it harms those kids, I'll curse your grave.
> (*Into the West*, 00:39:53, MPR1990D)

> 467) **By the power of God**, I'm after putting a curse on you that will go down through the ages.
> (*This is my Father*, 00:38:53, FW1930M)

> 468) **I swear to Jaysus**, I'll swing for you.
> (*Trojan Eddie*, 01:30:31, MJP1990M)

Some oaths in Irish English are quite inventive[283], spicing up existing religious expressions or invoking Satan, as can be seen in many of the following examples:

---

[283] Indeed, this inventiveness extends to the fact that a proper noun such as *Jaysus* can even be used as an adjective in Irish English. Share (2006: 85) cites the example "Get outta that Jaysus garden!" whereby *Jaysus* means something like 'bloody', 'feckin'" etc. Conor McPherson includes the example "Now would you ever give us a Jaysus fucking drink, you're gonna blow the whole Christmas atmosphere" in his play *The Seafarer*

469) **Sweet suffering Jesus!**
                                            (*Michael Collins*, 00:07:55, MMC1910C)

470) **Jesus sufferin' Christ!**
                                            (*My Left Foot*, 00:27:25, MMB1950D)

471) **Holy old Finbar**[284]!
                                            (*Darby O'Gill and the Little People*, 00:14:36, MDOG1800K)

472) **Holy Baholey!**
                                            (*About Adam*, 00:59:28, MH2000D)

473) **Holy Blessed God**, you're freezing with the cold, boy!
                                            (*Angela's Ashes*, 01:31:00, FMP1940L)

474) **Jesus tonight**, Maggie will have given me dinner to the cat.
                                            (*The Van*, 00:16:16, MB1990D)

475) Ah **the divil take you!** [285]
                                            (*Darby O'Gill and the Little People*, 00:55:33, MDOG1800K)

476) **Devil take me** if the lot of you is not possessed and damned.
                                            (*Ryan's Daughter*, 00:13:34, MFR1920W)

477) And **the divil's cure to you!**
                                            (*Widows' Peak*, 01:01:58, FMOH1930M)

478) **Glory be to the saints of joy**, this is a great day for Rathcullen.
                                            (*Darby O'Gill and the Little People*, 00:51:38, FBW1800K)

479) **Holy Mother of Divine God!**
                                            (*Into the West*, 00:15:20, FOW1990D)

480) **I swear by all that's holy**, I warned him to keep away from this house.
                                            (*The Informer*, 00:29:35, MG1920D)

Religious expressions from the Irish language also find their way into Irish English[286]. *Wirra* (or *wurra*), for example, is an exclamation of grief and comes from the Irish vocative *a Mhuire*, meaning 'Mary', the virgin mother (cf. Dolan 2006: 254). A related form is *wirrasthru*, also *wirrasthroo*, *wurrasthroo* or *wierasthru*, meaning 'alas'. This expression stems from the Irish *a Mhuire, is trua* (Mary, it's a pity). While these forms were used in earnest in the past, they are often used in a mocking fashion today, sometimes to make fun of somebody's misfortune (cf. McMahon 2004: 854). It is in just such a context that *wirra* is

---

(2006: 30). The film corpus also displays evidence of *Jaysus* being used as an adjective: "And what's the point in giving you a gun if they don't give you Jaysus bullets?" (*The Snapper*, 00:20:50, MFoC1990D).

[284] Finbar is an Irish name meaning 'fair head'. St Finbar is the patron saint of Cork.

[285] Oaths of the type "the devil take me/you/him/her etc" also appear in Bliss' corpus of texts (1979: 260).

[286] For more on oaths and ejaculations of Irish origin, see Bliss (1979: 256-62).

used below. Brian Connors, the King of the Leprechauns, feigns sympathy for having tricked Darby into making his second wish.

481) Oh, **wirra, wirra, wirra**!
(*Darby O'Gill and the Little People*, 00:57:39, MKB1800K)

A further point of note which is related to oaths and religious expressions is, as Taniguchi (1972: 124) observes, that in Irish English *and* is often used redundantly after expletives and swear words. This is borne out by evidence from the film corpus:

482) Begod, **and** he wouldn't.
(*How Harry Became a Tree*, 00:03:14, MH1920WW)

This redundant *and* can also appear after *indeed*, as can be seen in the following example from the same film:

483) Indeed **and** it was.
(*How Harry Became a Tree*, 00:19:38, MG1920WW)

In total, religious expressions of one form or another appear in all 50 of the films (100%) [see Table 47]. Given Ireland's status as a predominantly Catholic country, some readers may find it surprising that there are so many violations of the Third Commandment, with the Lord's name frequently "being used in vain" in Irish film. This surprise would certainly be justified, given the fact that even within the film industry the practice of using the Lord's name was severely frowned upon from the early days, so much so that the Motion Picture Production Code of 1930, also known as the Hays Code after the Chairman who implemented it, had strict rules governing, among other things, the use of religious expressions in films produced in the United States. One of the "Twelve Commandments", as the Code's sections were known, dealt specifically with the area of profanity and stated that "pointed profanity (this includes the words, God, Lord, Jesus, Christ – unless used reverently – Hell, S.O.B, damn, Gawd)… is forbidden" (Rockett 2004: 100). Some filmmakers got around this problem by employing euphemisms in their films, but Irish film censor Richard Hayes, who was a devout Catholic, also put a stop to this procedure during his time in office (1940-1954), removing euphemistic terms for *Jesus Christ* such as *Jeepers Creepers*, *Jeepers*, *Jumping Jeepers* and *Holy Jeepers* from a whole host of movies. What is more, during Hayes' reign, even reverential references to Jesus Christ remained on the cutting room floor. In his informative history on film censorship in Ireland, Rockett reports on the continued cutting of religious references of all sorts, including *Jeez*, *Jesus* and *Christ* throughout the 1950s, 60s and 70s, up to and including such iconic films as *Jaws* (Steven Spielberg, 1975) and *One Flew over the Cuckoo's Nest* (Milos Forman, 1975)[287].

Today, however, the use of the Lord's name is not an issue in Irish film nor indeed within Irish society, with the Irish English pronunciations of *Jesus*, namely ['dʒezəs] or ['dʒezɔz], even being regarded as less blasphemous than the original word. Nonetheless, Irish

---

[287] For more fascinating insights into Irish film censorship, see Rockett (2004).

English speakers still have a large number of euphemisms at their disposal when referring to the Holy family or other religious figures, should they need them.

Dolan (2006: 129) offers the following euphemisms for *Jesus*: *Bejapers*!, *Jabers*!, *Jeepers*!, *Jee-whiz*! *Jeez*! and *Janey Mac*![288], while Share (2003: 170) includes *Jakers*! as a further alternative. Examples of some of these forms from the film corpus include:

484) Ah, **Japers**[289], Annie is livid.

(*Waking Ned*, 00:35:21, MJ2000W)

485) **Janey Mac**!

(*The Snapper*, 00:49:01, FY1990D)

486) Oh, **Janey Mac**!

(*Waking Ned*, 00:12:25, MJ2000W)

487) I just saw it... I just saw it in a shop and I thought to myself, "**Janey**, that would look wonderful on Mags".

(*How Harry Became a Tree*, 00:56:21, MF1920WW)

488) **Jeenie Mac**!

(*Michael Collins*, 01:14:36, MMC1910C)

489) **Jayz**, the heat in here would kill ya!

(*The Van*, 01:03:02, ML1990D)

490) **Jeez**, they're trying to fucking kill me.

(*Michael Collins*, 00:15:55, MMC1910C)

491) **Jeez**, will you be careful where you're pointing that thing?

(*How Harry Became a Tree*, 01:10:10, MH1920WW)

Euphemisms are not restricted to references to Jesus, but are also used to refer to God. Dolan (2006: 19), for example, cites *Bedad*, *Begob* and *Begorra* as euphemistic forms of *by God*[290], but points out that *begorra* is "now restricted to Stage Irish"[291]. Some examples include:

492) **Bedad**, I think ya have more sense than I have meself.

(*The Quiet Man*, 01:04:48, MMF1930W)

493) **Begorrah**! He wasn't far wrong.

(*Darby O'Gill and the Little People*, 00:28:25, MKB1800K)

---

[288] *Janey Mac* or *Janey Mack* is more typically a Dublin interjection, used euphemistically instead of *Jesus* and is featured in the children's rhyme: "Janey Mack me shirt is black!/What will I do for Sunday?/Go to bed and cover your head,/And don't get up till Monday" (cf. Share 2003: 169 and McMahon 2004: 407).

[289] Unlike Dolan, Hickey does not attribute the etymology of *Japers* to an Irish pronunciation of the euphemism *Jeepers*, but rather to Middle English *jape* 'a practical joke' which itself had its origin in Old French. He states that it is used "as a general expression of incredulity, surprise or disapproval" (2007: 363).

[290] The form *Begod* also exists, although the name *God* is still easily recognisable in the structure, thus rendering it somewhat less effective for someone who wants to avoid taking the Lord's name in vain. Here is an example from the film corpus: "Ah, **Begod** that's much better" (*A Very Unlucky Leprechaun*, 00:17:39, MPM1990W).

[291] The notion of *begorra* as a Stage Irish expression is discussed further in Chapter 12.

A further form which appears in the film corpus is *by the hokey*, or more usually, *be the hokey*. Dolan (2006: 121) offers examples of the usage but states that the origin is obscure, while Share (2003: 22 and 157) suggests that it is a contraction of the expletive *Holy poker*, "the supposed implement of punishment employed in purgatory" – and he offers the example "be the holy poker, [...] she's stuck". This expression, *be the holy poker*, may also be the inspiration behind the examples from the film corpus given below:

> 494) Oh **be the holy**, where did ya get it Gypo? There's enough there to choke a horse, and me joking you about it a few minutes ago.
> (*The Informer*, 00:49:05, MSP1920D)

> 495) **Be the hokey**, this calls for a celebration.
> (*Evelyn*, 00:58:52, MBM1950D)

> 496) **By the hokey**, it did look bad.
> (*Darby O'Gill and the Little People*, 00:55:43, MDOG1800K)

6.2.5 *Arrah*

A further discourse marker of Irish English is *arrah*, which is adapted from the Irish *ara* or *arú* meaning 'But now!', 'Really!', or 'Truly!' (cf. Share 2003: 6, Dolan 2006: 10)[292]. According to Amador Moreno, *arrah* is used as a functional opener and, as is the case in the second example below, it can be combined with *and* when it introduces an interrogative (2005: 83). Like *sure*, it can have a host of different meanings, such as expressing impatience and disagreement (Hayden and Hartog 1909: 784) or indicating that something should not be taken too seriously (Dolan 2006: 10). Amador Moreno places *arrah* in Quirk's category of "attitudinal disjuncts", as it focuses "on the speaker's attitude towards the content of his or her utterance" (Amador Moreno 2005: 92).

Arrah only appears in 5 of the 50 films (10%) [see Table 48]. Below are some examples:

> 497) **Arrah**, go on. Sing one!
> (*When Brendan Met Trudy*, 00:07:57, FT2000C)

> 498) **Arrah**! And how was the chase, hmm?
> (*Darby O'Gill and the Little People*, 00:35:04, MDOG1800K)

The fact that there are only 5 occurrences in total would appear to confirm Hickey's observation that *arrah* is a discourse feature which is "old-fashioned" and "virtually obsolete" (2007: 371). However, the findings strike me as surprising nonetheless, as it is my contention that the feature is still quite common in Ireland and I would therefore have expected that Irish actors would have (if only subconsciously) incorporated it more frequently into their performances, in much the same way as they appear to have done with *sure*[293].

---

[292] A related expression is *yerra* which comes from the Irish word *dhera*, which itself is a combination of the vocative *a Dhia* (God) + *ara*. It is used to express disbelief, surprise, indifference etc. (cf. Dolan 2006: 257, Share 2003: 359). However, there are no examples of this in the film corpus.

[293] An example of the latter is visible in the movie *About Adam*, which shows the impact the eponymous character has on the lives of four siblings, with the same events in the story being seen over and over from four different perspectives. While one might assume that each scene was simply shot simultaneously from four

6.2.6 *Musha*

Musha, a further discourse feature of Irish English, which sometimes also appears as *maise* or *mhuise*, has its origin in the Irish *muise*, meaning 'indeed', 'well, well' or 'is that so?' and is itself derived from *más ea*, meaning 'if so' (cf. Dolan 2006: 160-1). The form also occasionally appears as *wisha* which also means 'indeed' or 'well' and comes from the Irish *muise mhuise* (a duplication of *muise*) (cf. Dolan 2006: 255). Bliss (1979: 260), however, suggests that *muise* may in fact represent "an arbitrary alteration of *Muire* 'Mary'; this latter derivation is made effectively certain by the existence of the form *mhuise* parallel to (*a*) *Mhuire* 'Mary!' with the lenition appropriate to the vocative". Below are examples of *musha* from the film corpus:

> 499) Ah, **musha**, me son. Sure, you must be starvin'.
> (*The Informer*, 00:16:37, FFM1920D)

> 500) Oh, **musha, musha**!
> (*The Quiet Man*, 00:47:31, MMOB1930W)

In total *musha* appears as a discourse marker in only 2 of the 50 films (4%) [see Table 49]. Interestingly, the feature only appears in the films which were produced the earliest, which would suggest that the feature is old-fashioned or possibly stereotypical. Support for the latter notion is evident in *Mary Poppins* (Robert Stevenson, 1964), a film which, however, is not included in the corpus, as it is set in Britain. The speech of the fox, the character who uses the feature in that movie, is a compendium of Stage Irish expressions, featuring "Musha Musha!", "Faith and Begorrah!", and "Saints preserve us!" in the space of fifteen seconds.

6.2.7 Summary of findings for discourse markers

As can be seen from the table, the average percentages of the Top 10 discourse features are not as high as those of the Top 10 grammar features (see page 119). However, unlike the grammar features, these discourse markers are less likely to occur in other dialects of English and, thus, they can be seen as more uniquely "Irish". Based on this point, it could be argued that discourse features do, indeed, reflect a dialect better than non-standard grammar features do.

It is interesting to note that some of the discourse markers are restricted to periods or places. *But*, for example only occurs as a tag in films produced after 1990 and only in those set in Dublin. *Musha*, on the other hand, is restricted to a period, only occurring in the two earliest productions in the corpus and, thus, not since the 1950s. Finally, while the tendency for Irish speakers to use *like* as a filler is a new phenomenon which has come from America,

---

different angles to show the different perspectives, this is not the case, as the dialogue differs marginally between scenes at one point, as is betrayed by the additional use of the word *sure* by one of the actresses. When we first see the scene the lines are as follows: "But, **sure**, I've hardly met him. You obviously know him much better" (*About Adam*, 00:34:29, FA2000D), whereas the same scene from a different angle goes as follows: "But, then, of course, I've hardly met him. I mean, you obviously know him much better" (*About Adam*, 01:04:53, FA2000D). This discovery is by no means meant as a criticism of the continuity of the film, but should hopefully highlight just how easily discourse markers such as *sure* can slip into the speech of Irish people. Given this, it is somewhat surprising that *arrah*, a similar feature, makes so few appearances in the corpus.

evidence in the film corpus shows that the Irish English use of *like* as a tag is not new and can even be found in the oldest film in the corpus from 1935.

Top 10 discourse features

Feature	% of films which display the feature
Religious expressions	100
Sure	92
Like as tag	42
Come here/here	40
What as tag	38
Repetitions in questions	34
So as tag	22
But as tag	10
Arrah	10
Musha	4

6.3 Lexicon

In order to be able to further contextualise the frequencies of the grammar and discourse features, it is useful to take a look at the frequencies of some typical Irish English lexical items. The rate for these features could be expected to be highest, as, according to Ives (1950: 171), "the easiest and one of the most effective methods of giving regional flavor to speech is the use of local expressions and names for things". These can very often be used in place of standard expressions or names and involve very little reworking of the script. For example, in an Irish context, one only has to substitute the words *Ma*, *Mam* or *Mammy* for the standard terms *Mum*, *Mummy*, *Mom* and *Mommy* to already lend the speech a certain air of Irishness. Similar substitutions can be done with *Da* for *Dad* or *Daddy*, *grand* for *fine*, *guard* for *police officer*, and *shite* for *shit*, with the cumulative result being a seemingly more Irish-sounding script. The following pages examine some of these typical Irish expressions or names for things, and then compare their frequencies with the aforementioned grammar and discourse features. The list is restricted to the most common terms which appear in the films[294], although, of course, the number of Irish English lexical items which could have been examined is considerably greater. The richness of Irish English vocabulary is due to the fact that, in addition to using Standard English terms, Irish English makes use of terms which have long since disappeared from the standard variety, as well as terms which are found in other

---

[294] Other terms which one might have expected to occur quite frequently in Irish English were not actually that common in the films. Examples include *banjax(ed)* 'to ruin, destroy' (Dolan 2006: 15) which has 5 appearances; *craic* meaning fun or 'entertaining conversation' (Dolan 2006: 65) also with 5 appearances; *yoke* 'any contrivance or implement; something whose name does not spring immediately to mind' (Dolan 2006: 257-8) with 6 appearances; and *gob* 'beak; mouth' (Dolan 2006: 109) with 6 appearances.

English dialects or have been borrowed or adapted from Irish[295]. For the sake of cohesion, the expressions and vocabulary items examined below have been grouped together into categories, such as, labels/terms of address, examples of Irish pronunciation which have become lexicalised, swear words/vulgarisms, and common adjectives or adverbs.

6.3.1 Labels/Terms of address

6.3.1.1 *Ma*, *Mam* and *Mammy*

The Irish word for mother is *mamaí*, which is often contracted to *mam* (Dolan 2006: 148)[296]. These terms have both found their way into Irish English, giving the forms *mammy*[297] and *mam*, as well as the shortened form *ma*. In films set in Ireland, these terms are very common, appearing in some form or other in 37 of the 50 movies (74%) [see Table 50]. Some examples include:

>501) **Ma**! **Ma**! Christy picked up the chalk.
>>(*My Left Foot*, 00:16:37, FSB1950D)

>502) My **ma** would beat the shite out of Mickah Wallace any day.
>>(*The Commitments*, 00:51:29, MO1990D)

>503) **Ma**, I'm not lonely. I'm not lonely, **Mam**!
>>(*Cowboys and Angels*, 00:19:55, MS2000L)

>504) My aunts wrote to my **mam's** mother to send money for the tickets.
>>(*Angela's Ashes*, 00:06:16, MN1990L)

>505) **Mam**, tell me the truth. You never liked Martin did you?
>>(*About Adam*, 01:15:20, FA2000D)

>506) **Mammy**! **Mam**, hold on! Wait!
>>(*The Boys and Girl from County Clare*, 00:45:51, FA1960Cl)

>507) **Mammy**, this is Kieran and Jack.
>>(*This is my Father*, 00:15:32, MT2000M)

>508) Now, it's just that when you meet the **mammy**, and you will, don't let on to her that I can change a tire[298].
>>(*Widows' Peak*, 00:14:36, MGDC1930M)

---

[295] For a brief, but excellent, overview of the lexicon of Irish English, see Bliss (1984: 140). Dictionaries of Irish English terms include those by Dolan (2006) and Share (2003).

[296] Interestingly, the Irish (Gaelic) pronunciation of *mamaí* is actually closer to American English's *Mommy* [mɑːmi] than to Irish English's *Mammy* [mæmi]/[mami].

[297] One of the films in the corpus, *Agnes Browne*, is actually an adaptation of a novel by Brendan O'Carroll entitled *The Mammy* (1994).

[298] Godfrey Doyle Counihan is very much a *mammy's boy* in this film and, thus, does not want his mother to know that he is independent and can live without her. In order to keep this a secret, he therefore makes his new American fiancée promise not to tell his mother that he can change a tire, to which she mockingly replies: "Mammy's the word!" (*Widows' Peak*, 00:17:48, FMB1930US), thus putting an Irish twist on the familiar idiom "Mum's the word".

A further derivation of *mammy* is the term *mammy-in-law* for *mother-in-law*, as seen in the following example from *The Van*:

> 509) There's a funny whiff off your **mammy-in-law**.
>
> (*The Van*, 00:13:35, MW1990D)

6.3.1.2 *Da*

Irish English does not have as many non-standard ways of describing/addressing fathers as it does for mothers. Nonetheless, the term *Da* features strongly in the film corpus.

> 510) I missed you, **Da**.
>
> (*Far and Away*, 01:39:41, MJD1890W)

> 511) Jesus, **Da**, what have you done?
>
> (*How Harry Became a Tree*, 01:04:00, MG1920WW)

> 512) **Da** was a bricklayer, Ma, and I'm a writer.
>
> (*My Left Foot*, 01:29:17, MCB1950D)

> 513) I just wanted to come home, **Da**! I just wanted to come home. I hate it here.
>
> (*The Magdalene Sisters*, 00:29:39, FUOC1960D)

> 514) I still think you should tell us who the **da** is.
>
> (*The Snapper*, 00:06:06, MDC1990D)

> 515) Tell your **da** his days are numbered.
>
> (*Trojan Eddie*, 01:24:40, MR1990M)

In total, *Da* appears in 24 of the 50 films (48%) [see Table 51]. While this number is relatively low compared to the numbers for *Ma*, *Mam* and *Mammy*, it is worth bearing in mind that the 74% rate for those forms was a combined total for three non-standard forms.

6.3.1.3 *Lad* and *Lads*

Although the terms of address/descriptors *lad* and *lads* are by no means exclusive to Irish English[299], they do appear very frequently in the variety, where Standard British and American English would be likely to use other forms, such as *bloke(s)*, *guy(s)* etc. It should be noted, however, that, by now, the use of *lad* (singular) or the diminutive form *laddie* as forms of address evokes Stage Irish connotations. *Lad*, for example, appears numerous times as a term of address in both *Far and Away* and *Darby O'Gill and the Little People*, two of the films deemed to be paragons of Oirishness. The form *good lad*, however, does not appear to bear the same negative connotations[300].

---

[299] According to Wright, *lad* is used 'as a familiar or affectionate term for a man; a husband, son, or boon companion, a fellow' (EDD s.v. lad, sb.[1]. 3) in various parts of the UK, but especially in the North of England and Scotland.

[300] An additional term, *boy*, pronounced [baɪ], can also be found in the corpus. It is used as a term of address or a filler, especially in Cork and Kerry. Examples of this usage from the films include: "Jesus, **boy**, I'm getting fierce hungry just looking at them" (*When Brendan Met Trudy*, 01:05:32, FT2000C), "Jaysus, I was all talk, **boy**" (*The Wind that Shakes the Barley*, 00:40:27, MD1920C), "Ah, 'tis a field worth fighting for, **boy**" (*The*

516) God bless you, **lad**.
   (*Far and Away*, 00:17:33, MDC1890W)

517) Well, **lad**, you took the words right out of me mouth.
   (*Darby O'Gill and the Little People*, 01:29:47, MDOG1800K)

518) Ah, you're a mess, **lad**.
   (*Ordinary Decent Criminal*, 00:09:26, MML1990D)

519) Jaysus, your eyes look atrocious, **lad**.
   (*Angela's Ashes*, 01:18:41, MUP1930L)

520) **Good lad**! There you go, what?
   (*The Snapper*, 00:26:38, MDC1990D)

521) Come on, Joe, there's a **good lad**.
   (*Ryan's Daughter*, 00:25:18, MTR1920W)

The plural form of address, *lads*, is heard very frequently in Irish English and appears widely throughout the film corpus. Examples include:

522) **Lads**, if I see yiz near Janine, I'm not jokin' ya, I'll kill yiz! Okay?
   (*Adam and Paul*, 00:18:04, MW2000D)

523) Do yourselves a favour, **lads**. Tell him!
   (*Mystics*, 00:38:48, MW2000D)

524) Listen, **lads**, when this band is happenin' you'll be fightin' women off.
   (*The Commitments*, 00:16:33, MJR1990D)

Interestingly, this form, which is generally thought to be masculine, can also be used when addressing females[301]. In *Trojan Eddie*, for example, Eddie addresses his young daughters as *lads* on a couple of occasions, even using the terms *lads* and *girls* together in one speech.

525) Go ahead upstairs, **lads**, will yez. Good girls.
   (*Trojan Eddie*, 00:28:20, MTE1990M)

Elsewhere, *lad* or *lads* is not used as a term of address, but rather when referring to someone who is not present, as in the following examples.

526) He's a fine strong **lad**.
   (*Darby O'Gill and the Little People*, 00:04:55, FMS1800K)

527) That **lad** of yours is goin' through hell.
   (*Evelyn*, 00:31:58, MBM1950D)

Field, 00:06:03, MBMC1950W), "Every year, **boy**, without fail" (*Trojan Eddie*, 00:13:16, FM1990M), "It's as close as you'd want to get, **boy**" (*Waking Ned*, 01:04:11, MD2000W).

[301] A similar semantic development has occurred with the American English use of *guys*.

528) If any of our **lads** come in, tell them to stay somewhere else.
(Michael Collins, 00:56:16, MMC1910C)

In total, *lad* or *lads* appear in 39 of the 50 films (78%) [see Table 52], placing them among the most common lexical items in the corpus.

Unusual examples
Share (2003: 184) notes that *lad* can be used with reference to "undifferentiated inanimate objects, usually in terms of grudging affection". There is also evidence of such usage in the film corpus. In the examples below, *lad* refers to a scar and a tree respectively.

529) See that **lad**. I got that climbin' out of the nurses' hostel window and 33 years later Mrs Headmaster thinks it's the sexiest thing about me.
(When Brendan Met Trudy, 00:56:40, MHM2000D)

530) Oh, there's nothing in the sky this **lad** need fear. Or under it neither.
(How Harry Became a Tree, 00:40:35, MH1920WW)

Despite observations by Dolan (2006: 135) and Share (2003: 184) that *the Lad* can be a euphemistic term for cancer; or even for the penis, there are no examples of such meanings in the film corpus.

Share also glosses the diminutive form *ladeen*, describing it as a term of affection (2003: 184). In the example from the film corpus, however, the diminutive form of *lad* does not express affection, but rather is more in keeping with Asián and McCullough's observation of the diminutive often being a term of contempt (1998: 43), as Finbar is speaking disparagingly of what he regards as a bunch of jumped-up soldiers wearing the new army uniforms.

531) These Free State **ladeens** up here are recruiting left, right and centre.
(The Wind that Shakes the Barley, 01:32:05, MF1920C)

The same applies to the use of the term *squireen* to address Red Will Danaher in the example from *The Quiet Man* below, where it is certainly meant by Fahy to be a term of contempt. Indeed, Dolan describes it as such, labelling the term "pejorative" (2006: 225).

532) F-A-H-Y. No 'E', **Squireen** Danaher.
(The Quiet Man, 00:24:10, MF1930W)

It is worth noting at this point that actual diminutive forms with *-een* are very rare in the corpus. The only examples are the aforementioned one from *The Wind that Shakes the Barley* and the ones from *A Very Unlucky Leprechaun* and *The Quiet Man* below.

533) Are you alright **loveen**?
(A Very Unlucky Leprechaun, 00:39:29, MPM1990W)

534) So we formed a little conspiracy, the Reverend Mister and Mrs Playfair, **Michaleen** Oge and, saints forgive us, myself.
(The Quiet Man, 00:49:00, MFL1930W)

Any other lexical items ending in -*een* which appear in the corpus are not diminutive expressions in the strictest sense, but rather diminutive expressions which by now have become lexicalised. After all, in the case of the words *sleveen, shebeen, gombeen* etc., if one were to remove the diminutive ending, what would remain would not be a lexeme.

535) What are you saying over there, Boland, you Dublin **jackeen**[302], ya?
(*Michael Collins*, 00:12:16, MMC1910C)

536) That **sleveen**[303] Kennedy, saying she kidnapped her own children.
(*A Love Divided*, 00:33:07, MA1950WX)

537) You're in front of Aunt Betty's, the finest **sheebeen**[304] in town and your little Katie is inside.
(*The Informer*, 00:54:34, MSP1920D)

538) Here, look at the **gombeen**[305] men, licking their lips already, Damien.
(*The Wind that Shakes the Barley*, 01:31:18, MDa1920D)

539) It's a drop of old **poteen**[306] I found in the bog.
(*Darby O'Gill and the Little People*, 00:36:05, MDOG1800K)

6.3.1.4 *Your man/woman/one*

One of the most common colloquial expressions in Irish English is the use of *your* together with *man, woman* or *one* to make reference to a specific individual, often someone who has already been thematised in the exchange (cf. Dolan 2006: 258 and Hickey 2005: 139). While *your man*[307] is used to refer to males, *your woman* and *your one* both refer to females, *one* being a typical Irish English referent for women[308]. *Your* is usually pronounced [jər], and is often spelled <yer> in the subtitles of these movies or in literary dialect representations of this structure. *Your* does not have a possessive function, and, in most cases, could be replaced by the demonstrative pronoun *that*, except when it is followed by a person's name, as in example 541 from *About Adam* below. In such cases, *your/yer* often serves as a filler until the speaker

---

[302] *Jackeen* is a pejorative term used by non-Dubliners to describe their compatriots from the capital. The label originally described 'a self-assertive Dubliner with pro-British leanings' and is a combination of Jack (the familiar name for John Bull, the personification of England) and the Irish diminutive suffix -*een* or a reference to the small Union Jack flags which were given to children during Queen Victoria's Dublin visit in 1900 (Dolan 2006: 129). As in example 535, the tautological expression *Dublin Jackeen* is often used in Irish English. The equivalent term used by Dubliners to describe Irish people who are not from Dublin is *culchie*, which is possibly derived from 'agricultural' or from the town of Kiltimagh in Co. Mayo "which is regarded as a remote place" (Dolan 2006: 70).
[303] A *sleveen* is 'a sly person, a trickster, a smooth-tongued rogue, a toady, a crooked person' (Dolan 2006: 215).
[304] A *shebeen* is 'an unlicensed liquor-house' (Dolan 2006: 209).
[305] A *gombeen* (-*man*) is 'a usurer, a loan-shark' (Dolan 2006: 111).
[306] *Poteen* is a home-made (illicit) spirit, once distilled from potatoes in a little pot (hence the name), and is distinct from 'parliament whiskey', on which duty has been paid (cf. Dolan 2006: 180).
[307] A similar, but unrelated, expression *your only man* is also used in Irish English and is perhaps most famous from its appearance in Flann O'Brien's poem "A pint of plain is your only man". According to Share, saying something is *your only man* means that it is 'the sine qua non, possessing a unique quality' (2003: 360). The feature is also evident in the film corpus: "The double-entry system is **your only man**. Believe me, Mr Hogan, you'll never regret it. Never" (*Circle of Friends*, 00:13:55, MSW1950D).
[308] The use of *one* in Irish English as a referent to females is discussed on the next page.

can recall the name of the person he is referring to. The use of this structure could potentially pose difficulties for those not familiar with it. An example from *The Van* goes as follows:

> 540) You messed it up for me with **your woman**.
>
> (*The Van*, 01:10:50, ML1990D)

For the uninitiated, the presence of the pronoun *your* in this sentence might suggest that the speaker, Larry, is angry at Bimbo for ruining his chances with Bimbo's lady friend. In reality, however, Larry is referring to a different lady whom he has been chatting up.

In total, *your man*, *your woman* or *your one* appear in 18 of the 50 films (36%) [see Table 53]. Further examples include:

> 541) So, by the time **yer man**, Adam, gets older, you know, it's starting to sink in to him, the significance of this wreck.
>
> (*About Adam*, 01:01:31, MH2000D)

> 542) Who's **your man** there with Billy?
>
> (*Ordinary Decent Criminal*, 00:26:57, MML1990D)

> 543) **Yer woman**, what's her name?
>
> (*When the Sky Falls*, 00:12:19, MDA1990D)

> 544) Lezzers. **Your women**. Them.
>
> (*The Van*, 01:05:57, ML1990D)

> 545) Shirley, come here, listen, you know **yer one** who's preggers, guess who's the da! Mr Burgess!
>
> (*The Snapper*, 00:44:49, FCG1990D)

> 546) Are you **your one** off the telly?
>
> (*Goldfish Memory*, 00:28:32, MTD2000D)

6.3.1.5 *One* as a referent for females

The aforementioned use of *one* to refer to females[309] is quite common in Irish English, and is not restricted to usage in the expression *your one*. In total, it appears in 20 of the 50 films (40%) [see Table 54]. As can be seen in the example below from *The Van*, the equivalent term for males is *fella*, which is also common in other varieties of English. Examples of *one* referring to a female include:

---

[309] Two additional terms often used in Irish English with regard to females are *strap* and *rip*. According to Bliss, *strap*, sometimes spelled *strapp*, means 'whore' and is of unknown origin, but may possibly be related to the Irish *striopach*, the origin of which is also unknown (cf. Bliss 1979: 263). The meaning of *strap* as 'whore' is too strong for modern usage, where the term is generally more synonymous with 'bitch', but can also be used to describe *bold* (i.e. *naughty*) girls. Indeed, this is one of the meanings cited by Dolan, who glosses *strap* as both 'an impudent girl' and 'a slut' (2006: 228) See also Share (2003: 315). The examples from *Widows' Peak* illustrate the possible range of uses. "God Almighty, for a **strap** of an Englishwoman, she'd talk the hind leg off a donkey" (*Widows' Peak*, 01:30:29, FMOH1930M), "Ah, Miss Grubb, why are you tempting me, you bold **strap** you?" (*Widows' Peak*, 00:20:23, FDC1930M). *Rip*, an English dialect term of abuse for a woman, (cf. Dolan 2006: 193 and Share 2003: 270) is also evident in two of the films. "And as for the other **rip**…" (*Widows' Peak*, 01:31:54, FDC1930M), "Oh, oh the **rip**" (*Widows' Peak*, 01:34:03, FDC1930M), "Go in and do what you're supposed to be doing. Ya **rip** ya!" (*Trojan Eddie*, 01:05:33, MGG1990M).

547) You stay away from that **one**.

(*Agnes Browne*, 00:25:04, FAB1960D)

548) You get some old **ones** are cute.

(*Intermission*, 00:42:56, MO2000D)

549) They only want young **ones** and young fellas that'll take those wages and wear the fucking uniforms.

(*The Van*, 00:19:57, ML1990D)

550) Yeah, sure, she's a slut, that **one**.

(*The Snapper*, 00:47:38, FJ1990D)

6.3.1.6 Guard(s)

The use of Irish English terms extends to the way the police are termed in Ireland. Police officers are known as *guards* there, which, according to Dolan, is a partial translation of the term *Garda Síochána* (Irish for "guard of the peace") and also a survival of the earlier official name, *Civic Guard*[310] (2006: 103 and 115). The terms *guard*, *guards*, *garda* and the plural *gardaí* all make appearances in the film corpus, very often in threats to call the police. In total these forms are evident in 17 of the 50 films (34%) [see Table 55].

551) Every villain and **guard** in Ireland will be watchin' ya.

(*Mystics*, 00:22:35, MLA2000D)

552) Now, get out of here before I call the **guard**.

(*Circle of Friends*, 01:28:25, FBH1950D)

553) Leave the bag down or I'm calling the **guards**.

(*Adam and Paul*, 00:25:45, FCO2000D)

554) Out ya go, the pair of ya, before I call the **guards**.

(*This is my Father*, 00:33:33, MOM1930M)

555) Now, lads, if the **Civic Guards** come around asking questions, we were here playing cards all night. Right, lads?

(*The Field*, 01:02:55, MBMC1950W)

556) I will not have the reputation of the **Garda Síochána** brought into disrepute by these shenanigans.

(*Ordinary Decent Criminal*, 00:18:07, MSG1990D)

557) The **Gardaí** will beat the fuckin' shite out of me. You know what they're like with perverts.

(*The General*, 01:42:19, Mga1990D)

---

[310] A further name for the police in Ireland, namely *peelers*, also makes an appearance in the film corpus. Policemen were named *peelers* after Robert Peel, the Chief Secretary for Ireland, who established the Peace Preservation Force in 1814 (cf. Dolan 2006: 174). An example from the corpus is: "The **peelers** aren't fighting back at all" (*The Wind that Shakes the Barley*, 00:54:58, MSB1920C).

6.3.2 Irish English pronunciations which have become lexicalised

6.3.2.1 *Eejit*

A further salient feature of Irish English vocabulary is the lexicalisation of the Irish pronunciations of Standard English words. One of the most well known is the use of *eejit* [ˈiːdʒət] for *idiot*. According to Dolan, "the pronunciation 'eejit' represents an approximation of the way the letters 'd' and 'i' are pronounced in Irish, in such words as 'DIA', sometimes carried over to Hiberno-English in such words as 'odious' [ˈoːdʒəs]" (2006: 83)[311]. He also adds that although *eejit* is the Irish pronunciation of *idiot*, the former is less pejorative than the latter. Below are some examples of the feature, which appears in 26 of the 50 films (52%) [see Table 56].

> 558) Would ya take a look at that **eejit**?
> *(This is my Father*, 00:29:42, MAD1930M)

> 559) If me mates saw me making a pure **eejit** out of meself at the Irish dancing, I'd be disgraced forever.
> *(Angela's Ashes*, 00:49:12, MN1990L)

> 560) He's not in there, you **eejit**!
> *(The Snapper*, 00:48:43, FSC1990D)

> 561) Two **eejits** tried to hold up the bank with a couple of pump guns.
> *(The Commitments*, 01:25:12, MR1990D)

6.3.2.2 *Oul(d)*

The same phenomenon of an Irish English pronunciation of a Standard English term becoming lexicalised is apparent in the words *ould* [aʊld] or *oul* [aʊl] for *old*. These pronunciations can be attributed to the influence of 17th century English (cf. Dolan 2006: 169)[312].

> 562) Lads, will we go to the **ould** dance? Say we will.
> *(Widows' Peak*, 01:01:35, FCG11930M)

> 563) Did you say a prayer for poor **ould** Kitty?
> *(Trojan Eddie*, 00:12:57, FK1990M)

> 564) Then I threw them out. Dirty **oul** things.
> *(Garage*, 00:42:35, MJ2000M)

> 565) This **oul** tree is not frightened of the bite of a storm.
> *(How Harry Became a Tree*, 00:40:28, MH1920WW)

---

[311] The received wisdom of the substratal influence on this pronunciation needs to be examined further, however, as in old-fashioned upper-class English speech the common pronunciation of words like *tremendous*, *hideous*, *tedious*, *medium*, and *India* was with /dʒ/, resulting in the respellings <tremenjus>, <hijjus>, <tejus>, <mejum>, and <Inja> in Kipling's writings, for example (cf. Rose 1997).

[312] A similar phenomenon exists in Scottish English, although according to Drury (2007), a difference exists between the Irish and Scottish pronunciations and spellings of *old*. *Auld* [ɔːld] is the Scottish spelling and rhymes with *called*, whereas the Irish form is *ould* [aʊld] and rhymes with *howled*.

Oul and *ould* are also often used together with the words *one*[313] (sometimes *wan*) and *fellow* (sometimes *fella*) when referring to old people generally, but particularly with regard to a person's parents (cf. Share 2003: 232-3), as in these examples from the corpus:

> 566) His **oul** one won't allow it.
> (*This is my Father*, 00:29:47, MAD21930M)

> 567) Fair play to ya, Christy! Your **oul** fella will never be dead.
> (*My Left Foot*, 01:20:45, MPM1950D)

In total, *oul* or *ould* appear in 31 of the 50 films (62%) [see Table 57], appearing across all periods and settings.

6.3.2.3 Shite

<Shite> [ʃaɪt] is the spelling used to reflect the Irish English pronunciation of the English noun *shit*, meaning 'faeces', or of the verb *shit*, meaning 'to defecate' (cf. Dolan 2006: 210). The term is very often used as an exclamation, and, according to Share, it is more commonly used than its English equivalent in the speech of Irish people (cf. 2003: 290). It should also be noted in this regard that the use of the word *shite* is deemed more socially acceptable than the use of the term *shit*.

> 568) **Shite**!
> (*The Snapper*, 00:44:40, MDC1990D)

> 569) **Shite**, we're late, Bimbo. Hurry up!
> (*The Van*, 00:35:14, ML1990D)

> 570) Go and **shite**!
> (*The Commitments*, 00:20:11, FSR1990D)

> 571) I need to have a **shite**.
> (*Adam and Paul*, 00:38:02, MP2000D)

> 572) I think we scared the **shite** out of her.
> (*Dead Meat*, 00:37:15, MD2000LM)

> 573) I fought for this country, and I look at you sacks of **shite** and I wonder if it was all worthwhile.
> (*A Love Divided*, 01:11:42, MA1950WX)

> 574) I don't want to read any more of his **shite**.
> (*Nora*, 01:08:44, FN1900G)

The film corpus also has an example of *shite* being used as a phrasal verb. The expression *to shite on about something* means 'to talk incessantly about something, usually something that the other person does not want to hear about'.

---

[313] For more on the role of *one* referring to women, see page 145.

575) What are you **shitin' on about**, man?
>
> (*Ordinary Decent Criminal*, 00:23:37, MA1990D)

In total, the word *shite* can be found in 27 of the 50 films (54%) [see Table 58]. The word also makes an appearance as part of the word *gobshite*, which is dealt with separately in the category of swear words and vulgarisms below.

6.3.2.4   *Feck, feckin'* and *fecker*

Feck [fek] and its variants are highly salient features of Irish English and are known as such throughout the English-speaking world. Dolan (2006: 91) cites *feck* as being a euphemism for *fuck* and indeed it is through the exclamations *feck!* and *feck off!* or the intensifier *feckin'* that people are most likely to be familiar with it[314]. However, as with *eejit* above, *feck* is deemed to be a good deal less vulgar than its root. Moreover, it is important to note that while *feck* can be used to replace *fuck* in many circumstances, as can be seen in the examples below, it cannot be used as a synonym for *fuck* in the sense of 'to have sexual intercourse'. Therefore an imaginary sentence like "I fecked her down the alley beside Supermac's" would not make sense in Irish English, or rather it would, but it would have a different meaning, namely 'I threw her down the alley beside Supermac's'. This latter understanding of the term is possible because, as Dolan (2006: 91) and Share (2003: 103-4) point out, *feck* also has the alternative meanings of 'to throw'[315] particularly when referring to 'a game of pitch and toss'. Furthermore, Share (2003: 104) notes that *feck* can act as an alternative for the verb *to steal* and he offers the etymology as "Old English *feccan*, fetch, seek, gain, take, or alternatively Germ. *fegen*, plunder" (Share 2006: 95). However, there is no evidence of such meanings in the film corpus. The forms *fecker* (sometimes shortened to *feck*) – "a term of abuse: perhaps a euphemism for 'fucker'" (Dolan: 2006:91) and *feckin'*, an adjective in the same vein do, however, appear in the movies.

576) Would you **feck** off?
>
> (*Agnes Browne*, 00:35:03, FAB1960D)

577) **Feck** off! Ask Lily to do the stall.
>
> (*The Wind that Shakes the Barley*, 01:35:30, MSB1920C)

578) I wouldn't give that **fecker** the skin of a fart. Do you hear me?
>
> (*Mystics*, 00:30:49, MLA2000D)

579) You're just like him, you drunken **feck**!
>
> (*Angela's Ashes*, 02:02:52, FA1930L)

580) All these **feckin'** questions! Look, I'm just lookin' for a ride, Dermot. I'm not tryin' to join the UN **feckin'** peace-keepin' force!
>
> (*The Matchmaker*, 00:15:03, MTon2000W)

---

[314] Familiarity with this feature outside of Ireland can be attributed to the frequency with which the word was used in the comedy series *Father Ted*, in which *feck* was a catchphrase of one of the protagonists.
[315] Although *feck* generally takes its lead from *fuck*, an interesting reverse example of *fuck* taking on the 'to throw' meaning of *feck* also exists in Irish English. The following is evidence from Conor McPherson's play *Port Authority*: "They were fucking beer cans at each other across the street" (2004: 175).

581) Now, we're all **feckin'** refugees. Amn't I right?
(When Brendan Met Trudy, 00:55:52, MHM2000D)

In total, *feck, feckin'* or *fecker* appears in 15 of the 50 films (30%) [see Table 59]. A reason for this number being lower than perhaps expected could be that an alternative euphemistic form is also in currency in Irish English and also finds its way into films in place of, or in addition to, *feck*. The form in question is *shag*, which will be dealt with below.

6.3.3 Swear words or vulgarisms

A very convenient way of lending "authenticity" to the speech in a film is to include swear words or vulgarisms which are typical of the dialect, as was the case with *shite* and *feck* above. This is evident in the film in the use of terms such as *arse, bollocks, bleedin', shag* and *gobshite* which feature strongly in Irish usage.

6.3.3.1 *Arse*

While the term *arse* is by no means exclusive to Irish English, it is nonetheless a very common lexical feature of the variety, appearing in 27 of the 50 movies[316] (54%) [see Table 60]. It should, of course, be noted that the /r/ is pronounced in Irish English, unlike in RP. Below are just a few examples of the usage of *arse* in the corpus.

582) Oh, so you didn't bother your **arse** finding out?
(When Brendan Met Trudy, 01:21:30, FT2000C)

583) You'd let them go barefoot before you'd get off your **arse**.
(Angela's Ashes, 00:31:46, FA1930L)

584) I was too soft to use the wooden spoon on your **arse** when you were growing up.
(Last of the High Kings, 00:05:41, FMG1970D)

585) I left a bruise on your **arse**, the size of a fucking melon, I'd say.
(Dead Meat, 00:46:40, MD2000LM)

6.3.3.2 *Bollocks/bollix*

As with *arse, bollocks*[317], sometimes spelled *bollix*, is not exclusive to Irish English. It does, however, appear very frequently in the variety and is, thus, worthy of examination. Dolan notes that it can be used as "an expression of anger, or used pejoratively in reference to a stupid person" (2006: 29). It can also be used to indicate that something is rubbish or nonsense, while, on other occasions, it also maintains its original meaning of 'testicles'. Examples of the various uses can be found in the film corpus.

---

[316] One of these appearances is in the form *lickarse*, which is the equivalent of an *ass-kisser* or a *brown-noser* in American English and refers to somebody who tries to gain favour with somebody through flattery or obsequious behaviour. In the example from *A Love Divided*, the *lickarse* is a cat which is purring in order to be let into the building.

[317] According to Dolan (2006: 29), the term comes from the Old English *beallucas*, meaning 'testicles'.

As an expression of anger:

    586) Ah, **bollocks**!
                                          (*Dead Meat*, 00:48:22, MC2000LM)

    587) **Bollocks**, Foxy! I was so looking forward to it.
                                              (*Mystics*, 00:55:20, FS2000D)

As a pejorative reference to a person:

    588) Well, he knew you and he said you're a **bollix**!
                                      (*Agnes Browne*, 01:18:59, MT11960D)

    589) Jeez, you're an awful **bollocks**, Cosgrave. Do you know that?
                                                    (*Nora*, 00:13:45, MG1900D)

As an indication of something being nonsense:

    590) Look, this is **bollocks**, man, I'm tellin' ya!
                                      (*Intermission*, 00:36:13, MG2000D)

    591) This anti-drug shit is all **bollix**. It's just a smoke screen.
                                      (*The General*, 01:01:49, MMC1990D)

    592) That's a load of **bollocks**.
                                      (*Veronica Guerin*, 01:08:23, MJT1990D)

To refer to testicles:

    593) I'll kick the **bollocks** off the both of yiz.
                                      (*This is my Father*, 00:33:16, MK1930M)

    594) I'd bite your **bollix** off, you come near me, you spotty fucker!
                                      (*The Commitments*, 00:28:28, FB1990D)

Additional uses:

The film corpus also shows evidence of different forms of *bollocks* being used as adjectives, as in examples 595-597, and as a verb, as in example 598.

    595) There's nothing wrong with my brain. It's the rest of me that's **bollocksed**.
                                      (*Inside I'm Dancing*, 00:08:19, MT2000D)

    596) And the strain on poor Dave there. Sure, look at him. He's **bollocksed**.
                                      (*Mystics*, 00:06:52, FMK2000D)

    597) The only **bollixin'** thing that's important is what this band's called.
                                      (*The Commitments*, 00:26:07, MJR1990D)

598) My cards are bought by men on their way home from work who give them to their wives, who give them a **bollocking**[318] for leaving the price on the back.
(*Waking Ned*, 00:14:14, FM2000W)

In total, *bollocks* appears in one form or another in 26 of the 50 films (52%) [see Table 61].

6.3.3.3   Bleedin'

While *bleedin'* is also common in British English as a swear word, its use in Ireland, at least based on the evidence in the film corpus, is almost exclusively limited to Dublin, where it appears as an adjective or an adverb. In total, it can be found in 16 of the 50 films (32%) [see Table 62], 15 of which are set in the capital. The remaining example is from *The Magdalene Sisters*, a movie set outside of the city, although the expression itself is used by a Dublin speaker. Given the high frequency of *bleedin'* in Dublin speech, screenwriters setting their film there would be well advised to include this feature in their characters' dialogue. Some examples of usage from the film corpus include:

599) What are youse **bleedin'** lookin' at?
(*The Commitments*, 00:27:28, FN1990D)

600) Jaysus, look at the size of that **bleedin'** dog!
(*The General*, 00:03:11, MYB1960D)

601) I dare ya, I **bleedin'** dare ya!
(*The Snapper*, 00:01:18, FSC1990D)

602) Hey, Tommy, get off the **bleedin'** bike. Come on.
(*Ordinary Decent Criminal*, 00:06:11, FLL1990D)

603) It's written outside the **bleedin'** police station.
(*When the Sky Falls*, 00:47:05, MSgt1990D)

6.3.3.4   Gobshite

Dolan (2006: 110) cites *gobshite* as being a pejorative term for a fool, with its etymology in the English dialect word *gob*, meaning 'mouth', and *shite*, the Irish English term for *shit* (see page 148). Share (2003: 130), on the other hand, attributes the etymology to a mixture of the British dialect *gawby*, *gooby* etc, meaning 'simpleton' or 'fool', and the Irish English term *shite*. Whatever the etymology, *gobshite* is evident in 16 of the 50 films (32%) [see Table 63].

604) Shut up, ya **gobshite**!
(*The Commitments*, 01:11:51, MD1990D)

605) And you, **gobshite**, you wash them dishes when you're finished!
(*The Snapper*, 01:07:05, MDC1990D)

606) This **gobshite** is the Minister for Education.
(*Evelyn*, 00:29:53, MLB1950D)

---

[318] This usage meaning 'to reprimand or tell someone off severely' is also listed in the OED (s.v. bollock, *v*. 2).

607) You plugged him, you little Free State **gobshite**!
(Michael Collins, 00:05:15, MMC1910C)

6.3.3.5   *Shag, shaggin'* **and** *shagger*

As mentioned above, *shag* shares the same function as *feck* in that it is a euphemism for *fuck*. Unlike *feck*, however, it can mean 'to have sexual intercourse' (cf. Dolan 2006: 208), as is also clear from examples 613-615 below. *Shag* and related forms appear in 10 of the 50 films (20%) [see Table 64].

608) **Shag** off, ya oul bollix.
(The Nephew, 00:08:16, MF1990D)

609) Just **shag** off, the pair of you.
(Far and Away, 00:04:33, MJD1890W)

610) You could have **shaggin'** killed me!
(High Spirits, 00:24:53, MDMC1980W)

611) Where's the rest of that **shaggin'** section?
(The Wind that Shakes the Barley, 00:15:00, MF1920C)

612) Let us all join our voices, all of us that is, except that ignorant crowd of **shaggers**, carrying on and canoodling down there in the back.
(Rat, 01:07:04, MFr2000M)

613) I'd **shag** the elephant man, before I'd let him near me again.
(The Snapper, 00:07:20, FJ1990D)

614) Did ya just catch Dempsey **shagging** his dog again?
(When the Sky Falls, 00:46:00, MSh1990D)

615) Ok. Do hurry, though. I'm dying for a **shag**.
(Mystics, 00:52:10, FS2000D)

6.3.4 Adjectives/adverbs with meanings different to those of Standard English

A number of adjectives or adverbs used in Irish English have different meanings than they do in the standard variety. Examples include *grand, bold* and *desperate*.

6.3.4.1   *Grand*

A renowned feature of Irish English is the use of the word *grand* as a general term of approval meaning 'fine' or 'splendid' (cf. Dolan 2006: 114 and Hickey 2005: 135). It can be employed as an adjective or an adverb and is to be found throughout the country. Indeed, it appears in 42 of the 50 films (84%) [see Table 65], making it the most common of the typically Irish English lexical items in the films.

616) **Grand** soft day, girls!
(Circle of Friends, 00:05:03, FMH1950D)

617) No, thanks. I'm **grand**.

(*The Dead*, 00:13:52, FMM1900D)

618) No buts, you'll be **grand**.

(*A Love Divided*, 00:14:00, MFR1950WX)

619) I've a **grand** bottle of whiskey there.

(*Dead Meat*, 00:59:38, MC2000LM)

620) Oh, you're doing **grand**. **Grand**.

(*Waking Ned*, 00:46:35, MJ2000W)

6.3.4.2   Bold

Bold, which in Standard English means 'courageous', has the primary meaning of 'naughty', 'mischievous', 'impudent' in Irish English (cf. Dolan 2006: 28), although the Standard English meaning can also be carried over into Irish English, but then the word is generally spelled <bould> and pronounced [baʋld][319]. Examples of the different uses and pronunciations are evident in *How Harry Became a Tree*. In the first example, *bold* means 'naughty', while, in the second, Gus is described as 'brave'.

621) What's going to happen to you and me if **bold** Gus Maloney kills your Daddy?

(*How Harry Became a Tree*, 01:11:34, FM1920WW)

622) And how's the **bould** Gus, and the new daughter-in-law?

(*How Harry Became a Tree*, 00:42:19, FOW1920WW)

Other cases of this Irish use of *bold* meaning 'naughty' are evident in the following examples:

623) **Bold** and cunning they are, but I'm up to them.

(*Darby O'Gill and the Little People*, 00:18:39, MDOG1800K)

624) Are you being **bold**, young lady?

(*Evelyn*, 00:15:10, FSrB1950D)

625) It's a **bold** one you are. And who gave you leave to be kissing me?

(*The Quiet Man*, 00:31:00, FMK1930W)

626) Miss Grubb, you **bold** thing, you're taking us home.

(*Widows' Peak*, 00:02:35, FDC1930M)

Bold meaning 'naughty' etc. appears in 6 of the 50 films (12%) [see Table 66], while the Irish English alternative *bould* conveying the standard English meaning 'brave' appears in only 1 of the 50 (2%).

---

[319] There is, however, also an example in the film corpus of *bold* being used with both the Standard English meaning and pronunciation: "Well, that's a **bold** stroke and no mistake, Maestro" (*A Man of No Importance*, 00:17:54, MCB1960D).

6.3.4.3 *Desperate*

Just like *bold* above, *desperate* has more than one meaning in Irish English. In addition to the standard meaning of 'having lost or abandoned hope' (OED: s.v. desperate, *adj.* A I 1), *desperate* has the Irish meaning of something being 'bad', 'terrible' or 'awful' (cf. Share 2003: 82). There are instances of *desperate* being used with the latter meaning in 12 of the 50 (24%) [see Table 67].
Examples include:

627) Isn't it **desperate?**[320]

(*Rat*, 00:05:17, FD2000D)

628) Oh, landlord, you're a **desperate**[321] man.

(*Ryan's Daughter*, 00:41:14, MP1920W)

629) It must be a **desperate** thing to be a doctor.

(*Circle of Friends*, 00:18:55, FBH1950D)

630) During August, the midges in the Highlands are **desperate**.

(*The Dead*, 00:54:47, FMM1900D)

631) You're a bit of a shite aren't you? It'd be a **desperate** party anyway.

(*When Brendan Met Trudy*, 00:06:39, FT2000C)

6.3.5 Summary of findings for lexical items

As was the case with the Top 10 discourse features, most of the Top 10 lexical items are less likely to occur in other dialects[322] than are the Top 10 grammar features, and thus they too can be seen as more likely to lend a more typically Irish air to a film. Unlike for the grammar and discourse features, for which trends were less obvious, the field of lexicon displayed some very striking findings. The most obvious of those is that swear words such as *feck*, *shite*, *arse*, *gobshite* and *shag* did not occur in films produced prior to 1988. This could be due to the aforementioned sensitivity towards swearing due to a fear of the film censor's scissors. Interestingly, those films set pre-1980 but produced since then regularly contain examples of the aforementioned swear words. Another trend related to period is that, again, those films produced pre-1988 do not feature the terms *ma, mam, mammy* or *da*. Instead the terms *mother* and *father* are used. This trend is most unusual, because the aforementioned Irish English terms were certainly used in Ireland in the past. Again, it is noticeable that in films made post 1988, but set in the past, the terms *ma, da* etc. very often occur. This trend also applies for the expressions *yer man, yer woman, yer one* and *bleedin'*, the last of which only occurs in Dublin speech.

---

[320] The realisation of *desperate* as ['dɛsprə] in this example from *Rat* reflects a typical phonetic reduction in Dublin English. According to Hickey (2005: 140), this pronunciation has even been lexicalised in that variety.

[321] From the context it is clear that the speaker is mockingly reprimanding the landlord, Mr Ryan, thus giving the word *desperate* its Irish English meaning.

[322] However, as already pointed out, *arse, bollocks* and *lad* are all also found outside of Ireland.

Top 10 lexical items

Feature	% of films which display the feature
Grand	84
Lad(s)	78
Ma, Mam, Mammy	74
Oul(d)	62
Shite	54
Arse	54
Eejit	52
Bollocks	52
Da	48
One for female	40

At this point it should be noted that although the liberal sprinkling of local lexical items adds greatly to the "Irishness" of a film, screenwriters also need to realise that the use of such terms may also serve a different function and, thus, could potentially be counterproductive. Commenting on this issue in literature, Paulin notes that a writer who employs region-specific terms "will create a form of closed, secret communication with readers who come from the same region. This will express something very near to a familiar relationship because every family has its hoard of relished words which express its members' sense of kinship. These words act as a kind of secret sign and serve to exclude the outside world" (1984: 191).

In order to avoid excluding outsiders completely, writers therefore need to strike a balance by choosing words which are exclusive, in so far as they are not used by non-Irish people, yet, at the same time, inclusive, in that non-Irish people are familiar with them[323]. In this regard, the choice of well-known words like *feck*, *grand*, *shite*, *eejit* etc., which Irish people use, but which non-Irish people know, serves the dual function of ensuring that the film language sounds that little bit more Irish to both Irish and non-Irish audiences alike.

Further testament to the fact that filmmakers try to be accommodating to their audience with regard to local expressions or terms is evident in the explanations which sometimes follow the use of Irish words in film. In *The Quiet Man*, for example, John Wayne's character says a line, which contains just such an explanation.

---

[323] Terms which are not familiar to outsiders pose possible comprehension difficulties, and not only for other native speakers of English. There is the additional problem of translating them for foreign language subtitles or dubbing. Renagh Holohan of *The Irish Times* has commented on this issue with regard to French subtitles for the Irish movie *I Went Down*. "A tirade of traditional exclamation ending with "B*****ks" was translated as "a rather wimpish "Mon Dieu!" and the French audience was informed "that one character said 'tu es un joueur de footbal', when in English he had described him as a 'head-the-ball'" (Holohan 1998). Speakers of Irish English, will recognise the problem with the translation, as, in Irish English, a *head-the-ball* is 'a crazy, happy-go-lucky sort of person' (Dolan 2006: 120) and not a footballer. For more on issues of dubbing and subtitling, see Herbst (1994), Maier (1997), Baker and Hochel (1998) and Gottlieb (1998).

632) I'll tell you why, Michaleen Oge Flynn, young small Michael Flynn, who used to wipe my runny nose when I was a kid, because I'm Sean Thornton and I was born in that little cottage over there, and I've come home and home I'm gonna stay.

(*The Quiet Man*, 00:06:55, MST1950US)

As MacHale has observed, Michaleen's name "has been given a full literal translation for the benefit of non-Irish speakers" (2000: 65). Later in the same film there is a similar instance of a translation for the benefit of a non Irish-speaking audience, when Michaleen utters the line "Will ya listen then and not be interruptin' the shaughraun, the matchmaker." (*The Quiet Man*, 00:36:30, MMF1930W) (cf. MacHale 2000: 105).

A comparable example is evident in *Darby O'Gill and the Little People*, when the *cóiste bodhair* appears. Darby says: "It's the cóiste bodhair, the death coach, send it away." (*Darby O'Gill and the Little People*, 01:22:39, MDOG1800K), conveniently adding the English translation for an international audience. It should be noted that of all the films in the corpus, this one has the highest percentage of Irish in it (the leprechauns speak a good deal of Irish amongst themselves and, in fits of anger, both Darby and King Brian use Irish curses). However, apart from this example of translation, they are not commented on as they are not crucial to understanding the story.

This practice of translation and/or explanation is familiar from other forms of literary dialect. For example, Amador Moreno comments on the insertion of parenthetical translations directly into the English texts in Patrick MacGill's novels for the benefit of non-Irish readers and she offers the following example: "They had reached a stile, and far in front the soft *caishin* (path) wound on by rock and rath across the broad expanse of moor" (*The Rat Pit*, narrator, p.98) (Amador Moreno 2006: 224). It goes without saying, however, that the use of Irish or Irish English terms followed by a Standard English explanation or translation can be a very awkward device, particularly in film, as rather than adding to the authenticity of the speech, it adds an additional layer of artificiality, as in real life Irish people would not translate such terms for each other.

6.4 Results

Although findings for the individual features have already been summarised and tables of the ten most common grammar, discourse and lexical features have been provided at the end of each section, the following gives a further summary of results based on the general trends in the corpus. Thus, rather than focusing on features up close, observing, for example, that the lexical item *bleedin'* appeared almost solely in films set in Dublin and only in those made in the last two decades, this part of the study will zoom out and explore general trends regarding the representation of Irish English in the films.

To that end, I have compiled the total frequency numbers of the different features of Irish English appearing in the films according to the year of production, the year in which the films were set, the locale of the setting, and according to whether they were Irish or Irish-related productions. By doing so, the films can be analysed diachronically, synchronically and regionally, as well as from the perspective of whether they were Irish or non-Irish productions. The findings are as follows:

The year of production (Table VII) does not appear to have any visible influence on the frequency of use of Irish English features, i.e. there is no indication that the total amount of Irish English features used has deteriorated or increased in any systematic way over time. Instead, the distribution of features appears to be quite random and thus it is possible, for example, for a film which contains 8 features (*A Very Unlucky Leprechaun*) to appear next to a film with 42 features (*The General*) from the same year.

The same lack of an obvious trend applies to the year in which a film is set (Table VIII). Again, as was the case above, random films occasionally display a very high or very low number of features, but these appear to be anomalies, which can generally be explained by the films either featuring large amounts of dialogue, thus increasing the likelihood of features appearing (cf. *Adam and Paul*, *Agnes Browne*, *The Snapper*), or by the fact that the amount of dialogue, at least that from Southern Irish English speakers, is very low (cf. *A Very Unlucky Leprechaun* and *Song for a Raggy Boy* in which the majority of the dialogue comes from American or Northern Irish characters respectively). Thus, the hypothesis that supraregionalisation, globalisation or the influence of the media might have led to an overall decline in the use of Irish English features over time is unfounded. What is more, the counterargument that the aforementioned factors may have even awakened a sense of pride in Irish English as a badge of Irishness and, thus, led to the retention of more dialect features is also unsupported by the evidence in the film corpus.

The locale of the setting of the films (Table IX), however, does appear to play a role in determining the overall number of features in a film, with more features appearing on average in the 25 films set in Dublin (30.16 features per film) than in the 25 which are set outside of the capital (23.88). One could, of course, argue that the inclusion of features which are generally associated with Dublin English, such as *yiz*, *youse*, *bleedin'*, and the use of *but* and *what* as tags, may have inflated the figures for the films set in Dublin. However, even if the numbers for these "Dublin" features were to be omitted from the calculations, the result would still be that films set in the capital have approximately 4 more features on average than those set outside the Pale. These findings are quite surprising, as the notion of "rural Ireland as real Ireland", as outlined in Chapter 3, would suggest that Irish English features would actually be more likely to occur outside of the capital city. Surprising as they are, these results can, nonetheless, be attributed to the fact that many of the films set in Dublin are comedies, which typically feature large amounts of dialogue, thus increasing the likelihood for features to occur. Examples include *The Snapper*, *The Van*, *The Commitments*, *Rat*, *Mystics*, *Agnes Browne*, *Intermission* and *Adam and Paul*, all of which have 35 or more features. In contrast, many of those films set outside the capital are concerned with the notion of tourists coming to Ireland and these non-Irish characters account for a great portion of the speech time in the movie, thus reducing the amount of time attributed to Irish English speech. The two most extreme examples of this are *High Spirits*, with 10 features and *A Very Unlucky Leprechaun*, with 8.

The final division of the films into Irish and Irish-related productions (Tables X and XI) reveals that there is very little difference with regard to the frequency of feature occurrence in the two categories, with Irish films displaying an average of 27.38 features per movie versus the Irish-related rate of 26.31. These findings show that although one might have expected Irish films to contain considerably more features than those from Britain or Hollywood, this is not the case.

Table VII

Films ordered according to the year of their production	Number of Features
The Informer (1935)	28
The Quiet Man (1952)	26
Darby O'Gill and the Little People (1959)	33
Ryan's Daughter (1970)	27
The Dead (1987)	16
High Spirits (1988)	10
My Left Foot (1989)	29
The Field (1990)	20
The Commitments (1991)	36
Far and Away (1992)	15
The Snapper (1993)	42
Into the West (1993)	26
A Man of No Importance (1994)	30
Widows' Peak (1994)	33
Circle of Friends (1995)	25
Last of the High Kings (1996)	25
The Van (1996)	38
Michael Collins (1996)	22
Trojan Eddie (1996)	31
The Matchmaker (1997)	25
The Nephew (1997)	26
This is my Father (1998)	31
Waking Ned (1998)	30
The General (1998)	42
A Very Unlucky Leprechaun (1998)	8
A Love Divided (1999)	24
Agnes Browne (1999)	41
Angela's Ashes (1999)	31
When the Sky Falls (2000)	31
About Adam (2000)	21
Ordinary Decent Criminal (2000)	35
When Brendan Met Trudy (2000)	20
Nora (2001)	25
Rat (2001)	40
How Harry Became a Tree (2001	35
The Magdalene Sisters (2002)	24
Mystics (2002)	36
Evelyn (2002)	30
Intermission (2003)	35
Song for a Raggy Boy (2003)	9
Veronica Guerin (2003)	27
Goldfish Memory (2003)	17
The Boys and Girl from County Clare (2003)	18
Cowboys and Angels (2003)	15
Adam and Paul (2004)	38
Dead Meat (2004)	20
Inside I'm Dancing (2004)	24
Irish Jam (2004)	24
The Wind that Shakes the Barley (2006)	27
Garage (2007)	30

Table VIII

	Films ordered according to the period they are set in	Number of features
1800-1900	Darby O'Gill and the Little People (1959)	33
	Far and Away (1992)	15
1900-1910	The Dead (1987)	16
	Nora (2001)	25
1920-1930	Ryan's Daughter (1970)	27
	Michael Collins (1996)	22
	The Informer (1935)	28
	The Wind that Shakes the Barley (2006)	27
	How Harry Became a Tree (2001)	35
1930-1940	Widows' Peak (1994)	33
	The Quiet Man (1952)	26
	This is my Father (1998)	31
	Song for a Raggy Boy (2003)	9
1950-1960	Circle of Friends (1995)	25
	My Left Foot (1989)	29
	The Field (1990)	20
	Angela's Ashes (1999)	31
	A Love Divided (1999)	24
	Evelyn (2002)	30
1960-1970	Agnes Browne (1999)	41
	The Magdalene Sisters (2002)	24
	A Man of No Importance (1994)	30
	The Boys and Girl from County Clare (2003)	18
1970-1980	Last of the High Kings (1996)	25
1980-1990	High Spirits (1988)	10
	The Commitments (1991)	36
1990-2000	The Snapper (1993)	42
	Into the West (1993)	26
	The Van (1996)	38
	Trojan Eddie (1996)	31
	The Matchmaker (1997)	25
	The Nephew (1997)	26
	Waking Ned (1998)	30
	A Very Unlucky Leprechaun (1998)	8
	The General (1998)	42
	Ordinary Decent Criminal (2000)	35
	When the Sky Falls (2000)	31
	Veronica Guerin (2003)	27
2000-	About Adam (2000)	21
	When Brendan Met Trudy (2000)	20
	Rat (2001)	40
	Mystics (2002)	36
	Intermission (2003)	35
	Goldfish Memory (2003)	17
	Cowboys and Angels (2003)	15
	Adam and Paul (2004)	38
	Dead Meat (2004)	20
	Inside I'm Dancing (2004)	24
	Irish Jam (2004)	24
	Garage (2007)	30

Table IX

	Films ordered according to the locale they are set in	Number of Features
Dublin	The Informer (1935)	28
	Michael Collins (1996)	22
	The Dead (1987)	16
	Agnes Browne (1999)	41
	Evelyn (2002)	30
	My Left Foot (1989)	29
	A Man of No Importance (1994)	30
	Last of the High Kings (1996)	25
	The Snapper (1993)	42
	Into the West (1993)	26
	The Commitments (1991)	36
	The Van (1996)	38
	The General (1998)	42
	Ordinary Decent Criminal (2000)	35
	When the Sky Falls (2000)	31
	Veronica Guerin (2003)	27
	About Adam (2000)	21
	When Brendan Met Trudy (2000)	20
	Rat (2001)	40
	Mystics (2002)	36
	Intermission (2003)	35
	Adam and Paul (2004)	38
	Goldfish Memory (2003)	17
	Inside I'm Dancing (2004)	24
	Nora (2001)	25
Wexford	A Love Divided (1999)	24
Wicklow	How Harry Became a Tree (2001)	35
Midlands	This is my Father (1998)	31
	Circle of Friends (1995)	25
	Widows' Peak (1994)	33
	The Magdalene Sisters (2002)	24
	Song for a Raggy Boy (2003)	9
	Trojan Eddie (1996)	31
	Garage (2007)	30
Kerry	Far and Away (1992)	15
	Ryan's Daughter (1970)	27
	Darby O'Gill and the Little People (1959)	33
Clare	The Boys and Girl from County Clare (2003)	18
Limerick	Angela's Ashes (1999)	31
	Cowboys and Angels (2003)	15
Cork	The Wind that Shakes the Barley (2006)	27
	The Nephew (1997)	26
Leitrim	Dead Meat (2004)	20
(unspecified)	The Field (1990)	20
	The Quiet Man (1952)	26
	A Very Unlucky Leprechaun (1998)	8
	The Matchmaker (1997)	25
	High Spirits (1988)	10
	Waking Ned (1998)	30
	Irish Jam (2004)	24

Table X

Irish films	Number of features
My Left Foot (1989)	*29*
The Field (1990)	*20*
The Commitments (1991)	*36*
Into the West (1993)	*26*
A Man of No Importance (1994)	*30*
Circle of Friends (1995)	*25*
Last of the High Kings (1996)	*25*
The Van (1996)	*38*
Michael Collins (1996)	*22*
Trojan Eddie (1996)	*31*
The Nephew (1997)	*26*
The General (1998)	*42*
A Very Unlucky Leprechaun (1998)	*8*
A Love Divided (1999)	*24*
Agnes Browne (1999)	*41*
Angela's Ashes (1999)	*31*
When the Sky Falls (2000)	*32*
About Adam (2000)	*21*
Ordinary Decent Criminal (2000)	*35*
When Brendan Met Trudy (2000)	*20*
Nora (2001)	*25*
Rat (2001)	*40*
How Harry Became a Tree (2001)	*35*
Mystics (2002)	*36*
Intermission (2003)	*35*
Song for a Raggy Boy (2003)	*9*
Veronica Guerin (2003)	*27*
Goldfish Memory (2003)	*17*
The Boys and Girl from County Clare (2003)	*18*
Cowboys and Angels (2003)	*15*
Inside I'm Dancing (2004)	*24*
Adam and Paul (2004)	*38*
Dead Meat (2004)	*20*
Garage (2007)	*30*

Table XI

Irish-related films	Number of features
The Informer (1935)	28
The Quiet Man (1952)	26
Darby O'Gill and the Little People (1959)	33
Ryan's Daughter (1970)	27
The Dead (1987)	16
High Spirits (1988)	10
Far and Away (1992)	15
The Snapper (1993)	42
Widows' Peak (1994)	33
The Matchmaker (1997)	25
This is my Father (1998)	31
Waking Ned (1998)	30
Evelyn (2002)	30
The Magdalene Sisters (2002)	24
Irish Jam (2004)	24
The Wind that Shakes the Barley (2006)	27

As we have seen, only one of the tables above, Table IX, displayed any sort of noticeable trend, namely that there were more features on average in films set in Dublin than there were in those set elsewhere. Otherwise, there were no obvious patterns in the frequency of the *total numbers* of Irish English features in the film corpus.

Seeing as this was the case, I deemed it important to examine the frequency of the *types* of features which appeared in the movies to ascertain whether there was a pattern there. By doing this, I could examine, for example, whether the discourse features were more frequent percentagewise than the grammar or lexical features, whether perhaps particular types of feature were more frequent in Irish, rather than in non-Irish, films, or whether there were trends in the usage of these features over time. In order to answer such questions, it was first of all necessary to break the total number of feature occurrences down into their constituent parts of grammar, discourse and lexical features, as can be seen in Table XII.

However, if one were to consider only the *actual numbers* for each category, as they are in Table XII, this would provide a skewed picture of the findings, as in the majority of the films the total number of grammar features is invariably higher than that for both discourse markers and lexical features. This is due to the simple fact that, in total, more grammar features were examined. Therefore, rather than looking at the *actual numbers* of feature appearances, it is more appropriate to look at *the percentage* of the possible[324] grammar, discourse and lexical features in each of the individual films in order to discover which types of feature were employed most frequently in a particular film. By subdividing the features in this way, one can compare like with like, regardless of the actual number of features present. This methodology is best illustrated with an example from the corpus. A film such as *The General*, for example, which displays a total of 42 features of Irish English, can therefore be described as having 22 of a possible 39 grammar features (56.41%), 7 of a possible 10

---

[324] "Possible" here refers to the 67 features which were the focus of this study. These were divided into 39 morphosyntactic, 10 discourse and 18 lexical features. Of course, it would have been "possible" in the strictest sense of the word to have found other features.

discourse features (70%), and 13 of a possible 18 lexical features (72.22%), while *A Very Unlucky Leprechaun*, which contains only 8 features in total, can be seen to have 5 of a possible 39 grammar features (12.82%), 2 of a possible 10 discourse features (20%) and 1 of a possible 18 lexical features (5.56%). These findings show that, although the number of grammar features in both films is ostensibly the highest, the type of features which were best represented in each case were actually discourse features. Having conducted similar calculations for all of the films, I compiled Tables XIII-XVI, which, like Tables VII-XI, reflect the year of production, the year the film is set, the setting and whether the film is an Irish or Irish-related production.

The first trend which can be observed in these tables is that, compared to the frequency of discourse and lexical features, the percentage of possible grammar features is generally lowest. If one looks at the films from the perspective of when they were produced (Table XIII), then this is particularly evident that the percentage of grammar features was highest in only 5 of the last 30 films made. It would be tempting to conclude from these findings that non-standard grammar features have become less frequent over time. However, that is not really the case. The truth is that many of the later films actually contain just as many grammar features as did earlier productions, but that nowadays the numbers of discourse and lexical features have simply increased[325], thus changing the relative frequency. In this regard, it is also worth noting that the relative percentage of lexical features in earlier films is automatically lower due to the fact that many of the swear words included in my lexical items list (*arse*, *shite* and *feck*) did not appear in films produced before 1989, perhaps due to censorship or a sense of propriety on the part of the filmmakers. However, in the case of films produced after 1989, but set in the past, such as *How Harry Became a Tree* or *This is my Father*, such terms appear and thus the relative percentage of lexical items in these films increases accordingly. This can be best seen in Table XIV, in which the films are ordered according to the period in which they are set.

Apart from that, Table XIV does not display any other obvious patterns, thus disproving the theory that the distribution of features might differ if one were to compare the year of production with the year in which the film is set.

Whereas Table IX above had shown that more features occurred, on average, in films set in Dublin than in those set elsewhere, Table XV, which also shows results according to where films are set, does not prove quite so insightful. The only apparent trend relating to feature type is that the percentage of lexical features is highest in almost two thirds of the films set in Dublin. Aside from that, no real pattern is apparent, with grammar features, for example, not proving to be any more likely to dominate along the west coast than in Dublin.

With regard to Irish versus Irish-related productions (Tables XVI and XVII), it is noticeable that discourse markers rarely dominate in the latter, whereas in 5 of the 7 most recent Irish films they were the features with the highest relative frequency. This trend was already hinted at earlier in the book, with discourse markers such as *come here* and *come here to me* rarely occurring in Irish-related movies. It should be noted again, however, that while discourse features may, proportionally, be the most frequent features in recent Irish films, this

---

[325] Indeed, the percentage of lexical features is highest in half of all the films in the corpus.

does not mean that there are actually more of them in contemporary films. They are only more frequent relative to the grammar or lexical features.

On the whole, the analysis of the features from a synchronic, diachronic and geographic perspective proved to be rather unsatisfactory, with no very obvious trends in feature usage over time or according to location. The same applied with regard to whether the films were Irish or Irish-related productions, so one can conclude that the language in the films in the corpus is actually quite homogenous. Any deviations from this homogeneity can be attributed more to methodological choices than to actual trends in language usage.

Table XII

Films ordered according to the year of their production	Number of grammar features	Number of discourse features	Number of lexical features	Total number of features
The Informer (1935)	21	4	3	28
The Quiet Man (1952)	19	4	3	26
Darby O'Gill & the Little People (1959)	23	5	5	33
Ryan's Daughter (1970)	22	2	3	27
The Dead (1987)	10	2	4	16
High Spirits (1988)	3	3	4	10
My Left Foot (1989)	17	3	9	29
The Field (1990)	14	2	4	20
The Commitments (1991)	19	5	12	36
Far and Away (1992)	8	2	5	15
The Snapper (1993)	20	7	15	42
Into the West (1993)	17	4	5	26
A Man of No Importance (1994)	16	4	10	30
Widows' Peak (1994)	22	4	7	33
Circle of Friends (1995)	15	3	7	25
Last of the High Kings (1996)	10	5	10	25
The Van (1996)	18	8	12	38
Michael Collins (1996)	10	5	7	22
Trojan Eddie (1996)	16	4	11	31
The Matchmaker (1997)	14	2	9	25
The Nephew (1997)	17	3	6	26
This is my Father (1998)	14	6	11	31
Waking Ned (1998)	17	3	10	30
The General (1998)	22	7	13	42
A Very Unlucky Leprechaun (1998)	5	2	1	8
A Love Divided (1999)	11	4	9	24
Agnes Browne (1999)	24	5	12	41
Angela's Ashes (1999)	16	4	11	31
When the Sky Falls (2000)	15	4	12	31
About Adam (2000)	12	2	7	21
Ordinary Decent Criminal (2000)	15	5	15	35
When Brendan Met Trudy (2000)	6	4	10	20
Nora (2001)	15	4	6	25
Rat (2001)	25	5	10	40
How Harry Became a Tree (2001)	20	4	11	35
The Magdalene Sisters (2002)	11	3	10	24
Mystics (2002)	22	2	12	36
Evelyn (2002)	12	6	12	30
Intermission (2003)	17	6	12	35
Song for a Raggy Boy (2003)	6	1	2	9
Veronica Guerin (2003)	11	5	11	27
Goldfish Memory (2003)	4	5	8	17
The Boys & Girl from Co. Clare (2003)	10	3	5	18
Cowboys and Angels (2003)	9	3	3	15
Adam and Paul (2004)	23	6	9	38
Dead Meat (2004)	10	4	6	20
Inside I'm Dancing (2004)	12	3	9	24
Irish Jam (2004)	14	1	9	24
The Wind that Shakes the Barley (2006)	16	4	7	27
Garage (2007)	21	4	5	30

Table XIII

Films ordered according to the year of their production	% of possible grammar features	% of possible discourse features	% of possible lexical features	% of total possible features
The Informer (1935)	53.85	40.00	16.67	41.79
The Quiet Man (1952)	48.72	40.00	16.67	38.81
Darby O'Gill & the Little People (1959)	58.97	50.00	27.78	49.25
Ryan's Daughter (1970)	56.41	20.00	16.67	40.30
The Dead (1987)	25.64	20.00	22.22	23.89
High Spirits (1988)	7.69	30.00	22.22	14.93
My Left Foot (1989)	43.59	30.00	50.00	43.28
The Field (1990)	35.90	20.00	22.22	29.85
The Commitments (1991)	48.72	50.00	66.67	53.73
Far and Away (1992)	20.51	20.00	27.78	22.39
The Snapper (1993)	51.28	70.00	83.33	62.69
Into the West (1993)	43.59	40.00	27.78	38.81
A Man of No Importance (1994)	41.03	40.00	55.56	44.78
Widows' Peak (1994)	56.41	40.00	38.89	49.25
Circle of Friends (1995)	40.54	30.00	38.89	37.31
Last of the High Kings (1996)	25.64	50.00	55.56	37.31
The Van (1996)	46.15	80.00	66.67	56.72
Michael Collins (1996)	25.64	50.00	38.89	32.84
Trojan Eddie (1996)	41.03	40.00	61.11	46.27
The Matchmaker (1997)	35.90	20.00	50.00	37.31
The Nephew (1997)	43.59	30.00	33.33	38.81
This is my Father (1998)	35.90	60.00	61.11	46.27
Waking Ned (1998)	43.59	30.00	55.56	44.78
The General (1998)	56.41	70.00	72.22	62.69
A Very Unlucky Leprechaun (1998)	12.82	20.00	5.56	11.94
A Love Divided (1999)	28.21	40.00	50.00	35.82
Agnes Browne (1999)	61.54	50.00	66.67	61.19
Angela's Ashes (1999)	41.03	40.00	61.11	46.27
When the Sky Falls (2000)	38.46	40.00	66.67	46.27
About Adam (2000)	30.77	20.00	38.89	31.34
Ordinary Decent Criminal (2000)	38.46	50.00	83.33	52.24
When Brendan Met Trudy (2000)	15.38	40.00	55.56	29.85
Nora (2001)	38.46	40.00	33.33	37.31
Rat (2001)	64.10	50.00	55.56	59.70
How Harry Became a Tree (2001)	51.28	40.00	61.11	52.24
The Magdalene Sisters (2002)	28.21	30.00	55.56	35.82
Mystics (2002)	56.41	20.00	66.67	53.73
Evelyn (2002)	30.77	60.00	66.67	44.78
Intermission (2003)	43.59	60.00	66.67	52.24
Song for a Raggy Boy (2003)	15.38	10.00	11.11	13.43
Veronica Guerin (2003)	28.21	50.00	61.11	40.30
Goldfish Memory (2003)	10.26	50.00	44.44	25.37
The Boys & Girl from Co. Clare (2003)	25.64	30.00	27.78	26.87
Cowboys and Angels (2003)	23.08	30.00	16.67	22.38
Adam and Paul (2004)	58.97	60.00	50.00	56.72
Dead Meat (2004)	25.64	40.00	33.33	29.85
Inside I'm Dancing (2004)	30.77	30.00	50.00	35.82
Irish Jam (2004)	35.90	10.00	50.00	35.82
The Wind that Shakes the Barley (2006)	41.03	40.00	38.89	40.30
Garage (2007)	53.85	40.00	27.78	44.78

Table XIV

Films ordered according to the period they are set in	% of possible grammar features	% of possible discourse features	% of possible lexical features	% of total possible features
Darby O'Gill & the Little People (1959)	58.97	50.00	27.78	49.25
Far and Away (1992)	20.51	20.00	27.78	22.39
The Dead (1987)	25.64	20.00	22.22	23.89
Nora (2001)	38.46	40.00	33.33	37.31
Ryan's Daughter (1970)	56.41	20.00	16.67	40.30
Michael Collins (1996)	25.64	50.00	38.89	32.84
The Informer (1935)	53.85	40.00	16.67	41.79
The Wind that Shakes the Barley (2006)	41.03	40.00	38.89	40.30
How Harry Became a Tree (2001)	51.28	40.00	61.11	52.24
Widows' Peak (1994)	56.41	40.00	38.89	49.25
The Quiet Man (1952)	48.72	40.00	16.67	38.81
This is my Father (1998)	35.90	60.00	61.11	46.27
Song for a Raggy Boy (2003)	15.38	10.00	11.11	13.43
Circle of Friends (1995)	40.54	30.00	38.89	37.31
My Left Foot (1989)	43.59	30.00	50.00	43.28
The Field (1990)	35.90	20.00	22.22	29.85
Angela's Ashes (1999)	41.03	40.00	61.11	46.27
A Love Divided (1999)	28.21	40.00	50.00	35.82
Evelyn (2002)	30.77	60.00	66.67	44.78
Agnes Browne (1999)	61.54	50.00	66.67	61.19
The Magdalene Sisters (2002)	28.21	30.00	55.56	35.82
A Man of No Importance (1994)	41.03	40.00	55.56	44.78
The Boys & Girl from Co. Clare (2003)	25.64	30.00	27.78	26.87
Last of the High Kings (1996)	25.64	50.00	55.56	37.31
High Spirits (1988)	7.69	30.00	22.22	14.93
The Commitments (1991)	48.72	50.00	66.67	53.73
The Snapper (1993)	51.28	70.00	83.33	64.17
Into the West (1993)	43.59	40.00	27.78	38.81
The Van (1996))	46.15	80.00	66.67	56.72
Trojan Eddie (1996)	41.03	40.00	61.11	46.27
The Matchmaker (1997)	35.90	20.00	50.00	37.31
The Nephew (1997)	43.59	30.00	33.33	38.81
Waking Ned (1998)	43.59	30.00	55.56	44.78
A Very Unlucky Leprechaun (1998)	12.82	20.00	5.56	11.94
The General (1998)	56.41	70.00	72.22	62.69
Ordinary Decent Criminal (2000)	38.46	50.00	83.33	52.24
When the Sky Falls (2000)	38.46	40.00	66.67	46.27
Veronica Guerin (2003)	28.21	50.00	61.11	40.30
About Adam (2000)	30.77	20.00	38.89	31.34
When Brendan Met Trudy (2000)	15.38	40.00	55.56	29.85
Rat (2001)	64.10	50.00	55.56	59.70
Mystics (2002)	56.41	20.00	66.67	53.73
Intermission (2003)	43.59	60.00	66.67	52.24
Goldfish Memory (2003)	10.26	50.00	44.44	25.37
Cowboys and Angels (2003)	23.08	30.00	16.67	22.38
Adam and Paul (2004)	58.97	60.00	50.00	56.72
Dead Meat (2004)	25.64	40.00	33.33	29.85
Inside I'm Dancing (2004)	30.77	30.00	50.00	35.82
Irish Jam (2004)	35.90	10.00	50.00	35.82
Garage (2007)	53.85	40.00	27.78	44.78

Table XV

	Films ordered according to the locale they are set in	% of possible grammar features	% of possible discourse features	% of possible lexical features	% of total possible features
Dublin	The Informer (1935)	53.85	40.00	16.67	41.79
	Michael Collins (1996)	25.64	50.00	38.89	32.84
	The Dead (1987)	25.64	20.00	22.22	23.89
	Agnes Browne (1999)	61.54	50.00	66.67	61.19
	Evelyn (2002)	30.77	60.00	66.67	44.78
	My Left Foot (1989)	43.59	30.00	50.00	43.28
	A Man of No Importance (1994)	41.03	40.00	55.56	44.78
	Last of the High Kings (1996)	25.64	50.00	55.56	37.31
	The Snapper (1993)	51.28	70.00	83.33	62.69
	Into the West (1993)	43.59	40.00	27.78	38.81
	The Commitments (1991)	48.72	50.00	66.67	53.73
	The Van (1996)	46.15	80.00	66.67	56.72
	The General (1998)	56.41	70.00	72.22	62.69
	Ordinary Decent Criminal (2000)	38.46	50.00	83.33	52.24
	When the Sky Falls (2000)	38.46	40.00	66.67	46.27
	Veronica Guerin (2003)	28.21	50.00	61.11	40.30
	About Adam (2000)	30.77	20.00	38.89	31.34
	When Brendan Met Trudy (2000)	15.38	40.00	55.56	29.85
	Rat (2001)	64.10	50.00	55.56	59.70
	Mystics (2002)	56.41	20.00	66.67	53.73
	Intermission (2003)	43.59	60.00	66.67	52.24
	Adam and Paul (2004)	58.97	60.00	50.00	56.72
	Goldfish Memory (2003)	10.26	50.00	44.44	25.37
	Inside I'm Dancing (2004)	30.77	30.00	50.00	35.82
	Nora (2001)	38.46	40.00	33.33	37.31
Wexford	A Love Divided (1999)	28.21	40.00	50.00	35.82
Wicklow	How Harry Became a Tree (2001)	51.28	40.00	61.11	52.24
Midlands	This is my Father (1998)	35.90	60.00	61.11	46.27
	Circle of Friends (1995)	40.54	30.00	38.89	37.31
	Widows' Peak (1994)	56.41	40.00	38.89	49.25
	The Magdalene Sisters (2002)	28.21	30.00	55.56	35.82
	Song for a Raggy Boy (2003)	15.38	10.00	11.11	13.43
	Trojan Eddie (1996)	41.03	40.00	61.11	46.27
	Garage (2007)	53.85	40.00	27.78	44.78
Kerry	Far and Away (1992)	20.51	20.00	27.78	22.39
	Ryan's Daughter (1970)	56.41	20.00	16.67	40.30
	Darby O'Gill & the Little People (1959)	58.97	50.00	27.78	49.25
Clare	The Boys & Girl from Co. Clare (2003)	25.64	30.00	27.78	26.87
Limerick	Angela's Ashes (1999)	41.03	40.00	61.11	46.27
	Cowboys and Angels (2003)	23.08	30.00	16.67	22.38
Cork	The Wind that Shakes the Barley (2006)	41.03	40.00	38.89	40.30
	The Nephew (1997)	43.59	30.00	33.33	38.81
Leitrim	Dead Meat (2004	25.64	40.00	33.33	29.85
(other)	The Field (1990)	35.90	20.00	22.22	29.85
	The Quiet Man (1952)	48.72	40.00	16.67	38.81
	A Very Unlucky Leprechaun (1998)	12.82	20.00	5.56	11.94
	The Matchmaker (1997)	35.90	20.00	50.00	37.31
	High Spirits (1988)	7.69	30.00	22.22	14.93
	Waking Ned (1998)	43.59	30.00	55.56	44.78
	Irish Jam (2004)	35.90	10.00	50.00	35.82

Table XVI

Irish films	% of possible grammar features	% of possible discourse features	% of possible lexical features	% of total possible features
My Left Foot (1989)	43.59	30.00	50.00	43.28
The Field (1990)	35.90	20.00	22.22	29.85
The Commitments (1991)	48.72	50.00	66.67	53.73
Into the West (1993)	43.59	40.00	27.78	38.81
A Man of No Importance (1994)	41.03	40.00	55.56	44.78
Widow's Peak (1994)	56.41	40.00	38.89	49.25
Circle of Friends (1995)	40.54	30.00	38.89	37.31
Last of the High Kings (1996)	25.64	50.00	55.56	37.31
The Van (1996)	46.15	80.00	66.67	56.72
Michael Collins (1996)	25.64	50.00	38.89	32.84
Trojan Eddie (1996)	41.03	40.00	61.11	46.27
The Nephew (1997)	43.59	30.00	33.33	38.81
The General (1998)	56.41	70.00	72.22	62.69
A Very Unlucky Leprechaun (1998)	12.82	20.00	5.56	11.94
A Love Divided (1999)	28.21	40.00	50.00	35.82
Agnes Browne (1999)	61.54	50.00	66.67	61.19
Angela's Ashes (1999)	41.03	40.00	61.11	46.27
When the Sky Falls (2000)	38.46	40.00	66.67	46.27
About Adam (2000)	30.77	20.00	38.89	31.34
Ordinary Decent Criminal (2000)	38.46	50.00	83.33	52.24
When Brendan Met Trudy (2000)	15.38	40.00	55.56	29.85
Nora (2001)	38.46	40.00	33.33	37.31
Rat (2001)	64.10	50.00	55.56	59.70
How Harry Became a Tree (2001)	51.28	40.00	61.11	52.24
Mystics (2002)	56.41	20.00	66.67	53.73
Evelyn (2002)	30.77	60.00	66.67	44.78
Intermission (2003)	43.59	60.00	66.67	52.24
Song for a Raggy Boy (2003)	15.38	10.00	11.11	13.43
Veronica Guerin (2003)	28.21	50.00	61.11	40.30
Goldfish Memory (2003)	10.26	50.00	44.44	25.37
The Boys & Girl from Co. Clare (2003)	25.64	30.00	27.78	26.87
Cowboys and Angels (2003)	23.08	30.00	16.67	22.38
Adam and Paul (2004)	58.97	60.00	50.00	56.72
Dead Meat (2004)	25.64	40.00	33.33	29.85
Inside I'm Dancing (2004)	30.77	30.00	50.00	35.82
Garage (2007)	53.85	40.00	27.78	44.78

Table XVII

Irish-related films	% of possible grammar features	% of possible discourse features	% of possible lexical features	% of total possible features
The Informer (1935)	53.85	40.00	16.67	41.79
The Quiet Man (1952)	48.72	40.00	16.67	38.81
Darby O'Gill & the Little People (1959)	58.97	50.00	27.78	49.25
Ryan's Daughter (1970)	56.41	20.00	16.67	40.30
The Dead (1987)	25.64	20.00	22.22	23.89
High Spirits (1988)	7.69	30.00	22.22	14.93
Far and Away (1992)	20.51	20.00	27.78	22.39
The Snapper (1993)	51.28	70.00	83.33	62.69
Widows' Peak (1994)	56.41	40.00	38.89	49.25
The Matchmaker (1997)	35.90	20.00	50.00	37.31
This is my Father (1998)	35.90	60.00	61.11	46.27
Waking Ned (1998)	43.59	30.00	55.56	44.78
The Magdalene Sisters (2002)	28.21	30.00	55.56	35.82
Evelyn (2002)	30.77	60.00	66.67	44.78
Irish Jam (2004)	35.90	10.00	50.00	35.82
The Wind that Shakes the Barley (2006)	41.03	40.00	38.89	40.30

7   Accent perception

Having arrived at results regarding the presence of grammar, discourse and lexical features of Irish English in film, I will now examine the accuracy of the Irish accents in those films, particularly those of non-Irish actors. However, before one can begin to judge the "authenticity" of accents in film, it is perhaps first of all useful to look at just how we perceive accents. After all, we have all at some time or another sat on a train or a bus and overheard a miniscule snatch of conversation between two complete strangers and recognised immediately where they were from. Depending on our previous exposure to the language being spoken, we would have been able to pinpoint their origin more precisely. What one person might have recognised as, for example, an Irish accent, another might more accurately have acknowledged as, say, a Dublin accent, whilst yet another may have been able to distinguish between a North Dublin and South Dublin accent. Nevertheless, despite the fact that we are able to do this, few of us know how we actually do it, or what it was that led us to our conclusions[326].

The following will therefore examine how we can make such accurate judgements about accents and yet not be able to say what it was exactly that led us to make them. It will explore how much input we actually need to be able to come to such decisions, and examine whether there are specific linguistic cues which inform our decisions more than others? (For example, are vowel sounds more likely to reveal accent than consonants, or is it perhaps a grammar feature or a lexical item, and nothing to do with pronunciation at all, that gives the game away?)

7.1   Is everybody able to perceive accent?

The ability to perceive, and distinguish between, accents is something which all humans share. Studies have shown that already as children we can perceive accent in our own language, and, what is more, we are also able to perceive non-native accents in other languages we have learned. One study which proved just that was conducted by Scovel in 1978. It set out to test whether there were differences in accent perception between adult native English speakers, child native English speakers, aphasic native English speakers and adult, non-native English speakers. All subjects were asked to listen to a recording of 20 individuals (10 native speakers of Standard American English and 10 non-native speakers who had been selected by EFL teachers for their excellent pronunciation) reading an 8-second-long passage containing all of the segmental phonemes of English. Scovel found that the adult native English speaking judges had a 97% accuracy rate for detecting a non-native accent, while for the children, the accuracy rate ranged from 78% for 5 year olds to 99% for 10 year olds. These figures show that the adult level of attainment is reached by children in a matter of only a few years, and are in keeping with a similar study of even younger children's ability to perceive accent, which was carried out by Mercer in 1975[327].

---

[326] Baugh has commented on this phenomenon before, correctly observing that "in spite of this ability for auditory discrimination, few of us can identify all of the particular linguistic cues and nuances that influence our capacity to detect dialect differences" (1996: 170).
[327] Mercer tested the ability of monolingual English-Canadian children, aged between 3 years and 6 months (3:6) and 5 years and 8 months (5:8), to distinguish between English and French, English and French-accented English and French and Greek. The findings showed that the youngest subjects, between the ages of 3:6 and 4:0, could distinguish between English and French, whereas those older than 4:6 could also differentiate between English and French-accented English. None of the children tested, however, could distinguish between the two foreign

Scovel's findings reveal that even his third group of respondents, aphasics with serious neurological damage, could still perceive non-native accent at a rate of 75-94%, while the final group, adult non-native speakers, who were divided into three sub-groups according to their ability in an English proficiency test, displayed an accuracy rate for identifying non-native accent which ranged from 57% for elementary students to 72% for advanced students. While the 57% rate for the elementary learner was the poorest performance of all judges, it was nevertheless still at a rate better than chance. All in all, Scovel's study shows that non-native accent can be detected by both native speakers and non-native speakers of different ages and abilities. Furthermore, based on the fact that both very young children and non-native speakers are less accurate in their judgements, it can be inferred that experience, in the form of exposure to native accent, would seem to be a determining factor in people's ability to detect accent.

7.2 Can some people judge accent better than others?

As outlined above, although everybody can *perceive* accent, experience, or lack thereof, is still an important factor in accent perception, particularly in the case of infants and non-native speakers. The role of experience is even more relevant, however, when it comes to successful accent *identification*, as can be seen in the results of a study of dialect recognition conducted by Williams *et al.* (1999) in Wales, in which teachers proved to be far more successful in their recognition of a variety of Welsh accents than were their pupils. The pupils' comparatively poor performance rate was attributed not to the teachers' superior education but to the pupils' simply having experienced "lower geographical mobility and less access to dialect speakers, face-to face or in the broadcast media" (Williams *et al.* 1999: 357).

Although these pupils (average age 14) certainly would have been able to perceive accent at an adult level (see Scovel's study above), when it came to actually identifying where the various accented speakers were from, they simply lacked experience or what Preston (1996) calls the "folk linguistic[328] awareness" to do so. Folk linguistic awareness can be identified on four different levels: availability, detail, accuracy, and control, which are in turn influenced by a series of factors, such as formal training and/or knowledge, publicity (e.g., popular culture, media exposure), correctness (transmitted formally or informally), and folk culture artefacts. Let us examine these more closely by looking at Preston's adapted version of his original 1996 definitions, with examples.

1) Availability: Folk respondents range in their attention to linguistic features from complete disregard for to frequent discussion of and even preoccupation with them.

---

languages (cf. Day 1982: 118). What is more, not only can children detect differences in language and varieties, there is also plenty of evidence to suggest that they are also already able to make judgements about them even before they commence primary education (cf. Day 1982: 116-31). This is of great interest with regard to language stereotyping in films and cartoons targeted at children and is addressed in Lippi-Green's fascinating study of the perpetuation of linguistic stereotypes through Disney's animated films (1997: 79-103).

[328] Folk linguistics, also known as perceptual dialectology, is a field of linguistics concerned with non-linguists' perception of language. While it was once a discipline which was treated with disdain due to its unscientific nature, it is now growing in popularity as linguists realise that it can be unwise to simply discount popular beliefs about language. In keeping with Niedzielski and Preston, the term "folk" is used throughout to refer to "those who are not trained professionals in the area under investigation" and it by no means refers to "rustic, ignorant, uneducated, backward, primitive, minority, isolated, marginalized, or lower status groups or individuals" (Niedzielski and Preston 2003: xviii).

2)		Accuracy: Folk respondents may accurately, partially accurately, or completely inaccurately represent linguistic facts (and their distribution).
3)		Detail: Folk respondents' characterizations may range from *global* (reflecting, for example, only a general awareness of a variety) to *detailed* (in which respondents cite specific details).
4)		Control: Folk respondents may have complete, partial, or no "imitative" control over linguistic features.

(Preston 1999: 360)

It is important to note that all of the categories represent clines or continua, on which lay respondents' degree of awareness can be marked. Furthermore, these clines are not interdependent. For example,

> A respondent who claims only a general awareness of a 'foreign accent' [limited 'availability' S.W.] may be capable of a completely faithful imitation of some of its characteristics ['accuracy' and 'control'] and a completely inaccurate imitation of others ['[in)accuracy coupled with a lack of 'control']. On the other hand, a respondent who is preoccupied with a variety [high 'availability'] might have no overt information about its linguistic makeup [lack of 'detail'] but be capable of performing a native-like imitation of it [high 'control'].

(Preston 1999: 360)

What is more, even in cases when people do have the linguistic awareness to identify where an accent is from, most of them are not able to verbalise what it is that makes the accent different. As early as in 1966, Labov recognised that one of the greatest problems with which the folk is confronted when it comes to discussing language is their lack of appropriate terminology. He describes this in the discussion of Hoenigwald's "A Proposal for the Study of Folk Linguistics" (Hoenigwald 1966: 23):

> 'Poverty-stricken' would be the best term for this vocabulary. The inadequacy of people's overt remarks about their own language is directly reflected in the fact that there are only a few words that they use to convey the subjective response that they feel.

In order to describe what they observe, the folk therefore have to use the language at their disposal or as McGregor suggests "non-linguists must devise their own technical jargons for talking about matters they have not previously had the opportunity to describe and discuss" (McGregor 1998: 49). Finding the right words to describe a phenomenon one had not previously had the opportunity, not to mention the inclination, to discuss can be a very difficult task and generally has one of two outcomes. In the first, the respondents are completely at a loss to explain their observations, which results in responses such as "I cannot describe it", "I don't know how to explain it", etc. This is evident in the example presented by Niedzielski and Preston in which a respondent said that an older relative spoke with a strong Polish accent, yet was completely unable to articulate what she thought constituted a Polish accent (cf. Niedzielski and Preston 2003: 12). The second outcome is not necessarily more helpful, because even if the folk do manage to articulate their perception of linguistic features, there is no guarantee that the vocabulary they use will be understood as they intend it. This is evident in one of the examples offered by Niedzielski and Preston, in which the respondent recounts how a friend of hers had described the differences between a Midwestern and a North Dakota accent:

> And she'd say you guys talk real funny. She said you talk up and down. And she said out in North Dakota we talk sideways. I said D. [the friend's name] Explain that to me what is up and down and sideways talk. She said that's the only way I can describe it.
> (Niedzielski and Preston 2003: 12)

This example hopefully shows that even when the folk are aware of differences and can articulate them somewhat, there is no guarantee that their explanations will be understood as they are intended.

This potential for misunderstanding lies in the fact that the terms used by lay people are not the same as those used by professional linguists, since "they are not used consistently by different individuals, nor are they defined in a rigorous manner" (McGregor 1998: 43). What is more, non-linguists often use umbrella terms for cues which linguists would normally subdivide into individual categories[329].

When terminology to describe the speech phenomenon is not available to respondents, they may simply resort to imitating the feature, in order to get their point across. Indeed, research by Niedzielski and Preston reveals that "mimicry appears to be the most productive means of eliciting the details of varieties from the folk" (2003: 111). This point is very important, particularly with regard to reviews, as writers regularly use respellings to imitate the poor accent present in the films. The following is an example regarding an Irish accent in the movie *P.S. I Love You* (Richard LaGravenese, 2007)[330].

> Lead actor Gerard Butler's 'Wicklow' accent is the worst advertisement for voice coaching in the history of moving pictures. 'Oive been writin' you lett-urrs,' he drawls as though auditioning for the part of the leprechaun in *Finian's Rainbow*.
> (*The Irish Times* December 15, 2007)

However, it is interesting to note that, despite the importance laid upon the "authenticity" or accuracy of imitations of accents in this book, Niedzielski and Preston have observed that the imitation of an accent need not be accurate to be effective. They came to this conclusion by conducting a very detailed linguistic analysis of one of their folk respondents' imitations of a Tennessee dialect. The analysis of the phrase "Y'all know what I'm talking about now, don't you", which can be seen in Niedzielski and Preston (2003: 114-115), shows that, segment-by-segment, the imitation is actually technically inept, but that the general impression it leaves is nonetheless successful – a case of the whole being better than the sum of its parts. This analysis suggests therefore that "a successful imitation need be neither complete nor accurate" (Niedzielski and Preston 2003: 116).[331]

In light of the fact that the imitation of the Tennessee accent was so technically inaccurate, one could validly question what it was that still led to the performance being regarded as a success, a question of some import to our analysis of Irish English in film as well. Niedzielski and Preston suggest that it was probably a nonsegmental, such as the slower tempo or rate of Southern speech – the famous "Southern drawl", which ensured the success

---

[329] McGregor (1998: 43), for example, notes that a descriptor such as "mumbly" can refer to loudness, speed and tension and, thus, may mean different things to different people.

[330] This movie is not included in the corpus, as it is partly set outside of Ireland.

[331] These findings are further proof that the clines of Preston's taxonomy of language awareness are independent of each other. The respondent clearly has quite a high degree of "availability" and "control" but "accuracy" is somewhat limited.

of the imitation. Alternatively, the poor segmental performance may have been compensated for by the imitator's use of a Southern lexical caricature (such as "y'all") or a Southern stock expression (such as "now", which also appeared in several other respondents' imitations of Southern speech) which seemed to lend some authenticity to the phrase. The use of stock phrases is very common among imitators as was shown by the number of respondents whose imitation of a Southern accent include some spin on the phrase "Y'all come down and see us sometime, (now) you hear" from the television show *The Beverly Hillbillies* . These findings, coupled with those taken from Internet criticism of films (Chapter 10), suggest that the power of popular cultural influences on language awareness, particularly with a view to imitative behaviour, should by no means be underestimated. They also put into question Preston's earlier findings from 1999 that popular cultural vehicles play a lesser role in language awareness than face-to-face contacts.

As outlined above, the analysis of imitations can be useful in determining the features that are thought to make an accent or dialect what it is. With the case of the Southern US dialect above, it was the drawl and the use of certain lexical items or stock phrases which seemed to play a role. In the film corpus, there are also examples of characters doing imitations of other characters' speech and these should signal what the imitators believe to be the salient features of that speech (cf. Hickey 2007: 8 and 19). There are two examples of Americans imitating Irish people, and two examples of Irish people assuming a brogue to mock Irish people from other parts of the country. It is interesting to see what the focus of each imitation is and what they may tell us about the different perceptions of Irish speech.

The first example of an American imitating the Irish comes from *The Matchmaker* and sees US Senator John McClory focusing on the linguistic stereotype of /ɔi/ for /ai/. The example is as follows:

> 633) [Hey, Marce, how are you doin' over there? How are my people doing?]
> [Your people?]
> Yeah, the Irish. You know, the **Oirish**!
>
> *(The Matchmaker*, 00:10:50, MMcC2000US)

The fact that this feature is erroneously believed to be typical of Irish English has also been identified by Taniguchi (1972: 249) and is discussed in Chapter 9.

The second example of an American imitation of Irish speech comes from *The Quiet Man*, where Sean Thornton both assumes an Irish accent and employs the Irish English expression *woman of the house* from the Irish *bean a' tí* (cf. Dolan 2006: 18-19) when addressing his new wife.

> 634) **Woman of the house**, where's me **tay**?
>
> *(The Quiet Man*, 01:46:38, MST1930US)

Later in the film, he does something similar, once again using *woman of the house*, as well as employing a definite article rather than a possessive pronoun before the noun *brother*, as is often the case in Irish English (see Chapter 6). One could argue that to make the imitation even more precise, he should have also inserted *for* in place of *to* and added a definite article before *supper*[332] (see Chapter 6.1.2.2).

> 635) **Woman of the house**, I've brought **the brother** home to supper.
> (*The Quiet Man*, 02:06:10, MST1930US)

Imitations of Irish English speech are not limited to non-Irish characters. Indeed, on two occasions, Irish characters make their speech seemingly more Irish by affecting a west of Ireland accent[333]. In the first, *The Matchmaker*, an Irish character, Sean, assumes a broader accent while in the presence of the locals on the Aran Islands. By exaggerating a brogue and peppering his speech with more Irish English features than he typically uses, he hopes to be accepted among the natives. The features which he uses to do this are the use of *would* rather than *should*, *clefting* and 'subordinating *and*'. According to Hickey, the use of 'subordinating and' is a frequent device employed by authors to represent the speech of rural speakers (cf. 2007: 264), What is more, clefting is seen as such a salient feature of Irish English that for many people it has taken on stereotypical connotations (Hickey 2007: 268). Thus, it lends itself well to imitations.

> 636) Ah, go on, **why wouldn't ya**? **Sure**, **'tis** a great judge that you'd be **and** you from the land of Perry Mason and all.
> (*The Matchmaker*, 00:41:52, MSea2000W)

In the second example of an Irish person doing an imitation, this time from the film *Nora*, Cosgrave changes his accent, not through any desire to fit in, but rather to make fun of the fact that James Joyce's lover is from the west of Ireland. He does so by reading out the last words of Nora's letter to Joyce in an affected Galway accent, complete with epenthesis in the word *girl* and the use of an exaggerated monophthongal /oː/ in the name Nora (see Chapter 9).

> 637) Your lovely **girl**, **Nora**.
> (*Nora*, 00:13:21, MC1900D)

The fact that Cosgrave's use of epenthesis is meant as a form of mockery is confirmed by Hickey's observation that "epenthetic pronunciations of such common words as girl are used by urbanites to imitate and ridicule rural accents" (Hickey 1989: 57).

From the above it should be clear that, although we can all perceive accent, our ability to articulate what we hear differs greatly, with many of us being forced to resort to making vague descriptions of accent or to offering impromptu imitations to reflect our observations. Such imitations, however, can prove extremely useful in establishing what it is exactly that constitutes an accent.

---

[332] This is exactly what Roddy Doyle did in adapting the title of the Sidney Poitier film *Guess Who's Coming to Dinner* (Stanley Kramer, 1967) for his short story "Guess Who's Coming for the Dinner?" (2007).
[333] This notion of the west of Ireland as real Ireland again supports the argument outlined in Chapter 3 on authenticity.

7.3 What, and how much, input is actually necessary for one to perceive accent?

We have seen that accent can be detected, and even identified, at high rates of accuracy by both adults and children, native and non-native speakers, and that experience proves to be a determining factor in such judgements. If we can all perceive accent, then what is it exactly that we perceive? What are the cues which reveal an accent? Are they more likely to be a) segmentals, b) suprasegmentals c) voice setting, or d) a mixture of all of the above?

The correct answer here would appear to be d) as there is really no consensus among linguists about just which cues carry the most weight. Studies by Wells (1982), Pennington and Richards (1986), Scovel (1988), and Markham (1995), for example, all tackle the question, but come up with no definitive answers. This book will not try to answer the question of what exactly it is we perceive, but instead will briefly summarise some of the research in this field so that the reader gains an insight into the complexities of the issue.

The lack of certainty, even among experts, on what it is that reveals an accent can probably be attributed to the fact that when we hear speech, the aforementioned cues, both segmental and suprasegmental, are usually all present together and, thus, it is difficult to say which one stands out among the others. Moreover, little of the research available has actually dealt with the question of what exactly it is that people perceive, but instead has focused simply on the overt detection of accent, or on attitude towards accent, often with regard to judging a person's personality, intelligence or reliability based on the way they speak. Furthermore, these studies were not always methodologically sound, as some of their shortcomings outlined briefly below will show.

One of the main problems with many tests of accent perception in the past lay in the fact that while listeners were supposed to be rating speech samples with regard to accent, non-standard dialect features were also often present in the samples, thus perhaps influencing the judgements. Therefore, in order to ensure that respondents were making their judgements based solely on the speakers' pronunciation, and not on grammatical or lexical cues, linguists devised a series of methods to eliminate all additional features which might otherwise have informed the judges that the speakers were non-native. A standard example of how this was done can be seen in the study by Asher and Garcia from 1969, the purpose of which was to compare the pronunciation of English sentences by Cuban immigrant children with that of American children. For the analysis, the children were not asked to speak freely on a topic, as had been the case in previous studies, but rather to repeat 4 sentences which were written in Standard English, so that there would be no variables other than accent to reveal their identity as non-native speakers[334].

However, even those changes were not good enough for linguists who were solely interested in the role which phonemes play in accent. Flege, for example, found that even removing possible grammatical and lexical cues still did not necessarily guarantee that the phonemes alone were responsible for accent detection. He observed that Asher and Garcia's

---

[334] This notion of controlling the linguistic stimuli, so that the listener is only focussing on pronunciation is also of interest with regard to Irish English in film. Are audience members irritated predominantly by poor accent or does it perhaps have something to do with clichéd expressions which may appear in the films (see Chapter 12). Personal experience in directing Irish plays in an EFL setting has revealed that syntactic and lexical cues included in scripts would appear to compensate for the lack of "authentic" Irish accents in a production, with audiences frequently commenting on how "Irish" the play sounded.

study and others like it (Lane 1963; Giles 1972; Brennan and Brennan 1981a/b) all invariably involved relatively long speech samples, ranging from phrases to paragraph-length passages and so "listeners' detection of accent may have been based solely on suprasegmental differences in timing, stress, and intonation rather than differences confined to the articulation of particular phonetic segments" (Flege 1984: 693)[335].

In order to remedy this problem, he decided to give respondents speech samples varying in length from a sentence to a word to a phoneme and he found that even with the most miniscule input they could still perceive non-native accents. The success rate ranged from 63% to 95% in forced-choice and paired-comparison tests, with accent detection proving to be slightly better for the relatively longer speech samples. Nonetheless, even when confronted with the shortest amount of input (the first 30 ms [milliseconds] of the word *two* – which is roughly equivalent to the release burst of /t/), the rate of detection was still considerably higher than chance.

Furthermore, in order to demonstrate that this ability to notice accent exists in the general population, separate studies were conducted with "sophisticated" listeners, who had extensive training in phonetics, and "unsophisticated" listeners, who had no training in linguistics or phonetics. In both cases, the listeners could correctly detect accent at statistically significant rates (cf. Flege 1984: 697)[336].

Flege's study clearly echoes Scovel's findings (above) in that it shows that even unsophisticated subjects can detect accent, and, what is more, that they can do so with a minimum of auditory input (30 milliseconds compared to Asher and Garcia's 8 seconds). Findings like Flege's, which show that "there is sufficient acoustic information present in a single phonetic segment to permit accent detection" (Flege 1984: 699), would certainly seem to lend support to the idea that listeners can perceive accent based on segmentals alone. This raises the question, however, as to whether that segment is more likely to be a consonant or a vowel? Let us take a look at the different schools of thought briefly.

---

[335] In addition to questionable methodology which was often employed in studies of accent perception, the results themselves are not always as reliable as they may seem. In Asher and Garcia's 1969 study of Cuban immigrants' pronunciation, the findings at first look promising, in that none of the 71 Cubans were judged to speak like natives, even if immigrants who had been in the United States longer had much less of an accent than their compatriots, thus showing the judges' perception to be very sensitive. However, the fact of the matter is that the judges also falsely perceived foreign accents among almost a quarter of the 30 American speakers who acted as a control. This consequently forces one to question the reliability of the apparent 100 per cent success rate of their initial judgements (cf. Oyama 1976: 36).

[336] It is perhaps important to note that respondents were only asked to detect foreign accent and not to actually identify it. Interestingly, during the informal debriefing after the experiment, only one of the twelve "unsophisticated" listeners was in fact able to correctly identify the language background of the non-native speakers as being French. This fact, plus the fact that the "unsophisticated" listeners were not familiar with French or French-accented English suggests that "they detected accent by comparing the speech samples to English phonetic norms, rather than identifying some known characteristics of French-accented English in the speech of the non-native talkers" (Flege 1984: 698). This finding supports the idea mentioned above that an ability to pinpoint where an accent is from is dependent on the degree of exposure one has had to that accent in the past.

7.4 Vowels versus consonants

> And the Gileadites took the passages of Jordan before the Ephraimites: and it was so, that when those Ephraimites which were escaped said, Let me go over; that the men of Gilead said unto him, Art thou an Ephraimite? If he said Nay; then said they unto him, Say now Shibboleth; and he said Sibboleth: for he could not frame to pronounce it right. Then they took him, and slew him at the passages of the Jordan: and there fell at that time of the Ephraimites forty and two thousand.
>
> Judges 12: 4-6. (Scovel 1988: 1 and Herman and Herman 1997: 13)

Despite the significant role that the consonants /s/ and /ʃ/ play in betraying the Ephraimites in this oft-quoted story from the Bible, research by Marks (1980) discovered that, on the whole, vowels appear to be a better indicator of accent. His study involved detailed analysis of the speech of two very fluent non-native speakers of English from Spain and Hungary. In his observation of their consonant and vowel errors, he noted that negative transfer[337] was greatest with regard to vowels.

> As far as consonants are concerned, native language transfer makes smaller contribution to foreign accent. However, it is interesting to note that the consonants which do seem to be affected by native language transfer are the sonorants: /l, r/. Both these consonants are the closest consonants to vowels in terms of the distribution of distinctive feature values on a distinctive feature matrix. This may indicate that perhaps native language transfer contributes most to foreign accent where it affects vowels and vowel-like sounds.
>
> (Marks 1980: 114-15)

While these findings certainly are credible, they must also be taken with a pinch of salt. Scovel (1988), for example, regards Marks' findings as plausible, but finds them to be inconclusive, since the study only involved two subjects, their native tongues were both European, and the possible influence of suprasegmental features was not examined (cf. Scovel 1988: 166-67). This, however, does not mean that there is no further support for the notion of vowels and vowel-like sounds playing the most important role in accent perception. Indeed, there are some very compelling arguments which point in that direction, particularly with regard to native accents of English.

The first of these is that, after conducting extensive comparisons of international varieties of English, Trudgill and Hannah discovered that varieties of English worldwide differ relatively little in their consonant systems and that most differences can be observed at the level of vowels (cf. 1994: 5). This notion had already been outlined by Wells (1982a: 74) and is one which is also familiar to dialect coaches such as Robert Blumenfeld who notes that "in accents native to English look first at vowels and diphthongs, because consonants tend to be very much the same in all accents native to English" (2000: 12).

A second reason for why listeners single out vowel sounds rather than consonants as being the main indicators of accent could be that vowels are simply more noticeable, by virtue of the fact that they are inherently louder than consonants because the energy used in producing them is not obstructed on its way out of the vocal tract (cf. Pennington 1996: 89).

Furthermore, it has been shown that vowels carry more information for the listener than consonants do. Werker and Polka state that: "As continuants, vowels are articulated more slowly, have more prominent and long-lasting acoustic cues and can be used to provide more

---

[337] For more on negative transfer, see: Chapter 8.2.1.

prosodic information than consonants. Thus vowels carry information about stress, speaker identity and emotional tone".

Finally, recognition of the importance of vowels is not restricted to linguists. Niedzielski and Preston (2003) show that even unsophisticated listeners appear to regard vowels as the key determinants of accent. As part of their research in folk linguistics, Niedzielski and Preston elicited hours of conversation from their subjects about language and came to the conclusion that vowels are of more importance to the folk than consonants, or at least that is what the respondents' overt comments would suggest. Niedzielski and Preston do concede, however, that this statement is only true with regard to overt comment on accents or dialects and that when it came to imitations of other varieties, consonants also played a role (cf. 2003: 113-117).

Although the above offers arguments for the importance of vowels and, to a lesser extent, consonants with regard to accent, evidence suggests that "accuracy at the segmental level is no longer the fundamental aim of teaching, since it is now known that accurate production of segmental features does not in itself characterize native-like pronunciation" (Pennington and Richards 1986: 218). This intriguing notion is supported by evidence from Niedzielski and Preston (2003: 116) which shows that one does not even have to produce the segments accurately to be judged to have good pronunciation, thereby answering a question posed by Flege as to whether native-like pronunciation at the level of phonetic implementation is even necessary for accent-free pronunciation (cf. Flege 1981: 446).

7.5   Suprasegmentals

In his article "Twenty Questions", Brown (1992: 11) suggests that the growing consensus among linguists is that "suprasegmental features are, if anything, more important than segmental in terms of intelligibility and the acquiring of a quasi-native accent[338]." Brown's opinion is echoed by both Gilbert (1980) and Markham (1997) among others[339], who summarise a number of studies on the role of suprasegmentals in determining accent and find that, at least with regard to second language learning, suprasegmentals are, indeed, more important in pronunciation than segments. Gilbert suggests that intonation, i.e. the prosodic elements of melody and rhythm are so important that "intonation errors are more apt to cause listener confusion than phonemic errors" (1980: 111). She goes on to cite a number of studies which support this notion[340], including one by Nash which suggests that "whereas phonemic interference involves the identification of meaning-bearing linguistic units, a necessary step in the decoding of the message, prosodic interference inhibits the transmission of meaning itself, often negating or contradicting the intentions of the speaker" (1971: 138). Markham found similar evidence in the studies he consulted and states that according to Bannert (1995), it would appear that prosodic non-nativeness is perceived as least acceptable by listeners. He further supports this argumentation with evidence from Johansson (1978) who noted that

---

[338] Brown's use of the term "quasi-native accent" is much more preferable to the word "authentic" which is so often used to describe accents. See Chapter 3 on authenticity.
[339] For further studies, see Van Els and De Bot 1987.
[340] See Leon and Martin 1972; Darwin 1975; Svensson 1971; Dooling 1974; and Knight 1975.

"prosodic errors in L1 Swedish speakers' English contributed more to the judgement of accent than did segmental errors" (Markham 1997: 101)[341].

Additional evidence which suggests that intonation is of paramount importance with regard to pronunciation is that, even when speech samples are artificially stripped of all segmental information, people can still identify languages based on their prosodic patterns alone (cf. Gilbert 1980: 113-16)[342]. While one could argue that all of the above arguments are based on second language acquisition and therefore perhaps not applicable to someone speaking with a new accent in his native language, Gilbert also offers evidence to suggest that prosody can indeed play an important role in one's mother tongue. She suggests that the reason why impersonators or impressionists are so competent in imitating people is that "stage mimics, like Danny Kaye, seem to 'have an ear' for prosodic patterns" (1980: 112). This theory certainly warrants further investigation and it would thus be very interesting to examine the performances of famous impressionists, such as Rory Bremner, Alistair McGowan, Frank Caliendo and Mario Rosenstock to find out whether their impressions are accurate due to their capturing of prosodic patterns or whether perhaps the real reason may be in the next category which is voice setting.

7.6 Voice setting

Although it has not been studied very widely or systematically (cf. Jenner 1992: 38), "voice setting" (Esling and Wong 1983) is, by no means, a new concept. In fact, it was identified as early as in the 1800s, but it has been in and out of fashion over time and its name has changed frequently over the years. According to Kelz (1971), who chronicled its history, "voice setting" was originally called "*Artikulationsbasis*" or "basis of articulation" by the German linguist Felix Franke. It has since been termed "*Operationsbasis*" (Sievers 1876) "organic basis" (Sweet 1877), "*Mundlage*" (Storm 1881), "articulatory basis" (Graff 1932), "articulatory setting" (Honikman 1964), "voice quality" (Laver 1980), "vocal setting" and "voice set" (Pennington 1996)[343]. What these terms have in common is that they all suggest that there is something else, besides segmentals and suprasegmentals, which plays a key role in how a person sounds. Indeed, these paralinguistic characteristics were described by Honikman as "the gross oral posture and mechanics, both external and internal, requisite as a framework for the comfortable, economic and fluent merging and integrating of the isolated sounds into that harmonious cognizable whole which constitutes the established pronunciation of a language" (1964: 276-7). In simpler terms, voice setting is the way in which the articulatory apparatus is normally set in order to produce the characteristic sounds of a particular language or, in the case of our study, accent. While the external articulatory settings are more noticeable, e.g. the characteristic rounding of the lips for French speakers or the

---

[341] However, in order to show the uncertainty within this field, Markham also cites a study by Grover, Jamieson & Dobrovolsky (1987) which ascertained that "the perception of non-nativeness was not cued by intonation, except where other cues (such as syntactic deviations) were present" (Markham 1997: 101). This notion also reflects the findings of a study of Vietnamese learners of English, by Cunningham (forthcoming). She shows that if the segments are not already in place, then the speech will already be so incomprehensible that intonation does not play a role.
[342] Gilbert found that, when given the processed speech samples, subjects could distinguish between Cantonese, Japanese and English at highly significant levels. For a similar study on English and Japanese, see Ramus und Mehler (1999).
[343] For more on these terms, see Kelz (1971: 194-8) and Pennington (1996: 156). For more on this phenomenon, see Laver (1980).

closely spread lips of Russian speakers, the internal articulatory settings, such as tongue position, are equally important in accurate accent production. Although the examples above apply to voice setting in different languages, its applications in the learning of different dialects within a language were recognised by Sievers as early as in 1876.

> [...] wer irgendwie in der Lage ist, mehrere Mundarten sich aneignen zu können, versäume ja nicht dies zu thun und die Abweichungen derselben systematisch zu studieren. Dabei leistet die oben erwähnte Artikulationsbasis die besten Dienste.
>
> (Sievers 1876: 115)

Indeed, according to Jenner and Bradford, correct voice setting automatically facilitates the accurate production of segmentals. By focussing on an internal setting whereby, for example, the tip of the tongue is on or near the upper teeth and the alveolar ridge, learners will automatically sound more English. Based on their experience in language teaching, Jenner and Bradford observe that "if the right degree of laxity and tongue-tip focus can be achieved through [...] consonant drills, the vowels largely take care of themselves, in that the internal shape is right" (1982: 41). This is again something which was observed by Sievers over eighty years earlier.

> Versuche ich als Mitteldeutscher z.B. eine prägnant norddeutsche Mundart wie etwa die holsteinische zu sprechen, so muß ein für allemal die Zunge etwas zurückgezogen und verbreitet werden; hat man diese Basis einmal gefunden versteht man sie beim Wechsel verschiedener Laute festzuhalten, so folgen die charakteristischen Lautnuancen der Mundart alle von selbst.
>
> (Sievers 1901: 114)

In order to illustrate how this voice setting manifests itself in practice, Esling and Wong offer an example of the characteristic features or voice setting which are typical[344] of the English spoken by an American male adult (Esling and Wong 1983: 90):

1. spread lips
2. open jaw
3. palatalised tongue body position
4. retroflex articulation
5. nasal voice
6. lowered larynx
7. creaky voice

The combination of all of these features, according to Jenner, has "important auditory effects which a listener (perhaps subconsciously) recognises and uses in the stereotyping of different accents" (1992: 41). He also adds that "if a native-like framework or 'setting' can be achieved, all that happens within it will also be perceived as native-like" (1992: 44).

Pennington (1996) is one of the greatest advocates of voice setting, seeing it as the foundation for everything else involved in accent. She sees pronunciation as a hierarchy in

---

[344] The idea that there is a typical American accent, or a typical accent of any kind, is, of course, problematic (cf. Chapter 3). The same applies to a typical voice setting. This was also observed by Viëtor, who noted that "eine allgemeine deutsche Artikulationsbasis ist freilich nur eine fast bedenkliche Abstraktion, da die Mundarten auch in dieser Hinsicht bedeutend voneinander abweichen; und ähnliches gilt vom Englischen und Französischen" (1910: 76).

which all of the aforementioned features have their position, with consonants being the least important and breath and voice setting proving to be the determining factors.

> The voice setting, which is manifested in the nature and volume of the breath stream passing through the glottis and in the posture of the articulators, can be thought of as the prosodic foundation on which intonation is pronounced. The general intonation pattern then sets the bounds for the rhythmic pattern of an utterance. Within this rhythmic pattern, individual stressed syllables occur and these, in turn, set the context for the production of the individual segments of speech.
>
> (Pennington 1996: 157)

As with all of the explanations which have been offered to explain accent, the concept of voice setting is not without its detractors. Scovel (1988), for example, is not convinced about the validity of the voice setting theory, as it is influenced by so many factors other than phonology, such as the speaker's age, sex, body size, emotional state, and even whether or not the speaker is suffering from a cold. He does, however, recognise the usefulness of voice setting with regard to foreign language teaching and, particularly, with regard to acting[345]. The latter point is of great interest for this study, and, thus, we shall now turn our attention to how actors learn a new accent for their roles.

---

[345] Dialect coaches sometimes make reference to voice setting in their acting manuals and cassettes/CDs (cf. Herman and Herman 1997; or Stern's cassette 1979). Stern, for example, refers to the Irish English voice setting as being breathy, with a distinctive lilt.

8 Dialect coaches and the factors influencing accent acquisition

8.1 The role of dialect coaches

From the early days of film, and indeed theatre, people have pretended to be people they are not. Men have played women, the young have played the old, and people of all nationalities have played each other. After all, acting is an art and like all art forms it is based on artifice. However, for many centuries a tradition has also existed which supports the notion that the goal of art is the imitation of nature, and thus that artists should strive to represent reality. Advocates of this belief contend that the motion picture has made it possible to achieve this ideal in an unprecedented way (cf. Mast 1992: 3). French film critic and film theorist André Bazin summed this philosophy up well:

> The realism of the cinema follows directly from its photographic nature. Not only does some marvel or some fantastic thing on the screen not undermine the reality of the image, on the contrary it is its most valid justification. Illusion in the cinema is not based as it is in the theater on convention tacitly accepted by the general public; rather, contrariwise, it is based on the inalienable realism of that which is shown.
>
> (1967: 108)

Thus, over time a cleft has slowly developed between the media of theatre and film, on the basis that the artifice which, for many people, still prevails in theatre[346] has been removed from film, leaving it seemingly less artificial and thus more realistic, or as Susan Sontag puts it: "Cinema, at once high art and popular art, is cast as the art of the authentic. Theatre, by contrast, means dressing up, pretense, lies" (Sontag 1966: 364). Evidence of this can be seen in the fact that in film, unlike in theatre[347], it is now unacceptable for a man to play the role of a woman, or vice versa, unless it is explicitly part of the plot, as is often the case in comedies[348]. The same applies to actors playing characters of another race. Images of white actors playing Othello in blackface or performing caricatured Asian roles, such as Mickey Rooney's distasteful portrayal of the Japanese neighbour in *Breakfast at Tiffany's* (Blake Edwards, 1961), have long since disappeared from the screen[349].

While the above examples show that the artifice of actors crossing the boundaries of gender and race is generally no longer acceptable for cinema audiences, there seems to be much less opposition to actors crossing the borders of region or nationality. For decades, film stars have played characters from different regions and countries, and audiences have willingly accepted this artifice, albeit on one condition. In a strange case of audiences wanting

---

[346] The artifice implicit in theatre was succinctly described by Charles Henry Woolbert, a professor at the University of Illinois, who observed that "the stage is irrevocably tied down to the necessity of being different from everyday life. Everything that appears on the stage is in some way an exaggeration of the life it portrays: lights, costumes, makeup, stage sets, action, dialog, and pronunciation ... Everything on the stage is illusion, including pronunciation" (cited in Knight 1997: 172).

[347] One could argue that such theatrical cross-dressing is more likely to occur in amateur or travelling productions and is often due to a scarcity of actors rather than by design. Whatever the reason, the practice is just as acceptable for audiences as, for example, a young actor playing an elderly man.

[348] See *Some Like It Hot* (Billy Wilder, 1959), *Tootsie* (Sydney Pollack, 1982) or *Mrs Doubtfire* (Chris Columbus, 1993).

[349] Having said that, at the time of writing, a white man, Robert Downey Jr., had just been nominated for an Academy Award for playing the role of a black man in the war comedy *Tropic Thunder* (Ben Stiller, 2008). Needless to say, this portrayal has fuelled great debate and made people reassess the (in)appropriateness of such a characterisation.

to have their cake and eat it too, they will accept artifice – for example, a Hollywood star in the role of a British character – , yet they still insist on a certain degree of realism – for the role in the film, the actor must approximate the accent of the locale. This seemingly contradictory stance with regard to realism is in keeping with an observation made by Umberto Eco in his 1975 essay "Travels in Hyperreality" which was quoted by Ruth Barton in her book *Acting Irish in Hollywood*.

> Umberto Eco distinguishes in West Coast America the abandonment of the 'real' for the 'authentic copy'. More perfect than the real, the copy replaces flaws with flawlessness, so much so that the viewer or participant in the spectacle will no longer feel any need for the original. America, he suggests is 'a country obsessed with realism, where if a reconstruction is to be credible, it must be absolutely iconic, a perfect likeness, a 'real' copy of the reality being represented.
>
> (Barton 2006: 181)

Based on this statement, the suggestion is that an audience will happily accept a copy in place of the original, but only as long as the reconstruction is an "authentic copy"[350]. In cases where the actor's accent is not "credible" or does not measure up to that of the locale in the film, the audience is often quick to reject it. Indeed, this rejection of poor accents has led to the compilation, both in the Internet and in reputable film magazines, of lists of actors who have been deemed to have the worst fake accents in cinema history[351]. Perhaps the most famous (or, rather, infamous) example is American actor Dick Van Dyke's oft-maligned portrayal of a Cockney chimney sweep in Disney's *Mary Poppins* (Robert Stevenson, 1964). However, his far-from-perfect likeness was only voted the second-worst accent in cinema history by British film magazine *Empire*, being outdone by Sean Connery's attempt at an Irish accent in *The Untouchables* (Brian De Palma, 1987)[352]. With so much attention being drawn to the quality of accents in film, it is therefore important for the actor to get them "right".

In the era of silent film, this was never a problem as the actor's voice was never heard and thus never betrayed his origins. With the advent of talkies, however, an actor's voice suddenly came to be of great importance; so much so that for many of the greatest stars of the silent era who were not blessed with a dulcet voice the introduction of sound was a death knell for their careers[353]. This fall from grace of some of the big names served as a warning for many other actors who promptly sought the help of voice coaches to train them to speak

---

[350] For more discussion of the inherent semantic and philosophical complications of the ludicrous term "authentic copy", see Chapter 3 on authenticity.

[351] For a list of sources featuring such lists, see Appendix 2.

[352] Ironically, despite it being voted the worst movie accent in history, Connery's accent is not regarded as the worst Irish accent of all time, polling only 3.8% of the votes in a 2007 survey by screenclick.com, an Irish video rental service (Retrieved: April 27, 2008). The dubious honour fell to Tom Cruise in *Far and Away* (56.6%). What is more, Connery's performance earned him both an Oscar and a Golden Globe Award, which would either suggest that an accurate accent is not everything, or confirm the widely held belief that many people cannot distinguish between a Scottish and an Irish accent in any case. "Many Americans are unfamiliar with the difference between Scottish and Irish sounds, and so you get Scottish-isms coming into Irish accents. Again, it's all about perception" (Moussoulides, personal communication 2005).

[353] In an article from 1930, Maurice L. Ahern wrote what could be seen as a sad epitaph to the stars of the silent era, as they literally tried to find their voice in the new medium: "With each syllable they utter, a friendly fan is lost to them" (Ahern 1930: 310).

properly. What follows is a brief history of the role of these voice coaches, dialect coaches or dialogue coaches, as they are also known[354].

While there are slight shades of meaning between these terms, all three have been used interchangeably in the industry. Technically, a voice coach is normally responsible for teaching proper breathing, voice projection and other elocution techniques, whereas a dialogue coach, in the early days of sound cinema in America, was traditionally somebody who helped actors to learn their lines and who ran dialogue with them. This role later developed into that of the dialect coach, who assisted actors in learning how to approximate various accents. The title, of course, is actually a misnomer and should really be "accent coach", as the coaches teach pronunciation, but not the grammar or other features of the dialects, which are already provided in the screenplay. For the purposes of this study, however, rather than using the terms interchangeably or coining the title "accent coach", I shall continue to use the more popular term "dialect coach".

While very few people can actually name dialect coaches who have worked or still work in the film industry, they are often surprised to hear that there is one dialect coach who is already familiar to them: Henry Higgins. This fictional character from George Bernard Shaw's *Pygmalion*, and from the subsequent film adaptation *My Fair Lady* (George Cukor, 1964), is the consummate dialect coach: He has a perfect ear for phonetics (he can distinguish between 130 distinct vowel sounds); he is able to accurately transcribe and reproduce all manner of sounds ("Cheer ap, Keptin; n' baw ya flahr orf a pore gel."); and, most importantly, he can prepare students to give a convincing performance (Eliza is successfully mistaken for a princess at the grand ball)[355]. The fictional character of Henry Higgins was in fact loosely based on a real linguist, the phonetician Henry Sweet, who was instrumental in the founding of the International Phonetic Alphabet. Sweet was the first of a long list of interconnected pupils and teachers, who have dominated the field of dialect coaching. Sweet taught William Tilly, who in turn instructed Edith Skinner, who herself was the mentor of Timothy Monich, who is one of Hollywood's busiest and most well-respected dialect coaches today.

The most famous of all of these coaches was Edith Skinner, the doyenne of American speech training, whose 1942 text *Speak with Distinction* is still a standard work for actors seeking help with their diction. Throughout her long career, Skinner cultivated and promoted a euphonic style of speech, with clipped British sounds, which can be heard in countless films from Hollywood's Golden Age and still survives today in the speech of actors, such as Kelsey Grammer and Kevin Kline, who studied under Skinner at the Juilliard School in New York.

Despite its venerability, what Skinner termed "Good American Speech" is certainly not without its detractors. In a *Los Angeles Times* article about Dudley Knight, a dialect coach

---

[354] These coaches should not be confused with speech therapists or speech pathologists, whose job is to help their clients to overcome some particular physiological problem in articulation. Voice/dialect/dialogue coaches, in contrast, are involved in various forms of accent modification and reduction, and work with clients who do not have physiological speech impediments. Some dialect coaches, such as Brendan Gunn, however, have worked in both fields. For Gunn, the processes involved are essentially the same: "You have a 'target', a 'realisation' and a 'set of variable parameters'. Obviously, speech therapy is more difficult, depending on the severity of what you're dealing with, but I use a lot of speech therapy techniques [again 'target', 'realisation' and a 'set of variable parameters'" (Gunn: personal communication, March 2005). For more about the potential parallels between the work of dialect coaches and speech pathologists, see Verdolini (1997: 225-35).

[355] The references in parentheses refer to pages 34, 22 and 95 of the Penguin/Klett Edition (2003) of Shaw's *Pygmalion*.

and one of Skinner's greatest critics, the journalist Mike Boehm paraphrases Knight's opposition to Skinner's "Good American Speech", calling it "a highfalutin, vaguely British mode of speaking" which she taught "as the standard, correct sound for actors to use in playing Shakespeare and other classic texts that do not call for a particular regional accent" (Boehm 2000). The words "highfalutin", "correct" and "regional" which are embedded in this quote deserve a closer look as they reveal a great deal about the arguments levelled at Skinner's standard speech, or at any standard for that matter.

The word "highfalutin" would suggest that the accent is pretentious or affected, implying class distinctions. Similarly, the word "correct" makes a clear qualitative judgement about the sounds an actor should be making, and suggests that any other speech is therefore "wrong". It also echoes the word "good" in Skinner's own term "Good American Speech" and implies that those who do not speak it must be using "Bad American Speech". Finally, the removal of "regional" accents from the actors' repertoire in order to gain some all encompassing "American Speech", (never mind the fact that it sounds "vaguely British") essentially robs actors of their own voice. It is exactly this flavourlessness, this non-regional, nondescript nature of the accent, which draws the most criticism from Knight. "In emphasizing 'Good American Speech' as an ideal, or at least as a primary dialect, they [Skinner and her protégées] hinder students' quest to find their own way of speaking, and perpetuate an idea of unified sound for actors that is outmoded in today's multicultural artistic world" (Boehm, 2000).

This "idea of unified sound for actors" is indeed outmoded and has been for a number of years. Modern audiences' demand for realism in film now also extends to realistic accents, making the "Good American Speech" of yesteryear almost obsolete today. Modern actors need to be flexible and the very regional accents which they were long encouraged to lose are now increasingly in demand. The main task of dialect coaches today is not to neutralise accents towards some bland standard, but rather to teach actors how to reproduce regional accents, be they Texan, Cockney, Glaswegian or, as in the case of this study, the various pronunciations of Irish English.

When it comes to Irish film, there has been a particularly strong need in recent years for dialect coaches. The tax incentives which were designed to encourage investment in the Irish film industry from the early 1990s were also ironically instrumental in ensuring that it was non-Irish actors who more often than not received leading roles in Irish films. In his book, *Power in the Eye*, Terry Byrne explains the reasons for this.

> In order to avail of the financial support of those foreign backers whose money is so essential, compromises have had to be made, frequently to the artistic and substantive aspects of a given project. Typically, this may take the form of casting decisions imposed from Britain or California, and the resulting films are those such as *Widows' Peak* and *Circle of Friends*. Hollywood backers, for example, will try to reduce their risk by ensuring that a film shot in Ireland has among its cast a number of names that are 'bankable' in the American market, and we can hardly expect otherwise. Such is the nature of that industry.
>
> (Byrne 1997: 189)

Thus, Irish actors are often overlooked and are replaced by bankable stars whose box-office appeal far outweighs their lack of Irishness, with producers believing that they can compensate for the latter by engaging the services of a dialect coach to make their Irish accents believable[356].

Over the course of my research, I have had the opportunity to conduct interviews with two of the Irish film industry's most accomplished dialect coaches, Brendan Gunn and Poll Moussoulides[357]. These two men regularly face the task of trying to equip foreign actors with credible Irish accents, and the content of my interviews with them will form the basis of some of the following discussion on the role of dialect coaches in film[358].

In the interest of brevity, rather than giving an in-depth description of how exactly dialect coaches teach actors to perform an accent, I will instead present a brief summary of the methods used by these coaches, and encourage the reader to consult Bonnie Raphael's excellent article "Preparing a Cast for a Dialect Show" (1984) for the definitive description of the processes involved.

When it comes to teaching somebody a new accent, the work of the dialect coach is not too dissimilar to that of the foreign-language teacher, insofar as they both try to equip their students with a range of completely new sounds, or combinations of sounds, which differ from those of the students' own sound system, irrespective of whether that system stems from a different language or merely a different variety. Much of the terminology and the techniques used by teachers of English as a Foreign or Second Language (EFL/ESL) can thus be applied to the work of dialect coaches.

One approach to teaching actors a foreign accent is the intuitive-imitative approach, which involves providing the actor with a model pronunciation and having him imitate it. This method "depends on the learner's ability to listen to and imitate the rhythms and sounds of the

---

[356] A quick glance at the casts of the movies in this corpus reveals a "who's who" of some of the film industry's most prominent names: Tom Cruise, Nicole Kidman, Kevin Spacey, Cate Blanchett, Daniel Day-Lewis, John Hurt, Julia Roberts, Alan Rickman, Joan Allen, Jon Voight, Mia Farrow, Robert Mitchum, Sean Connery, Ewan McGregor and Kate Hudson, who have all featured in Irish films and have all assumed Irish accents with varying degrees of success.

[357] In terms of Irish English, dialect coaching, and film, few people are as qualified as Brendan Gunn. Aside from being a renowned dialogue coach who has worked on over fifty films, Gunn has also conducted extensive research on various aspects of English as it is spoken in Ireland, boasting seven entries in Raymond Hickey's *A Source Book for Irish English* (Hickey 2002), including his Master's Thesis, *Aspects of intonation in the speech of the Cork urban area* (1985), his PhD thesis *The politic word* (1990), and several articles, such as "Social and political influences on phonological variation in Northern Irish English" (1984), and "'No Surrender': Existentialist sociolinguistics and politics in Northern Ireland" (1994). He was also involved in compiling the *Tape Recorded Survey of Irish English* for which he collected speech samples in the Cork area. He has taught Linguistics at the University of Ulster, Jordanstown, specialising in Phonetics and Dialectology, as well as teaching Human Communication and Speech Therapy at the Faculty of Social and Health Sciences there. Poll Moussoulides is also no stranger to the world of dialect coaching. A trained actor, he gravitated naturally into the world of dialect coaching for film through his work as Head of Voice at the Gaiety School of Acting and the Samuel Beckett Centre at Trinity College, Dublin. There he taught various aspects of speech production for over a decade and later in 2008 founded the Irish Voice Association. He too is well-versed in all aspects of Irish English, and has worked on over forty films, but admits that despite the fact that he is Irish, his non-Irish-sounding name (his father was Cypriot) can be an obstacle when people are seeking Irish dialect coaches. "When given the choice between a Murphy and a Moussoulides, most people will go with a Murphy" (Moussoulides: personal communication, March 2005). This again shows how people's perceptions of what they regard as typically Irish shape their notion of authenticity (cf. Chapter 3)

[358] Further insights into the work of the dialect coach were gained by consulting a number of works written by dialect coaches, such as Jerry Blunt (1967), Evangeline Machlin (1975), Lewis and Marguerite Herman (1997), Robert Blumenfeld (2000), Kimberly Mohne Hill (2002), Ginny Kopf (2003), and Paul Meier (2004).

target language [or, in this case, accent S.W.] without the intervention of any explicit information" and "also presupposes the availability of good models to listen to" (Celce-Murcia et al. 2000: 2). These good models can take a couple of forms. Either the dialect coach himself will be the model, or he can provide the actor with recordings of some other speaker speaking with the accent. Both options have their positive and negative sides, with the quality of the models playing a key role.

If the dialect coach himself happens to speak with the accent he is teaching, then the student has a perfect living model. However, if the dialect coach is, for example, American and is teaching an actor an Irish accent, then this may lead some people to question how accurate the end-product will be. After all, a copy of a copy is quality-wise usually a couple of steps removed from the original. On the other hand, some actors may find having a "non-native" dialect coach encouraging, as he is likely to know the potential stumbling blocks which the learner will face, and his own ability to imitate the new accent shows that it can, indeed, be done.

Alternatively, the dialect coach can furnish the actor with a recording of the required accent, the advantage of this being that the student has a model (or models)[359] to imitate, even in the absence of his teacher. Here again, however, one should distinguish between recordings which themselves are imitations of accents, such as dialect coach David Alan Stern's *Acting with an Accent* series (Stern 1979), and the real thing. Many dialect coaches, such as Poll Moussoulides, will tailor their recordings to the exact needs of the actor, collecting speech samples from local speakers of the same gender, age and social class as the character to be portrayed, thus giving them the most accurate input possible[360].

The other major approach adapted by dialect coaches from the world of foreign-language teaching is the analytic-linguistic approach, which employs teaching aids, such as the International Phonetic Alphabet (IPA), articulatory descriptions, diagrams of the vocal apparatus, contrastive information, and a host of other materials to supplement listening, imitation, and production. This approach was not designed to take the place of the intuitive-imitative approach, but rather to be employed in tandem with it. The result is that learners are not only provided with a model pronunciation, but that they are also given detailed linguistic information about the sounds they have to produce (cf. Celce-Mercia 2000: 2).

The IPA is very useful for this purpose, as it is well-established and internationally recognised, and once actors have learned it they can apply it to all future accent work. The disadvantage is that many actors have never learned this alphabet. Even when given a chance to learn it from a dialect coach, many are not willing to do so, or due to a tight shooting-schedule cannot afford to invest the time in learning what for them may seem to be a system of strange squiggles and dots. They much prefer to have an approximate orthographic

---

[359] Pennington suggests that as part of the process of elaborating and refining a person's new phonological system, "it may be of value to expose learners through listening material to a wide range of speakers' voices and types of discourse, as input to help shape their developing phonological targets" (1997: 78).
[360] Actors often also request recordings of the coaches saying the actual lines they will have to perform, and dialect coaches may reluctantly oblige. However, they are quick to stress that their job is not interpretive and that while they will happily say the lines with an accent, it is outside of their remit to interpret how these lines should be delivered. Such work is the responsibility of the actor and director. It was exactly this reluctance "to select a particular interpretation of a line, at the expense of others" (Crystal 2005: 33) which initially deterred David Crystal from providing the actors with a recording of him reading the lines from *Romeo and Juliet* in his experiment to recreate Shakespearean pronunciation for the stage. As is so often the case, however, he too later acquiesced and furnished the actors with the auditory material.

representation of the lines they have to say, using the regular English alphabet. While dialect coaches are usually accommodating to such requests, they, nevertheless, need to continue to provide a model pronunciation for the actor. Failure to do this can lead to potential misreading of respellings, as the following quote from Evangeline Machlin's manual for actors shows:

> Since many actors are unfamiliar with IPA, words heard on the tape with dialectal variant sounds are respelled phonetically in this manual, using the ordinary alphabet, not the IPA alphabet. The Southern 'I', for instance, is respelled 'Ah'. The New York-Brooklynese 'shirt' is heard as 'shoit', and is so respelled. The respelling for each variant is as phonetic as possible. But you must always remember that respelling is suggestive rather than exact as to the pronunciation it represents. It is the best that can be done to show dialectal pronunciations using the letters of the alphabet. The dialect pronunciations that you must learn are those HEARD ON THE TAPE. There only can you discover exactly what the respellings stand for. Guiding yourself by what you *hear* rather than by what you *see*, you will safeguard yourself against mistakes in dialect reproduction.
> (Machlin 1975: 2)

Machlin's advice highlights once again the age-old problem which has always befallen dialectal respellings, namely the shortcomings of a twenty-six letter alphabet in representing the forty-plus phonemes of the varieties of English[361].

In addition to offering actors a written model of what they have to say, either in IPA or literary dialect, dialect coaches also try to familiarise their students with the workings of the vocal apparatus, in the hopes that if they know where and how the sound is produced, they may be able to produce it themselves more easily. Again, it is often necessary for the coach to avoid using technical terminology, for the sake of actors who have no grounding in linguistics. Brendan Gunn describes the process of teaching American actors the typically Irish /l/ as follows:

> For example, most Americans have laterals which are somewhat velarised, so if I have in my head that they shouldn't be velarised, I'll tell them that. I won't say 'velarised' to them, I'll just say, 'Keep the back of your tongue down'. And if that doesn't work - some people say, 'Don't tell me physiological stuff, just go really light 'l'' – then, I'll try something else. Basically, I try to get what I have in my head translated into lay terms.[362]
> (Gunn, personal communication)

Whatever method they use, it is desirable, even if it is not always possible due to financial or logistical reasons, that the dialect coach also be present on set during the shooting of the film. The reason for this is that even if the dialect coach has been very successful at teaching the actor the required accent, fossilisation often sets in. This means that while the actor has reached a certain level of attainment, he will not progress beyond this point, and, worse still, if he has begun to make mistakes, he may just reinforce them through repetition.

---

[361] For further information on the shortcomings of literary dialect, see Chapter 2.

[362] In this respect, Gunn echoes the words of Scott Thornbury who describes the approach to teaching pronunciation as one of discovery, "whereby the learning takes place by induction rather than through explicit descriptions or models of voice setting features, on the premise that such descriptions, while useful for the teacher to refer to, are not very helpful for the learner. How, for example, does one lower one's larynx and palatize one's tongue position?" (1993: 131). In a similar vein, Judy Gilbert suggests that "explaining phonological stress rules might not be any more helpful to the pronunciation student than explaining the appropriate laws of physics to someone trying to learn to ride a bicycle" (1980: 111).

In the absence of a dialect coach for monitoring performance, a further method of ensuring accurate feedback is through the use of modern technology. Based on her own research and that of Leon and Martin (1972) and James (1976), Gilbert (1980: 112) advocates the use of technology in aiding pronunciation. She suggests that learners use "speech visualizer equipment" which enables them to compare the accuracy of their mimicry with that of a model by comparing the visual images of their own utterances with those of the model. Pennington (1997: 83) makes a similar suggestion and points to the work of de Bot and Mailfert (1982), and Champagne-Muzar, Schneidermann, and Bourdages (1993), among others. The implementation of such technology would certainly be a helpful means of ensuring accuracy, even in the absence of a dialect coach.

Given the presence of professional dialect coaches and their numerous methods to train actors, one can reasonably ask how it can still be that so many of these learned accents are deemed to be so bad? To find the answer to that question, we shall now look at the factors which determine successful accent acquisition.

8.2 Factors which determine successful accent learning

Much research has been conducted on the factors which are responsible for precise pronunciation among second and foreign language learners, and it is my contention that these factors are essentially the same as those which determine successful accent acquisition for the stage or screen. What follows is a summary of these determinants drawn from Celce-Murcia *et al.* (2000) and Nunan (1995), which has been amended slightly for the purpose of this study, with the term "language" being replaced by "accent" or "dialect" where appropriate[363]. The factors include: the influence of the learner's first language (or, in this case, accent), the learner's age, the amount of exposure to the target accent, the amount and type of prior pronunciation instruction, the actor's phonetic ability, his attitude toward the target accent and his motivation to achieve an accurate accent.

8.2.1 The influence of the learner's first language

Just as a foreign-language student's native sound system will invariably influence his pronunciation in the target language, an actor's attempt at an accent will also be influenced by his own sound system. The contrastive analysis hypothesis holds that "second language acquisition is filtered through the learner's first language, with the native language facilitating acquisition in those cases where the target structures are similar, and 'interfering' with acquisition in cases where the target structures are dissimilar or nonexistent" (Celce-Murcia *et al.* 2000: 20). This "interference", which is now more commonly referred to as "negative transfer," is thus supposed to be a determining factor in cases where accent acquisition is not so successful. As convincing as this hypothesis appears at first sight, it may not hold up to closer scrutiny.

There is, after all, a conflicting hypothesis, Flege's Speech Learning Model (SLM), which suggests that rather than facilitating acquisition, similar target structures actually impede it somewhat.

---

[363] In the direct quotations that follow, I shall leave the word "language" intact, in the interest of fidelity to the original. The reader should, however, insert the word "accent" in its place.

According to Flege (1992a), sounds are classed as 'new', 'similar' or 'identical' on the basis of the differences between L2 sounds and existing L1 sounds, and the model then predicts how the learner will behave. [...] (S)ounds which are classed as being similar to an existing L1 sound will succumb to equivalence classification and only be produced as the L1 sound – never as an authentic L2 sound - , whereas sounds judged to be new will be learnt successfully (in a native-like manner) by learners. Identical sounds will present no problem for the learner, as all necessary articulatory knowledge is already available in the L1.

(Markham, 1997: 107)

The SLM would imply that it is exactly those target structures which are classed as similar which betray an actor by revealing his or her true origins. A good example is Wallace Ford's American realisation of [æ] rather than the Irish English [a] when referring to the Black and Tans in *The Informer* (John Ford, 1935).

8.2.2 The learner's age

A further factor in determining the success of accent acquisition is the learner's age. There is a widely held belief that there is an optimum time for language acquisition and that once learners pass a certain age, they lose their ability to learn new languages to anything close to a near-native level. This belief is known as the critical period hypothesis (cf. Scovel 1969, 1988; Krashen 1973). It is thought that neuroplasticity – "the ability of the young brain to program and process new patterns of behaviour quickly and efficiently, and to relocate this programming and processing to different areas of the brain if there is congenital damage or injury incurred after birth" (Scovel 1988: 62) – is greatest in the brains of young children but then diminishes with age. For our purposes, it is interesting to note that this hypothesis distinguishes between a critical period for acquisition of grammar, pre-puberty, with a steady decline between the ages of twelve and sixteen, and one for the acquisition of near-native pronunciation, merely up to the age of six (cf. Ellis 1997: 68). The theory would suggest that it would be therefore nigh on impossible for an adult actor to ever learn a new accent to such a degree that it would sound native, which echoes Lippi-Green's assertion that a person's accent "is fixed or hard-wired in the mind, and once past a certain age it can only be very laboriously changed, to a very limited degree, regardless of commitment, intelligence, and resources" (Lippi-Green 1997: 241). Having said that, there are conflicting opinions on the validity of this critical period hypothesis, as a number of studies have revealed instances of adult foreign language learners, and, indeed, actors, who have attained excellent pronunciation, thus somewhat discrediting the theory (cf. Neufeld 1977, 1978, 1979, 1980, 1987; Kenworthy 1987; Knight 2000)[364]. Furthermore, as will become apparent, Lippi-Green

---

[364] Scovel (1988), however, debunks the results of studies such as Neufeld's 1977 attempt to teach native speakers of English to imitate ten target utterances in Japanese and Chinese so accurately so as to convince native Japanese and Chinese judges that they too were "native speakers" of these languages. He attacks the methodology employed, the interpretation of the results, as well as Neufeld's definition of how a subject was judged to be a native speaker. Furthermore, he raises an interesting point regarding the fact that, based on what they had been told in advance, the judges were "literally set up to hear native speakers of their mother tongues" (Scovel 1988: 159) and, thus, not surprisingly were more likely to award the judgement of native speaker to what they heard. (If one were to conduct similar research on non-native Irish English accents in film and were to give respondents a loaded question, then one could expect the results to be equally positive.) Given that many of Scovel's critics cite Neufeld's study as the prime example of adult learners being able to attain a native accent after all, by undermining this study so convincingly, Scovel would seem to have struck a winning blow for the critical period hypothesis. Furthermore, critics of the hypothesis are also confronted with the argument that the

may very well have underestimated the effects of "commitment, intelligence, and resources", which, in one way or another, are components of the other factors which determine the degree of accent acquisition.

8.2.3 Amount of exposure to the target accent

The first of these factors is the amount of exposure one has had to the target accent. It is generally agreed that learners acquire language primarily from the input they receive (cf. Postovsky 1974; Asher 1977; Krashen 1982). Therefore the amount of exposure they have to the target accent will play a crucial role in the degree of their success: accents which they have been regularly exposed to should be easier to learn. Even, in the absence of first-hand exposure to the target accent, the media can play a key role, ensuring that somebody, for example, who may never have been to Australia or never met an Australian, yet has had regular exposure to Australian television programmes, such as *Home and Away* and *Neighbours*, will, nonetheless, be able to imitate an Australian accent.

In cases where exposure to an accent is limited, so too will be the success. From an Irish perspective, therefore, the fact that so few Irish television programmes have been readily available to viewers in the UK and the US means that British and American actors lack the same degree of exposure to an Irish accent that an Irish actor who is exposed to many American and British movies and TV shows would have to those accents[365]. This would support an argument made by Michael Dorsey in *Volta Movie Magazine* regarding the poor quality Irish accents on offer from non-Irish actors.

> Why is it that the Hollywood Irish actors can effortlessly reproduce any number of European or American accents, but their British or American counterparts give an Irish accent all four provinces and a box of Lucky Charms wrapped up in forty shades of green? Be-da-hokey! Doff dat cap, Darby, tug dat forelock.
>
> (Dorsey 2000: 31)

Dorsey's comments would appear not only to criticise the quantity of exposure that British and American actors have to Irish accents, but also the quality of that exposure. The reference to "all four provinces" suggests that the accents assumed by foreign actors are often an amalgam of various regional Irish accents which when mixed together create an incredible whole. This opinion is corroborated by a review in the *RTE Guide* of Kevin Spacey's accent in the film *Ordinary Decent Criminal* (Thaddeus O'Sullivan, 2000). "Spacey's Irish accent is

---

critical period is not necessarily limited to neurological development or neuroplasticity alone. It is not merely a question of the mature brain not being able to process new phonological input, but rather that "phonological production is the only aspect of language performance that has a neuro-muscular basis" (Scovel 1988: 101), that is, motor skills are also affected by the critical period. Flege *et al.* have supported this notion, suggesting that "beyond a certain age, L2 learners may have difficulty at a motoric level in modifying pre-established patterns of articulation or in learning new patterns of speech articulation" (Flege *et al.* 1996: 48-9). This means that once our vocal apparatus has become accustomed to producing certain sounds, it requires great effort to recalibrate it. Indeed, studies have shown that adapting ones phonology after the critical period is very difficult, irrespective of whether it is for a completely new language or simply for a new dialect (cf. Scovel 1988: 171-75; Krashen and Seliger 1975: 28-29). In light of these findings, Scovel even goes so far as to suggest that "being a native speaker of English does not ensure that you will have an inordinate advantage in sounding like a native speaker of another dialect in English" (Scovel 1988: 172). Unfortunately, the corpus of Irish films does not feature any non-native speakers of English speaking with an Irish accent for whom we can test this hypothesis.

[365] The fact that Irish television and radio programmes can now be viewed and heard via the Internet means that, in theory, Irish accents can be accessed more easily by audiences worldwide than ever before.

something else, ranging as it does from the walls of Derry to Cork and back again to somewhere in Dublin" (Doherty 2000). Furthermore, *Lucky Charms*, *forty shades of green* and *Darby* are all references to Irish American creations, which are erroneously thought to be Irish, and so if actors are using these questionable sources as their model input, then their Irish accents will be equally questionable.[366]

8.2.4 The amount and type of prior pronunciation instruction

In addition to the amount of exposure to the target accent, the amount and type of prior pronunciation instruction is also a determinant of how accurate an actor's new accent will be. Some actors may have had extensive accent training at drama school or may have already played roles in plays which were written in dialect, thus making learning new accents easier as their ear and vocal apparatus are attuned to hearing and producing new sounds. However, it often arises, just as in EFL settings, that the instruction comes from a teacher whose own pronunciation differs greatly from the target norm, meaning that the coach's own negative transfer is passed onto the students. Moreover, many drama schools use manuals compiled by dialect coaches which aim to teach actors how to acquire a variety of accents, or dialects, as the case may be, yet which may be more detrimental to their acquiring a new accent than no prior instruction at all. These manuals are often poorly researched or so ambitious in their scope[367] that they often unintentionally propagate completely erroneous or stereotypical features. A selection of examples of such misinformation with regard to Irish English will be presented in Chapter 11, as a possible explanation for many of the erroneous features that appear in the films in the corpus.

8.2.5 The actor's phonetic ability

Another factor which influences an actor's ability to assume a new accent is his/her "ear" for accents, as it is often termed. This phenomenon has been variously called one's "phonetic coding ability" or "auditory discrimination ability" (Kenworthy 1987) and also one's "phonemic coding ability" (Carrol 1962, 1981). This ability is believed to have little to do with general intelligence or even language learning ability per se[368], and, indeed, there is a

---

[366] *Lucky Charms* is an American breakfast cereal which uses a leprechaun figure with a faux Irish accent in its advertising campaigns. *Forty Shades of Green* is a sentimental song written by American Country singer, Johnny Cash, about an emigrant reminiscing about the old sod, while *Darby* refers to Darby O'Gill, a character created by the Irish-American writer Hermione Templeton Kavanagh, who appears in a series of books written in dubious literary dialect (cf. Chapter 2 for an extract). The figure is best known from the Disney film *Darby O'Gill and the Little People* (Robert Stevenson, 1959), which was loosely based on Kavanagh's books and again features some debatable Irish accents.

[367] One such manual, *Foreign Dialects. A Manual for Actors, Directors, and Writers*, by Lewis Herman and Marguerite Shalett Herman, for example, ambitiously professes to teach actors all of the following "dialects": Cockney, British, Australian, Bermudan, Indian, Irish, Scottish, German, French, Italian, Spanish, Mexican, Filipino, Portuguese, Japanese, Chinese, Chinese pidgin English, Hawaiian, Beche Le Mar, Australian pidgin, Swedish, Norwegian, Russian, Lithuanian, Yugoslav, Czech, Finnish, Hungarian, Polish, Greek, and Yiddish (Herman and Herman 1997). The same authors also have published a separate volume on the various American dialects. However, these "dialects" are never accompanied by a recording, and, to make matters worse, the authors do not use the IPA, but instead offer faux transcriptions written in undecipherable respellings, such as "dUHd uhEE kUHI UHm, sEHzuhEE" which apparently is "'Did I kill him?' says I" in an Irish accent (Herman and Herman 1997: 68).

[368] It is worth noting that general intelligence or IQ is by no means a predictor of second language learning ability. Oyama states that IQ accounts for only about 18 to 20 per cent of the variance in student success in the foreign language classroom (cf. Oyama 1976: 34). By the same token, good second language learning ability is not a predictor of a good accent, as we have seen regarding the critical period hypothesis.

common belief among lay people, and even among dialect coaches, that this ability to learn accents may have more to do with the learner having, what they call, a "musical ear". For example, dialect coach Ginny Kopf suggests that those with an aptitude for music "will be better able to hear and copy the rhythms and pitch changes of different dialects" (Kopf 2000: 14), while Evangeline Machlin believes that "any actor who can sing a tune can learn to speak a dialect" (Machlin 1975: 1). However, Howard Gardner's seminal work on multiple intelligences offers evidence from in-depth research on the workings of the human brain, which highlights that the information-processing mechanisms for phonology are in fact located "close to the core of linguistic intelligence" and that "investigators working with both normal and brain-damaged humans have demonstrated beyond a reasonable doubt that the processes and mechanisms subserving human music and language are distinctive from one another" (Gardner 1984: 81, 117). Accordingly, in normal right-handed individuals, whose linguistic abilities are centred almost exclusively in the left hemisphere, and whose musical abilities, including sensitivity to pitch, are located in the right hemisphere, neural damage to the left hemisphere, through injuries or illness, will therefore affect a person's speech but not his musical ability (cf. Gardner 1984: 118).[369]

While we may have disproved the connection between having a "musical ear" and an ability for phonology, this does not mean that there is no validity to the notion of somebody having an "ear" for accents, which was mentioned above. Indeed, Flege *et al.* (1996) suggest that one of the main obstacles people encounter when learning pronunciation in a second language is that they simply cannot hear the phonetic nuances of the new language. This condition of "incorrect perception" is explained as follows:

> During L1 acquisition, speech perception becomes attuned to the phonetic elements of the L1. L2 learners may fail to perceive the phonetic details of L2 sounds and sound contrasts accurately owing to the assimilation of L2 sounds by L1 categories. Without accurate perceptual 'targets' to guide sensorimotor learning, production is destined to be inaccurate.
>
> (Flege *et al.* 1996: 48)[370]

As one can see, this issue is closely related to the aforementioned factor of the influence of the learner's first language. What is more, the learner's age can also play a role in this issue. Schneiderman and Desmarais state that research on phonetic perception shows that "adults and older children are less able to discriminate between speech sounds than infants when these sounds are not distinctive in the older subjects' first language [...] and that adults discriminate on the basis of the phonetic categories of their first language" (1988: 111).

---

[369] For further discussion on musical talent and foreign language learning ability see: Blickenstaff (1963) and Judd (1988).

[370] Flege *et al.* go on to state that due to the fact that adults are language-specific perceivers of speech, it is their assumption that "a larger proportion of production errors in a second language may have a perceptual basis" (1996: 66). It should be reiterated, however, that even if one is able to "hear" the nuances of a new language or accent, that does not necessarily mean that one will be able to accurately reproduce those sounds. As outlined already in 8.2.2., once pre-established patterns of articulation have been ingrained by the vocal apparatus, it is very difficult to modify them in order to learn new ones. Further discussion of the interplay between perception and production (or rather reproduction) can be found in Postovsky (1974).

8.2.6 The learner's attitude and sense of identity

A learner's attitude and sense of identity can also play important roles in the acquisition of accurate pronunciation. Indeed, Guiora (1972) argues that personality, or "language ego" as he calls it, is fundamental in the acquisition of a new language, and even more so with regard to pronunciation. "Speaking a foreign language entails the radical operation of learning and manipulating a new grammar, syntax and vocabulary and, at the extreme limits of proficiency, *modifying one of the basic modes of identification by the self and others, the way we sound*" [emphasis mine] (Guiora 1972: 144). This means that the extent to which we believe that our voices and our sense of identity are linked will be a determining factor in whether we are willing to change our voices. Schumann echoes Guiora's comments and calls this measure of our willingness to change "ego permeability" (Schumann 1975: 209-35). Based on this hypothesis, one could argue that actors should be good at learning new accents, as by the very nature of their job they should have a high degree of ego permeability, since they are constantly embodying new characters and assuming new personas[371].

What is more, actors may have another personality-related factor of accent acquisition in their favour, as it has been claimed that individuals who show a basic strong sensitivity to emotion perform better in phonetic acquisition (cf. Markham 1997: 25). If that is indeed the case, then one could certainly argue that actors should therefore be at an advantage, as they generally display this sensitivity to emotion, being able to call up feelings, and sometimes even tears, at will. This notion of empathy leading to superior accent acquisition is supported to a certain degree by the findings of a study by Taylor *et al.* (1969)[372]. However, this applies only to a certain degree, as it is interesting to note that the same study also suggests that, while actors indeed are often very adept at accent acquisition, it may not necessarily stem from their greater sense of empathy but can often be the result of a greater sense of narcissism. The study shows that achievement in pronunciation can be measured in two ways: 1) at a more general level ("General Authenticity") and 2) at a more precise segmental or suprasegmental level ("Specific Criteria"). Moreover, it demonstrates that different personality types play a determining role in our attainment of each. According to Taylor *et al.* (1969: 470), "people who are more aware of feelings [i.e. empathic people S.W.] are more sensitive to the details and specific aspects of the second language and reflect this in speaking".

Those subjects who scored highly on "General Authenticity", on the other hand, did not score highly regarding empathy. On the contrary. They were seen as "egocentric" and as people "who see interpersonal behaviour in terms of motivations and expectations". Their attitude is apparently reflected in their "ability to master the general impression of authenticity in speaking the second language, but it is devoid of the sensitivity to details which make it

---

[371] It might be worth noting, however, that, etymologically speaking, the words *embody* and *persona* only refer to the visible outward transformation of the actor, and do not necessarily suggest an audible change. If actors therefore lack the necessary degree of ego permeability and are not willing to also change the voice behind the mask, then their success with the new accent will be limited.

[372] The study examined the effects of empathy on two aspects of pronunciation: "General Authenticity" (the general impression of the accent created) and "Specific Criteria" (a more detailed evaluation of the accent pertaining to accent patterns or the pronunciation of certain sounds).

really accurate" (Taylor et al. 1969: 470)[373]. The implications for the actor are evident in Taylor et al.'s conclusion that

> The correlations between the intuitive measure and the ability to sound authentic when mimicking sentences, and the unrelated empathic measure and the ability to reproduce correctly the subtle details of the second language spontaneously points out important differential abilities in language pronunciation. This may explain the ability of most actors to imitate dialects when speculation as to their character is that they are more likely to be egocentric than empathic.
>
> (1969: 471)

Whether or not one agrees with Taylor et al.'s opinion about actors, it would appear to be the case that personality also plays a key role in accent acquisition.

8.2.7 The learner's motivation

The final, and for some the most crucial, determinant of success both in language learning and accent acquisition is motivation. Schumann (1986) and Gardner and Lambert (1972) distinguished between various forms of motivation in language learning, which are generally related to acculturation, or the extent to which the learner wants to integrate in the foreign-language community.

The first of these types of motivation is "integrative motivation" in which a learner desires to be integrated socially into the target culture, and thus learns the language. The second is "assimilative motivation" and is like the first, in that it involves a longing to be integrated. However, in the latter case, this longing is even greater, with the learner desiring to become indistinguishable from other members of the target speech community. Neither of these forms of motivation are necessarily those which drive actors who accept accent roles. They may have no personal desire at all to integrate with the community represented in the film, never mind completely assimilate there. What is more, the film may not even be shot in the actual target speech community being depicted: "Irish" films, such as *Waking Ned* and *Darby O'Gill and the Little People*, for example, were filmed on the Isle of Man and in Burbank, California respectively. Thus, the actors in those films would not even have had the chance to integrate or assimilate with the Irish people even if they had wanted to.

A better descriptor for an actor's motivation is perhaps "instrumental motivation", that is, the incentive involved when someone learns a new language (or accent) in order to attain a certain goal – to pass an examination or to get a job promotion. While this last type of motivation does not really involve acculturation, it does not mean that it is any less effective than the previous two. In fact, Lukmani (1972) has argued that the intensity of motivation is often as important as the type of motivation at play. Celce-Mercia echoes this notion, adding that "someone with extraordinarily high instrumental motivation (e.g. someone who wants to sound like a native speaker in order to function effectively as an actor or an espionage agent) may well achieve a better pronunciation than someone with integrative motivation that is quite positive yet less intense" (2000: 19)[374]. What better motivation could there be for a

---

[373] This finding is in keeping with Guiora's intuitive mode of comprehending (Guiora 1965; Guiora et al. 1965), the focus of which is "the opposite of empathy, self-directed rather than extended toward the other" (Taylor et al. 1969: 471).

[374] It is interesting, however, to note that, in the realm of psychology, the Yerkes-Dodson law states that "high motivation enhances performance on only relatively simple tasks, whereas it may hinder performance on

screen actor than the fact that if he fails to perform the accent properly, he runs the risk of embarrassing himself in front of millions of people? After all, in film, unlike in theatre, one's performance is not ephemeral, but rather is captured forever on celluloid.

As we have seen, there are numerous factors which can influence one's ability to successfully acquire a new accent. In this regard, it is interesting to question whether any of these individual factors has been proven to be more important than others. This notion was analysed in depth by Purcell and Suter (1980), who examined the following twelve factors[375] in relation to their influence on students' accuracy in their pronunciation of a second language, namely English: 1) First language, 2) Strength of Concern for Pronunciation Accuracy, 3) Percent of Conversation at Work or School, 4) Age of First Meaningful Conversation, 5) Years in an English-Speaking Country, 6) Aptitude for Oral Mimicry, 7) Intensive Classroom Training in English, 8) Formal Classroom Training in English, 9) Integrative Orientation, 10) Age of First Residence in English-Speaking Country, 11) Percent of Conversation at Home in English and 12) Residence with Native Speakers of English. The study found that the four most meaningful predictors of successful pronunciation accuracy were: First Language, Aptitude for Oral Mimicry, Residency, and Strength of Concern for Pronunciation Accuracy (Purcell and Suter 1980: 284-5). The contribution of the other factors was deemed negligible after the first four had been analysed using regression analysis. Obviously, not all of these factors realistically come into question for an actor preparing for a film role, with long term residence in the region or country in question or living with native speakers of that dialect unlikely to happen. However, seeing as it was one of the more influential factors in Purcell and Suter's study, it might be something for actors to bear in mind. Indeed, Tom Cruise and Nicole Kidman had an Irish couple come to live with them as preparation for their roles in *Far and Away*[376]. With little success, some would argue.

8.3 Defining successful accent acquisition

Having examined the possible reasons for success or failure in accent acquisition, it is important to take a moment to question what exactly we mean by "successful" accent acquisition, in the first place. In the world of Second Language Acquisition it generally implies being able to speak the target language in a native fashion, so that one does not draw attention to oneself as a non-native speaker[377]. The evidence given by Scovel (1988) suggests that for post-pubescent learners this is possible for grammar and lexicon, but is not possible for pronunciation. The result is what he termed the "Joseph Conrad phenomenon," named

---

difficult ones" (Oyama 1976: 27). This indeed proved to be the case in Oyama's study, where for many of the non-native speakers their increased monitoring of their own pronunciation while reading a paragraph actually led to poor performance (cf. Oyama 1976: 27). Attention will need to be paid to this aspect with regard to accent in film. Tasks which could be regarded as "difficult" include maintaining an accent during emotional scenes or action scenes, as well as imitating the timbre of a voice of a well-known figure.

[375] Suter (1987) had previously compiled these 12 factors from a possible 20 in a 1976 study. He had not attempted, however, to assess the relative importance of the 12.

[376] Cf. Entertainment Weekly http://www.ew.com/ew/article/0,,310539,00.html (Retrieved: April 24, 2008).

[377] However, in the world of Second Language Acquisition, this goal is no longer thought to be realistic. Kenworthy (1987) writes that "very few teachers today would claim that a pronunciation that is indistinguishable from that of a native speaker is necessary or even desirable for learners. Instead, it is generally accepted that intelligibility is the most sensible goal. [...] When we set intelligibility as our goal, rather than native-like pronunciation, in practical terms this means we are aiming for something 'close enough'" (Kenworthy 1987: 13). If teachers no longer expect perfect pronunciation and are happy with something "close enough", should audience expectations change accordingly and should we be more tolerant of actors' attempts at accents?

after the Polish-born English novelist who mastered the English language brilliantly, despite only beginning to learn it in his late teens, but whose strong foreign accent was a source of embarrassment to him and prevented him from lecturing publicly in English (Scovel 1969: 247).

With regard to actors, however, there is, in theory, little or no need for them to be able to master the grammar or lexicon of the language or dialect they have to perform, as essentially all they need to do is learn the lines they have been given in their script and deliver them verbatim to the camera. To that end, they do not, in theory, even have to be able to speak the language they are repeating. As far as their language skills are concerned, one could therefore argue that they have more in common with a parrot than with Joseph Conrad. Indeed their achievements could probably be best compared to those of the subjects in Neufeld's 1979 study which tested the success of English speakers learning ten target utterances in Chinese and Japanese.

In the case of Neufeld's subjects, they were tutored extensively to produce a small set of utterances, with the last of their five recordings being selected to be presented to the respondents who would be judging them. For many actors, the process is not much different, in that they too are tutored to achieve native-like accuracy for merely a limited number of target utterances[378]. The number of utterances to be mastered at any one time is also already automatically limited due to the slow process of shooting a film, and thus an actor, just like Neufeld's subjects, can focus on perfecting very short passages at any one time. What is more, the nature of filming several takes of every scene means that, again like Neufeld's speakers, actors also have multiple chances to get it right, if they or the filmmakers are not satisfied with their first attempts. Whether or not success in this short act of mimicry can be regarded as real success is open to debate, and most people would probably side with Gass and Selinker (1994: 240) who state that "performance on limited tasks is not equivalent to consistent performance in naturalistic situations" and that "the shorter and less demanding the task, the easier it is to feign." Be that as it may, for actors, unlike for second language learners, success in their few short speeches would appear to be more than enough.

It is, however, important for this study to distinguish between the achievements of actors working in the medium of film and those who work in theatre, as the criteria for judging the success of their accented performances are slightly different. While actors in theatre must also learn a limited number of target utterances, the number of these sentences is generally much larger and the actors need to be able to perform them all at once, chronologically, with no chance of repeating them for an audience if they slip up. In light of this fact, one could argue that their task is, therefore, all the more difficult and more likely to be open to criticism from audiences. The opposite, however, is the case.

Film actors are, in fact, the ones whose poor accents are more prone to criticism, for a number of reasons. Firstly, it is exactly because film actors' utterances are so short *and* because they have so many chances to get it right that audience tolerance of poor accents is very low. A second reason for such intolerance could be related to Bazin's "concept of presence" (Bazin 1967: 97-8). He suggests that the inherent presence of both the actor and the audience in a theatre means that the audience members feel for the actor should he forget a

---

[378] Actors, like Daniel Day-Lewis or Robert Carlyle, who immerse themselves in the accent in true Strasbergian "method" style for the duration of filming and who readily improvise dialogue in the target accent, both on set and off, are something of an exception (cf. Ryan 1989: 105 and Doyle 2000: 23).

line (or should his accent slip) and they are, thus, more forgiving. This relationship is not there between an audience in a cinema and an actor on the big screen[379].

Finally, the mere fact that film actors' performances are captured forever means that they can be subjected to multiple viewings and they can be witnessed by a much larger audience than an actor's once-off poor performance in the theatre. This in itself means that they are exposed to many more critical ears.

---

[379] Cf. Bazin (1967: 97-8). He later goes on to introduce the concept of the "pseudopresence" which exists during live television, whereby the actor is somehow with the viewers live in their sitting room, yet they are not present in the studio. He states that "the reciprocal actor-spectator relationship is incomplete in one direction" and that "this abstract presence is most noticeable when the actor fluffs his lines. Painful enough in the theater, it is intolerable on television since the spectator who can do nothing to help him is aware of the unnatural solitude of the actor. In the theater in similar circumstances a sort of understanding exists with the audience, which is a help to an actor in trouble. This kind of reciprocal relationship is impossible on television [and in the cinema. S.W.]." (Bazin 1967: 97-8). For more on the differences between acting in film and in theatre, see McDonald (1998).

9 Irish English accents in the film corpus

When it comes to describing the phonological features of Irish English, it is difficult to speak of a "typical" Irish accent, as, of course, there is potential for regional differences in pronunciation[380]. However, rather than becoming distracted by the individual features which distinguish the regional accents from one another, I shall, like Bliss (1977) and Wells (1982b), focus on those features which they have in common. In that respect, the accent being described can be regarded as some sort of a generic Irish one. It should be noted, however, that this accent is not quite equivalent to Hickey's "supraregional accent" (2004a: 28-29)[381], as the supraregional standard omits some of the conservative features which are quite common in rural speech and which shall be treated in my study.

It is worth noting, with regard to this study, that the notion of describing a generic accent is also in keeping with the aims of many dialect coach manuals, which freely admit to not professing to teach the actor a specific regional accent, but rather focus on an all-encompassing accent for the stage or screen. This philosophy is echoed in the introduction to Blunt's *Stage Dialects*.

> Were the stage dialectician under the same obligation as the phonetician or regional-speech expert, he would of necessity be concerned with the minutiae of each variant. But an actor's work, like the drama of which it is a part, is in this respect interpretive rather than scientific. The result is that, within the entities of the various dialects, the player seeks a standard which represents the variations.
>
> (Blunt 1967: 2)

In what follows, I shall examine what other linguists have thus far identified as common phonological features of Irish English, and I shall offer examples of such pronunciations from the film corpus. In each case, I shall include the approximate time of their occurrence in the movies, so that the reader can consult the respective DVDs at his or her leisure. This chapter begins by addressing consonants, before moving on to look at vowels. Seeing as so many of the films in the corpus are set in Dublin, I shall also include some brief descriptions and examples of particularly Dublin features. Chapter 10 will address features which are deemed to not belong to Irish English, but which are, nonetheless, used erroneously by actors in the films in the corpus.

9.1 Consonants

9.1.1 /θ/ and /ð/

The Irish English pronunciations of <th> are probably the most conspicuous features of the Irish accent[382]. According to Hickey, "in the main one can say that the dental fricatives of

---

[380] In the context of this study, it is even more difficult to speak of a typical accent, as even if there were such a thing, it would be susceptible to change over time, and in the case of when the films in the corpus are set this would be a time span of two centuries.
[381] Lexical sets for Hickey's supraregional standard and for a number of other common Southern Irish English accents can be found in Hickey (2004a: 55-59).
[382] Irish people's tendency to "mispronounce" <th> is all the more conspicuous, due to the fact that "as a class, the alveolar phonemes emerge as those which occur most frequently" in the English language (Gimson 1970: 219). What is more, the Irish habit of overusing the definite article, which is already the most common word in the English language, ensures that there are even more contexts for <th> to occur, and thus Irish people draw additional attention to what are supposed to be dental fricatives.

standard English are realised as stops in Irish English" (2005: 29). The reason for this realisation is that when Irish people were first exposed to the English language, they simply used the closest equivalents they had from Irish when producing English fricatives. These equivalents were the dental allophones of the non-palatal or coronal stops of Irish (cf. Bliss 1979: 232 and Hickey 2004a: 33). However, it is important to make a distinction between the stops produced for /θ/ and /ð/ in different parts of the country: the dental stops [t̪] and [d̪] are generally used in the west of Ireland compared to the alveolar stops [t] and [d], employed in the east and south (cf. Hickey 2004a: 33). Natives of Ireland can hear a clear difference between the dental and alveolar stops, and the use of the latter for the former is strongly stigmatised[383] (cf. Hickey 2004a: 59). Non-natives of Ireland, on the other hand, are often not able to hear this distinction and assume that [t] and [d] are used in all cases, when, in fact, [t̪] and [d̪] are the supraregional standards. This confusion has been exacerbated somewhat by the fact that representations of Irish pronunciation in literary dialect have, by necessity, had to comply with the constraints of a twenty-six-letter alphabet and, thus, the letters <t> and <d> have been understood to represent the alveolar pronunciation, even in cases where dental stops may have been meant[384].

Some examples of respellings of /θ/ and /ð/ using <t> and <d> are given below:

tink	trone	trut	bat	tirty
(think)	(throne)	(truth)	(bath)	(thirty)
wid	widout	de	dat	dis
(with)	(without)	(the)	(that)	(this)

(Taniguchi 1972: 237)

As outlined above, one cannot be sure whether the respellings listed by Taniguchi are supposed to suggest the supraregional [t̪] and [d̪] or rather [t] and [d]. However, in the film corpus, the distinction in pronunciation is clear. Below are some instances of the supraregional forms:

[t̪] and [d̪] for /θ/ and /ð/

[t̪]
638) For **theft**.

(*When the Sky Falls*, 00:06:56, FSH1990D)

---

[383] A look at the letters page of *The Irish Times* between November and December 2001 reveals a series of letters regarding the phenomenon. The debate was sparked by a letter criticising the "inability of some R[adio] T[elefis] E[ireann] presenters to pronounce the consonant 'th' correctly" which results in announcements such as "Arsenal four, Chelsea tree" (Feldman 2001). Correspondents to the newspaper were quick to either express their agreement with Feldman or to jump to the defence of the supposed "offenders" claiming the lack of [θ] and [ð] (or rather the presence of [t̪] and [d̪]) to be some sort of badge of honour, "linking us to our Gaelic past" and which should not be abandoned "in favour of a more bland, orthodox variety" (Riordan 2001).
[384] For more on the problems of misrepresentation in literary dialect, see Bliss (1979: 189).

       [t]
639) See ya **Thursday** so, David.

(Garage, 00:15:12, MJ2000M)

      [d]   [d]   [d]   [d]
640) He lives in **the**…**the**…wishing-well in **the**…in **the** courtyard.

(A Very Unlucky Leprechaun, 00:07:33, MPM1990W)

[t] and [d] for /θ/ and /ð/

As outlined above, the phonological feature with perhaps the highest degree of saliency in Irish English is the substitution (as well as the perceived substitution) of [t] and [d] for /θ/ and /ð/. In the film corpus, this substitution is evident in various positions in the following sentences:

In initial position:

              [d]   [t]
641) Do ya remember **them three**, Orla, years ago?

(Adam and Paul, 00:15:44, FM2000D)

            [d] [t]
642) Adam, Paul and Matthew. Like **the Three** Musketeers yez were.

(Adam and Paul, 00:15:58, FM2000D)

               [d]   [t]
643) Listen, I haven't managed to shift **that** other **thing** yet, like, ya know?

(Trojan Eddie, 00:02:33, MR1990M)

   [t]
644) I **think** I'll go for a bit of a swim meself.

(Trojan Eddie, 00:22:52, FK1990M)

   [t]
645) Oh, **thank** you for the zoo.

(A Man of No Importance, 00:44:33, FA1960M)

     [t]   [t]
646) Was it "**thick**"? "**Thick**" for droppin' the message, was it?

(The Wind that Shakes the Barley, 01:18:27, MTe1920C)

In medial position:

       [t]
647) It's all right. It's **nothin'**. I'm just being stupid.

(A Man of No Importance, 00:43:40, FA1960M)

   [t]
648) I did **nothin'** wrong.

(Intermission, 00:31:41, MBD2000D)

In final position:

                                [t]

649) Tell you the **truth**, your cabbages is the furthest thing from my mind.

                                           (*How Harry Became a Tree*, 00:37:11, MF1920WW)

                                [t]

650) Why choose when you can have **both**, boy?

                                         (*Ordinary Decent Criminal*, 00:06:01, MB1990C)

However, it is important to note that such pronunciations do not necessarily occur at every opportunity. In fact, there are examples of Irish actors using [d] or [t] in one <th> word in a sentence and then using the Standard English [θ] or [ð] in another. Below are some examples:

                            [t]   [θ]   [θ]

651) Well, it's a biblical **theme**. That's a good **thing**. A fine **thing**.

                                          (*A Man of No Importance*, 00:17:18, MFR1960W)

     [θ]   [t]

652) **Thirteen thousand** pounds.

                                         (*A Very Unlucky Leprechaun*, 00:13:00, MMMcG1990D)

Such evidence also shows that criticism of writers not being consistent in their respellings when employing literary dialect are not justified, as there can be a great deal of free variation both within the speech of different characters and within a single character's own speech.

9.1.2 [t̪] and [d̪] for /t/ and /d/

The Standard English plosives /t/ and /d/ differ from the corresponding pair in the Irish language, in that the latter are dentalised and are followed by quite a high degree of aspiration. These Irish sounds were carried over into the pronunciation of the first speakers who had contact with English, and still persist today, particularly before /r/. The reason for this is the equal-quality rule which exists in Irish, which stipulates that all the consonants in any consonant group must be of the same quality, i.e. all must be either palatal (/t, d, ʃ, ʒ, n, l/) or non-palatal (/t̪, d̪, s, z, r/). This quality is determined by the quality of the final consonant in the group. This phenomenon has also carried over into Irish English and is visible with regard to the group /tr, dr/ which are often realised as [t̪r, d̪r], as in [t̪rɪk] *trick* or [d̪rɑp] *drop*. The same applies when /r/ is syllabic as in [dɑːt̪r] *daughter* or [lad̪r] *ladder* (cf. Bliss 1984: 138)[385]. The result is that words featuring the clusters /tr/ and /dr/, as well as /tər/ and /dər/ are pronounced [t̪r] and [d̪r] or [t̪ər] and [d̪ər] respectively[386]. This is a very salient feature of Irish English and has often been imitated in literary dialect through the use of the letter <h> after the <t> or the <d> to suggest that aspirant quality. Taniguchi offers numerous examples of literary respellings which aim to reflect this pronunciation:

---

[385] Whilst Bliss omits schwa where <-ter> and <-der> occur, I shall include it in my transcriptions, in keeping with Hickey and others. Furthermore, I shall use square brackets in my transcriptions, unlike Bliss (1984).

[386] Hickey observes that "the /r/ is realised as a tap or slight trill due to the position of the tongue parallel to the escaping airstream (Bernoulli effect) and it (sic) frequently voiceless" (2004a: 38).

afther	betther	consthruction	flutther	misther
(after)	(better)	(construction)	(flutter)	(mister)
sthrip	sthrong	thrick	thruth	wather
(strip)	(strong)	(trick)	(truth)	(water)
dhrink	dhrunken	dhry	murrdher	ordher
(drink)	(drunken)	(dry)	(murder)	(order)

(Taniguchi 1972: 236)

There are also numerous examples of this realisation in the film corpus, as can be seen below:

[tr]
653) Well, the ignorant old bog-**trotter**!
(*Angela's Ashes*, 00:47:35, FGS1930L)

[tr]
654) Aye, I married a **Traveller** - ould Kitty, the Lord be good to her.
(*Trojan Eddie*, 00:21:13, MJP1990M)

[tr]
655) There's a great passin' **trade** nowadays. Passin'.
(*Garage*, 00:13:42, MJ2000M)

[tr]
656) **Strippin'** in front of that ould man.
(*Trojan Eddie*, 00:24:33, MD1990M)

[tr]   [tr]
657) **Country** girls is very lax in their morals. It's all that loose **straw** lying around.
(*A Man of No Importance*, 01:02:00, FRW1960D)

658) Tell me, is that fella Dermot O'Brien still codding tourists into marrying
[tr]
complete **strangers**?
(*The Matchmaker*, 00:36:00, MOH2000W)

[tr]   [tr]
659) Well, that's a bold **stroke** and no mistake, **Maestro**.
(*A Man of No Importance*, 00:17:54, MCB1960D)

[tər]
660) Aye, not for the **better**.
(*This is my Father*, 00:20:58, FT2000M)

[tər]
661) It doesn't **matter**.
(*A Man of No Importance*, 00:42:10, FA1960M)

[tˠəɾ]
662) Then go back to London and write us a **letter**.
(*Ryan's Daughter*, 00:11:12, FG1920W)

[tˠəɾ]
663) Two brown sauce sambos. Slap it on thick, no **butter**, two pints of Guinness.
(*Intermission*, 00:09:56, MO2000D)

[dˠəɾ]
664) Are these the same **outsiders** who drove us to the coffin ships and
[tˠəɾ]
scattered us to the four corners of the earth?
(*The Field*, 00:17:24, MBMC1950W)

[tˠəɾ]
665) A night on the **batter**.
(*The Van*, 01:04:43, ML1990D)

[tˠəɾ]
666) Kay Curley gave her a terrible **clatter** on the nose.
(*The Snapper*, 00:41:10, FRW21990D)

[tˠəɾ]
667) Jayz, poor Bimbo must be in **tatters**.
(*The Van*, 00:45:15, ML1990D)

[tˠəɾ]
668) As long as no one minds *Leprechaun Land* being under **water**.
(*Irish Jam*, 00:35:04, MP2000W)

[tˠəɾ]
669) Anyways, the pumps are old and contrary. I don't like to see the **punters** usin' them. Only break them they would.
(*Garage*, 00:22:47, MJ2000M)

[tˠəɾ]
670) If it's **entertainment** you want, try your hand at that fella.
(*The Nephew*, 00:30:38, MT1990C)

[tˠəɾ]
671) I've got two of me **daughters** livin' beyond in the States. One of them is married to a Yank. He's half an Apache. Lovely young lad. Great head of hair on him.
(*When Brendan Met Trudy*, 00:55:41, MHM2000D)

[tˠəɾ]   [tˠəɾ]   [tˠəɾ]
672) I mean, 25% is a **quarter**. You can't have a **quarter** of a **quarter**.
(*My Left Foot*, 00:16:06, MMB1950D)

[tˬər]
673) I could have strung the **bastard** up by the balls.
(*Garage*, 00:30:15, MSul2000M)

[tˬər]   [dˬər]
674) There's nothin' I like **better** than the glow of **murder** in a young fella's eyes.
(*Far and Away*, 00:11:41, MDD1880W)

[dˬər]
675) When I was a girl, years would go by without a **murder**.
(*This is my Father*, 00:20:51, FT2000M)

[dˬər] [tr]   [dˬr]   [tr]
676) I am **under instructions**. The **driver** of this **train** has been...
(*The Wind that Shakes the Barley*, 00:11:50, MTC1920C)

[dˬr]
677) And you can't lift him up on the seat in case he'd fall in and **drown**.
(*Rat*, 00:15:35, MM2000D)

[dˬr]
678) You know what I find fascinating, a mhúinteoir? **Dreams**.
(*Intermission*, 00:33:21, MRG2000D)

[dˬr]
679) Dave, would you ever **dry** up! I'm trying to study.
(*Mystics*, 00:08:32, ML2000D)

[dˬr]
680) Now, go and buy yourself a few sweets, eh...**drinks**.
(*The Snapper*, 00:33:04, MGB1990D)

9.1.3 Additional realisations of alveolar plosives

The fricativisation of /t/ sometimes occurs in intervocalic and word-final positions in Irish English, and is a remnant of Old English (cf. Taniguchi 1972: 236)[387]. While this being a survival of Old English is true for the Irish pronunciation of *height* as [haɪθ], the rule has also been transferred to other contexts as *drought* [drauθ][388] and the following instances from the film corpus, in which *throat* becomes [troːθ][389].

---

[387] Taniguchi suggests that this process also happens to /d/, although he does not offer any examples to support this. I have not been able to substantiate his claim.
[388] The literary dialect respelling of *drought* as <drouth> reflects this pronunciation (cf. Share 2006: 137).
[389] Strangely, given the fact that they are generally renowned for not realising <th> as [θ], Irish people often do so in circumstances where in RP it would be pronounced [t]. Such fricativisation regularly occurs in initial position in words such as *Thailand*, *thyme* and *Thames* and is possibly an example of hypercorrection.

[θ]
681) I'd come up with you, only I've an awful **throat** on me.
(*The Snapper*, 00:05:42, MDC1990D)

[θ]
682) Mad cow's a bit different though. Take the fucking **throat** off you.
(*Dead Meat*, 00:52:46, MC2000LM)

9.1.4 [ʃ] for /s/

There are a number of contexts where one can predict the substitution of /ʃ/ for /s/ in Irish English. These are strongly governed by the use of /ʃ/ in Irish, for which the aforementioned equal-quality rule stipulates that all the consonants in any consonant group must be of the same quality, i.e. all must be either palatal (/t, d, ʃ, ʒ, n, l/) or non-palatal (/t̪, d̪, s, z, r/). It is important again to note that this quality is determined by the quality of the final consonant in the group. This rule from Irish also applies whenever in Irish English the fricative /s/ is followed by one of the consonants which are similar to the Irish palatal consonants /t, n, l/. In those cases, /s/ is replaced by /ʃ/, as in [ʃtɑp] *stop*, [ʃnoː] *snow*, and [ʃloː] *slow* (cf. Bliss 1984: 139). This also happens before final /t/ and syllabic /n, l/, as in [beʃt] *best*, [lɪʃn] *listen*, and [reʃl] *wrestle*. In instances where English /s/ is followed by the cluster /tr/, however, this substitution does not occur, because, as was shown above, in Irish English speech /tr/ is itself realised as [t̺r], thus rendering the context for such a change obsolete. Thus one encounters [st̺rɑŋ] *strong* and [maːst̺r] *master* but not *[ʃtrɑŋ] or *[maːʃtr] (cf. Bliss 1984: 139).

When it comes to literary dialect representations of this feature, authors often do not appear to be aware of the constraints of the Irish English phonological system. For example, based on examples in literature, Taniguchi offers the following environments for the use of /ʃ/, not all of which are correct.

Before /uː/ or /w/
Taniguchi suggests that /ʃ/ can be used in place of /s/ before /uː/ or /w/ and he offers the following literary dialect examples:

conshume	purshue	reshume
(consume)	(pursue)	(resume)
shwear	shwim	shwum
(swear)	(swim)	(swum)

(Taniguchi 1972: 239)

However, Mr K.W. Heaslip, a native of Ireland, who Taniguchi had invited to comment on his findings, pointed out that while he and his colleagues agreed with the substitution of /ʃ/ for /s/ before /w/, they were not sure about the substitution before /uː/ (Taniguchi 1972: 239).

This also reflects my findings, which reveal that the substitution of /ʃ/ for /s/ before /w/ is possible as in the following example from the film corpus:

[ʃw]
683) Here with our arses fuckin' **swung** out in the wind.
(*Dead Meat*, 00:49:16, MC2000LM)

The substitution of /ʃ/ for /s/ before /uː/, however, does not appear in the films, thus confirming Mr Heaslip's assumptions. The fact that this combination does not occur appears to be in keeping with the rules of Irish. After all, in Irish the <s> before long /u/ in words like *súil* 'eye' and *súgradh* 'to play' etc is always pronounced as [s] and not [ʃ], due to the equal-quality rule which stipulates that broad (i.e. palatalized) consonants, like /s/, are always preceded or followed by the broad vowels <a>, <o> and <u> (/a/, /ɔː/, /ə/, /oː/, /ʊ/ and /uː/), while slender (i.e. velarized) consonants, like /ʃ/, always occur together with <e> and <i> (/e/, /eː/, /ɪ/, /iː/) (cf. MacMathúna and Nic Mhaolain 2006: xi and MacEoin 1993: 104-11).

Before /t/
One of the most frequent contexts for /s/ to be replaced by /ʃ/ is before /t/, as the following examples from Taniguchi and the film corpus show:

blasht (blast)	frosht (frost)	shtand (stand)	shtock (stock)	shtool (stool)	shtop (stop)
shtiff (stiff)	shtreet[390] (street)	resht (rest)	tashte (taste)	thirsht (thirst)	wansht (once)

(Taniguchi 1972: 239)

[ʃt]
684) It's on the band **stand**.
(*The Boys and Girl from County Clare*, 00:24:50, MJJ1960Cl)

[ʃt]
685) Then why do you **steal** my life and you make it somethin' else?
(*Nora*, 01:27:15, FN1900G)

[ʃt]
686) She'll be here. And **stop** pacing like that. You'll give yourself a heart attack.
(*The Boys and Girl from County Clare*, 00:37:20, FM1960Cl)

[ʃt]
687) No, I was just wonderin', like. I didn't realise you had a **stake** in the business.
(*Garage*, 00:17:45, MBr2000M)

---

[390] This cluster is not possible in Irish English due to the constraint explained on page 209.

[ʃt]
688) **Stone** mad.

(*Garage*, 00:20:06, MJ2000M)

[ʃ]   [ʃt]
689) Damn you for **listening**[391] to the **priest**.

(*The Field*, 01:40:13, MBMC1950W)

[ʃt]
690) Sir, we'd like the address, sir, to claim for the **assistance**.

(*Into the West*, 00:07:00, MMM1990D)

[ʃt]
691) **Best** I ever heard.

(*The Boys and Girl from County Clare*, 00:49:10, MJJ1960Cl)

[ʃt]
692) Ah, **blast** it!

(*Into the West*, 00:34:03, MI1990D)

[ʃt]
693) Ah, no. **Just** here to register.

(*The Boys and Girl from the County Clare*, 00:21:52, MJJ1960Cl)

[ʃt]
694) Oh, it's a fine night. The **finest** night of me life.

(*The Informer*, 00:46:20, MG1920D)

[ʃt]
695) We're **stuck**. You'll have to get out and push.

(*Dead Meat*, 00:48:32, MC2000LM)

In final sounds

polish, poleeish (police)	conversh (converse)	thish (this)	ish (is)

(Taniguchi 1972: 240)

The notion of /ʃ/ replacing /s/ in word-final position in Irish English is questionable, even if in Irish it is possible for /ʃ/ to appear after /iː/ and /ɪ/ as in *arís* meaning 'again' and *anois* meaning 'now'. Mr Heaslip and his Irish colleagues also cast doubt on the likelihood of hearing the forms above, which Taniguchi had discovered in Shakespeare's *Henry V*.

---

[391] Despite the <t> in *listening* being silent, /s/ is nonetheless palatalized in this context before syllabic /n/ (cf. Bliss 1984: 139).

In other combinations

shmall	shmoke	shplit	shpoil
(small)	(smoke)	(split)	(spoil)

(Taniguchi 1972: 240)

[ʃn]
696) We were playing **snap**, right lads?
(*The Field*, 01:02:58, MBMC1950W)

[ʃn]
697) Ah, you know me - a hardy **snipe**.
(*Trojan Eddie*, 00:15:02, MPMD1990M)

[ʃk]
698) This is **skelping**.
(*High Spirits*, 01:04:27, FMP1980W)

[ʃm]
699) Can you lend me the loan of a **small** pinch of tea?
(*Darby O'Gill and the Little People*, 00:01:52, FMS1800K)

[ʃm]
700) Oh, you can **smile** now, but who in this town would have you?
(*Darby O'Gill and the Little People*, 00:02:25, FMS1800K)

In the example below, one would probably expect *stars* to feature /ʃ/ rather than /s/, in keeping with the substitution which takes place in the word *sleeping*. However, one could argue that free variation is at play here.

701) You're all afraid that if you touch me you'll lose the soil under your feet
[ʃl]
and end up **sleeping** under the stars.
(*The Field*, 00:34:13, FTG1950W)

[ʃl]
702) You had better be, 'cause I'm goin' to **slap** every penny of that on you.
(*Trojan Eddie*, 00:55:14, MJP1990M)

Bliss (1979: 235) observes that "in the Irish consonant-cluster *rs* the *r* may induce in the *s* a retroflex articulation which gives it an acoustic resemblance to /ʃ/" and that this articulation may have found its way into Irish English. Evidence of this can be heard in the example:

      [ʃ]   [ʃ]
703) Drinkin', **cursin'** and fightin'. Drinkin', **cursin'** and fightin'. That's what erupted shortly after I left the dance at Temperance Hall last night.
(*This is my Father*, 00:35:30, MFR1930M)

Another variant affects the cluster /kst/ and can also be found in the films:

[kʃt]
704) Godfrey is not **next** or near the house.
(*Widows' Peak*, 00:02:45, FDC1930M)

[kʃt]
705) I could fix it for **sixty**.
(*Into the West*, 00:09:03, MPR1990D)

9.1.5 [ʒ] for /z/

The equal-quality substitution rule also applies to /z/, even though it is not a phoneme in Irish, with Irish English /z/ behaving in the same way as /s/ and, thus, being replaced by the voiced palato-alveolar fricative /ʒ/ when followed by /d, n, l/, as in [ˈwenʒdi] *Wednesday*, [ˈbɪʒnəs] *business*, [ˈpɔʒl] *puzzle* (cf. Bliss 1984: 139).

The Irish English substitution of /ʒ/ for /z/ is not addressed by Taniguchi in his work on literary dialect, but probably for very pragmatic reasons. His study focuses on respellings of Irish English pronunciation, but, unfortunately, a convenient and easily understandable respelling of /ʒ/ does not exist. Bliss addresses this in his examination of Irish English in literary dialect, noting that for the writer of literary dialect "some sounds cannot be indicated at all, since there is no appropriate orthography for them. The phoneme /ʒ/ is not very rare in English; it occurs in words like *leisure* and *vision*, and in foreign words like *rouge*; yet neither *s* nor *g* would in any way suggest the sound" (1979: 189). He later observes, however, that in a number of texts /z/ is respelled as <sh>, which was probably deemed by writers to be the most satisfactory approximation (cf. 1979: 238). Further words in which one might expect the substitution of /ʒ/ for /z/ include *cousin* and *dozen*, as well as the past participles of verbs which end in /z/. Below are two examples from the film corpus:

[ʒd]
706) No, it's **closed**.
(*Garage*, 00:23:17, FWIC2000M)

[ʒd]
707) The nerve of you to pretend to be **surprised** when you knew all along what that whoremaster was like.
(*How Harry Became a Tree*, 00:49.16, MH1920WW)

9.1.6 [ʍ] for /w/

The voiceless labio-velar /ʍ/[392] rather than /w/ has traditionally been used in Irish English in <wh-> words, such as *where*, *what*, *when*, *while* etc. Thus, terms such as *which* and *witch* or *whales* and *Wales* which are homophones in other varieties of English are not homophonous in Irish speech. In this regard, Irish English preserves a distinction from Early Modern

---
[392] This sound is sometimes represented by /hw/.

English. Having said that, Hickey has commented on a new trend to merge the pairs, resulting in a /w/ for both (2004a: 50 and 79). Below are some examples of the more traditional pronunciation:

       [ʍ]   [ʍ]
708) **Which** one of youse has ever seen me sellin' drugs? Come on! **Which** one of you?

                           (*The General*, 01:01:13, MN1990D)

                    [ʍ]
709) You've had that fax for two days. **When** do the rest of us get to see it?

                           (*Mystics*, 00:51:10, FL2000D)

   [ʍ]   [ʍ]
710) **Where** is she, then? **Where** is she?

                       (*Into the West*, 00:40:21, MPR1990D)

               [ʍ]
711) This is the life, **what**?

                       (*The Van*, 01:06:06, ML1990D)

In addition, the film corpus throws up an interesting example with regard to the use of /ʍ/ rather than /w/ in Irish English. The exchange is from *Widows' Peak* and results from Mrs Doyle-Counihan being asked too many questions.

        [ʍai] [ʍai] [wai]
712) *Mrs Doyle-Counihan*: **Why**? **Why**? "**Y**" is a crooked letter, pet.
Mrs Broom: What does that mean?
Mrs Doyle-Counihan: I haven't the remotest.

                   (*Widows' Peak*, 00:41:26, FDC1930M)

In the example, Mrs Doyle-Counihan employs a play on words, featuring the word *why* and the letter <y>. This pun works in other varieties of English in which the words are homophones; in Irish pronunciation, however, it does not make sense. Perhaps it is for this reason that Mrs Doyle Counihan admits to not knowing what the expression means. Her Irish pronunciation of <wh> is confirmed again later in the exchange:

    [ʍai]
713) **Why** don't you have a talk with her?

                   (*Widows' Peak*, 00:41:33, FDC1930M)

9.1.7 Clear [l] in all positions

One of the most characteristic features of Irish English pronunciation is the use of alveolar [l] in all positions (cf. Hickey 2004a: 49). Although this feature does not share the same saliency among the lay population as the consonants in the THINK and BREATHE lexical sets do, it has long been regarded by linguists as a very characteristic feature of Irish English. The use of alveolar [l] in all positions is thought to be a substratal feature, as it is also employed in almost all positions in the Irish language. Below are some examples of clear /l/ in positions in which one would expect a dark /l/:

                                        [l]
714) I don't want a drink. I want to sell the **field**.
  [l]
[The **field**?]
      [l]
Aye, the **field**. I need the best price I can get.
                                                                       (*The Field*, 00:06:03, FW1950W)

                        [l]   [l] [l]
715) Ladies, **Gentlemen**, your attention please! **Will all** the lovely ladies who are putting up their bonnets for the Inisfree Cup, please place their bonnets on the finishing line?
                                               (*The Quiet Man*, 00:49:46, MHF1930W)

9.1.8 Yod deletion

Although Hickey describes yod deletion as a typically Irish trait of pronunciation, this is somewhat overstating the case. Yod deletion certainly does occur in Irish English, but, geographically and phonotactically, its chances of occurring are quite limited. Geographically, it is most likely to occur in Dublin and parts of Munster, while phonotactically, as Hickey acknowledges, it can only appear in certain contexts. He correctly notes that it is possible after alveolar sonorants in stressed positions, e.g. *news* [nuːz], but not after labials, in unstressed positions or after non-sonorants (2005: 29). Thus terms like *mews*, *numerical* or *stew* which belong to the latter categories are pronounced [mjuːz], [njuːˈmerɪkəl] and [stjuː] rather than [muːz], [nuːˈmerɪkəl] and [stuː] (cf. Hickey 2004a: 83). What is more, Hickey points out that yod deletion in a word like *stupid* (i.e. pronouncing it [ˈstuːpɪd] rather than [ˈstjuːpɪd] or [ˈstʃuːpɪd])[393] "would be understood as a deliberate imitation of an American accent" (2005: 29).

    I would argue, however, that the perception among many Irish people of yod deletion being a conspicuous trait of an American accent is not restricted to occurrences after /t/, but that it also applies after /n/. This notion is nicely reflected in MacHale's respelling of the word *knew* in his comments on American actor Ward Bond's supposed Irish accent in *The Quiet Man*. He writes: "'Ah yes,' continues the priest in an excruciating brogue, 'I noo your people, Sean.'" (2002: 66). By respelling *knew* as <noo>, MacHale shows that this yodless realisation is not the normal way in which Irish people would pronounce the word.

    Given all of the aforementioned constraints outlined by Hickey, and the fact that the feature meets with a great deal of criticism even among Irish people, it can be argued that yod deletion is therefore perhaps not as typical a feature of the variety, as the literature suggests[394].

---

[393] As in other varieties of English, yod coalescence is very common in Irish English. This means, for example, that /dj/ before /uː/ has developed into a sibilant and is very often realised as [dʒ], with *dew* and *Jew*, for example, being realised as homophones (cf. Wells 1982b: 435 and Taniguchi 1972: 241).
[394] For more on this phenomenon, see Chapter 10.

Nonetheless, there are some examples of the phenomenon in the film corpus, as can be seen below.

        [nu:]
716) You owe me for a **new** pair of glasses.
(Cowboys and Angels, 01:06:03, MV2000L)

        [nu:]
717) It's an awful **nuisance**.
(Garage, 01:11:18, MJ2000M)

        [nu:]
718) I **knew** you wouldn' get that train.
(The Wind that Shakes the Barley, 00:14:25, MTe1920C)

        [nu:]
719) Ah, yes. I **knew** your people, Sean.
(The Quiet Man, 00:08:23, MFL1930W)

9.1.9 Rhoticism

On the whole, Irish English is a rhotic variety, with the /r/ being pronounced whenever it appears in writing. Although there is a slight exception in conservative popular Dublin English (cf. Hickey 2004a: 77), throughout the rest of the country, the /r/ is traditionally realised as a velarised alveolar continuant, which is in keeping with the type of /r/ to be found in the Irish language in the west and south west (cf. Hickey 2004a: 49)[395]. This rhotic nature of Irish English has long been reflected in the respellings used in literary dialect, with an additional <r> often being added in non-prevocalic positions to stress the point. Below are some examples from Taniguchi:

darrk	girrl	harrd	hearrt
(dark)	(girl)	(hard)	(heart)
murrdher	worrd	worrk	wurrk
(murder)	(word)	(work)	(work)

(Taniguchi 1972: 238)

This rhoticity is also to be found in the following examples from the film corpus. In RP, the <r> in the highlighted words would not be pronounced.

        [ɑ:r]   [ɜ:r]
720) He won a thousand pound on a scratch **card** last **Thursday**. The shock killed him.
(The Nephew, 00:20:16, MT1990C)

---

[395] It should be noted, however, that the retroflex /r/ which is used in fashionable Dublin speech has begun to spread throughout the country.

                                                                                 [ɚ]   [ɑːr]

721) She'll be here. And stop pacing like that. You'll give **yourself** a **heart** attack.

                        (*The Boys and Girl from County Clare*, 00:37:20, FM1960Cl)

                 [ɚ]   [ɚ]

722) I've **never** been with any lads, **ever**.

                                (*The Magdalene Sisters*, 00:38:44, FB1960D)

9.1.10   Nasal alveolarisation

A final observation on consonants, and one which is quite important, is that speakers of Irish English, like speakers of other varieties, generally tend to use /n/ rather than /ŋ/ in unstressed positions, particularly with regard to the continuous form of verbs and the noun *morning* (cf. Hickey 2007: 116). This phenomenon will already have been noticeable in the contractions used in many of the tables in the chapter on the grammar, lexis and discourse features of Irish English, and it can be heard in the following excellent example:

              [ɪn]   [ɪn]   [ɪn]   [ɪn]   [ɪn]   [ɪn]

723) **Drinkin', cursin'** and **fightin'**. **Drinkin', cursin'** and **fightin'**. That's what erupted shortly after I left the dance at Temperance Hall last night.

                                   (*This is my Father*, 00:35:30, MFR1930M)

9.2   Vowels

9.2.1   Raising of /ɛ/ to /ɪ/

According to Hickey (2004a: 32), the raising of /ɛ/ to /ɪ/ before nasals is the major segmental feature of the south-west of Ireland. This phenomenon, which he also calls "short E-raising" (2007: 302), is a survival from Middle English and is by no means limited to this area, also appearing up into Galway[396] and Mayo.

Below are a series of examples compiled by Taniguchi which show respellings from literature which are supposed to reflect this raising of /ɛ/ to /ɪ/ before nasals

Before <n>

agin (again/against)	attintion (attention)	binifit (benefit)	ind (end)
frind (friend)	hin (hen)	intintion (intention)	pincil (pencil)
rint (rent)	sintince (sentence)	thin (then)	wint (went)

                                                (Taniguchi 1972: 243)

---

[396] This raising is also evident outside of Ireland and can be found in dialects in the south of the United States.

Before <m>

| attimpt | rimimber | thim | timperance |
| (attempt) | (remember) | (them) | (temperance) |

(Taniguchi 1972: 243)

This realisation of [ɪ] rather than [ɛ] before nasals is not restricted to examples from literature, but is also evident in the following examples from the film corpus.

724) Ah, sure, after the Great War, I don't think anyone'd be foolish enough to
 [ɪ]
 do that ever **again**.[397]

(*This is my Father*, 00:56:12, MK1930M)

 [ɪ]
725) That's what comes of a man not yet threescore and **ten** matchin' his wits
 [ɪ]
fornenst[398] an intellectual gladiator 5,000 years old.

(*Darby O'Gill and the Little People*, 00:57:44, MKB1800K)

 [ɪ] [ɪ]
726) Wherever he **went** or wherever he played, he always **sent** me a postcard.

(*The Commitments*, 00:41:50, FJM1990D)

 [ɪ]
727) If you put half as much **energy** into your teachin', there'd be no stoppin' ya.

(*When Brendan Met Trudy*, 00:56:03, MHM2000D)

 [ɪ]
728) Well, you're blessed with a grand voice, Mrs **Kennedy**.

(*Waking Ned*, 00:06:35, FA2000W)

[ɪ]
729) **Dennis**, have you seen Pig Finn?

(*Waking Ned*, 00:08:58, MJ2000W)

As can be seen from the evidence below from both Taniguchi and from the film corpus, the raising of /ɛ/ to /ɪ/ is not solely limited to pre-nasal positions, even if the feature would normally be expected "to be restricted to environments in which it was phonetically natural, i.e. before nasals as these often trigger vowel raising due to their formant structure" (Hickey: 2004a: 33). Indeed, the phenomenon is to be found before alveolar plosives, velar

---

[397] The most common Irish English realisation of *again* is [əˈgɛn] rather than the RP [əˈgeɪn] (cf. Hickey 2007: 17). It is this Irish English realisation with [ɛ] which makes the raising to [ɪ] possible.

[398] In this context *fornenst* means 'against'. It typically means 'to', 'facing', 'in front of' and comes from Early Modern English *fore* 'in front' and *anent* 'towards' (cf. Dolan 2006: 96).

plosives, alveolar fricatives, and labio-dental fricatives. Taniguchi offers the following examples:

| git (get) | forgit (forget) | yit (yet) | yis (yes) | nixt (next) |

(Taniguchi 1972: 243)

Similar examples are evident in the film corpus:

[ɪ]
730) Well, I didn't really know myself until **yesterday**.
(*The Boys and Girl from County Clare*, 00:27:25, MJJ1960Cl)

[ɪ]
731) Come on. Sure, your sister's got the **kettle** on.
(*The Boys and Girl from County Clare*, 00:28:01, MJJ1960Cl)

[ɪ]
732) Ah, you know me. Pullin' the **divil** be the tail[399].
(*Mystics*, 00:37:39, MB2000D)

[ɪ]
733) I **never** thought I'd have the pleasure of seeing Your Lordship so soon.
(*Darby O'Gill and the Little People*, 00:13:41, MDOG1800K)

[ɪ]
734) It looks like a **pest** that I know ate it for his breakfast.
(*A Very Unlucky Leprechaun*, 00:05:37, MPM1990W)

[ɪ] [ɪ]
735) You see I'm after more than a **nest egg**, Jackie, and, as I'm the only that hasn't signed, I feel that there's some bargaining to be done.
(*Waking Ned*, 01:08:05, FL2000W)

9.2.2 Retention of /eː/ for Early Modern English <-ea-> words

The FLEECE-Merger which occurred in Early Modern English only partially applies to Irish English, with /eː/ still likely to be used instead of /iː/ in certain words, just as it was in Shakespeare's time (cf. Baugh and Cable 1993: 229). Thus, the following pairs are homophones in Irish English, with the first word always taking on the monophthongal /eː/ pronunciation of the second: *beast – baste, beat– bait, eat – ate, grease – grace, reap – rape, weak – wake*. Such pronunciations are, however, chiefly associated with rural or conservative

---

[399] The expression *pulling the devil by the tail* is used in Irish English with regard to people who are frequently in financial difficulty, yet somehow manage to cope. Share (2003: 256) defines it as 'living on one's wits; existing at the margins; surviving/getting by'.

working class urban accents and are recessive (cf. Wells 1982a 194ff.; Wells 1982b: 425; Bliss 1984: 139). The following are literary dialect respellings which reflect this feature:

aisy/asy (easy)	baste (beast)	bate (beat)	clane (clean)	lave/laive (leave)
mane (mean)	plaze (please)	say (sea)	snake (sneak)	tay (tea)

(Taniguchi 1972: 245)

The feature, which Hickey terms "unraised long E" (2007: 302), also appears very frequently in the film corpus:

[eː]
736) It'd want to be better than that **heap** of shite you gave me for the breakfast.
[eː]
The fuckin' dogs wouldn't **eat** it.
(*Trojan Eddie*, 00:17:56, MGG1990M)

[eː]
737) Yeah, he'd **beat** ya for just lookin' at me.
(*Trojan Eddie*, 00:18:28, FK1990M)

[eː]
738) Would ya **leave** me alone.
(*This is my Father*, 00:17:00, FT2000M)

[eː]
739) Can you lend me the loan of a small pinch of **tea**?
(*Darby O'Gill and the Little People*, 00:01:52, FMS1800K)

[eː]
740) Who took the **meat** out of this one?
(*The Field*, 00:26:06, MBMC1950W)

[eː]
741) I **mean** I took you off the street when no one else would even look at ya.
(*Trojan Eddie*, 01:29:13, MJP1990M)

[eː]
742) It must have been some **mean** customer whose dick produced a fucker like you.
(*When the Sky Falls*, 01:28:48, MSgt1990D)

[eː]
743) So I says to myself, "I'll **sneak** into town and I'll see me mother and I'll duck right out again".
(*The Informer*, 00:10:39, MFMP1920D)

This rule is not restricted to words spelled with <-ea-> but also applies to a number of other words which generally feature /iː/ in Standard English. Examples include:

                              [eː]
744) Your father was a great man for making a **reek**, Bull. Even the great storm
             [eː]
of '05 never knocked his **reek**.
                             (*The Field*, 00:24:37, MBi1950W)

                              [eː]
745) She's a harmless soul, a relic of oul **decency**.
                              (*Widows' Peak*, 00:47:23, MMG1930M)

                              [eː]
746) If your mother had married a proper, **decent** Limerick man, you wouldn't have stand-up, North-of-Ireland, Protestant hair.
                              (*Angela's Ashes*, 00:44:22, FGS1930L)

    [eː]
747) Well, **neither** do I.
                              (*A Very Unlucky Leprechaun*, 00:46:45, MPM1990W)

                    [eː]
748) No sign of it stoppin' **either**.
                              (*The Nephew*, 00:49:43, MT1990C)

[eː]
749) **Japers**[400], Annie.
                              (*Waking Ned*, 00:02:46, MJ2000W)

        [eː]
750) Ah, good **Jaysus**!
                              (*Intermission*, 00:51:27, MJ2000D)

               [eː]
751) Oh dear, oh dear. I have a **quare**[401] feelin' there's goin' to be a strange face in Heaven in the mornin'.
                              (*The Informer*, 01:03:13, MSP1920D)

This use of /eː/ for /iː/ does not mean, however, that writers of literary dialect have carte blanche when respelling Irish pronunciation. If one takes, for example, the short stories from 1903 which inspired the film *Darby O'Gill and the Little People*, they contain numerous instances of respellings, many of which are not correct. The following examples from just one page highlight the problem. While <wakeness> *weakness*, <taiche> *teach*, <disayses> *diseases*, <maysles> *measles*, and <aisily> *easily* are all justifiable respellings, the author also

---

[400] *Japers* is the Irish English realisation of *Jeepers*, a euphemism for *Jesus*. See Chapter 6.
[401] The word *quare* representing the Irish English pronunciation of *queer* has also become lexicalised. See page 82.

substitutes /eː/ in unstressed positions where /iː/ would not have occurred in the first place, such as <raymember> *remember*, <daytermined> *determined*, and <thraymendous> *tremendous* (cf. Templeton Kavanagh 2002: 78). Thus writers, and indeed actors, need to be careful about where they make this sound change. They would be wise to restrict themselves to the examples given or to consult linguistic studies on the phenomenon. Wells, for example, cites evidence from a study by Bertz (1975) on old-fashioned popular Dublin speech, which found that this use of /eː/ for /iː/ was most likely to occur in the words *leave, meat, eat, beat, cheat, tea, mean, easy, quay* and *treat* (as a verb), as well as in *either* or when using the name *Jesus*, albeit only in oaths. He also observes, however, that usage is recessive and often only used as a joke or "as a conscious Hibernicism" (Wells 1982b: 425).

9.2.3 /oː/ and /eː/ as monophthongs

The vowels in the GOAT and FACE lexical sets have both traditionally been realised as monophthongs in Irish English, although the former sometimes displays slightly diphthongised realisations, becoming [oʊ] in the supraregional variety and [əʊ] in fashionable Dublin English (cf. Collins 1997 and Hickey 2004a: 72). The FACE set is more stable, although it too may have a diphthongised realisation with a lower starting point in Dublin English (cf. Hickey 2004a: 73).

       [oː]
752) Thanks for the **coat**
              (*Into the West*, 00:38:55, MOR1990D)

         [oː]
753) Never turn up your **nose** at a free feed.
         (*How Harry Became a Tree*, 00:09:27, MH1920WW)

        [oː]
754) Why was I never on the **road**?
              (*Into the West*, 00:18:26, MOR1990D)

      [oː]
755) Jim's comin' **home**.
                (*Nora*, 01:13:07, FN1900G)

      [oː]
756) No, it's **closed**.
              (*Garage*, 00:23:17, FWIC2000M)

757) Was that the one danced for Herod and got the head of John the Baptist on
 [eː]
a **plate**?
           (*A Man of No Importance*, 00:10:35, FA1960M)

        [eː]
758) Mammy! Mam, hold on! **Wait**!
        (*The Boys and Girl from County Clare*, 00:45:51, FA1960Cl)

759) Get up off the parliamentary side of your arse and get a bit of colour in
[eː]
your **face**.
(*Michael Collins*, 00:18:23, MJC1910M)

9.2.4 Occasional pronunciation of /oː/ as [aʊ]

According to Wells (1982b: 427), the occasional pronunciation [aʊ] for /oː/ can be described as a "characteristically Irish oddity" which occurs "before /-ld/ in certain words, particularly *old* and *bold*." As can be seen from the examples in the films, this "OL-diphthongisation" (Hickey 2007: 302) can also occur in the words *hold* and *mould(y)*.

                  [aʊ]   [aʊ]
760) Ah you wicked **ould** divil. You murderin' **ould** hypocrite!
(*Darby O'Gill and the Little People*, 00:44:22, MKB1800K)

[aʊ]
761) **Hould** your whisht!⁴⁰²
(*Darby O'Gill and the Little People*, 00:38:41, MKB1800K)

[aʊ]
762) **Hould** on there!
(*Dead Meat*, 00:33:55, MD2000LM)

[aʊ]
763) The **bould**⁴⁰³ Harry, what can I do ya for?
(*How Harry Became a Tree*, 00:16:37, MF1920WW)

[aʊ]
764) Piss on your own bed, ya **mouldy** hoor⁴⁰⁴.
(*The Boys and Girl from County Clare*, 00:09:35, MJJ1960Cl)

Taniguchi also found evidence of respellings which suggested similar pronunciations. All of his examples are taken from Yeats' *Irish Fairy and Folk Tales*, and, while some of these, such as the pronunciation of *cold* as [kaʊld], can still frequently be heard, others, such as his

---

[402] *Hould your whisht* or simply *whisht* are Irish English ways of saying *stop*, *listen* or *be quiet*. The etymology of *whisht* is uncertain and may be from the obsolete English verb *whister*, meaning 'to whisper' or the Irish *éist* which literally means 'listen' but which by implication means 'please be silent' (cf. Dolan 2006: 253).
[403] Hickey has observed that the process of vernacularisation has led to a lexical split with regard to some words spelled <-old>. Although pronunciations with both /aʊ/ and /oː/ are available to Irish English speakers for the words *old* and *bold*, for example, the different realisations have different meanings, with the [aʊ] realisation of *old* often suggesting 'old + affectionate attachment', while the [aʊ] pronunciation of *bold* suggests 'daring + sneaking admiration' (cf. Hickey 2004b: 72). For more on the semantic differences between *bold* and *bould*, see page 154.
[404] The term *hoor* reflects the Irish English pronunciation of *whore*, which was also common in England during the sixteenth and seventeenth centuries. While this pronunciation has been retained in Ireland, the meaning has extended from 'prostitute' to refer to "any person, male or female, who is corrupt; and it may be used affectionately as well as pejoratively, especially when qualified by the adjective 'cute'"(Dolan 2006: 123). The word *cute* implies deviousness and a lack of scruples, and is often applied to politicians (cf. Share 2003: 159).

suggestions for *shoulder*, *sold*[405] and *told*, are falling out of use. Again, authors and actors need to exercise caution when it comes to this substitution, as it does not apply across the board for all <old> words. Thus, one would not expect *fold* or *gold* to be pronounced [faʊld] and [gaʊld]. It is also worth noting that the mixture of spellings with <ou> and <ow> in Taniguchi's examples once again illustrates the difficulties which authors face when trying to represent pronunciation. Out of context, the respelling <could> for [kaʊld], for instance, might easily be misread as the modal *could*.

ould	tould	showldher	could/cowld	hould	bowld
(old)	(told)	(shoulder)	(cold)	(hold)	(bold)

(Taniguchi 1972: 250)

9.2.5 /aː/ in BATH set

Unlike in Received Pronunciation, Irish English does not differentiate between the vowels in the BATH and TRAP lexical sets[406]. Thus instead of /ɑː/ and /æ/, Irish speakers use a long low central vowel, /aː/, for both. Thus, words such as *bland* and *glance* are realised as: [blaːnd] and [glaːns] respectively (cf. Hickey 2005: 29). This rule also carries into other members of the BATH lexical set, so that /aː/ is used in *answer*, *dance*, *laugh*, *rather* and (traditionally) in *father*. Below are some examples from the film corpus:

[aː]
765) We knew how to have a good **laugh**.
(*Nora*, 01:39:06, MNU1900G)

[aː]
766) At home, at this stage, everybody'd be up **dancin'** you know?
(*Nora*, 00:35:26, FN1900G)

[aː]
767) My **father** never beat me.
(*The Field*, 01:21:46, MT1950W)

[aː]
768) I think you'd better go inside now and see your **father**.
(*A Very Unlucky Leprechaun*, 01:12:07, MPM1990W)

[aː]
769) They're my **father's** rings.
(*Trojan Eddie*, 00:36:59, MJP1990M)

---

[405] Hickey offers an example of *sold* being pronounced [saʊl] by an elderly man (2007: 311). However, such pronunciations of that word have all but disappeared.
[406] Of course, Irish English is not unique in its not distinguishing between the BATH and TRAP lexical sets. In General American English, for example, both sets are realised as [æ].

[aː]
770) Her **father** is a chiropodist.
(*Garage*, 00:35:25, MJ2000M)

[aː]
771) Jesus, that's a stupid thing to **ask** in this place.
(*The Magdalene Sisters*, 01:02:34, FB1960D)

[aː]   [aː]
772) Sure, we **can't** take the **chance** that the widow might throw us out.
(*This is my Father*, 01:36:23, FMM1930M)

9.2.6 [ɑː] for /ʌ/

Another feature of Irish English pronunciation is the occasional pronunciation of /ʌ/ as [ɑː]. This pronunciation appears to be restricted to the lexical items *one* and *once* and has traditionally been reflected in the respellings <wan>, <wanst> or <wanse> (cf. Taniguchi 1972: 244). Below is an example of this pronunciation from the film corpus:

[ɑː]
773) Is there any **one** of ye man enough to dance with me?
(*The Field*, 00:34:29, FTG1950W)

9.2.7 Occasional pronunciation of [ɛ] for /a/

Observing spelling differences in his corpus of literary texts, Bliss observes that there are differences between Middle English <e> and <a> in a number of words, with seventeenth-century English not always preferring the form which is used in present-day English. "The words *then*, *when* and *thresh* had common forms with *a* (and the pronunciation of *thresh* preserves this form); on the other hand *than* and *gather* had common forms with *e*" (1979: 193). The occasional Irish English pronunciation of *gather* as [gɛðɚ] reflecting this older spelling can be heard in the following example from the film corpus:

[ɛ]
774) First you'll hear the **gatherin'** of the huntsmen and the bayin' of the hounds.
(*Darby O'Gill and the Little People*, 00:28:30, MDOG1800K)

The same phenomenon also appears to apply to the pronunciation of *catch*, with Hickey citing evidence of this form, which he calls "CATCH raising", in plays by Sean O'Casey (cf. 2005: 174; 2007: 302). Further examples of this earlier pronunciation are evident in the film corpus.

[ɛ]
775) If I hurry, I'll **catch** up with him.
(*Darby O'Gill and the Little People*, 00:55:17, MDOG1800K)

[ɛ]
776) And if I so much as **catch** you putting a wet foot on my property, I'll…I'll….
(*The Quiet Man*, 00:25:00, MRW1930W)

9.2.8 [ʊ] for /ʌ/

The opposition between /ʌ/ and /ʊ/ is rare in Ireland and, thus, words from the STRUT lexical set are generally pronounced like those from the FOOT set. This results in RP minimal pairs such as *stud* and *stood*, *luck* and *look*, *cud* and *could*, *putt* and *put*, and *tuck* and *took* all being realised as homophones involving /ʊ/ in Irish English (cf. Wells 1982b: 422-23). In the examples below, the highlighted words from the STRUT set are realised with the vowel from the FOOT set.

777) And another thing. Don't get too close to that other fella down there, if I
                  [ʊ]   [ʊ]
was you, because he don't **look** too **lucky** to me
                                           (*Trojan Eddie*, 01:08:32, MJP1990M)

                              [ʊ]
778) Them paintings, they brought us bad **luck**, Martin. We should get rid of them.
                                           (*The General*, 01:26:06, MN1990D)

                              [ʊ]
779) So did ye find out there's royalty in yer **blood**?
                                       (*This is my Father*, 00:21:22, MT2000M)

               [ʊ]
780) Did you ever taste **blood**?
                                             (*Rat*, 01:00:24, MH2000D)

     [ʊ]
781) He **stuck** his tongue in me ear once, and I'm not joking yez, I think he was trying to get it out the other one.
                                   (*The Snapper*, 00:08:29, FJ1990D)

9.2.9 Occasional pronunciation of /ʊ/ as [uː]

Despite the fact that /ʊ/ appears far more frequently in Irish English than in RP, due to the aforementioned merging of the STRUT and FOOT sets, not all words which are pronounced with /ʊ/ in standard accents are realised that way in Ireland. As in the north of England, certain words such as *book, cook, hook, nook, rook, brook, crook, cooker, cookie* and *Tootsie* are pronounced with /uː/ by many Irish people (cf. Kallen 1994: 177).

            [uː]
782) First a **book**, then a film.
                                                (*Rat*, 00:07:07, MP2000D)

           [uː]
783) A film of the **book**?
                                                (*Rat*, 00:07:09, FC2000D)

      [uː]   [uː]
784) A film of the **book**. And then a **book** of the film.

(*Rat*, 00:07:11, MP2000D)

              [uː]   [uː]
785) And do you know what's in his room? **Books**! Hundreds of **books** under lock and key.

(*A Man of No Importance*, 00:33:47, FL1960D)

   [uː]
786) There'll be no **cooking** done once it's started.

(*The Van*, 00:25:23, MB1990D)

787) Now, that is a beautiful[407] omelette, Alfred. It's a great gift to be able to [uː]
cook.

(*A Man of No Importance*, 00:40:25, FL1960D)

  [uː]
788) No **crooks** allowed, just crooked[408] cops.

(*The General*, 01:20:10, MMC1990D)

9.2.10 [ə] or [i] for the unstressed /oʊ/

Quite a common feature of Irish English pronunciation is the substitution of /ə/ or /i/ for the unstressed /oʊ/ at the end of words (cf. Hickey 2005: 169 and 174). The former can be seen in the following respellings from Taniguchi's literary dialect sources, in which <-ow> appears as <a> or <ah>, the best approximation of the schwa sound.

| arra | borra | fella/fellah | yella |
| (arrow) | (borrow) | (fellow) | (yellow) |

(Taniguchi 1972: 249)

There is also ample evidence of this "final-O-fronting" (Hickey 2007: 302) in the film corpus, but it is not restricted to words ending in the letters <ow>. Other words ending in /oʊ/, such as *piano* and *tomato* also undergo this change, as can be seen below in examples 795 and 796:

                        [ə]
789) See that. I got that lad climbin' out of the nurses' hostel **window** and 33 years later Mrs Headmaster thinks it's the sexiest thing about me.

(*When Brendan Met Trudy*, 00:56:40, MHM2000D)

---

[407] The pronunciation of *beautiful* as ['bjuːtifʊl], as can be heard in this sentence, is quite common in Dublin.
[408] Despite the presence of the word *crook* in *crooked*, the latter is not pronounced with /uː/ in Irish English.

[ə]
790) Ah, it's a **sorrow** that doesn't go away.
(*This is my Father*, 00:16:23, FT2000M)

[ə]
791) Oh, 'tis a bitter pill to **swallow**.
(*Irish Jam*, 00:52:21, MG2000W)

[ə]
792) And when he doesn't answer, tell the **widow**.
(*Mystics*, 00:19:02, ML2000D)

[ə]
793) Where they laid the coffin, the grass turned **yellow** and never grew again.
(*This is my Father*, 01:48:09, FT2000M)

[ə]   [ə]
794) **Tomorrow. Tomorrow** afternoon we'll talk more.
(*This is my Father*, 00:44:09, FT2000M)

[ə]
795) Well, I could fry up some **tomatoes**, if ye like.
(*This is my Father*, 00:15:23, MT2000M)

796) The day before she left she was in Katie Anderson's with her sister and that
[ə]
piano teacher.
(*A Love Divided*, 00:30:42, MC1950WX)

On other occasions, words ending in <ow> are pronounced with /i/. Whereas the /oʊ/ at the end of verbs, nouns and adjectives can sometimes be pronounced [ə], the [i] pronunciation appears only to apply to (some) verbs, namely *borrow*, *follow* and *swallow*, the latter pair having also been observed by Taniguchi. With verbs like *wallow* and *bellow*, for example, this phenomenon does not appear to be possible. Below are examples from both Taniguchi and the film corpus.

folly	swally
(follow)	(swallow)

(Taniguchi 1972: 249)

[i]
797) He has them X-rayed as they clock out, in case they **swallow** one.
(*The General*, 01:04:32, MMC1990D)

        [i]
798) Like they were **swallowin'** a lemon.

                                                     (*Rat*, 01:00:18, MH2000D)

         [i]
799) Like they **followed** us down here in case somebody died?

                                                     (*Mystics*, 01:07:15, MF2000D)

            [i]
800) They've 90 men **following** us.

                                                    (*The General*, 01:15:29, MMC1990D)

    [i]
801) **Follow** us over.

                                                    (*Intermission*, 00:50:43, ML2000D)

                                                                  [i]
802) I've been living from hand to mouth on whatever I could **borrow** from sailors and dockers.

                                                   (*The Informer*, 00:34:03, MG1920D)

9.2.11   [ai] for /ɔi/

In conservative varieties of Irish English, the onset of the diphthong /ɔi/ is quite open, with the result that it is realised as [ai] (cf. Hickey 2004a: 68). This leads to *oil* being pronounced as *aisle*, *boy* as *bye*, etc. These pronunciations are reflected in the respellings below from Taniguchi's corpus and in the subsequent examples from the film corpus.

bye	enj'y	bile
(boy)	(enjoy)	(boil)
j'in	p'int	spile
(join)	(point)	(spoil)

                                                             (Taniguchi 1972: 248)

        [ai]
803) About the **oils**.

                                                     (*Garage*, 00:02:21, MJ2000M)

    [ai]   [ai]
804) **Boys**, oh **boys**!

                                                   (*Garage*, 00:07:35, MJ2000M)

     [ai]
805) It's **boilin'**.

                                                   (*Garage*, 01:04:01, MJ2000M)

[ai]
806) Beyond that line, no **boy** is permitted to set foot.
(*Song for a Raggy Boy*, 00:17:22, MBJ1930)

[ai]
807) It's **pointin'** at Christy.
(*My Left Foot*, 00:32:12, FRG1950D)

9.2.12 [ɔi] for /ai/

According to Taniguchi, the substitution of [ɔi] for /ai/ in words like *Irish* "is believed by British and American writers to be one of (sic) characteristic sounds of Irish English" (1972: 249). It is, thus, no surprise that the spelling <Oirish> which echoes this pronunciation has become a byword for the Irish accent (or for a pseudo-Irish accent). Taniguchi explains that "to be more precise and exact regarding the sound value and nature, the substituted sound will be an intermediate sound between /ai/ and /ɔi/, which is sometimes heard as /ai/ and sometimes as /ɔi/" (1972: 249). In this regard, perception would appear to play an important role. While people may hear this sound as /ɔi/, this is not reflected in its production. In fact, Hickey suggests that the onset of the vowels is actually in the opposite direction to /ɔ/, and that "with the /ai/ diphthong, it is frequent to find centralisation or a raising and fronting of the onset" (2004a: 67). This centralisation, raising and fronting can especially be heard in the following Dublin examples, in which the realisation is [əɪ] rather than [ɔi].

[əɪ]
808) Number **19**, St Peter's Crescent.
(*Rat*, 00:04:26, MP2000D)

[əɪ]
809) Jaysus, Bosco, there's a **time** and a place!
(*Mystics*, 00:04:49, MMin2000D)

[əɪ]   [əɪ]
810) I'm a bit sick for that, **like**. I'm dying sick, **like**.
(*Adam and Paul*, 00:22:38, MP2000D)

[əɪ]
811) Here, I need something to **wipe** meself with.
(*Adam and Paul*, 00:38:50, MP2000D)

9.2.13 [i] for /ai/

In Irish English *my* and *by* are very often pronounced the same as *me* and *be*. According to Taniguchi (1972: 48), these are "vestiges of the pronunciations once common in ordinary English". These realisations are not restricted to *my* and *by*, but are also evident in related words, such as *meself* or the exclamations *Begod*, *Be the hokey*, *Bedad* and *Begorrah*. Below are some examples of the sound change from the film corpus:

[i]
812) Oh **by** the holy, where did ya get it Gypo? There's enough there to choke a horse, and me joking you about it a few minutes ago.
(*The Informer*, 00:49:05, MSP1920D)

[i]
813) Ah, you know me. Pullin' the divil **by** the tail.
(*Mystics*, 00:37:39, MB2000D)

[i]
814) I've got two of **my** daughters livin' beyond in the States. One of them is married to a Yank. He's half an Apache. Lovely young lad. Great head of hair on him.
(*When Brendan Met Trudy*, 00:55:41, MHM2000D)

[i]
815) Now, Jimmy, I want ya to follow **my** finger.
(*Irish Jam*, 00:38:28, MDR2000W)

9.2.14 Merger of CAUGHT and COT lexical sets

Just like in Midwestern American English (cf. Tottie 2002: 17), Irish English, and particularly Munster English, sometimes shows a merger in its back vowels, so that *caught* and *cot* are pronounced as homophones, both featuring /ɑ/ rather than /ɔ/. Two examples of this phenomenon from films set in Munster are given below:

[ɑ]
816) I was almost **caught** on the way over to ye.
(*The Wind that Shakes the Barley*, 00:18:07, FS1920C)

[ɑ]
817) We were **caught** in possession.
(*Cowboys and Angels*, 01:09:46, MS2000L)

9.2.15 Epenthesis

A common feature of Irish English is the presence of an intrusive epenthetic vowel in certain consonant clusters. According to Wells (1982b: 435), this schwa epenthesis is limited to environments where the preceding consonant is a plosive, liquid or nasal, and the following consonant is a liquid or a nasal.[409] Possible clusters and corresponding examples are therefore: between /l/ and /m/ (*film* [ˈfɪləm], *elm* [ˈɛləm]), between /r/ and /m/ (*arm* [ˈɑːrəm], *worm* [ˈwʌrəm]), between /r/ and /l/ (*girl* [gɚəl], *world* [ˈwʌrəld]), between /l/ and /n/ (*kiln* [ˈkɪlən]), between /r/ and /n/ (*turn* [tɚən]), between /b/ and /l/ (*Dublin* [ˈdʊbəlɪn]), between /t̪/ and /l/

---

[409] Again there is evidence of writers breaking this rule. In the short story "Darby O'Gill and the Leprechaun", Templeton Kavanagh correctly uses the respelling <worruld> to show epenthesis in *world* (2002: 27); however, she also suggests that there is epenthesis in *work* by respelling it <worruk> (2002: 19). Seeing as epenthesis is only possible before a liquid or a nasal, the latter respelling is wrong.

(*Kathleen* [ˈkatəliːn]) and /t̬/ and /r/ (*petrol* [ˈpɛt̬əɹəl]). Below are just a few instances of epenthesis in the film corpus:

Between /l/ and /m/

[ləm]
818) That was a very interesting **film**.
(*Circle of Friends*, 00:15:23, MSW1950D)

[ləm]
819) There's even talk about a **film**.
(*Last of the High Kings*, 00:12:50, MMG1970D)

[ləm]
820) That's an old **film**, that one.
(*Into the West*, 00:30:24, FMM1990D)

[ləm]
821) Oh, it'll be like that **film** *The Boys in their Hoods*.
(*Irish Jam*, 00:24:52, MG2000W)

The presence of epenthesis in the examples above is not at all surprising, as according to Bliss "in the word /filəm/ *film*, it is universal, even among educated speakers" (1984: 139).

Between /r/ and /m/

Literary dialect representations of epenthesis between /r/ and /m/ usually involve the insertion of the letter <u> after <r> to reflect the /ə/ sound.
Taniguchi offers the following examples from literature[410]:

arrum	ferrum	wurrum
(arm)	(firm)	(worm)

(Taniguchi 1972: 239)

The film corpus also displays a couple of examples in this context:

[rəm]
822) Do you think I'm a babe in **arms**?
(*Darby O'Gill and the Little People*, 00:10:38, MDOG1800K)

[rəm]
823) Where are you, you mongrel **worm**?
(*Rat*, 00:57:00, MFr2000M)

---

[410] Other environments for such a cluster are: *alarm, farm, firm, form, germ, harm, norm, term*, and *warm* (cf. Moylan 1996: 297).

Between /r/ and /n/:

In addition to finding epenthesis between /r/ and /m/, Taniguchi notes its presence between /r/ and /n/, and he offers the respelled example <borrun>, meaning 'born' (1972: 239). The film corpus also provides evidence of an intrusive vowel between /r/ and /n/, as can be seen in the example from *Into the West*.

        [rən]   [rən]
824) **Turn** Tír na nÓg! **Turn**!

                                  (*Into the West*, 01:24:00, MOR1990D)

Between /l/ and /n/

An example of epenthesis between /l/ and /n/ is also to be found in the film corpus, appearing in the word *kiln* [ˈkɪlən], meaning 'a furnace or oven used for calcining lime':

              [lən]
825) Nearby there was an old lime **kiln** with a tree growing out of it.
                               (*This is my Father*, 01:06:10, FT2000M)

D-Epenthesis can also occur in Irish English and is found between /r/ and /l/, in words such as *girl* and *world* (Wells 1982b: 435). Examples from the corpus are:

              [rdl]
826)   Now, now, now! She's a fine healthy **girl**, no patty fingers if you please.
                               (*The Quiet Man*, 01:02:00, MMF1930W)

              [rdld]
827) He was a good man, and the **world** was different then.
                               (*This is my Father*, 00:22:55, FT2000M)

828)   Well, the good part is that he's probably the oldest rat in the history of
[rdld]
the **world**.
                                              (*Rat*, 00:14:45, MM2000D)

9.2.16 Metathesis

Metathesis, whereby sounds in a word are interchanged, is another recognised feature of Irish English. According to Hickey, metathesis is most likely to occur in Irish English in clusters which consist of a short vowel and /r/, as in *pattern* [ˈpætrən] (cf. Hickey 2004a: 82), *lantern* [ˈlæntrən] (Hickey 1989: 56), *southern* [ˈsʊðrən] and *modern* [ˈmɑːdrən] (cf. Kallen 1994: 175; Share 2006: 64)[411]. Examples of metathesis from the film corpus are given below:

---

[411] Metathesis can frequently be heard on Tuesdays in County Mayo. That is the day when the weekly newspaper *The Western People* is printed and locals can be heard asking for the latest issue of "The Westren".

                                          [drən]
829) Yes, Mr Wilson, the accommodations are strictly **modern**.
                                        (*High Spirits*, 00:06:02, MPP1980W)

830) They're magical and eating just one will make a leprechaun lucky for a
    [dərd]
hundred years.
                                (*A Very Unlucky Leprechaun*, 00:07:28, MPM1990W)

                                              [tərl]
831) Non-belligerents will kindly remain **neutral**.
                                          (*The Quiet Man*, 01:58:28, MMF1930W)

Hickey also notes that metathesis can occur in clusters consisting of /s/ and /p/, such as hospital [ˈhɑstɪpəl], or in clusters with /k/ and /s/, as in [æks], the latter of which, he argues, is no longer attested in Irish English (2004a: 82). There are, however, other instances of metathesis in the film corpus, featuring the clusters /l/ and /t/ and /n/ and /k/, as can be seen in the following examples. However, the relatively high number of these examples in one film, albeit by different characters, suggests they may not be very representative and could be evidence of overuse for the sake of humour on the part of the screenwriter.[412]

832) If you don't produce him this instant, I'm calling the guards and having you
        [lət]
charged with **cruelty**.
                                                    (*Rat*, 01:09:26, FD2000D)

833) The story of a man who became a rat and a family who stood by him, in
    [lət]
love and **loyalty**.
                                                    (*Rat*, 01:19:22, MH2000D)

    [nɪkəlz]
834) Is it the **bronchials**, Hubert?
                                                    (*Rat*, 00:02:44, FD2000D)

9.3   Features of local Dublin pronunciation

Since so many films are set in and around Dublin, it is only appropriate to also include a description of the most salient features to be found in the pronunciation of Dublin speakers.

9.3.1 [uː] or [ɛː] for /ɜː/

The NURSE lexical set devised by Wells (1982) needs to be revised when looking at Irish English, and more specifically when looking at local Dublin English, which still displays features which were most likely established when English first came to Ireland prior to the 12th century. One such feature is the realisation of the RP NURSE lexical set as either [ɛː] or

---

[412] The forms <crulety> and <bronichals> also appear in Share (2006: 78 and 64).

[ʊː]. Hickey points out that, in local Dublin English, back vowels after /w/, as well as vowels which were originally short and high have developed into a vowel which is phonetically something like /ʊː/ when they come before tautosyllabic /r/, as in the words *first* [fʊː(ɹ)st], *turn* [tʊː(ɹ)n] and *work* [wʊː(ɹ)k], while words which originally had mid front vowels in this position are realised with [ɛː], as in *germ* [gɛː(ɹ)m] (cf. Hickey 2004a: 54 and 2005: 34). To reflect these differences, Hickey redefined Wells' NURSE lexical set and replaced it with his own sets: NURSE for the [ʊː] realisation and TERM for [ɛː]. The film corpus displays examples of each, sometimes with both types occurring in the same utterance, as in the following example.

                [ʊː]   [ɛː]

835) Mr Alfred **Byrne** presents *The Importance of Being **Earnest*** by Oscar Wilde.

                      (*A Man of No Importance*, 00:20:00, MCB1960D)

NURSE set /ʊː/

                                      [ʊː]

836) I mean Mary was a great cook and a great ironer of a **shirt**.

                      (*A Man of No Importance*, 00:52:37, MCB1960D)

            [ʊː]   [ʊː] [ʊː]

837) Martin Cahill, he's a **murderer**, a drug dealer and a **dirt bird**!

                              (*The General*, 00:33:26, MMC1990D)

    [ʊː]

838) Jason **Burke**.

                        (*When the Sky Falls*, 00:59:27, MSgt1990D)

                                [ʊː]

839) So I've decided I'm goin' to have to **hurt** you a bit.

                          (*Veronica Guerin*, 00:10:10, MMC1990D)

                            [ʊː]

840) You can't overfeed him or he'll **burst**.

                      (*Last of the High Kings*, 00:14:15, MMG1970D)

                              [ʊː]

841) Of course, Dublin's the finest city in the **world**, bar none - all the writers and playwriters and novelists that come out of it.

                    (*Last of the High Kings*, 00:37:23, MTD1970D)

842) I would have said it's about time some people here stood up to all this
    [ʊː]
church shite!

                          (*A Love Divided*, 00:32:49, ME1950WX)

   [ʊː]   [ʊː]
843) **Sir**, we'd like the address, **sir**, to claim for the assistance.
(Into the West, 00:07:00, MMM1990D)

TERM set [ɛː]

   [ɛː]
844) A **girl**.
(A Man of No Importance, 00:07:30, MA1960D)

                 [ɛː]
845) Maybe you need to be chatted up or something, **flirted** with.
(Intermission, 00:41:05, FK2000D)

           [ɛː]
846) Were you at any time aware of a **merging** of human and animal consciousness?
(Rat, 00:08:46, MP2000D)

                 [ɛː]
847) Permit me on your behalf to welcome her into our little **circle**.
(A Man of No Importance, 00:05:08, MA1960D)

      [ɛː]
848) I can't. You're makin' me **nervous**.
(The Van, 00:05:51, MB1990D)

849) Youse could take him on a provincial tour or lease him out to Fosset's
[ɛː]
circus.
(Rat, 00:14:57, MM2000D)

9.3.2 Vowel breaking

Long high vowels in local Dublin English are sometimes realised as two syllables in closed syllable contexts. This disyllabification process also applies to diphthongs with a high end point. In each case, the hiatus element between the syllables is either /j/ or /w/: /j/ in the case of front vowels, as in *clean* [kliʲən], and /w/ in the case of back vowels, as in *fool* [fuʷəl]. These same hiatus elements appear for the diphthongs, giving realisations such as: *time* [təʲəm] and *pound* [pɛʷən] (cf. Hickey 2004a: 45). Examples of vowel breaking are evident in the following sentences from the film corpus:

                    [miʲən]
850) Better be a bloke. Regular young fella. You know what I **mean**.
(A Man of No Importance, 00:15:35, MRo1960D)

   [stiʲəl]
851) To **steal**.
(The General, 01:03:55, MMC1990D)

[səʲəd]
852) Sharon, there's someone **outside**!

(*The Snapper*, 00:38:07, FK1990D)

[leʲən]
853) I'm not havin' a shite down a **lane**. I'm not a fuckin' dog.

(*About Adam*, 00:38:40, MP2000D)

[geʲəm]
854) It's a **game**.

(*The General*, 01:39:22, MMC1990D)

[neʲəmz]
855) Look at these **names**.

(*A Man of No Importance*, 00:20:41, MA1960D)

9.3.3 Fronting of /au/

Another feature of vowels in Dublin English is the fronting of /au/ in words like *down* to [dæʊn] or [dɛʊn] (Hickey 2004a: 45). This is evident in the film corpus in the following instances:

                                    [rɛʊnd]   [əˈbɛʊt]
856) What the fuck are you doin', goin' **round** telling people things **about** me?
[mɛʊθ]
Shootin' your fuckin' **mouth** off!

(*Adam and Paul*, 00:51:49, MC2000D)

[dɛʊn]
857) I've the plan written **down** and you're to stick with it, do you hear me?

(*Mystics*, 00:22:39, MLA2000D)

9.3.4 Fortition of dental fricatives

As outlined above, /θ/ and /ð/ are generally realised as [t] and [d] in Dublin English (see page 203). What is more, t-lenition is very common, with /t/ often being realised in weak positions as an apico-alveolar fricative rather than as a stop. Such lenition takes place along a cline and can vary from the aforementioned apico-alveolar fricative to an /ɹ/, then to /h/ and finally to deletion (Hickey 2004a: 45). Below are examples from the film corpus which display some of the various steps:

The use of [ɹ] for /t/

[ɹ]
858) Full of lovely gear and all **it is**.

(*Adam and Paul*, 00:17:23, FO2000D)

[ɹ]
859) Lads, mind that! Tell Noelie Lawrence dropped it in. He knows about it anyway, only keep **it** out of sight, will yiz?
(*Adam and Paul*, 00:59:07, ML2000D)

[ɹ]
860) So tell me **about it**.
(*Intermission*, 00:33:01, ML2000D)

[ɹ]
861) I was real **cut up** when I heard the news.
(*Mystics*, 00:04:43, MB2000D)

This lenition of /t/ to [ɹ] is most famously evident in one of the catch phrases used by Dublin-born chat show host Gay Byrne. He regularly professes to be "excira' and delira'", the Dublin pronunciation of "excited and delighted". Here one can observe both the lenition to /ɹ/ in the middle syllables as well as the deletion of the final plosive[413].

Glottalisation of lenited /t/

This process goes even further in Dublin English where it is often realised as [h] or as a glottal stop (cf. Kallen 1994: 178 and Hickey 2004a: 80)[414]. This phenomenon can occur in both medial and final position, as can be seen from the following examples from the film corpus.

In medial position:

[h]
862) I'm not askin' thirty for this **beautiful** machine.
(*Trojan Eddie*, 00:00:57, MTE1990M)

[ʔ]
863) Agnes **Loretta** Browne.
(*Agnes Browne*, 00:01:28, FAB1960D)

[ʔ]
864) How are ya, **Rita**?
(*Agnes Browne*, 00:19:03, FAB1960D)

[ʔ]
865) She has me wore out, that one. Always wanting her hair **plaited**.
(*Adam and Paul*, 00:12:09, FM2000D)

---

[413] For more, see Share (2003: 82).
[414] Hickey observes that the realisation of /t/ as [h] also extends to other varieties in Ireland with regard to the word *Saturday*, and he suggests that this may be attributable to influence from the Irish word for *Saturday*, *Sahairn*, which also has an intervocalic /h/ (Hickey 2004a: 80).

[?]
866) A box full of the **latest** videos.

(*Trojan Eddie*, 00:04:42, MTE1990M)

[?]
867) Thanks, Marian. You're a **sweetheart**.

(*Agnes Browne*, 00:08:35, FAB1960D)

In final position:

[?]
868) What's he doin' in the feckin' **toilet**?

(*Agnes Browne*, 00:09:35, FAB1960D)

[?]
869) Spendin' all your money on your **flat**.

(*Adam and Paul*, 00:41:46, MP2000D)

[?]
870) Isn't it **desperate**?

(*Rat*, 00:05:17, FD2000D)

In medial and final position:

[?]   [?]
871) Would have been **better** off if he'd never **set** eyes on yiz.

(*Adam and Paul*, 00:16:08, FO2000D)

[?]   [?]
872) I can't get pissed **tonigh'**. **Whatever** is wrong with me.

(*Garage*, 00:47:47, FC2000M)

This chapter has described the characteristic features of Irish accents, and offered numerous excellent examples of pronunciation from the film corpus. However, given the fact that many actors who appear in Irish roles are not Irish, it is almost inevitable that there are going to be instances in which non-Irish features find their way into the actors' performances. Building on the information just presented, the next chapter will take a look at the areas where actors are most likely to encounter problems when assuming Irish accents.

10 Evaluating accents

- You know, Homer, it's very easy to criticize.
- Fun, too.

                        Marge and Homer Simpson.

Having looked at the typical phonological features of Irish English, it is now possible to examine performances by non-Irish actors for evidence of where their accent falters. While voice setting may be one of the better indicators of accent (cf. Chapter 7.6), it is still a very abstract concept and is extremely difficult to explain, due to the fact that, as Jenner has observed, it probably functions on a "subconscious level" (1992: 41). Thus, trying to explain what, on a subconscious level, is problematic with many of the accented performances in the film corpus will not get us very far. Errors in segmentals, on the other hand, are identifiable and describable and therefore they will be evaluated in the current study. It should be quite easy to tell where non-Irish actors have gone wrong with their Irish accents, since as Hickey has pointed out, certain features of Irish English pronunciation, namely rhotacism, the presence of a monophthong in the FACE lexical set, the use of centralised /aː/, the use of plosive equivalents to English /θ/ and /ð/ and the retention of /ʍ/ are "so obvious that no possibility of confusion with the southern British standard is possible" (2005: 33). The same applies with regard to the distinction between Irish English and American English. Although these varieties do share rhotacism, the absence of any of the other features outlined above, or rather the presence of their American counterparts, should be more than adequate to betray an American accent in Irish film. The following pages take a look at a selection of the most common segmental errors made by both British and American actors in the films in the corpus.

[ɑː] and [æ] for [aː]

Some of the most obvious examples of segmental errors occur with regard to the vowel in the TRAP lexical set which is realised as [aː] in Irish English but as [æ] in both American English and RP. What is more, the distinction between the TRAP and BATH lexical sets which exists in RP does not apply in Irish English, with BATH being pronounced with [aː] in the Irish variety. Thus pronunciations of words from the BATH set with [ɑː], as in RP, would simply not be accurate. Below are some examples from the film corpus in which actors from abroad did not adhere to these rules.

The first few examples display the typical pronunciation problems which American actors may have, namely the use of [æ] instead of the more open Irish English [aː].

                        [æ]
873) Oh, maybe Laura was right. I just **can't** make my mind up.
                        (*About Adam*, 00:02:42, FL2000D)

      [æ]
874) Not so **fast**, you little snake, you can pay for the drinks yourself.
                        (*The Informer*, 01:02:52, FAB1920D)

                                                  [æ]

875) I looked you up first thing to find out if the **Tans** were still watchin' my mother's house.

                                                  (*The Informer*, 00:12:51, MFMP1920D)

                        [æ]   [æ]

876) If I get a **chance** to see **Gallagher**, I'll put the word[415] in for ya.

                                                      (*The Informer*, 00:13:00, MFMP1920D)

While examples 874 to 876 from *The Informer* showed American actors having difficulty with the pronunciation of the combined TRAP/BATH set in Irish English, British actors in that movie did not fare any better with it, with Margot Grahame, for example, continuing to use /ɑː/ in the BATH set.

                                                [ɑː]

877) Ah, Gypo, what's the use? I'm hungry and I **can't** pay me room rent.

                                                    (*The Informer*, 00:05:50, FK1920D)

                                                          [ɑː]

878) Miss McPhillip, for the sake of your own love, won't you be **asking** him to
      [ɑː]
give my man a **chance**?

                                                    (*The Informer*, 01:26:43, FK1920D)

Rhoticity

Another area in which British actors are likely to have difficulty in pronunciation is with regard to rhoticity. As was observed earlier, Irish English is a rhotic variety, in which the /r/ is traditionally realised as a velarised alveolar continuant; RP, on the other hand, is non-rhotic and, thus, the failure of British actors to employ rhoticity should be immediately apparent. Again, a number of instances of this occur in *The Informer*. It should be noted that the high frequency of quite blatant pronunciation mistakes in this particular film can be attributed to the fact that it was made in the 1930s, in the early days of sound films, when the actors probably would not have had a dialect coach on hand to correct such errors. However, given that an earlier silent version of the film, directed by Arthur Robison in 1929, had already been very poorly dubbed in order to cash in on the trend of "talkies", one would think that the producers might have learned their lesson. Patrick Sheeran makes the following observation regarding the terrible dubbing of the earlier film:

> It comes as quite a shock, when watching the film for the first time, to hear the English actor Warwick Ward (Dan Gallagher) suddenly break into speech halfway through and pronounce the recommisioned Captain Gallagher's words in a chiselled Knightsbridge accent. Those in the original audience who knew from the pages of *The Picturegoer* that leading lady Lya de Putti (Katie Fox) hardly spoke English must have been equally startled to hear her dainty, dubbed, upper-class tones. So too with the Swedish actor Lars

---

[415] This sentence includes yet another instance of the definite article being used where an indefinite article would be used in Standard English. See Chapter 6.

Hanson as Gypo Nolan: his lugubrious, dubbed received pronunciation, applied with a trowel, is greatly at variance with his working-class docker role.

(Sheeran 2002: 48-9)

While the situation in Ford's *The Informer* is not quite as bad as in Robison's, there are still examples in the former, in which the characters sound decidedly English, particularly due to their lack of the aforementioned rhoticity. Here are just a few examples:

[fɜːst]   [gɑːd]
879) He said he had to find him **first** to see if there was a **guard** on the house.
(*The Informer*, 00:57:22, FMMP1920D)

[tʃɜːtʃ]
880) Or did you rob a **church** or what?
(*The Informer*, 00:23:32, FK1920D)

[gɜːl]
881) I'm Katie Madden. I'm Gypo Nolan's **girl**.
(*The Informer*, 01:25: 20, FK1920D)

Although such glaring inaccuracies in pronunciation are less likely to appear in films today, they unfortunately did not stop in the 1930s. One of the worst examples of Irish pronunciation in the film corpus occurs in *A Very Unlucky Leprechaun* from 1998. The following passage taken from the movie is exemplary of the overall performance and is an exchange between Molly, a young American girl who has moved to Ireland, and Lucky, a leprechaun. Again the errors are very obvious, by nature of the fact that they relate to British actor Warwick Davis'[416] continuing to make a distinction between the aforementioned BATH and TRAP sets (even though in Irish English *can't, paragraph, half, ask* and *past* should all be pronounced with [aː] rather than [ɑː]) and his failing to employ rhoticity almost all of the time (*here, form* and *incur*). Where an actor fails to get the basics right, there is little hope for the rest of the accent.

882) *Molly*: How do I know you're telling me the truth?
                    [ɑː]   [ɪə]
Lucky: Well, didn't I tell ya? Leprechauns **can't** lie. See…it's right **here**.
   [ɑː]
Subsection C, **Paragraph** 2.
Molly: Gee, I didn't know being a leprechaun was so complicated.
                [ɑː]   [ɑː]
Lucky: <u>Ach</u>, you don't know the **half** of it. Now, I'll have to **ask** you to sign a
[ɔːm]
form.
Molly: What's it say?
                                [ɑː]
Lucky: Well, it releases me of all responsibility for any **past**, present, or future

---

[416] Given the fact that Davis frequently plays a leprechaun in the *Leprechaun* horror movie franchise, one could certainly expect him to make a better attempt at an Irish accent.

[ɜː]
injuries that you might **incur** while trying to obtain me pot of gold.
(*A Very Unlucky Leprechaun*, 00:24:42, ML1990W)

As can be seen, the pronunciation is really very poor, and even the substitution of an Irish discourse feature *ach* (cf. Dolan 2006: 2) or the use of *me* for *my*[417] can do nothing to save it.

Intrusive /r/

As well as omitting /r/ where it should be pronounced, some British actors actually insert it in contexts where it does not belong. According to dialect coach Brendan Gunn, this use of intrusive /r/ is one of the greatest potential pitfalls for British actors assuming roles in Irish films, as they focus so much on ensuring that their accent is rhotic that they erroneously add r-colouring in situations where this is inappropriate (Gunn, personal communication). A number of British actors use the feature in the context of the word *idea*, for example, which is a context known to be favourable for intrusive /r/ among speakers of British English dialects. A further context for this phenomenon is visible in *Circle of Friends*, in which Minnie Driver's otherwise impeccable accent slips slightly with her addition of an intrusive /r/ in the word *saw*.

[aɪˈdɪər]
883) That's the best **idea**.
(*Rat*, 01:12:01, FC2000D)

[aɪˈdɪər]
884) You have no **idea** at all.
(*Ryan's Daughter*, 00:28:37, FR1920W)

[sɔːr]
885) But on our way to the cottage we **saw** his son Simon riding his horse and looking grand as usual.
(*Circle of Friends*, 00:02:40, FBH1950D)

While British actors may have problems with the rhotic nature of Irish English, this does not pose a problem for most of their American counterparts, as most US accents, with the exception of some east coast ones, such as New York, Boston and Charleston, are rhotic. However, evidence from the film corpus shows problems with the realisation of [ɑːr] and a tendency to produce it as [ɔːr], so that *arse* rhymes with *horse*. These realisations confirm Wolfram's observation that "of the English vowels, the back /ɔ/ of *coffee* or *raw* and the front vowel /æ/[418] of *bad* and *ban* are probably the most dialectically sensitive vowels in the English language" (1991: 51). Examples of the erroneous realisation of [ɑːr] as [ɔːr] in the film corpus include:

---

[417] See Chapter 9.2.13.
[418] Evidence of the sensitivity of /æ/ can be seen on page 240.

[ɔːr]
886) He never says anything about it, but I know it would break his **heart** if I gave it up.
(*Circle of Friends*, 00:53:45, MJF1950D)

[ɔːr]
887) Her mother's not going to fall **apart** if she's left alone the odd night, is she?
(*Circle of Friends*, 01:10:26, MJF1950D)

[ɔːr]
888) We'll begin to settle our debt when we **harvest** the land.
(*Far and Away*, 00:06:55, MJD1890W)

[ɔːr]
889) I was too soft to use the wooden spoon on your **arse** when you were growing up.
(*Last of the High Kings*, 00:05:41, FMG1970D)

[ɔːr]
890) That's his **party** piece, isn't it, Ray?
(*Last of the High Kings*, 00:39:55, FMG1970D)

While it could (generously) be argued that these realisations are simply examples of what is known as the "Dort" accent or "Dortspeak"[419], this is extremely unlikely to be the case, and even if it was, this is not an accent which would have been heard in the 1800s, 1950s or even in the 1970s, when the films featuring the aforementioned examples are set[420]. This substitution of /ɔː/ for /ɑː/ does not appear to be limited to environments preceding /r/, but also appears in front of /ŋ/ in *Ordinary Decent Criminal*.

[ɔːŋ]
891) Don't ask me. I make 'em up as I go **along**.
(*Ordinary Decent Criminal*, 00:38:16, MML1990D)

[əʊ] for [oː]

The presence of monophthongs in the FACE and, particularly, the GOAT lexical sets are deemed to be typically Irish. Therefore examples of [əʊ] realisations instead are conspicuously RP and, thus, not very accurate. Again, *The Informer* is one of the main culprits in this regard, with the following sentences all sounding very RP. The problem is compounded in the final sentence, in that the word *heart* is also realised non-rhotically.

---

[419] This accent, which originated in the southside suburbs of Dublin, was named after the Dart, the Dublin Area Rapid Transport system which serves the area. The label was manipulated to "Dort" to reflect the "retracted and rounded vowel" which is typical of the accent (cf. Hickey 2005: 47-8).

[420] The realisation of [ɑːr] as [ɔːr] is not restricted to American actors. Irish actors who generally speak with a fashionable Dublin accent are also guilty of using this accent in settings which are inappropriate. This is the case with Orla Brady in *A Love Divided*. Even if her character is a wealthy Protestant in Wexford in the 1950s, and, thus, would not be expected to speak with a strong country brogue, her modern Dortspeak accent seems out of place. An example is in the sentence "So I told them that we were the parcel in a big game of pass the parcel" (*A Love Divided*, 00:50:47, FS1950WX), in which *parcel* is pronounced [pɔːrsəl].

[əʊ]
892) Katie, Katie! I've been lookin' all **over** for you. Where have you been?
(*The Informer*, 01:03:29, MG1920D)

[əʊ]   [əʊ]
893) I got **no** clothes. I got **no** money. I got nothin'.
(*The Informer*, 00:34:10, MG1920D)

[əʊ] [ɑːt]
894) Whatever happens to you happens to my **own heart**.
(*The Informer*, 00:57:54, FMMP1920D)

It should be pointed out, however, that there is a current tendency in fashionable Dublin English to realise the GOAT set as [əʊ]. Thus, if this realisation appears in films set today, it is understandable[421]. In the case of a movie like *The Informer*, however, which is set in working class Dublin in the 1920s, this accent is anachronistic. The same applies to *Evelyn* which is set in the 1950s. Although it is usually Pierce Brosnan who receives the brunt of the criticism for his accent in that movie, it is worth noting that the Dublin 4 accent of the girl playing his daughter is equally out of place in Fatima Mansions, a working-class, local authority housing complex in Dublin at that time. An example of her pronunciation is:

[əʊ]
895) Mammy's **going** shopping, Heidi. Would you like a nice new shoes and
[əʊ]
coat?
(*Evelyn*, 00:05:47, FE1950D)

[ɔi] for [ai]

As outlined in the previous chapter, the substitution of [ɔi] for [ai] in the PRICE set is falsely believed by non-Irish people to be one of the characteristic sounds of Irish English (cf. Taniguchi 1972: 249). This "Oirish" substitution is based on an error of perception, namely with [əɪ] being heard as, and later produced as, [ɔi]. However, the latter pronunciation with its back starting-point is not Irish, but, in fact, is more reminiscent of Cockney's [ɒɪ] (cf. Wells 1982b: 308) and it is for this reason that such pseudo-Irish pronunciations of the PRICE set often end up as sounding more British than Irish. Evidence of this is available in the number of film reviews which compare Ray Winstone's poor Irish accent in *Agnes Browne* with that of a character from the London-set Dickens' musical *Oliver!* (Carol Reed, 1968). Examples of such quotes include: "Ray Winstone, who sounds as if he has stepped off the set of *Oliver*" (*Evening Herald*)[422], "Winstone in Bill Sikes[423] mode" (*Time Out Film Guide*)[424], and "Winstone, offering up a possibly unique cockney-oirish crossover dialect" (*Empire*)[425].

---

[421] Indeed this realisation does occur in some modern films such as *Goldfish Memory*, *Cowboys and Angels* and *About Adam*.
[422] Brian Reddin, *Evening Herald*, 9th December 1999: 26-27
[423] Bill Sikes is the villain in *Oliver Twist*.
[424] http://www.timeout.com/film/reviews/77604/agnes_browne.html
[425] http://www.empireonline.com/reviews/ReviewsComplete.asp?FID=5521

The following example from *Agnes Browne*, in which *bye* is homophonous with *boy*, illustrates this phenomenon quite well.

        [ɔi]
896) Now, good **bye**, Mrs "lump sum".
                                 (*Agnes Browne*, 01:14:22, MB1960D)

There are additional examples. In the first, the name *Michael* is affected by this substitution, while in the second, *try*, *time* and *surprise* all feature the erroneous pronunciation.

              [ɔi]
897) That means no **Michael**.
                          (*Ordinary Decent Criminal*, 01:13:04, MSt1990D)

       [ɔi]   [ɔi]   [ɔi]
898) Now, **try** it again, except this **time surprise** me by going on two.
                        (*A Very Unlucky Leprechaun*, 00:26:10, ML1990W)

[w] for [ʍ]

As we have already seen in the previous examples from *A Very Unlucky Leprechaun*, the British actor playing the leprechaun produces one error after the other, appearing to be blissfully unaware of the features of Irish pronunciation. To make matters worse, the one time that he does appear to be familiar with a rule, he also manages to slip up. The feature involved is the use of /ʍ/. As already mentioned, although the actor appears to be conscious of the use of /ʍ/ in place of /w/ in Irish English[426], he, unfortunately, does not seem to be familiar with the contexts in which it is used, namely in words in which /w/ is spelled with <wh->. Instead he uses /ʍ/ for /w/ when pronouncing the word *one*, which is simply incorrect and a clear example of hypercorrection on the part of the actor.

                                                                   [ʍʌn]
899) I've an idea. I'll count to three and then you try and grab me. Ok? **One**, two, three!
                        (*A Very Unlucky Leprechaun*, 00:25:49, ML1990W)

Proof that this was not a once off mistake is evident later in the film when he again employs the word *one*.

        [ʍʌn]
900) Right. **One**, two.
                        (*A Very Unlucky Leprechaun*, 01:19:39, ML1990W)

[ʌ] for [ʊ]

As outlined in Chapter 9.2.8, the opposition between /ʌ/ and /ʊ/ is rare in Ireland, with words from the STRUT lexical set generally being pronounced like those from the FOOT set. Actors

---

[426] For more on this feature, see Chapter 9.1.6.

who fail to make these changes will sound non-Irish to Irish ears. Examples of such erroneous pronunciations include:

[ʌ]   [ʌ]
901) Ah, the **grudge**. The **grudge**.
(The Informer, 00:36:30, MG1920D)

[ʌ]   [uː]
902) Money! Some people have all the **luck**. **Look**[427] at that thing handing us the "ha! ha!"
(The Informer, 00:06:27, FK1920D)

[ʌ]
903) I couldn't do it, Frankie. Not in cold **blood**.
(The Informer, 00:11:49, MG1920D)

[ʌ]
904) Ah, but with a little **luck**, he'll never know.
(A Very Unlucky Leprechaun, 00:30:37, ML1990W)

Yod deletion

As already outlined in Chapter 9, yod deletion sometimes occurs in Irish English, although only after alveolar sonorants in stressed positions, with the result that when it does occur after non-sonorants, it sounds like an American affectation. This is best seen in *When the Sky Falls* where Patrick Bergin, whose character ticks all the boxes which suggest "Hollywood maverick cop", refers to his superiors as stupid morons.

[stuːpɪd]
905) **Stupid** morons.
(When the Sky Falls, 00:45:27, MSgt1990D)

This yod deletion could be intentional and meant to suggest that the character models himself on film icons like Dirty Harry, or it could simply be the consequence of an Irish actor having spent so much time in the USA that he has adapted some features of that country's pronunciation. Either way, the feature grates a little on Irish ears.

The films provide other examples in which the deletion of yod after the plosives /t/ and /d/ sounds very American to Irish ears. One example of it is evident in American actress Catherine O' Hara's yodless rendering of the word *tune* below:

[tuːn]
906) Or what about playing us a **tune**?
(Last of the High Kings, 00:40:00, FMG1970D)

---

[427] The pronunciation of [uː] for [ʊ] is not a feature of Irish English, but rather occurs in some Northern British dialects. In Irish English, *look* and *luck* are both pronounced with [ʊ].

Another instance can be seen in Ward Bond's accent in *The Quiet Man*. In the case of yod deletion already shown on page 215, Bond's omission of yod after /n/ could perhaps generously have been accepted as a feature of Irish English. After all, phonotactic rules permit it in that context. However, when he omits yod after /d/ later in the film, there can be no excuses and this has to be seen to be a slip back to American pronunciation. The offending sentence is as follows:

[duːti]
907) You do that, lad. It's your **duty**.
(*The Quiet Man*, 02:01:17, MFL1930W)

MacHale picks up on the inaccuracy of this pronunciation, stating that "there is a bit of a clanger here – Ward Bond gives us a very American pronunciation of 'dooty' rather than the Irish 'juty'" (2000: 229). The author's respelling here implies that he himself would use yod coalescence in such a context. When Bond proceeds to pronounce *duty* correctly seconds later, MacHale acknowledges that the latter attempt is "more Irish-sounding" (2000: 230). The second example is as follows:

[dʒuːti]   [dʒuːti]
908) Ah, we should, lad, yes we should. It's our **duty**. It's our **duty**.
(*The Quiet Man*, 02:01:45, MFL1930W)

The lowering of /ɪ/ to /ɛ/

In addition to actors sometimes displaying British or American segments in their roles in Irish movies, there is also evidence of actors confusing segments of Southern Irish English with segments of Northern Irish English. An example of this is in the lowering of /ɪ/ to /ɛ/ which is a feature of Ulster Scots (cf. Hickey 2004a: 37). This can be seen in the following sentence by Scottish actor Peter Mullan in *Ordinary Decent Criminal*:

[ɛ]
909) What was a big **thing** when you were eight, say?
(*Ordinary Decent Criminal*, 00:23:41, MSt1990D)

While this form is perfectly correct in Northern Ireland, it is out of place for a character supposedly from Dublin.

Shortening of /iː/ to /i/

Confusion regarding northern and southern features is also evident regarding the shortening of /iː/ to /i/. This short realisation of high vowels is a feature of Northern Irish English generally, but is particularly common in Belfast English (cf. Hickey 2004a: 37). An example appears in *Ordinary Decent Criminal* in the shortening of the /iː/ in *people* and *meet*.

[i]
910) Look at what they do to innocent **people**.
(*Ordinary Decent Criminal*, 00:04:25, MML1990D)

[i]
911) No, no, Peter. In fairness, you travelled a long way **to meet us**.
(*Ordinary Decent Criminal*, 00:50:14, MML1990D)

The examples offered above should have given the reader an impression of the most likely contexts in which non-Irish actors are likely to have difficulty with Irish accents. While a study into the prosody and voice setting of the accents in the films would no doubt have uncovered many more subtle errors, I believe that this brief survey of the main types of segmental errors has certainly laid the foundation for further studies on Irish accent in film.

11 Dialect coach handbooks as sources of poor accents

As was outlined in Chapter 8, the amount and quality of prior accent instruction can be a determining factor in the success or failure of an actor to master an accent, so much so that even though feature film productions generally have the budget to pay for highly-qualified dialect coaches to teach actors correct pronunciations, these coaches may have difficulty undoing the damage caused by the actors' prior exposure to misinformation or stereotypes regarding the accents.

Such misinformation and stereotypes can be the result of actors imitating existing examples of accents in the media, which themselves may be stereotypical or inaccurate. In other cases, actors who are aware of the pitfalls of imitating imitations may turn to what they assume will be more reliable sources of information, namely handbooks which are designed especially to teach actors accents, yet, as we shall see, these must also be approached with caution.

Dialect coach handbooks[428] have existed for decades now and are used to teach actors a whole host of accents for the stage and screen. Some titles include *Stage Dialects* (Blunt 1967), *Dialects for the Stage* (Machlin 1975), *Acting with an Accent* (Stern 1979), *Foreign Dialects. A Manual for Actors, Directors, and Writers* (Herman and Herman 1997), *Accents. A Manual for Actors* (Blumenfeld 2000), *Monologues in Dialect for Young Actors* (Mohne Hill 2002) and *The Dialect Handbook* (Kopf 2003). Unfortunately, many of these manuals can be just as misleading as existing examples of the accent in the media, as they too often take their lead from inauthentic media sources or are poorly researched.[429] What is more, none of the aforementioned books is dedicated solely to a single accent, but instead they all profess to teach actors the pronunciation of a host of different varieties. This broad range of accents, which some actors may see as the strength of such books, is also their greatest weakness, as these dialect handbooks are often so ambitious in their scope that the accuracy of the individual accent descriptions suffers. The following aims to examine just how accurate the accent descriptions in these books really are and to what extent these manuals contribute to perpetuating stereotypical Irish accents[430].

11.1 Perpetuation of cultural stereotypes

Dialect handbooks usually begin by offering a brief introduction to a country, its language and its people. Although these introductions are generally in the form of comments which may sound innocuous, quaint and charming, they nonetheless just serve to perpetuate stereotypes[431], as is the case in the following example related to Ireland:

---

[428] The term dialect manual is somewhat of a misnomer, as the majority of these books teach actors to acquire new accents rather than the other components of a dialect. Herman and Herman (1997), however, do also include sections on grammar and lexical changes for writers attempting to recreate the dialect in their plays and stories.

[429] To be fair, many of these manuals do offer very good advice on how to approach learning accents in general – Blunt deserves particular praise in this regard - and they also freely admit to the fact that artistic concerns should take precedent over realism. However, as we shall see, the frequency of the clichés and misinformation regarding Irish English must invariably lead one to question the general accuracy of the information in the manuals.

[430] I will take the liberty to quote from these books at length, so as not to be seen to be citing out of context.

[431] Lippi-Green (1997: 83-84) has already briefly commented on the skewed and stereotypical portrayals of certain nationalities which are evident in the original version of Herman and Herman's dialect coach manual from 1943. These clichéd and sometimes offensive descriptions of national character were removed from the 1997 edition of Herman and Herman's book, which is the one used in this study.

> The Irish people are warm, hospitable, and generous, and they are masters at conversation. Their speech is filled with proverbs, metaphors, clichés and quotations from plays, songs and films. There is a joy in speaking that comes through in the delivery. This is not to say that there are no sad people in Ireland; indeed, there is always a sense of deep-seated sorrow at the core of the Irish, but this sorrow is masked in the twinkling of the 'Irish eyes'.
>
> (Mohne Hill 2002: 56-7)

Such clichéd statements are made, despite Mohne Hill's claim in her introduction that

> The students at A.C.T. (American Conservatory Theatre) are taught that dialects are not to be taken lightly, as some silly voices they put on to 'be different'. Just as the essence of who you are is revealed in your personal speech pattern, so are your characters' souls revealed in their speech patterns. Dialects are to be respected. We study the region of the dialect to understand its place and its context. This deeper understanding makes us take responsibility for creating as true and realistic and deep a dialect as we possibly can. We strive to move beyond stereotype and generality.
>
> (Mohne Hill 2002: ix)

Other dialect coaches are far more cautious about misrepresenting Irish speech, with Blunt, for example, stating that one of the purposes of his book is "to make sure that the representation of each dialect is faithful to its primary sources, free from the multiple malpractices and the time ridden clichés which have always plagued this aspect of stage work" (1967: 7). Nonetheless, he, too, cannot resist referring to things which have absolutely no influence on language, namely leprechauns and Celtic mysticism:

> At once a hardy and fanciful and humorous people, the Irish, living close to nature in an environment hardly benign, have developed an elemental sensitivity to both the known and the unknown in the forces of nature. The imagination which, in the face of harsh and often cruel climatic conditions, could create leprechauns instead of ogres would more likely see and feel beauty than meanness in both natural and human relationships. A Celtic strain must be taken into account: an earlier Gaelic influence which went deep and stayed long; a mysticism which sought release in dance and song also left its impress on the rhythm of local utterance[432].
>
> (Blunt 1967: 75-76)

In keeping with her colleagues, Kopf also attributes the way Irish people speak to a host of non-linguistic factors. Note again the casual reference to leprechauns and elves, which, although not claimed to influence the way the Irish speak, nonetheless find their way into the text. What is more, the suggestion that "greenery" can have some sort of effect on the "melody" of a person's speech is truly absurd.

> The lilting melody that characterizes the Irish speech is reflective of the greenery of Ireland's rural past. Legends of leprechauns and elves, and tales of love and adventure, mystery and wonder, have been passed down generation to generation. The Irish people's romantic land is lush with rolling green hills and fields of wildflowers. The lilt of their accent could also come from the warmth and friendliness of the people.
>
> (Kopf 2003: 41)

---

[432] Surprisingly, something which does in fact play a role in the way Irish English sounds, i.e. the Irish language, is simply dismissed as irrelevant, with Blunt stating that "its presence, however, has had but little influence upon the speech we characterize as an Irish dialect, consequently it need not concern us now" (1967: 76).

Many of these notions had already been mentioned earlier in Kopf's book with regard to Northern Irish speech, where, again, there were repeated references to "rolling green hills" and "fields of wildflowers" and their supposed effect on language:

> The lilting melody that characterizes Northern Irish speech is reflective of the region's environment. Rolling green hills and fields of wildflowers stretch as far as the eye can see. Counties in the rural northwest, such as Donegal, have wild, undeveloped mountainous territory and a dramatic coastline. The land's thousands of acres of unproductive grass, heather, and peat bog are fit only for grazing sheep. Given this difficult environment, the strong upward lilt of the Northern Irish dialect seems to express tenacity to face frustration and hardship head-on with an 'irrepressible gaiety'[433].
>
> (Kopf 2003: 40)

Not content with associating the Irish accent with the influence of topography, Kopf goes on to attribute the Irish accent to the effects of climate and history on the Irish vocal apparatus.

> In Ireland, the weather is as unpredictable as the Irish themselves. If it is not raining, it is threatening to rain. Sheets of mist cause lack of definition that can shroud things, and make a person feel cut off from the world. In regions where the people protect themselves against inclement weather (snow, wind, rain), it is not uncommon to find that the mouth is more closed off, creating a dialect that has a smaller mouth opening. (Of course, a smaller mouth opening could also be the result of cultural factors, such as a history of repression or hardship).
>
> (2003: 40)

In this regard, Kopf is echoing comments by Mohne Hill, who also claims that "due to environmental conditions (cold, fog, wind), there is a lack of mouth opening and movement when the Irish produce sounds" (Mohne Hill 2002: 57). This notion that climate can affect pronunciation is not new, but, in fact, was originally championed by Johann Winckelmann and Johann Herder in the mid-eighteenth century. However, such a theory is nowadays regarded as "sheer ignorance" (Chambers 1995: 228)[434], and I believe the same can safely be said for the supposed influence of events like the Famine on the "lack of mouth opening" among the Irish.

In a final bid to explain why Irish people speak the way they do, Kopf draws a connection between Irish people's accents and their personalities, observing that "the unpredictable rhythms of their speech, the wide, emotional inflection, and the manner in which they "sit on" or stretch out stressed syllables can be linked to their fiery temperament" (2003: 42). Thankfully, she does not go so far as to draw connections between these "fiery temperaments" and the fiery red hair often associated with the Irish.

11.2 Respellings of sound changes

Having given some (spurious) background information about the country and its people, the dialect coach handbooks then outline a number of sound changes which need to be made if one is to acquire the appropriate accent. However, rather than explaining these changes using the internationally accepted IPA symbols, the authors very often employ

---

[433] Caulfield, Max. (1973) *The Irish Mystique*. Englewood Cliffs, N.J.: Prentice-Hall. 5.
[434] For more on this phenomenon, see Chambers (1995).

respellings of the kind one encounters in literary dialect. Their decision not to use the IPA is, on the one hand, understandable, seeing as many actors are not familiar with the phonetic alphabet and have little or no formal phonetic training. On the other hand, given the notorious problems involved in trying to represent the forty-plus phonemes of English using a twenty-six letter alphabet, the respellings used in the handbooks are very likely to be open to misunderstanding, as they are based on one of the standards or perhaps on some other regional accent[435]. Some examples of potentially confusing respellings are as follows:

shoowuhr AH:n' uhEEm nAH:t t'THoo AWool'!
(Sure, and I'm not too old!)

(Herman and Herman 1997: 82)

loyk oy sad t*e* yez, or yiz, dAts ray' *e* lee va'Ree tR<u>oo</u> An shawR y*e*l bay Af th*e*R nO *e*n d*e* tR<u>oo</u>th, or tsR<u>oo</u>t, or tR<u>oo</u>ts, *e*v it soom way' *e*R *e* LAng' d*e* Rawd a' nee we:'
(Like I said to yous, that's really very true, and sure you'll be after knowin' the truth of it, somewhere along the road anyway.)

(Blumenfeld 2000: 87)

To be fair, it should be acknowledged that Blumenfeld and the other dialect coaches do include a key to explain their respellings, and, in this respect, the actors learning the dialects will probably be able to make more sense of the respellings than someone reading the sentences as they are presented here. Nonetheless, since each coach uses a different system of respellings, actors working with different sources will have to familiarise themselves with each of the different codes. Given this fact, an agreement by coaches and actors to use the IPA, despite its perceived complexity, might be a better solution for all parties in the long term.

11.3 Misinformation

In addition to using respellings which, as we have seen, can be difficult to read, dialect coach manuals are often just plain wrong in the information they give about accents and dialects. This problem stems from the fact that such dialect manuals are often so ambitious in their scope (see Herman and Herman 1997) that it is almost impossible for the authors to be well-versed in so many different varieties. Not only are there blatant errors in the descriptions of linguistic features, as we shall see, but there are also basic mistakes with regard to geographical or cultural information which even non-experts would spot. Such errors lead one to question the usefulness of the manuals. A case in point is evident in Blumenfeld's treatment of Irish accents.

While Blumenfeld sensibly divides up the various accents of Ireland into different regions: "Northern Irish (Belfast)", "Border Accents", and "Southern Irish (Dublin; County Cork, etc)", he makes the major faux pas of including Derry in the latter section (2000: 86). While Republicans in Ireland may very well wish for a United Ireland so that Derry can

---

[435] To avoid such problems of interpretation, a minority of authors also include accompanying recordings with their books. However, the accuracy of the accents in such recordings also leaves something to be desired. Angela C. Pao has the following to say about Blumenfeld's recordings, in which he imitates all the accents himself: "accents are represented with varying degrees of refinement. In many cases, users of *Accents* might do well to follow the old adage 'Do as I say not as I do'" (2004: 368).

belong to Southern Ireland, there is absolutely no linguistic (or geographical) justification for its inclusion in that category.

What is more, he labels an accent as a "Kildare/County Clare accent", which he declares to be "some of the clearest Irish speech" (2000: 85). Those familiar with Ireland will find the term "Kildare/County Clare accent" to be a most unusual descriptor, as, both geographically and linguistically, these two counties are miles apart. Even if one were to generously argue that a Kildare/County Clare accent could be seen as an umbrella term for some sort of neutral or generic Irish accent (due to the fact that speakers from neither of these counties display the conspicuous features of, say, a Dublin or Kerry accent), the fact that, geographically, these places are on opposite sides of the country makes this choice of label very difficult to comprehend. Such blatant errors on a macro level lead one to call into question every other piece of information on Irish accents given by Blumenfeld. And with good reason. His book is a catalogue of errors.

He claims that Gaelic (Irish) is the "native tongue of perhaps one million people" today (2000: 80). This figure is incredibly inflated, as according to Hickey's calculations based on the 2006 census, "the percentage of native speakers in present-day Ireland would be between 0.4% and 0.5%, i.e. not more than 20,000 at the most" (http://www.uni-due.de/DI/Who_Speaks_Irish.htm). Even if the number of native speakers may have dropped between 2000, when Blumenfeld's book was published (in its third edition!), and 2006, when the census was conducted, there is no way that the number fell by 980,000 over a period of six years. What Blumenfeld presumably meant was that over a million people claim an ability to speak Irish. Indeed, the 2006 census suggested that 1,650,982 people claimed just this (http://www.uni-due.de/DI/Who_Speaks_Irish.htm)[436].

Blumenfeld's misinformation also extends to the most important aspects of all, namely his descriptions of phonological features of Irish English. He states that "the consonant 'l' is dark, liquid, and slightly retroflex" (2000: 82), despite the fact that this is in direct opposition to the standard description of Irish English as using an alveolar /l/ in all positions, due to influence from Irish which uses non-velar, non-palatal [l] (Hickey 2004a: 41)[437].

Blumenfeld also suggests that "in the south there is a heavily retroflex final 'R' and 'R' before another consonant" (2000: 82). However, if one consults the standard works on the variety, they state that the /r/ is traditionally realised as a velarised alveolar continuant in Irish English. In fact, the /r/ is only retroflex in Northern Irish English (Hickey 2004b: 81), which immediately disproves Blumenfeld's next claim, namely that Northern Irish English is "generally a non-rhotic accent" (2000: 83).

He then goes on to claim that "long 'ee' words like *tea* become like 'ay' in *say*; *tea* becomes 'tay'" and he offers the practice words "*tea, meat, Jesus, leave, here* (rhymes with

---

[436] Even then the number of people who speak Irish on a daily basis is small. According to census figures, "less than one person in 20 who claims to be able to speak Irish does so on a daily basis outside the educational system" (*The Irish Times*, October 5, 2007: 3)
[437] Incidentally, Herman and Herman make the same mistake as Blumenfeld regarding the typical clear /l/ of Irish English. They claim that "the Irish 'l' is sounded more liquidly than the American. Instead of the thin treatment, as in 'look', it is given the liquidity of the 'l' in 'valor'" (1997: 78). This again is incorrect, as in Irish English the opposite is the case: "/l/ is always 'clear' in quality; there is no trace of the dark [ɫ] normal in RP in such words as *fill, field*" (Bliss 1984: 138).

hair), beer, teach, reach, believe" (2000: 85). While this information applies to some of the practice words, this is certainly not true for all. *Here* does not rhyme with *hair*, nor *beer* with *bare*. This again is evidence of a dialect coach trying to apply a pattern across the board without being familiar with the rule or the etymology (cf. Bliss 1984: 139).

Blumenfeld also remarks that:

> On the southwest coast there is a particular phenomenon to consider: the semi-vowel "y" is sometimes inserted after an initial consonant, especially after "k" and "g". Car is pronounced "kyAR," and garden becomes "gyAR'din." Doctor is pronounced "dyak'teR."
>
> (2000: 86)

Although the palatalisation of velar plosives does exist in Ireland, it is not a feature of the accents of the southwest coast of Ireland, as Blumenfeld claims, but rather of Northern Irish English and of the border counties, as is reflected in the local pronunciation of County Cavan as ['kjævən]. The fact that this feature is not to be found in the south of Ireland is also confirmed by Hickey's singling out such palatalisation as "a conspicuous feature of northern Irish English" (2004: 39).[438]

Mohne Hill is also guilty of confusing the phonological features of Northern Irish English and Southern Irish English. For example, although she claims that the sound changes in her book should give the actor "a general, mostly West Ireland-sounding dialect" (2002: 56), the lowering of /ɪ/ to /ɛ/, which she offers as an example, is a feature of Ulster Scots (cf. Hickey 2004b: 78) and not of Southern Irish English. Below is Mohne Hill's example:

[ih] → [eh]
hill, different, dig, quick, thick → hehll, dehfrent, dehg, quehck, thehck

(2002: 59)

In the same vein, Herman and Herman also mix up Northern Irish English and Southern Irish English features. They focus on the same vowel as Mohne Hill, albeit on a different realisation of it, stating that this short vowel sound /ɪ/ as in *it, women, busy,* etc "is broadened in the Irish dialect into an 'UH,' as in 'sUHt' (sit)" (1997: 73). They highlight this substitution using a series of drill words:

UHt	(it)		mUHd'l	(middle)
sUHt	(sit)		lUhtTH'l	(little)
bUHl	(bill)		wUHm'n	(women)
		sUHvUHly'n	(civilian)	
		stTHUHmiyoolEH:t	(stimulate)	
		sUHnsAY:uhr	(sincere)	

(1997: 73)

While this centralisation of /ɪ/ to /ʊ/ does indeed occur in Irish English, it is once again a feature of Northern Irish English (cf. Hickey 2004a: 51), and should therefore be described as such to avoid confusion. If actors unquestioningly adopt all of these features from both the

---

[438] What is more, this palatalisation only occurs after velars and not after alveolars as Blumenfeld suggests.

Northern and Southern varieties, then their accent will invariably become some sort of mongrel mix.

Further inaccuracies are to be found in Herman and Herman with regard to the substitutions for /ɜː/ which occur in Dublin English. While they correctly identify that /ɜː/ is often pronounced [ʊː], they fail to make the distinction between those /ɜː/ words which are pronounced [ɛː] (e.g. girl) rather than [ʊː] (e.g. *bird*), as was illustrated in Chapter 9.3.1. They refer to the "ER" sound, as in *curb, earn, fir*, etc. and they state that "the vowel sound of this combination, when found in any of the 'er,' 'ir,' 'or,' and 'ur' combinations, is always sounded as 'UH' as a (sic) in: 'bUHruhd' (bird)" (1997: 75). They then offer the following drill words:

UHrn	(earn)	gUHruhl	(girl)
fUHr	(fir)	wUHruk	(work)
kUHrb	(curb)	dUHrthi	(dirty)
	sUHrTH'nli	(certainly)	
	flUHrtTHEH:sh's	(flirtatious)	
	oondUHstTHUHrb'd	(undisturbed)	

(1997: 75-6)

However, as mentioned above, their across the board substitution of /ʊː/ for /ɜː/ for all of the aforementioned terms is wrong. In fact, their substitution is only correct in four of the nine drill words given: *curb, work, dirty* and *undisturbed*.

Mohne Hill has similar problems with this feature, but instead of suggesting that /ɜː/ becomes /ʊː/ on all occasions, she goes to the other extreme stating that it always becomes /ɛː/. She suggests that all such words are pronounced as follows:

[er/ir] → [air]
girl, heard, bird → gairl, haird, baird

(Mohne Hill 2002: 59)

This error is also visible in one of her practice sentences, designed for actors to repeat while they are learning their accent: "The first bird is early and dirty" (2002: 61). The only word which should undergo the change "[er/ir] → [air]", as she calls it, is *early*. *First, bird* and *dirty*, on the other hand, are all pronounced with [ʊː] in Dublin English. When three quarters of the key words in Mohne Hill's list and over half of those in Herman and Herman's are incorrect, one is inclined to probe a little deeper for further errors. Unfortunately, one does not have to probe too deep.

Mohne Hill, for example, also goes on to perpetuate the notion that /ai/ is pronounced [ɔi] in Irish English, as can be seen in the following example:

[y] → [oy]
Ireland, my, kite → oyrland, moy, koyt (occasional change)

(2006: 60)

In this regard, she is not the only offender. Blumenfeld makes the same mistake, offering the respellings "moyl" and "tRoyl" for *mile* and *trial* (2000: 85). However, these substitutions of /ɔi/ for /ai/, as pointed out elsewhere in this book, are not accurate, and result in pseudo-Irish or, what are known as, "Oirish" accents.

Thankfully, Herman and Herman, are more accurate in their description of this feature, acknowledging that the frequent substitution of /ɔi/ for /ai/ by non-Irish people is erroneous.

> Perhaps the most identifying of all the vowel substitutions in the Irish dialect is the one made for this long 'i' (I). It is almost universally changed to 'OI,' ('AW-EE') as in 'nOIs.' But, actually, the substitution is not 'AW-EE' so much as 'uhEE' in which the initial 'uh' is only barely sounded while the long 'e' final sound is elongated slightly.
>
> (1997: 73)

However, Herman and Herman's accuracy with regard to this feature is cancelled out by their inaccuracy regarding one of the most important aspects of Irish English: the pronunciation of the BATH and TRAP lexical sets. While they recognise that there is no differentiation between the BATH and TRAP lexical sets in Irish English, they suggest that the pronunciation for both sets is [ɑː] rather than [aː] or [æ], stating that the pronunciation is "AH", as in the American pronunciation of *father*, *arm* and *park*, rather than "A:", as in the American pronunciation of *ask*, *draft* and *laugh* (1997: 70-1).

While one could argue that I may simply be misreading the Hermans' particular brand of respellings, and falling victim to one of the greatest perils of literary dialect, namely imposing my sound system on that of the writer[439], this is not the case. The authors clearly state in the introduction to the book that, since they are from the American Mid-West, their pronunciation of *ask* using their phonetic respellings is "A:sk" and not "AHsk", i.e. they say [æ] rather than [ɑː] (1997: 2). Therefore, by labelling the Irish English pronunciation of both lexical sets as "AH", they are essentially suggesting that the words in both are pronounced in Irish English as they would be in the BATH set in RP, namely with a low back vowel.[440] This, of course, is incorrect.

11.4 Recommendations of media representations of the accent

Misinformation in the dialect coach manuals is not restricted to the features of Irish accents. When it comes to recommending "primary" sources for learning the accents, many of the handbooks are just as unreliable.

Mohne Hill, for example, offers acting students some assistance with their Irish accents by referring them to some existing Irish film, television and audio references. The list of films is as follows:

Rural West Ireland:

Riders to the Sea
The Butcher Boy
Waking Ned Devine
Angela's Ashes

---

[439] For more on this issue, see Ives (1950: 162).
[440] Confirmation of the fact that their respelling "AH" is pronounced [ɑː] can be found in the chapters in Herman and Herman's handbook entitled "The British Dialect" (1997: 47-48) and "The Cockney Dialect" (1997: 19) in which the respelling for the BATH lexical set is indeed "AH".

Rural Northern Ireland (Donegal)

Dancing at Lughnasa
The Field
The Secret of Roan Inish
The Closer You Get

North Ireland (Belfast)

Michael Collins
In the Name of the Father
The Crying Game
Titanic Town

(2002: 58)

However, a quick look at the list reveals three quite obvious errors:

The Butcher Boy (Neil Jordan, 1998) does not belong on the Rural West Ireland list, as it is actually set in County Monaghan on the border to Northern Ireland and, thus, the speech therein displays many of the features of the Northern Irish accent[441]. It should therefore appear on the Rural Northern Ireland list with other films which share the same features.

The Field (Jim Sheridan, 1990), in contrast, is, in fact, set in the rural west of Ireland and does not display any of the features associated with Donegal or with rural Northern Ireland. Therefore it should appear on the first list rather than on the second.

Finally, *Michael Collins* (Neil Jordan, 1996) should not appear on the North Ireland (Belfast) list, as it is a biopic of the famous military and political leader from County Cork and is chiefly set in Dublin, the Midlands and Cork. Indeed, the only Belfast character in the film is MacBride, the Belfast detective who is sent to Dublin to capture Collins, but he is killed off after only 45 seconds of screen time, and thus the film is hardly a mine of information when it comes to Northern Irish accents. Mohne Hill's mistake would appear to have been her mistaking the actor, Liam Neeson, with the character, Michael Collins, as Neeson hails from Northern Ireland.

She does not appear to be alone in this regard. The authors of a number of the other manuals make exactly the same mistake, which arouses the suspicion that they may even be copying from one another. Blumenfeld, for example, also groups *Michael Collins* together with movies set in Northern Ireland, thereby implying that the accents are Northern:

> You should also see Carol Reed's magnificent film *Odd Man Out* (1947), with James Mason as a hunted Irish rebel leader; *The Crying Game* (1992) with Stephen Rea, for northern accents; and *Michael Collins* (1996) set during the 1916-1921 rebellion, with Liam Neeson in the title role.
>
> (Blumenfeld 2000: 81)

Kopf also sets great store in the fact that *Michael Collins* features "primary and secondary sources for Northern Irish", which as we have seen is not true. Furthermore, if as she claims, "Liam Neeson plays the title role but not the appropriate West Cork dialect" (2003: 131), then why recommend the film at all? Like Mohne Hill, Kopf also attributes "authentic rural Northern Irish" (2003: 131) accents to *The Field*, which, again, is not the

---

[441] It was for his very reason that the film was discounted from the film corpus for this study.

case, as the film is set in the west of Ireland and none of the characters bears the obvious trace of a Northern accent[442].

In addition to incorrectly advising actors regarding accents in Irish film, Kopf exacerbates this by suggesting that they listen to certain types of Irish music in order to get a flavour of the sounds of the variety. However, once again she is inaccurate in her choice of reference material, seeing as she writes that "the band, The Proclaimers, have the Northern Irish dialect" (2003: 132), when in fact they come from Scotland. Even if one were to argue that the accents in Northern Ireland and Scotland are somewhat similar, that does not really excuse the promotion of inauthentic primary sources, particularly when plenty of authentic ones exist.

As one can see, despite the best intentions of these dialect coaches, actors who are not familiar with the setting of the aforementioned films or with Irish accents in general may end up learning the wrong kind of accent for their role if they pay heed to these recommendations.

On the whole, one would have to say that, based on the evidence given here, the information given in such dialect coach manuals should certainly be taken with a pinch of salt – to say the least. After all, the errors listed were only those for Irish English. Who knows how reliable the information is for the other myriad accents included in such books?

In this regard, I believe that a detailed investigation into those other accents would prove very fruitful for further research. In the meantime, actors would probably be best advised to learn the IPA and to consult standard works on accents compiled by experienced linguists. Kortmann *et al.* (2004a), for example, contains a wealth of information on the typical accents of numerous varieties of English from all around the world, yet the quality of the information is never compromised by the quantity, since each chapter has been compiled by experts in their specific fields. A collaborative work such as this is considerably more accurate than the dialect coach handbooks mentioned above and clearly has practical applications, not only in classrooms but also in theatres and on film sets. What is more, actors who require original recordings of the different varieties will find these in the many ICE corpora or in the individual linguistic works which focus in depth on the accents of a particular variety. An example of the latter, which has proven invaluable in this study, is Hickey's *A Sound Atlas of Irish English* (2004a). By imitating the primary sources on the DVD which comes with the book, actors should be able to walk out on stage, confident in the fact that their accent is more Irish than "Oirish".

---

[442] The fact that Kopf clearly has difficulty differentiating between Northern and Southern Irish English renders her criticism of Blunt's *Stage Dialects* book a little hypocritical. She writes: "With Blunt's method, be aware that each dialect he teaches is a 'standard' (generic) one for the stage – he doesn't distinguish between the rural or urban, northern or southern speech of any of them. For example, Blunt teaches an Irish accent without differentiating it from that of Northern Ireland" (Kopf 2003: 22).

12 Additional reasons for the perception of poor accents in film

While this study has shown evidence of accents which are inaccurate on a segmental basis, not all examples of accents which have been widely criticised by both audiences and critics necessarily deserve the criticism they receive.

Indeed, it is my contention that very often audiences, and in this case Irish audiences in particular, deem an actor's accent to be inaccurate not on the basis of the accent itself, but because they react negatively towards other linguistic or, indeed, non-linguistic features. These features include: the actor's use (or perceived use) of stereotypical expressions which are falsely deemed to be typically Irish, the actor's physical appearance, and the phenomenon of accent hallucination on the part of the viewer. The fact that these elements, and not necessarily accent itself, play a role becomes very clear when one analyses both film reviews and what Preston describes as the "folk's" comments on the accents[443]. The first of these comments concern themselves with linguistic features, albeit ones which are not at all related to accent, namely stereotypical expressions or pat phrases.

12.1 Stereotypical expressions or pat phrases

The use (or perceived use) of stereotypical expressions which have entered the collective consciousness and are erroneously believed to be typically Irish is one of the major gripes of Irish cinema audiences. As was observed in the chapter on literary dialect and the figure of the Stage Irishman, the speech of Irish characters has traditionally been "spiced up" by the addition of pat phrases which by now have developed Stage Irish connotations. These include expressions such as *Top of the morning*, *Faith and Begorrah*, and *to be sure, to be sure*. Attention has been drawn to the inaccuracy of such "Irish" expressions before, perhaps most famously by George Bernard Shaw in his satirical play *John Bull's Other Island*, in which Doyle criticises Broadbent for having given money to the so-called "Irishman" Tim Haffigan:

> BROADBENT: [...] Why are you so down on every Irishman you meet, especially if he's a bit shabby? Poor devil! Surely a fellow-countryman may pass you the top of the morning without offence, even if his coat is a bit shiny at the seams.
> DOYLE [contemptuously]: The top of the morning! Did he call you a broth of a boy?
> BROADBENT [triumphantly]: Yes.
> DOYLE: And wished you more power to your elbow?
> BROADBENT: He did.
> DOYLE: And that your shadow might never be less?
> BROADBENT: Certainly.
>
> [...]
>
> DOYLE: [...] He's not an Irishman at all.
> BROADBENT: Not an Irishman! [He is so amazed by the statement that he straightens himself and brings the stool bolt upright].
> DOYLE: Born in Glasgow. Never was in Ireland in his life. I know all about him.
> BROADBENT: But he spoke – he behaved just like an Irishman.
> DOYLE: Like an Irishman!! Man alive, don't you know that all this top-o-the-morning and broth-of-a-boy and more-power-to-your-elbow business is got up in England to fool you, like the Albert Hall concerts of Irish music? No Irishman ever talks like that in

---

[443] For more on the usefulness of folk linguistics see Chapter 7.

Ireland, or ever did, or ever will. But when a thoroughly worthless Irishman comes to England, and finds the whole place full of romantic duffers like you, who will let him loaf and drink and sponge and brag as long as he flatters your sense of moral superiority by playing the fool and degrading himself and his country, he soon learns the antics that take you in. He picks them up at the theatre or the music hall.

(Shaw 1964: 80-1)

Bearing in mind Shaw's opposition to such terms, it is worth taking a brief look at where these terms come from and whether they are or ever were used in Ireland. Let us begin with the main offender. The expression *Top of the morning* has long been discussed in the press, with its Irishness invariably being called into question. A series of letters to *The Irish Times* in early 1952 tried to get to the heart of the matter, with the various authors claiming that, despite what people might like to think, the expression is actually Irish in origin (cf. *The Irish Times*, January 8, 1952). According to one contributor, the *Shorter Oxford English Dictionary* describes *Top of the morning* as an Irish greeting dating back to 1663. A second contributor claimed that an Irishman, the Kilkenny poet John Locke, was as responsible as anyone for spreading the now much-maligned feature, since his 1877 poem "Dawn on the Irish Coast" featured the expression in the final line of a number of its verses. One such verse reads as follows:

> O Ireland, isn't it grand you look –
> Like a bride in her rich adornin'!
> With all the pent up love of my heart,
> I bid you top of the mornin'!

(cited in McMahon 2004: 801)

Over forty years later, Diarmaid Ó Muirithe conducted further research into the expression's origin in his popular "The Words We Use" column in *The Irish Times*. Having examined the phrase's etymology, he came to the conclusion that *Top o' the mornin'* is "as English as cakes and ale" and he blamed "Boston-based John Boyle O'Reilly for spreading the expression through nationalist Ireland when he bade Ireland, which he found looking grand, the top of the morning in a popular sentimental poem" (1994: 26). In any case, no matter what its origin may be, it can be safely said that *Top of the mornin'* is universally regarded as a Stage Irish expression today and will not be heard in Ireland, unless spoken in jest or, as in *John Bull's Other Island*, when pandering to outsiders expectations of Irishness. The latter notion is confirmed by Slide, who states that "the phrase 'Top o' the Morning' is unknown in Ireland except among tour guides in Killarney anxious to please the American tourists" (1988: 110).

Faith (sometimes *faix*), meaning 'in truth' (Dolan 2006: 88), is another feature which is similarly loaded with Stage Irish connotations today, with its use being described by Share as generally ironic or as an example of a Paddyism (2003: 101)[444]. However, *faith* was, in fact, quite common as an oath or interjection in Standard English in the past, appearing in texts dating as far back as 1420 (cf. OED s.v. faith, *n*. 12. b). Its modern status as a Stage Irish term can possibly be attributed to its overuse in the speech of Irish characters in earlier literary dialect writing. Indeed, Bliss (1979: 259) cites *faith* or *'i' faith* as being the most

---

[444] McMahon and O'Donoghue echo this notion that the term is obsolete except for in Stage Irish contexts, stating that it is "now more likely to be used humorously or ironically". They add that "the variant 'faix' now seems very Oirish" (2004: 283).

popular oaths in his corpus of literary texts from 1600-1740. In addition to being used as an oath or interjection in its own right, *faith* is also frequently found in the Stage Irish expression *Faith and begorrah*.

The OED describes *begorrah* (also *begorra* and *begarra*)[445] as being an interjection or oath, which is an "Anglo-Irish alteration of the expletive *by God*", comparable to other dialect forms, such as *begar* and *begad* (OED s.v. begorra, *int.*). However, in keeping with the notion that *begorrah* has developed Stage Irish connotations, the OED does go on to add that it is "rarely heard in current speech". Terry Eagleton confirms this idea, observing that "if you hear anyone saying 'Begorrah' during your stay in Ireland, you can be sure he's an undercover agent for the Irish Tourist Board pandering to your false expectations" (2006: 25).

A further phrase mentioned in *John Bull's Other Island* which has disappeared from popular usage is *a broth of a boy*. This colloquial Irish expression signifying "the essence of what a boy should be, a downright good fellow" (OED s.v. broth, *n.* 3) can be found in texts from the mid-seventeenth century but was already in decline when it was critiqued by Shaw in 1907. Share (2003: 41) describes it as a "Paddyism", while MacMahon and O'Donoghue (2004: 127) state that it was "once entirely laudatory, but now has degenerated into an expression either pejorative or condescending".

The expression *more power to one's elbow* is generally used as an exclamation of encouragement in wishing someone to succeed (cf. OED s.v. elbow, *n.* 4.g.) and is attributed by Wright to the west and southwest of Ireland (EDD s.v. elbow, *phr.* 5). Unlike the previous features, it, or a shortened version of it – *more power to you* –, is still likely to be heard in Ireland (cf. McMahon and O'Donoghue 2004: 677).

However, somewhat surprisingly given the volume of discussion about these phrases and their associations with media representations of the Irish, these Stage Irish expressions almost never appear in the 50 films of the film corpus. Indeed, as the examples below show, the expressions *Top of the mornin'*, *Begorrah*, *Faith* and *More power to your elbow* appear in only one film each. *Broth of a boy* does not appear at all, at all[446].

912) **Top o' the mornin'** Father.
(*Ryan's Daughter*, 00:38:43, MP1920W)

913) **Begorrah**! He wasn't far wrong.
(*Darby O'Gill and the Little People*, 00:28:25, MKB1800W)

914) **Faith**, I know I can't sing a lick, but when I'm roarin like Doran's bull, it works up a killin' hunger in me.
(*Darby O'Gill and the Little People*, 00:48:54, MMB1800D)

915) **More power to your elbow**, Frankie.
(*Angela's Ashes*, 01:18:55, MUP1930L)

---

[445] Synonymous forms, *begob* and *begobs* are also cited (OED s.v. begob, *int.*).
[446] As noted in Chapter 6, repetitions like *at all, at all* and *to be sure, to be sure* are also regarded as Stage Irish. *At all at all* appears only once in the film corpus, while *to be sure, to be sure* does not occur in any of the films. The status of *to be sure, to be sure* as a clichéd term can also be seen in the title of a *Belfast Telegraph* article "Sure 'tis only a stereotype, to be sure, to be sure" http://www.belfasttelegraph.co.uk/entertainment/film-tv/news/article3515226.ece (Retrieved: July 1, 2008) which relates to the film *Far and Away*.

What is even more revealing than the absence of these expressions from the films is the fact that so many of the comments on poor Irish accents in film nevertheless incorporate these very terms, especially *Top o' the mornin'* or *Begorrah*, thereby implying the presence of Stage Irish features, which were not in the actual film[447]. Comments on Tom Cruise's performance in *Far and Away*, for example, often employ such terms, although, as already mentioned, these phrases do not appear in that film[448].

Below are some examples: the first two come from interviews by Sell (forthcoming) which asked informants whether they had ever seen a film in which a non-Irish person assumes an Irish accent. The third is from an Internet forum which addressed the notion of the worst accents on film.

Interviewer – And have you ever seen a film set in Ireland in which a foreign actor uses an Irish accent?
Respondent – Oh, my God! Have you ever heard of the movie *Far and Away*?
Interviewer – Yes.
Respondent – Tom Cruise and Nicole Kidman's **faith and begorrah** accents[449]. You'd be thinkin' "Oh, my God!" when you hear it.
(Female, 21 Galway, in: Sell, forthcoming)

Respondent – It's just, we don't talk like that.
Interviewer – Is it exaggerated?
Respondent – Yeah, a little bit, yeah, it's the usual ***Top o' the mornin' to you*** kind of thing. It's just you're, like, no, we don't speak like that. So, there's a bit of a stereotype to the Irish accent in general."
(Female, 25, Galway, in: Sell, forthcoming)

Has everyone forgotten about Tom 'Tommy Boy' Cruise in 'Far & Away'? Oh **begora** an' begod , sure isn't it a fantastic mornin' to be a lepracaun !
(lazyink[450], August 22, 2007)

---

[447] As Preston and Niedzielski have observed, the folk often include imitations of the accent or dialect to explain their point, and this is clearly also what happens in many people's observations, whether written or oral. Some of the quotes on the next few pages are taken from interviews conducted by my colleague Katrin Sell in the summer of 2007 in Galway City. I am indebted to her for including an additional question on accent in film for my purposes. Additional quotations have been garnered from internet forums which have addressed the notion of accent in films. These quotes have been taken over verbatim from their sources and, thus, sometimes contain quite a number of spelling errors. However, in the interest of faithfulness, I have not amended them in any way.

[448] Incidentally, this phenomenon of including stage Irish expressions in reviews is not only limited to films set in the Republic of Ireland. *The Devil's Own* (Alan J. Pakula, 1997) features Brad Pitt as a Northern Irish terrorist who goes on the run in the United States. Pitt's Irish accent was subjected to fierce criticism, which again very often featured the aforementioned terms associated with Stage Irishness. The following is just one example: "Devils Own.... OMG....Oscar nomination for worst OIrish accent ever. I was getting into it until THAT character appeared. I was waiting for the bearded leprechauns, fiddles, and Guinness to appear from nowhere. His script should have been limited to "Bejasus Begorrah Top o the morning to ya. A shure aren't I a great expert sitting ehre in jail". Ruined what would have been an alright film for me" (Posted by Dave Griffith 13/04/2007).
http://aims.ie.interact_discuss_displaythread.asp?ForumName=Games%20RoomandForumTag=games&ParentI D=71296 (Retrieved: July 1, 2008).

[449] It is interesting to note that whereas the term "Oirish accent" is at least based on a stereotypical sound change and, thus, can legitimately be used when describing accents, the terms "Faith and Begorrah accents" or Top o' the morning accents", which are frequently used in descriptions, actually refer to clichéd expressions and not pronunciation per se.

[450] http://deputy-dog.com/2007/08/21/13-of-the-worst-fake-accents-in-film/ (Retrieved: July 1, 2008).

The result of such comments is that even among those people who have never seen this film, but who read or hear these comments, there is already an expectation, based on stereotypical expressions, that the accent must be terrible. This is again substantiated in some of the Internet comments discussing accents.

> I haven't seen Tom Cruise's effort, but anyone who has seems to rate it among the very worst.
> (John 83[451], September 17, 2007)

What is more, as can be seen below, audiences appear to have picked up on one line of dialogue from the film *Far and Away* and they focus on that as the justification for Cruise's poor accent. However, it is worth asking the question whether the problem is not perhaps with the line itself rather than with the pronunciation.

> Far and Away - when i saw it in the early Nineties in a cinema in Galway when Tom Cruise says **"Aye Shannon you're a corker"** the cinema exploded with laughter - comedy gold, i always end up watching it on Tv just to see that bit, Niall Tobins stage Irish begorrah[452] accent is hilarious as well!!
> (Tim Landers[453], January 16, 2007)

> A movie which manages to belittle the plight of the Irish immigrant, mangle the Irish accent and trivialise Irish history in one fell swoop. When Tom Cruise fixed his slightly creepy gaze on Nicole Kidman and pronounced **"Yer a corker, Shannon"**, the groans from the audience were almost as loud as the sound of Joyce, Beckett and Yeats turning in their graves.
> (Declan McKenna[454], March 14, 2008)

> Ladies and gentlemen, I give you: "Far and Away". Oh. Dear. God. **"Aye Shannon, yer a corker"** - what? I mean, *what*? Tom Cruise and Nicole Kidman, you are found guilty of grievious bodily harm to the Irish accent.
> (Anacreon[455], January 23, 2001)

> Tom Cruises one in Far and Away. **"Jayz Shannon you're a corker"**
> (Pauro 76[456], September 17, 2007)

Ironically, the line which grated so much with Irish audiences was the very one which most struck a chord with the American film critic, Peter Travers, who works for *Rolling Stone*.

> '**You're a corker, Shannon,**' says Joseph in rapt admiration. '**What a corker you are.**' The delicate sweetness of that moment, magnetically played by Cruise and Kidman, represents the movie at in (sic) best.
> (Peter Travers[457], December 8, 2000)

---

[451] http://foot.ie/forums/showthread.php?t=71228 (Retrieved: July 1, 2008).
[452] Note again the use of the term *begorrah* with regard to this film, despite the fact that it does not appear in the movie.
[453] http://aims.ie/interact_discuss_displaythread.asp?ForumName=Games%20Room&ForumTag=games&ParentID=71296 (Retrieved: July 1, 2008)
[454] http://www.belfasttelegraph.co.uk/entertainment/film-tv/news/article3515226.ece (Retrieved: July 1, 2008).
[455] http://www.everything2.org/title/Irish%2520accent (Retrieved: July 1, 2008).
[456] http://foot.ie/forums/showthread.php?t=71228 (Retrieved: July 1, 2008).
[457] http://www.rollingstone.com/reviews/dvd/5948995/review/5948996/far_and_away (Retrieved: July 1, 2008).

This shows once again that, when it comes to expectations of authenticity, Irish and international audiences differ greatly. With regard to the controversial line from *Far and Away*, it would appear, based on my own enquiries and on the reaction of Irish audiences, that the word *corker* is not used in Ireland today[458]. That, of course, does not mean that the term might not have been popular at the time when the film was set, namely, in the late 1880s. Indeed, according to the OED, *corker* is first attested as appearing in 1882, and was a colloquial or dialect term which referred to "a person or thing of surpassing size or excellence, a stunner" (OED s.v. corker 2.b). Assuming that the latter meaning is intended, the description of Shannon as a *corker* is actually quite acceptable. The OED does, however, add that the term is "also used ironically" and this may be where the problem with Cruise's use of the word arises. He delivers the line so sincerely, "in rapt admiration", as Travers described it above, that this would appear to be his undoing.

Based on the evidence above, it is my contention that it was the line itself, coupled with the sincerity of its delivery, and not necessarily Cruise's actual accent which reduced audiences to groans and laughter. In this respect, audiences should remember Alan Lovell's comment that "there's a great need for a new framework for the discussion of acting that would show a greater awareness of the existence of scripts. How can you properly assess actors' performances without knowing what they had to work with?" (2005: 88). If one does take the time to look at the material Cruise had to work with, one finds that it is very much inspired by the Stage Irish tradition, with screenwriter Bob Dolman freely admitting in an interview that "if anything resembles the tone of this movie, it's Boucicault's work[459]" which he had drawn from (Dwyer 1991).

12.2 Non-linguistic factors

While critics and audiences alike have drawn attention to the linguistic shortcomings of many performances in Irish films, there is also evidence to suggest that it may not necessarily be the accents or the (perceived) use of Stage Irish expressions which detract from the perceived authenticity of the performance, but rather some other non-linguistic factors. For example, the *Historical Dictionary of Irish Cinema* (2007) features the following criticism of *Circle of Friends*, and, particularly, of American actor Chris O'Donnell:

> Inevitably, however, given the absence of Irish actors in lead roles, audiences were subjected to cringe-worthy attempts at local accents, some so bad as to obscure the dialogue. Chief among the culprits was Chris O'Donnell, clearly chosen to give the film international appeal, but always looking more like an American high school jock than what in the 1950s would have been a rare creature in Ireland – a university student.
> (Flynn and Brereton 2007: 58-9)

At first glance, it appears to be a run-of-the-mill criticism of poor accents in Irish film; mentioning, as it does, the "cringe-worthy attempt at local accents". However, if one looks at the choice of words a little more closely, there is another issue at play here. While Chris

---

[458] While Wright cites the term as being used in Ireland (as well as in Northumberland, the West Midlands, Lancashire, Yorkshire, Cheshire, Lincolnshire, East Anglia, and Warwickshire), it should be remembered that his dictionary was actually compiled between 1898 and 1905 when the term did indeed enjoy popularity (EDD s.v. corker, sb.¹.).

[459] Dion Boucicault (1820-1890) was famed for his plays, including what has been called "that most notorious of Stage Irish melodramas" - *The Colleen Bawn* (Kiberd 2005: 32).

O'Donnell is singled out as the chief culprit, there is a strong suggestion that this could have more to do with his appearance than with his accent. After all, the complaint is not that he *sounds* more like an American high school jock, but rather that he *looks* like one.

Closer scrutiny of reviews of other films reveals that writers' judgements may similarly be swayed by an actor's appearance rather than by his accent per se. For example, based on the following review, the credibility of Tom Cruise's performance in *Far and Away* would appear to have less to do with accent and more to do with dentistry.

> Any pretensions to plausibility are, however, fatally undermined by the presence of **Tom Cruise's perfect teeth.**
>
> (*O'Mahony, in: Film Ireland* (121), March/April 2008: 13)

It is significant therefore that, consciously or not, it is often non-linguistic elements which these reviewers make reference to when commenting on the elements which detract from the perceived authenticity of the actors' performances.

12.3 Accent hallucination

Another phenomenon which is certainly worth bearing in mind when evaluating accented performances in film is that of "accent hallucination". Accent hallucination occurs when "prejudice on the part of the hearer lead[s] to the perception of stigmatised forms (even where in reality these do not exist)" (Fought, 2006: 187-9). In her book, *Language and Ethnicity*, Fought offers a number of examples, including experiments by Williams (1983) and Rubin (1992), to show just how endemic accent hallucination can be. In Williams' study, a group of European-American student teachers viewed videotapes of three children (1 European-American, 1 African-American and 1 Mexican-American) with the task of rating the level of English they heard. Unbeknownst to the respondents, the voice they were hearing was always that of the same standard English-speaking child. Nonetheless, the speech of the African-American and Mexican-American children was consistently regarded as significantly more "non-standard" than that of the European-American. The same applied to Rubin's study which had students listen to a lecture while looking at a photograph which they were informed was of the speaker. Half of the group were shown a picture of a European-American, while the other half were given a picture of an Asian woman. As in Williams' experiment, the speaker was actually the same for all visual stimuli and again was a native speaker of English with no marked regional accent. However, as before, the students who were shown the picture of the Asian woman were more likely to rate her as having an Asian accent. Bearing such results in mind, it is worth considering the question of whether audiences who know that an actor is not Irish are perhaps also susceptible to accent hallucinations, thus projecting their preconceived notions[460] onto the actor's perhaps impeccable performance[461].

---

[460] This again echoes the notion of expectation playing a determining role in people's perception, as was already cited from Bailey (1991) in Chapter 5.

[461] Fought does, however, cite a study by Atagi (2003) which revealed that race may play more of a role in accent hallucination than foreign origin. "Overall, then, it seems that the more 'ethnically different' a speaker is perceived to be by the hearer, the more likely the hearer is to perceive an accent where none is present" (Fought, 2006: 189).

13 Conclusions

Given the amount of discussion in the media and among the general population regarding the poor quality of accents and dialects in film, this study set about measuring the authenticity of the representations of one such variety, namely Irish English. This proved to be quite a challenge, as, in addition to the inherent philosophical problem relating to the term authenticity itself, as described in Chapter 3, there was also a practical issue which complicated the process: in order to have been able to measure the accuracy of the dialect in the films, an appropriate yard stick would have been necessary. Unfortunately, no such thing exists, as "there is no 'ideal speaker' […] to whom other speakers can be said to measure up or not measure up" (Cohen Minnick 2004: 67). Given the absence of an ideal speaker, I turned my attention to ideal listeners instead, namely the 1017 Irish respondents who had judged the acceptability level of 57 features of Irish English for Hickey's *A Survey of Irish English Usage* (2004a). The logic behind this decision was that features which had been deemed by respondents to be most acceptable would also be the ones which could be regarded as most authentically Irish[462]. What is more, the features which were deemed most acceptable in the survey would also be the ones which would have been most likely to occur in the films[463].

Although Hickey's survey is not without its problems – it occasionally judges the acceptability of standard rather than non-standard features[464] –, it proved to be the best solution for my purposes, even allowing Ulster respondents to be filtered out, thus giving me a cohort of 815 judges from the three provinces in which the films are set.

On the whole, there was quite a high degree of correspondence between Hickey's findings and those of the film corpus, particularly at either end of the scale, with those features which had a high degree of acceptability in the survey usually also featuring strongly in the film corpus, and those which were regarded as problematic by Hickey's respondents also proving to be rare in the films. Although the actual percentage rates themselves differ greatly between the studies[465], the relative frequency of the features is generally comparable. For example, imperatives with the progressive form were among the most popular features in both the film corpus and in Hickey's survey, even if the 44% frequency rate for the feature in the film corpus (compared to the 90% rate in the *Survey*) belies this fact.

Seeing as the results for the individual features have already been summarised in Chapter 6, they will not be addressed again here. However, it should be clear from the findings just how useful a literary dialect corpus can be in the analysis of dialect features, in that they enable one to test the received wisdom regarding particular features and to investigate their occurrence with regard to period, setting and, perhaps most importantly, context.

---

[462] Problems with referring to degrees of authenticity have already been discussed in Chapter 3. However, I reserve the right to use the superlative in this context to reflect my thinking at the outset of this study.
[463] Admittedly, Hickey's survey reflects contemporary attitudes towards language, whereas a number of the films are set in the past. Nonetheless, I felt that since the majority of films had been produced and set post 1990, the comparison would be justified.
[464] For more on the methodological problems encountered in Hickey's survey, see page 115.
[465] Such disparity was to be expected as, after all, the results of the survey are not attestations but rather represent speakers' reactions to non-standard features (cf. Hickey 2007: 164).

While this study originally placed a great deal of emphasis on the behaviour of the features depending on the film's setting and period, it turned out in many cases that it was the context in which these features occur, and not where and when the films were made or set, which proved most interesting. Certain features like *amn't* appeared only in interrogatives, others such as *the 'be' perfect* occurred almost exclusively with certain verbs. Similarly, the lack of plural marking with quantity nouns applied almost exclusively to the word *pound*, while the unbound reflexives *himself/herself* were shown to have meanings far beyond the traditional 'master/mistress of the house' reading. With regard to the period and setting of the films, on the other hand, very few discernable patterns regarding feature occurrence were evident. Those patterns which were apparent showed that the last two decades have seen an increase in the percentage of possible local lexical and discourse features, meaning that the percentage of possible grammar features is almost always in the minority, even if the actual number of grammar features in the films has not necessarily decreased. What is more, when one looks at the ten most frequent grammar, discourse and lexical features, it is evident that many of the most frequent grammar features are not necessarily restricted to Irish English, but can be found in a number of English dialects worldwide. This is not the case for the majority of the discourse and lexical features examined, and, thus, screenwriters would be advised to focus predominantly on lexical and discourse items to make their scripts sound more exclusively Irish.

At the outset of this study, I decided to divide the films into Irish and Irish-related films in order to examine whether there was a difference in the frequency or type of features present in the different categories. The assumption that foreign films would have had significantly fewer Irish English features than their Irish counterparts proved unfounded, with the difference between their average rates being very marginal (1.07%) (see page 158). As far as the types of features in the two categories were concerned, there were also very few noticeable differences, with the exception that a couple of features, such as *'subordinating till'* and the use of *let* as an imperative, were restricted to Irish productions.

Suspicions that Irish-related productions would feature numerous stereotypical expressions, such as *Top o' the mornin'*, *faith* and *begorrah*, were also unfounded, although, admittedly, when these items did appear, it was always in Irish-related productions. However, with only one appearance each in the entire corpus, it would be very unfair to describe this as some sort of trend.

When it came to examining the accuracy of accents in the films, I first outlined the features of Irish English accents which one would expect to hear and illustrated them with examples. Then, using contrastive analysis, I examined where British and American actors might have encountered difficulty and offered examples of their erroneous pronunciations. As expected, these errors were predominantly with regard to vowels, particularly the BATH and TRAP lexical sets, and the use of diphthongs where Irish English traditionally has monophthongs. Rhoticity also proved to be a problem for a number of British actors, both with regard to its omission and with regard to the addition of intrusive /r/. However, even though I found some excellent examples of serious segmental errors, there were fewer obvious segmental errors in the films than originally expected. This could be testament to the good work of dialect coaches, who focus, first and foremost, on segmentals.

Nonetheless, despite the good work of dialect coaches, and even in the absence of obvious segmental errors, it was still possible to detect non-Irish accents on a number of occasions. The reason for this might have been, as discovered in Chapter 7, that voice setting is likely to be the main culprit in betraying accents. However, given the lack of research on this phenomenon in an Irish context, it would be useful to conduct further study into Irish voice setting(s) to find out what exactly it is that distinguishes it/them from those found in other varieties of English[466]. The result of such research would be that dialect coaches and actors would have something infinitely more helpful to work with than simply vague statements about a phenomenon which is believed to work on a subconscious level. On a related issue, given Niedzielski and Preston's (2003: 116) observation that people do not even have to produce segmentals correctly to be successful imitators, it would be interesting to also put this theory to the test. Rather than looking at failed attempts at accents, one could look instead at ones which people agree were a success, such as those by Cate Blanchett in *Veronica Guerin* and James McAvoy in *Inside I'm Dancing*, and examine them to see whether the segmentals are indeed correct or whether perhaps voice setting may have led to the performance being deemed a success. In this regard, it would also be interesting to contrast McAvoy's own voice setting in the bonus material on the DVD with that of his character Rory in the movie. His voice in the movie is much higher pitched than in real life, although not in the exaggerated fashion of so many Stage Irish brogues.

Given the limited scope of this study, a more in-depth analysis of individual accents in individual films was, unfortunately, not possible. However, such a study is already the focus of future research, with plans currently being made for collaborations with Una Cunningham and Peter Sundkvist at Dalarna University, Falun, Sweden, who have already conducted an in-depth study into Brad Pitt's Belfast accent in the movie *The Devil's Own*.

In a similar vein, a logical extension of this study would be to conduct a comparable quantitative and qualitative analysis of films set in Ulster, examining them first for particular dialect features and then exploring the accuracy of the accents. By doing so, one would gain a complete picture of the linguistic situation on the island of Ireland, or at least of how it is represented in the movies. Once again, one could compare and contrast the findings for the films with the acceptability ratings from Hickey's *A Survey of Irish English Usage*.

This study is the first of its kind to combine fields as varied as dialectology, literary dialect, second language acquisition and film studies, and, like so many pioneering studies, it has inevitably raised more questions than it has answered, thus, opening up new avenues for further interdisciplinary research. It has questioned the notions of authenticity and Irishness, explored the factors which influence accent perception and production, and highlighted how misinformation and stereotypes regarding Irish accents are perpetuated via dialect coach manuals and the media. In addition, it has offered hundreds of new examples of Irish English features in use, thus greatly expanding the existing pool of examples available for discussion and, who knows, possibly serving as a source of input for future film production.

---

[466] Hickey has come closest to describing this voice setting, stating that "there is a degree of indistinctiveness about southern Irish English, probably due to the amount of elision and assimilation found in the variety. In addition, the lenition of alveolar stops to fricative adds to the impression of slurred speech which is often conveyed" (2007: 11).

14 Bibliography

Abercrombie, David. (1956). "Teaching Pronunciation". In: Adam Brown, ed. (1991). *Teaching English Pronunciation: A Book of Readings*. London: Routledge. 87-95.

Abercrombie, David. (1967). *Elements of General Phonetics*. Edinburgh: University Press.

Acton, William. (1984). "Changing Fossilized Pronunciation". In: Adam Brown, ed. (1991). *Teaching English Pronunciation: A Book of Readings*. London: Routledge. 120-35.

Ahern, Maurice. (1930). "Hollywood Horizons". *Commonweal* 21 May 1930, reprinted in: Gerald Mast, ed. (1982). *The Movies in our Midst. Documents in the Cultural History of Film in America.* Chicago and London: The University of Chicago Press. 308-13.

Ahlqvist, Anders and Vera Capkova. (1997). *Dán Do Oide. Essays in Memory of Conn R. Ó Cléirigh*. Dublin: Institiúid Teangeolaíochta Éireann.

Amador Moreno, Carolina P. (2005). "Discourse Markers in Irish English: An Example from Literature". In: Anne Barron and Klaus P. Schneider, eds. (2005). *The Pragmatics of Irish English*. Berlin/New York: Mouton de Gruyter. 73-100.

Amador Moreno, Carolina P. (2006). *An Analysis of Hiberno-English in the Early Novels of Patrick MacGill. Bilingualism and Language Shift from Irish to English in County Donegal*. Lewiston, NY: The Edwin Mellen Press.

Amador Moreno, Carolina P. (2007). "How the Irish Speak English: A Conversation with T.P. Dolan". *Estudios Irlandeses* 2: 214-17.

Amor, Stuart. (2002). *Authenticity and Authentication in Language Learning. Distinctions, Orientations, Implications*. Frankfurt am Main: Peter Lang.

Anderwald, Lieselotte. (2004). "English in the Southeast of England: Morphology and Syntax". In: Bernd Kortmann, Kate Burridge, Rajend Mesthrie, Edgar W. Schneider and Clive Upton, eds. (2004b). *A Handbook of Varieties of English. Volume 2: Morphology and Syntax*. Berlin: Mouton de Gruyter. 175-95.

Asher, James J. and Ramiro Garcia. (1969/82). "The Optimal Age to Learn a Foreign Language". In: Stephen D. Krashen, Robin C. Scarcella, and Michael H. Long, eds. (1982). *Child-Adult Differences in Second Language Acquisition*. Rowley/London/Tokyo: Newbury House Publishers, Inc. 3-12.

Asher, James J. (1977). *Learning Another Language through Actions: The Complete Teachers' Guidebook*. Los Gatos, CA: Sky Oaks Productions.

Ashmore, Richard D. and Frances K. Del Boca. (1981). "Conceptual Approaches to Stereotypes and Stereotyping". In: David L. Hamilton, ed. (1981). *Cognitive Processes in Stereotyping and Intergroup Behavior*. Hillsdale, NJ: Lawrence Erlbaum Associates, Publishers. 1-35.

Asián, Anna and James McCullough. (1998). "Hiberno-English and the Teaching of Modern and Contemporary Irish Literature in an EFL Context". *Links and Letters* 5: 37-60.

Atagi, Eriko. (2003). "Are You a Native Speaker? The Role of Ethnic Background in the Hallucination of Foreign Accents on Native Speakers." Paper delivered at NWAVE 32, Philadelphia, PA.

Bailey, Guy, Natalie Maynor and Patricia Cukor Avila, eds. (1991). *The Emergence of Black English. Text and Commentary*. Amsterdam/Philadelphia: John Benjamins.

Bailey, Richard W. and Manfred Görlach, eds. (1982). *English as a World Language*. Cambridge.

Baker, Mona and Braňo Hochel. (1998). "Dubbing". In: Mona Baker, ed. (1998). *Routledge Encyclopedia of Translation Studies*. London and New York: Routledge. 74-6.

Baker, Mona, ed. (1998). *Routledge Encyclopaedia of Translation Studies*. London and New York: Routledge.

Ball, Martin. J. and James Fife, eds. (1993). *The Celtic Languages*. London: Routledge.

Bannert, Robert. (1995). "Intelligibility and Acceptability in Foreign Accented Swedish: the Effects of Rhythmical and Tonal Features". *Reports from the Department of Phonetics, Umeå University* 3: 7-29.

Bardovi-Harlig, Kathleen and Beverly Hartford, eds. (1997). *Beyond Methods. Components of Second Language Teacher Education*. New York: McGraw Hill.

Barron, Anne and Klaus P. Schneider, eds. (2005). *The Pragmatics of Irish English*. Berlin/New York: Mouton de Gruyter.

Barry, Kevin. (2001). *Ireland into Film: The Dead*. Cork: Cork University Press.

Barry, Michael. (1982). "The English Language in Ireland". In: Richard W. Bailey and Manfred Görlach, eds. *English as a World Language*. Cambridge: 84-133.

Bartley, James O. (1942). "The Development of a Stock Character: The Stage Irishman to 1800". *The Modern Language Review* 37 (4): 438-47.

Bartley, James O. (1954). *Teague, Shenkin and Sawney. Being an Historical Study of the Earliest Irish, Welsh and Scottish Characters in English Plays*. Cork: Cork University Press.

Bartley, James O. and D. L. Sims. (1949). "Pre-Nineteenth Century Stage Irish and Welsh Pronunciation". In: *Proceedings of the American Philosophical Society* 93 (5): 439-447.

Barton, Ruth. (2004). *Irish National Cinema*. London and New York: Routledge.

Barton, Ruth. (2006). *Acting Irish in Hollywood – From Fitzgerald to Farrell*. Dublin and Portland, OR: Irish Academic Press.

Barton, Ruth and Harvey O'Brien, eds. (2004). *Keeping it Real: Irish Film and Television*. London and New York: Wallflower.

Baugh, Albert C. and Thomas Cable. (1993). *A History of the English Language* (4th ed.). London: Routledge.

Baugh, John. (1996). "Perceptions within a Variable Paradigm: Black and White Racial Detection and Identification Based on Speech". In: Edgar W. Schneider, ed. (1996). *Focus on the USA*. Amsterdam/Philadelphia: John Benjamins. 169-82.

Bayley, Robert and Dennis R. Preston, eds. (1996). *Second Language Acquisition and Linguistic Variation*. Amsterdam/Philadelphia: John Benjamins.

Bazin, André. (1967). *What is Cinema? Volume I*. Berkeley and Los Angeles: University of California Press.

Bazin, André. (1971). *What is Cinema? Volume II*. Berkeley and Los Angeles: University of California Press.

Beal, Joan. (2004). "English Dialects in the North of England: Morphology and Syntax". In: Bernd Kortmann, Kate Burridge, Rajend Mesthrie, Edgar W. Schneider and Clive Upton, eds. (2004b). *A Handbook of Varieties of English. Volume 2: Morphology and Syntax*. Berlin: Mouton de Gruyter. 114-41.

Beile, Werner. (1986). "Authentizität als fremdsprachendidaktischer Begriff. Zum Problemfeld von Texten gesprochener Sprache". In: Rolf Ehnert and Hans-Eberhard Piepho, eds. (1986). *Fremdsprachen lernen mit Medien*. München: Max Hueber Verlag. 96-7.

Bendix, Regina. (1997). *In Search of Authenticity*. Madison: The University of Wisconsin Press.

Berg, Jan, Hans-Otto Hügel and Hajo Kürzenberger, eds. (1997). *Authentizität als Darstellung*. Hildesheim: Hildesheim University.

Bertz, Siegfried. (1975) Der Dubliner Stadtdialekt. Eine synchronische Beschreibung der Struktur und Variabilität des heutigen Dubliner Englischen. I. Phonologie. Doctoral Dissertation. University of Freiburg i. Br.

Biggar, Francis. J. (1897). *Our Ulster Accent and Ulster Provincialisms*. Belfast: Religious Tract and Book Depot.

Blackburn, Ruth M. (1971). "Dialects in Eugene O'Neill's Plays". In: Juanita V. Williamson and Virginia M. Burke, eds. (1971). *A Various Language. Perspectives on American Dialects*. New York: Holt, Rinehart and Winston, Inc. 230-41.

Blake, Norman. (1981). *Non-Standard Language in English Literature*. London: André Deutsch.

Blickenstaff, Channing B. (1963). "Musical Talents and Foreign Language Learning Ability". *The Modern Language Journal* 47 (8): 359-63.

Bliss, Alan. (1971). "The Language of Synge". In: Maurice Harmon, ed. (1972). *J.M. Synge Centenary Papers 1971*. Dublin: The Dolmen Press. 35-62.

Bliss, Alan. (1977). "The Emergence of Modern English Dialects in Ireland". In: Diarmaid Ó Muirithe, ed. (1977). *The English Language in Ireland*. Cork: Mercier. 7-19.

Bliss, Alan. (1979). *Spoken English in Ireland 1600-1740*. Dublin: The Dolmen Press.

Bliss, Alan. (1984). "English in the South of Ireland". In: Peter Trudgill, ed. (1984). *Language in the British Isles*. Cambridge: Cambridge University Press. 135-51.

Blumenfeld, Robert. (2000). *Accents. A Manual for Actors* (3rd ed.). New York: Limelight Editions.

Blunt, Jerry. (1967). *Stage Dialects*. New York: Harper & Row, Publishers.

Boehm, Mike. (2000). "In the Cause of Freer Speech". *Los Angeles Times* (Sunday "Calendar"), 3 December.

Boorman, John. (1998). *The General (Screenplay)*. London: Faber and Faber.

Bradac, James J., Aaron Castelan Cargile and Jennifer S. Hallett. (2001). "Language Attitudes: Retrospect, Conspect, and Prospect". In: W. Peter Robinson and Howard

Giles, eds. (2001). *The New Handbook of Language and Social Psychology*. Chichester: John Wiley & Sons. 137-55.

Brennan, Eileen and John Brennan. (1981a). "Accent Scaling and Language Attitudes: Reactions to Mexican American speech". *Language and Speech* 24: 207-21.

Brennan, Eileen and John Brennan. (1981b). "Measurements of Accent and Attitude toward Mexican American speech". *Journal of Psycholinguistic Research* 10: 487-501.

Bright, William, ed. (1966) *Sociolinguistics. Proceedings of the UCLA Sociolinguistics Conference, 1964*. The Hague. Mouton and Co.

Brook, George L. (1965). "Dialect and Literature". In: George L. Brook. (1965). *English Dialects*. London. Andre Deutsch. 184-209.

Brook, George L. (1965). *English Dialects*. London. Andre Deutsch.

Brown, Adam, ed. (1991). *Teaching English Pronunciation: A Book of Readings*. London: Routledge.

Brown, Adam. (1992). "Twenty Questions". In: Adam Brown, ed. (1992). *Approaches to Pronunciation Teaching. Modern English Publications in Association with The British Council*. London: Macmillan Publishers Ltd. 1-17.

Brown, Adam, ed. (1992). *Approaches to Pronunciation Teaching. Modern English Publications in Association with The British Council*. London: Macmillan Publishers Ltd.

Burchfield, Robert, ed. (1994). *The Cambridge History of the English Language. Volume V. English in Britain and Overseas: Origins and Development*. Cambridge: Cambridge University Press.

Byrne, J.G. (2000). "Letter to the Editor". *The Irish Times*, 20 January.

Byrne, Terry. (1997). *Power in the Eye. An Introduction to Contemporary Irish Film*. Lanham, MD and London: The Scarecrow Press, Inc.

Carroll, John B. (1962). "The Prediction of Success in Intensive Foreign Language Teaching". In: Robert Glaser, ed. (1962). *Training, Research, and Education*. Pittsburgh: University of Pittsburgh Press. 87-136.

Carroll, John B. (1981). "Twenty-five Years of Research on Foreign Language Aptitude". In: Karl C. Diller, ed. (1981). *Individual Differences and Universals in Language Learning Aptitude*. Rowley, MA: Newbury House. 83-118.

Caulfield, Max. (1973). *The Irish Mystique*. Englewood Cliffs, NJ: Prentice-Hall.

Celce-Murcia, Marianne, Donna M. Brinton and Janet M. Goodwin. (2000). *Teaching Pronunciation. A Reference for Teachers of English to Speakers of Other Languages*. Cambridge: Cambridge University Press.

Chambers, Jack K. (2001). "Vernacular Universals". In: Josep M. Fontana, Louise McNally, M. Teresa Turrell and Enric Vallduvi, eds. (2001). *ICLaVE 1: Proceedings of the First International Conference on Language Variation in Europe*. Barcelona: Universitat Pompeu Fabra. 52-60.

Chambers, Jack K. (1995). *Sociolinguistic Theory. Linguistic Variation and its Social Significance*. Oxford: Blackwell.

Chambers, Jack K. and Peter Trudgill. (1998). *Dialectology* (2nd ed.). Cambridge: Cambridge University Press.

Champagne-Muzar, Cécile, Eta I. Schneidermann and Johanne S. Bourdages. (1993). "Second Language Accent: The Role of the Pedagogical Environment". *IRAL: International Review of Applied Linguistics in Language Teaching* 31: 143-60.

Cheng, Vincent J. (2004). *Inauthentic. The Anxiety over Culture and Identity.* New Brunswick, NJ: Rutgers University Press.

Cheshire, Jenny. (1981). "Variation in the Use of Ain't in an Urban British English Dialect". In: Peter Trudgill and Jack K. Chambers, eds. (1991). *Dialects of English. Studies in Grammatical Variation.* London and New York: Longman. 54-73.

Cheshire, Jenny, Viv Edwards and Pamela Whittle. (1989). "Urban British Dialect Grammar". *English World Wide* 10: 185-225.

Cheshire, Jenny, ed. (1991). *English Around the World: Sociolinguistic Perspectives.* Cambridge: Cambridge University Press.

Cleary, Joe and Claire Connolly, eds. (2005). *The Cambridge Companion to Modern Irish Culture.* Cambridge: Cambridge University Press.

Cohen, Antoine and Sieb G. Notteboom, eds. (1975). *Structure and Process in Speech Perception.* Berlin: Springer-Verlag.

Cohen Minnick, Lisa. (2004). *Dialect and Dichotomy. Literary Representations of African American Speech.* Tuscaloosa: The University of Alabama Press.

Collins, Alma. (1997). "Diphthongisation of (o) in Claddagh Hiberno-English". In: Jeffrey Kallen, ed. (1997). *Focus on Ireland.* Amsterdam: John Benjamins. 153-70.

Collins, Beverley and Inger M. Mees. (2003). *Practical Phonetics and Phonology: A Resource Book for Students.* London: Routledge.

Connaughton, Shane and Jim Sheridan. (1989). *My Left Foot (Screenplay).* London: Faber and Faber.

Corner, John. (1996). *The Art of Record: A Critical Introduction to Documentary.* Manchester: Manchester University Press.

Corrigan, Karen. (1997). "Contact Vernacular Grammar". In: Anders Ahlqvist and Vera Capkova, eds. (1997). *Dán Do Oide. Essays in Memory of Conn R. Ó Cléirigh.* Dublin: Institiúid Teangeolaíochta Éireann. 75-93.

Coupland, Nikolas, Angie Williams and Peter Garrett. (1999). "'Welshness' and 'Englishness' as Attitudinal Dimensions of English Language Varieties in Wales". In: Dennis R. Preston, ed. (1999). *Handbook of Perceptual Dialectology (Volume 1).* Amsterdam/Philadelphia: John Benjamins. 333-43.

Cronin, Michael and Cormac Ó Cuilleanáin, eds. (2003). *The Languages of Ireland.* Dublin: Four Courts Press.

Cronin, Michael. (2006). *Ireland Into Film: The Barrytown Trilogy.* Cork: Cork University Press.

Crystal, David. (2005). *Pronouncing Shakespeare: The Globe Experiment.* Cambridge: Cambridge University Press.

Cunningham, Una. (forthcoming). "Quality, Quantity and Intelligibility of Vowels in Vietnamese-accented English". Paper delivered at *Accents 2008*. (University of Lodz, 12-14 December 2008).

Darwin, Chris. (1975). "On the Dynamic Use of Prosody in Speech Perception". In: Antonie Cohen and Sieb G. Notteboom, eds. (1975). *Structure and Process in Speech Perception*. Berlin: Springer-Verlag. 178-194.

Day, Richard R. (1982). "Children's Attitude toward Language". In: Ellen Bouchard Ryan and Howard Giles, eds. (1982). *Attitudes towards Language Variation*. London: Edward Arnold. 116-31.

De Bot, Kees, and Kate Mailfert. (1982). "The Teaching of Intonation: Fundamental Research and Classroom Applications". *TESOL Quarterly* 16: 71-77.

Delahunty, Gerald. (1977). "Dialect and Local Accents". In: Diarmaid Ó Muirithe, ed. (1977). *The English Language in Ireland*. Cork: Mercier. 127-49.

Diller, Karl C., ed. (1981). *Individual Differences and Universals in Language Learning Aptitude*. Rowley, MA: Newbury House.

Doherty, Michael. (2000). "General Mayhem". *RTE Guide*, 14 January.

Dolan, Terence P., ed. (1990). *The English of the Irish*. Special Issue of *Irish University Review* 20 (1).

Dolan, Terence P. (2003). "Translating Irelands: the English Language in the Irish Context". In: Michael Cronin and Cormac Ó Cuilleanáin, eds. (2003). *The Languages of Ireland*. Dublin: Four Courts Press. 78-93.

Dolan, Terence P., ed. (2006). *A Dictionary of Hiberno-English*. (2nd ed.). Dublin: Gill and Macmillan.

Dooling, D. James. (1974). "Rhythm and Syntax in Sentence Perception". *Journal of Verbal Learning and Verbal Behaviour* 13 (3): 255-64.

Dorsey, Michael. (2000). "Casting Couch". *Volta Movie Magazine* 2 (2): 31.

Doyle, Diarmuid. (2000). "Method to his Madness". *The Sunday Tribune*. 9 January.

Doyle, Roddy. (1992). *The Barrytown Trilogy*. New York: Penguin.

Doyle, Roddy. (2007). "Guess Who's Coming for the Dinner". In: Roddy Doyle. (2007). *The Deportees and Other Stories*. New York: Viking. 1-26.

Doyle, Roddy. (2007). *The Deportees and Other Stories*. New York: Viking.

Drury, Michael. (2007). "Mind your Oul' Hiberno-English". *The Irish Times*. 10 April.

Dublin Evening Mail. (1930). 12 August.

Duggan, George. C. (1937/1969). *The Stage Irishman: A History of the Irish Play and Stage Characters from the Earliest Times*. New York and London: Benjamin Blom.

Dwyer, Michael. (1991). "Romantic Comedy Comes to Ireland". *The Irish Times*, 27 September.

Dwyer, Michael. (1998). "Wake up and Smell the Blarney". *The Irish Times (Weekend)*, 5 December.

Eagleton, Terry. (2006). *The Truth about the Irish*. Dublin: New Island Books.

Eco, Umberto. (1975). "Travels in Hyperreality". In: Umberto Eco (1986). *Faith in Fakes. Essays*. London: Secker and Warburg. 3-58.

Eco, Umberto. (1986). *Faith in Fakes. Essays*. London: Secker and Warburg.

Edensor, Kizzi. (2009). "Dialect in Films: Examples of South Yorkshire Grammatical and Lexical Features From Ken Loach Films". In: *Dialectologia 3* (2009). 1-21.

Edwards, John. (1977). "Students' Reactions to Irish Regional Accents". *Language and Speech* 20 (1): 280-86.

Edwards, John. (1982). "Language Attitudes and their Implications among English Speakers". In: Ellen Bouchard Ryan and Howard Giles, eds. (1982). *Attitudes towards Language Variation*. London: Edward Arnold. 20-33.

Edwards, John. (1984). "Irish and English in Ireland". In: Peter Trudgill, ed. (1984). *Language in the British Isles*. Cambridge: Cambridge University Press. 480-98.

Edwards, John and Maryanne Jacobsen. (1987). "Standard and Regional Standard Speech: Distinctions and Similarities". *Language in Society* 16: 369-80.

Ehnert, Rolf and Hans-Eberhard Piepho, eds. (1986). *Fremdsprachen lernen mit Medien*. München: Max Hueber Verlag.

Eisikovits, Edina. (1991). "Variation in the Lexical Verb in Inner-Sydney English". In: Peter Trudgill and Jack K. Chambers, eds. (1991). *Dialects of English. Studies in Grammatical Variation*. London and New York: Longman. 120-42.

Ellis, Rod. (1997). *Second Language Acquisition*. Oxford: Oxford University Press.

Erdmann, Peter. (1979). *Inversion im heutigen Englisch*. Heidelberg: Winter.

Esling, John. H. and Rita F. Wong. (1983). "Voice Quality Settings and the Teaching of Pronunciation". *TESOL Quarterly* 17 (1): 89-95.

Esling, John. H. (1987). "Methodology for Voice Setting Awareness in Language Classes". *Revue de Phonétique Appliqué* 85: 449-73.

Fasold, Ralph, ed. (1983). *Variation in the Form and Use of Language: A Sociolinguistics Reader*. Georgetown: Georgetown University Press.

Feldman, Victor. (2001). "English on the Air". *The Irish Times*, 16 November.

Ferguson, Charles A., Lise Menn and Carol Stoel-Gammon, eds. (1992). *Phonological Development: Models, Research, Implications*. Timonium, MD. York Press.

Filppula, Markku. (1986). *Some Aspects of Hiberno-English in a Functional Sentence Perspective*. Joensuu: University of Joensuu Publications in the Humanities.

Filppula, Markku. (1991). "Urban and Rural Varieties of Hiberno-English". In: Jenny Cheshire, ed. (1991). *English around the World: Sociolinguistic Perspectives*. Cambridge: Cambridge University Press. 51- 60.

Filppula, Markku. (1999). *The Grammar of Irish English. Language in Hibernian style*. London: Routledge.

Filppula, Markku, Juhani Klemola, Marjatta Palander and Esa Penttilä, eds. (2005). *Dialects Across Borders. Selected Papers From The 11th International Conference On Methods In Dialectology (Methods XI), Joensuu, August 2002*. Amsterdam/Philadelphia: John Benjamins.

Fischer-Lichte, Erika, Christian Horn, Isabel Pflug and Matthias Warstat, eds. (2007). *Inszenierung von Authentizität* (2nd ed.). Tübingen: A. Francke Verlag Tübingen und Basel.

Flege, James Emil. (1981). "The Phonological Basis of Foreign Accent: A Hypothesis". *TESOL Quarterly* 15 (4): 443-55.

Flege, James Emil. (1984). "The Detection of French Accent by American Listeners". *Journal of the Acoustical Society of America (JASA)* 76 (3): 692-707.

Flege, James Emil. (1988). "Factors Affecting Degree of Perceived Foreign Accent in English Sentences". *Journal of the Acoustical Society of America (JASA)* 84 (1): 70-79.

Flege, James Emil and James M. Hillenbrand. (1987). "Differential Use of Closure Voicing and Release Burst as Cue to Stop Voicing by Native Speakers of French and English". *Journal of Phonetics* 15. 203-08.

Flege, James Emil. (1992a). "The Intelligibility of English Vowels Spoken by British and Dutch Talkers". In: Raymond D. Kent, ed. (1992). *Intelligibility in Speech Disorders: Theory, Measurement, and Management. Volume 1*. Philadelphia: John Benjamins. 157-232.

Flege, James Emil. (1992b). "Speech Learning in a Second Language". In: Charles A. Ferguson, Lise Menn and Carol Stoel-Gammon, eds. (1992) *Phonological Development: Models, Research, Implications*. Timonium, MD: York Press. 565-604.

Flege, James Emil. (1995). "Second Language Speech Learning: Theory, Findings and Problems". In: Winfred Strange, ed. (1995). *Speech Perception and Linguistic Experience: Theoretical and Methodological Issues*. Timonium, MD: York Press. 233-77.

Flege, James Emil, Murray J. Munro and Ian R.A. MacKay. (1996). "Factors Affecting the Production of Word-Initial Consonants in a Second Language". In: Robert Bayley and Dennis R. Preston, eds. (1996). *Second Language Acquisition and Linguistic Variation*. Amsterdam/Philadelphia: John Benjamins. 47-73.

Flynn Roderick and Patrick Brereton, eds. (2007). *Historical Dictionary of Irish Cinema*. Lanham, MD: The Scarecrow Press.

Foley, Cian. (2008). *For Focal Sake. A 32 County Guide to Irish Slang*. Waterford: UpTheDeise Enterprises.

Fontana, Josep M., Louise McNally, M. Teresa Turrell and Enric Vallduvi, eds. (2001). *ICLaVE 1: Proceedings of the First International Conference on Language Variation in Europe*. Barcelona: Universitat Pompeu Fabra.

Foster, Roy, ed. (1989). *The Oxford Illustrated History of Ireland*. Oxford: Oxford University Press.

Foster, Roy. (1989). "Ascendancy and Union". In: Roy Foster, ed. (1989). *The Oxford Illustrated History of Ireland*. Oxford: Oxford University Press. 161-212.

Fought, Carmen. (2006). *Language and Ethnicity*. Cambridge: Cambridge University Press.

Fryd, Mark. (1992). "Some Remarks on 'after –ing' in Hiberno-English". *L'Irlande et ses Langues. Actes du Colloque 1992 de la Société Française d'Études Irlandaises.* 53-61.

Gardner, Howard. (1984). *Frames of Mind. The Theory of Multiple Intelligences.* London: Heinemann.

Gardner, Robert C. (1985). *Social Psychology and Second Language Learning: The Role of Attitudes and Motivation.* London: Edward Arnold.

Gardner, Robert C. and Wallace E. Lambert (1972). *Attitudes and Motivation in Second-Language Learning.* Rowley, MA: Newbury House.

Garvin, John. (1977). "The Anglo-Irish Idiom in the Works of Major Irish Writers". In: Diarmaid Ó Muirithe, ed. (1977). *The English Language in Ireland.* Cork: Mercier. 100-14.

Gass, Susan M. and Larry Selinker. (1994). *Second Language Acquisition. An Introductory Course.* Hillsdale, New Jersey: Lawrence Erlbaum Associates, Publishers.

Gibbons, Luke. (2002). *Ireland into Film: The Quiet Man.* Cork: Cork University Press.

Gibbons, Luke. (1996). *Transformations in Irish Culture.* Cork: Cork University Press.

Gibbons, Luke. (2005). "Projecting the Nation: Cinema and Culture". In: Joe Cleary and Claire Connolly, eds. (2005). *The Cambridge Companion to Modern Irish Culture.* Cambridge: Cambridge University Press. 206-24.

Gilbert, Judy B. (1978). "Gadgets: Non-Verbal Tools for Teaching Pronunciation". In: Adam Brown, ed. (1991). *Teaching English Pronunciation: A Book of Readings.* London: Routledge.

Gilbert, Judy B. (1980). "Prosodic Development: Some Pilot Studies". In: Robin C. Scarcella and Stephen D. Krashen, eds. (1980). *Research in Second Language Acquisition.* Rowley, MA: Newbury House Publishers, Inc. 110-117.

Giles, Howard. (1972). "The Effect of Stimulus Mildness-Broadness in the Evaluation of Accents". *Language and Speech* 15: 262-69.

Gimson, Alfred. C. (1970). *An Introduction to the Pronunciation of English.* London: Edward Arnold.

Glaser, Robert, ed. (1962). *Training, Research, and Education.* Pittsburgh: University of Pittsburgh Press.

Görlach, Manfred. (1999). *English in Nineteenth-Century England: An Introduction.* Cambridge: Cambridge University Press.

Gottlieb, Henrik. (1998). "Subtitling". In: Mona Baker, ed. (1998). *Routledge Encyclopaedia of Translation Studies.* London and New York: Routledge. 244-8.

Graff, Willem L. (1932). *Language and Languages. An Introduction to Linguistics.* New York/London. D. Appleton and Company.

Greene, David. (1979). "Perfects and Perfectives in Modern Irish". *Eriu* 30: 122-41.

Grover, Cinthia, Donald G. Jamieson and Michael B. Dobrovolsky. (1987). "Intonation in English, French and German: Perception and Production". *Language and Speech* 30 (3): 277-96.

Guiora, Alexander Z. (1965). "On Clinical Diagnosis and Prediction". *Psychological Reports* 17: 779-84.

Guiora, Alexander Z. (1972). "Construct Validity and Transpositional Research: Toward an Empirical Study of Psychoanalytic Concepts". *Comprehensive Psychiatry* 13 (2): 139-50.

Guiora, Alexander Z., R. Bolin, C. Dutton and R. Meer. (1965). "Intuition: A Preliminary Statement". *Psychiatric Quarterly [Supplement]* 39: 110-22.

Guiora, Alexander Z., Benjamin Beit-Hallami, Robert C. L. Brannon, Cecilia Y. Dull and Thomas Scovel. (1972). "The Effects of Experimentally Induced Changes in Ego States on Pronunciation Ability in a Second Language: An Exploratory Study". *Comprehensive Psychiatry* 13 (5): 421-8.

Halliday, Michael A.K. and Ruqaiya Hasan. (1976). *Cohesion in English*. London: Longman.

Hampton, Marion and Barbara Acker, eds. (1997). *The Vocal Vision. Views on Voice by 24 Leading Teachers, Coaches and Directors*. New York: Applause.

Harris, John. (1984a). "Syntactic Variation and Dialect Divergence". *Journal of Linguistics* 20: 303-27.

Harris, John. (1984b). "English in the North of Ireland". In: Peter Trudgill, ed. (1984). *Language in the British Isles*. Cambridge: Cambridge University Press. 115-34.

Harris, John, David Little and David Singleton, eds. (1985). *Perspectives on the English Language in Ireland*. Dublin: Trinity College Dublin.

Harris, John. (1991a). "Conservatism Versus Substratal Transfer in Irish English". In: Peter Trudgill and Jack K. Chambers, eds. (1991). *Dialects of English. Studies in Grammatical Variation*. London and New York: Longman. 191-212.

Harris, John. (1991b). "Ireland". In Jenny Cheshire, ed. (1991). *English around the World: Sociolinguistic Perspectives*. Cambridge: Cambridge University Press. 37-50.

Harris, John. (1993). "The Grammar of Irish English". In: James Milroy and Lesley Milroy, eds. (1993). *Real English. The Grammar of English Dialects in the British Isles*. London and New York: Longman. 139-86.

Hayden, Mary and Marcus Hartog. (1909). "The Irish Dialect of English: its Origins and Vocabulary". *Fortnightly Review, New Series* 85: 933-47.

Henry, Alison. (1992). "Infinitives in a *for-to* dialect". *Natural Language and Linguistic Theory* 10: 279-301.

Henry, Patrick Leo. (1957). *An Anglo-Irish Dialect of North Roscommon. Phonology, Accidence, Syntax*. Dublin: Department of English, University College Dublin.

Henry, Patrick Leo. (1977). "Anglo Irish and its Irish background". In: Diarmaid Ó Muirithe, ed. (1977). *The English Language in Ireland*. Cork: Mercier. 20-36.

Herbst, Thomas. (1994). *Linguistische Aspekte der Synchronisation von Fernsehserien: Phonetik, Textlinguistik, Übersetzungstheorie*. Tübingen: Max Niemeyer Verlag.

Herman, Lewis and Marguerite Shalett Herman. (1947). *Manual of American Dialects for Radio, Stage, Screen and Television*. Chicago and New York: Ziff Davis Publishing Company.

Herman, Lewis and Marguerite Shalett Herman. (1997). *Foreign Dialects. A Manual for Actors, Directors, and Writers*. New York and London: Routledge.

Herr, Cheryl. (2002). *Ireland into Film: The Field*. Cork: Cork University Press.

Hickey, Raymond. (1983). "Remarks on Pronominal Usage in Hiberno-English". *Studia Anglica Posnaniensia* 15: 47-53.

Hickey, Raymond. (1989). "R-Coloured Vowels in Irish English". *Journal of the International Phonetic Association* 15. 44-58.

Hickey, Raymond. (2002). *A Source Book for Irish English*. Amsterdam: John Benjamins.

Hickey, Raymond. (2004a). *A Sound Atlas of Irish English*. Berlin: Mouton de Gruyter.

Hickey, Raymond. (2004b). "Irish English: Phonology". In: Bernd Kortmann, Kate Burridge, Rajend Mesthrie, Edgar W. Schneider and Clive Upton, eds. (2004a). *A Handbook of Varieties of English. Volume 1: Phonology*. Berlin: Mouton de Gruyter. 68-97.

Hickey, Raymond. (2005). *Dublin English: Evolution and Change*. Amsterdam: John Benjamins.

Hickey, Raymond. (2007). *Irish English. History and Present-Day Forms*. Cambridge: Cambridge University Press.

Hill, John and Pamela Church Gibson, eds. (1998). *The Oxford Guide to Film Studies*. Oxford: Oxford University Press.

Hoenigswald, Henry M. (1966). "A Proposal for the Study of Folk Linguistics" and "Discussion". In: William Bright, ed. (1966). *Sociolinguistics. Proceedings of the UCLA Sociolinguistics Conference, 1964*. The Hague: Mouton and Co. 16-26.

Hogan, James. (1927). *The English Language in Ireland*. Dublin: Educational Company of Ireland.

Holohan, Renagh. (1998). "Pardon my French". *The Irish Times*. 14 February.

Honikman, Beatrice. (1964). "Articulatory Settings". In: Adam Brown, ed. (1991). *Teaching English Pronunciation: A Book of Readings*. London: Routledge. 276-87.

Hutson, Arthur E. (1947). "Gaelic loan-words in American". *American Speech* 22: 18-23.

Ihalainen, Ossi. (1991). "Periphrastic Do in Affirmative Sentences in the Dialect of East Somerset." In: Peter Trudgill and Jack K. Chambers, eds. (1991). *Dialects of English. Studies in Grammatical Variation*. London: Longman.148-60.

Ihalainen, Ossi. (1994). "The Dialects of England since 1776". In: Robert Burchfield, ed. (1994). *The Cambridge History of the English Language. Volume V. English in Britain and Overseas: Origins and Development*. Cambridge: Cambridge University Press. 197-224.

Ingle, Róisín. (2007). "Author of Her Own Destiny". *The Irish Times*. 15 December.

Ioup, Georgette and Steven H. Weinberger, eds. (1987). *Interlanguage Phonology: the Acquisition of a Second Language Sound System*. Cambridge, MA: Newbury House.

Ives, Sumner. (1950). "A Theory of Literary Dialect". In: Juanita V. Williamson and Virginia M. Burke, eds. (1971). *A Various Language. Perspectives on American Dialects*. New York: Holt, Rinehart and Winston, Inc. 145-77.

James, Eric. (1976). "The Acquisition of Prosodic Features of Speech Using a Speech Visualizer". *International Review of Applied Linguistics in Language Teaching* 14 (3): 227-43.

Jenner, Bryan. (1987). "Articulation and Phonation in Non-Native English: The Example of Dutch English". *Journal of the International Phonetic Association* 17 (2): 125-38.

Jenner, Bryan. (1992). "The English Voice". In: Adam Brown, ed. (1992). *Approaches to Pronunciation Teaching. Modern English Publications in Association with The British Council*. London: Macmillan Publishers Ltd. 38-46.

Jenner, Bryan. (2001). "'Articulatory Setting'. Genealogies of an Idea". In: *Historiographia Linguistica* 28 (2): 121-141.

Jenner, Bryan and Barbara Bradford. (1982). "Teaching Pronunciation". *Modern English Teacher* 10 (2): 38-41.

Johansson, Stig. (1978). *Studies in Error Gravity. Gothenburg Studies in English 44.*

Johnson, Ellen and Stephanie Chastain. (2003). "Two Views of One Place: The Dialect of Putnam County, Georgia, in the Works of Joel Chandler Harris and Alice Walker". *Southern Journal of Linguistics. 2003 SouthEastern Conference on Linguistics.* 174-86.

Johnstone, Barbara. (1991). "Discourse-Level Aspects of Dialect in Fiction: A Southern American Example". *Language and Style* 24 (4): 461-71.

Jones, Gavin. (1999). *Strange Talk – The Politics of Dialect Literature in Gilded Age America*. Berkley and Los Angeles: University of California Press.

Jones, Rodney H. and Stephen Evans. (1995). "Teaching Pronunciation through Voice Quality". *ELT Journal* 49 (3). Oxford: Oxford University Press. 244-51.

Jordan, Neil. (1996). *Michael Collins. Screenplay and Film Diary*. New York: Plume/Penguin Books.

Joyce, Patrick Weston. (1988). *English as we Speak it in Ireland*. London: Longmans, Green and Co.

Judd, Tedd. (1988). "The Varieties of Musical Talent". In: Loraine K. Obler and Deborah Fein, eds. (1988). *The Exceptional Brain. Neuropsychology of Talent and Special Abilities*. New York and London: The Guilford Press. 127-55.

Kallen, Jeffrey L. (1985). "The Co-Occurrence of Do and Be in Hiberno-English". In: John Harris, David Little and David Singleton, eds. (1985). *Perspectives on the English Language in Ireland*. Dublin: Trinity College Dublin. 133-47.

Kallen, Jeffrey L. (1991). "Sociolinguistic Variation and Methodology: 'After' as a Dublin Variable". In: Jenny Cheshire, ed. (1991). *English around the World: Sociolinguistic Perspectives*. Cambridge: Cambridge University Press. 61-74.

Kallen, Jeffrey L. (1994). "English in Ireland". In: Robert Burchfield, ed. (1994). *The Cambridge History of the English Language. Volume V. English in Britain and Overseas: Origins and Development*. Cambridge: Cambridge University Press. 148-96.

Kallen, Jeffrey L. (1997). "Irish English: Context and Contacts". In: Jeffrey L. Kallen, ed. (1997). *Focus on Ireland*. Amsterdam: John Benjamins. 1-33.

Kallen, Jeffrey L., ed. (1997). *Focus on Ireland*. Amsterdam: John Benjamins.

Kelz, Heinrich P. (1971). "Articulatory Basis and Second Language Teaching". *Phonetica* 24: 193-221.

Kent, Raymond D., ed. (1992). *Intelligibility in Speech Disorders: Theory, Measurement, and Management. Volume 1*. Philadelphia: John Benjamins.

Kenworthy, Joanne. (1987). *Teaching English Pronunciation*. London: Longman.

Kiberd, Declan. (1996). "The Periphery and the Center". *The South Atlantic Quarterly* 95 (1): 5-21.

Kiberd, Declan. (2005). *The Irish Writer and the World*. Cambridge: Cambridge University Press.

Kiely, Benedict. (1977). "Dialect and Literature". In: Diarmaid Ó Muirithe, ed. (1977). *The English Language in Ireland*. Cork: Mercier. 100-14.

King, Barry. (1985). "Articulating Stardom". *Screen* 26 (5): 27-50.

Kirby, Anthony and James MacKillop. (1999). "Selected Filmography of Irish and Irish-Related Feature Films". In: James MacKillop, ed. (1999). *Contemporary Irish Cinema. From The Quiet Man to Dancing at Lughnasa*. New York: Syracuse University Press. 182-231.

Kirk, John M. (1997). "Irish English and Contemporary Literary Writing". In: Jeffrey L. Kallen, ed. (1997). *Focus on Ireland*. Amsterdam: John Benjamins. 189-206

Kirk, John M. (1999). "Contemporary Irish Writing and a Model of Speech Realism". In: Irma Taavitsainen, Gunnel Melchers and Päivi Pahta, eds. (1999). *Writing in Nonstandard English*. Amsterdam: John Benjamins. 45-61.

Kirk, John M., Jeffrey L. Kallen, Orla Lowry, and Anne Rooney. (2003). "Issues Arising from the Compilation of ICE-Ireland". In: *Belfast Working Papers in Language & Linguistics* 16. University of Ulster. 23-41.

Klemola, Juhani, Merja Kytö, and Matti Rissanen, eds. (1996). *Speech Past and Present. Studies in English Dialectology in Memory of Ossi Ihalainen*. Frankfurt am Main: Peter Lang.

Knaller, Susanne. (2007). *Ein Wort aus der Fremde. Geschichte und Theorie des Begriffs Authentizität*. Heidelberg: Universitätsverlag Winter.

Knight, Dudley. (1997). "Standard Speech. The Ongoing Debate". In: Marion Hampton and Barbara Acker, eds. (1997). *The Vocal Vision. Views on Voice by 24 Leading Teachers, Coaches and Directors*. New York: Applause. 155-83.

Knight, Michael. (1975). "Teaching Pronunciation". *Zielsprache Englisch* 1. 1-6.

Kopf, Ginny. (2003). *The Dialect Handbook. Learning, Researching and Performing a Dialect Role* (2nd ed.). Orlando, Florida: Voiceprint Publishing.

Kortmann, Bernd, Kate Burridge, Rajend Mesthrie, Edgar W. Schneider and Clive Upton, eds. (2004a). *A Handbook of Varieties of English. Volume 1: Phonology*. Berlin: Mouton de Gruyter.

Kortmann, Bernd, Kate Burridge, Rajend Mesthrie, Edgar W. Schneider and Clive Upton, eds. (2004b). *A Handbook of Varieties of English. Volume 2: Morphology and Syntax*. Berlin: Mouton de Gruyter.

Kortmann, Bernd and Benedikt Szmrecsanyi. (2004). "Global Synopsis: Morphological and Syntactic Variation in English". In: Bernd Kortmann, Kate Burridge, Rajend Mesthrie, Edgar W. Schneider and Clive Upton, eds. (2004b). *A Handbook of Varieties of English. Volume 2: Morphology and Syntax.* Berlin: Mouton de Gruyter. 1142-202.

Kozloff, Sarah. (2000). *Overhearing Film Dialogue.* Berkeley and Los Angeles: University of California Press.

Krapp, George Philip. (1925). "The Psychology of Dialect Writings". In: Juanita V. Williamson and Virginia M. Burke, eds. (1971). *A Various Language. Perspectives on American Dialects.* New York: Holt, Rinehart and Winston, Inc. 22-9.

Krashen, Stephen D. (1973). "Lateralisation, Language Learning, and the Critical Period: Some New Evidence". *Language Learning* 23 (1): 63-74.

Krashen, Stephen D. (1982). *Principles and Practice in Second Language Acquisition.* Oxford: Pergamon Institute.

Krashen, Stephen D. and Herbert W. Seliger (1975). "Maturational Constraints on Second Dialect Acquisition". *Language Sciences* 38: 28-29.

Krashen, Stephen D., Robin C. Scarcella and Michael H. Long, eds. (1982). *Child-Adult Differences in Second Language Acquisition.* Rowley/London/Tokyo: Newbury House Publishers, Inc.

Krause, David, ed. (1964). *The Dolmen Boucicault.* Dublin: The Dolmen Press.

Krug, Manfred. (2007) "Modern Methodologies and Changing Standards in English Linguistics". In: María Losada Friend, Pilar Ron Vaz, Sonia Hernández Santano and Jorge Casanova, eds. (2007) *Proceedings of the 30th International AEDEAN Conference.* Servicio de Publicaciones de la Universidad de Huelva. [CD-Rom].

Labov, William. (1972). *Language in the Inner City.* Philadelphia: University of Pennsylvania Press.

Labov, William. (1978). *Sociolinguistic Patterns.* Oxford: Basil Blackwell.

Lane, Harlan. (1963). "Foreign Accent and Speech Distortion". *The Journal of the Acoustical Society of America* 35: 451-53.

Lass, Roger. (1990) "Early Mainland Residues in Southern Hiberno-English". *Irish University Review. A Journal of Irish Studies. The English of the Irish. Special Issue.* 20 (1): 137-48.

Laver, John. (1980). *The Phonetic Description of Voice Quality.* Cambridge: Cambridge University Press.

Laverty, Paul. (2006). *The Wind that Shakes the Barley. A Screenplay by Paul Laverty, Directed by Ken Loach.* Cork: Galley Head Press.

Leather, Jonathan and Allan James, eds. (1990). *New Sounds 90, Proceedings of the 1990 Amsterdam Symposium on the Acquisition of Second Language Speech (University of Amsterdam, 9-12 April 1990).* Universiteit van Amsterdam.

Leon, Pierre and Philippe Martin. (1972). "Applied Linguistics and the Teaching of Intonation". *Modern Language Journal* 56 (3): 139-44.

Lindsey, Geoff. (1990). "Quantity and Quality in British and American Vowel Systems". In: Susan Ramsaran, ed. (1990) *Studies in the Pronunciation of English: A*

Commemorative Volume in Honour of A.C. Gimson. London and New York: Routledge. 110-18.

Lippi-Green, Rosina. (1997). "Teaching Children How to Discriminate: What We Learn from the Big Bad Wolf". In: Rosina Lippi-Green. (1997). *English with an Accent. Language, Ideology, and Discrimination in the United States*. New York: Routledge. 79-103.

Lippi-Green, Rosina. (1997). *English with an Accent. Language, Ideology, and Discrimination in the United States*. New York: Routledge.

Lovell, Alan. (2005). "Sensitive to Technique". In: *Sight and Sound* 15 (4). 88.

Lukmani, Yasmeen M. (1972). "Motivation to Learn and Learning Proficiency". *Language Learning* 22: 261-73.

Mac Eoin, Gearóid. (1993). "Irish". In: Martin. J. Ball and James Fife, eds. (1993). *The Celtic Languages*. London: Routledge.

MacHale, Des. (2000). *The Complete Guide to The Quiet Man*. Belfast: Appletree Press.

MacKillop, James, ed. (1999). *Contemporary Irish Cinema. From The Quiet Man to Dancing at Lughnasa*. New York: Syracuse University Press.

Mac Mathúna, Séamus and Maire Nic Mhaolain, eds. (2006). *Collins Irish Dictionary. Express Edition*. Glasgow: Harper Collins.

McArthur, Colin. (2003). *Brigadoon, Braveheart and the Scots. Distortions of Scotland in Hollywood Cinema*. London & New York: I.B. Taurus.

McCafferty, Kevin. (2003). "'I'll Bee After Telling Dee de Raison…': Be After V-ing as a Future Gram in Irish English, 1601-1750". In: Hildegard L.C. Tristram, ed. (2003). *The Celtic Englishes III*. Heidelberg: Universitätsverlag Winter. 298-317.

McCawley, James D. (1971). "Tense and Time Reference in English". In: Charles J. Filmore and Terence D. Langendoen, eds. *Studies in Linguistic Semantics*. New York: Holt, Rinehart & Winston. 96-113.

McCourt, Frank. (1996). *Angela's Ashes. A Memoir of a Childhood*. London: Flamingo.

McDonald, Paul. (1998). "Film Acting". In: John Hill and Pamela Church Gibson, eds. (1998). *The Oxford Guide to Film Studies*. Oxford: Oxford University Press. 30-5.

McGregor, Graham. (1998). "Whaddaweknow? Language Awareness and Non-Linguists' Accounts of Everyday Speech Activities". *Language Awareness* 7 (1): 32-51.

McIlroy, Brian. (2003a). "Hollywood East? A Cautionary Tale of Irish Film Distribution in North America.". In: Jerry White, ed. (2003). *Canadian Journal of Irish Studies*. 29 (2) Fall 2003: University of Alberta. 46-52.

McIlroy, Brian. (2003b). "A Film Apparatchik Speaks. An Interview with Rod Stoneman.". In: Jerry White, ed. (2003). *Canadian Journal of Irish Studies*. 29 (2) Fall 2003: University of Alberta. 53-61.

McIlroy, Brian, ed. (2007). *Genre and Cinema. Ireland and Transnationalism*. New York: Routledge.

McLoone, Martin. (2000). *Irish Film. The Emergence of a Contemporary Cinema*. London: British Film Institute.

McLoone, Martin (2006). "National Cinema in Ireland". In: Valentina Vitali and Paul Willemen, eds. (2006). *Theorising National Cinema*. London: British Film Institute. 88-99.

McLoone, Martin. (2008). *Film, Media and Popular Culture in Ireland. Cityscapes, Landscapes, Soundscapes*. Dublin: Irish Academic Press.

McMahon, Sean and Jo O'Donoghue, eds. (2004). *Brewer's Dictionary of Irish Phrase and Fable*. London: Weidenfeld & Nicholson.

McPherson, Conor. (2004). *Plays: Two*. London: Nick Hern Books.

McPherson, Conor. (2006). *The Seafarer*. London: Nick Hern Books.

Machlin, Evangeline. (1975). *Dialects for the Stage*. New York: Theatre Arts Books.

Maier, Wolfgang. (1997). *Spielfilmsynchronisation*. Frankfurt am Main. Peter Lang.

Mair, Christian. (2003). "Kreolismen und verbales Identitätsmanagement im geschriebenen jamaikanischen Englisch". In: Elisabeth Vogel, Antonia Napp and Wolfram Lutterer, eds. (2003). *Zwischen Ausgrenzung und Hybridisierung*. Würzburg: Ergon. 79-96.

Major, Roy C. (1987). "Measuring Pronunciation Accuracy Using Computerized Techniques". *Language Testing* 4 (2): 155-69.

Malcolm, Derek. (1992). "An Epic out of its Time". *The Guardian*, 30 July: 30.

Markham, Duncan. (1997). *Phonetic Imitation, Accent, and the Learner*. Lund: Lund University Press.

Marks, J. (1980). *Foreign Accent and the Interlanguage Hypothesis*. Unpublished M.A. thesis: University of Toronto.

Mast, Gerald, ed. (1982). *The Movies in our Midst. Documents in the Cultural History of Film in America*. Chicago and London: The University of Chicago Press.

Mast, Gerald, Marshall Cohen and Leo Braudy, eds. (1992). *Film Theory and Criticism. Introductory Readings*. (4th ed.). New York and Oxford: Oxford University Press.

Matossian, Lou Ann and Lisa Giles-Klein, eds. (1980). *Language in Society* 9 Cambridge: Cambridge University Press.

Meier, Paul. (2004). *Accents and Dialects for Stage and Screen*. McLouth, KS: Paul Meier Dialect Services.

Mercer Gene V. (1975). "The Development of Children's Ability to Discriminate between Languages and Varieties of the Same Language". Unpublished M.A. thesis. McGill University, Montreal.

Milroy, James and Lesley Milroy, eds. (1993). *Real English. The Grammar of English Dialects in the British Isles*. London and New York: Longman.

Mohne Hill, Kimberly, ed. (2002). *Monologues in Dialect for Young Actors*. Hanover, NH: Smith and Kraus.

Montague, John, ed. (1974). *The Faber Book of Irish Verse*. London: Faber & Faber.

Moore, Timothy E., ed. (1973). *Cognitive Development and the Acquisition of Language*. New York and London: Academic Press.

Moylan, Séamus. (1996). *The Language of Kilkenny. Lexicon, Semantics, Structures.* Dublin: Geography Publications.

Murphy, Gerard. "English 'Brogue' Meaning 'Irish accent'". *Éigse* 3: 231-6.

Nash, Rose. (1971). "Phonemic and Prosodic Interference and their Effects on Intelligibility". *International Congress of Phonetic Sciences. 1971, 7*: 138-9.

Nelson Francis, W. (1985). "Amn't I, or the Hole in the Pattern". In: Wolfgang Viereck, ed. (1985). *Varieties of English Around the World. Focus On: England and Wales.* Amsterdam/Philadelphia: John Benjamins. 141-52.

Neufeld, Gerald G. (1977). "Language Learning Ability in Adults: A Study on the Acquisition of Prosodic and Articulatory Features". *Working Papers in Bilingualism* 12: 45-60.

Neufeld, Gerald G. (1978). "On the Acquisition of Prosodic and Articulatory Features in Adult Language Learning". *The Canadian Modern Language Review* 34 (2): 163-74.

Neufeld, Gerald G. (1979). "Towards a Theory of Language Learning Ability". *Language Learning* 29 (2): 227-241.

Neufeld, Gerald G. (1980). "On the Adult's Ability to Acquire Phonology". *TESOL Quarterly* 3: 285-98.

Neufeld, Gerald G. (1987). "On the Acquisition of Prosodic and Articulatory Features in Adult Language Learning". In: Georgette Ioup and Steven H. Weinberger, eds. (1987). *Interlanguage Phonology: the Acquisition of a Second Language Sound System.* Cambridge, MA: Newbury House. 321-32.

Niedzielski, Nancy A. and Dennis R. Preston. (2003). *Folk Linguistics.* Berlin/New York: Mouton de Gruyter.

Nunan, David. (1995). *Language Teaching Methodology. A Textbook for Teachers.* Hertfordshire: Phoenix ELT.

O'Carroll, Brendan. (1994). *The Mammy.* Dublin: The O'Brien Press.

O'Cassidy, Teresa L. (2004). "Accent, Linguistic Discrimination, Stereotyping and West Virginia in Film". Unpublished M.A. thesis. West Virginia: Marshall University.

O'Connor, Áine. (1996). *Leading Hollywood.* Dublin and London: Wolfhound Press.

O'Flaherty, Liam. (1925/1999). *The Informer.* Dublin: Wolfhound Press.

O'Mahony, Patrick and Gerard Delanty. (1998). *Rethinking Irish History. Nationalism, Identity and Ideology.* London: Macmillan Press.

Ó Muirithe, Diarmaid, ed. (1977). *The English Language in Ireland.* Cork: Mercier.

Ó Muirithe, Diarmaid. (1994). "The Words We Use". *The Irish Times.* 1 October.

O'Rahilly, Thomas Francis. (1926). *Irish Dialects Past and Present.* Dublin: Browne and Nolan.

Ó Sé, Diarmuid. (1992). "The Perfect in Modern Irish". *Ériu* 43: 39-67.

O'Toole, Fintan. (1985). "Going West: The Country versus the City in Irish Writing". *The Crane Bag* 9 (2): 111-16.

Odlin, Terence. (1997). "Bilingualism and Substrate Influence: a Look at Clefts and Reflexives". In: Jeffrey L. Kallen, ed. (1997). *Focus on Ireland*. Amsterdam: John Benjamins. 35-50.

Olson, Linda L. and S. Jay Samuels. (1973). "The Relationship between Age and Accuracy of Foreign Language Pronunciation". In: Stephen D. Krashen, Robin C. Scarcella and Michael H. Long, eds. (1982). *Child-Adult Differences in Second Language Acquisition*. Rowley/London/Tokyo: Newbury House Publishers, Inc. 67-75.

Oyama, Susan. (1976). "A Sensitive Period for the Acquisition of a Nonnative Phonological System". In: Stephen D. Krashen, Robin C. Scarcella and Michael H. Long, eds. (1982). *Child-Adult Differences in Second Language Acquisition*. Rowley/London/Tokyo: Newbury House Publishers, Inc. 20-38.

Oyama, Susan. (1978). "The Sensitive Period and Comprehension of Speech". In: Stephen D. Krashen, Robin C. Scarcella and Michael H. Long, eds. (1982). *Child-Adult Differences in Second Language Acquisition*. Rowley/London/Tokyo: Newbury House Publishers, Inc. 39-51.

Page, Norman. (1988). *Speech in the English Novel*. London: Macmillan.

Pao, Angela C. (2004). "False Accents: Embodied Dialects and the Characterization of Ethnicity and Nationality". In: *Theatre Topics* 14 (1): 353-72.

Paulin, Tom. (1984). "A New Look at the Language Question". In: Tom Paulin. (1984). *Ireland and the English Crisis*. Newcastle-upon-Tyne, Bloodaxe Books. 178-93.

Pennington, Martha C. and Jack C. Richards. (1986). "Pronunciation Revisited". *TESOL Quarterly* 20 (2): 207-25.

Pennington, Martha C. (1996). *Phonology in English Language Teaching: An International Approach*. London and New York: Longman.

Pennington, Martha C. (1997). "Phonology in Language Teaching: Essentials of Theory and Practice". In: Kathleen Bardovi-Harlig and Beverly Hartford, eds. (1997). *Beyond Methods. Components of Second Language Teacher Education*. New York: McGraw Hill. 67-87.

Perry Curtis, Jr., L. (1971). *Apes and Angels. The Irishman in Victorian Caricature*. Newton Abbot, Devon: David and Charles.

Pettitt, Lance. (2000). *Screening Ireland. Film and Television Representation*. Manchester: Manchester University Press.

Postovsky, Valerian A. (1974). "Effects of Delay in Oral Practice at the Beginning of Second Language Learning". *The Modern Language Journal* 58 (5/6): 229-39.

Preston, Dennis R. (1989). *Perceptual Dialectology. Nonlinguists' Views of Areal Linguistics*. Dordrecht, Holland: Foris Publications.

Preston, Dennis R. (1996). "Whaddyaknow?: The Modes of Folk Linguistic Awareness". *Language Awareness* 5 (1): 40-74.

Preston, Dennis R., ed. (1999). *Handbook of Perceptual Dialectology (Volume 1)*. Amsterdam/Philadelphia: John Benjamins.

Purcell, Edward T. and Richard W. Suter. (1980). "Predictors of Pronunciation Accuracy: A Reexamination". *Language Learning* 30 (2): 271-87.

Quirk, Randolph, Sidney Greenbaum, Geoffrey Leech and Jan Svartik. (1985). *A Grammar of Contemporary English*. London: Longman.

Rains, Stephanie. (2007). *The Irish-American in Popular Culture 1945-2000*. Dublin: Irish Academic Press.

Ramisch, Heinrich. (1988). *The Variation of English in Guernsey/Channel Islands*. Frankfurt am Main: Peter Lang.

Ramsaran, Susan, ed. (1990). *Studies in the Pronunciation of English: A Commemorative Volume in Honour of A.C. Gimson*. London and New York: Routledge.

Ramus, Franck and Jacques Mehler. (1999). "Language Identification with Suprasegmental Cues: A Study Based on Speech Resynthesis". *Journal of the Acoustic Society of America (JASA)* 105 (1): 512-21.

Raphael, Bonnie N. (1984). "Preparing a Cast for a Dialect Show". *Communication Education* 33 (1): 43-51.

Riordan, Vincent. (2001). "English on the Air". *The Irish Times*, 22 November.

Robinson, W. Peter and Howard Giles, eds. (2001). *The New Handbook of Language and Social Psychology*. Chichester: John Wiley & Sons.

Roche, Billy. (1997). *Trojan Eddie. A Screenplay by Billy Roche*. London: Methuen.

Rockett, Kevin, John Hill and Luke Gibbons. (1988). *Cinema and Ireland*. London: Routledge.

Rockett, Kevin, ed. (1996). *The Irish Filmography. Fiction Films 1896-1996*. Dublin: Red Mountain Media.

Rockett, Kevin. (2004). *Irish Film Censorship. A Cultural Journey from Silent Cinema to Internet Pornography*. Dublin: Four Courts Press.

Ronan, Patricia. (2005). "The After-Perfect in Irish English". In: Markku Filppula, Juhanii Klemola, Marjatta Palander and Esa Penttilä, eds. (2005). *Dialects Across Borders. Selected Papers From The 11th International Conference On Methods In Dialectology (Methods XI), Joensuu, August 2002*. Amsterdam/Philadelphia: John Benjamins. 253-70.

Rosch, Eleanor. (1973). "On the Internal Structure of Perceptual and Semantic Categories". In: Timothy E. Moore, ed. (1973). *Cognitive Development and the Acquisition of Language*. New York and London: Academic Press. 111-44.

Rosch, Eleanor. (1978). "Principles of Categorization". In: Eleanor Rosch and Barbara B. Lloyd, eds. (1978). *Cognition and Categorization*. Hillsdale, NJ: Lawrence Erlbaum Associates, Publishers. 27-48.

Rosch, Eleanor and Barbara B. Lloyd, eds. (1978). *Cognition and Categorization*. Hillsdale, NJ: Lawrence Erlbaum Associates, Publishers.

Rose, D.C. (1997). "Tremenjus". *The Irish Times*. 18 July.

Rouvel, Kristof. (1997). "Zur Unterscheidung der Begriffe Glaubwürdigkeit, Wahrhaftigkeit und Authentizität". In: Jan Berg, Hans-Otto Hügel and Hajo Kürzenberger, eds. (1997). *Authentizität als Darstellung*. Hildesheim: Hildesheim University. 216-26.

Rubidge, Sarah. (1996). "Does Authenticity Matter? The Case for and against Authenticity in the Performing Arts". In: Patrick Campbell, ed. (1996). *Analysing Performance – A Critical Reader*. Manchester and New York: Manchester University Press. 219-33.

Rubin, Donald L. (1992). "Nonlanguage Factors Affecting Undergraduates' Judgements of Nonnative English-Speaking Teaching Assistants". *Research in Higher Education* 33 (4): 511-31.

Ryan, Ellen Bouchard and Howard Giles, eds. (1982). *Attitudes towards Language Variation*. London: Edward Arnold.

Ryan, Rob. (1989). "Day Glow". *Arena* (Autumn) 102-05.

Sabban, Annette. (1982). *Gälisch-Englischer Sprachkontakt. Zur Variabilität des Englischen im gälischsprachigen Gebiet Schottlands. Eine empirische Studie*. Heidelberg: Julius Groos Verlag.

Savard, Jean-Guy and Lorne Laforge, eds. (1981). *Proceedings of the 5th Congress of L'Association Internationale de Linguistique Appliquée*. Québec: Les Presses de l'Université Laval.

Scarcella, Robin C. and Stephen D. Krashen, eds. (1980). *Research in Second Language Acquisition*. Rowley, MA: Newbury House Publishers, Inc.

Schiffrin, Deborah. (2001). "Discourse Markers: Language, Meaning and Context". In: Deborah Schiffrin, Heidi E. Hamilton and Deborah Tannen, eds. (2001). *Handbook of Discourse Analysis*. Malden, MA. Blackwell. 54-75.

Schiffrin, Deborah, Heidi E. Hamilton and Deborah Tannen, eds. (2001). *Handbook of Discourse Analysis*. Malden, MA. Blackwell.

Schneiderman, Eta I. and Chantal Desmaris. (1988). "A Neuropsychological Substrate for Talent in Second-Language Acquisition". In: Loraine K. Obler and Deborah Fein, eds. (1988). *The Exceptional Brain. Neuropsychology of Talent and Special Abilities*. New York and London: The Guilford Press. 103-126.

Schumann, John H. (1975). "Affective Factors and the Problem of Age in Second Language Acquisition". *Language Learning* 25 (2): 209-35.

Schumann, John H. (1986). "Research on the Acculturation Model for Second Language Acquisition". *Journal of Multilingual and Multicultural Development* 7 (5): 379-92.

Schwarz, Daniel R. ed. (1994) *The Dead. James Joyce*. New York: Bedford Books of St Martin's Press:

Scott, Temple. ed. (1905). *The Prose Works of Jonathan Swift D.D. Volume 7 (Historical and Political Tracts)*. London: George Bell and Sons.

Scovel, Thomas. (1969). "Foreign Accent: Language Acquisition and Cerebral Dominance". *Language Learning* 28 (1): 143-8.

Scovel, Thomas. (1978). "The Recognition of Foreign Accents in English and its Implications for Psycholinguistic Theories of Language Acquisition". In: Jean-Guy Savard and Lorne Laforge, eds. (1981). *Proceedings of the 5th Congress of L'Association Internationale de Linguistique Appliquée*. Québec: Les Presses de l'Université Laval. 389-401.

Scovel, Thomas. (1988). *A Time to Speak. A Psycholinguistic Inquiry into the Critical Period for Human Speech*. Cambridge and New York: Newbury House Publishers.

Seger, Linda. (1992). *The Art of Adaptation. Turning Fact and Fiction into Film.* New York: Henry Holt and Company.

Sell, Katrin. (forthcoming). "A Sociolinguistic Approach to Spoken Irish English in Galway City". (Working title).

Share, Bernard. (2003). *Slanguage. A Dictionary of Irish Slang.* Dublin: Gill and Macmillan.

Share, Bernard. (2006). *Dublinese. Know what I mean?* Cork: The Collins Press.

Shaw, George Bernard. (1964). *John Bull's Other Ireland.* London: Constable and Company.

Shaw, George Bernard. (2003). *Pygmalion.* Harmondsmith, Middlesex: Penguin Books/Ernst Klett Verlag.

Sheeran, Patrick F. (2002). *Ireland into Film: The Informer.* Cork: Cork University Press.

Shorrocks, Graham. (1996). "Non-Standard Dialect Literature and Popular Culture". In: Juhani Klemola, Merja Kytö, and Matti Rissanen, eds. (1996). *Speech Past and Present. Studies in English Dialectology in Memory of Ossi Ihalainen.* Frankfurt am Main: Peter Lang. 385-411.

Shuken, Cynthia. (1984). "Highland and Island English". In: Peter Trudgill, ed. (1984). *Language in the British Isles.* Cambridge: Cambridge University Press. 152-66.

Sievers, Eduard. (1876). *Grundzüge der Lautphysiologie.* Leipzig: Breitkopf & Härtel.

Sievers, Eduard. (1901). *Grundzüge der Phonetik.* Leipzig: Breitkopf & Härtel.

Simms, Katharine. (1989). "The Norman Invasion and the Gaelic Recovery". In: Roy Foster, ed. (1989). *The Oxford Illustrated History of Ireland.* Oxford: Oxford University Press. 53-103.

Skinner, Edith. (1942 and 2000). *Speak with Distinction.* New York: Applause Books.

Slide, Anthony. (1988). *The Cinema and Ireland.* Jefferson, NC and London: McFarland & Company, Inc.

Snow, Catherine E. and Marian Hoefnagel-Höhle. (1977). "Age Differences in the Pronunciation of Foreign Sounds". In: Stephen D. Krashen, Robin C. Scarcella, and Michael H. Long, eds. (1982). *Child-Adult Differences in Second Language Acquisition.* Rowley/London/Tokyo: Newbury House Publishers, Inc. 84-92.

Sontag, Susan. (1966). "Film and Theatre". In: Gerald Mast, Marshall Cohen and Leo Braudy, eds. (1992). *Film Theory and Criticism. Introductory Readings.* (4th ed.). New York and Oxford: Oxford University Press. 362-74.

Sponsel, Daniel, ed. (2007). *Der schöne Schein des Wirklichen. Zur Authentizität im Film.* Constance: UVK Verlagsgesellschaft mBH.

Stenström, Anna-Brita. (1984). *Questions and Responses in English Conversation.* Malmö: Gleerup/Liber.

Stern, David Allan. (1979). *Acting with an Accent.* [Cassette]. Lydonville, VT: Dialect Accent Specialists, Inc.

Stockwell, Peter. (2007). *Sociolinguistics. A Resource Book for Students.* London and New York: Routledge.

Stoney, Francis Sadlier. (1895). *Don't Pat: A Manual of Irishisms by Colonel O'Critical.* Dublin: McGee William.

Storm, Johan. (1881). *Englische Philologie.* Heilbronn: Henninger.

Strange, Winifred, ed. (1995). *Speech Perception and Linguistic Experience: Theoretical and Methodological Issues.* Timonium, MD: York Press.

Strick, Philip. (1993). *Sight and Sound,* February: 52-3.

Sullivan, James P. (1980). "The Validity of Literary Dialect: Evidence from the Theatrical Portrayal of Hiberno-English Forms". In: Lou Ann Matossian and Lisa Giles-Klein, eds. (1980). *Language in Society* 9. Cambridge: Cambridge University Press. 195-219.

Svensson, Stig-Göran. (1971). "A Preliminary Study of the Role of Prosodic Parameters in Speech Perception". *Speech Transmission Laboratory Quarterly Progress and Status Report KTH 2/3.* Stockholm: Royal Institute of Technology. 24-42.

Sweet, Henry. (1877). *A Handbook of Phonetics.* Oxford: Frowde.

Swift, Jonathan. (1728). "On Barbarous Denominations in Ireland". In: Temple Scott, ed. (1905). *The Prose Works of Jonathan Swift D.D. Volume 7 (Historical and Political Tracts).* London: George Bell and Sons. 340-50.

Taniguchi, Jiro. (1972). *A Grammatical Analysis of Artistic Representation of Irish English with a Brief Discussion of Sounds and Spelling.* Tokyo: Shinozaki Shorin.

Taylor, Linda L., Alexander Z. Guiora, John C. Catford and Harlan L. Lane. (1969). "The Role of Personality Variables in Second Language Behavior". *Comprehensive Psychiatry* 10 (6): 463-74.

Templeton Kavanagh, Herminie. (2002). *Darby O'Gill and the Good People.* Manchester, NH: Sophia Institute Press.

Templeton Kavanagh, Herminie. (2003). *Darby O'Gill and the Crocks of Gold and Other Irish Tales.* Manchester, NH: Sophia Institute Press.

Thomas, Alan R. (1985). "Welsh English: A Grammatical Conspectus". In: Wolfgang Viereck, ed. (1985). *Varieties of English Around the World. Focus On: England and Wales.* Amsterdam/Philadelphia: John Benjamins. 213-21

Thompson, Ben. (1995). *Sight and Sound,* May: 42.

Thornbury, Scott. (1993). "Having a Good Jaw: Voice Setting Phonology". *ELT Journal* 47 (2). Oxford: Oxford University Press. 126-31.

Tilling, Philip M. (1985). "A Tape Recorded Survey of Irish English in its Context". In Dónall Ó Baoill, ed. (1985). *Papers on Irish English. Irish Association for Applied Linguistics.* 16-26.

Todd, Loreto. (1992). "Irish English". In: Tom McArthur, ed. (1992). *The Oxford Companion to the English Language.* Oxford: Oxford University Press. 529-30.

Tottie, Gunnel. (2002). *An Introduction to American English.* Oxford: Blackwell.

Tristram, Hildegard L.C., ed. (2003). *The Celtic Englishes III.* Heidelberg: Winter.

Trudgill, Peter, ed. (1978). *Sociolinguistic Patterns in British English.* London: Edward Arnold.

Trudgill, Peter. (1983). *On Dialect. Social and Geographical Perspectives.* Oxford: Basil Blackwell.

Trudgill, Peter, ed. (1984). *Language in the British Isles.* Cambridge: Cambridge University Press.

Trudgill, Peter. (1994). *Dialects.* London and New York: Longman.

Trudgill, Peter and Jack K. Chambers, eds. (1991). *Dialects of English. Studies in Grammatical Variation.* London and New York: Longman.

Trudgill, Peter and Jean Hannah. (1994). *International English. A Guide to the Varieties of Standard English.* London: Edward Arnold.

Truninger, Annelise. (1976). *Paddy and the Paycock. A Study of the Stage Irishman from Shakespeare to O'Casey.* Bern: Franke Verlag.

Verdolini, Katherine. (1997). "Interface between Theatre Voice and Speech Trainer and Speech-Language Pathologist". In: Marion Hampton and Barbara Acker, eds. (1997). *The Vocal Vision. Views on Voice by 24 Leading Teachers, Coaches and Directors.* New York: Applause. 225-35.

Viereck, Wolfgang, ed. (1985). *Varieties of English Around the World. Focus On: England and Wales.* Amsterdam/Philadelphia: John Benjamins.

Viereck, Wolfgang, Karin Viereck and Heinrich Ramisch. (2002). *Dtv Atlas. Englische Sprache.* Munich: Dtv.

Viëtor, Wilhelm. (1910). *Kleine Phonetik des Deutschen, Englischen und Französischen.* Leipzig: Reisland.

Vitali, Valentina and Paul Willemen, eds. (2006). *Theorising National Cinema.* London: British Film Institute.

Van Els, Theo and Kees de Bot. (1987). "The Role of Intonation in Foreign Accent". *The Modern Language Journal* 71 (2): 147-55.

Vogel, Elisabeth, Antonia Napp and Wolfram Lutterer, eds. (2003). *Zwischen Ausgrenzung und Hybridisierung.* Würzburg: Ergon.

Wall, Richard. (1990). "Dialect in Irish Literature: The Hermetic Core". In: Terence P. Dolan, ed. (1990). *The English of the Irish. Irish University Review* 20 (1): 8-18.

Walsh, Stephen. (1999). "Actor's Life". In: *Film Ireland* 69: 17.

Waters, Maureen. (1984). *The Comic Irishman.* Albany, NY: State University of New York Press.

Welch, Robert. (1996). *The Oxford Companion to Irish Literature.* Oxford: Clarendon Press.

Wells, John. C. (1982a). *Accents of English 1. An Introduction.* Cambridge: Cambridge University Press.

Wells, John. C. (1982b). *Accents of English 2. The British Isles.* Cambridge: Cambridge University Press.

Wenk, Brian. J. (1979). "Articulatory Settings and De-Fossilisation". *The Interlanguage Studies Bulletin* 4: 202-20.

Wenk, Brian. J. (1983). "Articulatory Setting and the Acquisition of Second Language Phonology". *Revue de Phonétique Appliquée* 65: 51-65.

Werker, Janet F. and Linda Polka. (1993). "Developmental Changes in Speech Perception: New Challenges and New Directions". *Journal of Phonetics* 21: 83-101.

White, Jerry, ed. (2003). *Canadian Journal of Irish Studies* 29 (2) Fall 2003: University of Alberta.

Williams, Angie, Peter Garrett and Nikolas Coupland. (1999). "Dialect Recognition". In: Dennis R. Preston, ed. (1999). *Handbook of Perceptual Dialectology (Volume 1)*. Amsterdam/Philadelphia: John Benjamins. 345-58.

Williams, Frederick. (1983). "Some Research Notes on Dialect Attitudes and Stereotypes". In: Ralph Fasold, ed. (1983). *Variation in the Form and Use of Language: A Sociolinguistics Reader*. 354-69.

Williamson, Juanita V. and Virginia M. Burke, eds. (1971). *A Various Language. Perspectives on American Dialects*. New York: Holt, Rinehart and Winston, Inc.

Wolfram, Walt. (1991). *Dialects and American English*. New Jersey: Prentice Hall.

Wright, Joseph, ed. (1898-1905). *The English Dialect Dictionary*. London: Oxford University Press.

Internet Sources:

Hickey, Raymond. (2008) http://www.uni-due.de/DI/Who_Speaks_Irish.htm. (Retrieved December 3, 2008).

Camden, William. (1610). *Britannia*. http://www.philological.bham.ac.uk/cambrit/irelandeng 3.html#mores1. (Retrieved: December 3, 2008).

Knight, Dudley. (2000). "Standards". The Voice and Speech Review 1 (1). http://www.fitzmauricevoice.com/standardsarticle.htm. (Retrieved: September 27, 2004).

Regan, Mary. (2008). *The Irish Examiner*. 21 January. http://archives.tcm.ie/irishexaminer/2008/01/21/story53174.asp (Retrieved: January 23, 2008).

McGuckian, Etain. (2006). "Tom Cruise's Oirish Accent was Far and Away the Worst". http://www.unison.ie on January 26, 2006. (Retrieved: January 30, 2006).

http://aims.ie/interact_discuss_displaythread.asp?ForumName=Games%20Room&ForumTag =games&ParentID=71296 (Retrieved: July 1, 2008).

http://archive.thenorthernecho.co.uk/2003/2/20/103201.html (Retrieved: June 10, 2008).

http://deputy-dog.com/2007/08/21/13-of-the-worst-fake-accents-in-film/ (Retrieved: July 1, 2008).

http://foot.ie/forums/showthread.php?t=71228 (Retrieved: July 1, 2008).

http://www.belfasttelegraph.co.uk/entertainment/film-tv/news/article3515226.ece (Retrieved: July 1, 2008).

http://www.empireonline.com/reviews/ReviewsComplete.asp?FID=5521 (Retrieved: January 21, 2008).

http://www.evertype.com/standards/euro/open-letter.pdf. (Retrieved: March 30, 2008).

http://www.everything2.org/title/Irish%2520accent (Retrieved: July 1, 2008).

http://www.ew.com/ew/article/0,,310539,00.html (Retrieved: April 24, 2008).

http://www.filmboard.ie/section_481.php (Retrieved: June 19, 2005).

http://www.oed.com

http://www.rollingstone.com/reviews/dvd/5948995/review/5948996/far_and_away (Retrieved: July 1, 2008).

http://www.spiegel.de/international/germany/0,1518,523341,00.html (Retrieved: June 10, 2008).

http://www.timeout.com/film/reviews/77604/agnes_browne.html (Retrieved: January 21, 2008).

15 Appendix 1

Questionnaire for *A Survey of Irish English Usage*

Informants and classification

Test person   male   female
               under 18   18-30   over 30   over 40

Home county:

How do you find the following sentences (in casual speech among your friends)?

no problem   a bit strange   unacceptable   something else, short comment

(Informants could tick one of the above boxes depending on how they felt about the structure in question. In a very few cases, informants added a short comment. In the questionnaire the boxes were to be found after each sentence below.)

Test sentences used for the survey
- (1) What are youse up to?
- (2) What were yez up to?
- (3) Are ye going out tonight?
- (4) Amn't I leaving soon anyway?
- (5) Aren't I right after all?
- (6) Them shoes are too small for me.
- (7) She does be worrying about the children.
- (8) They bees up late at night.
- (9) I gets awful anxious about the kids at night.
- (10) His uncle does be a hard worker.
- (11) She's after spilling the milk.
- (12) She has the housework done.
- (13) I know her for five years now.
- (14) Some farmers has little or no cattle.
- (15) John and his wife plays bingo at the weekend.
- (16) There was two men on the road.
- (17) He was born here so he mustn't be Scottish.
- (18) I seen him yesterday.
- (19) They done all the work for us.
- (20) He went to Dublin for to buy a car.
- (21) They're finished the work now.
- (22) She allowed him drive the car.
- (23) They used make me stay in my room for hours.
- (24) Will he come see us in the spring?
- (25) He don't like me staying up late.
- (26) I suppose he have his work done now.
- (27) It looks as if it might rain, doesn't it?
- (28) Don't be teasing your brother.
- (29) Do you have any matches on you?

(30) She a teacher in the new college.
(31) He might could come after all.
(32) My hair needs washed.
(33) He's not interested in no cars.
(34) Everyone didn't want to hear them.
(35) I'll not wait any longer for him.
(36) She never rang yesterday evening.
(37) I know a farmer that rears sheep.
(38) I know a farmer rears sheep.
(39) I know a farmer what rears sheep.
(40) It's to Glasgow he's going tomorrow.
(41) We went for a walk and it raining.
(42) She asked him was he interested.
(43) He asked who had she spoken to.
(44) He likes the life in Galway.
(45) The fire went out on him.
(46) He crashed the car on her.
(47) She has to go to the hospital for a check-up.
(48) Their youngest son is good at the maths.
(49) I suppose the both of us should go.
(50) He paid twenty pound for the meal.
(51) Himself is not in today.
(52) The work is real difficult.
(53) Come here till I tell you.
(54) She's hard-working, like.
(55) He's gone to the races, but?
(56) Did you use to cycle to school?
(57) I shall have to leave soon.

16 Appendix 2

Sources of Internet Criticism Regarding Accents in Film

http://forum.dvdtalk.com/showthread.php?t=302392
(Retrieved: 24 June, 2008).

http://www.cinematical.com/2007/11/27/cinematical-seven-when-good-actors-do-bad-accents/
(Retrieved: 24 June, 2008).

http://www.empireonline.com/empireblog/Post.asp?id=167
(Retrieved: 24 June, 2008).

http://www.helium.com/items/179371-worst-movie-accents
(Retrieved: 24 June, 2008).

http://www.movies.msn.com/movies/2007fallmovieguide/badaccents/
(Retrieved: 24 June, 2008).

http://www.nervepop.com/nerveblog/screengrabblog.aspx?id=107e9985
(Retrieved: 24 June, 2008).

http://www.screenhead.com/reviews/the-best-and-worst-irish-accents-in-cinema/
(Retrieved: 24 June, 2008).

http://www.telegraph.co.uk/arts/main.jhtml?xml=/arts/2007/09/08/bfaccents108.xml
(Retrieved: 24 June, 2008).

17 Appendix 3

Table 1: Habitual aspect *do* + *verb (infinitive)*
Table 2: Habitual aspect *do* + *be* + *verb (-ing)*
Table 3: Habitual aspect *bees*
Table 4: The 'after' perfect
Table 5: The 'medial object' perfect
Table 6: The 'be' perfect
Table 7: The 'extended-now' perfect
Table 8: The 'indefinite anterior' perfect
Table 9: Simplified strong verb patterns *seen*
Table 10: Simplified strong verb patterns *done*
Table 11: Lack of *do* support
Table 12: *Will* for *shall*
Table 13: Overuse of progressive form
Table 14: Imperatives with progressive form
Table 15: Plural subject-verb concord
Table 16: Singular existential
Table 17: *For to* infinitives
Table 18: Plurals of quantity nouns
Table 19: Non-standard use of the definite article
Table 20: Unbound reflexive pronouns *himself/herself*
Table 21: Unbound reflexive pronouns *myself/yourself/yourselves*
Table 22: Adverb marking
Table 23: Negative concord
Table 24: Lack of negator contraction
Table 25: Word order in indirect questions *Yes/No* questions
Table 26: Word order in indirect questions *WH-* questions
Table 27: Responses to *Yes/No* questions
Table 28: Relative clause marking *that*
Table 29: Relative clause marking *zero relative*
Table 30: Relative clause marking *what*
Table 31: Focusing devices *'it' clefting*
Table 32: Focusing devices *topicalisation*
Table 33: 'Subordinating *and*'
Table 34: 'Subordinating *till*'
Table 35: Second person plural *ye*
Table 36: Second person plural *youse*
Table 37: Second person plural *yez/yiz*
Table 38: Negation of auxiliary *amn't*
Table 39: Demonstrative pronoun *them*
Table 40: Discourse marker *sure*
Table 41: Sentence-final markers *but*
Table 42: Sentence-final markers *what*
Table 43: Sentence-final markers *like*
Table 44: Sentence-final tags *so*
Table 45: Repetition for emphasis
Table 46: Discourse markers *come here/here*
Table 47: Religious expressions
Table 48: Discourse markers *arrah*
Table 49: Discourse markers *musha*
Table 50: Lexical features *ma/mam/mammy*

Table 51: Lexical features *da*
Table 52: Lexical features *lad/lads*
Table 53: Lexical features *your man/your woman/your one*
Table 54: Lexical features *one* for females
Table 55: Lexical features *guard/guards/gardai*
Table 56: Lexical features *eejit*
Table 57: Lexical features *oul/ould*
Table 58: Lexical features *shite*
Table 59: Lexical features *feck/feckin'/fecker*
Table 60: Lexical features *arse*
Table 61: Lexical features *bollocks/bollix*
Table 62: Lexical features *bleedin'*
Table 63: Lexical features *gobshite*
Table 64: Lexical features *shag/shaggin'/shagger*
Table 65: Lexical features *grand*
Table 66: Lexical features *bold*
Table 67: Lexical features *desperate*

	Film	Time	Speaker	Example of usage
1	The Informer			
2	The Quiet Man			
3	Darby O' Gill and the Little People			
4	Ryan's Daughter			
5	The Dead			
6	High Spirits			
7	My Left Foot			
8	The Field			
9	The Commitments			
10	Far and Away			
11	The Snapper			
12	Into the West			
13	A Man of No Importance	00:03:55	MMOB1960D	I **do love** this bit about the city.
14	Widows' Peak	00:08:45	FMOH1930M	People do pay me compliments on my roses. I **do tell** them there's not a ha'porth of skill involved.
15	Circle of Friends			
16	Last of the High Kings			
17	The Van			
18	Michael Collins			
19	Trojan Eddie			
20	The Matchmaker			
21	The Nephew			
22	This is my Father			
23	Waking Ned			
24	The General			
25	A Very Unlucky Leprechaun			

Table 1: Habitual aspect: *do* + *verb* (*infinitive*)

26	A Love Divided			
27	Agnes Browne	00:17:34	FCB1960D	But, Mammy, people do get worms in their poo. Mary Dowdall told me. And they **do be** mad long.
28	Angela's Ashes			
29	When the Sky Falls			
30	About Adam			
31	Ordinary Decent Criminal			
32	When Brendan Met Trudy			
33	Nora			
34	Rat	01:08:01	FC2000D	No, we have a little one at home and it **does be** lonely.
35	How Harry Became A Tree			
36	The Magdalene Sisters			
37	Mystics	00:05:56	ML2000D	So, just to be sure that you come back again next week, coz sometimes you **do be** lonely here ….
38	Evelyn			
39	Intermission			
40	Song for a Raggy Boy			
41	Veronica Guerin			
42	Goldfish Memory			
43	The Boys and Girl from County Clare			
44	Cowboys and Angels			
45	Adam and Paul	00:17:19	FO2000D	And she **does keep** that flat lovely and all.
46	Dead Meat			
47	Inside I'm Dancing			
48	Irish Jam			
49	The Wind that Shakes the Barley			
50	Garage			
				Total: 6/50

Table 1: Habitual aspect: *do* + *verb* (*infinitive*)

	Film	Time	Speaker	Example of usage
1	The Informer			
2	The Quiet Man			
3	Darby O' Gill and the Little People			
4	Ryan's Daughter			
5	The Dead			
6	High Spirits			
7	My Left Foot			
8	The Field			
9	The Commitments			
10	Far and Away			
11	The Snapper			
12	Into the West			
13	A Man of No Importance			
14	Widows' Peak			
15	Circle of Friends			
16	Last of the High Kings			
17	The Van			
18	Michael Collins			
19	Trojan Eddie			
20	The Matchmaker			
21	The Nephew			
22	This is my Father			
23	Waking Ned			
24	The General			
25	A Very Unlucky Leprechaun			

Table 2: Habitual aspect: *do* + *be* + *verb* (*-ing*)

26	A Love Divided			
27	Agnes Browne			
28	Angela's Ashes			
29	When the Sky Falls			
30	About Adam			
31	Ordinary Decent Criminal			
32	When Brendan Met Trudy			
33	Nora			
34	Rat			
35	How Harry Became A Tree			
36	The Magdalene Sisters			
37	Mystics			
38	Evelyn			
39	Intermission			
40	Song for a Raggy Boy			
41	Veronica Guerin			
42	Goldfish Memory			
43	The Boys and Girl from County Clare			
44	Cowboys and Angels			
45	Adam and Paul			
46	Dead Meat	00:41:28	FF2000LM	They **do be** peepin' from the gorse bushes.
47	Inside I'm Dancing			
48	Irish Jam			
49	The Wind that Shakes the Barley			
50	Garage			
	Total: 1/50			

Table 2: Habitual aspect: *do* + *be* + *verb* (*-ing*)

Film	Time	Speaker	Example of usage
1 The Informer			
2 The Quiet Man			
3 Darby O' Gill and the Little People			
4 Ryan's Daughter			
5 The Dead			
6 High Spirits			
7 My Left Foot			
8 The Field			
9 The Commitments			
10 Far and Away			
11 The Snapper			
12 Into the West			
13 A Man of No Importance			
14 Widows' Peak			
15 Circle of Friends			
16 Last of the High Kings			
17 The Van			
18 Michael Collins			
19 Trojan Eddie			
20 The Matchmaker			
21 The Nephew			
22 This is my Father			
23 Waking Ned			
24 The General			
25 A Very Unlucky Leprechaun			

Table 3: Habitual aspect: *bees*

26	A Love Divided		
27	Agnes Browne		
28	Angela's Ashes		
29	When the Sky Falls		
30	About Adam		
31	Ordinary Decent Criminal		
32	When Brendan Met Trudy		
33	Nora		
34	Rat		
35	How Harry Became A Tree		
36	The Magdalene Sisters		
37	Mystics		
38	Evelyn		
39	Intermission		
40	Song for a Raggy Boy		
41	Veronica Guerin		
42	Goldfish Memory		
43	The Boys and Girl from County Clare		
44	Cowboys and Angels		
45	Adam and Paul		
46	Dead Meat	00:42:16	MC2000LM	You'd wonder what **bees** scraping through their heads.
47	Inside I'm Dancing		
48	Irish Jam		
49	The Wind that Shakes the Barley		
50	Garage		
		Total: 1/50	

Table 3: Habitual aspect: *bees*

	Film	Time	Speaker	Example of usage
1	The Informer	01:12:50	MBK1920D	I'm certain about the time. It was just about half six. **I was after passing** …
2	The Quiet Man			
3	Darby O' Gill and the Little People	00:13:17	MMB1800D	Someone's **after poaching** rabbits.
4	Ryan's Daughter	01:01:13	MFR1920W	He'll be **after catching** a few flounders.
5	The Dead			
6	High Spirits			
7	My Left Foot	00:50:46	FNM1970D	I'm just **after telling** you I don't smoke.
8	The Field			
9	The Commitments	01:04:25	ML1990D	Yo, Elvis, me man, look what your daddy's **after doin'** to my trumpet. And who's gonna pay to get her cleaned?
10	Far and Away			
11	The Snapper	00:36:11	MDa1990D	Pat says his da **is after running away** from home.
12	Into the West			
13	A Man of No Importance			
14	Widows' Peak			
15	Circle of Friends	00:05:20	MSW1950D	I'm just **after telling** your father, Benny, "You won't be letting go of her. She won't be led astray in the big city like some".
16	Last of the High Kings			
17	The Van	00:25:08	MB1990D	The more I look at it, the more I think **we're after getting** a bargain.
18	Michael Collins			
19	Trojan Eddie	00:27:39	FM1990M	Such a night as **I'm after puttin'** in with her here!
20	The Matchmaker			
21	The Nephew	00:34:01	MT1990C	I left that fella fencin' this mornin'; when I went back he **was after shaggin' off** on me.
22	This is my Father	00:38:53	FW1930M	By the power of God, I'm **after putting** a curse on you that will go down through the ages.
23	Waking Ned			
24	The General	01:53:57	Mga1990D	Fuck, Jesus, Martin! You're **after smashin'** me fuckin' kneecap.
25	A Very Unlucky Leprechaun			

Table 4: The 'after' perfect

26	A Love Divided			
27	Agnes Browne	00:20:38	FSV1960D	Fresh? Sure, it's **after pinchin'** me on the arse twice already.
28	Angela's Ashes			
29	When the Sky Falls			
30	About Adam	00:31:33	FLF2000D	McCormack is only **after saying** to me that....
31	Ordinary Decent Criminal	00:56:28	MA1990D	I bet the guards are sitting there thinking "What the fuck **are we after lettin'** ourselves in for?"
32	When Brendan Met Trudy	01:05:05	FT2000C	He's **after designing** his own place somewhere.
33	Nora	00:43:04	FN1900G	I am so sorry, and **I'm after waking** the baby up as well.
34	Rat	00:04:22	FLG2000D	Ah, look, you're **after putting** me off.
35	How Harry Became A Tree	00:48:53	MH1920WW	That George O'Flaherty **is after seducing** my daughter-in-law.
36	The Magdalene Sisters			
37	Mystics	00:10:07	ML2000D	**I'm after getting** a tip for a horse at Leopardstown.
38	Evelyn			
39	Intermission	01:21:25	ML2000D	Look what you're **after making** me do!
40	Song for a Raggy Boy			
41	Veronica Guerin			
42	Goldfish Memory			
43	The Boys and Girl from County Clare			
44	Cowboys and Angels			
45	Adam and Paul	00:01:48	MA2000D	Some fucker's **after gluing** me to this thing.
46	Dead Meat	00:38:37	MC2000LM	Where are ye **after coming** out of?
47	Inside I'm Dancing			
48	Irish Jam			
49	The Wind that Shakes the Barley	00:58:37	MOIC1920C	Teddy O' Donovan's **after takin'** Mister Sweeney off us. He's taken him out the front door of the court.
50	Garage			
				Total: 24/50

Table 4: The 'after' perfect

	Film	Time	Speaker	Example of usage
1	The Informer	01:08:43	MG1920D	I **had** a drop **taken** before I came here and I didn't know what I was sayin', but now I remember.
2	The Quiet Man			
3	Darby O' Gill and the Little People			
4	Ryan's Daughter			
5	The Dead			
6	High Spirits			
7	My Left Foot	01:16:30	FMB1950D	You **have** me heart **broken**, Christy Brown.
8	The Field			
9	The Commitments			
10	Far and Away			
11	The Snapper			
12	Into the West			
13	A Man of No Importance	00:08:10	FL1960D	Art **has** your head **put astray**. And mine as well.
14	Widows' Peak	00:49:36	FMOH1930M	And she's you **fooled** as well.
15	Circle of Friends			
16	Last of the High Kings			
17	The Van			
18	Michael Collins			
19	Trojan Eddie	00:30:58	FB1990M	No, I've me money **saved** and all. We could have a great time out there, sure.
20	The Matchmaker			
21	The Nephew	00:47:22	MT1990C	Because she was far too young for him and he **had** her **mesmerised**.
22	This is my Father			
23	Waking Ned			
24	The General			
25	A Very Unlucky Leprechaun			

Table 5: The 'medial object' perfect

26	A Love Divided			
27	Agnes Browne	00:48:42	MT2196OD	I **have** four crates of lemonade bottles **collected**. You can have them; that's **ten** bob.
28	Angela's Ashes			
29	When the Sky Falls			
30	About Adam			
31	Ordinary Decent Criminal			
32	When Brendan Met Trudy			
33	Nora	00:57:42	MSJ1900D	No, I **have** the mind **made up** and it's not working out with all of us on top of each other like this.
34	Rat	01:10:49	FC2000D	You **have** us **destroyed** now.
35	How Harry Became A Tree			
36	The Magdalene Sisters			
37	Mystics			
38	Evelyn			
39	Intermission			
40	Song for a Raggy Boy			
41	Veronica Guerin			
42	Goldfish Memory			
43	The Boys and Girl from County Clare			
44	Cowboys and Angels			
45	Adam and Paul	00:45:22	FJ2000D	Well it's amazing you **haven't** anything **robbed** or fuckin' **broken**.
46	Dead Meat			
47	Inside I'm Dancing			
48	Irish Jam			
49	The Wind that Shakes the Barley			
50	Garage			
				Total: 10/50

Table 5: The 'medial object' perfect

	Film	Time	Speaker	Example of Usage
1	The Informer			
2	The Quiet Man			
3	Darby O' Gill and the Little People			
4	Ryan's Daughter			
5	The Dead			
6	High Spirits			
7	My Left Foot			
8	The Field			
9	The Commitments	01:26:56	MJR1990D	And why **aren't youse changed**?
10	Far and Away			
11	The Snapper			
12	Into the West			
13	A Man of No Importance			
14	Widows' Peak			
15	Circle of Friends			
16	Last of the High Kings			
17	The Van	00:17:52	MW1990D	Shite. Where **are they gone**?
18	Michael Collins			
19	Trojan Eddie			
20	The Matchmaker			
21	The Nephew			
22	This is my Father			
23	Waking Ned			
24	The General			
25	A Very Unlucky Leprechaun			

Table 6: The 'be' perfect

26	A Love Divided	01:22:31	MS1950WX	The whole place **is gone** mad. I've never seen anything like it.
27	Agnes Browne	00:21:06	FCB1960D	Mammy, **is** Daddy **gone** to Heaven forever?
28	Angela's Ashes	01:00:36	MF1940L	[...] a man who drinks the money for a new baby **is gone** beyond the beyonds.
29	When the Sky Falls			
30	About Adam			
31	Ordinary Decent Criminal			
32	When Brendan Met Trudy			
33	Nora			
34	Rat			
35	How Harry Became A Tree			
36	The Magdalene Sisters			
37	Mystics	01:06:34	MMic2000D	We're **finished** with these ones.
38	Evelyn			
39	Intermission			
40	Song for a Raggy Boy			
41	Veronica Guerin			
42	Goldfish Memory			
43	The Boys and Girl from County Clare			
44	Cowboys and Angels			
45	Adam and Paul	01:12:47	FJ2000D	It's **gone cold** now, **isn't** it?
46	Dead Meat			
47	Inside I'm Dancing			
48	Irish Jam			
49	The Wind that Shakes the Barley			
50	Garage			
				Total: 7/50

Table 6: The 'be' perfect

	Film	Time	Speaker	Example of usage
1	The Informer			
2	The Quiet Man			
3	Darby O' Gill and the Little People	00:45:31	FK1800W	But **he's a lonely man since me mother died**.
4	Ryan's Daughter	01:23:20	MFR1920K	Well, **they're not mourning long**.
5	The Dead	00:07:32	FL1900D	Oh, no, sir. **I'm done schooling this year and more**.
6	High Spirits			
7	My Left Foot	00:09:15	MTB1950D	It's all right. **I'm up! I'm up! I'm up! I'm up ages!**
8	The Field			
9	The Commitments	00:30:42	MDuf1990D	**Everything's shite since Roy Orbison died**.
10	Far and Away			
11	The Snapper			
12	Into the West	00:51:15	MTT1990M	**He's not the same since the wife died**.
13	A Man of No Importance			
14	Widows' Peak	01:10:11	FDC1930M	Such a stranger **you are these two weeks**.
15	Circle of Friends	00:16:22	MFR1950D	**How long is it since your last confession?**
16	Last of the High Kings			
17	The Van			
18	Michael Collins			
19	Trojan Eddie			
20	The Matchmaker			
21	The Nephew	00:45:24	MFr1990C	And **how long is it since your last confession?**
22	This is my Father	01:39:40	FMM1930M	If it's nothin' serious, **why are you here twice in two days?**
23	Waking Ned	01:06:14	MM2000W	Oh, God, no. **They're all down since the storm**.
24	The General	01:34:05	MMC1990D	**Is she minding them on her own since the missus died?**
25	A Very Unlucky Leprechaun			

Table 7: The extended-now perfect

#	Title	Time	Code	Quote
26	A Love Divided			
27	Agnes Browne	00:03:04	FM1960D	I know him years, love. Never seen him look so bad. Dead. Definitely dead.
28	Angela's Ashes			
29	When the Sky Falls	00:46:06	MSgt1990D	I'm too long in this game to be made a fool of by this scum.
30	About Adam	00:29:56	FLF2000D	Since when are you smoking?
31	Ordinary Decent Criminal	00:19:51	MML1990D	No, he's out a couple of years.
32	When Brendan Met Trudy			
33	Nora	00:46:43	FN1900G	He's only born. He hasn't had a chance to look like anyone yet.
34	Rat			
35	How Harry Became A Tree			
36	The Magdalene Sisters			
37	Mystics	00:49:02	MD2000D	Well, it's a while since we've had a visit from Foley and the guards.
38	Evelyn			
39	Intermission	00:48:26	FOW2000D	I'm coming here for long enough not to need these lies.
40	Song for a Raggy Boy			
41	Veronica Guerin			
42	Goldfish Memory			
43	The Boys and Girl from County Clare	01:12:04	FM1960CI	Sure, you hardly know him more than a day.
44	Cowboys and Angels			
45	Adam and Paul			
46	Dead Meat			
47	Inside I'm Dancing			
48	Irish Jam			
49	The Wind that Shakes the Barley	00:52:10	MD1920C	I know Chris Reilly since he was a child.
50	Garage	00:48:55	MJ2000M	Pauline all right since?
				Total: 22/50

Table 7: The 'extended-now' perfect

	Film	Time	Speaker	Example of Usage
1	The Informer	00:37:22	MDG1920D	I never heard that.
2	The Quiet Man	01:29:36	FMK1930W	Did you ever see such a…why, it looks like it could fly!
3	Darby O' Gill and the Little People	00:39:18	MDOG1800K	Did you ever hear the like of it?
4	Ryan's Daughter	01:25:20	MTR1920W	You met my daughter, then?
5	The Dead	00:16:22	FMM1900D	Oh, the most beautiful big fish you ever saw.
6	High Spirits			
7	My Left Foot	01:18:20	MMB1950D	Sure, I was never able to take it easy.
8	The Field	00:53:39	MBMC1950W	I never harmed the woman in my life.
9	The Commitments	00:45:08	MFR1990D	Did you talk to the committee? [I have, yes, and they've agreed in principle]
10	Far and Away	00:07:09	MJD1890W	We thought you died, Da.
11	The Snapper			
12	Into the West	01:01:08	FK1990M	Them two boys never forgot the tricks of the Travellers.
13	A Man of No Importance	00:55:41	MFR1960W	[We've done the minutes] Oh, yes. So we did.
14	Widows' Peak	01:30:14	FMOH1930M	Such an aggravating young woman I never met.
15	Circle of Friends	00:59:10	MJF1950D	I never knew such a good girl to her parents.
16	Last of the High Kings	00:56:33	MF1970D	Since when were you a smoker?
17	The Van	00:08:24	ML1990D	I never heard of him.
18	Michael Collins	00:03:25	MMC1910C	The game is over Harry. We lost again.
19	Trojan Eddie	00:58:44	MG1990M	Jaysus, I'm terrible sorry about this, John. Disgraced the family, she did. And as for that other fella…he's dead.
20	The Matchmaker	00:15:22	MDer2000W	The mammy just died.
21	The Nephew	01:01:35	FA1990C	Chad, you're the same person you ever were.
22	This is my Father	00:50:00	FF1930M	I saw it five times.
23	Waking Ned	00:38:43	MB2000W	Oh, Maurice, you're a bad boy. I told you time and time again not to be playing with matches.
24	The General			
25	A Very Unlucky Leprechaun	00:15:26	FFC1990D	And you can have your own pigeon loft like you always wanted.

Table 8: The 'indefinite anterior' perfect

26	A Love Divided			
27	Agnes Browne	00:36:00	FM1960D	I didn't go to him yet.
28	Angela's Ashes	01:39:48	MOF1950L	I never heard of a sin like that, Father.
29	When the Sky Falls	00:42:35	ME1990D	And since when did one of your foot soldiers decide to become adamant?
30	About Adam	00:16:56	FL2000D	He's the best fella I ever went out with.
31	Ordinary Decent Criminal	01:05:41	FCL1990D	You really think they'll ever let you get away, Michael, **after all you did**?
32	When Brendan Met Trudy	00:35:35	FT2000C	Return of the Clammy Feet. **Did you ever see** that one, Brendan?
33	Nora	01:37:52	FN1900G	A bigger bollocks **never put** an arm through a coat.
34	Rat	00:18:20	MF2000D	I never heard of Matt Flynn.
35	How Harry Became A Tree	00:45:48	MH1920WW	If I wasn't in there, sure, you wouldn't have got your eyesight back.
36	The Magdalene Sisters	00:17:16	FSB1960D	Did no one ever tell you that it's bad manners to interrupt?
37	Mystics	00:32:53	MD2000D	That's the most money we ever had.
38	Evelyn	00:05:08	MG1950D	We never died of winter yet.
39	Intermission	01:37:58	FN2000D	Oh, no, I saw this one.
40	Song for a Raggy Boy	00:13:58	MMF1930	Did you ever read a book you didn't rob?
41	Veronica Guerin	00:25:42	MJT1990D	For a few hundred grand, **you murdered** all of us.
42	Goldfish Memory			
43	The Boys and Girl from County Clare	01:20:21	MM1960CI	I never heard you soundin' better. Did you know that?
44	Cowboys and Angels	00:01:09	MS2000L	Have you ever felt that life was passing you by? **Did you ever feel** like there was something missing?
45	Adam and Paul	00:56:24	MP2000D	I think you took a wrong turn. That last turn, if you **took** that, you'd be at the flats.
46	Dead Meat			
47	Inside I'm Dancing	01:28:02	MROS2000D	I never liked you.
48	Irish Jam	00:04:00	MFR2000W	Since when were you a **pacifist**?
49	The Wind that Shakes the Barley	00:51:10	MN1920C	He cost us three lives already.
50	Garage	00:33:38	MD2000M	Did you always work here, Josie?
				Total: 44/50

Table 8: The 'indefinite anterior' perfect

	Film	Time	Speaker	Example of usage
1	The Informer	00:16:51	FMMP1920D	You're sure nobody **seen** you?
2	The Quiet Man			
3	Darby O' Gill and the Little People			
4	Ryan's Daughter	00:15:38	MFR1920W	I just **seen** your Rosy loafing about the beach again.
5	The Dead			
6	High Spirits			
7	My Left Foot			
8	The Field			
9	The Commitments	00:27:01	MO1990D	I just **seen** Imelda Quirke's arse comin' down a ladder!
10	Far and Away			
11	The Snapper	00:41:00	FRW21990D	Yer woman hit her. You **seen** it yourself.
12	Into the West	00:19:20	FOW1990D	It's in there. I **seen** it meself. Look!
13	A Man of No Importance			
14	Widows' Peak			
15	Circle of Friends			
16	Last of the High Kings			
17	The Van	00:14:45	ML1990D	Has to be here. I **seen** it landing.
18	Michael Collins			
19	Trojan Eddie			
20	The Matchmaker			
21	The Nephew			
22	This is my Father			
23	Waking Ned			
24	The General	01:55:30	MMC1990D	Where's Tina? I **seen** her talking to a copper yesterday.
25	A Very Unlucky Leprechaun			

Table 9: Simplified strong verb patterns: *seen*

26	A Love Divided			
27	Agnes Browne	00:48:18	MMB1960D	I **seen** her looking at a frock in Clery's - it's dear though.
28	Angela's Ashes	00:41:36	MMM1930L	I **seen** it three times already.
29	When the Sky Falls			
30	About Adam			
31	Ordinary Decent Criminal			
32	When Brendan Met Trudy			
33	Nora			
34	Rat	01:01:56	MP2000D	The doctor only **seen** a rat, Conchita.
35	How Harry Became A Tree			
36	The Magdalene Sisters			
37	Mystics			
38	Evelyn			
39	Intermission			
40	Song for a Raggy Boy			
41	Veronica Guerin			
42	Goldfish Memory			
43	The Boys and Girl from County Clare			
44	Cowboys and Angels			
45	Adam and Paul	00:12:13	FO2000D	That's coz she probably **seen** it on the telly or somethin'
46	Dead Meat			
47	Inside I'm Dancing			
48	Irish Jam			
49	The Wind that Shakes the Barley			
50	Garage	00:30:25	MSui2000M	I **seen** him humpin' her out the back window, but I'd no shoes or pants on, so I couldn't get to them quick enough.
	Total: 12/50			

Table 9: Simplified strong verb patterns: *seen*

	Film	Time	Speaker	Example of usage
1	The Informer	01:21:52	MG1920D	I **done** it for you. That's what I couldn't tell to Gallagher.
2	The Quiet Man			
3	Darby O' Gill and the Little People	00:17:35	MDOG1800K	That was a grand bit of work you **done**, so it was, aye.
4	Ryan's Daughter			
5	The Dead			
6	High Spirits			
7	My Left Foot			
8	The Field			
9	The Commitments			
10	Far and Away			
11	The Snapper	00:49:34	FWIP1990D	He **done** it deliberately.
12	Into the West			
13	A Man of No Importance			
14	Widows' Peak			
15	Circle of Friends			
16	Last of the High Kings			
17	The Van	01:02:44	MYG1990D	Did you see what he **done**?
18	Michael Collins			
19	Trojan Eddie	01:23:55	MR1990M	I know I **done** some quare things on you in me time [...], but there was things I didn't do on you too, ya know?
20	The Matchmaker			
21	The Nephew			
22	This is my Father			
23	Waking Ned			
24	The General	01:42:48	MMC1990D	I condemn him for what he **done**, Mrs Duggan.
25	A Very Unlucky Leprechaun			

Table 10: Simplified strong verb patterns: *done*

#	Title	Time	Code	Quote
26	A Love Divided			
27	Agnes Browne	00:38:33	FM1960D	Do ya know what they **done** to me? They shaved me.
28	Angela's Ashes			
29	When the Sky Falls	00:05:34	MS1990D	Drugs **done** that to Dublin, Mrs Hamilton.
30	About Adam			
31	Ordinary Decent Criminal			
32	When Brendan Met Trudy			
33	Nora			
34	Rat			
35	How Harry Became A Tree			
36	The Magdalene Sisters			
37	Mystics			
38	Evelyn			
39	Intermission			
40	Song for a Raggy Boy			
41	Veronica Guerin	00:35:28	MCF1990D	I bet you any money the Monk **done** that.
42	Goldfish Memory			
43	The Boys and Girl from County Clare			
44	Cowboys and Angels			
45	Adam and Paul			
46	Dead Meat			
47	Inside I'm Dancing			
48	Irish Jam			
49	The Wind that Shakes the Barley			
50	Garage	00:31:30	MSul2000M	The kids would never forgive me, if they knew I **done** that.
	Total: 10/50			

Table 10: Simplified strong verb patterns: *done*

	Film	Time	Speaker	Example of usage
1	The Informer	00:05:59	FK1920D	**Have you** the price of a flop on you?
2	The Quiet Man	00:24:18	MRW1930W	What right **has he** to land that he's never worked?
3	Darby O' Gill and the Little People	00:11:46	MFR1800K	Now, if I had a horse, which **I haven't**, I'd go for it myself, which I won't.
4	Ryan's Daughter	00:09:51	MFR1920W	**Have you** nothing to do?
5	The Dead	00:27:47	FG1900D	What row **had you** with Molly Ivors?
6	High Spirits			
7	My Left Foot	01:27:58	MCB1950D	What **have you** for dessert, Mam? Mam, what **have you** for dessert?
8	The Field	00:27:43	MBMC1950W	**Have you** no word of Irish from that school of yours?
9	The Commitments			
10	Far and Away	00:07:56	MMD1890W	You have all kinds of oddities clattering around in your brain. So **had I** when I was as young as you.
11	The Snapper	01:20:24	FJ1990D	**Have we** the money to pay for this?
12	Into the West	01:09:21	FK1990M	What **have we** in the end? Only each other.
13	A Man of No Importance			
14	Widows' Peak	00:51:11	MMC1930M	**Has it** to do with the past?
15	Circle of Friends	01:04:11	FNM1950D	But **he hasn't** a chance to be bad. Benny, we don't let him out of our sight.
16	Last of the High Kings			
17	The Van			
18	Michael Collins	00:08:29	MMC1910C	Sure, **haven't I** a civil war to run?
19	Trojan Eddie			
20	The Matchmaker	01:26:54	MDer2000W	**Have we** a deal?
21	The Nephew	00:02:56	MP1990C	**Have you** any letters?
22	This is my Father	01:28:23	MPo1930M	**Have you** family there?
23	Waking Ned			
24	The General	00:18:47	MIK1990D	I'm a poor fella. **I haven't** much. Debts up to here. But I can sleep at night.
25	A Very Unlucky Leprechaun			

Table 11: Lack of do support

26	A Love Divided	00:24:31	FS1950WX	Have you a desk for this one, Anna?
27	Agnes Browne	00:41:05	FM1960D	[I have good news as well] Have you?
28	Angela's Ashes			
29	When the Sky Falls			
30	About Adam	00:52:13	MA2000D	Has she her own phone or is it a payphone in the hall?
31	Ordinary Decent Criminal	00:54:27	MML1990D	Of course, you've no mountains in Holland, sure ya haven't.
32	When Brendan Met Trudy			
33	Nora	00:27:00	MJ1900D	I haven't a penny until I get an advance from Berlitz.
34	Rat	01:01:45	FC2000D	Haven't we Father Geraldo as a witness?
35	How Harry Became A Tree	00:17:29	MH1920WW	Haven't you enough money already to build this boil on the arse of Skillet?
36	The Magdalene Sisters			
37	Mystics	00:18:13	MD2000D	Look, oul son, we never died o' winter yet. Haven't you all the names?
38	Evelyn			
39	Intermission	00:37:47	MG2000D	Has nobody any balls these days?
40	Song for a Raggy Boy			
41	Veronica Guerin			
42	Goldfish Memory			
43	The Boys and Girl from County Clare	00:46:00	FA1960CI	Has this to do with my father?
44	Cowboys and Angels	00:30:38	MJ2000L	I hadn't the balls to do anything different.
45	Adam and Paul	00:02:48	MP2000D	What money have you?
46	Dead Meat			
47	Inside I'm Dancing	01:30:14	FS2000D	Yet because he's seen as a rebel, you believe he hasn't the responsibility to live independently.
48	Irish Jam			
49	The Wind that Shakes the Barley	01:01:22	MDa1920D	Have you a blade of grass to your name?
50	Garage	00:24:26	MD2000M	Have you coffee?
				Total: 32/50

Table 11: Lack of *do* support

	Film	Time	Speaker	Example of usage
1	The Informer			
2	The Quiet Man	00:51:18	MMF1930W	Father, **will** I tell him?
3	Darby O' Gill and the Little People	01:13:30	MDOG1800K	**Will** I get you a drink, sir?
4	Ryan's Daughter	00:19:53	MS1920W	**Will** I get it out?
5	The Dead			
6	High Spirits			
7	My Left Foot			
8	The Field	00:19:01	MBMC1950W	**Will** I take care of this, Sergeant, or **will** you?
9	The Commitments			
10	Far and Away			
11	The Snapper	00:14:48	FJ1990D	Let's get pissed, **will** we?
12	Into the West	00:23:49	MAG1990D	**Will** I shoot him, Inspector Bolger?
13	A Man of No Importance			
14	Widows' Peak	01:01:35	FCG11930M	Lads, **will** we go to the ould dance? Ah, say we **will**.
15	Circle of Friends	00:15:25	MSW1950D	**Will** we go to Sullivan's for a bag of chips?
16	Last of the High Kings			
17	The Van	00:39:17	FD1990D	**Will** I open it?
18	Michael Collins			
19	Trojan Eddie			
20	The Matchmaker			
21	The Nephew			
22	This is my Father	00:50:28	MK1930M	**Will** we take a look at this ocean, **will** we?
23	Waking Ned	01:07:00	FA2000W	**Will** I make you a nice cup of tea, Lizzy?
24	The General	00:03:57	MYMC1960D	**Will** I bring them back then, **will** I?
25	A Very Unlucky Leprechaun			

Table 12: *Will* for *shall*

26	A Love Divided			
27	Agnes Browne	00:21:49	FAB1960D	Hey Marion, **will** I wear me tiara?
28	Angela's Ashes			
29	When the Sky Falls	00:03:35	MS1990D	**Will** we go for a spin, Mrs. Hamilton?
30	About Adam	00:27:00	FLa2000D	**Will** I? I will, yes, I'll buy it.
31	Ordinary Decent Criminal	00:54:49	MML1990D	Fantastic, we might stop for a pint, **will** we? Are you thirsty?
32	When Brendan Met Trudy			
33	Nora			
34	Rat	01:11:55	FC2000D	Where **will** we send him, Felix?
35	How Harry Became A Tree			
36	The Magdalene Sisters			
37	Mystics			
38	Evelyn			
39	Intermission			
40	Song for a Raggy Boy			
41	Veronica Guerin			
42	Goldfish Memory			
43	The Boys and Girl from County Clare	00:51:12	FMS1960Cl	**Will** I put the kettle on?
44	Cowboys and Angels			
45	Adam and Paul	00:11:19	MP2000D	**Will** I kick the ball, will I?
46	Dead Meat			
47	Inside I'm Dancing	00:51:51	FS2000D	**Will** I do your hair?
48	Irish Jam			
49	The Wind that Shakes the Barley			
50	Garage	00:03:53	MJ2000M	**Will** I move them oils then?
				Total: 21/50

Table 12: *Will* for *shall*

	Film	Time	Speaker	Example of usage
1	The Informer	01:26:09	FK1920D	Wouldn't you **be wanting** mercy then?And won't you **be giving** it to me now?
2	The Quiet Man	00:03:25	MMC1930W	Ah, Inisfree, I'd **be bringing** you there myself, only I've got to drive the train.
3	Darby O' Gill and the Little People	00:26:51	MKB1800K	And if you're the fine daycent man that I think you are, you'll **be showin'** me a little bit of gratitude.
4	Ryan's Daughter	01:02:30	MFR1920W	What more **are you wanting** now?
5	The Dead	00:15:05	FMM1900D	I got my own little room there on the ground floor, overlooking the garden. So I don't need to **be climbing** the stairs.
6	High Spirits			
7	My Left Foot			
8	The Field	01:18:58	FMC1950W	**Are you hearing** me?
9	The Commitments	00:09:43	FMR1990D	Listen, Jimmy, I've more things to **be doin'** than ironin' shirts for you every day o' the week.
10	Far and Away	02:07:36	MJD1890W	But you could be sure I won't **be dying** twice.
11	The Snapper	00:28:38	ML1990D	You wouldn't want to **be getting** worked up about it.
12	Into the West			
13	A Man of No Importance			
14	Widows' Peak			
15	Circle of Friends	00:01:15	FBH1950D	The whole village was there when my two best friends and I **were having** our confirmation day.
16	Last of the High Kings			
17	The Van			
18	Michael Collins			
19	Trojan Eddie	00:21:30	FK1990M	I don't like the road, meself. When I get married, **I'm wanting** to live in a house.
20	The Matchmaker	01:05:34	MOH2000W	I wouldn't go there. Sure, all the men would **be trying** to ride me.
21	The Nephew	00:15:22	MT1990C	Hold on to that. You'll **be needin'** it.
22	This is my Father	01:28:58	FW1930M	You're in no position to **be setting** terms with me.
23	Waking Ned	00:40:23	MJ2000W	I do. I do. Is it Ned **you're wanting**?
24	The General			
25	A Very Unlucky Leprechaun			

Table 13: Overuse of progressive form

26	A Love Divided		
27	Agnes Browne	00:01:13	FSS1960D	Your husband. **Is he working**?
28	Angela's Ashes	00:08:21	MIRA1930D	We can't **be handing** out money to every man who wanders in here saying he did his bit for Ireland.
29	When the Sky Falls	00:48:29	FSH1990D	**I'm wondering**, Mickey, what it is that makes you nervous?
30	About Adam	01:15:49	FM2000D	I didn't want to **be sticking** my oar in.
31	Ordinary Decent Criminal	01:14:09	FCL1990D	You can't **be fallin'** out with friends like him.
32	When Brendan Met Trudy			
33	Nora	00:55:27	FN1900G	It fills in the time. I can't always **be sitting** in that room.
34	Rat	00:49:14	FC2000D	We don't want to **be letting** ourselves down.
35	How Harry Became A Tree	00:11:31	MH1920WW	I told him you were too old to **be getting** married.
36	The Magdalene Sisters	01:10:20	MIC1960D	**Are you wanting** a lift or what?
37	Mystics	00:22:27	MLA2000D	Let me guess. You'll **be wanting** to know where I stashed the diamonds?
38	Evelyn	01:24:40	FB1950D	You'll **be needing** a housekeeper now, won't you?
39	Intermission	00:53:04	MO2000D	She may be older, but she's sporty, and **I'm taking** exception to that description.
40	Song for a Raggy Boy			
41	Veronica Guerin			
42	Goldfish Memory			
43	The Boys and Girl from County Clare			
44	Cowboys and Angels			
45	Adam and Paul	00:29:33	MK2000D	Hey, if we were black, you wouldn't **be throwin'** us out.
46	Dead Meat			
47	Inside I'm Dancing	00:39:20	MROS2000D	For some strange reason he thought it was demeaning to **be seeking** out the gobshite that flushed him at birth.
48	Irish Jam	00:15:15	MBMN2000W	I'll volunteer. After all, it's a real man she'll **be needing**, O'Malley.
49	The Wind that Shakes the Barley			
50	Garage			
				Total: 30/50

Table 13: Overuse of progressive form

	Film	Time	Speaker	Example of usage
1	The Informer	00:51:24	MSP1920D	Now, now! **Don't be disrespecting** me friend Gypo or you'll have me to settle with.
2	The Quiet Man	01:21:52	FMK1930W	**Don't be shaming** me, please, in front of your friends.
3	Darby O' Gill and the Little People			
4	Ryan's Daughter			
5	The Dead			
6	High Spirits			
7	My Left Foot	00:17:36	MMB1950D	Ah, **don't be gettin'** notions into your head, woman. The child's a cripple. Face facts.
8	The Field			
9	The Commitments	01:16:38	MJR1990D	It's all right. **Don't be worryin'**.
10	Far and Away	00:12:20	MDD1980W	And **don't you be pretending** you know what Captain Moonlight means, coz you don't.
11	The Snapper			
12	Into the West			
13	A Man of No Importance	00:02:19	MRo1960D	**Don't be dirtying** that nice clean bus now with your elbows.
14	Widows' Peak			
15	Circle of Friends			
16	Last of the High Kings			
17	The Van			
18	Michael Collins			
19	Trojan Eddie	01:05:22	MGG1990M	I tell ya, **don't be annoying** my fuckin' head anymore, now.
20	The Matchmaker	01:05:14	MOH2000W	**Don't be talking** about the shit bucket in front of strangers.
21	The Nephew	00:34:02	FB1990C	**Don't be rubbin'** your head at me.
22	This is my Father	00:48:27	MMM1930M	Get into bed, boy, and **don't be doing** any work!
23	Waking Ned	01:16:52	MLM2000D	**Don't be spending** all your money in one go.
24	The General			
25	A Very Unlucky Leprechaun	00:05:03	MPM1990W	Ah, **don't be criticising** the garden before you've seen it.

Table 14: Imperatives with progressive form

#	Title	Time	Code	Text
26	A Love Divided	00:36:27	MB1950WX	Now, **don't** you **be worrying** about lawyers.
27	Agnes Browne	00:18:52	FAB1960D	Now, go on. Off. **Don't be annoying** me.
28	Angela's Ashes	01:25:31	FA1930L	Go and see a man, but **don't be coming** home here drunk, singing your stupid songs.
29	When the Sky Falls			
30	About Adam			
31	Ordinary Decent Criminal			
32	When Brendan Met Trudy			
33	Nora	01:16:48	MJJ1900D	Well, then **don't be coming** around here complaining about it.
34	Rat	00:03:37	MH2000D	Ah, **don't be starting**, Conchita. I'm suffering.
34	How Harry Became A Tree	00:09:08	MG1920W	Ah, Jesus, Da. **Don't be annoying** him.
36	The Magdalene Sisters	01:21:12	FSB1960D	**Don't be giving** me any trouble.
37	Mystics			
38	Evelyn			
39	Intermission			
40	Song for a Raggy Boy			
41	Veronica Guerin			
42	Goldfish Memory			
43	The Boys and Girl from County Clare			
44	Cowboys and Angels			
45	Adam and Paul	01:10:06	FO2000D	Ma, **don't be buyin'** them nothin'.
46	Dead Meat			
47	Inside I'm Dancing			
48	Irish Jam	00:03:33	FM2000W	**Don't** you **be getting** your hands dirty. You're a man of the cloth.
49	The Wind that Shakes the Barley	01:32:53	MR1920C	**Don't be rushing** ahead.
50	Garage			
				Total: 22/50

Table 14: Imperatives with progressive form

	Film	Time	Speaker	Example of usage
1	The Informer	01:02:19	MSP1920D	I know who they are! **Them is** the Republican Army. The Republican Army!
2	The Quiet Man	00:13:10	MMF1930W	Maybe you don't know it's a privilege reserved for courting couples, and then only when **the banns has been read**.
3	Darby O' Gill and the Little People			
4	Ryan's Daughter	00:50:58	MS1920W	**Them fellas has** an elegant sense of humour.
5	The Dead	00:07:46	FL1900D	**The men that is** now is only all palaver and what they can get out of ya.
6	High Spirits	00:19:00	MDMC1980W	Julia, **where's me bandages**?
7	My Left Foot	01:17:11	FMB1950D	**Christy and me is** buildin' a room.
8	The Field	00:21:37	MBMC1950W	**Our souls is** buried down there.
9	The Commitments	01:42:34	MD1990D	**My chords was** good.
10	Far and Away			
11	The Snapper	00:22:45	FSC1990D	[How are your movements?] Not bad, **how's yours**?
12	Into the West	00:10:23	MPR1990D	You listen to me. **Them boys is** stayin' here.
13	A Man of No Importance	01:02:00	FRW1960D	**Country girls is** very lax in their morals. It's all that loose straw lying around.
14	Widows' Peak	00:20:12	FDC1930M	No, wait. **Where is my manners**?
15	Circle of Friends			
16	Last of the High Kings	00:36:05	MF1970D	So, **who's Erin and Rainbow**?
17	The Van			
18	Michael Collins	00:08:42	MMC1910C	**How's the men**?
19	Trojan Eddie			
20	The Matchmaker			
21	The Nephew	00:50:26	MP1990C	**What's "beats"**?
22	This is my Father			
23	Waking Ned	00:15:47	FM2000W	**The pigs is** all you know.
24	The General	00:51:17	MJ1990D	Half **them fuckers is** havin' you on, Martin. They're lyin' bastards.
25	A Very Unlucky Leprechaun			

Table 15: Plural subject-verb concord

#	Title	Time	Code	Quote
26	A Love Divided	00:31:39	FS1950WX	Who's good girls? Who's my good girls?
27	Agnes Browne	00:26:31	FAB1960D	Now where's **these** fuckin' monkeys?
28	Angela's Ashes	01:45:55	MPat1950L	Some things **is** most peculiar, Frankie.
29	When the Sky Falls	00:05:55	MS1990D	Drugs **is** for jungle bunnies and wankers generally, not me.
30	About Adam			
31	Ordinary Decent Criminal	01:27:23	MML1990D	Is that tins of corned beef you have there?
32	When Brendan Met Trudy			
33	Nora			
34	Rat	00:44:18	FC2000D	The wild ones **is** jealous of the beauty of the budgie.
35	How Harry Became A Tree	00:37:11	MF1920WW	Tell you the truth, **your cabbages is** the furthest thing from my mind.
36	The Magdalene Sisters			
37	Mystics	00:59:27	ML2000D	If Foley makes a capture, **who's going to be the star witnesses** for the prosecution?
38	Evelyn	00:03:56	MM1950D	Daddy, **where's the carriages**?
39	Intermission	01:11:37	MBD2000D	Me and her's based on more than that.
40	Song for a Raggy Boy			
41	Veronica Guerin	00:40:49	MCM1990D	But **drugs is** just not his scene, Veronica.
42	Goldfish Memory			
43	The Boys and Girl from County Clare			
44	Cowboys and Angels			
45	Adam and Paul			
46	Dead Meat			
47	Inside I'm Dancing			
48	Irish Jam			
49	The Wind that Shakes the Barley	00:41:31	MDa1920D	**Where's the other fellas**?
50	Garage	01:07:00	MSgt2000M	Things **is** bad enough without making them worse.
				Total: 30/50

Table 15: Plural subject-verb concord

	Film	Time	Speaker	Example of usage
1	The Informer	00:20:55	MBM1920D	**There's a lot of things** I'd like, if I could afford it.
2	The Quiet Man	00:02:50	MB1930W	**There's many** knows Knockanore that **doesn't** know Inisfree.
3	Darby O' Gill and the Little People			
4	Ryan's Daughter			
5	The Dead			
6	High Spirits	01:07:03	MDMC1980W	Mr Plunkett, I think **there's some people** want to have a word with you.
7	My Left Foot	00:07:48	FNH1950D	**There's been some complications.**
8	The Field			
9	The Commitments	00:09:47	FMR1990D	**There's more people** in the house, ya know.
10	Far and Away			
11	The Snapper	00:06:28	MDC1990D	**There's your pals** over there.
12	Into the West	01:19:46	MOR1990D	**There's no pictures,** Tito.
13	A Man of No Importance			
14	Widows' Peak	00:25:32	MGDC1930M	**There's too many little jobs** to be done around the house.
15	Circle of Friends	01:28:32	MSW1950D	I would have married you, Benny. And **there's not many** would say that, fat cow that you are.
16	Last of the High Kings	00:14:10	MMG1970D	Frankie, **there's special instructions** for feeding that fish.
17	The Van	00:21:47	MW1990D	**There's three more** behind there.
18	Michael Collins			
19	Trojan Eddie	01:23:55	MR1990M	I know I done some quare things on you in me time [...], but **there was things** I didn't do on you too, ya know?
20	The Matchmaker	00:36:33	MOH2000W	Now, **there's no McGlorys** in this area.
21	The Nephew			
22	This is my Father			
23	Waking Ned	00:34:02	MPat2000W	I'm looking to settle down, Brendy, and **there's plenty of girls** who would jump at the chance.
24	The General	01:12:27	MIK1990D	Do you think **there's buyers** out there for that kind of stuff?
25	A Very Unlucky Leprechaun			

Table 16: Singular existential

26	A Love Divided	00:14:43	MFR1950WX	Well, Sheila, **there's no minds** to be made up.
27	Agnes Browne	00:18:35	MMB1960D	**There's hairs** growin' on it.
28	Angela's Ashes			
29	When the Sky Falls			
30	About Adam			
31	Ordinary Decent Criminal	01:08:47	MH1990D	**There's no lord mayors** beggin' to do you favours anymore.
32	When Brendan Met Trudy			
33	Nora	00:52:20	MSJ1900D	Anyway, **there's my classes** to consider, Jim. We need that money.
34	Rat	01:17:27	MP2000D	Marietta, **there's times** in life when you have to be cruel to be...
35	How Harry Became A Tree			
36	The Magdalene Sisters	01:32:53	FK1960D	Well, **there was an awful lot of us** and we were poor.
37	Mystics	01:15:18	MS2000D	I didn't know **there was flights** to Spain from Malin.
38	Evelyn	00:28:11	MDES1950D	**There's no bloody laws** in this country that's gonna keep my daughter away from me.
39	Intermission	00:39:05	MH2000D	**There's a couple of jars** smashed in that lane, John. Clean them up, will ya!
40	Song for a Raggy Boy	01:06:37	MDB1930	**There's eight** more of us at home. They won't even fuckin' notice.
41	Veronica Guerin	00:09:07	FVG1990D	I hear **there's some dodgy scangers** about.
42	Goldfish Memory	00:28:37	FR2000D	Ah, no, sure, we'll wait. **There's only another ten minutes**.
43	The Boys and Girl from County Clare	00:52:36	MJJ1960CI	**There's no hairs** growing on your knees, that's for sure.
44	Cowboys and Angels	00:12:05	MV2000L	**There's only so many sleepless nights** and weeks of unwashed dishes you can take.
45	Adam and Paul	00:49:50	MA2000D	**There's loads** of "sixteens".
46	Dead Meat	00:20:40	MD2000LM	Well, **there was reports** of an infection spreading around here.
47	Inside I'm Dancing			
48	Irish Jam			
49	The Wind that Shakes the Barley	00:18:14	FS1920C	**There was about eight or nine** of them.
50	Garage	01:11:02	MJ2000M	**There's spots** in it.
				Total: 33/50

Table 16: Singular existential

#	Film	Time	Speaker	Example of usage
1	The Informer			
2	The Quiet Man	00:03:42	FBW1930W	Me sister's third young one is living at Inisfree, and she'd be only too happy **for to** show you the road.
3	Darby O' Gill and the Little People	01:12:47	MIP1800K	[What for?] **For to** hold the gold.
4	Ryan's Daughter			
5	The Dead			
6	High Spirits			
7	My Left Foot			
8	The Field			
9	The Commitments			
10	Far and Away			
11	The Snapper			
12	Into the West			
13	A Man of No Importance			
14	Widows' Peak			
15	Circle of Friends			
16	Last of the High Kings			
17	The Van			
18	Michael Collins			
19	Trojan Eddie			
20	The Matchmaker			
21	The Nephew			
22	This is my Father			
23	Waking Ned			
24	The General			
25	A Very Unlucky Leprechaun			

Table 17. *For to* infinitives

26	A Love Divided				
27	Agnes Browne				
28	Angela's Ashes				
29	When the Sky Falls				
30	About Adam				
31	Ordinary Decent Criminal				
32	When Brendan Met Trudy				
33	Nora				
34	Rat				
35	How Harry Became A Tree				
36	The Magdalene Sisters				
37	Mystics				
38	Evelyn				
39	Intermission				
40	Song for a Raggy Boy				
41	Veronica Guerin				
42	Goldfish Memory				
43	The Boys and Girl from County Clare				
44	Cowboys and Angels				
45	Adam and Paul				
46	Dead Meat				
47	Inside I'm Dancing				
48	Irish Jam				
49	The Wind that Shakes the Barley				
50	Garage				
	Total: 2/50				

Table 17: *For to* infinitives

	Film	Time	Speaker	Example of usage
1	The Informer			
2	The Quiet Man			
3	Darby O' Gill and the Little People			
4	Ryan's Daughter	00:22:32	FR1920W	Then, I'll just take some potatoes. Five **pound**.
5	The Dead			
6	High Spirits			
7	My Left Foot	01:28:54	FMB1950D	Eight hundred **pound**.
8	The Field	00:49:27	MBMC1950W	A hundred **pound**. Close the sale.
9	The Commitments			
10	Far and Away			
11	The Snapper			
12	Into the West	00:35:35	MCT1990D	I'll give you twenty **pound** or I'll give you a kick up the arse!
13	A Man of No Importance			
14	Widows' Peak			
15	Circle of Friends	00:11:59	MNM1950D	Forty-two **pound** a month?
16	Last of the High Kings			
17	The Van	01:07:44	MBT1990D	It's twenty-seven **pound** please.
18	Michael Collins			
19	Trojan Eddie			
20	The Matchmaker			
21	The Nephew	00:20:16	MT1990C	He won a thousand **pound** on a scratch card last Thursday. The shock killed him.
22	This is my Father			
23	Waking Ned			
24	The General	01:04:27	MMC1990D	Pays blackies about two **pound** a week to dig them out for him.
25	A Very Unlucky Leprechaun			

Table 18: Plurals of quantity nouns

#	Title	Time	Code	Quote
26	A Love Divided			
27	Agnes Browne	00:48:38	MMB1960D	That's four **pound** ten bob.
28	Angela's Ashes			
29	When the Sky Falls			
30	About Adam			
31	Ordinary Decent Criminal			
32	When Brendan Met Trudy			
33	Nora			
34	Rat	00:37:32	MF2000D	I was shown a fine range of white buck rats at two **pound** a head.
35	How Harry Became A Tree			
36	The Magdalene Sisters			
37	Mystics	00:41:32	MCh2000D	That'll be sixty-four **pound** in old money.
38	Evelyn			
39	Intermission			
40	Song for a Raggy Boy			
41	Veronica Guerin			
42	Goldfish Memory			
43	The Boys and Girl from County Clare			
44	Cowboys and Angels			
45	Adam and Paul			
46	Dead Meat	00:42:34	MC2000LM	I've known him now twenty **year**. T'wasn't an aisy thing to do either.
47	Inside I'm Dancing			
48	Irish Jam			
49	The Wind that Shakes the Barley			
50	Garage			
				Total: 12/50

Table 18: Plurals of quantity nouns

	Film	Time	Speaker	Example of usage
1	The Informer	00:42:11	MSP1920D	With me own two eyes, I saw Gypo knock **the** Scrapper Maloney flyin' across the road like a man divin' off the bull wall.
2	The Quiet Man	01:33:55	FMK1930W	Father, could I … could I tell you in **the** Irish?
3	Darby O' Gill and the Little People	00:15:57	MDOG1800K	Mr McBride is coming to resort with us for a fortnight, so throw a couple of extra spuds in the pot for **the** supper…
4	Ryan's Daughter	00:18:34	MS1920W	She'd been at **the** teaching for over 50 years.
5	The Dead	00:09:42	FG1900D	And forcing Eve to eat **the** stirabout, the poor child, she simply hates the sight of it.
6	High Spirits			
7	My Left Foot	00:33:47	FMB1950D	This is a fine time of **the** night to be comin' in.
8	The Field	00:26:19	MBMC1950W	I'll have to talk to **the** wife about it.
9	The Commitments	00:43:11	FB1990D	Me da's in **the** fuckin' hospital.
10	Far and Away			
11	The Snapper	01:11:56	MDC1990D	It's for **the** wife.
12	Into the West	00:07:00	MMM1990D	Sir, we'd like **the** address, sir, to claim for **the** assistance.
13	A Man of No Importance	00:11:53	MMC1960D	Ah, Alfred. Something for **the** sister? Sweetbread, it's good for a delicate tum.
14	Widows' Peak	01:04:38	MMC1930M	A few more steps and a good night's sleep and you'll be as right as **the** rain.
15	Circle of Friends	00:16:35	FBH1950D	They want me to go to **the** university but they want me to stay their whole child as well.
16	Last of the High Kings	00:05:02	FMG1970D	Look at the state of ya - eyes falling out of your head with **the** drink.
17	The Van	00:16:52	MG1990C	There's eighteen of us in **the** one area phone book.
18	Michael Collins	00:28:04	MTDC1910D	So, it's **the** drink, is it?
19	Trojan Eddie	00:17:56	MGG1990M	It'd want to be better than that heap of shite you gave me for **the** breakfast. The fuckin' dogs wouldn't eat it.
20	The Matchmaker	00:15:22	MDer2000W	**The** mammy just died.
21	The Nephew	00:09:29	MP1990C	Get up there beside **the** uncle.
22	This is my Father	00:16:43	FT2000M	**The** Widow Flynn.
23	Waking Ned	00:12:14	MD2000W	Morning, boys, how's **the** heads?
24	The General	01:34:08	Mga1990D	[Is she minding them on her own since **the** missus died?] Ah, it won't do her no harm. **The** granny comes in during the day.
25	A Very Unlucky Leprechaun	00:24:35	ML1990W	Ach, you don't know **the** half of it.

Table 19: Non-standard use of the definite article

26	A Love Divided		
27	Agnes Browne	00:29:47	FM1960D	It was like getting 10 early numbers in **the** bingo.
28	Angela's Ashes	00:27:50	FA1930L	Only I'm worried about sleeping in beds that people might have died in. Especially if they died of **the** consumption.
29	When the Sky Falls	01:18:02	MSgt1990D	Tattoo was arrested in **the** hospital for the murder of Jamie Thornton.
30	About Adam	01:19:01	FA2000D	Mind **the** hair!
31	Ordinary Decent Criminal	00:32:19	MML1990D	Tony'll take you to **the** hospital.
32	When Brendan Met Trudy	01:13:10	FT2000C	There's no point in **the** both of us getting caught.
33	Nora	00:57:42	MSJ1900D	No, I have **the** mind made up and it's not working out with all of us on top of each other like this.
34	Rat	00:00:17	MH2000D	Seventy years ago, me grandfather, Hubert Flynn I, set out from his home in **the** County Wexford …
35	How Harry Became A Tree	00:42:19	FOW1920WW	And how's **the** bould Gus, and the new daughter-in-law?
36	The Magdalene Sisters	01:31:48	FK1960D	They wanted to send me to **the** hospital, but I said no, I wanted to stay here with the sisters and my friends.
37	Mystics	00:08:16	MD2000D	**The** mammy was dead chuffed though. That's what matters.
38	Evelyn	00:37:15	FB1950D	No, Desmond. I said you have to give up **the** drink.
39	Intermission			
40	Song for a Raggy Boy			
41	Veronica Guerin	00:16:45	MJT1990D	You're way off the mark, Veronica. Martin Cahill isn't into **the** drugs. Neither am I.
42	Goldfish Memory			
43	The Boys and Girl from County Clare	01:14:12	MJJ1960CI	Well, when you've got **the** music, you've got friends for life. It's why I'm never alone.
44	Cowboys and Angels	00:34:57	MDD2000D	Watch where you put **the** hands. Fingerprints.
45	Adam and Paul	00:09:39	MG2000D	Just in here, like. Bit of **the** oul skills training with the young fella.
46	Dead Meat	00:44:20	MC2000LM	I took half **the** jaw off her there with the hurl.
47	Inside I'm Dancing			
48	Irish Jam			
49	The Wind that Shakes the Barley	00:31:05	MD1920C	Look at me. Just keep **the** head back.
50	Garage	01:01:41	MJ2000M	Ye're **the** busy men this hour on a Sunday mornin'.
				Total: 42/50

Table 19: Non-standard use of the definite article

	Film	Time	Speaker	Example of usage
1	The Informer			
2	The Quiet Man	00:02:04	MFL1930W	A fine soft day in the spring it was, when the train pulled into Castletown, 3 hours late as usual, and **himself** got off.
3	Darby O' Gill and the Little People			
4	Ryan's Daughter	00:40:57	MTR1920W	And **himself**, no doubt at this very moment walking the broad streets of Dublin.
5	The Dead			
6	High Spirits			
7	My Left Foot			
8	The Field			
9	The Commitments			
10	Far and Away			
11	The Snapper	00:50:11	MSgt1990D	That depends on **himself**.
12	Into the West			
13	A Man of No Importance			
14	Widows' Peak	00:03:59	MMC1930M	The woman is incomplete until **himself** is six feet under.
15	Circle of Friends			
16	Last of the High Kings			
17	The Van			
18	Michael Collins			
19	Trojan Eddie	00:18:36	MD1990M	**Himself** and Raymie knocked off a post office one time, ya know.
20	The Matchmaker			
21	The Nephew	00:28:36	FB1990C	It might have been **herself** singing.
22	This is my Father			
23	Waking Ned	01:16:57	MLM2000D	Look after **himself**, now.
24	The General	01:12:01	MCM1990D	Just **himself**.
25	A Very Unlucky Leprechaun			

Table 20: Unbound reflexive pronouns: *himself/herself*

26	A Love Divided			
27	Agnes Browne			
28	Angela's Ashes			
29	When the Sky Falls			
30	About Adam			
31	Ordinary Decent Criminal			
32	When Brendan Met Trudy			
33	Nora			
34	Rat	00:27:25	FD2000D	Oh, God. Is that **himself**?
35	How Harry Became A Tree			
36	The Magdalene Sisters			
37	Mystics	00:20:30	MD2000D	Could I just say that, like, it's entirely up to **himself**.
38	Evelyn			
39	Intermission			
40	Song for a Raggy Boy			
41	Veronica Guerin			
42	Goldfish Memory			
43	The Boys and Girl from County Clare			
44	Cowboys and Angels			
45	Adam and Paul			
46	Dead Meat			
47	Inside I'm Dancing			
48	Irish Jam	00:17:15	MFR2000W	Will ya raise your glasses to **himself**, our new landlord, the long-lost son of Ireland.
49	The Wind that Shakes the Barley	01:34:39	MD1920C	Maybe a drop for **himself**.
50	Garage			
				Total: 12/50

Table 20: Unbound reflexive pronouns: *himself/herself*

	Film	Time	Speaker	Example of usage
1	The Informer			
2	The Quiet Man	00:08:00	MFL1930W	Now, then, here comes **myself**, that's me there. […], that tall, saintly-looking man, Peter Lonergan, Parish Priest.
3	Darby O' Gill and the Little People	00:45:40	MMB1800D	Well, what about **yourself**? Don't you get lonely?
4	Ryan's Daughter	00:40:43	MP1920W	That's **yourself**, landlord.
5	The Dead			
6	High Spirits			
7	My Left Foot			
8	The Field			
9	The Commitments			
10	Far and Away	00:16:55	MDC1890W	Then you're a man of business like **myself**.
11	The Snapper	00:32:46	MGB1990D	That's for **yourself**, Sharon.
12	Into the West			
13	A Man of No Importance			
14	Widows' Peak	01:28:49	MRM1930M	Good woman **yourself**!
15	Circle of Friends			
16	Last of the High Kings	01:01:28	MJF1970D	I know there have been various allegations made about **meself**. And I know the names of all the alligators.
17	The Van			
18	Michael Collins	01:26:46	MMC1910C	Are **we** discussing the treaty or discussing **myself**?
19	Trojan Eddie	00:30:16	FB1990M	Your mother and **meself** were droolin' over these the other day.
20	The Matchmaker	00:10:00	MSea2000W	I'd say I'd be five minutes, I'd say. And then the dog and then **yourself**.
21	The Nephew	00:45:21	MFr1990C	Is that **yourself**, Chad?
22	This is my Father	01:36:17	MK1930M	What was between Fiona and **myself** is over now.
23	Waking Ned	00:09:37	FA2000W	Well, hello, Mrs Kennedy! Don't be afraid, it's only **myself** I've been baking.
24	The General	01:55:03	MMC1990D	Only **meself** and Noel knew where they were.
25	A Very Unlucky Leprechaun	00:39:27	MPM1990W	Miss Molly, is it **yourself**?

Table 21: Unbound reflexives: *myself/yourself/yourselves*

26	A Love Divided		
27	Agnes Browne	00:21:33	FM1960D	And what about **yourself**?
28	Angela's Ashes		
29	When the Sky Falls	00:05:45	MS1990D	Anyone with a drop of the buccaneering spirit, like **meself**,...
30	About Adam	01:08:53	MH2000D	Why don't you hit the sack, and **meself** and Adam will just go downstairs and have a couple of small ones [...]?
31	Ordinary Decent Criminal		
32	When Brendan Met Trudy		
33	Nora	00:16:43	FN1900G	You want me to talk to noone but **yourself**.
34	Rat	00:22:56	MP2000D	I couldn't help hearing the little discussion **yourself** and Marietta were having.
35	How Harry Became A Tree	00:37:09	MH1920WW	**Meself** and Gus are picking ours today and taking them to market Saturday.
36	The Magdalene Sisters	01:25:12	FSB1960D	Now, like **yourselves**, I don't know what the film is, but I know it's not a Western.
37	Mystics	00:14:01	MD2000D	It'd be a real honour to reunite **yourself** and Big Mac across the great divide.
38	Evelyn		
39	Intermission	00:01:19	ML2000D	Take **meself**, for example. You ever see me before?
40	Song for a Raggy Boy		
41	Veronica Guerin	00:43:39	MJG1990D	**Myself** and Geraldine are planning to make this the largest and finest equestrian centre in all of Ireland.
42	Goldfish Memory	00:43:02	FI2000D	I'm grand and **yourself**?
43	The Boys and Girl from County Clare		
44	Cowboys and Angels	00:47:11	MBU2000L	We're always on the lookout for young professionals like **yourself**.
45	Adam and Paul		
46	Dead Meat	00:38:44	MD2000LM	Listen, I know **yourself**.
47	Inside I'm Dancing		
48	Irish Jam		
49	The Wind that Shakes the Barley	01:25:17	MR1920C	And maybe if I was a politician like **yourselves**, I could say whatever I want, but I'm not.
50	Garage		
				Total: 29/50

Table 21: Unbound reflexives: *myself/yourself/yourselves*

	Film	Time	Speaker	Example of usage
1	The Informer	00:10:10	MG1920D	Nothin', Frankie. You came up to me so **sudden**, like.
2	The Quiet Man			
3	Darby O' Gill and the Little People	00:26:11	MDOG1800W	And who makes the men tip their hats **respectful** to every swirl of dust?
4	Ryan's Daughter	01:23:30	MFR1920W	Does she think he killed himself **deliberate**?
5	The Dead			
6	High Spirits	01:07:31	ME1980W	He looks **terrible** angry too.
7	My Left Foot			
8	The Field			
9	The Commitments	00:16:40	MD1990D	[How did he take it?] Not too **bad**.
10	Far and Away			
11	The Snapper			
12	Into the West	01:05:42	MOR1990D	Come in **quick**.
13	A Man of No Importance	00:44:00	FA1960M	But I know you won't judge me too **harsh**.
14	Widows' Peak	01:13:53	FMOH1930M	You promised that no one in the town would ever mention it or think **bad** of me, that it would be looked after.
15	Circle of Friends	00:16:56	FBH1950D	I do love them, Father, but I'm finding it **awful** hard to honour them.
16	Last of the High Kings	00:45:25	MF1970D	It's spelled completely **different**.
17	The Van	00:29:38	MB1990D	I know that. I never said **different**.
18	Michael Collins			
19	Trojan Eddie	00:58:44	MG1990M	Jaysus, I'm **terrible** sorry about this John. Disgraced the family, she did. And as for that other fella…he's dead.
20	The Matchmaker	00:20:20	FLii2000W	And you have the right to a kick in the arse if you don't get out of here **quick**.
21	The Nephew	00:48:52	MPe1990W	I always tried to treat you **nice**.
22	This is my Father			
23	Waking Ned	00:31:23	MM2000W	The floor will need to be cleaned **proper** before we go.
24	The General	00:44:07	MMC1990D	Me and Noel have to go. Stay here. The bags'll be picked up later and hidden **safe**.
25	A Very Unlucky Leprechaun			

Table 22: Adverb marking

#	Title	Time	Code	Quote
26	A Love Divided			
27	Agnes Browne			
28	Angela's Ashes			
29	When the Sky Falls			
30	About Adam			
31	Ordinary Decent Criminal			
32	When Brendan Met Trudy	00:35:50	FT2000C	Brendan, come **quick**!
33	Nora	00:39:16	FN1900G	If someone hurt you, and I was there, I'd hurt them back so **bad**, I'm telling you.
34	Rat	00:27:48	FD2000D	Give him little delicacies, talk **soft** to him, bring him into bed in the mornings.
35	How Harry Became A Tree	00:03:08	MG1920W	One of them big fellas wouldn't cut down **easy**.
36	The Magdalene Sisters			
37	Mystics	00:04:43	MB2000D	I was **real** cut up when I heard the news.
38	Evelyn	01:04:17	FE1950D	I don't think it's fair that I should be treated **special** just because my daddy's gettin' famous.
39	Intermission			
40	Song for a Raggy Boy			
41	Veronica Guerin			
42	Goldfish Memory			
43	The Boys and Girl from County Clare			
44	Cowboys and Angels	00:28:46	MS2000L	You could start by not speaking **bad** about me to her
45	Adam and Paul	00:57:28	MA2000D	Some young fellas are after robbin' a car. **Near** fuckin killed us they did.
46	Dead Meat	00:37:18	FLG2000L	They hurt my dad real **bad**
47	Inside I'm Dancing	00:48:45	MROS2000D	You're doing really **good**.
48	Irish Jam	00:24:31	FM2000W	Are you alright granda? You're **awful** quiet.
49	The Wind that Shakes the Barley	00:49:47	FP21920C	It's an **awful** long walk.
50	Garage	00:30:25	MSul2000M	I seen him humpin' her out the back window but I'd no shoes or pants on so I couldn't get to them **quick** enough.
				Total: 29/50

Table 22: Adverb marking

	Film	Time	Speaker	Example of usage
1	The Informer			
2	The Quiet Man			
3	Darby O' Gill and the Little People	01:01:07	MDOG1800K	Ah, she **doesn't** want the gold **nor** the manor house **neither**.
4	Ryan's Daughter			
5	The Dead			
6	High Spirits			
7	My Left Foot			
8	The Field			
9	The Commitments	01:14:08	MJR1990D	And we **don't** need your poxy wheels **neither**.
10	Far and Away			
11	The Snapper			
12	Into the West			
13	A Man of No Importance			
14	Widows' Peak			
15	Circle of Friends			
16	Last of the High Kings			
17	The Van			
18	Michael Collins			
19	Trojan Eddie	00:34:38	MPMD1990M	Why London? I **don't** know **no one** over there.
20	The Matchmaker			
21	The Nephew			
22	This is my Father			
23	Waking Ned			
24	The General	01:23:51	Mga1990D	Look, we **can't** pull **no** strokes with them watchin'.
25	A Very Unlucky Leprechaun			

Table 23: Negative concord

#	Title	Time	Code	Quote
26	A Love Divided			
27	Agnes Browne	00:30:20	FM1960D	I **wasn't** sad or **nothing**. I just cried.
28	Angela's Ashes			
29	When the Sky Falls			
30	About Adam			
31	Ordinary Decent Criminal			
32	When Brendan Met Trudy			
33	Nora			
34	Rat	00:06:20	FM2000D	I'm **not** saying **no** more.
35	How Harry Became A Tree			
36	The Magdalene Sisters			
37	Mystics			
38	Evelyn			
39	Intermission			
40	Song for a Raggy Boy			
41	Veronica Guerin	00:43:15	MJT1990D	Don't know **nothing** about him.
42	Goldfish Memory			
43	The Boys and Girl from County Clare			
44	Cowboys and Angels			
45	Adam and Paul	00:25:46	MA2000D	I **wasn't** fuckin' doin' **nothin'**!
46	Dead Meat			
47	Inside I'm Dancing			
48	Irish Jam	00:28:37	MBMN2000W	I **don't** see **nothin'** of the sort.
49	The Wind that Shakes the Barley			
50	Garage	00:31:25	MSuI2000M	Say **nothin'** to **noone** you.
				Total: 10/50

Table 23: Negative concord

	Film	Time	Speaker	Example of usage
1	The Informer			
2	The Quiet Man			
3	Darby O' Gill and the Little People	00:03:50	MLF1800K	Oh, I'll not be stopping here long enough for that.
4	Ryan's Daughter	00:39:51	FMMC1920W	They'll not start without her.
5	The Dead			
6	High Spirits			
7	My Left Foot			
8	The Field	00:26:25	MBi1950W	You've not said a word to each other for twenty years, Bull.
9	The Commitments			
10	Far and Away			
11	The Snapper			
12	Into the West			
13	A Man of No Importance	00:11:11	MA1960D	She's not absolutely agreed, but I'm certain she'll do it.
14	Widows' Peak	01:14:25	FMOH1930M	And youse kept your word, I'll not deny it.
15	Circle of Friends			
16	Last of the High Kings			
17	The Van			
18	Michael Collins			
19	Trojan Eddie			
20	The Matchmaker			
21	The Nephew			
22	This is my Father	01:25:11	MK1930M	I'll not deny any statement she'll make.
23	Waking Ned	01:21:46	FM2000W	You'll not tell a soul now?
24	The General			
25	A Very Unlucky Leprechaun			

Table 24: Lack of negator contraction

26	A Love Divided	00:49:55	MT1950W	Thanks Andy, but **I'll not** stay where I'm not wanted.
27	Agnes Browne			
28	Angela's Ashes			
29	When the Sky Falls	01:34:36	MD1990D	**We'll not** bother shooting you in the leg then, shitface.
30	About Adam			
31	Ordinary Decent Criminal			
32	When Brendan Met Trudy			
33	Nora			
34	Rat			
35	How Harry Became A Tree	01:19:22	MG1920WW	**You'll not** put me in the ground, nor Eileen.
36	The Magdalene Sisters	00:38:42	FB1960D	**I've not** committed any crime.
37	Mystics			
38	Evelyn			
39	Intermission			
40	Song for a Raggy Boy	00:19:34	MBJ1930	**He'll not** disrupt an entire class again because he feels like it.
41	Veronica Guerin	00:29:47	MBM1990D	**You'll not** be so big the next time you meet me with a bally [balaclava] on.
42	Goldfish Memory			
43	The Boys and Girl from County Clare			
44	Cowboys and Angels			
45	Adam and Paul			
46	Dead Meat			
47	Inside I'm Dancing			
48	Irish Jam	00:53:49	MFR2000W	You know, Da, **I've not** seen Maureen this happy for years.
49	The Wind that Shakes the Barley			
50	Garage			
				Total: 14/50

Table 24: Lack of negator contraction

	Film	Time	Speaker	Example of usage
1	The Informer			
2	The Quiet Man			
3	Darby O' Gill and the Little People	01:10:16	FMS1800K	I wonder does she know?
4	Ryan's Daughter			
5	The Dead			
6	High Spirits			
7	My Left Foot	01:33:09	MCB1950D	I asked ya did ya love him, Mary?
8	The Field			
9	The Commitments			
10	Far and Away			
11	The Snapper	00:04:28	FKC1990D	He wants to know do you want to have an abortion?
12	Into the West			
13	A Man of No Importance			
14	Widows' Peak			
15	Circle of Friends			
16	Last of the High Kings			
17	The Van	01:07:29	FIP1990D	He wants to know do you want to taste it first?
18	Michael Collins			
19	Trojan Eddie			
20	The Matchmaker			
21	The Nephew			
22	This is my Father			
23	Waking Ned			
24	The General			
25	A Very Unlucky Leprechaun			

Table 25: Word order in indirect questions: Yes/No questions

#	Title	Time	Code	Quote
26	A Love Divided			
27	Agnes Browne			
28	Angela's Ashes	01:51:19	MN1990L	**I wonder should I go in.** I might get the consumption. And that'll be the end of me and I'll never get to America.
29	When the Sky Falls			
30	About Adam	01:03:52	FA2000D	**I wonder has he any taste** in clothes.
31	Ordinary Decent Criminal			
32	When Brendan Met Trudy			
33	Nora	01:02:29	FN1900G	Read out the part where **he asks is Giorgio really his son**.
34	Rat			
35	How Harry Became A Tree	00:37:14	MF1920WW	**I came up to ask you would you let Eileen stay** with us a bit longer? Margaret's not well; it's her first child.
36	The Magdalene Sisters			
37	Mystics			
38	Evelyn			
39	Intermission			
40	Song for a Raggy Boy			
41	Veronica Guerin			
42	Goldfish Memory			
43	The Boys and Girl from County Clare			
44	Cowboys and Angels			
45	Adam and Paul	00:20:43	MP2000D	**We were just waitin' to see is what's-his-name around**
46	Dead Meat			
47	Inside I'm Dancing			
48	Irish Jam			
49	The Wind that Shakes the Barley			
50	Garage	00:46:54	MBr2000M	Regina, run over there and **ask your mammy is she matchin' collar and cuffs**.
				Total: 10/50

Table 25: Word order in indirect questions: Yes/No questions

	Film	Time	Speaker	Example of usage
1	The Informer			
2	The Quiet Man			
3	Darby O' Gill and the Little People	00:34:10	MDOG1800K	You'll find out **who's the knowledgeable one**.
4	Ryan's Daughter	00:15:19	MFR1920W	I don't know **what's the matter** with the youngsters in this place.
5	The Dead			
6	High Spirits			
7	My Left Foot			
8	The Field			
9	The Commitments			
10	Far and Away	00:40:34	FSC1890W	May I ask **what are you doing** sitting at my table?
11	The Snapper	00:44:49	FCG1990D	Shirley, come here, listen, you know yer one who's preggers, **guess who's the da!** Mr Burgess!
12	Into the West			
13	A Man of No Importance	00:17:00	MFR1960W	Do ya think **will ye manage** it this time?
14	Widows' Peak			
15	Circle of Friends			
16	Last of the High Kings			
17	The Van			
18	Michael Collins	01:08:55	MED1910W	We'll see **who is the big fella**.
19	Trojan Eddie			
20	The Matchmaker			
21	The Nephew			
22	This is my Father			
23	Waking Ned			
24	The General	00:02:14	MI1990D	Inspector, **the press want to know why was there** no Gardaí presence.
25	A Very Unlucky Leprechaun			

Table 26: Word order in indirect questions: *WH-* questions

26	A Love Divided	
27	Agnes Browne	
28	Angela's Ashes	
29	When the Sky Falls	
30	About Adam	
31	Ordinary Decent Criminal	
32	When Brendan Met Trudy	
33	Nora	
34	Rat	
35	How Harry Became A Tree	
36	The Magdalene Sisters	
37	Mystics	
38	Evelyn	
39	Intermission	
40	Song for a Raggy Boy	
41	Veronica Guerin	
42	Goldfish Memory	
43	The Boys and Girl from County Clare	
44	Cowboys and Angels	
45	Adam and Paul	
46	Dead Meat	
47	Inside I'm Dancing	
48	Irish Jam	
49	The Wind that Shakes the Barley	
50	Garage	
	Total: 7/50	

Table 26: Word order in indirect questions: *WH-* questions

	Film	Time	Speaker	Example of usage
1	The Informer	00:34:31	MDG1920D	[Do you mean that?] **Indeed, I do**, Gypo.
2	The Quiet Man	00:50:00	FMK1930W	[Will you not be putting up your bonnet, Mary Kate?] **Indeed, I will not**.
3	Darby O' Gill and the Little People	00:46:30	FK1800K	[Are you wearing your holy medal?] **I am**.
4	Ryan's Daughter	00:31:13	MTR1920W	[Did you cut the wire?] **I did**
5	The Dead	00:11:54	MG1990D	[Is my mother here?] **She is**.
6	High Spirits			
7	My Left Foot	00:28:16	FNM1970D	[Is he ok?] **He's grand**.
8	The Field	00:20:11	MBi1950W	[Did you tell the tinkers about the donkey, Bird?] **I did not tell the tinkers**.
9	The Commitments	00:42:47	FMML1990D	[Is Bernie in?] **She is. Come on in**.
10	Far and Away			
11	The Snapper	00:55:06	FJ1990D	[Do they believe me?] **They do, yeah**. I think they do.
12	Into the West	00:37:00	MPR1990D	[Do you know where your boys are?] **No, I don't know where they are**, sir. I don't know.
13	A Man of No Importance	00:45:04	FA1960M	[The love that dare not speak its name. Do you know what that is?] **I don't**, Mr Byrne, to be honest.
14	Widows' Peak	00:36:00	FMF1930M	[Are you there, Mrs Fogarty?] **I am**.
15	Circle of Friends	00:22:04	MMF1950D	[You don't miss much do you, Dad?] **I do not**.
16	Last of the High Kings	00:23:17	MF1970D	[Do you give me your solemn word?] **I do**.
17	The Van	00:32:58	MB1990D	[Are you sure she's a painting student?] **She is, yeah**. In a college, Maggie says.
18	Michael Collins	00:48:23	FKK1910M	[Will you write?] **I will**.
19	Trojan Eddie	00:01:32	MD1990M	[Did I say a fiver?] **You did**.
20	The Matchmaker	00:14:45	MSea2000W	[Sean, will you help him?] **I will**.
21	The Nephew			
22	This is my Father	01:18:10	MK1930M	[Would you run away with me?] **I would**.
23	Waking Ned	00:06:16	MJ2000W	[Does Annie know?] **She does**.
24	The General	00:16:31	FWIB1990D	[Is this where you get the banker's drafts?] **Yes, it is indeed**.
25	A Very Unlucky Leprechaun	00:07:45	MPM1990W	[Is that it over there?] **Oh, that's it over there now**.

Table 27: Responses to Yes/No questions

#	Title	Time	Code	Quote
26	A Love Divided	00:02:50	MS1950WX	[Do you mean it?] **I mean it.**
27	Agnes Browne	00:21:19	FAB1960D	[Does that mean we won't be going to the zoo this year?] Ah, **no, it doesn't.** Sure, I'll take yiz.
28	Angela's Ashes	01:30:55	MOF1950L	[Is that you, Frankie?] **Tis,** Mrs Purcell.
29	When the Sky Falls	00:35:22	FSH1990D	[Do you know the Rave Club?] **I do.**
30	About Adam	00:36:49	MA2000D	[I know this sounds really silly, but, em, did I see you in Brown Thomas the other day?] **Yes. Yes, you did.** Laura.
31	Ordinary Decent Criminal	00:05:54	MB1990C	[Is that them? Is that the two sisters?] **That's them, all right.** boy
32	When Brendan Met Trudy	01:15:18	MG2000G	[You're from Galway, aren't you?] **I am.**
33	Nora			
34	Rat	00:25:57	FC2000D	[Is this himself?] **It is,** Mick.
35	How Harry Became A Tree	00:43:35	MH1920WW	[Can it not wait until morning?] **It can not.**
36	The Magdalene Sisters			
37	Mystics	00:30:35	FF2000D	[Were you at Mass?] **I was.** Of course I was.
38	Evelyn	00:01:49	FE1950D	[Evelyn, did Jesus have a big sister?] **No, Dermot, he didn't.** He wasn't as lucky as you.
39	Intermission	00:12:09	MSe2000D	[Have you not got a sign that says "Toilets for patrons use only"?] **I do.**
40	Song for a Raggy Boy	00:40:51	MMF1930	[Do you want to leave us, Mr Franklin?] **No, Father. I don't.**
41	Veronica Guerin	00:18:31	FFC1990D	[Are you Frances Cahill?] **I am**
42	Goldfish Memory	00:45:51	FK2000D	[Is that its real name?] **It is, yeah.**
43	The Boys and Girl from County Clare	00:26:57	MJ1960CI	[Jimmy? Jimmy's here?] **He is.** Yes, he is.
44	Cowboys and Angels	00:24:58	MS2000L	[You can skin up, can't you?] **Sure I can.**
45	Adam and Paul	00:17:06	FM2000D	[Was Janine there, Marian? This morning?] **She was.** Not that it's any of your business.
46	Dead Meat	01:01:17	MC2000LM	[Was she a nurse?] **She was.**
47	Inside I'm Dancing			
48	Irish Jam			
49	The Wind that Shakes the Barley	00:50:54	MD1920C	[Were they tortured?] **They were.**
50	Garage	00:03:02	MJ2000M	[We're set so?] **Indeed we are set.** We're set. We're ready for anything.
				Total: 43/50

Table 27: Responses to Yes/No questions

	Film	Time	Speaker	Example of usage
1	The Informer	00:37:20	MG1920D	She was in trouble. And wasn't Frankie the boyo that was named!
2	The Quiet Man	00:02:50	MB1930W	There's many knows Knockanore that doesn't know Inisfree.
3	Darby O' Gill and the Little People	01:27:53	MMB1800D	What kind of man are you at all that doesn't believe in the little people?
4	Ryan's Daughter	00:40:57	MTR1920W	Red Tim himself that 1,000 secret policemen have been hunting for these last five years.
5	The Dead	00:32:30	FAK1900D	I don't think it's very honourable of the Pope to throw the women out of the choirs that's been there for years…
6	High Spirits			
7	My Left Foot			
8	The Field	00:58:20	MBMC1950W	No collar, uniform or weapon will protect the man that stands in my way.
9	The Commitments	00:21:35	MMR1990D	Wait till you see the little bollix that's out the back askin' for ya.
10	Far and Away	00:30:00	MJD1890W	You're the bastard that burned my father's house.
11	The Snapper	01:16:35	FSC1990D	Excuse me, I'm the one that's pregnant.
12	Into the West	00:12:00	MGR1990D	Now. Oisin was the most handsome traveller that ever lived.
13	A Man of No Importance			
14	Widows' Peak	00:28:11	FMad1930M	I swear on the grave of my mother that's dead and gone…
15	Circle of Friends			
16	Last of the High Kings	00:37:23	MTD1970D	Dublin's the finest city in the world, bar none - all the writers and playwriters and novelists that come out of it.
17	The Van	00:19:57	ML1990D	They only want young ones and young fellas that'll take those wages and wear the fucking uniforms.
18	Michael Collins	00:10:51	MMC1910C	I'm the fucker that asked to meet Dev.
19	Trojan Eddie			
20	The Matchmaker			
21	The Nephew	00:20:10	MT1990C	Lucky Mick Millane. The most unfortunate man that ever lived.
22	This is my Father			
23	Waking Ned	00:12:53	FA2000W	I thought it would be you boys that would have the heads this morning, not me.
24	The General	01:29:32	MMC1990D	And I was the one that didn't stick needles in himself, huh?
25	A Very Unlucky Leprechaun	00:05:37	MPM1990W	It looks like a pest that I know ate it for his breakfast.

Table 28: Relative clause marking: *that*

26	A Love Divided	00:16:20	FS1950WX	It's Sean and me **that**'ll be deciding where she's going to school, not Fr Stafford.
27	Agnes Browne			
28	Angela's Ashes	01:47:40	FAA1930L	Get up and put the kettle on for your poor Uncle Pat **that** fell down the worse for drink.
29	When the Sky Falls			
30	About Adam	00:09:24	FL2000D	Wouldn't it be deadly though if it turns out to be me **that** has this great passion she's always goin on about?
31	Ordinary Decent Criminal	00:48:57	MN1990D	Obviously someone **that** likes a gag. Someone **that** likes a joke.
32	When Brendan Met Trudy			
33	Nora	01:27:08	FN1900G	Oh, doesn't it occur to you that I couldn't bear to see my life twisted and made strange to me **that**'s livin' it?
34	Rat	00:20:29	FC2000D	What way is that to talk to a walkin' saint **that** never had a bad thought in his life?
35	How Harry Became A Tree	00:58:25	FE1920WW	All you've done is fed gossip to them **that** should know better.
36	The Magdalene Sisters	00:32:44	MDB1960D	So they're all hookers and whores **that** work in there?
37	Mystics	01:18:19	ML2000D	That place is full of lonely oul Paddies **that**'d be only too glad to talk to their nearest and dearest.
38	Evelyn			
39	Intermission	01:18:44	MBD2000D	You're the one **that** loves her. You go back.
40	Song for a Raggy Boy	01:25:03	MMF1930	There are those here **that** will tell you that Liam Mercier died of an illness.
41	Veronica Guerin	00:53:43	MJT1990D	Relax, will ya? She's convinced it was Gerry Hutch **that** done it.
42	Goldfish Memory	00:17:53	ME2000D	Oh, your man **that** had the affair with that woman from the newspaper.
43	The Boys and Girl from County Clare	01:20:50	MJJ1960CI	I'd say it's him **that** needs the medicine.
44	Cowboys and Angels			
45	Adam and Paul			
46	Dead Meat			
47	Inside I'm Dancing	00:32:40	MROS2000D	... interfering, dried-up oul bitches **that** wouldn't know responsibility if it bit them on their fat arses.
48	Irish Jam	00:33:32	FBM2000W	Oh, it's Kathleen **that** likes him, is it?
49	The Wind that Shakes the Barley			
50	Garage	01:07:53	MSgt2000M	It wasn't him **that** complained.
				Total: 35/50

Table 28: Relative clause marking: *that*

	Film	Time	Speaker	Example of usage
1	The Informer	00:53:37	MSP1920D	And if there's anyone here **Ø thinks** he's a match with his fists, will he kindly step up.
2	The Quiet Man	00:22:05	MMF1930W	Well, he's a nice quiet peace-loving **man Ø come** home to Ireland to forget his troubles.
3	Darby O' Gill and the Little People	00:02:35	FMS1800K	There's not a **gorsoon Ø doesn't** want you, but who among them dare look at you with the grand house you live in?
4	Ryan's Daughter	00:26:30	MTR1920W	No, it was that wife of **his Ø knocked** all the spirit out of him.
5	The Dead			
6	High Spirits			
7	My Left Foot			
8	The Field			
9	The Commitments	01:27:21	MJR1990D	Someone's comin' in **tonight Ø could** make a big difference to us.
10	Far and Away			
11	The Snapper	00:28:56	MDC1990D	It was **Lester Ø told** me.
12	Into the West			
13	A Man of No Importance	00:10:35	FA1960M	Was that the **one Ø danced** for Herod and got the head of John the Baptist on a plate?
14	Widows' Peak			
15	Circle of Friends	01:01:40	MSW1950D	It isn't **everyone Ø can** grasp it right away.
16	Last of the High Kings			
17	The Van			
18	Michael Collins			
19	Trojan Eddie			
20	The Matchmaker	00:32:24	MDer2000W	There's a **fella Ø lives** on Inishmore, it's one of the Aran Islands, called O'Hara. He's full of stories and information.
21	The Nephew	00:34:18	MT1990C	There's another **fella Ø wants** watchin'.
22	This is my Father	00:15:30	MT2000M	Ah look, it's **Mammy Ø come** to inspect the guests.
23	Waking Ned			
24	The General	00:57:53	FFC1990D	How many other men do you **know Ø don't** drink or smoke or hang around with other women?
25	A Very Unlucky Leprechaun			

Table 29: Relative clause marking: *zero relative*

26	A Love Divided			
27	Agnes Browne			
28	Angela's Ashes	01:58:43	FMF1950L	There are people in the lunatic **asylum Ø can** read and write. Can you write a letter?
29	When the Sky Falls	01:14:55	FSH1990D	It was **O' Fagan Ø shot** me, not Cosgrave.
30	About Adam			
31	Ordinary Decent Criminal	00:08:35	MML1990D	It's fellas like **you Ø make** the world go around.
32	When Brendan Met Trudy			
33	Nora			
34	Rat	00:24:57	FC2000D	Is there anybody **here Ø was** a friend of Hubert Flynn's?
35	How Harry Became A Tree	00:17:21	MF1920WW	It was **you Ø put** them on the table, Harry.
36	The Magdalene Sisters			
37	Mystics	00:11:35	MS2000D	You know it was **Larry Ø did** the Cork Security job?
38	Evelyn			
39	Intermission	00:08:28	MJ2000D	You don't just hook up with the next **fella Ø walks** by.
40	Song for a Raggy Boy			
41	Veronica Guerin			
42	Goldfish Memory			
43	The Boys and Girl from County Clare			
44	Cowboys and Angels			
45	Adam and Paul			
46	Dead Meat			
47	Inside I'm Dancing			
48	Irish Jam	00:28:15	MG2000W	[...] as recently as the '50s, there were many **guest houses Ø had** signs up saying "No Blacks, No Dogs, No Irish".
49	The Wind that Shakes the Barley			
50	Garage			
	Total: 20/50			

Table 29: Relative clause marking: zero *relative*

Film	Time	Speaker	Example of usage
1 The Informer			
2 The Quiet Man			
3 Darby O' Gill and the Little People			
4 Ryan's Daughter	00:03:21	MS1920W	Well, it's not the cuttlefish **what** I told you to look for.
5 The Dead			
6 High Spirits			
7 My Left Foot			
8 The Field			
9 The Commitments			
10 Far and Away			
11 The Snapper			
12 Into the West			
13 A Man of No Importance			
14 Widows' Peak			
15 Circle of Friends			
16 Last of the High Kings			
17 The Van			
18 Michael Collins			
19 Trojan Eddie			
20 The Matchmaker			
21 The Nephew			
22 This is my Father			
23 Waking Ned			
24 The General			
25 A Very Unlucky Leprechaun			

Table 30: Relative clause marking: *what*

26	A Love Divided		
27	Agnes Browne		
28	Angela's Ashes		
29	When the Sky Falls		
30	About Adam		
31	Ordinary Decent Criminal		
32	When Brendan Met Trudy		
33	Nora		
34	Rat		
35	How Harry Became A Tree		
36	The Magdalene Sisters		
37	Mystics		
38	Evelyn		
39	Intermission		
40	Song for a Raggy Boy		
41	Veronica Guerin		
42	Goldfish Memory		
43	The Boys and Girl from County Clare		
44	Cowboys and Angels		
45	Adam and Paul		
46	Dead Meat		
47	Inside I'm Dancing		
48	Irish Jam		
49	The Wind that Shakes the Barley		
50	Garage	00:03:55	MJ2000M	Them oils onto the new stand **what** I got off the rep.
			Total: 2/50

Table 30: Relative clause marking: *what*

	Film	Time	Speaker	Example of usage
1	The Informer	00:31:14	MT1920K	**Is it** afraid of the commandant you are?
2	The Quiet Man	00:13:00	MMF1930W	**It's** a bold sinful man you are, Sean Thornton.
3	Darby O' Gill and the Little People	01:16:50	MDOG1800K	**Is it** drunk you are?
4	Ryan's Daughter			
5	The Dead			
6	High Spirits			
7	My Left Foot	00:30:00	MBB1950D	**It's** like the bleedin' fire of hell that one is.
8	The Field	01:35:24	MBMC1950W	**Is it** your mouth those words are coming out of?
9	The Commitments			
10	Far and Away			
11	The Snapper	00:30:41	FMB1990D	**Is it** George you want, Sharon?
12	Into the West	00:34:50	MOR1990D	**Is it** us they're after?
13	A Man of No Importance	00:52:02	MCB1960D	Ah, **it's** better you're getting.
14	Widows' Peak	01:03:00	MMC1930M	If **it's** a drink you want, it's down there. Good lad.
15	Circle of Friends	01:01:40	MSW1950D	**It isn't** everyone can grasp it right away.
16	Last of the High Kings			
17	The Van			
18	Michael Collins			
19	Trojan Eddie			
20	The Matchmaker	00:41:52	MSea2000W	Sure, **'tis** a great judge that you'd be and you from the land of Perry Mason and all.
21	The Nephew			
22	This is my Father			
23	Waking Ned	00:40:23	MJ2000W	I do. I do. **Is it** Ned you're wanting?
24	The General			
25	A Very Unlucky Leprechaun			

Table 31: Focusing devices: *'it' clefting*

#	Title	Time	Code	Quote
26	A Love Divided	00:16:20	FS1950WX	**It's** Sean and me that'll be deciding where she's going to school, not Fr Stafford.
27	Agnes Browne			
28	Angela's Ashes	01:32:55	ML1940L	**It's** four weeks behind in the rent you are, and now this.
29	When the Sky Falls	01:13:42	FM1990D	**It was** O' Fagan shot you.
30	About Adam			
31	Ordinary Decent Criminal			
32	When Brendan Met Trudy			
33	Nora	00:06:10	MC1900D	**It's** always me that's caught.
34	Rat	00:15:28	MM2000D	**It's** training he wants.
35	How Harry Became A Tree	00:17:21	MF1920WW	**It was** you put them on the table, Harry.
36	The Magdalene Sisters	00:12:26	MFR1960D	**It's** a grievous sin you have commited.
37	Mystics	01:18:55	MMic2000D	**It's** Mammy I'm sorry for.
38	Evelyn	00:35:16	FB1950D	**It's** not a housekeeper you need, it's a barkeeper.
39	Intermission	00:09:53	MO2000D	I thought **it was** her wanted to take a break.
40	Song for a Raggy Boy			
41	Veronica Guerin			
42	Goldfish Memory			
43	The Boys and Girl from County Clare	00:44:32	MJ1960CI	Oh, **is it** a bet you call it?
44	Cowboys and Angels			
45	Adam and Paul			
46	Dead Meat			
47	Inside I'm Dancing	01:16:43	FS2000D	Oh, **it's** the truth you want, is it?
48	Irish Jam	00:03:30	MFR2000W	**It's** a good kick up the arse you need.
49	The Wind that Shakes the Barley			
50	Garage	01:07:53	MSgt2000M	**It wasn't** him that complained.
				Total: 26/50

Table 31: Focusing devices: *'It' clefting*

	Film	Time	Speaker	Example of usage
1	The Informer	01:15:12	MB1920D	He did. He did, the poor man. **A pound note he gave me**.
2	The Quiet Man	00:02:04	MFL1930W	**A fine soft day in the spring it was**, when the train pulled into Castletown, [...], and himself got off.
3	Darby O' Gill and the Little People	00:18:39	MDOG1800K	**Bold and cunning they are**, but I'm up to them.
4	Ryan's Daughter	00:26:39	MTR1920W	**Oh, pure she was.**
5	The Dead	00:07:16	FAK1900D	**A fine pair of bellows he has**.
6	High Spirits			
7	My Left Foot	01:20:15	MBM1950D	**Seven pounds five shillings and sixpence he owed**, Missus.
8	The Field	01:01:13	MBi1950W	**Spending money like water he was**, Bull.
9	The Commitments	00:14:47	MMR1990D	**In the bath he is**. Interviewing himself.
10	Far and Away	01:00:54	FSC1890W	**Me, he adored**. He worshipped me.
11	The Snapper			
12	Into the West			
13	A Man of No Importance	00:21:18	MCB1960D	**A Morris Minor, was it, he got?**
14	Widows' Peak	01:30:14	FMOH1930M	**Such an aggravating young woman I never met**.
15	Circle of Friends			
16	Last of the High Kings	00:04:37	MF1970D	**Seventeen years I've been waiting for this day**.
17	The Van	00:53:46	MOM1990D	Shocking. **Filthy dirty it is**.
18	Michael Collins			
19	Trojan Eddie	01:13:45	MTE1990M	**Fascinated me he did**.
20	The Matchmaker			
21	The Nephew	00:34:19	FB1990C	**A father he needs**.
22	This is my Father			
23	Waking Ned			
24	The General			
25	A Very Unlucky Leprechaun			

Table 32: Focusing devices: *topicalisation*

#	Title	Time	Code	Quote
26	A Love Divided			
27	Agnes Browne	00:12:15	MB1960D	**A fine man so he was.**
28	Angela's Ashes	01:45:43	MPat1950L	**The world champion he is**, Uncle Pat.
29	When the Sky Falls	00:03:51	MMC1930M	**Fresh and well she's looking.**
30	About Adam			
31	Ordinary Decent Criminal	00:12:33	MML1990D	**Like savages they were.**
32	When Brendan Met Trudy			
33	Nora	00:49:01	FN1900G	**A fine brother you have.**
34	Rat			
35	How Harry Became A Tree			
36	The Magdalene Sisters			
37	Mystics	00:50:21	MD2000D	**Yards of it there was.**
38	Evelyn	01:09:43	FSrB1950D	**Throttling me he was.**
39	Intermission	01:36:04	MO2000D	**Keep it to myself I will. Cherish it. Relish it I will.**
40	Song for a Raggy Boy			
41	Veronica Guerin			
42	Goldfish Memory			
43	The Boys and Girl from County Clare			
44	Cowboys and Angels			
45	Adam and Paul	00:45:59	FJ2000D	**Hoping to see yez there she was.** Asking, you know, where yiz were and things.
46	Dead Meat			
47	Inside I'm Dancing	00:30:54	MROS2000D	**Some fuckin' lawyer you are.**
48	Irish Jam			
49	The Wind that Shakes the Barley	00:23:09	MIP1920C	**Handpicked they were**, by a personal friend of that bollocks, Churchill.
50	Garage	00:22:47	MJ2000M	Anyways, the pumps are old and contrary. I don't like to see the punters usin' them. **Only break them they would**

Total: 27/50

Table 32: Focusing devices: *topicalisation*

	Film	Time	Speaker	Example of usage
1	The Informer	01:10:50	MM1920D	I remember I heard the Angelus beginning to strike **and** me on me way down the stairs.
2	The Quiet Man	01:46:55	MMF1930W	She came tapping at my door **and** the sun not up.
3	Darby O' Gill and the Little People	01:00:30	MKB1800K	How can I give the order **and** me tied up in a sack?
4	Ryan's Daughter	00:40:57	MTR1920W	Red Tim [...] that 1,000 [...] policemen have been hunting [...], **and** himself [...] walking the [...] streets of Dublin.
5	The Dead			
6	High Spirits			
7	My Left Foot			
8	The Field			
9	The Commitments			
10	Far and Away			
11	The Snapper			
12	Into the West	00:53:10	MSgt1990D	Dancin' like an animal **and** your children out on the road without a mother to look after them.
13	A Man of No Importance			
14	Widows' Peak			
15	Circle of Friends			
16	Last of the High Kings			
17	The Van			
18	Michael Collins			
19	Trojan Eddie			
20	The Matchmaker	01:05:48	MOH2000W	Don't you be speaking out of turn you brazen hussy **and** you coming in here at all hours of the night ...
21	The Nephew			
22	This is my Father			
23	Waking Ned			
24	The General			
25	A Very Unlucky Leprechaun			

Table 33: 'Subordinating *and*'

26	A Love Divided		
27	Agnes Browne		
28	Angela's Ashes	01:45:40	MPat1950L	That's not right, him hittin' a wee boy **and** him being heavyweight champion of America and all.
29	When the Sky Falls		
30	About Adam		
31	Ordinary Decent Criminal		
32	When Brendan Met Trudy		
33	Nora		
34	Rat		
35	How Harry Became A Tree		
36	The Magdalene Sisters		
37	Mystics		
38	Evelyn		
39	Intermission	00:29:02	FD2000D	Ma found her, it was like two or three days later, and "the stink" she said, flies crawling over her **and** her hysterical.
40	Song for a Raggy Boy		
41	Veronica Guerin		
42	Goldfish Memory		
43	The Boys and Girl from County Clare		
44	Cowboys and Angels		
45	Adam and Paul	00:57:36	MN2000D	That's all I need now is the cops callin' around here **and** everything I have in there fuckin' robbed.
46	Dead Meat		
47	Inside I'm Dancing		
48	Irish Jam		
49	The Wind that Shakes the Barley		
50	Garage	00:46:47	MV2000M	Well, I don't think it's right having them children there **and** she like that.
	Total: 10/50		

Table 33: 'Subordinating *and*'

	Film	Time	Speaker	Example of usage
1	The Informer			
2	The Quiet Man			
3	Darby O' Gill and the Little People			
4	Ryan's Daughter			
5	The Dead			
6	High Spirits			
7	My Left Foot	00:17:59	MMB1950D	Come on *till* ya see.
8	The Field			
9	The Commitments			
10	Far and Away			
11	The Snapper			
12	Into the West			
13	A Man of No Importance	00:37:59	FL1960D	Come here *till* I have a quick word with you for a minute.
14	Widows' Peak			
15	Circle of Friends			
16	Last of the High Kings			
17	The Van			
18	Michael Collins			
19	Trojan Eddie			
20	The Matchmaker			
21	The Nephew			
22	This is my Father			
23	Waking Ned			
24	The General			
25	A Very Unlucky Leprechaun			

Table 34: 'Subordinating *till*'

26	A Love Divided	00:10:18	MP1950WX	Come here till I tell ya.
27	Agnes Browne			
28	Angela's Ashes			
29	When the Sky Falls			
30	About Adam			
31	Ordinary Decent Criminal			
32	When Brendan Met Trudy			
33	Nora			
34	Rat	00:28:11	FD2000D	Come here till I see ya, Hubert.
35	How Harry Became A Tree	01:05:08	MH1920WW	Come here till I tell you what you saw.
36	The Magdalene Sisters			
37	Mystics			
38	Evelyn			
39	Intermission			
40	Song for a Raggy Boy			
41	Veronica Guerin			
42	Goldfish Memory			
43	The Boys and Girl from County Clare			
44	Cowboys and Angels			
45	Adam and Paul	00:54:35	MA2000D	Climb onto the front there till we open it from the outside.
46	Dead Meat			
47	Inside I'm Dancing	00:41:22	MCW2000M	Come on in now till I show you.
48	Irish Jam			
49	The Wind that Shakes the Barley			
50	Garage	00:09:15	FC2000M	Come on in now, Josie, till I get rid of you.
				Total: 8/50

Table 34: 'Subordinating *till*'

	Film	Time	Speaker	Example of usage
1	The Informer	00:16:32	MFMP1920D	I was so homesick to see you, I'd have walked down the middle of O'Connell St. to get a glimpse of the two of **ye**.
2	The Quiet Man	01:14:54	MRW1930W	You lied, didn't you? You lied, didn't you? **Ye** all lied.
3	Darby O' Gill and the Little People	01:00:24	MDOG1800K	If he lays a finger on Katie, I'll kill ya dead and murder **ye** entirely.
4	Ryan's Daughter			
5	The Dead	00:05:30	FAK1990D	Do you want to go into the dancing first or do **ye** want to have a refreshment?
6	High Spirits			
7	My Left Foot			
8	The Field	00:18:32	MFR1950W	Will **ye** stop fighting among yourselves?
9	The Commitments			
10	Far and Away			
11	The Snapper			
12	Into the West	01:24:34	MPR1990D	Oh, I missed **ye**, boys. I missed **ye**.
13	A Man of No Importance	00:16:58	MFR1960W	So **ye**'re trying it again this year?
14	Widows' Peak	00:35:36	MAM1930M	Now, now, now. Everybody, stay where **ye** are.
15	Circle of Friends			
16	Last of the High Kings			
17	The Van	00:47:32	MG1990C	Oh, Jaysus, he'll crack, lads, I'm telling **ye**.
18	Michael Collins	00:16:17	MMC1910C	I'll make a fucking army out of **ye**, if it's the last thing I do.
19	Trojan Eddie	00:13:15	FB1990M	How are **ye**, lads?
20	The Matchmaker			
21	The Nephew	00:07:30	MT1990C	You all knew Karen. I'd like **ye** to drink to her memory and to my nephew from America.
22	This is my Father	00:16:09	FT2000M	I'll tell **ye** two things for nothin'.
23	Waking Ned	01:07:36	FL2000W	Did **ye** know that if you report a fraud to the Lotto, you get ten per cent of the winnings?
24	The General			
25	A Very Unlucky Leprechaun			

Table 35: Second person plural: ye

26	A Love Divided			
27	Agnes Browne			
28	Angela's Ashes	01:32:31	ML1940L	I rented **ye** two rooms up here and one is gone.
29	When the Sky Falls			
30	About Adam			
31	Ordinary Decent Criminal			
32	When Brendan Met Trudy			
33	Nora			
34	Rat	00:57:34	MFF2000D	If **ye** have rosary beads, hang on tight to them.
35	How Harry Became A Tree	00:51:26	FE1920WW	No, **ye** all seem to know already or think **ye** do, so why don't I just leave it up to your own dirty minds?
36	The Magdalene Sisters	00:08:24	FB1960D	Get off, I'll never tell **ye**.
37	Mystics			
38	Evelyn	01:21:15	FSrF1950D	Children, don't **ye** stop praying now!
39	Intermission			
40	Song for a Raggy Boy	00:10:16	MMF1930	So if any of **ye** want to challenge me, I suggest you do it now.
41	Veronica Guerin			
42	Goldfish Memory			
43	The Boys and Girl from County Clare	01:10:03	MJ1960CI	Would the pair of **ye** stop picking on me?
44	Cowboys and Angels			
45	Adam and Paul	00:45:06	FJ2000D	How the fuck did **ye** get in?
46	Dead Meat	00:38:37	MC2000LM	Where are **ye** after coming out of?
47	Inside I'm Dancing			
48	Irish Jam	00:02:33	MFR2000W	Hush, now. Will **ye** all be quiet? Be quiet!
49	The Wind that Shakes the Barley	01:25:24	MR1920C	And the only question I want you to answer today is are **ye** men of your word?
50	Garage	00:07:11	MJ2000M	That's what **ye** all love.
				Total: 26/50

Table 35: Second person plural: ye

Film	Time	Speaker	Example of usage
1 The Informer			
2 The Quiet Man			
3 Darby O' Gill and the Little People			
4 Ryan's Daughter			
5 The Dead			
6 High Spirits			
7 My Left Foot			
8 The Field			
9 The Commitments	00:27:28	FN1990D	What are **youse** bleedin' lookin' at?
10 Far and Away			
11 The Snapper	00:27:00	MDa1990D	**Youse** are messin'!
12 Into the West			
13 A Man of No Importance			
14 Widows' Peak	00:51:03	FDC1930M	She trusts you, in her innocence. I don't, not as far as I could throw you, or the whole seed and breed of **youse**.
15 Circle of Friends	00:07:57	FNM1950D	It's lovely to see **youse** again.
16 Last of the High Kings			
17 The Van	00:55:51	MOM1990D	Which of **youse** is Bimbo's?
18 Michael Collins			
19 Trojan Eddie			
20 The Matchmaker			
21 The Nephew			
22 This is my Father			
23 Waking Ned			
24 The General	00:51:43	MMC1990D	**Youse** drug addicts are always short of money.
25 A Very Unlucky Leprechaun			

Table 36: Second person plural: youse

#	Title	Time	Code	Quote
26	A Love Divided			
27	Agnes Browne	00:25:37	FAB1960D	I don't have enough money to feed the lot of **youse**, never mind feeding the bloody ducks.
28	Angela's Ashes			
29	When the Sky Falls			
30	About Adam			
31	Ordinary Decent Criminal	00:11:58	MML1990D	So one day, this is before **youse** were born, I was comin' home after workin' hard all day and I saw them …
32	When Brendan Met Trudy			
33	Nora			
34	Rat	01:11:28	FM2000D	**Youse** don't care anything about Daddy.
35	How Harry Became A Tree	00:53:39	MH1920WW	Are **youse** listening to me?
36	The Magdalene Sisters	00:27:35	FK1960D	That's what's wrong with **youse**. You're completely selfish.
37	Mystics	00:31:21	MLA2000D	It'll set **youse** up for life.
38	Evelyn	00:03:26	MDES1950D	Go on, off to bed with the lot of **youse**.
39	Intermission	00:05:43	MH2000D	Are **youse** not clockin' back on?
40	Song for a Raggy Boy			
41	Veronica Guerin	00:30:23	MJM1990D	Do you know what? I make more in a week than **youse** fuckers earn in a month.
42	Goldfish Memory			
43	The Boys and Girl from County Clare			
44	Cowboys and Angels			
45	Adam and Paul	00:18:14	MG2000D	So, are **youse** two goin' down The Bunker later?
46	Dead Meat			
47	Inside I'm Dancing	00:43:12	MIM2000D	Will I have to push **youse** two fellas around all day?
48	Irish Jam	00:22:12	FM2000W	Shouldn't **youse** not be getting back to the zoo before it closes up for the night?
49	The Wind that Shakes the Barley			
50	Garage			
				Total: 18/50

Table 36: Second person plural: *youse*

Film	Time	Speaker	Example of usage
1 The Informer	00:53:17	MSP1920D	What did I tell **yiz**? What did I tell **yiz**? He's as rich as crazy!
2 The Quiet Man	02:07:13	MFL1930W	I want **yez** all to cheer like Protestants.
3 Darby O' Gill and the Little People			
4 Ryan's Daughter			
5 The Dead			
6 High Spirits			
7 My Left Foot	00:18:59	FMB1950D	Are **yez** all deaf or what?
8 The Field			
9 The Commitments	01:44:18	FI1990D	Not one of **yiz** has ever seen me as anythin' but a bum and a skirt!
10 Far and Away			
11 The Snapper	00:13:16	FSC1990D	I'm pregnant. Did I tell **yiz**?
12 Into the West	00:04:40	MPR1990D	Now, I'm not going to tell **yez** again.
13 A Man of No Importance			
14 Widows' Peak	01:14:35	FMOH1930M	I suppose I reminded **yiz** of how good **yiz** were and how Christian.
15 Circle of Friends	00:10:53	MJF1950D	See **yez**.
16 Last of the High Kings	00:29:06	MD1970D	I'm not moving. I told **yiz**.
17 The Van	01:05:45	ML1990D	How are **yiz**, girls?
18 Michael Collins	00:15:47	MMC1910C	Grab that bag, one of **yez**.
19 Trojan Eddie	00:28:20	MTE1990M	Go ahead upstairs, lads, will **yez**. Good girls.
20 The Matchmaker	00:24:18	MJim2000W	See **yez**!
21 The Nephew			
22 This is my Father	01:23:36	FMF1930M	Kieran O'Dea, get the hell off my property, or I'll evict the lot of **yiz**.
23 Waking Ned			
24 The General	00:10:58	MMC1990D	Fuck off, the lot of **yiz**. **Yiz** are all oppressors of the poor.
25 A Very Unlucky Leprechaun			

Table 37: Second person plural: yez/yiz

26 A Love Divided	00:33:15	ME1950WX	Jesus, Sean, could the pair of **yiz** not have sorted this out yourselves?
27 Agnes Browne	01:17:03	FAB1960D	No, **yiz** are doing things my way till **yiz** are men.
28 Angela's Ashes	00:53:32	MQ1940L	You climb up the spout there and each of **yiz** have a look.
29 When the Sky Falls	00:47:38	MJ1990D	What are **yiz** doing?
30 About Adam			
31 Ordinary Decent Criminal	00:36:17	MBi1990D	How are **yiz**?
32 When Brendan Met Trudy			
33 Nora			
34 Rat	01:16:59	FD2000D	Did **yiz** look under the floorboards, Sergeant?
35 How Harry Became A Tree	00:53:47	MH1920WW	Fuck **yiz**, then!
36 The Magdalene Sisters			
37 Mystics	00:05:41	ML2000D	Quiet now, the both of **yiz**.
38 Evelyn	00:55:48	MJOL1950D	Sorry to interrupt **yiz**.
39 Intermission	00:06:05	MH2000D	Get back on that floor, **yiz** little pups!
40 Song for a Raggy Boy			
41 Veronica Guerin			
42 Goldfish Memory			
43 The Boys and Girl from County Clare			
44 Cowboys and Angels	00:21:54	FWIH2000L	Hi **yiz**!
45 Adam and Paul	00:18:04	MW2000D	Lads, if I see **yiz** near Janine, I'm not jokin ya, I'll kill **yiz**! Okay?
46 Dead Meat			
47 Inside I'm Dancing	00:43:41	MIM22000D	Do **yiz** ever dress up? I mean as animals, or whatever.
48 Irish Jam	00:57:42	MFR2000W	Now, as **yiz** all know, we have a new addition to our little family.
49 The Wind that Shakes the Barley	01:29:07	MDa1920D	It's a short quote, men, but I won't keep **yiz**.
50 Garage			
			Total: 30/50

Table 37: Second person plural: *yez/yiz*

	Film	Time	Speaker	Example of usage
1	The Informer			
2	The Quiet Man			
3	Darby O' Gill and the Little People			
4	Ryan's Daughter			
5	The Dead			
6	High Spirits			
7	My Left Foot			
8	The Field			
9	The Commitments			
10	Far and Away			
11	The Snapper			
12	Into the West			
13	A Man of No Importance			
14	Widows' Peak	00:22:46	FDC1930M	Ladies, amn't I right?
15	Circle of Friends			
16	Last of the High Kings			
17	The Van			
18	Michael Collins			
19	Trojan Eddie			
20	The Matchmaker			
21	The Nephew			
22	This is my Father			
23	Waking Ned			
24	The General			
25	A Very Unlucky Leprechaun			

Table 38: Negation of auxiliary *amn't*

26	A Love Divided			
27	Agnes Browne	00:54:41	FM1960D	Sure, don't you know I'll be there? Sure, **amn't** I always there when you're having a good time?
28	Angela's Ashes			
29	When the Sky Falls			
30	About Adam	01:19:07	FA2000D	Look, everybody does something like that before they get married. Sure, you'd be mad not to. **Amn't** I right, Laura?
31	Ordinary Decent Criminal			
32	When Brendan Met Trudy	00:26:31	MB2000D	Making good progress. Good, good progress. **Amn't** I right?
33	Nora			
34	Rat			
35	How Harry Became A Tree			
36	The Magdalene Sisters			
37	Mystics			
38	Evelyn			
39	Intermission			
40	Song for a Raggy Boy			
41	Veronica Guerin			
42	Goldfish Memory			
43	The Boys and Girl from County Clare			
44	Cowboys and Angels			
45	Adam and Paul			
46	Dead Meat			
47	Inside I'm Dancing			
48	Irish Jam			
49	The Wind that Shakes the Barley			
50	Garage			
				Total: 4/50

Table 38: Negation of auxiliary *amn't*

	Film	Time	Speaker	Example of usage
1	The Informer	01:02:19	MSP1920D	I know who they are! **Them** is the Republican Army. The Republican Army!
2	The Quiet Man			
3	Darby O' Gill and the Little People	00:18:11	MDOG1800K	**Them** as I heard it from give it no name.
4	Ryan's Daughter	00:39:21	MFR1920W	And if **them** two's tinkers, I'm the Bishop of Cork.
5	The Dead			
6	High Spirits			
7	My Left Foot	00:30:50	FFN1950D	Stay away from **them** sheets.
8	The Field	01:00:13	MBi1950W	They're the Judases of this nation, **them** same priests!
9	The Commitments	00:42:58	FB1990D	Move **them** washing there if you want to sit down.
10	Far and Away			
11	The Snapper	00:46:40	FSC1990D	It was one of **them** Spanish sailors.
12	Into the West	00:10:23	MPR1990D	You listen to me. **Them** boys is stayin' here.
13	A Man of No Importance	00:27:19	FL1960D	The cut of **them** girls.
14	Widows' Peak	01:01:00	MCB11930M	It must be one of **them** mirages.
15	Circle of Friends			
16	Last of the High Kings			
17	The Van	00:29:00	ML1990D	It took me ages to make **them** chips.
18	Michael Collins			
19	Trojan Eddie			
20	The Matchmaker	00:51:13	MG2000W	And, listen, I'll throw in one of **them** as a little gift.
21	The Nephew			
22	This is my Father			
23	Waking Ned	00:07:08	FM2000W	Finn, darlin', you know I would, if it wasn't for the smell of **them** pigs.
24	The General	00:06:03	MMC1990D	**Them** flats is right opposite the cop shop.
25	A Very Unlucky Leprechaun			

Table 39: Demonstrative pronoun: *them*

#	Title	Time	Code	Quote
26	A Love Divided			
27	Agnes Browne	00:08:32	FM1960D	I'll drop by later, love, help ya bath **them** kids.
28	Angela's Ashes			
29	When the Sky Falls	00:09:05	MK1990D	You get me a story even vaguely like that, and I'll dance over **them** tables bollock naked.
30	About Adam			
31	Ordinary Decent Criminal			
32	When Brendan Met Trudy			
33	Nora			
34	Rat			
35	How Harry Became A Tree	00:03:08	MG1920WW	One of **them** big fellas wouldn't cut down easy.
36	The Magdalene Sisters			
37	Mystics	00:27:00	FL2000D	Ah, sure, **them** days are gone.
38	Evelyn			
39	Intermission	00:19:05	MG2000D	You like **them** artistes? Their music?
40	Song for a Raggy Boy			
41	Veronica Guerin			
42	Goldfish Memory			
43	The Boys and Girl from County Clare			
44	Cowboys and Angels	00:55:15	MBU2000L	You brought 400 of **them** back from Dublin.
45	Adam and Paul	00:14:20	FM2000D	Orla, give **them** two a can before my heart breaks.
46	Dead Meat			
47	Inside I'm Dancing	00:22:58	MDM2000M	Not with **them** boots, you're not.
48	Irish Jam	00:22:03	MBMN2000W	Would ya like some help with **them** groceries? Or would ya prefer himself to be carrying **them** for you?
49	The Wind that Shakes the Barley	00:22:59	MIP1920C	A pound a day, lads. A pound a day. That's what they're paying **them** bastards.
50	Garage	00:28:25	MV2000M	Wipe down **them** tables there Li, like a good girl.
				Total: 25/50

Table 39: Demonstrative pronoun: *them*

	Film	Time	Speaker	Example of usage
1	The Informer	01:30:23	FFM1920D	**Sure**, you didn't know what you were doing.
2	The Quiet Man	00:22:15	MMF1930W	**Sure**, yes, yes, he's a millionaire, you know, like all the Yanks.
3	Darby O' Gill and the Little People	01:17:13	MMB1800D	She was in a tearin' rage at me and **sure** it was your fault for not telling her the truth in the first place.
4	Ryan's Daughter	00:13:22	FMC1920W	Ah, **sure**, it's only a bit of fun, Father.
5	The Dead	00:55:03	FAK1900D	Ah, **sure**, God love him. **Sure**, he wasn't so bad this year.
6	High Spirits	01:12:26	MC1980W	**Sure**, they don't drink whiskey.
7	My Left Foot	00:14:44	FWN1950D	Ah, **sure**, he has the mind of a three-year-old.
8	The Field	00:05:52	MBMC1950W	If we knew how to keep the women happy, **sure**, we'd still be in Paradise.
9	The Commitments			
10	Far and Away	00:12:56	MDD1980W	**Sure**, Joseph, it was too good to be kept a secret.
11	The Snapper	00:29:36	FSC1990D	**Sure**, men are always saying things like that about girls.
12	Into the West			
13	A Man of No Importance	00:10:21	FA1960M	But, **sure**, I can't act.
14	Widows' Peak	00:59:00	MMC1930M	**Sure**, all you need is a denture and a bit of bridgework.
15	Circle of Friends	01:26:53	MSW1950D	**Sure**, I'm doing you a favour. Not many men would take you on at all.
16	Last of the High Kings	00:37:10	MTD1970D	Milwaukee? **Sure**, I know it well.
17	The Van	00:57:14	FM1990D	He doesn't really like me, **sure** he doesn't.
18	Michael Collins	00:07:06	MMC1910C	They wouldn't kill me in my own county, **sure**.
19	Trojan Eddie	00:09:58	MR1990M	I've already sold it, **sure**, and spent the money.
20	The Matchmaker	01:13:40	MJim2000W	No, no. **Sure**, the festival's not over yet.
21	The Nephew	00:25:24	MIP21990C	Oh, **sure**, 'tis well known. Goes back hundreds of years.
22	This is my Father	01:25:50	MGard1930M	On Sunday. **Sure**, we'll have to get Mass first. **Sure**, we might as well leave it off till Monday then.
23	Waking Ned	01:07:18	FA2000W	**Sure**, the whole village is waiting for the news.
24	The General	00:06:02	MMC1990D	Kevin Street? **Sure**, that's a deliberate insult to a criminal.
25	A Very Unlucky Leprechaun	00:05:11	MPM1990W	I know, but, **sure**, looks aren't everything.

Table 40: Discourse marker: *sure*

26	A Love Divided	00:18:46	MS1950WX	Sure, I lashed it half way to Dublin.
27	Agnes Browne	00:54:41	FM1960D	Sure, don't you know I'll be there. Sure, amn't I always there when you're having a good time.
28	Angela's Ashes	01:47:19	MUP1930L	Sure, the drink never hurt anyone, did it?
29	When the Sky Falls	01:04:55	MTH1990D	Sure, I'll be back for the second half.
30	About Adam	00:34:29	FA2000D	But, sure, I've hardly met him. You obviously know him much better.
31	Ordinary Decent Criminal	00:24:05	MA1990D	But, sure, me da probably robbed the fuckin' things anyway.
32	When Brendan Met Trudy	00:37:46	FT2000C	Ah, sure, Brendan, I wouldn't know a Montessori if it came and bit me on the arse.
33	Nora	01:39:00	FNM1900G	Go on, sure. You haven't had a real chance to have a talk together.
34	Rat	00:26:26	FM2000D	Ah, sure, what harm, Ma?
35	How Harry Became A Tree	00:04:03	MH1920WW	Sure, it's good for the roots.
36	The Magdalene Sisters	00:59:45	FC1960D	If I died of the flu, it wouldn't be your fault, sure it wouldn't.
37	Mystics	00:33:40	MD2000D	Ah, sure, we get all sorts, Inspector.
38	Evelyn	00:05:01	MG1950D	Ah, sure, look on the bright side, son.
39	Intermission	01:21:09	ML2000D	Now, tell me. You're after blowing your cover, sure.
40	Song for a Raggy Boy			
41	Veronica Guerin	00:10:05	MMC1990D	And then I thought to myself, you know, sure, people get killed every day, and nobody gives a shite.
42	Goldfish Memory	00:28:55	FH2000D	Sure, we can get pissed as easily here as in Nirvana.
43	The Boys and Girl from County Clare	00:28:01	MJJ1960CI	Come on. Sure, your sister's got the kettle on.
44	Cowboys and Angels	01:10:04	MG32000L	You'll be brought before the inspector first thing in the morning and charged, and after that, sure, I couldn't tell ya.
45	Adam and Paul	00:15:48	FO2000D	Sure, didn't they practically live in our house.
46	Dead Meat	00:45:21	FF2000LM	Sure, they don't want anyone to know what's going on.
47	Inside I'm Dancing	00:19:18	MROS2000D	No. Sure, it's for funding the needs of the disabled. I'm disabled and I need a drink.
48	Irish Jam			
49	The Wind that Shakes the Barley	00:41:05	MD1920C	But, sure, by the time he came back he was a man.
50	Garage	00:10:08	MJ2000M	He's in there all the time, sure.
				Total: 46/50

Table 40: Discourse marker: *sure*

	Film	Time	Speaker	Example of usage
1	The Informer			
2	The Quiet Man			
3	Darby O' Gill and the Little People			
4	Ryan's Daughter			
5	The Dead			
6	High Spirits			
7	My Left Foot			
8	The Field			
9	The Commitments			
10	Far and Away			
11	The Snapper	00:57:50	MDC1990D	I tell you, **but**, I gave as good as I got.
12	Into the West			
13	A Man of No Importance			
14	Widows' Peak			
15	Circle of Friends			
16	Last of the High Kings			
17	The Van	00:15:48	ML1990D	You have to hand it to the Vietnamese, **but**
18	Michael Collins	00:38:10	MA1910D	Just wanted to make sure he wouldn't get up, **but**.
19	Trojan Eddie			
20	The Matchmaker			
21	The Nephew			
22	This is my Father			
23	Waking Ned			
24	The General	01:16:29	MMC1990D	He used to like them pan-fried, **but**.
25	A Very Unlucky Leprechaun			

Table 41: Sentence-final markers: *but*

26	A Love Divided		
27	Agnes Browne		
28	Angela's Ashes		
29	When the Sky Falls		
30	About Adam		
31	Ordinary Decent Criminal		
32	When Brendan Met Trudy		
33	Nora		
34	Rat		
35	How Harry Became A Tree		
36	The Magdalene Sisters		
37	Mystics		
38	Evelyn		
39	Intermission		
40	Song for a Raggy Boy		
41	Veronica Guerin		
42	Goldfish Memory		
43	The Boys and Girl from County Clare		
44	Cowboys and Angels		
45	Adam and Paul	00:56:05 MP2000D	They're goin' to fuckin' kill us. Not lookin' out was bad, then stealin' their car, **but**.
46	Dead Meat		
47	Inside I'm Dancing		
48	Irish Jam		
49	The Wind that Shakes the Barley		
50	Garage		
		Total: 5/50	

Table 41: Sentence-final markers: *but*

Film	Time	Speaker	Example of usage
1 The Informer			
2 The Quiet Man	00:18:37	MFe1930D	There now, there now, isn't that grand, isn't that grand now, **what**?
3 Darby O' Gill and the Little People			
4 Ryan's Daughter			
5 The Dead			
6 High Spirits	01:15:12	MDMC1980W	It's a bloody good thing we ignored it, **what**?
7 My Left Foot	01:23:54	MBB1950D	Poor Tom, **what**?
8 The Field			
9 The Commitments	00:08:35	MO1990D	Dublin soul, **wha**?
10 Far and Away			
11 The Snapper	00:49:57	MDC1990D	An Irish sailor wasn't good enough for you, **what**?
12 Into the West			
13 A Man of No Importance			
14 Widows' Peak	00:59:10	MMC1930M	You'll be sailing this boat till your 100. Another 80 years, **what**?
15 Circle of Friends			
16 Last of the High Kings	01:00:30	MJF1970D	You'll never catch us in coalition, **what**?
17 The Van	01:06:06	ML1990D	This is the life, **what**?
18 Michael Collins	00:38:34	MMC1910C	Christ, pure genius, **what**?
19 Trojan Eddie			
20 The Matchmaker			
21 The Nephew			
22 This is my Father	01:28:06	MPo1930M	Hi, Kieran. A busy day, **what**?
23 Waking Ned			
24 The General	00:58:12	FFC1990D	Keep it in the family, **what**?
25 A Very Unlucky Leprechaun			

Table 42: Sentence-final markers: *what*

#	Title	Time	Code	Quote
26	A Love Divided	00:17:14	MFR1950WX	Ah, we didn't know you played like that, **what**?
27	Agnes Browne	00:27:22	MMB1960D	Yeah, well. See you tomorrow, **wha**?
28	Angela's Ashes			
29	When the Sky Falls			
30	About Adam			
31	Ordinary Decent Criminal			
32	When Brendan Met Trudy			
33	Nora			
34	Rat			
35	How Harry Became A Tree	00:19:37	MH1920WW	It was a hard oul years work all the same, **what**?
36	The Magdalene Sisters			
37	Mystics			
38	Evelyn	00:04:33	MG1950D	One for everyone, **what**?
39	Intermission	00:05:00	MJ2000D	Next time, **wha**?
40	Song for a Raggy Boy			
41	Veronica Guerin	00:15:47	MGM1990D	Look who's got himself a new girlfriend, **what**?
42	Goldfish Memory	00:26:46	MC2000C	Yeah, she's some chick, **what**?
43	The Boys and Girl from County Clare			
44	Cowboys and Angels			
45	Adam and Paul			
46	Dead Meat	00:40:58	MC2000LM	Grand, now I'm sucking diesel, **wha**?
47	Inside I'm Dancing			
48	Irish Jam			
49	The Wind that Shakes the Barley			
50	Garage			
				Total: 19/50

Table 42: Sentence-final markers: *what*

	Film	Time	Speaker	Example of usage
1	The Informer	00:10:10	MG1920D	Nothin', Frankie. You came up to me so sudden, **like**.
2	The Quiet Man			
3	Darby O' Gill and the Little People			
4	Ryan's Daughter			
5	The Dead			
6	High Spirits			
7	My Left Foot			
8	The Field			
9	The Commitments	00:17:06	MJR1990D	Be in a band. Back up singer, **like**.
10	Far and Away			
11	The Snapper	00:14:57	ML1990D	Your Sharon, **like**?
12	Into the West			
13	A Man of No Importance	00:38:28	FL1960D	And you need a bit of nourishment, **like**, you know. A girl on your own.
14	Widows' Peak			
15	Circle of Friends			
16	Last of the High Kings	00:27:37	MD1970D	I was just wondering, ahm, if you'd like to go out with me, **like**?
17	The Van	00:16:25	MG1990C	So up I goes to the hatch, **like**.
18	Michael Collins			
19	Trojan Eddie	00:02:50	MJP1990M	I mean, what am I supposed to think, **like**?
20	The Matchmaker			
21	The Nephew			
22	This is my Father	00:51:57	MK1930M	So I always had the kind of a notion of joining the navy, **like**, ya know.
23	Waking Ned			
24	The General	00:56:00	MMC1990D	We all have our hobbies, **like**, you know.
25	A Very Unlucky Leprechaun			

Table 43: Sentence-final markers: *like*

#	Title	Time	Code	Quote
26	A Love Divided			
27	Agnes Browne			
28	Angela's Ashes			
29	When the Sky Falls	00:48:07	MMOF1990D	He's a bit of a lad, but I wouldn't necessarily finger him for drugs, **like**.
30	About Adam			
31	Ordinary Decent Criminal	00:46:35	MML1990D	I think we can give them the runaround any time we like 'cause they're only eejits. Mentioning no names, **like**.
32	When Brendan Met Trudy	00:07:07	FT2000C	What, hymns, **like**?
33	Nora	00:55:48	FN1900G	We were only young, **like**.
34	Rat	00:11:39	FC2000D	And he was lying there, **like**, letting on that he didn't hear me.
35	How Harry Became A Tree			
36	The Magdalene Sisters			
37	Mystics			
38	Evelyn	00:11:10	MDES1950D	Well, sir, my father Henry, who's sitting over here, and meself, we're settin' up a bit of a tour of the Dublin pubs, **like**.
39	Intermission	00:34:10	MRG2000D	Number twos, **like**. In a little toilet outside the GPO.
40	Song for a Raggy Boy			
41	Veronica Guerin			
42	Goldfish Memory	01:11:34	FI2000D	Look, do you want to be my girlfriend for the next week? Exclusive, **like**?
43	The Boys and Girl from County Clare			
44	Cowboys and Angels	00:17:12	FG2000L	No money. Living at home with my parents again. A bit of a shock, **like**.
45	Adam and Paul	00:10:57	MP2000D	Ah, just hangin' around, **like**, you know. Just layin low, **like**.
46	Dead Meat			
47	Inside I'm Dancing			
48	Irish Jam			
49	The Wind that Shakes the Barley	00:51:06	MC1920C	Ah, Jesus Christ, lads. He's only a young fella, **like**.
50	Garage	00:48:42	FC2000M	It's only oul roll-on … deodorant, **like**.
				Total: 21/50

Table 43: Sentence-final markers: *like*

	Film	Time	Speaker	Example of usage
1	The Informer			
2	The Quiet Man			
3	Darby O' Gill and the Little People	00:17:35	MDOG1800K	That was a grand bit of work you done, **so it was**, aye.
4	Ryan's Daughter			
5	The Dead			
6	High Spirits			
7	My Left Foot			
8	The Field			
9	The Commitments			
10	Far and Away			
11	The Snapper			
12	Into the West	00:40:28	MPR1990D	I don't see her turnin' me heart upside down with a little smile, **so I don't**.
13	A Man of No Importance			
14	Widows' Peak	00:04:29	MMC1930M	I date on women, **so I do**.
15	Circle of Friends	00:38:47	FAH1950D	Sure, you're practically one of the family now, **so you are**.
16	Last of the High Kings			
17	The Van	00:11:18	MB1990D	You wouldn't know what to wear, **so you wouldn't**.
18	Michael Collins			
19	Trojan Eddie	00:06:59	MTE1990M	I tell yeh, if I didn't have to hand this over every day I'd be laughin' altogether, **so I would**.
20	The Matchmaker			
21	The Nephew			
22	This is my Father			
23	Waking Ned			
24	The General			
25	A Very Unlucky Leprechaun			

Table 44: Sentence-final tags: so

26	A Love Divided			
27	Agnes Browne	00:12:15	MB1960D	A fine man, **so he was**.
28	Angela's Ashes	00:04:04	MN1990L	Dad said he would get a job soon, **so he will**, and buy her dresses of silk and shoes with silver buckles.
29	When the Sky Falls			
30	About Adam			
31	Ordinary Decent Criminal			
32	When Brendan Met Trudy			
33	Nora	01:13:19	FN1900G	Then I threatened to have Lucia baptised, **so I did**. He'll be home inside a week.
34	Rat	01:12:12	FM2000D	He's got Mammy's head turned, **so he has**.
35	How Harry Became A Tree			
36	The Magdalene Sisters			
37	Mystics			
38	Evelyn	00:44:39	MDES1950D	Well, I really appreciate your help, **so I do**.
39	Intermission			
40	Song for a Raggy Boy			
41	Veronica Guerin			
42	Goldfish Memory			
43	The Boys and Girl from County Clare			
44	Cowboys and Angels			
45	Adam and Paul			
46	Dead Meat			
47	Inside I'm Dancing			
48	Irish Jam			
49	The Wind that Shakes the Barley			
50	Garage			
				Total: 11/50

Table 44: Sentence-final tags: so

	Film	Time	Speaker	Example of usage
1	The Informer			
2	The Quiet Man			
3	Darby O' Gill and the Little People			
4	Ryan's Daughter			
5	The Dead			
6	High Spirits			
7	My Left Foot			
8	The Field			
9	The Commitments	01:26:01	MD1990D	Did your granny knit that suit, **did she**?
10	Far and Away			
11	The Snapper	01:22:23	MS1990D	Does it really hurt you, Sharon, **does it**?
12	Into the West	00:40:50	MPR1990D	Do ya want me to make a big traveller thing out of it, **do ya**? Is that what ya want?
13	A Man of No Importance			
14	Widows' Peak			
15	Circle of Friends			
16	Last of the High Kings			
17	The Van	01:12:34	ML1990D	Is he downstairs, **is he**?
18	Michael Collins			
19	Trojan Eddie			
20	The Matchmaker			
21	The Nephew	01:06:30	MPe1990C	Was that for my benefit, **was it**?
22	This is my Father	00:50:28	MK1930M	Will we take a look at this ocean, **will we**?
23	Waking Ned			
24	The General	01:48:50	MMC1990D	Did the church let you down, **did it**?
25	A Very Unlucky Leprechaun			

Table 45: Repetition for emphasis

#	Title	Time	Code	Quote
26	A Love Divided			
27	Agnes Browne	00:23:39	MB1960D	Is he lookin' for the vampire, **is he**?
28	Angela's Ashes	00:33:37	MMB1930L	Did you come to school without shoes, **did ya**?
29	When the Sky Falls	00:50:05	MMOF1990D	Mary, will ya come here, **will ya**?
30	About Adam			
31	Ordinary Decent Criminal	00:31:24	MML1990D	I mean, would you trust them, Tom, **would ya**?
32	When Brendan Met Trudy			
33	Nora			
34	Rat			
35	How Harry Became A Tree			
36	The Magdalene Sisters	00:09:32	FB1960D	Do you spend all your time hanging around playgrounds, **do ye**?
37	Mystics			
38	Evelyn	00:07:17	MDES1950D	Is it the bastard I saw her with in the pub, **is it**?
39	Intermission	00:34:23	FN2000D	Did you not hear him, **did you not**?
40	Song for a Raggy Boy			
41	Veronica Guerin	00:49:33	FVG1990D	Do you think I want to do this, **do you**?
42	Goldfish Memory			
43	The Boys and Girl from County Clare			
44	Cowboys and Angels			
45	Adam and Paul	00:11:19	MP2000D	Will I kick the ball, **will I**?
46	Dead Meat			
47	Inside I'm Dancing			
48	Irish Jam			
49	The Wind that Shakes the Barley	00:31:17	MD1920C	Do I know you, **do I**?
50	Garage			
	Total: 17/50			

Table 45: Repetition for emphasis

	Film	Time	Speaker	Example of usage
1	The Informer			
2	The Quiet Man			
3	Darby O' Gill and the Little People	00:15:38	MDOG1800K	Now, **here**, wouldn't it be a shame to put his lordship to the expense of a room in the pub [...] ?
4	Ryan's Daughter			
5	The Dead			
6	High Spirits			
7	My Left Foot			
8	The Field			
9	The Commitments	01:06:00	FMQ1990D	**Here**, let's get in out o' the cold.
10	Far and Away			
11	The Snapper	00:08:11	FM1990D	**Come here**, Jackie. Was he passionate?
12	Into the West			
13	A Man of No Importance	00:37:59	FL1960D	**Come here** till I have a quick word with you for a minute?
14	Widows' Peak			
15	Circle of Friends			
16	Last of the High Kings	01:08:44	MN1970D	**Come here**, your ma is a fruitcake like the rest of your freaking family.
17	The Van	00:03:35	MW1990D	**Come here**, **come here**. This lump sum, how much will you be getting?
18	Michael Collins			
19	Trojan Eddie			
20	The Matchmaker			
21	The Nephew			
22	This is my Father			
23	Waking Ned	00:21:39	MJ2000W	**Here**, wait a minute. What if it's you?
24	The General	00:59:50	MMC1990D	**Here**, let me get me dole money and I'll see what can be done.
25	A Very Unlucky Leprechaun			

Table 46: Discourse markers: *come here/here*

26	A Love Divided	00:10:18	MP1950WX	**Come here** till I tell ya.
27	Agnes Browne			
28	Angela's Ashes			
29	When the Sky Falls			
30	About Adam			
31	Ordinary Decent Criminal	00:26:48	MBi1990D	**Come here to me**, listen, go on upstairs, right, and I'll be with you in a few minutes. All right, chicken?
32	When Brendan Met Trudy			
33	Nora			
34	Rat	00:28:11	FD2000D	**Come here** till I see ya, Hubert.
34	How Harry Became A Tree	01:05:08	MH1920WW	**Come here** till I tell you what you saw.
36	The Magdalene Sisters			
37	Mystics			
38	Evelyn			
39	Intermission	01:21:54	FSa2000D	**Come here**, if you want to leave your job, do you know what I say? Leave your fucking job.
40	Song for a Raggy Boy			
41	Veronica Guerin	00:44:52	MGG1990D	Ah, **here**, we'll want something stronger than that.
42	Goldfish Memory	00:53:21	MTD2000D	**Here**, I'm a busy man!
43	The Boys and Girl from County Clare	00:23:11	MCO1960D	**Come here to me**, your brother is on his way.
44	Cowboys and Angels			
45	Adam and Paul	00:20:17	MP2000D	**Here**, are you not freezing in that bag, no?
46	Dead Meat	01:03:12	MD2000LM	**Here**, do you hear that?
47	Inside I'm Dancing	00:51:12	FS2000D	**Here**, listen to this.
48	Irish Jam			
49	The Wind that Shakes the Barley			
50	Garage	00:10:20	FC2000M	**Here**, Josie, take a punnet of them apples for yourself.
				Total: 20/50

Table 46: Discourse markers: *come here/here*

	Film	Time	Speaker	Example of usage
1	The Informer	00:16:20	FFM1920D	Oh, **praise be to God**, you've come back to us!
2	The Quiet Man	00:07:21	MMF1930W	**Saints preserve us**, what do they feed you Irishmen on in Pittsburgh?
3	Darby O' Gill and the Little People	00:51:38	FBW1800K	**Glory be to the saints of joy**, this is a great day for Rathcullen.
4	Ryan's Daughter	01:03:28	MFR1920W	**Glory be to God**, why must there be? Because Rosy Ryan wants it?
5	The Dead	00:13:18	MB1900D	Ah, sure, **God help me**, it's the doctor's orders.
6	High Spirits	00:50:34	FMP1980W	**Sweet Jesus**, what happened to you?
7	My Left Foot	00:27:25	MMB1950D	**Jesus Sufferin Christ!**
8	The Field	01:11:24	MBMC1950W	Go home, Yank. **For the love of God**, go home.
9	The Commitments	00:37:00	FI1990D	**Good Jaysus!**
10	Far and Away	01:51:55	MJD1890W	**Sweet Mary and Jesus and all the saints preserve us!**
11	The Snapper	00:41:40	MDC1990D	Ah, **Jaysus Christ!**
12	Into the West	00:15:20	FOW1990D	**Holy Mother of Divine God!**
13	A Man of No Importance	00:26:50	FL1960D	Ah, Daddy, **Lord rest him**. Devoted to St Blaze, wasn't he?
14	Widows' Peak	01:20:44	FDC1930M	Oh, **the saints protect her** this day.
15	Circle of Friends	00:23:35	FBH1950D	Oh, **Jesus, Mary and Joseph**, I look like the prow of a ship!
16	Last of the High Kings	01:04:16	MJF1970D	**Lord God**, there must be somwhere cozier where we could….
17	The Van	00:16:16	MB1990D	**Jesus tonight**, Maggie will have given me dinner to the cat.
18	Michael Collins	00:58:52	MVH1910D	**Sweet mother of God!**
19	Trojan Eddie	00:12:20	MG1990M	Poor oul Kitty. **God be good to her**, huh? Ya keep the grave lovely anyway, John. Fair play to ya.
20	The Matchmaker	00:27:00	FSar2000W	**God Almighty**, if their mother were still alive, she'd kill herself.
21	The Nephew	01:10:35	FB1990C	**Holy Divine God!**
22	This is my Father	00:41:44	FT1930M	**God save all here!**
23	Waking Ned	00:46:48	MJ2000W	Oh, **holy mother of God!**
24	The General	01:43:12	FMD1990D	Well, we don't live in Hollyfield now, **thanks be to God**.
25	A Very Unlucky Leprechaun	00:17:39	MPM1990W	Ah, **Begod** that's much better.

Table 47: Religious expressions

26	A Love Divided	00:15:47	MS1950WX	**Sufferin Jesus**, I'll do it.
27	Agnes Browne	00:34:28	FAB1960D	**God bless you**, Mr Foley.
28	Angela's Ashes	00:03:08	FA1930L	**Sweet Jesus in Heaven**, Malachy.
29	When the Sky Falls	00:04:48	MC1990D	**Christ**!
30	About Adam	01:09:21	FA2000D	Well it's the spare-room for me tonight, **thank Christ**!
31	Ordinary Decent Criminal	01:15:56	MSh1990D	**Mother of Christ**!
32	When Brendan Met Trudy	00:48:32	MB2000D	Oh, would you, **Christ**, now, **Jesus**, just stop that ABC drivel!
33	Nora	00:16:19	MNF1900G	**Jim, for Jaysus' sake!**
34	Rat	00:27:15	FC2000D	**Sacred heart!**
34	How Harry Became A Tree	00:17:02	MH1920W	As my Annie, **God rest her soul**, always said, "The future of this country, if it has any future at all, lies in cabbages".
36	The Magdalene Sisters	00:26:56	FK1960D	**Jesus, Mary and Holy St Joseph**, get them away from me.
37	Mystics	00:46:20	FF2000D	**In the name of Jaysus**, Larry, what is it?
38	Evelyn	01:01:19	MBM1950D	**Holy Jesus!** This thing'll never catch on.
39	Intermission	00:25:17	FM2000D	**Jesus, Mary and Joseph!**
40	Song for a Raggy Boy	00:44:38	MMF1930	**Jesus Christ**, Mercier, I thought you had a brain in your head!
41	Veronica Guerin	01:02:41	FBG1990D	**Jesus! Jesus**, what happened to you?
42	Goldfish Memory	01:11:56	MT2000D	**Mother of Divine Jesus!**
43	The Boys and Girl from County Clare	00:49:29	MJ1960Cl	**Jaysus!**
44	Cowboys and Angels	00:30:10	MJ2000L	My poor mother, **the Lord have mercy on her**, she was over the moon.
45	Adam and Paul	00:11:21	MG2000D	Ah, **Jaysus!** Would ya leave the young fella alone?
46	Dead Meat	00:42:13	MC2000LM	**Lord bless us and save us**. You'd nearly...you'd nearly say they were better off dead.
47	Inside I'm Dancing	00:07:54	MT2000D	Use your card, **for Christ's sake!**
48	Irish Jam	00:52:57	MG2000W	Oh, **God forbid!** I'm no racist.
49	The Wind that Shakes the Barley	00:50:48	MC1920C	Oh, **Jesus Christ Almighty!**
50	Garage	00:31:26	MJ2000M	Oh, **Lord**, no.
				Total: 50/50

Table 47: Religious expressions

Film	Time	Speaker	Example of usage
1 The Informer			
2 The Quiet Man			
3 Darby O' Gill and the Little People	00:35:04	MDOG1800K	**Arrah!** And how was the chase, hmm?
4 Ryan's Daughter			
5 The Dead			
6 High Spirits			
7 My Left Foot			
8 The Field			
9 The Commitments			
10 Far and Away			
11 The Snapper			
12 Into the West	01:13:34	MTR1990D	**Arrah**, I suppose it just blew away to nothin'.
13 A Man of No Importance			
14 Widows' Peak			
15 Circle of Friends			
16 Last of the High Kings			
17 The Van			
18 Michael Collins	00:06:09	MJC1910M	**Arrah**, he'd never get out of there alive.
19 Trojan Eddie			
20 The Matchmaker			
21 The Nephew			
22 This is my Father	01:25:43	MSgt1930M	And if you're missin', **arrah**, I suppose sure it'll be dark, there'll be no point in lookin' until the next day, I suppose.
23 Waking Ned			
24 The General			
25 A Very Unlucky Leprechaun			

Table 48: Discourse markers: *arrah*

#	Title			
26	A Love Divided			
27	Agnes Browne			
28	Angela's Ashes			
29	When the Sky Falls			
30	About Adam			
31	Ordinary Decent Criminal			
32	When Brendan Met Trudy	00:07:57	FT2000C	**Arrah**, go on. Sing one!
33	Nora			
34	Rat			
35	How Harry Became A Tree			
36	The Magdalene Sisters			
37	Mystics			
38	Evelyn			
39	Intermission			
40	Song for a Raggy Boy			
41	Veronica Guerin			
42	Goldfish Memory			
43	The Boys and Girl from County Clare			
44	Cowboys and Angels			
45	Adam and Paul			
46	Dead Meat			
47	Inside I'm Dancing			
48	Irish Jam			
49	The Wind that Shakes the Barley			
50	Garage			
	Total: 5/50			

Table 48: Discourse markers: *arrah*

	Film	Time	Speaker	Example of usage
1	The Informer	00:16:37	FFM1920D	Ah, **musha**, me son, sure you must be starvin'.
2	The Quiet Man	00:47:31	MMOB1930W	Oh, **musha, musha!**
3	Darby O' Gill and the Little People			
4	Ryan's Daughter			
5	The Dead			
6	High Spirits			
7	My Left Foot			
8	The Field			
9	The Commitments			
10	Far and Away			
11	The Snapper			
12	Into the West			
13	A Man of No Importance			
14	Widows' Peak			
15	Circle of Friends			
16	Last of the High Kings			
17	The Van			
18	Michael Collins			
19	Trojan Eddie			
20	The Matchmaker			
21	The Nephew			
22	This is my Father			
23	Waking Ned			
24	The General			
25	A Very Unlucky Leprechaun			

Table 49: Discourse markers: *musha*

#	Title	
26	A Love Divided	
27	Agnes Browne	
28	Angela's Ashes	
29	When the Sky Falls	
30	About Adam	
31	Ordinary Decent Criminal	
32	When Brendan Met Trudy	
33	Nora	
34	Rat	
35	How Harry Became A Tree	
36	The Magdalene Sisters	
37	Mystics	
38	Evelyn	
39	Intermission	
40	Song for a Raggy Boy	
41	Veronica Guerin	
42	Goldfish Memory	
43	The Boys and Girl from County Clare	
44	Cowboys and Angels	
45	Adam and Paul	
46	Dead Meat	
47	Inside I'm Dancing	
48	Irish Jam	
49	The Wind that Shakes the Barley	
50	Garage	
	Total: 2/50	

Table 49: Discourse markers: *musha*

	Film	Time	Speaker	Example of usage
1	The Informer			
2	The Quiet Man			
3	Darby O' Gill and the Little People			
4	Ryan's Daughter			
5	The Dead	00:17:17	MF1900D	Hello, **Ma**!
6	High Spirits	00:11:40	MDMC1980W	Oh, **Mammy**!
7	My Left Foot	00:49:20	FSB1950D	Look after me **ma** for me.
8	The Field	01:04:22	MT1950W	Why don't you and **ma** talk?
9	The Commitments	00:46:14	F1990D	Jesus, my **ma** would crease me if she thought I was a sex machine.
10	Far and Away			
11	The Snapper	00:06:11	MDC1990D	Your **mammy** took it very well.
12	Into the West	00:38:55	MOR1990D	What did **Mammy** look like?
13	A Man of No Importance	00:15:11	MRo1960D	Me **mam** puts in beef.
14	Widows' Peak	00:13:58	MGDC1930M	The **mammy** and I live up the hill from you.
15	Circle of Friends	01:09:22	FNM1950D	No, **Mam**. I'm going out.
16	Last of the High Kings	00:10:15	MF1970D	And that's my mother, **Ma**.
17	The Van	00:13:35	MW1990D	There's a funny whiff off your **mammy-in-law**.
18	Michael Collins			
19	Trojan Eddie	00:39:15	MJP1990M	When my family - my dada and my **mam** - came in….
20	The Matchmaker	01:01:37	MBoy2000W	**Ma**'s going to kill me.
21	The Nephew	01:10:37	MD1990C	What do you think, **Ma**?
22	This is my Father	00:20:57	MT2000M	Ah, the world's changed, **Mammy**.
23	Waking Ned			
24	The General	00:35:57	FW1990D	Go back to sleep, **Ma**.
25	A Very Unlucky Leprechaun			

Table 50: Lexical features: *ma/mam/mammy*

#	Title	Time	Code	Quote
26	A Love Divided	00:12:11	FE1950WX	**Mammy** said the dinner will only be fit for pigs.
27	Agnes Browne	00:06:19	MFB1960D	Ma! **Mammy**!
28	Angela's Ashes	00:06:16	MN1990L	My aunts wrote to my **mam**'s mother to send money for the tickets.
29	When the Sky Falls	01:04:42	FSH1990D	You be good, and **mammy** and daddy will pick you up in the morning.
30	About Adam	00:13:37	FM2000D	His Dad was always promising his **mam** that, when they had a bit of money to splash out, he'd buy her one.
31	Ordinary Decent Criminal	00:12:11	MML1990D	…. so your **ma** and me and Lisa, we barricaded ourselves in and **we** wouldn't come out.
32	When Brendan Met Trudy	00:26:45	FSA2000D	Samantha, your **Mammy** wants ya.
33	Nora			
34	Rat	00:54:16	FM2000D	**Mammy**!
35	How Harry Became A Tree	01:19:21	MG1920WW	You put Pat in the ground and you put **Mam** in after him.
36	The Magdalene Sisters	00:08:02	MMB1960D	**Ma**! Where's Father Doyle taking Margaret?
37	Mystics	00:08:16	MD2000D	The **mammy** was dead chuffed though. That's what matters.
38	Evelyn	00:05:55	FE1950D	**Mammy**, come back. It's St Stephen's Day the shops are shut.
39	Intermission	00:15:37	FD2000D	Sorry, **Ma**!
40	Song for a Raggy Boy			
41	Veronica Guerin	00:36:46	FVG1990D	You're getting too big for your old **ma**.
42	Goldfish Memory	00:04:52	MT2000D	God save us from Irish **mammies**!
43	The Boys and Girl from County Clare	00:45:51	FA1960CI	**Mammy**! **Mam**, hold on! Wait!
44	Cowboys and Angels	00:19:55	MS2000L	**Ma**, I'm not lonely. I'm not lonely, **Mam**!
45	Adam and Paul	01:09:26	FO2000D	You alright, **Ma**?
46	Dead Meat			
47	Inside I'm Dancing			
48	Irish Jam			
49	The Wind that Shakes the Barley	00:02:57	MD1920C	I want to go up above and see Peggy and your **mam**.
50	Garage	00:46:54	MBr2000M	Regina, run over there and ask your **mammy** is she matchin' collar and cuffs.
				Total: 37/50

Table 50: Lexical features: *ma/mam/mammy*

	Film	Time	Speaker	Example of usage
1	The Informer			
2	The Quiet Man			
3	Darby O' Gill and the Little People			
4	Ryan's Daughter			
5	The Dead			
6	High Spirits			
7	My Left Foot	01:23:42	MBB1950D	I think it's brilliant. It's the image of **Da**.
8	The Field	00:27:36	MT1950W	What are they saying, **Da**?
9	The Commitments	00:21:57	MJR1990D	You're the same age as me **da**.
10	Far and Away	01:39:34	MJD1890W	**Da**, is that you?
11	The Snapper	00:06:06	MDC1990D	I still think you should tell us who the **da** is.
12	Into the West	00:28:04	MTR1990D	Please, **Da**!
13	A Man of No Importance			
14	Widows' Peak			
15	Circle of Friends	00:03:04	FBH1950D	I don't think me ma and **da** would let me.
16	Last of the High Kings	00:06:32	MF1970D	It's **Da**!
17	The Van	01:00:59	MK1990D	**Da**! Lookit!
18	Michael Collins			
19	Trojan Eddie	00:18:26	MD1990M	Her **da** is a bare-knuckle boxer, you know.
20	The Matchmaker			
21	The Nephew			
22	This is my Father			
23	Waking Ned	00:39:03	MB2000W	Jeez, man, you're not the **da**!
24	The General	00:07:38	MMC1990D	Your **da's** here.
25	A Very Unlucky Leprechaun			

Table 51: Lexical features: *da*

26	A Love Divided			
27	Agnes Browne	00:33:29	MMB1960D	It was good enough for me **da**.
28	Angela's Ashes	01:25:15	MF1940L	You drank the money, **Da**.
29	When the Sky Falls			
30	About Adam			
31	Ordinary Decent Criminal	00:05:49	FLL1990D	Say hello to your **da**.
32	When Brendan Met Trudy			
33	Nora			
34	Rat	00:32:07	FM2000D	You shouldn't have done that, **Da**.
35	How Harry Became A Tree	00:03:59	MG1920WW	Jesus, **Da**, will ya wait until the rain stops?
36	The Magdalene Sisters	00:30:35	FUOC1960D	Please don't leave me here, **Da**!
37	Mystics	00:04:23	ML2000D	And tell **Da** to go easy on the hard stuff.
38	Evelyn	00:04:30	MDES1950D	Happy Christmas, **Da**!
39	Intermission	00:19:46	MG2000D	Me **da** used to say "Hate your opponent [...] Hate him and you'll never give less than 100%."
40	Song for a Raggy Boy			
41	Veronica Guerin			
42	Goldfish Memory	01:16:58	MC2000C	Jesus, I thought it was your **da**!
43	The Boys and Girl from County Clare			
44	Cowboys and Angels			
45	Adam and Paul			
46	Dead Meat			
47	Inside I'm Dancing	00:16:50	MROS2000D	Is that your **da**?
48	Irish Jam	00:20:00	FM2000W	Once there was a time, my **da** would always say before tellin' us stories that would send me off to my dreams.
49	The Wind that Shakes the Barley			
50	Garage			
				Total: 24/50

Table 51: Lexical features: *da*

	Film	Time	Speaker	Example of usage
1	The Informer	01:26:23	FK1920D	Poor **lad**.
2	The Quiet Man			
3	Darby O' Gill and the Little People	00:04:55	FMS1800K	He's a fine strong **lad**.
4	Ryan's Daughter	00:22:58	MFR1920W	Charles, what do they say they'll do with the **lads** they've got in prison?
5	The Dead			
6	High Spirits			
7	My Left Foot	01:17:34	MMB1950D	Right, **lads**. You bring in some more bricks, mix up a bit of muck.
8	The Field	01:02:55	MBMC1950W	Now, **lads**, if the civic guards come around asking questions, we were here playing cards all night. Right **lads**!
9	The Commitments	00:16:33	MJR1990D	Listen, **lads**, when this band is happenin', you'll be fightin' women off.
10	Far and Away	00:05:20	MDD1980W	**Lads**, your father's been damaged!
11	The Snapper	00:34:39	MGB1990D	I was just messing with the **lads**.
12	Into the West			
13	A Man of No Importance	00:16:04	MRo1960D	Acting's stupid. The **lads**'d rag the arse off of me if I came on acting.
14	Widows' Peak	01:03:00	MMC1930M	If it's a drink you want, it's down there. Good **lad**.
15	Circle of Friends			
16	Last of the High Kings	00:03:51	MMF1970D	Hey **lads**, come on get down!
17	The Van	00:47:32	MG1990D	Oh, Jaysus, he'll crack, **lads**, I'm telling you.
18	Michael Collins	00:48:49	MMC1910C	**Lads**, **lads**. Can a man not say goodbye to his wife in peace?
19	Trojan Eddie	00:28:20	MTE1990M	Go ahead upstairs, **lads**, will yez. Good girls.
20	The Matchmaker			
21	The Nephew	00:19:17	MPe1990C	You're goin' to give these two **lads** here a heart attack.
22	This is my Father	00:30:01	MAD1930M	Well, here goes, **lads**. Wish me luck.
23	Waking Ned			
24	The General	01:26:14	MN1990D	Oh, my Jaysus, don't go messin' with them **lads**.
25	A Very Unlucky Leprechaun	00:32:31	MCW1990W	Ah, come on, **lads**. You can blow harder than that.

Table 52: Lexical features: *lad/lads*

26	A Love Divided	00:11:53	MA1950WX	There you go, **lads**.
27	Agnes Browne			
28	Angela's Ashes	01:18:41	MUP1930L	Jaysus, your eyes look atrocious, **lad**.
29	When the Sky Falls	00:12:36	MDA21990D	Look at this, **lads**.
30	About Adam			
31	Ordinary Decent Criminal	00:49:39	MGS1990D	I'm sorry but we'd look like fools presenting that idea to the top **lads** in Interpol.
32	When Brendan Met Trudy	00:17:21	FT2000C	This is the **lad** I was telling you about.
33	Nora	00:57:15	MJJ1900D	Where are you going, you fine, big **lad**?
34	Rat	00:26:07	MMI2000D	Give him some air, **lads**.
35	How Harry Became A Tree	00:40:35	MH1920WW	Oh, there's nothing in the sky this **lad** need fear. Or under it neither.
36	The Magdalene Sisters	00:38:44	FB1960D	I've never been with any **lads**, ever.
37	Mystics	00:38:48	MW2000D	Do yourselves a favour, **lads**. Tell him!
38	Evelyn	00:48:09	MTC1950D	Anyway, **lads**, your case is interesting.
39	Intermission	00:16:09	MRO2000C	All right, you **lads** ready?
40	Song for a Raggy Boy	01:07:08	MDB1930	I'll see ya, **lads**.
41	Veronica Guerin	00:56:56	FPO1990D	Those **lads** go to meetings with their probation officers in BMWs and Mercedes.
42	Goldfish Memory			
43	The Boys and Girl from County Clare	00:41:26	MO1960CI	Right, **lads**. We're ready for you.
44	Cowboys and Angels	00:56:12	MK2000L	Listen, there's no problem, **lads**. He's with me, ok?
45	Adam and Paul	00:18:04	MW2000D	**Lads**, if I see yiz near Janine, I'm not jokin ya, I'll kill yiz! Okay?
46	Dead Meat			
47	Inside I'm Dancing	00:20:28	FGIP2000D	Thanks for the drinks, **lads**. We have to head off.
48	Irish Jam	00:27:19	MG2000W	Oh, good evening, **lads**. And what's goin' on?
49	The Wind that Shakes the Barley	00:51:06	MC1920C	Ah, Jesus Christ, **lads**. He's only a young fella, like.
50	Garage	01:07:10	MSgt2000M	I'll just have to copy this and see how the **lads** are getting on.
				Total: 39/50

Table 52: Lexical features: *lad/lads*

	Film	Time	Speaker	Example of usage
1	The Informer			
2	The Quiet Man			
3	Darby O' Gill and the Little People			
4	Ryan's Daughter			
5	The Dead			
6	High Spirits			
7	My Left Foot			
8	The Field			
9	The Commitments	01:06:31	MS1990D	Mickah, would you get **yer man** off the piano here?
10	Far and Away			
11	The Snapper	00:28:47	MDC1990D	You know **yer man**, George Burges?
12	Into the West			
13	A Man of No Importance			
14	Widows' Peak			
15	Circle of Friends			
16	Last of the High Kings			
17	The Van	01:20:14	MB1990D	If it hadn't been **your man**, it would have been something else.
18	Michael Collins	00:08:29	MMC1910C	So, tell me, how long has **your man** been there for?
19	Trojan Eddie			
20	The Matchmaker	00:58:15	FMa2000W	Now, who's **yer man** in the suit?
21	The Nephew			
22	This is my Father			
23	Waking Ned	01:21:20	MJ2000W	I was just looking at **your man** there…Al Capone.
24	The General	01:04:47	MMC1990D	It's a shoppin' list. She's sendin' **yer woman** down to the shop for a package of cornflakes.
25	A Very Unlucky Leprechaun			

Table 53: Lexical features: *your man/your woman/your one*

#	Title	Time	Code	Quote
26	A Love Divided			
27	Agnes Browne	00:45:21	FSW1960D	**Yer man** looks like he's making his move.
28	Angela's Ashes			
29	When the Sky Falls	00:12:19	MDA1990D	**Yer woman**, what's her name?
30	About Adam	01:01:31	MH2000D	So, by the time **yer man**, Adam, gets older, you know, it's starting to sink in to him, the significance of this wreck.
31	Ordinary Decent Criminal	00:48:51	MN1990D	He's imitating the painting, Sir. Same as **yer man**, Judas, there.
32	When Brendan Met Trudy			
33	Nora	01:16:20	FE1900D	**Yer man** who wanted to paint you?
34	Rat			
35	How Harry Became A Tree			
36	The Magdalene Sisters			
37	Mystics	00:46:09	MW2000D	It's **your man**, chancing his arm.
38	Evelyn	00:23:30	MDES1950D	Who's **yer man** in the sharp suit over there?
39	Intermission	00:56:17	MR2000D	Look at **yer woman's** make up.
40	Song for a Raggy Boy			
41	Veronica Guerin	00:23:51	MJG1990D	**Yer man**, Martin Cahill, thinks over half a million quid is owed him.
42	Goldfish Memory	00:28:32	MTD2000D	Are you **your one** off the telly?
43	The Boys and Girl from County Clare			
44	Cowboys and Angels			
45	Adam and Paul			
46	Dead Meat			
47	Inside I'm Dancing	01:12:24	MZS2000D	Who's **yer man**?
48	Irish Jam			
49	The Wind that Shakes the Barley			
50	Garage			
			Total: 18/50	

Table 53: Lexical features: *your man/your woman/your one*

	Film	Time	Speaker	Example of usage
1	The Informer			
2	The Quiet Man	00:03:42	FBW1930W	Me sister's third young **one** is living at Inisfree, and she'd be only too happy for to show you the road.
3	Darby O' Gill and the Little People			
4	Ryan's Daughter			
5	The Dead	00:15:12	MF1900D	Have you heard the latest about old man Gallagher and the young **one**?
6	High Spirits			
7	My Left Foot			
8	The Field			
9	The Commitments			
10	Far and Away			
11	The Snapper	00:05:10	MDC1990D	Sure, the O'Neill young **ones** are after having kids, the pair of them.
12	Into the West			
13	A Man of No Importance	00:10:35	FA1960M	Was that the **one** danced for Herod and got the head of John the Baptist on a plate?
14	Widows' Peak	00:05:15	MMC1930M	The first day I clapped eyes on that **one**, I made up my mind.
15	Circle of Friends	00:21:44	MMF1950D	That **one** had a nice soft look about her. Nice eyes, beautiful hair, a lovely smile, a fine set of teeth on her.
16	Last of the High Kings	00:14:37	FMG1970D	Lots of pretty young **ones** floating round you.
17	The Van	00:03:01	MB1990D	Marie's young **one** has epilepsy, did I tell ya?
18	Michael Collins			
19	Trojan Eddie	00:27:36	FM1990M	She's no bloody good that **one**.
20	The Matchmaker			
21	The Nephew			
22	This is my Father	00:29:47	MAD21930M	His oul **one** won't allow it.
23	Waking Ned	00:12:50	FA2000W	That Mrs Kennedy is a fine **one** for the champagne.
24	The General	01:05:05	Mga1990D	Look at the knockers on that **one**.
25	A Very Unlucky Leprechaun			

Table 54: Lexical features: *one* for females

26	A Love Divided	00:24:31	FS1950WX	Have you a desk for this **one**, Anna?
27	Agnes Browne	00:25:15	FAB1960D	That **one**'s getting as cheeky since she started hanging out with Mary Dowdall.
28	Angela's Ashes			
29	When the Sky Falls			
30	About Adam			
31	Ordinary Decent Criminal	00:19:20	MGM1990D	You know you drive like a bleedin' oul **one**.
32	When Brendan Met Trudy			
33	Nora			
34	Rat			
35	How Harry Became A Tree	00:06:00	MH1920WW	You have a new **one**, I see.
36	The Magdalene Sisters			
37	Mystics			
38	Evelyn			
39	Intermission	01:20:50	ML2000D	Now, who's this crazy oul **one**?
40	Song for a Raggy Boy			
41	Veronica Guerin			
42	Goldfish Memory	00:28:32	MTD2000D	Are you your **one** off the telly?
43	The Boys and Girl from County Clare			
44	Cowboys and Angels			
45	Adam and Paul	00:12:09	FM2000D	She has me wore out, that **one**. Always wanting her hair plaited.
46	Dead Meat	00:41:00	FF2000LM	Is there something wrong with that **one** back there?
47	Inside I'm Dancing			
48	Irish Jam			
49	The Wind that Shakes the Barley			
50	Garage			
				Total: 20/50

Table 54: Lexical features: *one* for females

	Film	Time	Speaker	Example of usage
1	The Informer			
2	The Quiet Man			
3	Darby O' Gill and the Little People			
4	Ryan's Daughter			
5	The Dead			
6	High Spirits			
7	My Left Foot			
8	The Field	01:02:55	MBMC1950W	Now, lads, if the **Civic Guards** come around asking questions, we were here playing cards all night. Right, lads?
9	The Commitments			
10	Far and Away			
11	The Snapper			
12	Into the West			
13	A Man of No Importance			
14	Widows' Peak			
15	Circle of Friends	01:28:25	FBH1950D	Now, get out of here before I call the **guard**.
16	Last of the High Kings			
17	The Van			
18	Michael Collins			
19	Trojan Eddie			
20	The Matchmaker			
21	The Nephew			
22	This is my Father	01:23:02	FMF1930M	The **guards** are going to be here for you later today.
23	Waking Ned			
24	The General	01:32:01	MN1990D	The **guards** have more guns than us, Martin.
25	A Very Unlucky Leprechaun			

Table 55: Lexical features: *guard/guards/gardaí*

26	A Love Divided	00:29:58	MC1950WX	The **guards** think she got the train to Belfast.
27	Agnes Browne			
28	Angela's Ashes			
29	When the Sky Falls	00:06:28	FSH1990D	So why do the **guards** follow your car?
30	About Adam			
31	Ordinary Decent Criminal	00:18:07	MSG1990D	I will not have the reputation of the **Garda Síochána** brought into disrepute by these shenanigans.
32	When Brendan Met Trudy	00:30:38	MMOC2000D	The **Gardaí** at Rathmines have issued an identikit of the black balaclava worn by the assailant.
33	Nora			
34	Rat	00:04:39	FW2000D	Get away now before I call the **guards**.
35	How Harry Became A Tree			
36	The Magdalene Sisters	00:09:41	FT1960D	Right, lads, that's enough. Move it or I'll call the **guards**.
37	Mystics	00:11:18	FF2000D	Christmas came early for the **guards** this year, Sean.
38	Evelyn	00:54:48	MHC1950D	Desmond Doyle struggles with the **gardaí** for possession of his children.
39	Intermission	00:19:35	MG2000D	I could have turned pro, except for I joined the **guards**. Made crime me calling.
40	Song for a Raggy Boy			
41	Veronica Guerin	00:09:46	MMC1990D	What did you have to go and shoot your mouth off to the **guards** about me for?
42	Goldfish Memory	01:03:16	FP2000D	I'll call the **guards** on you.
43	The Boys and Girl from County Clare			
44	Cowboys and Angels			
45	Adam and Paul	00:25:49	FCO2000D	Someone call the **guards** now.
46	Dead Meat			
47	Inside I'm Dancing	00:23:37	MDM2000M	How are you, **Garda**?
48	Irish Jam			
49	The Wind that Shakes the Barley			
50	Garage			
				Total: 17/50

Table 55: Lexical features: *guard/guards/gardaí*

	Film	Time	Speaker	Example of usage
1	The Informer			
2	The Quiet Man			
3	Darby O' Gill and the Little People	01:13:20	MDOG1800K	... he told me there was only one man in the town who was happy altogether - the village **eejit**.
4	Ryan's Daughter			
5	The Dead			
6	High Spirits			
7	My Left Foot			
8	The Field			
9	The Commitments	01:08:42	MB1990D	And you, George Michael, if you ever call me a fuckin' **eejit** again, you'll go home with a drumstick stuck up your hole!
10	Far and Away			
11	The Snapper	00:39:31	FMB1990D	Dirty-lookin' **eejit**!
12	Into the West			
13	A Man of No Importance			
14	Widows' Peak			
15	Circle of Friends	01:06:04	MBM1950D	Nasey, you dirty-lookin' **eejit**, now look what you're after doing.
16	Last of the High Kings	00:16:23	MN1970D	Gallo, you big **eejit**! What do you think you're like?
17	The Van	01:25:42	ML1990D	Where are you, you fuckin' **eejit** you?
18	Michael Collins			
19	Trojan Eddie	01:31:08	MJP1990M	Trojan Eddie? Trojan fuckin' **eejit**!
20	The Matchmaker	00:27:40	FSar2000W	I mean, why would you give up a good career like that to chase your brother around the hotel like an **eejit**?
21	The Nephew			
22	This is my Father	00:39:01	MP1930M	You're making **eejits** of us.
23	Waking Ned	00:22:11	MJ2000W	Stupid **eejit**!
24	The General			
25	A Very Unlucky Leprechaun			

Table 56: Lexical features: *eejit*

26	A Love Divided	00:04:55	FS1950WX	Sean Cloney, ya **eejit**, we're late for church!
27	Agnes Browne	00:12:16	MB1960D	He was an **eejit**.
28	Angela's Ashes	02:03:11	FA1930L	You've a mouth on you worse than your drunken **eejit** father.
29	When the Sky Falls	00:38:30	MDA1990D	Quit the messin', ya fuckin' **eejit**, ya!
30	About Adam	00:18:35	FL2000D	Just hope I don't make a complete **eejit** of meself.
31	Ordinary Decent Criminal	00:46:35	MML1990D	In fact, I think we can give them the runaround any time we like 'cause they're only **eejits**
32	When Brendan Met Trudy	01:12:03	FT2000C	Oh, ya **eejit**.
33	Nora			
34	Rat			
35	How Harry Became A Tree	00:46:10	MH1920WW	You fuckin **eejit**!
36	The Magdalene Sisters			
37	Mystics			
38	Evelyn	00:35:48	FB1950D	I knew you were up to something, you big **eejit**.
39	Intermission	00:54:31	FSG2000D	Fucking **eejit**!
40	Song for a Raggy Boy			
41	Veronica Guerin	00:30:18	MJM1990D	Bunch of fuckin' **eejits**. Working and paying taxes.
42	Goldfish Memory	00:09:21	MR2000D	Fuckin' **eejit**.
43	The Boys and Girl from County Clare	00:44:03	MJJ1960CI	Not to me, ya **eejit**. Him!
44	Cowboys and Angels			
45	Adam and Paul	00:16:00	FM2000D	Now look at yiz. Yiz are like the two…fuckin' **eejits**
46	Dead Meat	00:39:54	MC2000LM	Bit of a fucking **eejit** by the looks of it.
47	Inside I'm Dancing			
48	Irish Jam	00:15:30	MBMN2000W	What are you two **eejits** laughin' at?
49	The Wind that Shakes the Barley			
50	Garage			
				Total: 26/50

Table 56: Lexical features: *eejit*

	Film	Time	Speaker	Example of usage
1	The Informer	00:53:30	MSP1920D	Music for me **oul** friend and bosom companion.
2	The Quiet Man			
3	Darby O' Gill and the Little People	00:44:22	MKB1800K	Ah you wicked **ould** divil. You murderin' **ould** hypocrite!
4	Ryan's Daughter			
5	The Dead			
6	High Spirits			
7	My Left Foot	00:17:16	MMB1950D	That's only an **oul** squiggle.
8	The Field			
9	The Commitments			
10	Far and Away	00:08:35	MMD1890W	And, by God, if you manage it, your **ould** da will be smiling down on you from Heaven above.
11	The Snapper	00:34:24	MDC1990D	You should be ashamed of yourself. An **oul** fella like you.
12	Into the West			
13	A Man of No Importance	00:10:32	MRM1960D	Get out of the way, ya dozy **oul** bollocks ya!
14	Widows' Peak	00:47:23	MMG1930M	She's a harmless soul, a relic of **oul** daycency.
15	Circle of Friends			
16	Last of the High Kings	00:38:33	MTD1970D	Jeez, must have been a long **ould** flight.
17	The Van			
18	Michael Collins	00:07:37	MMC1910C	You're like an **oul** clockin' hen, fussin' all the time.
19	Trojan Eddie	00:09:56	MR1990M	I got this big **oul** antique wardrobe off them a couple of weeks ago there.
20	The Matchmaker	01:22:28	FLii2000W	I'm goin' to miss you, ya **ould** bastard.
21	The Nephew	00:08:16	MF1990D	Shag off, ya **oul** bollix.
22	This is my Father	00:22:02	MT2000M	That's just an **oul** expression.
23	Waking Ned	00:05:20	MM2000W	Now, Jackie, would I spend me time sitting on this **ould** beach if I was a millionaire?
24	The General	01:18:49	MMC1990D	Ah there she is. Still at the **oul** writin'.
25	A Very Unlucky Leprechaun			

Table 57: Lexical features: *oul/ould*

#	Title	Time	Code	Quote
26	A Love Divided	00:11:58	MA1950WX	How is that bad-tempered **oul** horse of Tom's anyway?
27	Agnes Browne			
28	Angela's Ashes	02:00:38	FA1930L	That **oul** bitch Finnucane sent her a threatening letter. Look!
29	When the Sky Falls			
30	About Adam			
31	Ordinary Decent Criminal	00:16:58	MN2000D	Don't tell me you were off banging some other **oul** slag.
32	When Brendan Met Trudy			
33	Nora	00:40:42	FN1900G	The **oul** bitch.
34	Rat	00:27:22	FD2000D	Poor **oul** Conchita. I'm sorry for your trouble.
35	How Harry Became A Tree	00:19:37	MH1920WW	It was a hard **oul** years work all the same, what?
36	The Magdalene Sisters	01:32:00	FB1960D	What are you rambling on about, you **oul** witch?
37	Mystics	00:11:14	MV2000D	Good riddance to him, anyway, the **ould** bollix.
38	Evelyn	00:31:49	MG1950D	Ah, poor **oul** Dessie's been going through a rough **oul** time lately.
39	Intermission	00:22:45	FM2000D	Would you not get yourself a bit of imac or something and get rid of that **oul** ronnie your cultivatin'?
40	Song for a Raggy Boy			
41	Veronica Guerin	00:50:24	FVG1990D	You drive like an **oul** granny.
42	Goldfish Memory	00:28:21	MTD2000D	Ah, well, now, it's a busy **oul** night.
43	The Boys and Girl from County Clare			
44	Cowboys and Angels			
45	Adam and Paul	00:09:39	MG2000D	Just in here, like. Bit of the **oul** skills training with the young fella.
46	Dead Meat			
47	Inside I'm Dancing	00:32:40	MROS2000D	You've rejected my application three times on the unsupported word of interfering, dried-up **oul** bitches…
48	Irish Jam	00:02:49	MG2000W	That **oul** scrooge.
49	The Wind that Shakes the Barley			
50	Garage	01:06:42	MJ2000M	I could send the mother a letter, tell her I'm sorry and no harm done. Nothing, like. Just innocent **oul** craic is all.
				Total: 31/50

Table 57: Lexical features: *oul/ould*

	Film	Time	Speaker	Example of usage
1	The Informer			
2	The Quiet Man			
3	Darby O' Gill and the Little People			
4	Ryan's Daughter			
5	The Dead			
6	High Spirits			
7	My Left Foot			
8	The Field			
9	The Commitments	01:00:54	FB1990D	Will you stop talkin' **shite**, Joey?
10	Far and Away			
11	The Snapper	00:59:15	MDC1990D	They're only a shower of **shites**!
12	Into the West			
13	A Man of No Importance	01:29:47	MRo1960D	Ah, don't mind that old **shite** Carson. He had me transferred.
14	Widows' Peak			
15	Circle of Friends			
16	Last of the High Kings	00:16:32	MN1970D	You, ya little **shite**! Take it back!
17	The Van	00:31:47	ML1990D	I nearly did a **shite** in me trousers.
18	Michael Collins			
19	Trojan Eddie	00:17:56	MGG1990M	It'd want to be better than that heap of **shite** you gave me for the breakfast. The fuckin' dogs wouldn't eat it.
20	The Matchmaker	00:15:52	MTon2000W	Dermot, what kind of **shite** is this?
21	The Nephew			
22	This is my Father	00:26:45	MK1930M	**Shite**!
23	Waking Ned			
24	The General	01:42:19	Mga1990D	The Gardaí will beat the fuckin' **shite** out of me. You know what they're like with perverts.
25	A Very Unlucky Leprechaun			

Table 58: Lexical features: *shite*

#	Title	Time	Code	Quote
26	A Love Divided	00:32:49	MA1950WX	I would have said it's about time some people here stood up to all this church **shite**!
27	Agnes Browne	00:46:40	FAB1960D	Marion Monks, you go and **shite**!
28	Angela's Ashes	01:42:42	MLG1950L	I'm telling you, that boy is a little **shite**.
29	When the Sky Falls	00:13:18	MMOF1990D	Take this **shite** with you.
30	About Adam	00:59:39	FA2000D	We don't need to talk **shite**.
31	Ordinary Decent Criminal	00:52:27	MA1990D	I couldn't give a **shite**, man, to be honest with you.
32	When Brendan Met Trudy	00:06:39	FT2000C	You're a bit of a **shite** aren't you? It'd be a desperate party anyway.
33	Nora	00:51:45	MSJ1900D	For Christ's sake, Jim, you are half blind from that **shite** already. Would you not think of the work?
34	Rat	00:20:25	FM2000D	You're gonna be a priest and you're called after twelve popes and you want to kill your da, ya little **shite**.
35	How Harry Became A Tree	01:04:04	MH1920WW	You're my witness. You saw him turn on me and beat seven shades of **shite** out of me.
36	The Magdalene Sisters	01:33:35	FB1960D	The sisters don't give a **shite** about you and neither do I.
37	Mystics			
38	Evelyn	00:46:00	MDES1950D	Oh, by the way, Minister, your paintwork's **shite**.
39	Intermission	01:04:52	ML2000D	Vitamins and **shite**.
40	Song for a Raggy Boy			
41	Veronica Guerin	01:07:00	FVG1990D	Gilligan got you to feed me that **shite** about Hutch.
42	Goldfish Memory			
43	The Boys and Girl from County Clare			
44	Cowboys and Angels			
45	Adam and Paul	00:38:40	MP2000D	I'm not havin' a **shite** down a lane. I'm not a fuckin' dog.
46	Dead Meat	00:46:10	MC2000LM	Yeah, I bet you didn't expect this **shite** this morning, did you?
47	Inside I'm Dancing	01:02:16	MROS2000D	If it wasn't for me, you'd still be sitting in your own **shite** in Carrigmore, spelling out toilet on that piece of card.
48	Irish Jam	00:05:30	MBMN2000W	Well, I think it's **shite**.
49	The Wind that Shakes the Barley			
50	Garage			
				Total: 27/50

Table 58: Lexical features: *shite*

	Film	Time	Speaker	Example of usage
1	The Informer			
2	The Quiet Man			
3	Darby O' Gill and the Little People			
4	Ryan's Daughter			
5	The Dead			
6	High Spirits			
7	My Left Foot	01:12:11	MP1950D	Where's the **feckin'** brake on this stupid thing?
8	The Field			
9	The Commitments			
10	Far and Away			
11	The Snapper	00:53:00	FSC1990D	Would you ever, **feck** off!
12	Into the West			
13	A Man of No Importance	00:58:36	MCB1960D	I told him to **feck** off or I'd burst him.
14	Widows' Peak			
15	Circle of Friends			
16	Last of the High Kings			
17	The Van			
18	Michael Collins			
19	Trojan Eddie	01:29:17	MJP1990M	A **feckin'** little jailbird, bejesus.
20	The Matchmaker	00:33:20	MFis2000W	Oh God, another **feckin'** Yank as well. Who am I, huh? Aristotle O' **feckin'** nasis, huh?
21	The Nephew			
22	This is my Father	00:43:08	MK1930M	I didn't put the poteen in the **feckin'** punch.
23	Waking Ned			
24	The General			
25	A Very Unlucky Leprechaun			

Table 59: Lexical features: *feck/feckin'/fecker*

26	A Love Divided			
27	Agnes Browne	01:03:44	FAB1960D	Don't mind about me. You watch the **feckin'** road.
28	Angela's Ashes	00:31:46	FA1930L	You'd let them go barefoot before you'd get off your arse. Useless **feck** that you are.
29	When the Sky Falls			
30	About Adam	00:07:42	FL2000D	Yes, go, I wish you'd all just **feck** off.
31	Ordinary Decent Criminal			
32	When Brendan Met Trudy	00:55:30	MHM2000D	I told them all to **feck** off.
33	Nora			
34	Rat			
35	How Harry Became A Tree			
36	The Magdalene Sisters			
37	Mystics	00:30:49	MLA2000D	I wouldn't give that **fecker** the skin of a fart. Do you hear me?
38	Evelyn			
39	Intermission	00:44:51	FOW2000D	I mean, **feck** it, a woman my age in a place like this, what's the point in lying? That's my philosophy - the truth!
40	Song for a Raggy Boy			
41	Veronica Guerin			
42	Goldfish Memory			
43	The Boys and Girl from County Clare	00:34:11	MFF1960CI	There'll be no **feckin'** ice cream for you, that's for sure.
44	Cowboys and Angels			
45	Adam and Paul			
46	Dead Meat			
47	Inside I'm Dancing			
48	Irish Jam	00:16:52	MBMN2000W	That's fine coz the bloody Yank can pull the **feckin'** balance out of his **feckin'** arse.
49	The Wind that Shakes the Barley	01:23:03	MVIC1920C	I don't have any **feckin'** king!
50	Garage			
				Total: 15/50

Table 59: Lexical features: *feck/feckin'/fecker*

	Film	Time	Speaker	Example of usage
1	The Informer			
2	The Quiet Man			
3	Darby O' Gill and the Little People			
4	Ryan's Daughter			
5	The Dead			
6	High Spirits			
7	My Left Foot	01:38:04	MCB1950D	Get in the car before I kick your **arse**.
8	The Field			
9	The Commitments	00:27:01	MO1990D	I just seen Imelda Quirke's **arse** comin' down a ladder!
10	Far and Away			
11	The Snapper	01:09:41	MDC1990D	If it looked like Burgess's **arse**, I'd still love it.
12	Into the West	00:35:35	MCT1990D	I'll give you 20 pound or I'll give you a kick up the **arse!**
13	A Man of No Importance	00:16:04	MRo1960D	Acting's stupid. The lads'd rag the **arse** off of me if I came on acting.
14	Widows' Peak			
15	Circle of Friends			
16	Last of the High Kings	00:05:41	FMG1970D	I was too soft to use the wooden spoon on your **arse** when you were growing up.
17	The Van	01:14:28	ML1990D	I should tell him to stick his wages up his **arse**.
18	Michael Collins	00:18:23	MJC1910M	Get up off the parliamentary side of your **arse** and get a bit of colour in your face.
19	Trojan Eddie	00:24:57	MD1990M	So you needn't bother your **arse** flattering yourself there, girl.
20	The Matchmaker	00:20:20	FLii2000W	And you have the right to a kick in the **arse**, if you don't get out of here quick.
21	The Nephew			
22	This is my Father			
23	Waking Ned	00:39:11	MPai2000W	Christ, man, the stink on your donkey's **arse** is almost as bad as yourself.
24	The General	01:50:13	MSupt1990D	He's making a horse's **arse** of you.
25	A Very Unlucky Leprechaun			

Table 60: Lexical features: *arse*

26	A Love Divided	01:17:01	MA1950D	Plunkett, ya bloody, scabby little lick**arse**, I'll let you in, but no whingin'.
27	Agnes Browne	00:20:38	FSV1960D	Fresh? Sure, it's after pinchin' me on the **arse** twice already.
28	Angela's Ashes	00:25:29	MMIP1930D	Jaysus, if that was my son, I'd kick his **arse** from here to County Kerry.
29	When the Sky Falls	01:06:00	FSH1990D	You'd lose your **arse**, if it wasn't in your trousers.
30	About Adam			
31	Ordinary Decent Criminal	00:59:27	MN1990D	Right, Michael. We're up your **arse** now.
32	When Brendan Met Trudy	00:06:06	FT2000C	You're lyin' through your **arse**.
33	Nora			
34	Rat			
35	How Harry Became A Tree	00:17:29	MH1920WW	Haven't you enough money already to build this boil on the **arse** of Skillet?
36	The Magdalene Sisters	00:35:00	FB1960D	Well, you can shove it up your not-so-friendly **arse**.
37	Mystics			
38	Evelyn	00:51:10	MTC1950D	We had to give the minister a kick up his fat **arse**.
39	Intermission			
40	Song for a Raggy Boy			
41	Veronica Guerin	00:33:44	MJT1990D	You're talking out of your **arse**, Veronica.
42	Goldfish Memory			
43	The Boys and Girl from County Clare			
44	Cowboys and Angels			
45	Adam and Paul			
46	Dead Meat	00:40:21	MC2000LM	Are ya getting in or are ya gonna stand there with your **arses** hanging out?
47	Inside I'm Dancing	00:04:16	MROS2000D	You can shake me hand or kiss me **arse**, but don't expect me to reciprocate.
48	Irish Jam	00:22:15	FM2000W	Or perhaps a swift kick up the **arse** would get ya there quicker?
49	The Wind that Shakes the Barley	00:14:31	MT1920C	Because I would have kicked your **arse** if you had.
50	Garage	01:03:39	MSgt2000M	Yeah, well if she does ring, tell her I'm working here till 6, and she better get her **arse** down here.
				Total: 27/50

Table 60: Lexical features: *arse*

	Film	Time	Speaker	Example of usage
1	The Informer			
2	The Quiet Man			
3	Darby O' Gill and the Little People			
4	Ryan's Daughter			
5	The Dead	01:12:43	MDMC1980W	Ether, me **bollocks**.
6	High Spirits			
7	My Left Foot			
8	The Field			
9	The Commitments	00:26:07	MJR1990D	The only **bollixin'** thing that's important is what this band's called.
10	Far and Away			
11	The Snapper	00:59:00	MDC1990D	And feck it all, you're my daughter, and as long as you live in this house, I won't let **bollixes** say things about you!
12	Into the West			
13	A Man of No Importance	00:10:32	MRM1960D	Get out of the way, ya dozy oul **bollocks** ya!
14	Widows' Peak	00:05:36	FW1930M	Back that at a hundred to eight, ya **bollocks** ya!
15	Circle of Friends			
16	Last of the High Kings			
17	The Van	01:06:17	ML1990D	Wankers and **bollockses** wear white socks.
18	Michael Collins			
19	Trojan Eddie	01:01:32	MTE1990M	**Bollocks!**
20	The Matchmaker	00:26:57	MDec2000W	You're working tonight, Sean. You lazy little **bollocks**.
21	The Nephew	00:08:16	MF1990D	Shag off, ya oul **bollix**.
22	This is my Father	00:33:16	MK1930M	I'll beat the **bollocks** off the both of yiz.
23	Waking Ned	00:15:13	FM2000W	It's **bollocks**, Finn!
24	The General	01:01:49	MMC1990D	This anti-drug shit is all **bollix**. It's just a smoke screen.
25	A Very Unlucky Leprechaun			

Table 61: Lexical features: *bollocks/bollix*

26	A Love Divided		
27	Agnes Browne	01:18:59	MT1196OD	Well, he knew you and he said you're a **bollix**!
28	Angela's Ashes	01:52:49	MOF1950L	Fuck off, ya **bollocks**.
29	When the Sky Falls	00:44:02	FSH1990D	Well, **bollocks** to that!
30	About Adam			
31	Ordinary Decent Criminal	00:20:54	MA1990D	**Bollocks**, man!
32	When Brendan Met Trudy			
33	Nora	01:37:52	FN1900G	A bigger **bollocks** never put an arm through a coat.
34	Rat	01:17:34	MP2000D	Right, you little **bollix**.
35	How Harry Became A Tree			
36	The Magdalene Sisters	00:09:40	MDG1960D	**Bollocks**.
37	Mystics	00:06:52	FMK2000D	And the strain on poor Dave there. Sure, look at him. He's **bollocksed**.
38	Evelyn			
39	Intermission	00:36:13	MG2000D	Look, this is **bollocks**, man, I'm tellin' ya!
40	Song for a Raggy Boy	00:29:54	MDB1930	I think you're a stupid **bollix**.
41	Veronica Guerin	00:24:03	MJG1990D	When a scumbag like Martin Cahill is down on his luck, that's when you kick him in the **bollix**.
42	Goldfish Memory			
43	The Boys and Girl from County Clare			
44	Cowboys and Angels			
45	Adam and Paul			
46	Dead Meat	00:48:22	MC2000LM	Ah, **bollocks**.
47	Inside I'm Dancing	00:08:19	MT2000D	There's nothing wrong with my brain. It's the rest of me that's **bollocksed**.
48	Irish Jam			
49	The Wind that Shakes the Barley	01:43:32	MD1920C	John Bull has got his hand down your pants and his fist round your **bollocks** and you can't see it.
50	Garage			
				Total: 26/50

Table 61: Lexical features: *bollocks/bollix*

	Film	Time	Speaker	Example of usage
1	The Informer			
2	The Quiet Man			
3	Darby O' Gill and the Little People			
4	Ryan's Daughter			
5	The Dead			
6	High Spirits			
7	My Left Foot	00:30:00	MBB1950D	It's like the **bleedin'** fire of hell, that one is.
8	The Field			
9	The Commitments	00:44:54	MJR1990D	Poxiest **bleedin'** lyrics ever written.
10	Far and Away			
11	The Snapper	00:15:17	MP1990D	I'm not gonna buy the food, the nappies or the little **bleedin'** track suits.
12	Into the West	01:13:09	MOR1990D	I'm **bleedin'** freezin'.
13	A Man of No Importance	01:13:51	MIC1960D	Dozy **bleedin'** queer!
14	Widows' Peak			
15	Circle of Friends			
16	Last of the High Kings	00:10:05	FFS1970D	**Bleedin'** stupid.
17	The Van	00:03:29	MS1990D	Now, now, now. There's no **bleedin'** need for that.
18	Michael Collins	01:35:49	MIV1910D	Come on, get out of the **bleedin'** way!
19	Trojan Eddie			
20	The Matchmaker			
21	The Nephew			
22	This is my Father			
23	Waking Ned			
24	The General	01:00:47	MMC1990D	Get out, Curley, ya **bleedin'** drug pusher.
25	A Very Unlucky Leprechaun			

Table 62: Lexical features: *bleedin'*

#	Title	Time	Code	Quote
26	A Love Divided			
27	Agnes Browne	00:28:47	FAB1960D	What's to **bleedin'** miss?
28	Angela's Ashes			
29	When the Sky Falls	00:46:37	MSgt1990D	If I had my way, I'd put them all up against a wall and blow their **bleedin'** brains out.
30	About Adam			
31	Ordinary Decent Criminal	00:19:20	MGM1990D	You know you drive like a **bleedin'** oul one.
32	When Brendan Met Trudy			
33	Nora			
34	Rat			
35	How Harry Became A Tree			
36	The Magdalene Sisters	00:08:36	FYG1960D	Where's the **bleedin'** brush?
37	Mystics	00:05:16	MB2000D	Get your **bleedin'** hands off me, you bollix!
38	Evelyn			
39	Intermission			
40	Song for a Raggy Boy			
41	Veronica Guerin	00:42:50	MJT1990D	I run a **bleedin'** garage, Veronica. I provide loads of cars to people.
42	Goldfish Memory			
43	The Boys and Girl from County Clare			
44	Cowboys and Angels			
45	Adam and Paul	00:59:01	MTV2000D	What did you **bleedin'** call me?
46	Dead Meat			
47	Inside I'm Dancing			
48	Irish Jam			
49	The Wind that Shakes the Barley			
50	Garage			
	Total: 16/50			

Table 62: Lexical features: *bleedin'*

	Film	Time	Speaker	Example of usage
1	The Informer			
2	The Quiet Man			
3	Darby O' Gill and the Little People			
4	Ryan's Daughter			
5	The Dead			
6	High Spirits	00:31:10	MPP1980W	It's an unholy trinity of a muckraker, a **gobshite** and a hoor's melt.
7	My Left Foot	00:15:13	FWN1950D	Ya, poor, unfortunate **gobshite**.
8	The Field			
9	The Commitments	01:02:54	FB1990D	You'll have to wait longer than that to get near me, you fuckin' **gobshite**!
10	Far and Away			
11	The Snapper	00:03:26	MDC1990D	Jesus, do you hear that **gobshite**?
12	Into the West			
13	A Man of No Importance			
14	Widows' Peak			
15	Circle of Friends			
16	Last of the High Kings	00:29:55	MF1970D	Davy, come down out of that you **gobshite**.
17	The Van			
18	Michael Collins	00:16:30	MMC1910C	Won't do to keep the **gobshites** waiting.
19	Trojan Eddie			
20	The Matchmaker			
21	The Nephew			
22	This is my Father	00:37:59	FF1930M	I'd be delighted, the pair of **gobshites**.
23	Waking Ned	00:12:09	FL2000W	You little **gobshite**!
24	The General			
25	A Very Unlucky Leprechaun			

Table 63: Lexical features: *gobshite*

#	Title	Time	Code	Quote
26	A Love Divided			
27	Agnes Browne	00:09:41	FAB1960D	Marion, you go on with these, while I see what's up with the little **gobshite**.
28	Angela's Ashes			
29	When the Sky Falls	00:27:05	MH1990D	Fucking **gobshite**.
30	About Adam			
31	Ordinary Decent Criminal	00:16:43	MC1990D	Give us an answer, you fucking **gobshite**!
32	When Brendan Met Trudy	00:48:04	MB2000D	Yes, this is Sunset Boulevard. You see the body of a young, wet **gobshite**.
33	Nora			
34	Rat			
35	How Harry Became A Tree	00:46:40	MH1920WW	**Gobshite**!
36	The Magdalene Sisters			
37	Mystics	00:44:57	MD2000D	**Gobshite**!
38	Evelyn	00:29:49	MDES1950D	Who is this **gobshite**?
39	Intermission			
40	Song for a Raggy Boy			
41	Veronica Guerin			
42	Goldfish Memory			
43	The Boys and Girl from County Clare			
44	Cowboys and Angels			
45	Adam and Paul			
46	Dead Meat			
47	Inside I'm Dancing	00:39:20	MROS2000D	For some strange reason he thought it was demeaning to seek out the **gobshite** that flushed him at birth.
48	Irish Jam			
49	The Wind that Shakes the Barley			
50	Garage			
				Total: 16/50

Table 63: Lexical features: *gobshite*

	Film	Time	Speaker	Example of usage
1	The Informer			
2	The Quiet Man			
3	Darby O' Gill and the Little People			
4	Ryan's Daughter			
5	The Dead			
6	High Spirits	01:12:36	MDMC1980W	You don't **shaggin'** know, do you?
7	My Left Foot			
8	The Field			
9	The Commitments	01:06:41	MBM1990D	They're takin' up half the **shaggin'** pub!
10	Far and Away	00:04:33	MJD1890W	Just **shag** off, the pair of you.
11	The Snapper	01:12:31	MDC1990D	I can't wait to see the **shaggin'** electric bill.
12	Into the West			
13	A Man of No Importance			
14	Widows' Peak			
15	Circle of Friends			
16	Last of the High Kings			
17	The Van			
18	Michael Collins			
19	Trojan Eddie			
20	The Matchmaker			
21	The Nephew	00:08:16	MF1990D	**Shag** off, ya oul bollix.
22	This is my Father			
23	Waking Ned			
24	The General			
25	A Very Unlucky Leprechaun			

Table 64: Lexical features: *shag/shaggin'/shagger*

26	A Love Divided			
27	Agnes Browne			
28	Angela's Ashes			
29	When the Sky Falls	00:12:54	MDA1990D	That's **shag** all use around here. Press wankers!
30	About Adam	01:12:50	FA2000D	What you need is a good **shag**.
31	Ordinary Decent Criminal			
32	When Brendan Met Trudy			
33	Nora			
34	Rat	01:07:04	MF2000D	Let us all join our voices, all of us that is, except that ignorant crowd of **shaggers** …
35	How Harry Became A Tree			
36	The Magdalene Sisters			
37	Mystics	00:11:55	FF2000D	I'm going to have to **shag** off now. I've a reputation to maintain.
38	Evelyn			
39	Intermission			
40	Song for a Raggy Boy			
41	Veronica Guerin			
42	Goldfish Memory			
43	The Boys and Girl from County Clare			
44	Cowboys and Angels			
45	Adam and Paul			
46	Dead Meat			
47	Inside I'm Dancing			
48	Irish Jam			
49	The Wind that Shakes the Barley	00:15:00	MF1920C	Where's the rest of that **shaggin'** section?
50	Garage			
				Total: 10/50

Table 64: Lexical features: *shag/shagair/shaggin'/shagger*

	Film	Time	Speaker	Example of usage
1	The Informer	00:35:09	MG1920D	Ah, that's **grand** stuff!
2	The Quiet Man	00:18:37	MFe1930D	There now. There now, isn't that **grand**? Isn't that **grand** now, what?
3	Darby O' Gill and the Little People	00:04:18	MLF1800K	That Katie's a **grand** girl. Almost makes up for her father.
4	Ryan's Daughter	01:31:01	MFR1920W	**Grand** day for a journey.
5	The Dead	00:40:15	MF1900D	I think he has a **grand** voice.
6	High Spirits			
7	My Left Foot	00:28:16	FNM1970D	He's **grand**.
8	The Field			
9	The Commitments			
10	Far and Away	01:05:37	MJD1890W	I'm feeling **grand** tonight.
11	The Snapper	00:06:38	MDC1990D	Go on, you might as well. I'll be **grand**.
12	Into the West	01:31:00	MPR1990D	That's right, son. **Grand**.
13	A Man of No Importance	01:16:54	MA1960D	I'm **grand** thanks. I'm **grand**!
14	Widows' Peak	01:08:34	FRW1930M	Isn't that a **grand** class of a day?
15	Circle of Friends	00:40:12	MSW1950D	That would tie things up just **grand** now, don't you think so?
16	Last of the High Kings			
17	The Van	00:47:29	MW1990D	He'll be **grand**. He takes all Arsenal's pennos.
18	Michael Collins	00:24:53	MMC1910C	**Grand** evening.
19	Trojan Eddie	00:49:27	MTE1990M	Oh, yeah. Sure, **grand**. Lovely.
20	The Matchmaker	01:14:06	MJim2000W	I'm fine. I'm **grand**.
21	The Nephew	00:19:09	MIP1990C	God, isn't that a **grand** sight?
22	This is my Father	01:24:33	MSgt1930M	Kieran, **grand** day!
23	Waking Ned	00:06:35	FA2000W	Well, you're blessed with a **grand** voice, Mrs Kennedy.
24	The General	00:41:18	MJ1990D	No, look, it's **grand**. It's been sorted out.
25	A Very Unlucky Leprechaun			

Table 65: Lexical features: *grand*

26	A Love Divided	00:14:00	MFR1950WX	No buts, you'll be **grand**.
27	Agnes Browne	00:11:18	FAB1960D	Isn't this **grand**?
28	Angela's Ashes	01:05:43	FV1940L	You're a **grand** soldier, Frankie.
29	When the Sky Falls	00:22:37	MD1990D	Half twelve. That's **grand**.
30	About Adam	00:01:00	FL2000D	No, we're **grand**. We were just finishing up anyway.
31	Ordinary Decent Criminal	01:27:38	FSW1990D	That's a **grand** bike you have. I wish I had your speed.
32	When Brendan Met Trudy	00:28:27	FT2000C	It's not so bad. It'll be **grand**.
33	Nora	00:04:37	MJJ1900D	Good. **Grand**. I'll see you there.
34	Rat	00:13:14	MP2000D	Look, I'm **grand** where I am.
35	How Harry Became A Tree	00:59:17	MH1920WW	Ah, well, that's **grand**. That's settled then.
36	The Magdalene Sisters	01:46:13	FB1960D	**Grand**.
37	Mystics	00:37:50	MD2000D	Ah, no, no thanks. We're **grand**.
38	Evelyn	00:35:33	FB1950D	You think all you have to do is smile with that cheeky twinkle in your eye and everything will be **grand**.
39	Intermission			
40	Song for a Raggy Boy			
41	Veronica Guerin	01:06:15	MJT1990D	I'm **grand**. Get you a drink?
42	Goldfish Memory	00:43:02	FI2000D	I'm **grand** and yourself?
43	The Boys and Girl from County Clare	00:06:07	MJJ1960CI	That's **grand**. Well it's a start anyway.
44	Cowboys and Angels	00:48:51	MJ2000L	Listen to the voice of experience, son. You get a few pints down you and you'll be **grand**.
45	Adam and Paul	00:07:06	MA2000D	You're **grand**. Put your head between your legs.
46	Dead Meat	00:42:10	MC2000LM	She'd be telling you she'd only herself to look after and she was doing **grand** ....
47	Inside I'm Dancing			
48	Irish Jam	00:05:29	FM2000W	Well, I think it's a **grand** idea. I'm with you, Michael.
49	The Wind that Shakes the Barley	00:30:52	MT1920C	Kevin, you're **grand**. Let me look.
50	Garage	01:10:57	MMG2000M	I'm sure it's **grand**, Josie.
				Total: 42/50

Table 65: Lexical features: *grand*

	Film	Time	Speaker	Example of usage
1	The Informer			
2	The Quiet Man	00:13:00	MMF1930W	It's a **bold**, sinful man you are, Sean Thornton.
3	Darby O' Gill and the Little People	00:18:31	MMB1800D	Well, aren't they the **bold** creatures?
4	Ryan's Daughter			
5	The Dead			
6	High Spirits			
7	My Left Foot			
8	The Field			
9	The Commitments			
10	Far and Away			
11	The Snapper			
12	Into the West			
13	A Man of No Importance			
14	Widows' Peak	00:20:23	FDC1930M	Ah, Miss Grubb, why are you tempting me, you **bold** strap you?
15	Circle of Friends			
16	Last of the High Kings			
17	The Van			
18	Michael Collins			
19	Trojan Eddie			
20	The Matchmaker			
21	The Nephew			
22	This is my Father			
23	Waking Ned			
24	The General			
25	A Very Unlucky Leprechaun			

Table 66: Lexical features: *bold*

26	A Love Divided			
27	Agnes Browne			
28	Angela's Ashes			
29	When the Sky Falls			
30	About Adam			
31	Ordinary Decent Criminal			
32	When Brendan Met Trudy			
33	Nora			
34	Rat			
35	How Harry Became A Tree	01:11:34	FM1920WW	What's going to happen to you and me if **bold** Gus Maloney kills your Daddy?
36	The Magdalene Sisters			
37	Mystics			
38	Evelyn	00:15:10	FSrB1950D	Are you being **bold**, young lady?
39	Intermission	00:12:50	MG2000D	If I find out that you've been in any way **bold**. I'm going to nab you.
40	Song for a Raggy Boy			
41	Veronica Guerin			
42	Goldfish Memory			
43	The Boys and Girl from County Clare			
44	Cowboys and Angels			
45	Adam and Paul			
46	Dead Meat			
47	Inside I'm Dancing			
48	Irish Jam			
49	The Wind that Shakes the Barley			
50	Garage			
				Total: 6/50

Table 66: Lexical features: *bold*

	Film	Time	Speaker	Example of usage
1	The Informer			
2	The Quiet Man			
3	Darby O' Gill and the Little People			
4	Ryan's Daughter	00:41:14	MP1920W	Oh, landlord, you're a **desperate** man.
5	The Dead	00:54:47	FMM1900D	During August, the midges in the Highlands are **desperate**.
6	High Spirits			
7	My Left Foot			
8	The Field			
9	The Commitments	00:47:32	MO1990D	That's a **desperate** place!
10	Far and Away			
11	The Snapper			
12	Into the West			
13	A Man of No Importance			
14	Widows' Peak			
15	Circle of Friends	00:18:55	FBH1950D	It must be a **desperate** thing to be a doctor.
16	Last of the High Kings			
17	The Van	00:14:23	MB1990D	God, this is **desperate**.
18	Michael Collins			
19	Trojan Eddie			
20	The Matchmaker			
21	The Nephew			
22	This is my Father			
23	Waking Ned	00:52:55	MJ2000W	It's **desperate**.
24	The General	01:15:09	MMC1990D	**Desperate**, isn't it?
25	A Very Unlucky Leprechaun			

Table 67: Lexical features: *desperate*

26	A Love Divided			
27	Agnes Browne			
28	Angela's Ashes	01:22:36	FA1930L	The Irish sea's **desperate** this time of year.
29	When the Sky Falls			
30	About Adam			
31	Ordinary Decent Criminal	00:01:56	MMB1990D	**Desperate. Desperate** altogether.
32	When Brendan Met Trudy	00:06:39	FT2000C	You're a bit of a shite aren't you? It'd be a **desperate** party anyway.
33	Nora			
34	Rat	00:27:01	FC2000D	Isn't that **desperate**?
35	How Harry Became A Tree			
36	The Magdalene Sisters			
37	Mystics			
38	Evelyn			
39	Intermission			
40	Song for a Raggy Boy			
41	Veronica Guerin			
42	Goldfish Memory			
43	The Boys and Girl from County Clare			
44	Cowboys and Angels			
45	Adam and Paul			
46	Dead Meat			
47	Inside I'm Dancing			
48	Irish Jam	00:28:57	MG2000W	Oh, I know it. And I've a **desperate** thirst and I'm goin' to quench it.
49	The Wind that Shakes the Barley			
50	Garage			
				Total: 12/50

Table 67: Lexical features: *desperate*

GRAZER BEITRÄGE ZUR ENGLISCHEN PHILOLOGIE

Band 1 Peter Bierbaumer: Der botanische Wortschatz des Altenglischen. 1. Teil: Das Læcebōc. 1975.

Band 2 Peter Bierbaumer: Der botanische Wortschatz des Altenglischen. 2. Teil: Lācnunga, Herbarium Apuleii, Peri Didaxeon. 1976.

Band 3 Peter Bierbaumer: Der botanische Wortschatz des Altenglischen: 3. Teil: Der botanische Wortschatz in altenglischen Glossen. 1979.

Band 4 Gerd Sieper: Fachsprachliche Korpusanalyse und Wortschatzauswahl. 1980.

Band 5 Rüdiger Pfeiffer-Rupp: Studien zu Subkategorisierung und semantischen Relationen. 1977.

Band 6 Bernhard Kettemann: Aspekte der natürlichen generativen Phonologie eines amerikanisch-englischen Dialektes. 1978.

BAMBERGER BEITRÄGE ZUR ENGLISCHEN SPRACHWISSENSCHAFT
UNIVERSITY OF BAMBERG STUDIES IN ENGLISH LINGUISTICS
(Die Reihe wird unter neuer Reihenbezeichnung ab Band 7 weitergeführt)

Band 7 Günter Radden: Ein Profil soziolinguistischer Variation in einer amerikanischen Kleinstadt. 1979.

Band 8 Karin Viereck: Englisches Wortgut, seine Häufigkeit und Integration in der österreichischen und bundesdeutschen Pressesprache. 1980.

Band 9 John Oakeshott-Taylor: Acoustic Variability and its Perception. The effects of context on selected acoustic parameters of English words and their perceptual consequences. 1980.

Band 10 Edgar W. Schneider: Morphologische und syntaktische Variablen im amerikanischen Early Black English. 1981.

Band 11 Val Jones-Sargent: Tyne Bytes. A Computerised Sociolinguistic Study of Tyneside. 1983.

Band 12 Lee Pederson: East Tennessee Folk Speech. A Synopsis. 1983.

Band 13 Cornelia Zelinsky-Wibbelt: Die semantische Belastung von submorphematischen Einheiten im Englischen. Eine empirisch-strukturelle Untersuchung. 1983.

Band 14 Rolf Bremann: Soziolinguistische Untersuchungen zum Englisch von Cornwall. 1984.

Band 15 Wolf-Dietrich Bald and Horst Weinstock (eds.): Medieval Studies Conference Aachen 1983. Language and Literature. 1984.

Band 16 Clausdirk Pollner: Englisch in Livingston. Ausgewählte sprachliche Erscheinungen in einer schottischen New Town. 1985.

Band 17 Adam Jaworski: A linguistic picture of women's position in society. A Polish-English contrastive study. 1986.

Band 18 Mark Newbrook: Sociolinguistic reflexes of dialect interference in West Wirral. 1986.

Band 19 George Townsend Dorrill: Black and White Speech in the Southern United States. Evidence from the Linguistic Atlas of the Middle and South Atlantic States. 1986.

Band 20 Birgit Meseck: Studien zur konservativ-restaurativen Sprachkritik in Amerika. 1987.

Band 21 Barbara Kryk: On Deixis in English and Polish: The Role of Demonstrative Pronouns. 1987.

Band 22 Sándor Rot: On Crucial Problems of the English Verb. 1988.

Band 23 Stephen J. Nagle: Inferential Change and Syntactic Modality in English. 1989.

Band 24 Heinrich Ramisch: The Variation of English in Guernsey/Channel Islands. 1989.

Band 25 Ronald R. Butters: The Death of Black English. Divergence and Convergence in Black and White Vernaculars. 1989.

Band 26 Włodzimierz Sobkowiak: Metaphonology of English Paronomasic Puns. 1991.

Band 27 Robert J. Penhallurick: The Anglo-Welsh Dialects of North Wales. A Survey of Conservative Rural Spoken English in the Counties of Gwynedd and Clwyd. 1991.

Band 28 Merja Kytö: Variation and Diachrony, with Early American English in Focus. Studies on CAN/MAY and SHALL/WILL. 1991.

Band 29 Sándor Rot: Language Contact. 1991.

Band 30 Agnieszka Kiełkiewicz-Janowiak: A Socio-Historical Study in Address: Polish and English. 1992.

Band 31 Stanisław Puppel: The Dynamics of Speech Production. 1992.

Band 32 Anna Zbierska-Sawala: Early Middle English Word Formation. Semantic Aspects of Derivational Affixation in the AB Language. 1993.

Band 33 Nadine Van den Eynden: Syntactic Variation and Unconscious Linguistic Change. A study of adjectival relative clauses in the dialect of Dorset. 1993.

Band 34 Marcin Krygier: The Disintegration of the English Strong Verb System. 1994.

Band 35 Caroline Macafee: Traditional Dialect in the Modern World. A Glasgow Case Study. 1994.

Band 36 Robert Penhallurick: Gowerland and its language. A history of the English speech of the Gower Peninsula, South Wales. 1994.

Band 37 Monika Klages-Kubitzki: Article Usage in English. A Computer-based Self-teaching Programme on the Basis of a Functional Theory of Reference. 1995.

Band 38 Juhani Klemola / Merja Kytö / Matti Rissanen (eds.): Speech Past and Present. Studies in English Dialectology in Memory of Ossi Ihalainen. 1996.

Band 39 Piotr Gąsiorowski: The Phonology of Old English Stress and Metrical Structure. 1997.

Band 40 Marcin Krygier: From Regularity to Anomaly. Inflectional i-Umlaut in Middle English. 1997.

Band 41 Graham Shorrocks: A Grammar of the Dialect of the Bolton Area. Part I. Introduction, Phonology. 1998.

Band 42 Graham Shorrocks: A Grammar of the Dialect of the Bolton Area. Part II. Morphology and Syntax. 1999.

Band 43 Mats Rydén / Ingrid Tieken-Boon van Ostade / Merja Kytö (eds.): A Reader in Early Modern English. 1998.

Band 44 Herbert Grabes (ed.): Innovation and Continuity in English Studies. A Critical Jubilee. 2001.

Band 45 Kinga Nettmann-Multanowska: English Loanwords in Polish and German after 1945: Orthography and Morphology. 2003.

Band 46 Birgit Eder: Ausgewählte Verwandtschaftsbezeichnungen in den Sprachen Europas untersucht anhand der Datensammlungen des *Atlas Linguarum Europae*. 2004.

Band 47 Gabriele Knappe: Idioms and Fixed Expressions in English Language Study before 1800. A Contribution to English Historical Phraseology. 2004.

Band 48 Gabriele Knappe (Hrsg.): Englische Sprachwissenschaft und Mediävistik: Standpunkte – Perspektiven – Neue Wege. English Linguistics and Medieval Studies: Positions – Perspectives – New Approaches. Proceedings of the Conference in Bamberg, May 21–22, 2004. 2005.

Band 49 Wolfgang Viereck: Selected Writings – Ausgewählte Schriften. English Linguistic and Cultural History – English Dialectology. Englische Sprach- und Kulturgeschichte – Englische Dialektologie. 2005.

Band 50 Wolfgang Viereck: Selected Writings – Ausgewählte Schriften. History of Science, English Surnames, American English, Languages in Contact, Language and School, *Atlas Linguarum Europae*. Wissenschaftsgeschichte, Englische Familiennamen, Amerikanisches Englisch, Sprachen in Kontakt, Sprache und Schule, *Atlas Linguarum Europae*. 2005.

Band 51 Herbert Grabes / Wolfgang Viereck (eds.): The Wider Scope of English. Papers in English Language and Literature from the Bamberg Conference of the International Association of University Professors of English. 2006.

Band 52 Stephanie Barker / Stefankai Spoerlein / Tobias Vetter / Wolfgang Viereck: An Atlas of English Surnames. 2007.

Band 53 Shane Walshe: Irish English as Represented in Film. 2009

www.peterlang.de